*...sociated in the preparation of this volume were:* J. R. FREDLAND ...D HENRY H. ADAMS, *Assistant Editors; and* HENRY H. ADAMS, ...MES A. ARNOLD, WILLIAM M. BELOTE, EDWIN M. HALL, ...NSTON B. LEWIS, PHILIP K. LUNDEBERG, E. B. POTTER, *and* H. O. WERNER.

# THE GRE
## SEA W

The Story of Naval
in World

# THE GREAT
# SEA WAR

## The Story of Naval Action
## in World War II

Edited by E. B. POTTER
*U.S. Naval Academy*

*and*

**CHESTER W. NIMITZ**
*Fleet Admiral, USN*

*New York*

BRAMHALL HOUSE

The *Great Sea War* is adapted from the naval
history of World War II as told in *Sea Power*.

This edition is published by Bramhall House,
a division of Clarkson N. Potter, Inc.,
by arrangement with Prentice-Hall, Inc.
(B)

Library of Congress Catalog Card Number: 60–53441
Printed in the United States of America
36491–T

# A WORD TO THE READER . . . .

## from Fleet Admiral Chester W. Nimitz, USN

World War II is almost beyond comparison with any previous conflict. It was fought with more weapons of more different sorts, by more men involved in a greater variety of operations, in more areas of the world than any other war in history.

Because World War II was in truth worldwide, it was basically a naval war. The Allied navies carried the Allied armies across the seas to scores of hostile shores, played a major (often the sole) part in isolating the prospective beachheads, thrust aside and decimated opposing fleets, put the invaders ashore in the teeth of enemy defenses, supported them with naval gunfire and carrier aircraft, and kept them supplied and reinforced in spite of enemy attacks from the air, surface, and subsurface. In carrying out such missions, the United States Navy grew into a vast, complex organization operating from land, sea, and air to project and maintain military power beyond the oceans.

The basically naval nature of World War II was obvious in the Pacific Ocean Areas, where the United States Navy controlled every man and every weapon of all Allied services and nationalities—with the sole exception of the Marianas-based B-29's, which the Navy serviced but did not command. In the European theater of operations, the magnitude of the naval contribution was not so obvious, for here the supreme command was Army and here armies campaigned across vast stretches of territory. But in the European theater also it was the navies that brought the armies to the beaches, landed them, and kept them supplied. And it was the navies that brought in, or protected the ships that brought in, most of the aircraft and bombs and all of the aviation fuel for land-based air operations. In the European theater too the invading forces came more and more to depend upon the navies to isolate the beachheads and to support the landing forces. Moreover, while the Allied armies were closing the pincers on the enemy in North Africa, fighting their way up the rough spine of Italy, and surging across the plains of Europe, the Allied navies were carrying on equally far-flung and unremitting warfare on the seas. Had our navies not been victorious over enemy fleets, over enemy surface raiders, and, above all, over the U-boat, the Allied armies would have been without the means of achieving victory ashore.

v

Today the United States is at the center of a system of alliances involving more nations than were banded together to defeat the Axis powers. The linking element in this system of international pacts is the sea. It is important for all Americans and their friends in all lands to understand how the United States and her allies used the sea to win the victory in World War II. *The Great Sea War* explains clearly, accurately, and vividly how it was done.

*Chester W. Nimitz*
*Fleet Admiral, USN*

# Preface

The authors of *The Great Sea War* have undertaken to present within a limited space a clear and understandable narrative of the most complex and widespread of all naval conflicts. They have kept in mind that war is more than a succession of battles and campaigns. It is on the one hand an intellectual problem and on the other, high drama. The authors have devoted considerable space to explaining the reasons for strategic and tactical decisions. But they have not forgotten that warfare is a conflict not only of ideas and of weapons but also of men, with their personal tragedies and triumphs.

To attain clarity, the authors have treated one facet of the war at a time, even at some violence to chronology. The story of the war against Germany and Italy is completed before the story of the war against Japan begins. The narrative of Atlantic surface operations has a chapter to itself. This is followed by the story of the Mediterranean campaign up to the turning point of the Battle of El Alamein and the Allied landings in Northwest Africa. The Atlantic submarine war next has a chapter to itself, and this is followed by three chapters covering the successful Allied landings in Africa and Europe, and the subsequent navy-supported land operations that led to the defeat of Italy and Germany. In the story of the Pacific war, the operations in the various areas are segregated as far as is possible without obscuring their close interrelationship.

The authors have omitted all details except those necessary to understanding or that are of special interest in themselves. They have avoided excessive repetition by treating at length only one operation of a particular sort, usually the first to take place. Thus in the Atlantic theater the assault on Morocco, and in the Pacific theater the assault on Tarawa, are presented in considerable detail. Subsequent amphibious assaults are described only in so far as they differed from the pattern set in these. The Battle of Midway, with a chapter to itself, establishes the pattern for carrier battles, enabling the authors to treat subsequent carrier battles at lesser length—up to the Battle for Leyte Gulf, which, because of its complexity and the controversial decisions involved, also is treated at chapter length.

Thus by segregation of campaigns and selection of details the authors have striven to avoid sketchiness and clutter while compressing six years of worldwide naval conflict into a single volume. In order to provide a complete picture, they have carried the story far beyond the shoreline and described the major land campaigns in broad outline. *The Great Sea War* is in fact a general history of World War II with emphasis on the sea power aspect.

To achieve continuity, uniformity of style, and uniformity of treatment, the authors have worked together as a closely knit research and writing team. This has been possible, first, because they have similar professional backgrounds. All saw service in World War II, mostly in the naval reserve. Since then they have been associated as teachers of naval history at the United States Naval Academy. Here they have tested their ideas on each other through several years of discussion and of writing together. Most of them participated in writing an earlier preliminary study, *The United States and World Sea Power* (Prentice-Hall, Inc., 1955), passages of which have been incorporated into the present book. Second, the efforts of each author have been subjected to intensive analysis and criticism by his colleagues and by professional officers. Every page of *The Great Sea War* reflects the influence of Fleet Admiral Chester W. Nimitz USN, who was closely associated with the project from beginning to end. Lastly, the authors, besides coordinating their efforts under editorial guidance, have submitted their finished work to unlimited editing. There are numerous instances where it would be difficult to specify where one writer's work leaves off and another's begins, or to separate editorial work from original composition.

While taking full responsibility for errors of fact and interpretation, the authors wish to express their gratitude to all who have helped them complete this work.

*The Great Sea War*, while in preparation, was read and criticized by a number of the major participants in the operations described. The following officers reviewed portions of the typescript covering their own experiences and provided the authors with detailed comment and marginal notes: the late Fleet Admiral William F. Halsey USN (Ret.), Admiral Raymond A. Spruance USN (Ret.), Admiral H. Kent Hewitt USN (Ret.), Admiral Thomas C. Kinkaid USN (Ret.), Admiral Robert B. Carney USN (Ret.), Lieutenant General Julian C. Smith USMC (Ret.), Vice Admiral Charles A. Lockwood USN (Ret.), Vice Admiral Stanton A. Merrill USN (Ret.), and Captain Ralph Weymouth USN.

The following officers read portions of the typescript and gave helpful advice: the late Vice Admiral Eliot H. Bryant USN (Ret.), Rear Admiral Walter C. Ansel USN (Ret.), and Commander F. Barley RNVR (Ret.) and Lieutenant Commander D. W. Waters RN (Ret.) both of the Historical Section, British Admiralty.

So many persons have been helpful in supplying information that a comprehensive listing is impossible, but prominent among them are

General of the Army Douglas MacArthur usa; Grand Admiral Erich Raeder, formerly Commander in Chief of the German navy; Admiral Arleigh A. Burke, Chief of Naval Operations, U.S. Navy; Vice Admiral Friedrich Ruge, Chief of Naval Operations, German Federal Navy; Vice Admiral Giuseppi Fioravanzo, Director of the Historical Division of the Italian navy; Lieutenant Commander P. K. Kemp rn (Ret.), Archivist and Head of the Historical Section, British Admiralty; Commander G. A. Titterton rn (Ret.), Historical Section, British Admiralty; and M. Jacques Mordal, Historical Section, Ministry of the French *Marine*.

Professor Vernon Tate, Head Librarian of the United States Naval Academy, his predecessor, the late Louis H. Bolander, and their staffs have been unstintingly helpful, as have Rear Admiral Ernest M. Eller usn (Ret.), Director of Naval History, and his staff.

The charts and diagrams were drawn, largely from authors' sketches, by Mr. William M. Shannon and Mr. Albert Jones, both of the U.S. Naval Academy.

*The Great Sea War* is adapted from the naval history of World War II as told in *Sea Power* (Prentice-Hall, Inc., 1960), a general history of sea warfare covering 2,500 years. The adaptation, extensive in places, makes *The Great Sea War* an independent volume, complete in itself. Like *Sea Power*, it is addressed both to the expert and to the general public.

Much of the material in *The Great Sea War* is based upon original research, particularly among official documents. Some is based on correspondence and interviews with participants. A great deal however is drawn from the numerous histories and memoirs of World War II already published. Of these, *History of United States Naval Operations in World War II*, by Samuel Eliot Morison, and *The War at Sea*, by Captain S. W. Roskill rn (Ret.) have proved most useful. Readers desiring to know the source of quotations and special data in *The Great Sea War* should consult the footnotes in *Sea Power*.

The authors and Admiral Nimitz wish to emphasize that *Sea Power* is in no sense an official history. It was conceived and written as a private enterprise. The opinions expressed are the writers' own.

# Illustration Acknowledgments

The maps, charts, tables, and diagrams used in this book are necessarily compiled from information drawn from many sources. In some instances one source has been the primary basis for an illustration. The authors therefore wish to acknowledge these sources for the illustrations appearing on the following pages: page 21, adapted from Antony Martienssen, *Hitler and His Admirals* (New York: E. P. Dutton & Co., 1949); page 32, adapted, with the permission of the Controller of H.M. Stationery Office, from Captain S. W. Roskill RN, *The War at Sea, 1939-1945*, vol. II (London: Her Majesty's Stationery Office, 1956); page 96, adapted from David W. Waters, "The Philosophy and Conduct of Maritime War," *Journal of the Royal Navy Scientific Service*, July 1958; pages 107 and 186, adapted from Dwight D. Eisenhower, *Crusade in Europe*, copyright 1948 by Doubleday and Company, Inc., by permission of the publisher; page 196, adapted from Allan Westcott, ed., *American Sea Power since 1775* (Chicago: J. B. Lippincott Company, 1952); pages 92, 116, 209, 268, 350, and 351, adapted with the permission of the author from Samuel Eliot Morison, *History of United States Naval Operations in World War II*, vols. I, II, III, V, and VIII (Boston: Little, Brown & Company, 1948-1953); pages 162 and 165, adapted from Chester Wilmot, *The Struggle for Europe* (New York: Harper and Brothers, Publishers, 1952); page 170, adapted from Department of Military Art and Engineering, United States Military Academy, Atlas for *A Military History of World War II* (West Point, 1953); page 177, adapted from Alfred Stanford, *Force Mulberry* (New York: William Morrow and Company, 1951); page 326, adapted from Philip A. Crowl and Edmund G. Love, *Seizure of the Gilberts and Marshalls* (Washington: Office of the Chief of Military History, Department of the Army, 1955).

# Table of Contents

# 1

# Atlantic Surface Operations

"It is peace in our time," said Britain's Prime Minister, Neville Chamberlain, when he returned from the Munich conference with Adolf Hitler. Less than a year later, at 0445 on September 1, 1939, Nazi armies hurled themselves against Poland, and the holocaust of World War II began. The danger signs had been unmistakable from the latter part of August, when Hitler signed with Russia a non-aggression pact that freed him from the danger of Soviet intervention. England and France had mutual aid treaties with Poland, but Hitler had no reason to suspect that they would honor them any more than they had fulfilled their Munich-repudiated moral obligations to Czechoslovakia.

The German *Führer* planned a swift campaign that would smash Poland while Britain and France vacillated. He thus would present them with a *fait accompli*. But he failed to consider the change in temper of both leaders and people in the two western countries. This time he would be opposed with force to the utmost, on land, on sea, and in the air. The British presented the Germans an ultimatum during the evening of September 1 and issued a final warning at 0900 on the 3rd. At 1115 on September 3, 1939, in a broadcast to the nation, Prime Minister Chamberlain announced that His Majesty's Government was at war with Germany. France followed suit that afternoon. The same day a round-faced, chubby man of dynamic fighting spirit returned as First Lord of the British Admiralty, an office he had relinquished 24 years earlier. A signal was flashed to the fleet: "Winston is back."

There was little that Britain or France could do to aid Poland. Germany unleashed a new kind of warfare on the Polish plains, a war of rapid movement, heavily mechanized, in which tanks were used to spearhead long lines of advance and to encircle whole armies. Overhead, the *Luftwaffe* swept the ineffectual Polish Air Force from the skies, and then roared in with Stukas and Messerschmitts to wipe out Polish infantry strong points in the way of the onrushing German divisions. In a few

1

weeks all was over on the Polish front. Here the *Blitzkrieg,* or lightning war, tactics had done their work. But all was not over in the West. Though British and French mobilization had come too late to help Poland, Britain and France laid plans to meet any westward thrusts of the German *Wehrmacht*—Britain primarily through the use of her sea power; France by means of her armies sheltered behind the Maginot Line.

Hitler had no wish to face a real war with Britain and France—at that time. He accepted the Russian occupation of half of Poland in an effort to keep the war localized. He hoped that he could persuade Britain and France to accept the situation and agree to peace, thus affording him time to build up his navy for a war in the West in 1944 or 1945. Hence, after the Polish operation had been completed, Hitler refrained from any offensive action on the Western Front, a measure of restraint that brought about what has been called the "Phony War." Through the winter of 1939-40 German troops in the Siegfried Line faced French troops in the Maginot Line with only small skirmishes relieving the monotony.

## The War Begins at Sea

Near the end of 1938, Grand Admiral Erich Raeder, *Oberbefehlshaber der Kriegsmarine,* had presented Hitler with a choice of plans. One, based on the assumption that war was imminent, called for most of Germany's naval resources to be devoted to weapons of commerce warfare —U-boats, raiders, minelayers, and coast defense forces. The other, known as PLAN Z, was a long-range program, based on the assumption that war was not to be expected for ten years. Under this plan, Germany would build a surface fleet of ships so superior to those of the Royal Navy that she could wrest mastery of the oceans from Britain.

Hitler informed Raeder that he should proceed on the basis of PLAN Z. The reason for this decision, sorely mistaken in the light of subsequent events, is difficult to fathom. Hitler valued the big ships for their political influence. He also appears to have been seized with a desire to emulate and perhaps outstrip Great Britain, little anticipating that his projects on the Continent would involve him in war with her. When he overreached himself in Poland, he was stunned by the British ultimatum. Not until 1940 did he give up hope of Britain's agreeing to peace.

Whatever the reason for Hitler's decision, it left his navy in no condition for war. By the end of 1939 PLAN Z was well launched, but the fleet would not be combat-ready before 1945. Experiments had yet to be evaluated. Only interim ship types had been completed. Having begun by laying down conventional vessels, the Germans were gradually introducing bolder experiments. To ensure long radius of action they depended heavily on diesel propulsion, but in 1939 some German ships had mixed power plants, using both diesel and steam.

At the outbreak of war, the German navy comprised the following units: two battleships, *Scharnhorst* and *Gneisenau*, completed; two battleships, *Bismarck* and *Tirpitz*, nearing completion; three 10,000-ton, 11-inch "pocket battleships," *Deutschland*, *Scheer*, and *Graf Spee*; three heavy cruisers, *Hipper*, *Prinz Eugen*, and *Blücher*; and six light cruisers, *Karlsruhe*, *Köln*, *Leipzig*, *Nürnberg*, *Emden*, and *Königsberg*. Twenty-six merchant ships had been converted into armed merchant cruisers. A respectable number of destroyers, torpedo boats, minesweepers, and auxiliaries completed the surface fleet. German submarine warfare, which was directed by Admiral Karl Dönitz, began operations with only 57 U-boats. Twenty-one submarines, the *Graf Spee*, and the *Deutschland* were at sea in waiting areas even before the outbreak of war.

The Germans at sea struck hard from the first. The day England entered the war, the British passenger liner *Athenia* was sunk by *U-30*, whose commander could not resist the temptation when he found her in his periscope sights. Dönitz, Raeder, and Hitler all issued denials of German responsibility—in good faith because they could not believe a U-boat commander had disobeyed their orders to spare passenger ships. In less good faith was Propaganda Minister Goebbels' declaration that Churchill had engineered the whole thing himself in the hope of involving the United States in the war.

British naval strategy was necessarily almost the converse of Germany's. The Royal Navy promptly blockaded the German North Sea coast and the exits from the Baltic by means of the Home Fleet based on Scapa Flow. Britain's most vital task however was to ensure that ships bringing more than 40 million tons of cargo a year entered British ports and discharged their cargoes. Oddly enough, pre-war British planning to attain that goal overlooked the lessons of World War I. Reviving the old misconception that convoys are less efficient in delivering goods than independently routed ships, the Admiralty planned to continue independent sailings. The sinking of the *Athenia* however changed Admiralty minds, and convoys were quickly instituted.

The first convoy sailed for Halifax on September 8. Its escort accompanied it for 300 miles, then picked up an inbound convoy and brought it safely to United Kingdom ports. This was the early pattern of convoy operations, because shortage of escorts did not permit protection far beyond the British coast. During the first two years of the war moreover, because of the activity of German surface raiders, the Admiralty considered it necessary to provide each convoy with a heavy escort, a battleship or cruiser if possible, otherwise a converted, armed passenger liner.

That the threat from German surface raiders was real was soon made apparent by the activities of the *Deutschland* and the *Graf Spee*. By the middle of October the *Deutschland* had sunk two merchant ships and committed a first class diplomatic blunder by seizing the American freighter *City of Flint*. Under a prize crew, the *City of Flint* sailed to Murmansk, in North Russia. Later, en route to Germany via Norwegian territorial waters, she was intercepted by the Norwegians and returned to her master. The incident caused much anti-German sentiment in the United States. It was also the first incident to attract Hitler's attention, militarily, to Norway. On her return to Germany, the *Deutschland* was renamed *Lützow* lest home morale suffer should a ship named *Deutschland* be lost.

## The Battle of the River Plate, December 13, 1939

The *Graf Spee* operated in the area between Pernambuco and Cape Town, although in November she slipped over into the Indian Ocean south of Madagascar for a brief period. On the way back, she met her supply ship *Altmark,* refueled, transferred prisoners, and then resumed her search for victims. The effectiveness of her cruise, completely apart from the 50,000 tons she sank, is shown in the number of Allied ships assigned to chase her. Out of Freetown, the British naval base on the western bulge of Africa, operated the carrier *Ark Royal* and the battle cruiser *Renown;* from Dakar two French heavy cruisers and the British carrier *Hermes* joined the search. The heavy cruisers *Sussex* and *Shropshire* were poised at the Cape of Good Hope, and up and down the east coast of South America ranged Commodore Sir Henry Harwood's force consisting of the two heavy cruisers *Cumberland* and *Exeter* and the light cruisers *Ajax* and H.M.N.Z.S. *Achilles.*

Commodore Harwood's group, less the *Cumberland,* which was refitting in the Falklands, on December 13 succeeded in intercepting the *Graf Spee* in the approaches to the River Plate. The contact presented Harwood a ticklish tactical problem. The *Graf Spee's* six 11-inch guns outranged the cruiser guns by about 8,000 yards. None of the cruisers could long withstand her fire. Their only opportunity would be to come in from widely diverging angles in order to force the *Graf Spee* to divide her fire. The cruisers would not be able to reply until they had passed through the danger zone from about 30,000 yards, the effective range of the *Graf Spee's* guns, to about 22,000 yards, the effective limit of the cruisers' main batteries. If the *Graf Spee* had been properly handled, she would have turned directly away from the cruisers, forcing them to a stern chase. Even with their speed advantage of about five knots, it would have taken the cruisers nearly half an hour to pass through the danger zone. Probably they would never have made it. But Captain Hans Langsdorff thought he had a cruiser and two destroyers to deal with. Since they stood between him and the open sea, he ran down to meet

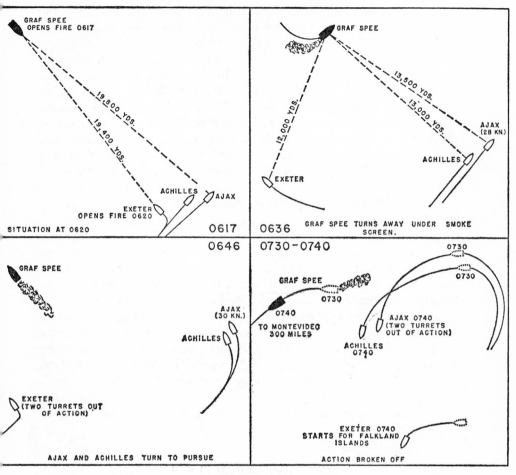

BATTLE OF THE RIVER PLATE, DECEMBER 13, 1939

them and to break his way through to freedom. The three British cruisers were in column, the *Ajax* leading and the *Exeter* in the rear. At 0617 the *Graf Spee* opened fire, whereupon the *Exeter* made a turn to port to engage from the south, while the two light cruisers held their northerly course to engage the enemy's opposite bow. On the completion of her turn, at 0620, the *Exeter* opened fire at a range of 19,400 yards. The *Ajax* and *Achilles* commenced fire a few minutes later, and the 6- and 8-inch shells from all three ships began to hit effectively. The *Graf Spee's* shells also took their toll. Soon the *Exeter* received a hit that knocked out her "B" turret, destroyed bridge communications, and killed or wounded nearly everyone on the bridge. The German then shifted fire to the two light cruisers and turned away under a smoke screen, apparently to make for the River Plate. As the *Ajax* turned in pursuit, the *Graf Spee* once more shifted fire to the *Exeter*, again under control. By 0725, both the *Exeter*'s forward turrets were out of action, and at 0730 power was lost to the after turret. Meanwhile the *Ajax* had two turrets put out of action, and Commodore Harwood decided to break off until night, when he would have a chance to make a torpedo attack. The *Exeter* started on the long voyage to the Falklands, while the wounded *Graf Spee* set her course for Montevideo, dogged by the *Ajax* and *Achilles*. Occasional exchanges of fire occurred all day, but neither side attempted to renew the battle. A little after midnight, the *Graf Spee* entered Montevideo. There Langsdorff hoped to effect repairs and force his way clear at a later date. He had chosen Montevideo on the advice of his navigator and was not aware of the political situation whereby he would have received a much more sympathetic welcome in Buenos Aires, farther up the river.

Frenzied diplomatic activities on the part of the German consular representatives were unsuccessful in getting permission for the *Graf Spee* to remain in port longer than 72 hours. British propaganda was more successful in giving the impression of a large British fleet just offshore. Actually only the *Cumberland* had joined the battered *Ajax* and *Achilles*. From Berlin Langsdorff received the option of fighting his way out or scuttling his ship. Shortage of ammunition decided him to take the latter course. Having landed wounded, prisoners, and most of his crew, he got underway on the afternoon of December 17. The British cruisers went to action stations, but before they could engage her, the *Graf Spee*'s skeleton crew abandoned her just before she blew up. Langsdorff shot himself shortly afterward. Thereafter for several months the Germans abandoned the use of surface raiders.

## Other Operations at Sea

While the *Graf Spee* was still finding victims, other units of the German navy had been active. Most striking was the penetration of Scapa Flow on the night of October 14 by the *U-47* under the command of Lieutenant Günther Prien, who was to become one of Germany's U-boat aces. Prien successfully navigated the tortuous channel and sank the battleship *Royal Oak* with the loss of 786 of her officers and men. In late November the two German battleships *Scharnhorst* and *Gneisenau* passed out into the Atlantic through the North Sea, primarily to cover the return of the *Deutschland* from her mid-Atlantic raiding, and incidentally to see what they could pick up in the way of British merchant shipping. They came upon H.M.S. *Rawalpindi*, a converted passenger liner armed with four old 6-inch guns and carried on the Admiralty List as an armed merchant cruiser. Her commander, thinking he had found the *Deutschland*, was under no illusions about the outcome of such an encounter, but he accepted the odds against him. The *Scharnhorst* opened fire and the *Rawalpindi* replied as best she could. In a few minutes, the British ship was reduced to a helpless wreck. Before she sank, the cruisers *Newcastle* and *Delhi* arrived on the scene, but only to lose contact with the Germans in the darkness and heavy rain. The British Home Fleet sortied from Scapa Flow, but the two Germans, their presence revealed and hence their usefulness lost, headed for home, slipping through the British cordon. The hopeless fight of the *Rawalpindi* had not been in vain, since the two powerful raiders were driven from the sea before they could get into the commerce areas.

## The *Altmark* Affair

The German supply ship *Altmark*, which had replenished the *Graf Spee* shortly before her final action off Montevideo, was serving as a floating prison for some 300 British seamen taken by the pocket battleship. The British were anxious to capture the *Altmark*, but she successfully hid in the South Atlantic for nearly two months. Gambling that the search had died down, she attempted to make her way back to Germany. She was favored by the weather and was not sighted until February 14, in Norwegian territorial waters. A flotilla of destroyers under Captain Philip Vian in H.M.S. *Cossack* intercepted her at Jossing Fiord but took no further action pending a directive from the Admiralty. When Vian received his instructions, he sent two destroyers with orders for a boarding party to examine the vessel. Two Norwegian gunboats met the small force and told Vian that the *Altmark* was unarmed, had been examined, and had received permission to proceed to Germany, making use of Norwegian territorial waters. Accordingly the destroyers withdrew for further instructions.

Churchill now sent orders for Vian to board the *Altmark*, using force if necessary in self-defense. While the Norwegian authorities continued their protests, the *Altmark* made the first belligerent move by getting under way and attempting to ram the *Cossack*, which evaded the clumsy attempt and then ran alongside the German ship and sent over a boarding party. After a sharp hand-to-hand fight, the German crew surrendered. Examination revealed that the British prisoners were battened down in storerooms and that the ship had two pompoms and four machine guns.

Although the British action was a violation of Norway's neutrality, Norway's position was by no means clear. The *Altmark* had not, in fact, been searched, claiming immunity by reason of the special service flag which made her a naval auxiliary. The British claimed that she was not on "innocent passage," since she was returning from war operations and had prisoners on board, and that it was up to Norway to enforce her own neutral rights. Yet Norway was in the unhappy position of not daring to enforce her rights against her two powerful belligerent neighbors. Although most of her people were sympathetic with the Allied cause, they feared Germany and her ever-present threat of action. Hence Norway made strong protests to Britain over the *Altmark* affair, hoping, no doubt, thereby to stave off German counter-action.

## The Invasion of Norway

Norwegian hopes of being allowed to remain on the sidelines of the war were vain. A glance at the map gives a partial reason; from the Norwegian coast the British naval base at Scapa Flow can be outflanked. If Germany intended to operate either U-boats or surface units in the open Atlantic, she could get them out more easily from Norwegian than from German bases. But another feature, not so readily apparent, made use of Norwegian waters even more vital to Germany. Norway's coast, extending from Egersund to North Cape, offers a 1,000-mile-long sheltered passage between the offshore islands and the mainland. This passage, known as the Leads, has served Norway as a means of communication since Viking times; it also served the Germans in the two world wars. Ignoring Norwegian neutrality, German ships could take advantage of their own air cover in traversing the Skagerrak or Kattegat, make a dash across the narrow seas between the Skaw and Kristiansand or Egersund, and then follow the Leads until they chose to make a break through to the Atlantic.

Yet the use of the Leads by warships was only a small part of the story. The principal reason for the German invasion of Norway can be given in the single word, *iron*. Annually Germany imported 15 million tons of iron ore, and of this total, nearly 75 per cent came from Scandinavia. In summer this ore was carried through the Baltic Sea from the Swedish port of Lulea to Germany, safe from the Royal Navy, which could not penetrate the Skagerrak. But the Baltic freezes in winter, and then the iron ore had to be transported overland to the Norwegian town of Narvik. Forty-one per cent of Scandinavian iron came by this route. Thus Norway was vital to Germany.

Admiral Raeder early brought the Norwegian situation to Hitler's attention, but argued that Norway's neutrality was to the advantage of Germany, provided it was respected by the British. Yet, realizing that Britain would not allow such a gaping hole in her blockade to go unplugged, Raeder ordered the naval staff, the *Seekriegsleitung* (SKL), to prepare plans for the invasion of Norway, should it be necessary. In an attempt to win his goal by peaceable means, he arranged for a meeting between Hitler and the strongly pro-German Vidkun Quisling, who he mistakenly believed could win control of the Storting, the Norwegian

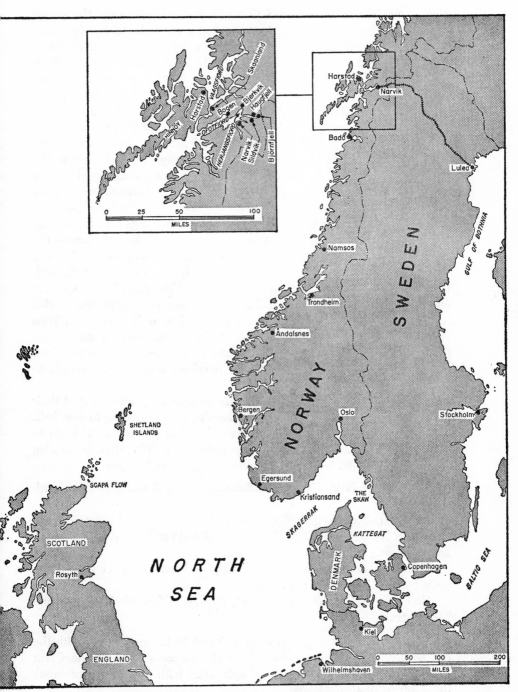

**NORWEGIAN CAMPAIGN, APRIL–JUNE 1940**

parliament. The winter proved that events would not take the course that Raeder hoped. Quisling, instead of offering help to the Germans, began to ask for aid himself. The *City of Flint* and the *Altmark* affairs indicated that the Leads were not as safe as they had seemed. Then intelligence reports reached Berlin indicating that the British were planning to mine the Leads. The Germans believed that the Norwegians would acquiesce. Hence on March 1, 1940, Hitler issued the order for Operation WESERUBUNG, the invasion of Norway and Denmark.

The operation violated every principle of naval strategy except one—surprise. The invasion force would make its way across the sea in the face of the power of the foremost navy in the world and would land at several widely separated points, some nearly a thousand miles from German bases. It would have to establish and maintain itself and fend off the inevitable British counterattack. Yet these things had to be done if Norway was to be captured. One feature gave the key to success—the geography of the area. After the initial assault, German supply lines could be maintained through the Kattegat with only a short dash through the Skagerrak from the Skaw to Oslo Fiord. In this area, close to German air bases in the north, the Royal Navy could not operate. To protect this route the Germans decided to occupy Denmark as well as Norway. Thus Raeder and the SKL estimated that if the initial landings could take place without excessive loss, then the positions could be maintained through sea transport to Oslo and by overland transport from Oslo to the various occupied positions.

The Germans committed their entire surface navy and most of their U-boats to the Norwegian operation. Raeder fully expected to lose half. Dönitz, to his intense annoyance, was ordered to provide 25 U-boats to be stationed off Norway. He had to strip the North Atlantic hunting grounds to comply. Surface ships were assigned as follows:

Group I, Narvik: *Gneisenau, Scharnhorst,* and ten destroyers with 2,000 troops.

Group II, Trondheim: *Hipper,* four destroyers, and 1,700 troops.

Group III, Bergen: *Köln, Königsberg,* the old training cruiser *Bremse,* small vessels (E-boats) and 900 troops.

Group IV, Kristiansand and Arendal: *Karlsruhe,* a depot ship, a torpedo boat flotilla, and 1,400 troops.

Group V, Oslo: *Blücher, Lützow, Emden,* a few small vessels, and 2,000 troops.

In addition, two naval groups were assigned to Denmark. One with the old battleship *Schleswig-Holstein* had the responsibility for the Great Belt area, while a smaller group of light craft with 1,000 men undertook the capture of Copenhagen.

All landings were to be carried out simultaneously in the early morning of April 9, 1940. While the German preparations were going forward, the British, in one of the major coincidences of the war, were themselves planning operations in Norway. To attempt to stop the German use of the Leads, the Admiralty planned to lay mine fields off Narvik, announcing their intention to the Norwegian government simultaneously with the act. This operation was scheduled for the night of April 6, and had it been carried out then, it might well have balked the German scheme. Anticipating that the Germans might react vigorously to the mining, even to the extent of an invasion of Norway, the British had a small expeditionary force embarked in ships to proceed with the minelaying forces. However, because of last minute difficulties, the undertaking was postponed for 48 hours, and as intelligence of German activity reached London, the Cabinet decided to disembark the troops until the situation was "clarified." Thus, when the German expedition sailed, the troops so sorely needed for prompt counteraction in Norway were in England.

The opening event of the Norwegian drama took place at sea on April 8 with a chance encounter between a German destroyer and the British destroyer *Glowworm*. Before either ship was seriously damaged, the German heavy cruiser *Hipper* from the Trondheim group appeared on the scene, Gallantly the *Glowworm* attacked the newcomer, making effective use of smoke. At length, in a sinking condition, she rammed her adversary, tearing a hole in the cruiser's side. As the *Glowworm* fell away, she blew up and sank. The Germans rescued some 40 survivors. Her captain was posthumously awarded the Victoria Cross.

The next act took place about 0330 on the morning of April 9, when the battle cruiser *Renown* encountered the *Gneisenau* and *Scharnhorst* in a brief, inconclusive engagement. To the British, the circumstances did not seem to indicate a major German assault on Norway, although the Admiralty believed that these forces might be bound for Narvik. The Norwegians also did not consider the events ominous, nor had they taken warning from the sinking of the German transport *Rio de Janeiro* by a submarine a few hours earlier off Kristiansand. When these warnings were misinterpreted, the situation passed its critical moment. The German gamble was beginning to succeed.

Denmark offered little resistance. A thousand soldiers landed in Copenhagen, and a smaller detachment on the western side of the island quickly seized key positions and communications. Before the Danes realized what was happening, they were under the Nazi heel.

In Oslo the Germans received one of their most serious setbacks. They had to traverse the 70-mile-long Oslo Fiord, where they could not expect to escape observation, even at night. Near the naval base at Horton, some 25 miles south of Oslo, the Fiord narrows to about 200 yards, and here the naval guns were alert. Promptly opening fire, the Norwegians at 0623 sank the cruiser *Blücher* with shells and torpedoes. While the

German naval attaché waited anxiously on the pier at Oslo, the German assault forces landed south of Horton and seized it from the rear. This accomplished, they pressed on. In the meantime Fornebo Airfield at Oslo had been seized by airborne troops, and the city was soon under control of the Germans. The King, however, had removed the government to Hammar, 100 miles to the north.

At most other points the landings were unopposed or met little serious resistance, except that the guns at Bergen heavily damaged and immobilized light cruiser *Königsberg*, allowing British naval aircraft to sink her the next day. At Narvik, far to the north, the German invasion force was opposed only by the Norwegian coastal defense ships *Eidsvold* and *Norge*, which were sunk after a gallant but futile resistance. Then the ten destroyers proceeded up the Fiord to land their troops, while the two battleships carried out their mission of general support.

It seemed that Operation WESERUBUNG had succeeded beyond the most optimistic expectations of its planners. The losses had been very light and all objectives were in German hands by the end of April 9. It was now up to the Army to exploit the opportunities won for them by the Navy. The Navy still had the tasks of getting its warships out of Norwegian waters and of maintaining the supply lines to Norway.

The first counterattack came at Narvik. The British Admiralty, recognizing the supreme importance of this port, prepared to act as swiftly as possible. Believing that only one destroyer had entered Narvik, they ordered Captain B. A. W. Warburton-Lee, commanding a destroyer flotilla: "Proceed to Narvik and sink or capture enemy ship. It is at your discretion to land forces, if you think you can recapture Narvik from the number of enemy present." Later, learning that the Germans were stronger than had been anticipated, they gave Warburton-Lee the option of canceling the operation if he believed German defenses made it impracticable. His reply was characteristic of the traditions of the Royal Navy: "Going into action."

Accompanied by the destroyers *Hunter, Havock, Hotspur,* and *Hostile,* Captain Warburton-Lee in the *Hardy* entered Ofot Fiord before dawn. In the approach phase, the *Hotspur* and *Hostile* engaged the shore batteries while the other three ships pressed into the port. There they found not one, but five German destroyers and several merchant ships. In the first attack, the *Hardy* torpedoed German destroyer *Wilhelm Heidkamp,* killing the German commodore. Another German destroyer was sunk by gunfire and a third was beached. Recovering from their surprise, the Germans opened fire and straddled but failed to hit the *Havock.* The British ships then retired under a smoke screen. Shortly they returned for a second attack, augmented by the *Hostile* and *Hotspur,* the latter sinking two merchant ships. The British pressed home a third attack, but this time the fortunes changed. Warburton-Lee discovered three fresh

German destroyers coming down on him from Herjangs Fiord. At a range of 10,000 yards he opened fire and turned away. The British ships then commenced a retirement, keeping up a running fire, but ran into an ambush at Ballangen Fiord, where two more destroyers were awaiting them. The *Georg Thiel* engaged the *Hardy*, which shortly afterward took a hit on the bridge that killed Warburton-Lee. The *Hardy* sank a few minutes later. Making a swing to the left, the *Georg Thiel* launched a spread of torpedoes at the *Hunter*, which also sank. The *Hotspur* and *Hostile* were both damaged, but, together with the *Havock*, made their way to the open sea. The damage the Germans had sustained made them helpless to follow or to carry out their planned retirement to Germany. On the way out, the three surviving British destroyers encountered German ammunition ship *Rauenfels*. After a few salvos from their guns, the German blew up in a tremendous explosion.

A few days later, on April 13, a heavy British naval force including battleship *Warspite* and carrier *Furious* finished off the work begun by Warburton-Lee, sinking all eight destroyers that had survived his attack. The lesson of these two battles was plain. Warburton-Lee, much outnumbered, had accepted action in an area where the speed and maneuverability of his ships were restricted and in an area that afforded many chances for ambush. Effecting tactical surprise on his arrival, he did considerable damage, but was surprised himself by being caught between two forces, one of which blocked his way to the open sea. In the second battle, the British properly used overwhelming force to ensure completion of the job.

In general, British reaction to the German operations in Norway was marked by indecision and improvisation. Keenly conscious that the Germans had flouted Britain's sea power, the British eagerly sought a way to hit back at the invaders. The situation called for rapid, decisive countermeasures, for the German forces were the most vulnerable immediately following the landings. Until road and rail communications were opened from Oslo to the several points of German occupation, troops had to live on the materials already provided them. The sea could not serve for supply in face of an alerted British Home Fleet. While the Germans worked feverishly to build internal communications in Norway, the British Cabinet lost critical days in trying to decide where to counterattack. With most of their troops already committed to the French front, there were very few available for operations in Norway, although the French were willing to supplement the British contingent with a brigade of Chasseurs Alpins and two brigades of the Foreign Legion. Where the Allied troops could best be placed was the big strategic problem facing the Cabinet. Two main possibilities offered themselves, Narvik and Trondheim. As has already been noted, Narvik was of supreme importance, since it controlled the export of iron ore from

Norway and Sweden. Also, in view of the success already won there by the naval forces, Narvik appealed to several key officials, including Churchill. On the other hand, Trondheim had its adherents because here Norway narrows to only a few miles and all land communications to the north can be controlled from that city. The Cabinet started to follow up the naval successes in the Narvik area, but when this operation was barely under way, the government shifted the point of the main attack to the Trondheim area.

## Narvik

The first detachment of troops sailed for Narvik on April 12, 1940, with troops under the command of Major General Mackesy, while the naval forces in support were under Admiral of the Fleet Lord Cork and Orrery. General Mackesy's instructions contained the following points:

> It is clearly illegal to bombard a populated area in the hope of hitting a legitimate target which is known to be in the area, but which cannot be precisely located and identified.

● ● ●

> The object of the force will be to eject the Germans from the Narvik area and establish control of Narvik itself. . . . Your initial task will be to establish your force at Harstad, ensure the cooperation of Norwegian forces that may be there, and obtain the information necessary to enable you to plan further operations. It is not intended that you should land in the face of opposition. . . . The decision whether to land or not will be taken by the senior naval officer in consultation with you. If landing is impossible at Harstad, some other suitable locality should be tried. A landing must be carried out when you have sufficient troops.

The cautious tone of these instructions seems to have impressed itself so deeply upon General Mackesy's mind that he took little account of a more aggressive suggestion in a personal letter from General Ironside, Chief of the Imperial General Staff: "You may have a chance of taking advantage of naval action and should do so if you can. Boldness is required."

The manner in which the Narvik attack was planned clearly reveals British unpreparedness for conducting amphibious operations. Mackesy's instructions emphasized caution, when boldness was needed. Mackesy and Cork were made equal commanders, with no clear-cut definition of their individual or joint responsibilities. Most curious of all was the choice of Harstad for the initial landing. Forces at Harstad could not interdict German supplies to Narvik, the main objective, and to attack Narvik from Harstad would require further amphibious operations.

While the expedition was en route to Harstad, Cork received a dispatch from the Commander in Chief of the Home Fleet suggesting that, in view of the success of the attack by the *Warspite* and *Furious,* a direct assault on Narvik could be carried out. Cork urged Mackesy to make the attempt, but the General refused, pointing to his instructions with regard to bombing civilian areas. Further pressed, Mackesy insisted that the German defenses at Narvik were too strong to be forced by means of naval bombardment. Finally, he admitted that his transports were not combat loaded. In the face of Mackesy's opposition and unpreparedness, Cork had no alternative but to proceed with the original plan.

Next came a dispatch from the Cabinet urging the bolder course on Mackesy:

> Your proposals involve damaging deadlock at Narvik and the neutralisation of one of our best brigades. We cannot send you the Chasseurs Alpins. The *Warspite* will be needed elsewhere in two or three days. Full consideration should, therefore, be given by you to an assault upon Narvik covered by the *Warspite* and the destroyers, which might also operate at Rombaks Fiord. The capture of the port and town would be an important success. We should like to receive from you the reasons why this is not possible, and your estimate of the degree of resistance to be expected on the waterfront. Matter most urgent.

Mackesy remained adamant, and the landing at Harstad proceeded. Once ashore, he announced that he was unable to advance on Narvik until the snow melted and until he had built up his supplies. Thus while the Germans strengthened Narvik, British troops at Harstad suffered attrition from the cold and from *Luftwaffe* attacks that seriously imperiled attempts at supply and reinforcement.

## Trondheim

Meanwhile the British cabinet had turned its attention to Trondheim. The plan called for a main assault at Trondheim itself, with subsidiary landings at Namsos, a hundred miles to the north, and at Åndalsnes, a hundred miles to the south. The landing at Namsos took place under heavy German air attack on April 15, and that at Åndalsnes three days later. The main landing at Trondheim was to follow April 22. But on the 18th, the Chiefs of Staff began to have reservations about the Trondheim landing, emphasizing the tremendous risks of the long approach up the Fiord. They recommended instead that the landings at Namsos and Åndalsnes be developed into main drives, to capture Trondheim overland by a double envelopment. At length this view prevailed, in spite of the opposition of Churchill and of Admiral of the Fleet Sir Roger Keyes, who offered to take some older ships into Trondheim himself. The counsel of caution once more carried the day.

## The Allied Evacuation From Norway

It soon became evident that the Allies could not maintain their beach-heads at Namsos and Åndalsnes in the face of growing German air power operating from captured Norwegian airfields. British and French cruisers and destroyers could bring in supplies and reinforcements by night, but during the day the *Luftwaffe* ruled the air, bombing the Allied bases into rubble and interdicting Allied communications. British carriers attempted to provide fighter support, but there were not enough carriers to operate aircraft continuously and not enough fighters to provide simultaneous protection for the carriers, other naval forces in the area, and the troops ashore. An attempt by a squadron of fighters from H.M.S. *Glorious* to operate from a frozen lake while the carrier pulled out of German bomber range resulted in the prompt destruction of the fighters. The Allies had no alternative to evacuating their forces in late April and early May, leaving the Germans in possession of all of southern and central Norway.

There remained however the British toehold at Harstad, in the north. On April 20, the Cabinet, exasperated by General Mackesy's repeated delays, appointed Lord Cork to over-all command of the operations against Narvik. Finally, in mid-May, the British made their assault, not directly against Narvik, but against Bjerkvik, to the north, with the intention of building up a force there and then attacking Narvik across Rombaks Fiord. The Bjerkvik operation, supported by planes from the *Ark Royal*, was a complete success. By now airfields had been prepared ashore for use by the R.A.F., and carriers *Glorious* and *Furious* ferried in enough fighters to offset the growing German air power in the area through the next stage in the campaign.

By this time however Germany had invaded the Low Countries and France, and total Allied defeat was imminent on the Western Front. Accordingly fresh instructions went to British forces in the Narvik area: capture the city, destroy the installations, and prepare for evacuation. Narvik fell to the British on May 28, following a successful crossing of Rombaks Fiord the preceding day. The evacuation took place soon afterward, being completed by June 8, in three convoys transporting 24,000 men and quantities of equipment and supplies.

To oppose this evacuation Raeder sent the *Scharnhorst* and the *Gneisenau* to the northern area. Known as Operation JUNO, this sweep had the further purpose of covering the movement of other elements of the German fleet to Trondheim. With the British Home Fleet committed to support of the Narvik evacuation, the German ships reached Trondheim safely. The *Scharnhorst* and *Gneisenau* surprised and sank the *Glorious* before she had a chance to get her planes into the air, together with her two escorting destroyers, which made gallant efforts to save their charge. In addition the Germans sank two merchant ships and an antisubmarine trawler. The remainder of the Allied Expeditionary Force reached England safely.

Thus ended the Norwegian campaign. Brilliantly conceived and executed by the Germans, it showed what could be accomplished by a ruthless nation, willing to take any advantage of friendship and neutrality. Germany's use of the sea routes across areas theoretically commanded by British sea power showed what an inferior naval force can accomplish through surprise. Once the Germans had made good their beachheads they no longer had to rely on surprise, for they could supply and reinforce their forces via the Kattegat, immune to Allied attack, and then overland in Norway.

The British operations in Norway had to be undertaken, if only for political reasons, but they cost Britain more prestige than they gained. The Belgians, the French, and, later, the Greeks remembered Norway when their own days of crisis arrived.

## The Fall of France

The disastrous Allied expedition into Norway brought about the fall of the British government. On May 10, 1940, the day that Hitler struck at the Low Countries, Neville Chamberlain yielded the office of Prime Minister to Winston Churchill, who set out to form a National Government with ministers representing all parties, in contrast to the Conservative Government of his predecessor. Under Churchill's leadership the war was pursued with vigor and courage through the darkest hours, when Britain stood alone.

Neither Holland nor Belgium was able to make a significant resistance to the *Blitzkrieg* of the Nazi forces pouring across the Rhine. Hitler, finally abandoning all hopes of a compromise peace with the West, had hurled his armies through the Low Countries, as the Kaiser had done a quarter of a century before. The Allies were forced back at point after point, overwhelmed as the Poles had been by a combination of air power and panzer (armored) divisions. Although the French and British air forces occasionally achieved local superiority, they were never able to stop the onrushing Germans. Despite French protests, the British retained 25 air squadrons for home defense, refusing to commit everything to what was rapidly becoming a lost cause.

By again advancing through Belgium, as in World War I, the Germans simply passed around the left flank of the Maginot Line. Then the panzer divisions, followed up by motorized infantry, drove westward from Sedan to the English Channel, trapping the British Expeditionary Force in Belgium and Northern France. As early as May 20, the Admiralty, recognizing that a supreme effort was now needed to save the army, began to organize shipping for an evacuation from Dunkirk, on the French coast near the Belgian border. British private boat owners spontaneously aided naval efforts, volunteering themselves and their craft for service. The Lords of Admiralty accepted these gladly, but there was hard naval planning as well. They hoped to rescue about 45,000 men in two days.

Hitler, believing that the *Luftwaffe* would render escape impossible, ordered his panzer forces to stop short of Dunkirk—partly in fear that he was over-extended and partly to give Air Marshal Hermann Goering's planes the glory of wiping out the would-be evacuees. Goering intended to paralyze the troops on the beach by repeated bombing and to sink the rescue ships as fast as they appeared. He reckoned however without three factors. First, bombing of the troops was ineffective, the soft sand absorbing much of the force of the explosions. Second, the Royal Air Force was fully committed to protecting the Dunkirk beachhead; even the British Metropolitan Air Force, the last reserve that had been withheld from the defense of France, entered the battle. Third, the presence of evacuation ships and craft in such large numbers provided simply too many targets. Pleasure boats, fishing craft, destroyers, minesweepers, trawlers—ships and boats of all types—shuttled from Dunkirk beach to English ports and then back to reload. When the operation was completed, 338,226 men had been safely delivered to England by 861 vessels, with a total loss of 243 vessels sunk and many damaged. Less spectacularly, nearly half a million British and French, soldiers and civilians, were lifted from other French ports during the last hours of France's freedom.

On June 11, in order to participate in the German victory, Italy declared war on France and Britain, and Italian troops crossed the French border. Paris fell to the Germans on June 14, and the next day Premier Paul Reynaud requested the British government to release France from her pledge not to make separate terms with Germany. The British agreed on the condition that the French fleet would not fall into the hands of the common enemy. Determined to fight on, Britain urged France to continue the battle from her colonies in North Africa and from overseas. Churchill even went the length of offering France union with England, the two people to share common citizenship. The French Assembly rejected this appeal and could see no way to comply with Britain's requests for continuation of the war. Churchill and Reynaud advised General Weygand to surrender in the field, as this would not tie the hands of the French government. Weygand refused. He would not surrender, said he, unless an armistice were negotiated by the national government. Such a national armistice would of course be binding on all French armed forces, not simply on the army as Churchill and Reynaud desired. For the French navy to continue the war from overseas would be a violation of the armistice terms, and Germany would be able to undertake whatever measures she saw fit in retaliation. Weygand of course was imposing his desires on the political level, but Premier Reynaud did not relieve him. Reynaud was in fact in no position to take any action, for the next day, June 16, he was forced to resign, being succeeded by Marshal Philippe Pétain, who immediately appealed for an armistice. The Germans put the capstone on French humiliation by conducting the armistice proceedings in the same railroad car that had been used for the German Armistice in 1918. France was divided into two zones: occupied France, the Atlantic front and all of the northern part including Paris; and unoccupied France, with a government under Pétain but dominated by the Nazi sympathizer Pierre Laval and his associates.

Meanwhile Admiral François Darlan, Commander in Chief of the French navy, who had pledged his word of honor that the French fleet would not fall intact into the hands of the Germans, sent all ships the following message in code:

> I refer to the clauses of the armistice now being telegraphed in plain language by other channels. I am taking advantage of the last coded messages I can send in order to make known my views on this matter.
>
> First—The demobilized warships are to stay French, under the French flag, with reduced French crews, remaining in French metropolitan or colonial ports.
>
> Second—Secret preparations for auto-sabotage are to be made in order that an enemy or foreigner seizing a vessel by force shall not be able to make use of it.
>
> Third—Should the Armistice Commission charged with interpreting the text come to a decision different from that in paragraph one, warships are without further orders to be dispatched to the United States or, alternatively, scuttled, provided that no other action is possible to preserve them from the enemy. Under no circumstances are they to fall into enemy hands intact.
>
> Fourth—Ships that seek refuge abroad are not to be used in operations against Germany or Italy without prior orders from the Commander in Chief.

The armistice terms as finally announced provided that French ships were to be assembled in ports to be specified, either in France or in French colonies under German or Italian control. Germany solemnly declared it her intention not to make use of the French ships herself or to claim them at the conclusion of peace. On the other hand, the armistice provided that French Atlantic bases must be placed completely at the disposal of the Germans for U-boat operations. Italian terms were almost identical with the German. The armistice with both Germany and Italy became effective at 0035 on June 25, 1940.

Despite French assurances and despite their knowledge of the general provisions concerning the French fleet, the British felt far from satisfied that the French navy would in fact be kept from Axis hands. Some French ships were already in British ports—two battleships, four light cruisers, a few submarines, eight destroyers, and about 200 mine-sweepers and antisubmarine vessels. But a large number of vessels were in French national or colonial ports, where the Germans might gain control of them.

The situation confronted the British with a dilemma. Hourly expect-ing invasion, hard put to fulfill existing naval commitments, they were in no shape to cope with a fleet the size of that remaining to France. Having no knowledge of Darlan's orders of June 24, the British felt that they could not stake their national security on the word of their enemies. Noting that the ships would be under Axis control and that the armistice could be voided at any time by Germany on grounds of "noncompliance," the British War Cabinet reluctantly decided to take whatever measures were necessary to see that the French fleet did not fall into Axis hands, accepting the risk that their action might bring France into the war against them. On July 3, 1940, all French ships at Plymouth and Portsmouth were seized. Some of the French sailors volunteered to man their former vessels and serve under the Free French flag, taking as their commander General Charles de Gaulle, who had established himself as head of the Free French Government in Exile in opposition to the German-dominated Vichy government of Marshal Pétain.

The resolution of the problem of the French fleet in the Mediter-ranean brought tragedy, as will be recounted in the next chapter. To immobilize the French battleship *Richelieu* at Dakar, on the western bulge of Africa, the British carrier *Hermes* approached and sent in six torpedo-bombers which attacked the battleship, doing enough damage to keep her off the seas for a year. Two French cruisers and a carrier in the West Indies were neutralized through the diplomatic efforts of Presi-dent Roosevelt. Thus, while attaining only partial success, the British were able to preserve their tenuous command of the sea, but at a cost of embittering their former French allies. This unfortunate by-product of their operations was to exact its toll at the time of Operation TORCH, the invasion of North Africa in late 1942.

## German Plans for the Invasion of England: Operation Sea Lion

Jubilant over his swift conquest of France and confident that Britain would capitulate in a few weeks, Hitler at first paid scant attention to any idea of invading England. In this belief he was encouraged by *Luftwaffe* commander Hermann Goering. Admiral Raeder however feared the situation was such that Hitler might suddenly order a cross-

Channel attack. Raeder regarded Britain as the chief foe, but had little confidence in the success of an invasion, since he felt that he had inadequate time and resources to stage it. Although his exploratory soundings got no response, Raeder went ahead with preliminary planning in order not to be caught off guard when it became obvious even to Hitler and Goering that Britain had no intention of surrendering. Raeder understood the difficulties far better than the army commanders, who commenced to show an interest in invading England, for they had millions of victorious troops on hand and no place to go with them. They eyed the English Channel and thought that crossing it would present no more problems than crossing a very wide river. Encouraged by the army, Hitler on July 16, 1940, issued a directive for the invasion of England, Operation SEA LION.

This directive, drawn up by the army, showed little grasp of the naval problems involved. It ordered that the landing be made on a broad front extending from Ramsgate to a point near the Isle of Wight, a front of approximately 200 miles, and that it be ready to jump off by August 13. Patiently Raeder explained that landing on such a scale would require many harbors for preparation of the invasion fleet, that the French ones were too damaged for use, that the concentration of shipping in these harbors would infallibly reveal the plan to the British, and that in any

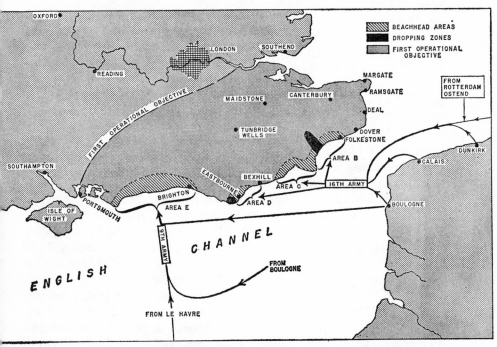

GERMAN PLANS FOR INVADING ENGLAND, SUMMER 1940

event Germany did not have anything like the number of ships the operation would require. Raeder emphasized that the assault must be on a narrow front where there could be a reasonable hope of maintaining a supply line across the Channel. From his point of view the only possible landing sites lay between Dover and Beachy Head. On hearing this proposal, the Chief of the Army General Staff retorted, "I might just as well put the troops that have landed straight through a sausage machine." The Naval Chief of Staff replied that he wanted to put the troops ashore and not at the bottom of the sea.

Hitler finally had to intervene personally to resolve the conflict. The plan, as finally worked out, was for landings in four main areas: Folkstone-Dungeness, Dungeness-Cliff's End, Bexhill-Beachy Head, and Brighton-Selsey Bill. This compromise pleased no one, but both the army and the navy proceeded to draw up their plans in accordance with it.

In the meantime, everything depended on the *Luftwaffe*. All agreed that command of the air was an absolute prerequisite to an invasion attempt. The *Luftwaffe* unleashed heavy attacks against air installations in the south of England and other points to gain superiority over the R.A.F. The air effort was also intended to force Britain to sue for peace. The hope of sweeping the R.A.F. from the skies was vain. The British refusal to commit the 25 home defense squadrons to the Battle of France now paid off in the air "Battle of Britain." The British pilots shot down nearly two planes to each loss of their own. During the early critical period of the air war, the month of August 1940, the *Luftwaffe* was never able to whittle the R.A.F. strength down to an acceptable level for risking Operation SEA LION.

The day of decision for SEA LION was September 14, 1940. At a meeting of the Grand Council, after hearing reports from his commanders in chief, Hitler decided against giving the order to launch the invasion, scheduled for September 28. This decision meant that there was little prospect that SEA LION could be staged that year, since suitable tide and moon conditions could not be expected until October 24. Then bad weather could be expected to interfere.

On October 12, 1940 Hitler postponed the cross-Channel attack indefinitely, but continued preparations for invasion in order to maintain pressure on the British. On December 18 he, in effect, canceled Operation SEA LION altogether by issuing an alert for Operation BARBAROSSA: "The *Wehrmacht* must be prepared, even before the end of the war against England, to overthrow Russia in a quick campaign."

Before Hitler could launch his attack on the Soviet Union, he was obliged to divert forces to North Africa and to Greece. He planned the campaign against Russia in order to remove a potential enemy and to capture a new source of materials and manpower. He moved forces to the Mediterranean theater in order to rescue defeated Italian troops and to shore up the Axis position there. But he also saw both operations as means toward ultimately bringing Britain to terms. In this context, his attack on Russia was intended to eliminate a possible British ally. His North African campaign grew into a drive against the Suez Canal via Egypt, to be followed by a drive against India via Iran. As Hitler thus strategically faced east, an undefeated and defiant Britain behind his back obliged him to retain 49 divisions in western Europe to guard the Atlantic Coast. This overextending of her military strength was at length to prove fatal to Germany.

The point especially to be noted is that Hitler was attempting *simultaneously* to duplicate Napoleon's campaigns of 1798 and 1812, and for much of the same reasons. Both of Napoleon's campaigns had ultimately ended in failure. An additional factor in the strategic picture of 1941 was that Great Britain could look to the United States for support. Hitler's armies marched into Russia on June 21. The United States immediately extended Lend-Lease aid to the Soviet Union. Six months later, as the Russian winter stalled the German drive, the United States was in the war on the side of Britain and Russia. What Churchill called "the Grand Alliance" was complete.

We must now backtrack to consider the continuing war at sea and on the Atlantic front.

## Dakar

Repulsed from the Continent, Britain reverted to her traditional peripheral strategy, using her sea-conferred mobility to probe for soft spots. Despite the immobilization of the battleship *Richelieu*, the British Cabinet remained uneasy with Dakar in the hands of the Vichy French government. For Dakar, on the westernmost point of Africa, commands the narrows of the Atlantic. Should it be taken over by the Germans for use as a base for submarines and surface raiders, Dakar could pose a real threat to British commerce and to British military transport around Africa to Egypt. Accordingly the Cabinet ordered an offensive operation to "liberate" Dakar into the hands of the Free French. The landing, which presumably would not be seriously resisted, was to be carried out by 4,200 British and 2,700 Free French troops, the latter under the direct command of General de Gaulle. The landing operation was to be supported by a naval force of two battleships, a carrier, and several cruisers and destroyers under Vice Admiral J. H. D. Cunningham. Transports and support in early September 1940 proceeded toward the British port of Freetown, southeast of Dakar, which was to be the advanced base of operations.

Through coincidence and mismanagement the Dakar operation came to naught. The coincidence was that just at this time a Vichy force of three cruisers and three destroyers set out from Toulon for Libreville, French Equatorial Africa. Through diplomatic sources the British Admiralty learned of this departure, and a British destroyer sighted and briefly shadowed the Vichy force in the Straits of Gibraltar. Yet nothing immediately was done to prevent the arrival of these reinforcements in the vicinity of Dakar. The significance of the movement was not immediately perceived at the Admiralty. Admiral Sir James Somerville, commanding naval Force H, and Sir Dudley North, Commander North Atlantic Station, both at Gibraltar, each assumed that the other had orders from the Admiralty to intercept the Vichy ships. When at last the Admiralty awakened to the situation, the ships were far down the African coast. Cunningham, belatedly alerted, succeeded only in chasing two of the cruisers into the port of Dakar, where they added to the defense force, though Dakar had not been their destination.

On September 23, 1940, Cunningham at last stood off Dakar. Instead of finding a ready welcome for de Gaulle and his troops, he was met by determined resistance. A landing attempt was repulsed. British bombardment of the harbor on the 24th and 25th achieved little. On the contrary, the immobilized *Richelieu* and the two Vichy cruisers, firing through a smoke screen laid by a destroyer, made most of the hits. On the 25th, the British battleship *Resolution,* already battered by four shells, was heavily damaged by a torpedo fired from a Vichy submarine. On receiving news of this, the Admiralty ordered the action broken off. The operation seemed to the world to be a prime example of confusion, delay, and muddle.

Although the Dakar attack failed, the flexibility of the War Cabinet enabled Britain to retrieve something from the operation. By landing de Gaulle and his Free French forces at Douala in Cameroons, the British barred the Vichy French from a proposed penetration into French Equatorial Africa—thus removing a threat to Freetown and providing the British with an important air base in Central Africa.

### German Surface Raiders in 1940

The pocket battleship *Scheer* made her debut into Atlantic waters in October 1940, followed a month later by the heavy cruiser *Hipper.* Both cruised the North Atlantic in an effort to break up the convoys from Halifax to the British Isles.

On November 5 the *Scheer* encountered the independently-routed British merchantman *Mopan,* which she sank after taking off the crew. As the *Mopan* was going down, the masts of Convoy HX-84, consisting of 37 ships, loomed over the horizon. The requirements of the Mediterranean theater at that time were such that Convoy HX-84 was being escorted by only one vessel, the armed merchant cruiser *Jervis Bay.*

Here was a situation made to order for the *Scheer.* With her speed and firepower she was apparently in a position to sink the greater part of the convoy. Two things balked her: the lateness of the hour and the fight put up by the *Jervis Bay*. While the convoy scattered, making smoke, the escort radioed an alarm and closed the pocket battleship at top speed. The 6-inch guns of the *Jervis Bay* were of course no match for the 11-inch guns of her opponent, but the hour it took the *Scheer* to finish her off saved most of the convoy. The pocket battleship was able to overtake and sink only five of the 37 vessels before nightfall ended the chase. After dark the *Scheer* fled the area to elude the British forces which the Germans knew would be converging from all directions in response to the *Jervis Bay*'s radio warning. Evidently ships in convoy, even when poorly escorted, were safer than ships sailing out of convoy. The *Scheer* steamed rapidly south, refueled from a supply ship, made a brief appearance in the West Indies, and then disappeared into the South Atlantic and Indian Oceans, returning to Kiel in April 1941, having sunk 16 ships totaling 99,000 tons.

The *Hipper* achieved little. She attacked a convoy near the Azores, only to find it escorted by four British cruisers. After a brief action, the *Hipper* managed to shake off pursuit and make her way back home.

### The *Bismarck* Breaks Out

In the spring of 1941, the *Hipper, Scharnhorst,* and *Gneisenau* again made brief sweeps into the Atlantic, sinking more than 20,000 tons in two months of operation. The *Hipper* returned to Germany, but in late March the two battleships were at Brest, a strategically located port from which to launch further raiding operations.

Admiral Raeder had now conceived the most ambitious raider operation of the Atlantic war. In the Baltic lay the great battleship *Bismarck,* newly completed, and the heavy cruiser *Prinz Eugen.* Raeder planned to send these vessels out into the Atlantic, where they would be joined by the *Scharnhorst* and *Gneisenau.* The powerful squadron thus formed, supplemented with a stepped-up U-boat campaign, could be counted on to paralyze British shipping. In preparation for this operation, supply ships and tankers were dispatched ahead to prearranged rendezvous areas far from shipping areas, and German merchantmen disguised as neutrals combed the convoy routes in search of information.

But damage suffered by the *Scharnhorst* on her last cruise could not be repaired in time, and in April the *Gneisenau* was put out of action by a torpedo from a British aircraft. Yet, not to delay the operation, for which extensive preparations had been made, Raeder ordered the *Bismarck* and the *Prinz Eugen* to Bergen, Norway. Here they were to await thick weather and then break out into the Atlantic, the long way around north of Iceland. The *Scharnhorst* was to join them as soon as her damages were repaired.

The *Bismarck* and the *Prinz Eugen,* while passing through the Kattegat, were sighted by a Swedish cruiser. Sweden passed the word to England, and British reconnaissance aircraft got a look at the two raiders as they neared Bergen. The British Admiralty correctly estimated the German intention and made plans to forestall it. Eleven convoys, including one troop convoy, were in the Atlantic or about to sail. A concentration of German naval strength against them would have been calamitous.

The Admiralty was particularly concerned about the *Bismarck*. In the spring of 1941 she was the most powerful battleship in commission. Mounting eight 15-inch guns in her main battery, she had a secondary battery of twelve 5.9's and an antiaircraft battery of sixteen 4.1's. Her armor was the most advanced on any capital ship, amounting to 16,000 tons dead weight. She had skillfully designed compartmentation to prevent flooding. All the available resources of the Royal Navy were required to track her down and sink her.

The weather closed down on the Norwegian coast as the *Bismarck* and the *Prinz Eugen* reached Bergen. On May 22 a British aircraft in a daring reconnaissance ascertained that the raiders had departed. Admiral Sir John Tovey, Commander in Chief of the British Home Fleet, who was anxiously awaiting news of their movements, immediately took steps to intercept. The Admiralty placed at his disposal all the heavy ships that could be spared. Tovey had with him at Scapa Flow the battleships *King George V*, flagship, and *Prince of Wales* and the battle cruiser *Hood* in addition to destroyers and cruisers. In England were the carrier *Victorious*, which had not yet had her working-up cruise, and the battle cruiser *Repulse*. At Gibraltar, under the command of Admiral Sir James Somerville, were the battle cruiser *Renown* and the carrier *Ark Royal*. The battleships *Rodney* and *Ramillies* were on duty escorting convoys in the Atlantic, and the battleship *Revenge* was at Halifax. All these ships played some part in tracking down and sinking the *Bismarck*.

In order to keep the various routes available to the *Bismarck* under observation and to have a force capable of striking at any of them, Tovey had to divide his force to cover all possible contingencies. Bad weather hampered his efforts. Because he had to keep the least likely passages under the lightest observation, he covered the passage between the Orkneys and the Faroes only by air search. He stationed a cruiser force in the passage between the Faroes and Iceland and headed thither himself in the *King George V* with the *Victorious* and *Repulse*. The heavy cruisers *Suffolk* and *Norfolk* patrolled the Denmark Strait, between Iceland and Greenland, supported by the *Prince of Wales* and *Hood*, en route at high speed from Scapa Flow, under the command of Vice Admiral L. E. Holland in the *Hood*.

First contact with the raiders was made in the early evening of May 23 in the Denmark Strait by the *Norfolk* and *Suffolk* under the command of Rear Admiral Wake-Walker. The *Suffolk*, which made the sighting,

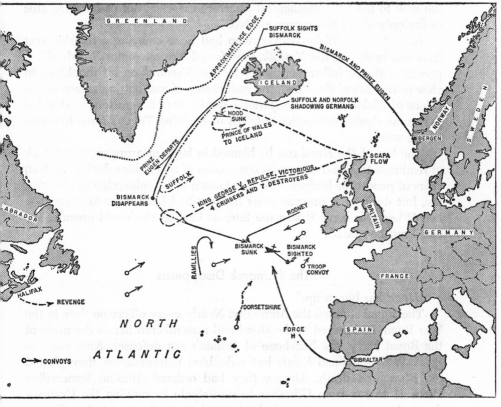

## THE CHASE OF THE BISMARCK

immediately took refuge in a fog bank and began tracking the Germans by radar. All night the two cruisers hung on to the German warships, broadcasting information that would enable the big ships to bring them into action.

On board the battle cruiser *Hood*, Admiral Holland calculated his intercept course and prepared for action at any time after 0140, May 24. Contact was not made until 0535, whereupon the *Hood* and the new battleship *Prince of Wales* advanced into action. Admiral Holland, maneuvering both his ships together, ordered a head-on approach which denied him the use of their after guns. The Germans opened fire, concentrating on the *Hood*. To confuse their aim and to bring his after turrets to bear, Holland ordered a 20-degree turn to port, but scarcely had the ships begun to swing in response to the signal when the *Hood* disintegrated, hit in the magazine by a shell from the *Bismarck*. The *Prince of Wales* had to swing hard a-starboard to avoid the floating wreckage of the *Hood*. The situation had dramatically reversed. Tactical superiority had passed to the Germans. To make matters worse, the *Prince of Wales*, too new to have the mechanical difficulties worked out of her, was able to fire only about three guns a salvo.

Rear Admiral Wake-Walker, who had been enjoying a ringside seat from the bridge of the *Norfolk*, now found himself senior British officer present with the full responsibility for the *Bismarck* on his shoulders. In view of the loss of the *Hood*, the inefficiency of and battle damage to the *Prince of Wales*, and the comparative weakness of his cruisers, he decided to resume shadowing tactics in hopes of enabling Tovey's force to arrive on the scene.

The loss of the *Hood* can be blamed in large measure on British lack of readiness to spend money on conversion of older ships during the lean years of peacetime budgets. She was known to be vulnerable to plunging fire, but during the pre-war years nothing had been done to strengthen her. When war came it was too late; as long as she could operate, she could not be spared.

## The *Bismarck* Disappears

"*Hood* has blown up."

The signal stunned the Admiralty. Nearly every officer on duty in the War Room had served in the *Hood* and remembered her as the pride of the Royal Navy, the backbone of Britain's sea defenses. Now she was gone. With saddened hearts but redoubled determination they plotted the *Bismarck*'s death. Already they had ordered Admiral Somerville's Force H to sea from Gibraltar to participate in running the Germans down. Now they summoned the battleships *Rodney* and *Ramillies* to break off from convoys and join in the chase. The battleship *Revenge* raised steam and proceeded with all possible speed from Halifax.

After being dogged all day by the *Norfolk*, *Suffolk*, and *Prince of Wales*, the *Bismarck* suddenly turned on the *Suffolk*, which opened range rapidly. This move was made to cover the departure of the *Prinz Eugen*, which escaped to the south and entered Brest ten days later. Once again the game of shadowing went on. Since the ships were by this time entering known U-boat waters, all British vessels were zigzagging. On the outward leg of one of these zigzags, the *Suffolk* lost radar contact and failed to regain it. Once more the *Bismarck* was loose. Three courses of action seemed to be open to her. She was known to be trailing oil from the encounter with the *Hood* and *Prince of Wales*. She might be in need of repairs. If so, she would head for Germany or for one of two French ports, Brest or St. Nazaire. Alternately, she might be heading for a rendezvous with a supply ship and then on to operations in whatever quarter of the globe she chose. When radio-direction-finder signals led Tovey to believe that she was heading for the North Sea and Germany, he steamed north for several hours to attempt an interception. Both he and the Admiralty had begun to have misgivings about this course of action, when a recomputation of the direction-finder bearings aboard the *King George V* revealed a strong probability that the *Bismarck* was heading for a French port. A new dispatch from the Admiralty plotted the German battleship as being within a 50-mile radius of the position lat. 55° 15′ N, long. 32° 00′ W, about 600 miles southeast of Cape Farewell on the southern tip of Greenland. Tovey accordingly turned to attempt to intercept the *Bismarck's* probable course toward Brest, but his cruisers and the carrier *Victorious* held for home, being too short of fuel to continue. Tovey also ordered the damaged *Prince of Wales* to proceed to England. Convoys were diverted to get them out of the probable danger area. The *Rodney's* course toward the North Sea was not immediately corrected, and she crossed ahead of the *Bismarck* on the afternoon of May 25. If she had been alerted, she could easily have made an interception. As it was, Somerville's Force H, consisting of carrier *Ark Royal*, battle cruiser *Renown*, and escorting ships, was now the only British force in position to do so.

Realizing that the shortage of fuel for the smaller ships would soon leave the larger vessels exposed to submarine attack, the Admiralty decided that five destroyers could be spared from the Convoy WS-8B and one from the Irish Sea Patrol and sent them under Captain Vian of the *Altmark* affair to rendezvous with Tovey. During the night all forces raced toward the *Bismarck's* most probable position.

### Bismarckdämmerung

By the morning of May 26, the pursuers began to lose hope. The wind had increased during the night, forcing Somerville's ships to slow from 25 to 17 knots. The flight deck of the *Ark Royal* was pitching between 53 and 55 feet, but in spite of the difficulties and dangers of air operations, a search patrol set out from the carrier at 0835. Still no word of the *Bismarck*. Suddenly at 1030, a Catalina flying patrol from the Coastal Air Command broadcast a sighting of a battleship in position lat. 49° 33′ N, long. 21° 50′ W, approximately 750 miles west of Brest, steering course 150 at 20 knots. On all ships, plotting officers hurried with their work. It was no British battleship. The *Bismarck* was found.

On receipt of the news, Captain Vian in destroyer *Cossack* decided to disregard his instructions to rendezvous with Admiral Tovey and turned with his five destroyers to intercept the *Bismarck*. Swordfish aircraft from the *Ark Royal* took over shadowing the German, but her position was too far ahead of any of the forces to make interception likely. Only an air strike from the *Ark Royal* could hope to slow her down until the heavy ships could come up. The strike preparations began immediately, while the cruiser *Sheffield* darted away at high speed to take up a station shadowing the Nazi battleship. Then came near-tragedy. The pilots, improperly briefed, attacked the *Sheffield*, which had accompanied them from Gibraltar, under the impression that she was the *Bismarck*. Only highly skilled shiphandling and a belated radio warning averted a calamity. The next two strikes found the *Bismarck*, for the *Sheffield* had gone ahead and already located her. The pilots of these strikes had been briefed to fly to the *Sheffield* and take their departure from her. She would coach them on the target, which she did with alacrity. The results of this strike were at first uncertain, and early reports led Tovey to believe that no significant damage had been done. However, he eventually learned that the *Bismarck* was heading in a northerly direction. Since this course was directly into the teeth of her enemies, the conclusion could only be that either the ship was having rudder difficulties or that damage was forcing her to take the heavy seas on her bow. In fact, both conjectures were true. The *Bismarck* had been hit in her steering engine compartment, and her rudders were jammed full over. Only by maneuvering with her engines could she avoid circling. Also a following sea would threaten further flooding because of the weakened bulkheads of the steering engine compartment. There was no choice. The *Bismarck* had to head into the sea. She was obliged at last to face her gathering enemies.

Darkness fell, and with it came Captain Vian and his destroyers to assist the *Sheffield* in shadowing. Vian saw no objection to attempting to put a few torpedoes into her as well. His first concerted attack the *Bismarck* drove off without damage either to herself or the destroyers. Captain Vian then stationed one destroyer on each bow and one on each quarter and himself took position astern. During the night each destroyer made several torpedo attacks on the *Bismarck* but made no hits because each time fire from the battleship forced the attacking destroyer to break off the action before it could get to effective torpedo launching position.

Raeder had been making every effort to save the *Bismarck*. He summoned all available submarines to the area, but those closest had already expended all their torpedoes and could only watch impotently. By an odd chance, one U-boat passed within 400 yards of the *Ark Royal*, but having fired her last torpedo the previous day, was powerless to harm the British carrier.

By morning the heavy British ships reached the scene of action. At 0847 the battleships *Rodney* and *King George V* exchanged the first salvos with the *Bismarck* at a range of 25,000 yards. The *Bismarck*, although badly crippled, still had magnificent endurance and splendid fire control. Her third salvo straddled the *Rodney*, but soon the weight of British firepower began to tell, hitting the *Bismarck's* main battery director early in the action so that the accuracy of her fire diminished appreciably. Soon the *Bismarck* was a helpless wreck, rolling sluggishly in the trough of the sea. But she refused to sink. At length Admiral Tovey, with barely enough fuel to get home, had to break off. Cruiser *Dorsetshire* requested permission to expend her last three torpedoes on the *Bismarck* before leaving, and as her third torpedo hit, the *Bismarck* slowly rolled over and disappeared beneath the waves. The *Hood* had been avenged.

The loss of the *Bismarck* put an end to German use of major combat ships for attack on transoceanic commerce. Raeder's standing with Hitler took a decided drop. German commerce warfare on the high seas thereafter was left to Dönitz' U-boats and a few disguised merchant raiders.

## The Channel Dash

British pride in the Royal Navy's achievement in hunting down and destroying the mighty *Bismarck* was somewhat quenched early the following year when the Germans brought home the last of their big surface raiders under the very noses of the Admiralty. After the *Bismarck* episode, the *Scharnhorst, Gneisenau,* and *Prinz Eugen* had remained at Brest. Despite damaging air attacks staged from Britain, all three were repaired and ready for operations by February 1942. Noting this, the British Admiralty anticipated that they would soon put to sea in an effort to regain home ports.

Hitler, convinced that the Allies were about to attack Norway, desired to concentrate all his naval strength there. Hence he ordered the three ships at Brest to make a break for home. They were not to proceed by way of the open Atlantic, which had proved a grave for the *Bismarck,* but use the shortest route, through the English Channel. Coming this way they would at least have strong land-based fighter support.

The Germans estimated that if they could maintain complete secrecy and leave Brest after dark, they would be through the most dangerous waters before the British could organize their defenses. With the Home Fleet far away at Scapa Flow, the German ships could expect opposition only from light surface forces, air attacks, and mine fields. Carefully sweeping the Channel route, the Germans prepared to give maximum air cover and provided the big ships with an escort of six destroyers and three torpedo boats. Eighteen more torpedo boats would join the escort as the force swept past Le Havre.

The *Scharnhorst, Gneisenau,* and *Prinz Eugen,* under command of Vice Admiral Ciliax, left Brest after dark on February 11, 1942. The night departure ran contrary to British estimates, for the Admiralty had assumed that the Germans would leave Brest during the day in order to pass through the Straits of Dover in darkness. The Royal Air Force had night reconnaissance planes over the Brest area, but radar failed to function in the only two planes that might have detected the German departure. Worse, R.A.F. headquarters failed to notify the Admiralty of the

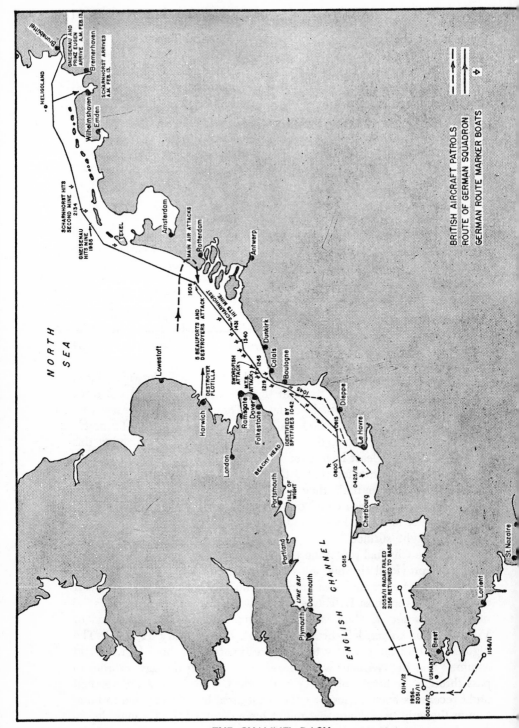

**THE CHANNEL DASH**

BRITISH AIRCRAFT PATROLS
ROUTE OF GERMAN SQUADRON
GERMAN ROUTE MARKER BOATS

breakdown. Finally, at 1100 on the 12th, an R.A.F. plane made radar contact through thickening weather with the German force, but even this contact was incorrectly evaluated. By the time a corrected report of the contact reached the Admiralty, the German ships had already passed through the Straits into the North Sea. The British attacked with coastal guns, torpedo boats, and with hundreds of aircraft without slowing down the fleeing Germans in the least. Tempestuous weather defeated a British destroyer attack. Unscathed, the three big German vessels reached waters off the Dutch coast. Here at last they ran into trouble: both the *Scharnhorst* and the *Gneisenau* hit British-laid mines. While the damage to the *Gneisenau* was minor, the *Scharnhorst* was out of action for months.

The failure to stop the Germans aroused great indignation in Britain. "Vice-Admiral Ciliax has succeeded where the Duke of Medina Sidonia failed," thundered the London *Times,* referring to the ill-fated Spanish Armada of 1588. "Nothing more mortifying to the pride of sea power has happened in Home waters since the 17th century." Nevertheless there were compensating advantages. The threat from Brest to Atlantic convoys had been eliminated. More important, the ineffectiveness of the Royal Navy's air striking power had been so clearly revealed that the Navy at long last began to receive its share of up-to-date aircraft, formerly exclusively the prerogative of the R.A.F.

## St. Nazaire

The month following the German Channel dash, the Royal Navy recovered much of its lost prestige by a raid on St. Nazaire. The port was an important U-boat base and contained a lock that could be used as a drydock, the only one outside Germany capable of receiving the battleship *Tirpitz.* To destroy this lock and to damage U-boat installations, the British readied one of their former American destroyers, H.M.S. *Campbeltown* (ex-U.S.S. *Buchanan*), as an explosive blockship to ram and destroy the lock gates. To support the operation and to destroy harbor facilities, a group of motor launches carried a raiding force of Commandos. Entering the Loire late at night on March 27, 1942, the group under Commander R. E. D. Ryder made recognition signals, thereby gaining four valuable minutes during the final approach. When the *Campbeltown* had only 1,000 yards to go, all German batteries opened fire. Her captain increased to full speed and rammed the lock squarely, bringing her time-set explosive charge into perfect position. The crew was taken off in motor launches. Meanwhile the Commandos had fought their way ashore with great difficulty and set about blowing up port and lock machinery. With the main objective achieved, Ryder gave the recall signal, and the survivors made good their escape with the loss of three motor launches on the way home. The next morning, while a group of senior German naval officers were inspecting the *Campbeltown* to plan her removal, the demolition charges blew up, wrecking the lock gate and wiping out the inspection party.

## Dieppe

A raid on Dieppe conducted on August 19, 1942 was intended not only to inflict damage but also to test amphibious techniques. Some 5,000 Canadian troops participated. Counting heavily on surprise, the army refused naval gunfire support; hence only eight destroyers with 4-inch guns accompanied the troops. Through a chance encounter with a small German coastal convoy, the raiders on one flank lost surprise and were repulsed with heavy losses, the few men who got ashore being quickly killed or captured. The other flank met with success, but the main assault on Dieppe itself also failed. The presence of a battleship would, in the opinion of the Naval Force Commander, have "probably turned the tide in our favour." The Canadians lost some 3,350 men, or 67 per cent of the troops involved. The raid, while discouraging to ideas of cross-Channel operations in 1942 and 1943, did reveal many weaknesses in amphibious planning which had to be rectified before the forthcoming major landings in Africa and Europe.

## Reorganization of the German Navy

The German surface ships were gradually transferred to bases in Norway, where they could repel the invasion Hitler feared and where they would be in a position to strike at Arctic convoys to North Russia. In the early morning hours of December 31, 1942, a German raiding force composed of the pocket battleship *Lützow*, the heavy cruiser *Hipper*, and six destroyers made contact with a convoy meagerly protected by five destroyers, two corvettes, and one trawler. The Germans split up, the *Hipper* with two destroyers attacking the escort, the *Lützow* and four destroyers making for the helpless convoy. Then ensued one of the most amazing actions of the war. Captain R. S. V. Sherbrooke managed his tiny escort force so brilliantly and so aggressively that the entire German force had to turn to deal with him. For more than an hour he held the attention of the Germans, losing only one destroyer, while the convoy escaped into the fog. On the arrival of the British cruisers *Sheffield* and *Jamaica*, the Germans obeyed their standing order to avoid engaging major forces and retired. The convoy reached Russia without the loss of a ship. The Germans lost a destroyer and sustained heavy damage to the *Hipper*. The most important damage however was not to the ships but to the German navy, for this action caused a major reorganization in the German naval high command.

When word of the action reached Hitler, he stormed and raged. He would have all the heavy ships scrapped, he declared, so that their steel could be used by the army and the *Luftwaffe* and their personnel could be sent to man the submarines, which were the only naval forces carrying on a useful fight. He ordered Admiral Raeder to report to him to receive the scrapping order in person, but Raeder managed to get the meeting postponed until January 6. As he waited for Hitler to cool off, he prepared for him a kind of child's guide to sea power, pointing out the importance of the German heavy ships in tying down the British navy. But in the meantime, Goering had got Hitler's ear. Goering had always been intensely jealous of Raeder and sought any method of encompassing his ruin. A braggart, a schemer, and an unscrupulous liar, Goering proposed to win the war with his *Luftwaffe* alone. He had promised to reduce Britain by air attack, and he had failed. He had promised to reduce Russia by air attack, and he had failed. He had promised to keep the German forces in Russia supplied, and he had failed. He had promised to keep German forces in North Africa supplied, and he had failed. He had promised to destroy Allied shipping to Britain, and he had failed. He had promised to himself that he would scuttle Raeder, and he succeeded. Goering promised that his *Luftwaffe* could do, and do better, all that the surface ships could do, and Raeder was out. He resigned on January 30, 1943 and was succeeded by Dönitz. The contrast between the two men was great. Dönitz was an ardent Nazi; Raeder a professional naval officer, generally aloof from politics. Dönitz was a man of action; Raeder, something of a naval philosopher and historian.

When Dönitz took command of the German navy, he was convinced that Hitler's position was sound. This conviction lasted only a few months. When he began to see the war as a whole in contrast to the limited view he had had as U-boat admiral, he realized that Raeder was right; there was more to sea power than submarines. He succeeded in persuading Hitler to reverse the order, so that no ships were scrapped. The rescued ships however were not immediately used significantly. Nearly a year passed before the next major use of a surface ship occurred, once more against the North Russian convoys.

## The *Scharnhorst's* Last Cruise

On Christmas Eve of 1943, the *Scharnhorst* set out from Norway to intercept a convoy bound for North Russia. But the convoy had been diverted to the northward, and the battleship met instead a cruiser scouting force of the British Home Fleet. In the morning of December 26, H.M.S. *Belfast* made radar contact with the German and opened fire, joined by the *Sheffield* and the *Norfolk*, but foul weather so reduced the speed of the British cruisers that they soon lost contact. Vice Admiral Robert Burnett, judging that the *Scharnhorst* would make for the convoy,

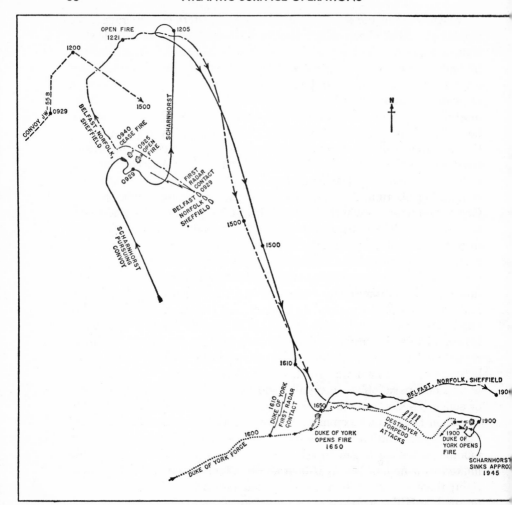

THE SINKING OF THE *SCHARNHORST*, DECEMBER 26, 1943

headed to intercept and again made radar contact a little after noon. Destroyers which Burnett now sent in to attack with torpedoes were defeated by high seas, but the threat was enough to make the battleship head for Norway. This suited Burnett exactly, for the German line of retirement provided a perfect intercept course for the battleship *Duke of York* and the cruiser *Jamaica*, under command of Admiral Sir Bruce Fraser, who had relieved Sir John Tovey as Commander in Chief of the British Home Fleet. The *Belfast*, *Sheffield*, and *Norfolk* made no further attempt to engage, contenting themselves with shadowing the German. By late afternoon the two British forces were both in the area of expected contact. Because in those latitudes it was already pitch dark, Burnett illuminated with starshell, whereupon the *Duke of York* and the *Jamaica* sighted the *Scharnhorst* and immediately engaged at 12,000 yards. A high-speed eastward chase developed until the 14-inch shells of the British battleship began to take effect, and the *Scharnhorst* lost speed. British destroyers then further slowed her with torpedo attacks. Ordered to sink her with torpedoes, the *Belfast* and the *Jamaica* attacked in concert with destroyers and sent the *Scharnhorst* down off North Cape a little before 2000.

That the *Scharnhorst* was mishandled is evident. She was superior to the three British cruisers which first engaged her and stood a good chance of fighting it out with them to a successful conclusion. If she had done so and then continued toward the convoy, interception by the *Duke of York* would have been impossible, at least until after the *Scharnhorst* had wreaked havoc among the freighters. Her running to the south to regain the Norwegian ports meant that she was running toward the most likely route for the approach of British reinforcements. In running for safety, the *Scharnhorst* adopted the course that offered the least probability of inflicting damage to the British and offered the greatest risk to herself. She had been sent out with a specific task, that of inflicting the maximum damage to the convoy. Her abandonment of her task meant that she was expended uselessly, with no gain to compensate for her loss.

## The End of the *Tirpitz*

The chief remaining German surface ship was the huge battleship *Tirpitz* at anchor in Kaa Fiord, an inlet of Alten Fiord far in the north of Norway. Here she was a particular threat to the North Russian convoys. On the night of September 19–20, 1943, three months before the *Scharnhorst* was sunk, the *Tirpitz* had been attacked by British midget submarines. Four midgets, known as X-craft, survivors of six that had been towed across the North Sea by fleet submarines, penetrated the outer fiord. There the *X-10*, beset with misfortunes, turned back. The other three pressed on. One was never heard from again. The other two, *X-6*, commanded by Lieutenant D. Cameron RNR, and *X-7*, Lieutenant B. C. G. Place RN, placed time charges beneath the keel of the *Tirpitz*. Although the Germans discovered and captured the crews of these two midgets, they were unable to move the *Tirpitz* sufficiently to avoid the consequences of the explosion, which unseated her main engine and did heavy damage to her rudders and steering engine.

Following the sinking of the *Scharnhorst*, and when Allied intelligence reports revealed that the Germans had nearly completed repairs to the *Tirpitz*, the British determined to hit her again lest she attack North Russian convoys or make a break for the open Atlantic as the *Bismarck* had done. This time the Admiralty decided to employ carriers.

After receiving special training, flyers from H.M. carriers *Victorious, Furious, Pursuer, Searcher,* and *Emperor* prepared to launch their attack. Sailing from England on March 30, 1944, in order to coordinate with a convoy bound for Russia, they attacked in the early morning of April 3. The *Victorious* and the *Furious* carried bombers, while the other three carriers provided the fighter escort. Attacking in two waves, the planes scored 15 hits, doing extensive damage without however impairing the ability of the *Tirpitz* to steam, for the bombs could not penetrate the eight inches of steel that formed her armor deck.

After the worst of the damage had been repaired, the ship was still not completely seaworthy, and as the dockyards in Germany were too battered to repair her, the Germans decided to move her to Tromsö, north of Narvik, where she might be employed as a floating battery. Tromsö was within range of the R.A.F. long-range bombers. On November 12, 1944, Lancasters capsized her by direct hits with six-ton bombs. This time there was no question of repair. The *Tirpitz* was gone.

# 2

# The Struggle for the Mediterranean

As war approached in 1939, Britain and France, recognizing the vital importance of the Mediterranean theater, laid joint plans to exploit its strategic opportunities and to deny them to the Axis. Britain traditionally considered the Mediterranean her lifeline to the Suez Canal and the Far East, while France considered it the main high road to her colonies in Algeria, Tunisia, and French Morocco. To a great extent the safety of British and French commerce and installations depended on the role Italy would assume in the war. On the assumption that Italy would be an active participant, the Anglo-French allies agreed that British naval forces would assume responsibility for the eastern half and French naval forces the western half of the Mediterranean. At the outbreak of war, the British had a strong Mediterranean Fleet. In addition to their major base at Alexandria, they had secondary establishments at Malta and Gibraltar. The French had three battleships, eleven cruisers, 33 destroyers, and 45 submarines disposed at Toulon, Oran, Mers-el-Kebir, Bizerte, Morocco, and Dakar.

Ever since the Italian invasion of Ethiopia in 1935, the Italian navy had been operating on a quasi-war footing. When the Italians went into Albania in April 1939, the British, not having anticipated the move, hurriedly concentrated their Mediterranean Fleet at Alexandria. In May Hitler and Mussolini proclaimed a Pact of Steel, promising to aid each other in any military action. This dramatic public announcement was secretly modified by the Cavallero Memorandum in which Mussolini informed Hitler that he would not be ready for war for three years and asked him to postpone military action until 1942. Although Hitler agreed in principle, on August 11 the German foreign minister informed his Italian opposite number that Germany was about to attack Poland. Mussolini, mindful of his obligations under the Pact of Steel, sent a lengthy request for raw materials for Germany to supply to Italy. Hitler refused the requested items and informed Mussolini that he would not be

39

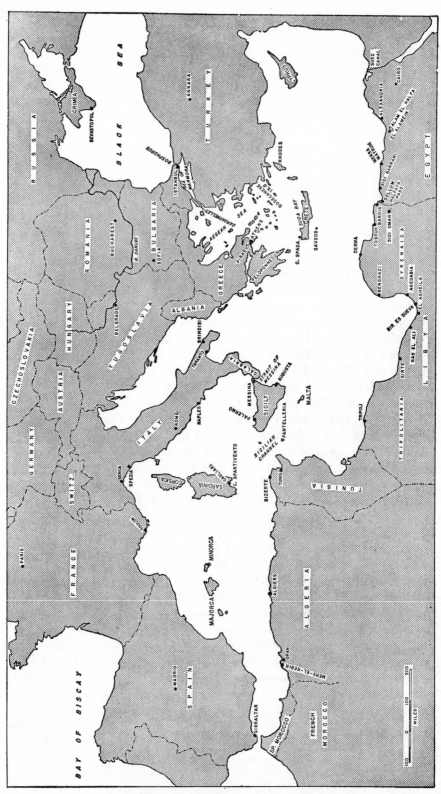

THE MEDITERRANEAN THEATER

requested to enter the war. Consequently, when Germany invaded Poland on September 1, 1939, Mussolini proclaimed Italy's nonbelligerence.

In the face of this unexpected development, the British, urgently requiring ships in other theaters, left the Mediterranean largely on a caretaker basis. Withdrawing most of their ships for service elsewhere, they depended on the French to keep order and to assist the few remaining British ships in enforcing Allied Shipping Control measures. Meanwhile the British bent every effort toward strengthening their positions in the Middle East. In Egypt they had, in addition to the naval base at Alexandria, a body of troops and a Royal Air Force command, stationed there in accordance with the Anglo-Egyptian Treaty of 1936. Because the Egyptian government had done little to build up its armed forces and facilities, the British made great efforts during the winter of 1939–40 to make good the deficiencies.

By spring of 1940 Mussolini was chafing under Allied shipping restrictions and was anxious to extend Italian influence and territory. For years he had dreamed of restoring a Roman Empire in the Mediterranean; his conquests of Ethiopia and of Albania had been moves in this direction. Now he dreamed of an Empire which would challenge in splendor that of the Caesars. He sought means of expelling the two great powers he saw as standing in his way—Britain and France. Meeting Hitler at the Brenner Pass in March 1940, he promised to intervene on the German side at the appropriate time. Soon thereafter he announced to the King and to his military leaders his concept of a "parallel war," which would assist Germany indirectly but which would be designed primarily to further Italian interests. As he watched the rapid success of the Germans in Norway and France, Mussolini made hurried plans to join the war before it should be too late. "To participate in the peace," he proclaimed, "one must participate in the war."

As the British began to see signs that Italy's nonbelligerency might soon shift to outright war, they reviewed their earlier policy of non-provocation of Italy, proposing to substitute a show of force. But Mussolini had already made up his mind. On April 17 he was restrained from a declaration of war only by the strong protests of Marshal Badoglio, chief of the Italian armed forces, on the grounds of unreadiness. Unobtrusively the British began to return strength to the Mediterranean. They resumed responsibility for the eastern Mediterranean, and on April 29, 1940 issued an order that Allied merchant ships bound to or from India or elsewhere in the East would be routed around the Cape of Good Hope. Simultaneously reinforcements for all three services began to appear at British bases in and around the Mediterranean. On the arrival at the end of May of four battleships and the aircraft carrier *Eagle,* Sir Andrew B. Cunningham, Commander in Chief Mediterranean Fleet, shifted his flag from Malta to the *Warspite* and his base of operations to Alexandria. In

June seven cruisers and a force of destroyers arrived. Also under Admiral Cunningham at Alexandria was a French force commanded by Vice Admiral René Godfroy, consisting of battleship *Lorraine*, three heavy cruisers, one light cruiser, three destroyers, and six submarines.

## Italy Enters the War

Marshal Badoglio had been right when he told Mussolini that the Italian armed forces were not ready for war. The army was not fully mobilized and was in a poor state of training, while the Italian air force, although strong on paper, had little operational experience. The navy was feeling the consequences of insufficient maintenance and insufficient replacement of ships. The Italian armed forces were inefficiently organized for naval war in the Mediterranean. The three service commands, *Superesercito* (army), *Superareo* (air force), and *Supermarina* (navy), were co-equal but subordinated to the supreme headquarters, *Comando Supremo*. The officers in *Comando Supremo* tended to hold the continental viewpoint of the army and the strategic bombing concepts of the air force; hence they had little sympathy for naval problems and little appreciation of naval opportunities. When the Italian air force was organized in 1923, the navy had been directed to give up all of its aviation to the new service. The navy thus had no control over the aircraft it needed to carry out its missions. Nor did it have any aircraft carriers, for both *Comando Supremo* and Mussolini considered Italy itself to be a gigantic aircraft carrier. Since planes operating from Italian air bases would be able to cover the central Mediterranean, *Comando Supremo* argued that the air force could perfectly well perform all the tasks usually allotted to naval aviation. Air force pilots however were not trained for naval tasks, and the air force, like the *Luftwaffe* and all other major air forces in the war, wished to conduct the fighting in accordance with its own strategic concepts. Thus, when the navy requested aircraft for support of naval operations, the planes were all too frequently allocated elsewhere. The navy controlled only units for naval reconnaissance, and even these planes were flown by air force pilots.

The Italian navy at the outbreak of war consisted of six battleships (of which only two, the *Cavour* and the *Giulio Cesare*, were actually in service), seven heavy and twelve light cruisers, and some 50 destroyers. In addition Italy had 108 submarines, nearly double Germany's total. Two older battleships, the *Duilio* and *Doria*, were being modernized and would join the fleet shortly, while four fast new battleships, the *Littorio, Vittorio Veneto, Roma*, and *Impero*, were in various stages of construction. The first two of these were nearly ready for service, but the others would require several years to complete. In the Red Sea at Massawa the Italians had a small force of seven destroyers and eight submarines which would be able to pose a threat to Britain's shipping to and from the Suez Canal. Class for class, the Italian ships were more lightly armored but faster than their Allied counterparts. These high-speed characteristics and comparatively small fuel capacity gave them a severely restricted combat radius.

The chief Italian naval base was at Taranto, with subordinate bases at Naples, Spezia, and Brindisi in Italy; Augusta and Palermo in Sicily; Cagliari in Sardinia; and Tripoli and Benghazi in Libya. Generally the Italian navy envisioned its strategy in war as defensive in the eastern and western Mediterranean, while in the central Mediterranean it must at all costs protect shipping between Italy and her armies in Libya. Italian naval doctrine prescribed weakening the Allied fleets by raids and by submarine and frogman attack while avoiding encounters with superior forces.

As May wore on, the British recognized that France might be forced from the war and anticipated that Mussolini would wish to join the attack on France so that he might have a place at the victors' feast. In addition to building up the Mediterranean Fleet, the War Cabinet understood that Britain might have to assume responsibility for the western Mediterranean as well as the eastern and took steps to provide a naval force to be based on Gibraltar. Also abandoning the non-provocation policy, the British on May 23 ordered that all Italian merchant ships should be stopped for contraband-control searches. On June 6, Mussolini announced that all waters within twelve miles of Italian territory were dangerous to navigation. Forewarned by this announcement, Admiral Cunningham had most of the Mediterranean Fleet at sea when Italy's declaration of war against Britain and France became effective at one minute after midnight on June 11, 1940.

Cunningham's initial sweep, by which he hoped to surprise units of the Italian navy, met with no success, while an Italian submarine sank the British cruiser *Calypso*. The first two days of the war however cost Italy 130,000 tons of merchant shipping through capture, scuttling, or internment. On June 14, a force of French cruisers bombarded Genoa, the French cooperating in the war against Italy for 15 days until their own surrender to Germany took place.

With France's surrender, as told in the preceding chapter, Britain's concern over the French fleet became acute. The British situation in the Mediterranean in a short month had gone from overwhelming superiority to nearly hopeless inferiority. Instead of having two powerful forces watching a non-belligerent, the British now had the care of the entire Inland Sea with a hostile Italy and the strong possibility that the powerful French ships would be used against them. The War Cabinet therefore ordered its commanders in the Mediterranean to take action.

In anticipation of having to assume responsibility for the western Mediterranean, the Admiralty had already assembled a force at Gibraltar designated as Force H, including the battleships *Valiant* and *Resolution,* the battle cruiser *Hood,* the aircraft carrier *Ark Royal,* two cruisers, and eleven destroyers. Vice Admiral Sir James F. Somerville, its commander, received orders from the War Cabinet to present to the commander of the French detachment at Mers-el-Kebir, the naval anchorage of Oran, the following proposals:

> A. Sail with us and continue to fight for victory against the Germans and Italians.
> B. Sail with reduced crews under our control to a British port. . . .
> C. Alternatively, if you feel bound to stipulate that your ships should not be used against Germans or Italians, since this would break the Armistice, then sail them with us with reduced crews to some French port in the West Indies—Martinique, for instance, where they can be demilitarised to our satisfaction, or perhaps be entrusted to the United States of America, and remain safely until the end of the war, the crews being repatriated.
>
> If you refuse these fair offers, I must with profound regret require you to sink your ships within six hours. Finally, failing the above, I have the orders of His Majesty's Government to use whatever force may be necessary to prevent your ships from falling into German or Italian hands.

On Admiralty orders, Somerville took his entire force to Mers-el-Kebir, arriving early on the morning of July 3, 1940. Sending Captain C. S. Holland, former British naval attaché in Paris, and a personal friend of the French commander, Admiral Marcel Gensoul, to deliver his note, Somerville waited off shore. Sensing an ultimatum, Gensoul refused to receive Holland, but sent his flag lieutenant to represent him. In reply to the British note, Gensoul wrote that previous French assurances still held good, that under no circumstances would French ships be allowed to fall into Axis hands, and that French ships would defend themselves by force. Gensoul felt that he could accept none of the alternatives offered him without breaking the armistice; accordingly he informed his government only that he had been offered an ultimatum. As Admiral Darlan was not available, his chief of staff ordered forces at Toulon and Algiers to Mers-el-Kebir. Meanwhile all participants attempted to find a solution. In the afternoon Gensoul received Holland, proposing a gentleman's agreement, but Somerville, alerted to the coming of French reinforcements, set a final deadline. Unable to accept any of the French counterproposals, Holland withdrew and at 1756 Somerville opened fire, the first shots fired by the British against the French since Waterloo.

The French fleet at Mers-el-Kebir had, during the negotiations, seized the opportunity to prepare for battle. It included four battleships and six super destroyers, as well as a seaplane tender. During the brief action, which included a carrier air strike, three French battleships were either sunk or beached, while the battleship *Strasbourg* made good her escape and reached Toulon undamaged.

At Alexandria the personal friendship between Admirals Cunningham and Godfroy averted tragedy. Cunningham had an advantage over Somerville in that he did not have to fear the arrival of reinforcements, and he was in a position to demand more latitude from his government than Somerville had had. On July 5, the two commanders worked out a gentleman's agreement by which Godfroy would discharge fuel, remove firing mechanisms from his guns, and make no attempt to break out to sea. Cunningham, for his part, agreed to undertake no measures to seize the French ships by force as had been done in England. Thus there remained under Vichy control in the Mediterranean one battleship, one aircraft carrier, four heavy and eight light cruisers, 30 destroyers, and 70 submarines.

Enraged by this attack by their former allies, the French Vichy government ordered reprisal measures against the British. On July 5 French planes attacked Gibraltar, but the bombs all fell harmlessly in the harbor. On July 8 the Vichy government severed diplomatic relations with Britain but did not declare war.

Thus at terrific cost the British had ensured themselves against a significant part of the French fleet. The risk had been great; the full cost would not be known for years.

## Britain Against Italy in the Mediterranean

The entry of Italy into the war created serious doubt in the minds of the British on whether they could hold Malta. Its defenses were pitifully weak, promised guns and aircraft having been sent elsewhere to meet desperate needs of the moment. Its proximity to Italy made it of negligible value as a naval base. It could however prove of inestimable value as an air base from which to attack Italian shipping to Libya. Italy lost no time in attempting to knock Malta out altogether, sending 36 raids against the island during June. As a result the submarines which had been based there were forced to leave, and women and children were evacuated. During the next two and a half years, Malta remained under siege, but always a menace to Axis shipping in the Mediterranean.

While covering the evacuation convoys, the British Mediterranean Fleet had its first action with the Italian fleet off Calabria, the toe of the Italian boot. Disposed in three groups, the British had a scouting unit of five light cruisers in the van, followed by the battleship *Warspite*, Cunningham's flagship, screened by five destroyers. Some miles astern were the older battleships *Malaya* and *Royal Sovereign* with the carrier *Eagle*, carrying 19 planes, and escorted by ten more destroyers. As a diversion, Force H made a sweep of the western Mediterranean.

The Italian force, heading northward toward Italy after escorting a convoy to Benghazi, consisted of battleships *Giulio Cesare* and *Cavour*, six heavy cruisers, twelve light cruisers, and destroyers—under command of Admiral Angelo Campioni, Commander in Chief of the Italian Fleet. This force had been especially strengthened in expectation of battle on the return trip.

A strike launched from the *Eagle* failed to find the battleships and expended its torpedoes fruitlessly against the cruisers. The course of the Italians suggested to Cunningham that they were covering movements to Libya; accordingly he maneuvered to get between the Italian force and its base at Taranto. In the afternoon the British light cruisers came upon the Italian cruisers. Heavily outnumbered and outranged, the British fought on until the *Warspite* came to the rescue. Soon thereafter the *Warspite* sighted the two Italian battleships and engaged them at 26,000 yards. After a few rounds, the Italian flagship *Giulio Cesare* received a hit at the base of the forward funnel. Campioni then sent his destroyers in for a torpedo attack and retired behind a smoke screen, to head for Messina. Firing now became general and the battle more confused as the British attempted to cut off the Italian retreat. By 1700 superiority in speed enabled the Italians to make good their escape, and Cunningham, unwilling to risk running into a submarine ambush within 25 miles of the Italian coast, broke off pursuit. Meanwhile two convoys to Alexandria had sailed from Malta, taking advantage of the diversion caused by the battle. Cunningham's force covered their passage, absorbing air attacks which otherwise would have been directed against the merchant ships.

The action off Calabria seemed to prove the soundness of Cunningham's aggressive policy. Although the Italian battleships mounted lighter main battery guns than the British battleships, they had more of them, and the two Italian battleships could have engaged the British flagship closely before the two slower British battleships could have got into action. The Italian force was greatly superior in cruisers. Yet Campioni did not press his advantage. Although the British had a carrier within striking range, it had played an ineffective role. Italian land-based air, on the other hand, had been poorly coordinated, arriving after the battle and then attacking the Italian instead of the British fleet. Happily for the Italians, their airmen's bombing was as inaccurate as their recognition, and no ship was hit.

Italian reluctance to engage approximately equal forces was displayed again on July 19 in the Battle of Cape Spada, when three British destroyers on an antisubmarine sweep northwest of Crete ran into two Italian light cruisers. The destroyers fell back upon the support of the Australian light cruiser *Sydney* and another destroyer, which were to the northward of them. When the Italians sighted the *Sydney* they retired to the southwest, although they had superiority in 6-inch guns and only a slight inferiority in smaller calibers. In the pursuit the *Sydney* sank the cruiser *Bartolomeo Colleoni;* her damaged consort, the *Bande Neri,* managed to reach Tobruk.

After these actions the Admiralty and Cunningham effected a re-definition of the responsibilities for the Mediterranean. Since the Italians had many interests in the eastern half of the area and since the British forces in Egypt and the Middle East required constant support, the eastern fleet was made stronger, while Force H at Gibraltar would be a raiding force, available for operations in the Mediterranean and, under Admiralty control, in the Atlantic. The Flag Officer Commanding North Atlantic, Admiral Sir Dudley North at Gibraltar, could also call upon Force H for assistance in preventing enemy ships from passing the Straits. Cunningham desired to rid himself of his two slow *Royal Sovereigns* and wanted instead a total force of three or four faster *Queen Elizabeths,* including the *Valiant,* which had radar. He also requested an increased number of heavy cruisers to enable him to cope with the Italian preponderance in that type of ship. He particularly desired the carrier *Illustrious* to supplement the inadequate *Eagle.* The redistribution of strength, called Operation HATS, took place in late August and early September unopposed except by moderate air attacks. Cunningham took advantage of the operation to send a small convoy into Malta.

## The Italian Offensive in Libya

On September 7, 1940, Mussolini ordered Marshal Graziani, commander of the Italian army in Libya, to begin a land offensive against Egypt. On September 14 the Italians captured the important port city of Sidi Barrani but were unable to go farther because the British navy began to harass their sea-borne supply routes by attacks on Benghazi, Sollum, Bardia, and Sidi Barrani itself. British submarines had met with little success because Italian ships clung as far as possible to shallow coastal waters, where it was difficult for British submarines to operate successfully. Nor was there adequate air strength on Malta. Until December the Italians lost no ships on the Italy-Libya run either from submarine or air attack while they delivered 692,403 tons to Libya during the year. Until Malta could be built up, the British were helpless to interdict this traffic.

## Italy Invades Greece

Against the advice of his naval officers, Mussolini on October 15, 1940, at a meeting with army and political leaders, issued orders for the invasion of Greece. He kept his intention to attack a secret from Hitler, who he knew would not approve.

The Greeks had long feared an Italian invasion of their country, but were determined to avoid giving a pretext. Hence they refused to allow the British to send aid ahead of time, to send military advisers, or even to be informed of the Greek strategy of defense. Thus on October 28, when Italian troops crossed the Greek frontier, the British, with slender resources, were faced with a difficult decision. To maintain their position with neutrals in the Middle East, they were obliged to support Greece in her struggle. Any troops that might be sent to Greece would have to be drawn from General Archibald Wavell's forces in Egypt. The problem of air support was equally difficult. The entire British position in the Middle East might be lost if the defenses of Egypt were weakened.

In view of these considerations, the British War Cabinet agreed to sent munitions and money and an R.A.F. contingent. Also by arrangement with the Greek government, the British established a naval fueling base on Crete. The Greeks as it turned out did not at the time need troop assistance, for the Italian offensive stalled on November 8, and a few days later a Greek counteroffensive pushed the invaders back to the Albanian border. Thus in both his North African venture and in his Greek invasion, Mussolini, because of inadequate planning and inadequate support, failed in his attempt to make political expediency promote military success. Instead of winning glory, Mussolini became a laughingstock.

## The Carrier Raid on Taranto

In view of the reluctance of the Italian navy to accept decisive action at sea, Cunningham sought to attack their ships at their Taranto base. Originally scheduled for October 21, Trafalgar Day, the operation was twice postponed because of other urgent commitments and because of damage to the *Illustrious*. The delays proved to be fortunate for the British, for when the raid finally took place late at night on November 11, all six of the Italian battleships were in port.

At the last moment the *Eagle* developed defects and had to be left behind. Five of her Swordfish planes were transferred to the *Illustrious*, which arrived at the launching point with 21 aircraft. The latest reconnaissance photographs, flown aboard the carrier on the afternoon of November 11, revealed the position of every Italian unit. As the first wave of twelve planes neared its target, four bombers split off to make a diversion in the inner harbor, and two other planes broke away to drop flares to the east in order to silhouette the battleships for the six torpedo planes. The first attack worked perfectly, the flares showing the targets clearly to the torpedo-plane pilots, who scored hits on the *Cavour* and *Littorio*, at the cost of one plane. A second wave of eight planes an hour later used identical tactics. This wave scored a hit on the *Duilio* and two more on the *Littorio*. This wave also lost one aircraft.

The attack reduced the Italian fleet to three available battleships, the *Giulio Cesare, Vittorio Veneto,* and *Doria*. The *Cavour* never went to sea again, while the *Littorio* and *Duilio* were out of action for some months. The surviving Italian major ships abandoned Taranto as a fleet base, moving to Naples immediately after the attack. Italian air reconnaissance had completely failed to spot the British forces moving up for the attack or the Malta convoy which took advantage of the diversion caused by fleet movements for the Taranto raid. The British gained an additional dividend from the operation, for a light force wiped out a small convoy of four ships bound for Brindisi.

### Germany to the Rescue

As a result of the Greek success in repelling the Italian invaders and of their own success in the Taranto operation, the British found their Mediterranean situation much improved. On December 9, General Wavell opened an offensive out of Egypt, capturing Sollum on the 16th, Bardia and Tobruk in January, and reaching Benghazi on February 1. By February 9 the entire bulge of Cyrenaica was in British hands, and Wavell's forces stood before El Agheila at the threshold of Tripolitania.

Throughout the winter of 1940–41, the Mediterranean Fleet had assumed the task of moving supplies from Egypt to Wavell's advancing army. An Inshore Squadron carried the brunt of this labor, its small ships suffering heavy losses to aircraft based in Sicily. Its operations were a brilliant example of the flexibility of sea power in bringing essential materials to an army advancing along a seacoast. The supplies needed were difficult if not impossible of transport along the sand trails and inadequate roads of the Western Desert.

In the face of repeated Italian setbacks, in Greece, in North Africa, and at sea, the OKW (*Oberkommando der Wehrmacht*—the German High Command) held a series of meetings to consider what could be done to retrieve the situation. As early as November 12, 1940, Hitler had decided that it would be necessary to extricate Italy from the consequences of her "regrettable blunder" in Greece. But at the same time, Germany was busy with other commitments, including exploratory staff discussions for Operation BARBAROSSA, the invasion of Russia. Once the officers of the OKW turned their attention to the Mediterranean, they proposed to do what was necessary to make the Inland Sea an Axis lake. First, they planned to give direct troop support to Italy in Greece and Albania, coming down through Romania and Bulgaria in order to insure that the output of the Romanian oil fields would come to Germany. The second part of the plan, Operation FELIX, envisioned having Spain enter the war against Britain. If Spain would not take this step, diplomatic arrangements would be made to allow German troops free passage of Spanish soil in order to capture Gibraltar. A part of this operation was the capture of the Canary and Cape Verde Islands in order to control the entrances to the Mediterranean. If France objected to the passage of German troops for this purpose, all France was to be occupied. Third, Germany planned to send a *Luftwaffe* corps to Italy to cooperate with the Italian air force. Finally, they would send mechanized infantry to Africa, to be designated the *Afrika Korps,* under command of General Erwin Rommel.

During December and January, German *Fliegerkorps X* (Tenth Air Fleet) of some 500 planes, especially trained in attack on ships, moved from Norway to airfields in Calabria and Sicily. Its tasks were to protect Axis shipping with North Africa, prevent the passage of British convoys through the central Mediterranean, and neutralize Malta by air attack.

After a part of the German air reinforcements had already arrived, a British convoy of four cargo ships escorted by two battleships, one aircraft carrier, four cruisers, and destroyers of Force H passed Gibraltar January 6 en route to Malta and Greece. About the same time the battleships *Warspite* and *Valiant,* the carrier *Illustrious,* and seven destroyers of the Mediterranean Fleet sailed from Alexandria to meet the convoy and cover other convoy movements between Malta and Alexandria. In support of the operation Malta-based aircraft attacked the Italian fleet at Naples on the 8th, damaging the battleship *Giulio Cesare* and forcing her and the *Vittorio Veneto* to move to the small base at Spezia well away from the strategic area. This attack left the *Vittorio Veneto* the only serviceable Italian battleship. On the evening of the 9th, after daylight attacks by Italian aircraft from Sardinia, the Gibraltar force turned back undamaged, leaving the convoy with three cruisers and several destroyers to proceed to Malta. That night the cruisers drove off an attack by Italian destroyers, sinking one of them, but a British destroyer struck a mine and had to be towed to Malta. The next day an Italian force from Spezia searched the western Mediterranean for Force H, which had long since passed out of reach.

Around noon on January 10 the Alexandria force, which had joined the convoy from Gibraltar during the night, was attacked west of Malta by about 50 Stuka dive bombers from Sicily. Unlike the Italian pilots, who attacked from high level, the Germans pressed home their attacks with great skill through very heavy antiaircraft fire. Concentrating on the *Illustrious,* they hit the carrier several times. Steering with her engines, the *Illustrious* headed for Malta, and despite an afternoon attack which started large fires, managed to make port that evening. Next day, en route to Alexandria, the cruisers *Gloucester* and *Southampton* were damaged by air attack, the latter so badly that she had to be sunk by her own force.

At Malta the *Illustrious* became the target of numerous air attacks. Nevertheless, the naval constructors succeeded in making temporary repairs to her, and on the night of January 23 she slipped out of the harbor and reached Alexandria without further damage. Since the *Illus-*

*trious* had to go to the United States for permanent repairs and the *Eagle* was unserviceable, the Mediterranean Fleet would be without a carrier until the arrival of the *Formidable,* which the Admiralty had immediately ordered transferred from the South Atlantic.

While maintaining air attacks on Malta at the rate of three or four a day, the *Luftwaffe* did not neglect the eastern end of the Mediterranean. At the end of January German aircraft from the Dodecanese Islands began dropping magnetic mines in the Suez Canal in such numbers that it had to be closed intermittently throughout the month of February. Thus in the brief space of one month the intervention of the German air force had dramatically reversed the situation in the Mediterranean.

To send ships through the Mediterranean was to subject them to extreme peril. The only feasible route to maintain supply for Britain's Middle Eastern army was the long one around the Cape of Good Hope, through the Red Sea and the Suez Canal. Regular Cape convoys designated WS (for Winston's Specials) brought men, stores, tanks, and ammunition to the Middle East Command. Yet this route was by no means secure. In addition to the obvious threat from the Germans in the Atlantic, the Italians had substantial forces southeast of Suez, with seven destroyers, two motor torpedo boats, and eight submarines based at Kisimayo on the Indian Ocean and at Massawa on the Red Sea. In January 1941 British forces from Kenya and the Sudan began a campaign with fleet support to drive the Italians out of East Africa. In February the Italians abandoned the port of Kisimayo, and in early April British forces took Massawa while torpedo planes from the *Eagle* sank two Italian destroyers and drove one ashore. The remaining Italian naval forces in East Africa scuttled themselves or fled the area. As a result, the President of the United States was able under the Neutrality Act to proclaim the Red Sea open to American shipping, and British convoys had security from attack near their destinations.

In the next few months the British Mediterranean Fleet endured its most severe trial. When the Germans intervened in Greece, the Greek government accepted the active participation of British troops and air forces in the mainland fighting. Although reinforcement of Greece meant that General Wavell's drive had to be stopped short of the Tripolitan border, the War Cabinet felt that the political reasons for aiding Greece outweighed all other considerations. The Mediterranean Fleet, shouldering the responsibilities for transport and protection of three divisions and an armored brigade with their supplies, had to commit so much of its strength to the Aegean that it could spare little attention for Italian convoys to Libya. The result was nearly fatal to the British position in North Africa, for during the month of March, Italian ships carried General Rommel's *Afrika Korps* across the Mediterranean.

The first British convoy sailed for Piraeus March 5, others following every three days. Italian explosive motor boats sank a British cruiser in Suda Bay on the night of March 26, and a few days later an Italian submarine sank another. During a period of about six weeks however the fleet carried 58,000 troops with their equipment and supplies to Greece without loss.

## The Battle of Cape Matapan, March 28–29, 1941

Pressed by the Germans, the Italian navy planned to employ their last operational battleship, the *Vittorio Veneto,* with eight cruisers and a number of destroyers to strike at British convoys to Greece. Commanded by Admiral Angelo Iachino, the force sailed under the misapprehension that the British could oppose them with only one battleship, for *Fliegerkorps X* claimed to have put the *Warspite* and *Barham* out of action.

During the morning of March 27 air search and cover by the German and Italian landbased air forces proved ineffective, and about noon the Italian naval force was shadowed by a British flying boat about 80 miles east of Sicily. Worried by these developments, the Italian naval command ordered the northern cruiser group to rejoin the main body before it could make its assigned sweep. On the morning of March 28 the *Vittorio Veneto,* screened by destroyers, was south of the west end of Crete steering southeast with a division of three cruisers and destroyers seven miles in the van and a northern group of five cruisers and destroyers 25 miles to eastward.

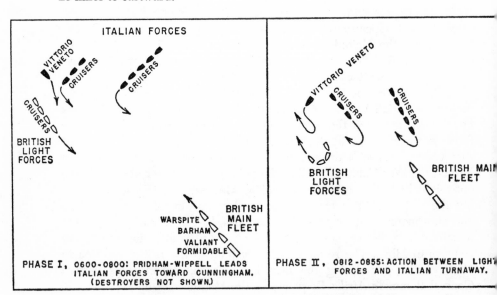

BATTLE OF CAPE MATAPAN, MARCH 28, 1941

Warned by the British intelligence service in Italy, Admiral Cunningham had taken measures to counter the Italian thrust. Clearing convoys from the way, he ordered Vice Admiral H. D. Pridham-Wippell to leave Greece with his cruiser-destroyer force and rendezvous with him south of Crete on the morning of March 28. Cunningham himself sortied from Alexandria in the *Warspite* with the *Valiant*, the *Barham*, the recently arrived carrier *Formidable*, and nine destroyers after dark on the 27th.

At dawn on the 28th search planes from the *Formidable* sighted the Italian cruiser group and almost simultaneously a scout plane from the *Vittorio Veneto* spotted Pridham-Wippell's light forces. A few moments later, Pridham-Wippell sighted another Italian light force. As at the Battle of Jutland, neither commander knew of the presence of heavy forces nearby. Also, as Beatty had done at Jutland, Pridham-Wippell turned to lead the group he had just sighted toward Cunningham's battleships, a running fight continuing for nearly an hour, with no hits on either side. At 0855 Iachino directed his light forces to break off the action, as they were nearing the range of British shore-based air. Pridham-Wippell followed their retirement in order to keep in touch. To prevent his light forces from running into a trap, Cunningham ordered the *Formidable* to make a torpedo strike on the unengaged group of Italian cruisers. The planes however had so far to go that before they arrived on the scene the next dramatic development occurred. At 1100 a lookout in the *Orion*, Pridham-Wippell's flagship, spotted the *Vittorio Veneto*, which immediately opened accurate fire with her 15-inch guns. Caught between the *Vittorio Veneto* and the cruisers, Pridham-Wippell turned south behind a smoke screen. At this point the *Formidable's* torpedo planes arrived and attacked the Italian battleship. Although they scored no hits, they caused Iachino to break off the chase and set a course for home at 25 knots, with the British in pursuit.

For the next few hours the *Formidable* made repeated strikes in an effort to slow the Italian force so that the British battleships could come up. At 1520 a torpedo hit stopped the *Vittorio Veneto* temporarily, but an hour and a half later she was making 19 knots. Cunningham meanwhile had ordered Pridham-Wippell to press on at 30 knots with his cruisers and attempt to make visual contact with the fleeing Italian force. The battle fleet followed at its top speed of 24 knots. Because the British underestimated the speed of the *Vittorio Veneto* by four knots, their intercept courses were wide of the mark. Against just such a contingency Cunningham ordered another strike by the *Formidable's* planes, which stopped the cruiser *Pola*, the Italian main body continuing its run for home.

After these events the battle lost form. Misjudging the course and speed of the enemy, Pridham-Wippell failed to maintain contact after passing the crippled *Pola*. The battleships coming up later first mistook as British an Italian cruiser force returning to the aid of her helpless sister. Quickly rectifying that error, the battle fleet engaged the Italian group, sinking three cruisers, including the *Pola,* and two destroyers. The remainder of the Italian force made its way safely to port.

The British had achieved a considerable tactical victory at almost no cost to themselves. Although the *Vittorio Veneto* escaped them, they had sunk three Italian cruisers and two destroyers. One British cruiser had been slightly damaged, and one plane and pilot were lost. Belated air attacks by the *Luftwaffe* failed to do any additional damage to the British force.

The disproportionate victory provided a much needed lift to the morale of the Alexandria fleet and the British public at a time when the Mediterranean situation seemed dark. It had the important strategic consequence that the Italian fleet did not venture from the safety of its ports to interfere with British naval operations in the waters around Greece and Crete.

## The Loss of Greece and Crete

British troops did not remain long in Greece. From Bulgaria the German army had invaded southern Yugoslavia and Greece on April 6. To the 800 supporting aircraft of *Fliegerkorps IV,* the Royal Air Force could oppose only 80 operational planes plus two long-ranged bomber squadrons flying night missions from Egypt. Outflanked and outnumbered, the Greek and Yugoslav armies retreated. Yugoslavia capitulated on April 17. The Greeks had already decided that their cause was lost. The Greek King informally suggested that, to spare the country the ravages of further fighting, the British send no more troops and evacuate those already there. The War Cabinet immediately agreed to evacuate the mainland, and all British troops began to fall back on embarkation ports. On April 24 the Greeks surrendered. On the same night the British evacuation began.

For this task, even more difficult than Dunkirk, the Mediterranean Fleet had available seven cruisers, 20 destroyers, 21 transports, and a number of small craft. The port of Piraeus having been destroyed by the explosion of an ammunition

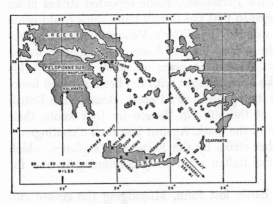

**SOUTHERN GREECE AND CRETE**

ship early in April, the evacuation had to be managed from three beaches in the Athens area and three in the Peloponnesus. To avoid air attack, the evacuating ships were ordered not to approach the beaches until one hour after dark and to leave by 0300. For six days the operation continued, with no air cover, with embarkation ports widely separated, and with less effective organization than at Dunkirk. Ship losses were heavy. Yet at the end over 50,000 British troops were saved. In addition, one cruiser, six destroyers, and four submarines of the Greek navy escaped to Alexandria.

Although the British had been forced out of Greece, they determined to save Crete. Its strategic position for controlling shipping in the eastern Mediterranean made the War Cabinet take the decision to hold it at all costs. A large number of troops evacuated from Greece served to stiffen the island's defenses, although loss of replacement parts caused the evacuation of all planes except for those the fleet might be able to provide. On the other hand, Crete lay within easy reach—60 miles—of the newly established German airfields in Greece and of an Italian strip on Scarpanto, only 45 miles to the east.

At dawn on May 20 the expected German assault came. The primary attack was made by 16,000 airborne troops of *Fliegerkorps XI* transported in 530 planes and 100 gliders, while following up were 7,000 reserve troops to be transported by sea. At 0800 gliders towed by transport planes landed troops west of Maleme airfield, and 15 minutes later parachute troops began to drop to the east. By the end of the day 5,000 airborne troops of the Seventh Airborne Division had landed, and Maleme field, though still under British artillery fire, was partly in German hands. Retimo and Heraklion fields had also been attacked, but less strongly, and the British forces there had held. Next day the Germans used Maleme airfield to build up their forces, even though many of their aircraft had to crash-land on the shell-pocked field.

For the sea defense of Crete Admiral Cunningham divided his forces into three groups. To the east and west of Crete two cruiser-destroyer forces were stationed during daylight hours with orders to carry out sweeps north of the island at night or when enemy forces were known to be at sea. The main body, including the *Valiant,* the *Warspite,* a cruiser, and eight destroyers, provided general support. On the night of May 21, a cruiser force which swept around the west end of the island met a German invasion flotilla of small craft 20 miles to the northward and sank about 15 of them, drowning some 4,000 troops. Low on ammunition, the cruisers withdrew to the westward to join the battleship force. Meanwhile another British cruiser force sweeping to the northwest sank several small vessels of another German convoy and drove it off.

Since it was now daylight and the British ships were low on ammunition and already under heavy air attack, their commander, satisfied that the convoy was retiring, did not pursue it but instead retired to the southwest and asked for support from the battleship force. Before the forces could join, two cruisers were damaged, and at 1330 the battleship *Warspite* was hit and a destroyer was sunk by Axis planes. Of two cruisers sent to help the stricken destroyer, one was sunk by air attack in Kithira Strait at 1550. About an hour later another British battleship was damaged, and in the next two and one half hours another cruiser was hit twice and finally sunk. During this night and day of wild activity, no German soldier reached Crete. Yet, although the Mediterranean Fleet had prevented the seaborne invasion of the island, on May 22 German airborne forces made Maleme airfield operational and began landing 20 troop-carrying planes and towed gliders an hour.

During the next few days the British forces fared badly on sea and land. On May 23 two destroyers en route to Alexandria were sunk by air attack. On the 26th while making an air strike against Scarpanto airfield, the carrier *Formidable* and a destroyer were badly damaged. Ashore, German troops broke through to Suda Bay, and the British troops there began to retire across the mountains to Sphakia on the south coast. Late that night the British decided to evacuate their forces from Crete. Next morning the *Barham* was damaged while covering the retirement of lighter forces from Suda Bay.

Like the withdrawal from Greece, the evacuation of Crete had to be carried out during darkness. On May 28 three cruisers and six destroyers manned by exhausted crews sailed from Alexandria for the Heraklion area in response to Cunningham's signal "Stick it out, we must never let the Army down." Although one cruiser was hit and forced to retire during the approach, the rest of the force embarked 4,000 troops that night. Homeward bound a damaged destroyer lost steering control and had to be abandoned, and air attacks sank a destroyer and damaged another and two cruisers. A bomb that exploded on the crowded mess deck of cruiser *Orion* killed or wounded 540 troops. In the whole force a total of 800 troops were killed, wounded, or captured.

Evacuation from Sphakia on the south coast was naturally less costly. During the night of May 29 four cruisers, a fast transport, and three destroyers picked up 7,000 troops and got away with damage to only one cruiser. Meanwhile the British forces in the Retimo area had surrendered. The next night 4,000 more troops were evacuated from Sphakia with the loss of still another cruiser.

In all the Royal Navy saved about 17,000 troops from Crete, at a cost to itself of three cruisers and six destroyers sunk; one aircraft carrier, three battleships, six cruisers, and seven destroyers damaged, and just over 2,000 caualties. Although the British had suffered about 13,000 casualties, their stubborn defense had cost the Germans 400 planes and

15,000 to 20,000 troops, including 5,000 men of their only airborne division. The British defense of Crete actually saved Malta, for after their Cretan experience the Germans had no airborne force available for further operations.

But the post-Crete situation of the Mediterranean Fleet was not a happy one. Despite the arrival of reinforcements consisting of a battleship, two cruisers, and six new destroyers in early May, at the beginning of June only two battleships, three cruisers, and 17 destroyers were operational. The British supply line from Alexandria to Malta was now flanked to the northward by German air forces based on Crete. As Malta grew weaker from lack of supplies, the Axis supply line to North Africa would become more secure.

Another threat to the eastern flank of the British army in Egypt and the fuel supply of the Royal Navy had developed meanwhile in the Middle East. In early April the pro-Axis Rashid Ali seized control of the government of Iraq. On the 18th, British naval forces under the Commander in Chief India supported a landing at Basra which quickly forced Rashid Ali to flee to Iran. By mutual agreement British and Russian forces moved into Iran in August to prevent its seizure by the Germans.

In Syria German agents, encouraged by the anti-British feelings of the Vichy-minded French colonial government, had been active. Here the French had a small naval force of two super destroyers armed with five 5.5-inch guns and capable of 40 knots, three submarines, a sloop, and a patrol vessel. To oppose these the British Mediterranean Fleet sent two cruisers and four destroyers to Haifa, Palestine. In early June a fast attack transport supported by another cruiser and two more destroyers landed British troops in Syria while other British and Free French forces advanced from Palestine. Three days later an armistice was signed. Before the fighting ended at sea, however, one of the French super destroyers heavily damaged a British destroyer, and French aircraft severely damaged two others. Reinforced by two more cruisers, British ships and naval aircraft sank a super destroyer en route to Syria with arms for the French and damaged the two that were already there. They also sank a submarine and two merchant ships.

## Rommel Takes the Offensive

While the British vainly attempted to save Greece and Crete, disaster loomed on the Egyptian border. Although the *Afrika Korps* had arrived during March, 1941, at first Rommel was concerned only with halting Wavell's drive toward Tripoli. Rommel himself had arrived in February and had devoted himself to stiffening the Italian defenses. Establishing a base at Tripoli, Rommel organized a group of small coasting ships to transport supplies from Tripoli to the port of Sirte, and later Ras el Ali some 250 miles to the east, a move necessitated by the fact that the Italians had never built a railway along the coast. Field Marshal Walther von Brauchitsch, Commander in Chief of the German army, had informed Rommel that there was to be no question of a major German offensive in North Africa and that he could expect no reinforcements. Rommel realized however that limited objectives could not be held in the desert, and that if he were to carry out his instructions to take Benghazi, he could not hold it, but must take all of Cyrenaica in order to obtain a position where he could secure his flanks.

Although Rommel's orders were not to begin even a limited offensive until the end of May, he feared that the delay would enable the British to strengthen the El Agheila-Bir es Sueva position, so he launched his attack on April 2. Wavell, who had sent part of his forces to Greece, and who had been forced to relieve his most experienced troops in Libya with inexperienced units fresh from home, could not withstand the precision of Rommel's advance and gave permission to fall back to Benghazi, or farther if necessary.

Agedabia fell to the Germans on the first day of their offensive, and reports came to Rommel that Benghazi had been evacuated. At this point, the Italian Commander in Chief, General Graziani, attempted to assert his authority and stop Rommel's advance as exceeding instructions from Rome and as impossible of support in the precarious supply situation. Rommel refused to consider wasting his opportunity. While the two men argued, Rommel received a dispatch from the OKW giving him complete freedom of action. After this, the *Afrika Korps* moved rapidly, seizing Benghazi the following day. Cutting across the bulge of Cyrenaica, Rommel reached Derna on April 8, capturing the city and some 800 men.

Immediately Rommel drove on toward Tobruk, which the British were busily reinforcing by sea through the efforts of the Inshore Squadron. After several unsuccessful attacks on Tobruk, thwarted by stubborn British resistance, the necessity for using inexperienced Italian troops, and the preoccupation of the *Luftwaffe* with strategic bombing rather than tactical support, Rommel decided to by-pass Tobruk and drive for Sollum, just over the Egyptian border where he expected to stabilize his front. By the end of May the *Afrika Korps* had established a strong position in the Sollum-Halfaya-Sidi Omar triangle, where it sought to build supplies for an offensive into Egypt.

The arrival in May of a special convoy, code-named Tiger, laden with 238 tanks, the first successful passage in several months of merchant ships from Gibraltar to Alexandria, made it possible for General Wavell to mount a counteroffensive against Rommel's position. Covered by maximum tactical air support, the drive, Operation BATTLEAXE, opened June 15. After heavy fighting, the attack failed, and General Wavell was replaced as Commander in Chief of the British Armies in the Middle East by General Sir Claude Auchinleck. The North African front thereupon stabilized for some months, neither the British nor the Germans having sufficient strength to mount an offensive. Further, while Tobruk remained in British hands Rommel could not advance to the important outpost of Mersa Matruh, whose airstrip would have enabled him to strike at Alexandria, Cairo, and the Suez Canal.

Off North Africa the Inshore Squadron kept up the supply of beleaguered Tobruk throughout the spring and summer. In August the overworked ships of the Tobruk Run were further burdened by the task of removing from Tobruk and replacing with others 19,000 Australian troops which the Dominion Government desired at home for defense against the Japanese threat. By the end of October the Inshore Squadron had completed the exchange and at the same time had delivered about 8,000 tons of stores for the garrison. Finally in November Auchinleck launched an offensive that raised the siege of Tobruk on December 10 and reached Benghazi two weeks later. In the 242 days of the Tobruk siege, the Inshore Squadron had brought in some 33,000 troops, 92 guns, 72 tanks, and 34,000 tons of supplies. During the same period its ships had removed 34,000 troops, 7,500 wounded, and 7,000 prisoners. The entire support operation had cost two destroyers, one minelayer, 24 small naval vessels, and six merchant ships sunk, with damage to seven destroyers, one attack transport, 19 smaller naval vessels, and seven merchant ships.

## The Battle of Supplies

During the summer of 1941, both sides in North Africa undertook to build up strength. The Germans, consolidating their gains in Greece, Crete, and Cyrenaica, used the maximum of Axis shipping capacity to send troops and supplies to North Africa. To oppose this flow of goods to Rommel, the British had to depend on Malta.

Situated almost at the mid-point of the Mediterranean, Malta not only served as a way station for ships passing between Gibraltar and Alexandria; it also sat squarely athwart the normal sea routes between Italy and Libya. Fighter planes and bombers based on Malta forced Axis shipping to make wide detours beyond the range of air strikes, effectively cutting down the efficiency of transport to North Africa. As a fleet base, Malta could threaten Italian and German convoys, forcing the Italian fleet to provide heavy escorts and to accept action under unfavorable conditions of air cover. When Malta was strong, nearly two fifths of Axis shipping for North Africa went to the bottom; when the island was weak, over 95 per cent arrived safely. The chart on page 62 shows this story graphically.

To keep Malta supplied, the British decided to send strongly escorted

THE IMPORTANCE OF MALTA

convoys approximately once a month. They had to provide heavy cover in view of heavy attacks to be expected from the Italian and German air forces and because of the danger of opposition by the Italian fleet. As a rule two convoys were run simultaneously, one from Gibraltar and one from Alexandria. Force H would escort the Gibraltar convoy as far as the Sicilian Channel, while the Mediterranean Fleet gave the Alexandria convoy protection right through to Malta. Despite all the British could do, convoys often were unable to win through under the blistering attacks from the skies.

As a result of the losses incurred in the Greek campaign, no surface ships could be spared for Malta during the late spring and summer, but in other respects the Malta situation greatly improved, largely because of the transfer in June of *Fliegerkorps X* from Sicily to Greece to replace half of *Fliegerkorps IV*, which was being transferred to Russia. Meanwhile British submarines and aircraft kept up the work of interdicting Axis communications to North Africa. In the first six months of 1940, the Axis shipped some 2,372,000 tons of material, losing not quite 80,000 tons for a loss rate of 3.4 per cent. In the second half of the year, while shipping only some 1,750,000 tons, they lost nearly 400,000 for a loss rate of 22.7 per cent.

To strengthen Malta's offensive capability, in October 1941 two cruisers and two destroyers dispatched from England were based on the island and designated Force K. On the night of November 8 they intercepted a Tripoli-bound convoy of seven German supply ships protected by two Italian cruisers and six destroyers, sinking all seven supply ships and one of the escorting destroyers. A British submarine sank another of the Italian destroyers the next day. About two weeks later a cruiser and a destroyer of Force K found two tankers escorted by two destroyers and sank both tankers while the escort escaped. At the end of November Force K was reinforced by two more cruisers and destroyers. In the middle of December four destroyers of Force K caught two Italian cruisers in the desperate expedient of rushing gasoline to Tripoli and turned them into blazing torches.

On November 18, 1941, the British Eighth Army began another offensive, advancing rapidly to Benghazi. Because of heavy losses in Axis shipping and lack of reinforcements, Rommel was forced to retreat after a masterly stand. He pulled all the way back to Agedabia before increased strength enabled him to resume the offensive.

The success of Force K and other Malta forces and the loss of Cyrenaica caused the German High Command to take a renewed look at the Mediterranean problem. Although Hitler was bemused with his campaign in Russia, others, especially Raeder, were fully aware of the strategic importance of the Mediterranean. The SKL (German naval staff) urged measures to strengthen Italy's use of her fleet to protect the shipping to North Africa. But when these matters came to Hitler's attention in August 1941, he ordered instead that U-boats be sent to the Mediterranean, against the advice of Raeder and Dönitz, who wished to maintain the Atlantic attack at full strength. The first two waves of boats made the passage of the Straits of Gibraltar in September and November

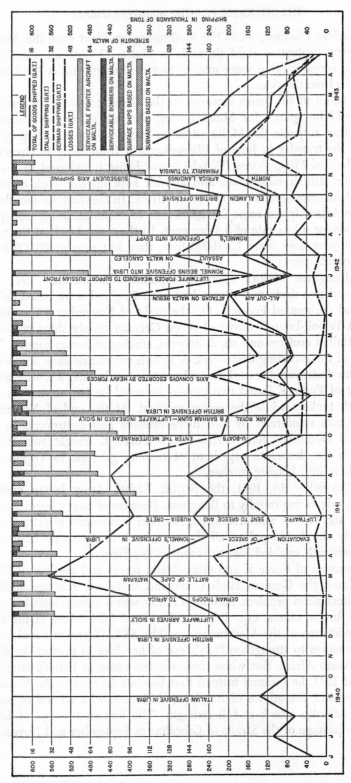

EFFECT OF THE STRENGTH OF MALTA ON AXIS TRANS-MEDITERRANEAN SHIPPING

1941, and soon thereafter made their presence felt dramatically. On November 11, *U-81* sank the *Ark Royal,* and twelve days later *U-331* sent the *Barham* to the bottom. In maneuvering to escape after the attack, the U-boat lost control and went to a depth of 820 feet safely, 490 feet deeper than her designed depth.

Other German efforts to stiffen the Mediterranean Theater followed. In December Hitler sent Field Marshal Albert Kesselring to Italy as Commander in Chief South with orders to gain and hold sea and air supremacy in the Sicilian Channel. At the same time Hitler sent *Fliegerkorps II* to Sicily.

To hold up their end of the struggle, the Italians agreed to provide heavy ship support for vital convoys and to attempt further attacks on British harbors. On December 19, 1941, Italian submarine *Scire* launched three two-man torpedoes (midget submarines with detachable warheads) in Alexandria which severely damaged the British battleships *Queen Elizabeth* and *Valiant.* About the same time *U-81*, the killer of the *Ark Royal,* damaged the *Malaya,* leaving the Mediterranean Fleet without a single serviceable heavy ship. Nor could replacements be provided, for Japan had entered the war, and her planes had sent the *Prince of Wales* and the *Repulse* to the bottom only a few days before.

To make matters worse, on December 19, three cruisers and four destroyers of Force K ran into a mine field off Tripoli which sank one destroyer and one cruiser and damaged two other cruisers. As a result of this disaster a big Axis convoy reached Tripoli safely.

Because of these increased Axis measures and severe British losses, the Axis shipping picture in the central Mediterranean improved enormously, enabling Rommel to resume the offensive in North Africa and recapture Cyrenaica during the first two months of 1942. Simultaneously the Axis intensified the air assault on Malta.

Despite the arrival of additional fighters for the defense of the island on November 11, the scale of attack more than doubled to 175 raids in December. In the first four months of 1942, as German air reinforcements poured into Sicily, the monthly total of raids ranged between two and three hundred. At the end of March British carrier *Eagle,* which had been flying in twelve Spitfires at a time, was laid up for repairs. Early in April, at the personal request of Churchill, President Roosevelt made the United States carrier *Wasp* available to fly in its much larger capacity of about 60 Spitfires, but these were all destroyed within a few days. That month the tonnage of bombs dropped on Malta reached a high of 6,700, and the British were forced to withdraw the surface ships that were still operational. Submarines ran in fuel and ammunition, but in early May the last Malta-based submarines retired to Alexandria. A second *Wasp* trip delivered 60 more Spitfires on May 9, just in time for a series of costly air battles on that day and the next.

At the end of these battles, Marshal Kesselring considered that his task of neutralizing Malta had been accomplished.

In March 1942 the supply situation at Malta became so desperate that all British North African forces concerted their efforts to get a convoy through. The Eighth Army made diversionary attacks upon Axis airfields near Tobruk. The Royal Air Force attacked airfields in Cyrenaica and Crete, carried out air reconnaissance and strikes from Libya and Malta, and provided air cover for the convoy to the limit of its endurance. Royal Air Force planes and a naval air squadron bombed the Libyan port of Derna on the nights of March 20 and 21. The weakened Mediterranean Fleet could provide only three cruisers and ten destroyers for cover and an antiaircraft cruiser and six destroyers for escort of the four-ship convoy. Six other destroyers made an antisubmarine sweep along the North African coast, in the course of which one destroyer was sunk; the remaining five, together with a cruiser and destroyer from Malta, reinforced the covering group.

During the morning of March 22 the convoy suffered intermittent air attacks without damage. In the afternoon an Italian force under Admiral Iachino consisting of the battleship *Littorio*, three cruisers, and four destroyers intercepted the British force north of Sirte. By adroit maneuvering, the use of smoke screens, and threatening destroyer attacks, the British admiral was able to keep between his convoy and the Italian force and hold off the superior enemy until sundown, when again Iachino retired to avoid a night action. Two of the four supply ships arived safely at Malta. Yet there was more honor than profit in the victory, for subsequent heavy air attacks upon the harbor sank the other two ships at their moorings after only 5,000 of their 26,000 tons of cargo had been landed.

In June, with Malta reduced to near starvation, the Admiralty made another desperate effort to send in two convoys, one each from Alexandria and Gibraltar. The first, of eleven ships, was escorted by seven cruisers and 26 destroyers with several smaller warships and the ancient, unarmed battleship *Centurion* pretending to be a capital ship. Nine submarines took station to the north of the convoy track to intercept the Italian fleet if it should leave port. Maximum air support covered the convoy as it advanced.

In spite of aircraft and submarines, the Italian fleet came on, losing one cruiser to a submarine, and suffering damage to the *Littorio* from an aircraft torpedo. Although the Italian fleet never made contact, Admiral Sir Philip Vian had to order the convoy to return to Alexandria since his ships had exhausted their ammunition fighting off air attacks.

The eastbound convoy, from Gibraltar, had better luck. Once it reached the Sardinian Narrows it came under heavy air attack, and then in the Sicilian Narrows it encountered a force of Italian destroyers. But, after heavy fighting, two of the six merchant ships won through, bringing temporary respite to Malta.

## The Axis Plan to Seize Malta

In the spring of 1942 German and Italian leaders agreed that for their North African ventures to succeed in winning through to Suez and making possible the acquisition of Iranian oil fields, they must first neutralize or capture Malta. Forces based there still exacted a toll of Axis shipping. Accordingly Hitler and Mussolini, meeting at Berchtesgaden late in April, agreed to launch an assault on Malta in July, after Rommel's forthcoming offensive. Rommel was to stop at the Egyptian border so that the *Luftwaffe* planes could be employed for the Malta operation. The plan provided for newly trained German airborne troops to be supported by Italian naval forces and seaborne troops. Hitler, never wholly supporting this operation, constantly sought an excuse to avoid it. He hoped that Rommel would be able to capture Tobruk, which the Axis might then use as a supply port for ships routed via Crete, beyond attack radius of aircraft based on Malta.

On May 26, Rommel resumed his offensive. His forces reached Tobruk on June 19 and broke through the defense perimeter the next day. On June 21, Tobruk fell. For this accomplishment Hitler promoted Rommel to field marshal. Rommel remarked, "I would rather he had given me one more division." The Germans in seizing Tobruk captured vast quantities of stores. In view of this unexpected windfall and with the port of Tobruk now available, Rommel requested permission to take advantage of his momentum and drive into Egypt. Hitler, seeing a chance to avoid the assault on Malta, wrote Mussolini a letter in which he described the Egyptian opportunities in glowing terms and urged him to agree to allow Rommel to attempt to capture Suez. Mussolini acquiesced. Shortly thereafter the Malta operation was postponed until September and then canceled.

Rommel drove hard, seizing Mersa Matruh and its important air base. Then an incredible thing happened. Hitler diverted reinforcements scheduled for Africa to the Russian front. Of the 60,000 tons of supply Rommel had requested for June, only 3,000 were sent. He was able to keep going only by seizing British materials. At one point 85 per cent of his transport consisted of captured British vehicles. He was obliged to call a halt at El Alamein, only 60 miles from Alexandria.

## The Turn of the Tide

Once again the supply race was on. While the Axis had to undertake only a three-day voyage to send material to North Africa, the British had to depend on the three-month voyage around the Cape of Good Hope.

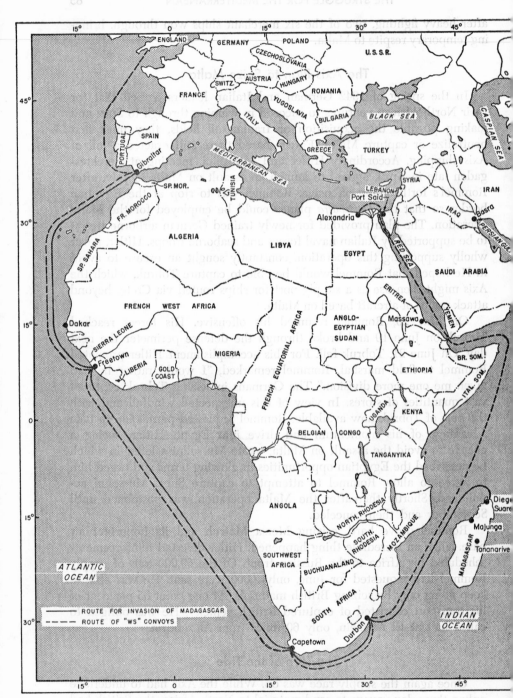

**THE MADAGASCAR OPERATION, MAY 1942**

ROUTE FOR INVASION OF MADAGASCAR
ROUTE OF "WS" CONVOYS

Rommel chiefly required food, fuel, and light vehicles, while the British desperately needed tanks. When Tobruk fell, the United States sent 300 brand-new Sherman tanks and 100 self-propelled 105 mm. guns.

Ever since Japan had entered the war and begun operations in the Indian Ocean, the British had been haunted by fears of an Axis base being established at Diego Suarez on Madagascar. From this base German or Japanese naval or air forces could not only threaten India but operate against the vital WS convoys to Egypt. Madagascar belonged to France, but the British had little faith in the Vichy Government, especially after reports of Admiral Darlan's visit to Germany at the beginning of the year and after Vichy's virtual cession of French Indo-China to Japan. Vichy clearly wished to be aligned with the winning side and still believed in an ultimate Axis triumph.

Heavy ships for Operation IRONCLAD, the capture of Madagascar, came from Force H, and included two aircraft carriers, the *Illustrious* and *Indomitable,* as well as the battleship *Ramillies,* two cruisers, eleven destroyers, with smaller craft, and 15 transports and assault vessels. Force H was replaced at Gibraltar by ships from the Home Fleet, which was in turn reinforced by American heavy ships temporarily transferred to Scapa Flow.

The assault on Diego Suarez took place at 0430 on May 5, 1942. After an uncertain start, a flanking attack by 50 marines turned the edge of the defenses, and within a few hours Diego Suarez was in British hands. A few weeks later the British also took Majunga and Tananarive. Once the Vichy officials had been supplanted, the people of the island generally supported the Allied cause.

With the danger to the Cape route cleared up, reinforcement of the British Middle Eastern position proceeded rapidly. In Egypt the British had approximately 630,000 men, and Churchill became impatient for a desert offensive. Shortly after the fall of Tobruk, he made up his mind to go to Cairo to see for himself why General Auchinleck delayed his scheduled attack on Rommel. He found Auchinleck so concerned with his responsibilities for the entire Middle Eastern area that he had not recognized the full importance of North Africa. After many discussions, Churchill decided to split the Middle East command in two, to relieve Auchinleck, and to give the new Near East Command to General Sir Harold Alexander and the Eighth Army to General Sir Bernard L. Montgomery. The latter, immediately on taking over on August 13, began to reorganize and retrain his forces to meet the expected German attack on the El Alamein position and for an eventual offensive. Montgomery planned not merely to roll the Germans back on their supply lines as previous British offensives had done but to destroy them as a fighting force so that they could not be turned against the forthcoming Anglo-American landings in North Africa.

Meanwhile the air reinforcement of Malta continued. Serviceable aircraft on hand rose from a low of 23 in May to 169 in September. Even more important than the increase in numbers was the greatly extended range of the new torpedo planes being delivered. In 1939 the effective attack radius of Malta-based torpedo planes had been only 100 miles; in 1942 it had increased to 400 miles. Now it was impossible for Axis shipping to avoid attacks, even by the most circuitous routing. Even in the harbors of Bardia, Tobruk, and Mersa Matruh, ships suffered heavy attack. Axis coastal shipping also met heavy losses. Thus while Rommel attempted to build up stores for resuming his offensive before September, the supplies he received barely covered his daily requirements for his infantry forces, and not half of what he needed for the Panzer Army. Only captured British supplies alleviated the situation.

Rommel knew that if he was to win a break-through at El Alamein, he would have to attack before the expected British heavy reinforcements could arrive in September. The Italian *Comando Supremo* promised heavy shipments of oil and gasoline, and Kesselring agreed to fly in 500 gallons of gasoline a day during the offensive. Accepting these promises, Rommel took the risk and on the night of August 30–31, 1942, hurled an attack at the ridge of Alam el Halfa, hoping to outflank the El Alamein defenses. Montgomery refused to be drawn out and contented himself with allowing Rommel's drive to spend itself against his strong defensive positions while the R.A.F. made punishing attacks on the German armor. None of Rommel's promised fuel oil or gasoline arrived, and on September 2, Rommel called off the attack.

"With the failure of this offensive," wrote Rommel, "our last chance of gaining the Suez Canal had gone. We could now expect that the full production of British industry and, more important, the enormous industrial potential of America . . . would finally turn the tide against us."

When Rommel withdrew on September 3, Montgomery did not pursue him. With his own supply line to the eastward secure, Montgomery continued to build up his forces for a massive offensive which began at El Alamein on October 23, 1942. After eleven days of furious fighting, the Eighth Army finally broke through and rolled on to the westward. Tobruk was in British hands again on November 13 and Benghazi on the 24th. On December 15 the Eighth Army reached El Agheila, and Rommel was in retreat toward Tunisia. Far to the westward British and American forces that had landed in Morocco and Algeria were advancing upon his rear. The tide of war in the Mediterranean had turned for the last time.

# 3

# The Battle of the Atlantic

"The only thing that ever really frightened me during the war was the U-boat peril." So wrote Winston Churchill after the victory. From the Allied point of view, the Battle of the Atlantic was being won when nothing was happening. Every time a convoy arrived in port, the battle was that much nearer victory. When a dramatic action took place at sea, the Allied cause came that much nearer defeat. Victory was won by many people, by merchant seamen who sailed in the freighters and tankers, by stevedores who loaded and unloaded them, by seamen, ratings, and officers who manned the escorting vessels and aircraft, by shipyard workers who built both merchant ships and escorts, and by thousands of people on both sides of the Atlantic who plotted U-boat positions, routed convoys, organized sailing lists, experimented with new devices, and analyzed the results of previous actions.

The most curious thing about the Battle of the Atlantic is that neither side really prepared for it. Although the Anglo-German Naval Treaty of 1935 allowed Germany under certain conditions to build her U-boat arm up to parity with that of Great Britain, the Germans constructed few boats because their building yards were fully occupied in preparing surface ships under PLAN Z. Thus Germany began the war with only 56 operational U-boats, of which only 22 were suitable for Atlantic service; of the remainder, ten had not completed operational readiness tests, and 24 were 250-ton boats of short radius, suitable only for North Sea operations.

Britain had allowed preparations for antisubmarine warfare to lapse into the status of a minor activity. The Admiralty had abolished its Mine Sweeping, Antisubmarine, and Trade Divisions. Britain built few small ships for antisubmarine work, for the Admiralty set forth the policy that in the event of another war "the convoy system will only be introduced when the balance of advantage is in its favour and when sinkings are so great that the country no longer feels justified in allowing ships to sail by themselves but feels that, for the protection of their crews, the convoy system is necessary. . . . It is simply a matter of expediency . . . [that] as convoy will not be needed immediately on the outbreak of war it will give us time to improvise protection, while orders are given to build the sloops which we shall eventually require." Because efficient convoy escorts could not be improvised, most of the escorts early in the war were hurriedly adapted from fishing trawlers and other small craft, ill-suited for the rigorous duties they had to undertake. Fortunately with asdic, and the parallel development of sonar in the United States, both the British and the Americans had a reliable underwater detector which, in the hands of an experienced operator, showed the direction and also the range of a submerged submarine out to approximately 1,500 yards. However the U-boats were later to adopt night surfaced attacks, thereby largely nullifying the advantage of asdic. In 1937 the Admiralty had regained full control of the Fleet Air Arm. Although this move had been made for the sake of fleet carrier operations, the Royal Navy could now integrate the Fleet Air Arm efforts into its anti-submarine warfare operations. At the same time the navy also attained close cooperation with the R.A.F. Coastal Command in matters pertaining to the protection of shipping. This harmonious partnership proved a decisive factor in the Atlantic struggle.

## Phase I: U-Boat Operations Until the Fall of France

When hostilities began in September 1939, Dönitz was obliged to operate with only a handful of boats rather than the 300 he considered a minimum. Yet one of this handful, *U-30*, by torpedoing the *Athenia* on the opening day of the war, provided an apparent indication of German intentions regarding the resumption of unrestricted U-boat warfare and abruptly dispelled the British Admiralty's hesitation in adopting the convoy system. On August 26, the Admiralty had assumed control of all British merchant shipping, and immediately after the *Athenia* sinking ordered convoys to be established over the principal routes for ships of speeds between nine and 14.9 knots. Ships outside these limits sailed independently. Later in the war, slower ships were included in slow convoys of about six to seven knots. Escort endurance precluded close support beyond 15° W or beyond 47° N for Gibraltar and Sierra Leone convoys. East Coast convoys operated successfully throughout the war with a loss rate of one tenth of one per cent. In October convoys between Britain and Norway began and continued with no losses until the invasion of Norway. Meanwhile a Dover mine barrage closed the Strait to German U-boats.

The success of these measures contrasts sharply with so-called "offensive" operations against U-boats. H.M. aircraft carrier *Ark Royal* on antisubmarine patrol narrowly avoided torpedoes on September 14; three days later *U-29* sank the 22,500-ton carrier *Courageous* patrolling with an inadequate screen off the Irish coast. Remembering the mythical success of the North Sea Mine Barrage of World War I, the British planned a similar barrage in World War II. After the fall of Norway, it was laid between Iceland and Scotland. It destroyed one U-boat, but otherwise did not affect U-boat movements at all.

The Germans too resorted to minelaying on a large scale, employing the *Luftwaffe*, surface vessels, and U-boats to sow their offensive mine fields in harbor entrances, estuaries, and shallows of the English Channel and the North Sea. These mines were of a magnetic impulse type, impossible to sweep by normal methods. On November 23, 1939, the British recovered a German magnetic mine which a plane had dropped in the mud flats in the Thames Estuary. Examination disclosed the operating principle, and the British were able partly to counter the magnetic impulse feature by means of an electrically charged cable running horizontally around each ship. This device, known as a "degaussing cable," cut to some extent into the effectiveness of the German minelaying campaign. Nonetheless, in the first four months of the war, German mines caused serious dislocations to coastal shipping and sank 79 merchant ships totaling 262,697 Gross Register Tons, almost all sailing independently.*

Meanwhile the convoys came through. U-boats sank 153,879 tons of Allied and neutral shipping in September, yet not one of their 41 victims was sailing under escort. By the end of 1939 the Royal Navy had escorted 5,756 vessels with the loss of only twelve ships, four being claimed by U-boats; during the same period 102 independently routed merchant vessels had been lost. Dönitz had lost nine U-boats, nearly a sixth of his strength. As he later revealed in his postwar *Essay on the Conduct of the War at Sea*, "U-boats at sea in operational areas during the winter 1939–40 never exceeded ten in number and at times fell as low as two."

Because of wide fluctuations in escort availability, screening dispositions changed frequently. Theoretically the best defense against U-boat assault was a formation that completely enclosed the merchant ships. These were disposed on a broad front with short flanks, a formation which reduced the U-boat's opportunities for beam attacks. To protect a convoy with a perimeter of seven miles (e.g. ten columns of four ships, columns 600 yards apart, ships in column 400 yards apart, as was the practice in 1939–40) escort commanders initially adopted the box screen of World War I, stationing an escort on each corner of the merchant

---

* Gross Register Ton, abbreviated G.R.T., is an internationally accepted measure of the carrying capacity of a cargo ship, computed on the basis of 100 cubic feet of cargo space per ton. Warship tonnage is measured in displacement tons. A freighter of 3,000 G.R.T. would have about 5,000 tons displacement.

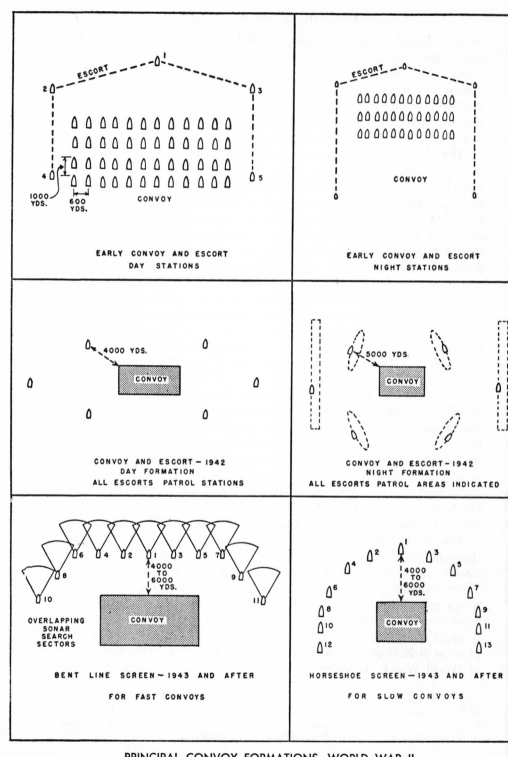

EARLY CONVOY AND ESCORT
DAY STATIONS

EARLY CONVOY AND ESCORT
NIGHT STATIONS

CONVOY AND ESCORT — 1942
DAY FORMATION
ALL ESCORTS PATROL STATIONS

CONVOY AND ESCORT — 1942
NIGHT FORMATION
ALL ESCORTS PATROL AREAS INDICATED

BENT LINE SCREEN — 1943 AND AFTER

FOR FAST CONVOYS

HORSESHOE SCREEN — 1943 AND AFTER

FOR SLOW CONVOYS

PRINCIPAL CONVOY FORMATIONS, WORLD WAR II

formation and ordering any additional units into the arc directly ahead. Early in World War II it was customary to employ cruisers or battleships in the escort, but when the threat of surface raiders diminished, the practice was abandoned as too dangerous to the large ships.

A typical early transatlantic convoy was made up of 30 to 40 merchant ships steaming in from nine to twelve columns. The customary rectangular formation with a broad front was adopted for several reasons. First, it reduced a U-boat's opportunities to attack from the advantageous beam positions; second, it was the most convenient one for inter-ship visual communication; third, it reduced the tendency of ships in the rear of a long column to surge up on the ships ahead; and fourth, it was the best compromise formation for controlling, with few escorts, the largest number of ships with the least risk of collision. Furthermore, it gave the escorts the most favorable opportunities both to deter U-boats from attacking and for attacking the threatening U-boats. Grouping of ships does, obviously, bunch targets, but a "browning shot," one fired in the general direction of a convoy, is unlikely to find a target if the ships are adequately spaced. Also the risk that a U-boat might slip through the defenses submerged by day or surfaced by night and sink a number of ships with a single salvo can likewise be reduced by appropriate inter-ship spacing.

Early British doctrine called for a prompt "hold-down" on an attacking U-boat. Such tactics, though successful in limiting convoy losses before the advent of wolf pack operations, seldom produced a kill, because there were so few escorts with each convoy, and most of these were of such relatively low speed that they were obliged to rejoin their convoy before they could gain the opportunity of delivering a *coup de grâce*. Thus a U-boat that had evaded its attackers could often resume stalking the same convoy. Dönitz' submariners favored night surfaced attacks from 45 degrees on either bow of the convoy, ensuring a short torpedo run that afforded the merchantmen little time for evasive action. Evolving British escort doctrine called for heavier bow defenses, ultimately producing in 1942 the "bent-line" screen, which provided strong protection on the bows while deploying additional warships directly ahead to intercept "down-the-throat" approaches. The problem of how to frustrate browning shots bedeviled escort commanders until 1942, when, using shipboard radar and H/F D/F (high frequency radio direction finder), they were able to extend their screens to ranges of 4,000 to 6,000 yards from the main body. At the same time the interval between columns was increased from 600 to 1,000 yards, a measure which reduced by about 50 per cent the probability of a browning shot hitting a ship, while increasing the perimeter of the convoy by less than 8 per cent.

U-boat mining operations in British waters during the first quarter of

1940 offered little indication of the intensified campaign that Admiral Dönitz was soon to unleash. Continuing their concentration in the South-western Approaches, German U-boats sank 85 ships aggregating 280,829 tons during January and February; only seven of their victims were in convoy, and these sinkings from convoy were achieved only at the cost of three U-boats. In the next three months, merchant ship losses declined as a result of a major redeployment of Dönitz' flotillas for the invasion of Norway, to which some 25 boats were committed.

In the ultimate success of the Norwegian invasion the U-boats played no part, being frustrated by widespread torpedo failures. Off Narvik, Günther Prien launched repeated attacks on anchored transports and cruisers, only to have all his magnetic torpedoes run deep. An exhaustive analysis of such unsuccessful attacks convinced the SKL (German naval staff) that torpedo failures had prevented U-boats from claiming one or more battleships, seven cruisers, and a number of destroyers and transports. Subsequent investigations, which resulted in a shakeup of the German Torpedo Inspectorate, revealed that the magnetic torpedo had an unreliable detonator as well as a tendency to run well below the selected depth settings. These were virtually the same by-products of inadequate testing that were soon to plague American submariners in the Pacific. Unfortunately for the Allies, the Germans rectified their deficiencies much more promptly than the Americans did.

Humiliating as the northern operations proved for BdU (*Befehlshaber der U-Boote*—Commander Submarines), the spring of 1940 laid substantial foundations for Dönitz' subsequent months of triumph in the Atlantic. The acquisition of Norway's entire coastline and the subsequent conquest of the Low Countries and France gave to Hitler the means of turning Britain's maritime flanks. While secondary U-boat havens were being established in Norway, Dönitz personally supervised the creation of heavily fortified bases on the French Atlantic coast at Brest, Lorient, St. Nazaire, La Rochelle, and Bordeaux. Possession of these French bases meant a reduction of over 50 per cent in the transit time of U-boats to their Atlantic hunting grounds. Unfortunately for Britain, the R.A.F. was so heavily engaged over the Channel that it was unable to disrupt the construction of massive concrete "pens" in these Biscay ports, with the result that they were strengthened to the point of invulnerability. Late in July *Luftwaffe* support added to the strategic effectiveness of these French bases.

## Phase II: The Mid-Atlantic Offensive Based on French Ports

In July 1940 U-boats began operating from French bases. The reduction in cruising time to patrol stations had the effect of increasing the number of U-boats available in the operating areas. Thus Dönitz was able to make an attack on convoys by the tactical innovation of *Rudel-taktik*, or wolf pack operations. Still preferring to attack independent shipping, the U-boats nevertheless now had a means of forcing their way through the escorts to the body of the convoy. The toll of Allied shipping mounted ominously, exceeding 500,000 tons in June; U-boats accounted for 58 merchantmen of 284,113 tons, largely in the vulnerable Southwestern Approaches. These June sinkings were but a prelude to the French-based "Golden Age," of the *U-Waffe*, a four-month campaign in which Dönitz' wolf packs, abetted by the *Luftwaffe*, unleashed their first crippling assaults on North Atlantic convoys. Midway in July BdU concentrated his strength in the waters off Rockall Bank, 260 miles west of Scotland, and for the first time employed wolf pack tactics. When a U-boat made contact with a convoy it would not attack immediately, but would trail, decks awash, well behind the target, while it reported the convoy's course, speed, and composition to BdU headquarters in France. BdU would then assume tactical command, ordering the other boats of the pack to make contact with the shadower. On the scene, the senior commander would then take over, attempting to coordinate a night surfaced attack that would swamp the escort and then annihilate the convoy. Dönitz, soon concluding that effective control of pack attacks was impossible on the scene, began directing the operations by radio from U-boat command headquarters.

In order to assist in the new campaign, Italy dispatched some 27 submarines to the Atlantic to cooperate with the Germans against merchant shipping. With German assistance, the Italians established a submarine base at Bordeaux, from which the Italian boats operated under German strategic command. At first the Germans attempted to integrate the Italians into pack warfare, but because the Mediterranean boats were slow and unhandy, the results were less than ideal. At length the Italians were allocated the waters south of 45° N as their operating area. Because most Allied traffic operated north of this parallel, the Italians found few targets.

The British were hard pressed to meet the new threats. Casualties to destroyers and other escorts during the Norwegian campaign and the Dunkirk evacuation had been heavy. Since at that time there was a daily average of 2,000 British merchant ships at sea, the need for escorts was desperate. Additional destroyers were ordered and two new types were authorized—corvettes and frigates. The former were vessels of less than 1,000 tons, mounting one or two 4-inch guns, equipped with depth charges and asdic. Corvettes were unsuited for operations in the North Atlantic, yet they had to be used there because nothing else could be provided in time. The new frigates, appearing considerably later, were much larger and had better sea-keeping qualities than the corvettes. These two types, assisted by trawlers, luggers, and other small vessels, bore the brunt of escort work in the North Atlantic for half the war. To tide them over the difficult times ahead, Churchill as early as May 1940 requested the loan of some 50 American destroyers for convoy work.

In July 1940 the British extended the limits of close escort of convoy from 15° W to 17° W for transatlantic convoys, a move that served to nullify a part of the gain of the U-boats' time on station. On the other hand, escorts of ocean convoys were severely weakened by withdrawal of larger escort ships to be used in anti-invasion patrol during the summer of 1940. Some convoys sailed protected by a single escort. Sinkings naturally mounted as summer wore on. The following table for seven months in 1940 shows the results of pack operations and of weakening convoy escorts. The sinking figures are losses in tons from all causes.

| March | April | May | June |
|-------|-------|-----|------|
| 107,009 | 158,218 | 288,461 | 585,496 |

| July | August | September |
|------|--------|-----------|
| 386,913 | 397,229 | 448,621 |

In October, to try to cut down the slaughter, the Admiralty again extended the westward limits of ocean convoy escort, this time to 19° W. The benefit of this move however was largely lost by the reduction in the upper speed limit of convoys in order to permit more ships to sail independently. In spite of Admiralty arguments to the contrary, an economic committee, worried about decreasing amounts of cargo reaching Britain, in November persuaded the War Cabinet to permit faster ships to sail independently in order to make swifter passages. The Admiralty clearly realized that some ships might make individual voyages more quickly, but they also realized that the ships had to remain afloat if they were to deliver cargoes, and knowing that individual ships got sunk more quickly than convoyed vessels, predicted that these ships would soon be delivering fewer cargoes. In the event, the Admiralty was proved right by differential statistics of losses. Though the economic experts insisted on counting stragglers from convoys as sailing in convoy, independent losses by their count were still twice those of ships under escort. Not until June 1941 was the upper speed limit of 15 knots restored.

U-boats preferred to enjoy the easy kills of independent ships rather than employ wolf pack tactics to tangle with convoys, however inadequately they might be escorted. For a five-week period in late 1940, not a single ocean convoy was molested, yet independent losses soared. In the mid-Atlantic, not only were ships unescorted, but also the U-boats had immunity from air attack. In spite of long-range air patrols from Britain and from Canada, there remained a broad stretch of the central

North Atlantic which land-based aircraft simply could not reach. In this "Black Pit" the U-boats reaped a rich harvest among ships sailing independently. As convoy escort was extended westward, the U-boats perforce had to make pack attacks on escorted convoys. Most heavily hit was eastbound SC-7, a slow 34-ship convoy intercepted some 250 miles northwest of Bloody Foreland, north Ireland. Attacking at dusk, Lieutenant Commander Otto Kretschmer in *U-99* with six other experienced boats penetrated the four-ship screen, sinking 17 merchantmen in a midnight melee. Scarcely had this "Night of the Long Knives" ended, when weakly escorted HX-79, a fast 49-ship convoy, ran afoul of Günther Prien's *U-47* and five others which again swamped the defense and claimed an additional 14 victims. Several boats had already exhausted their torpedoes and had begun homeward passage when eastbound HX-79A entered these same waters, at the cost of seven more merchantmen.

These one-sided encounters climaxed Dönitz' first determined foray into the Northwestern Approaches, the "Happy Time" in which his U-boats sank 217 merchant vessels, totaling over 1,100,000 tons, at the cost of only six boats. Such success firmly convinced BdU of the bright prospects of wolf pack operations, yet, because of the limited number of boats available and their need for replenishment, they could not maintain this attrition rate. Less than half a dozen U-boats patrolled off Rockall during the last two months of 1940, and heavy weather frustrated efforts to locate the increasingly evasive British convoys. Allied merchant tonnage losses from U-boat attack declined to an average of some 180,000 tons during November and December. By Christmas 1940 only one U-boat lurked in the Northwestern Approaches, and when Dönitz reckoned accounts at the end of the year, he discovered that construction had barely made good the loss of 31 boats since the war's outbreak.

In the spring of 1941, the *U-Waffe* achieved increased success. Late in February, Dönitz dispatched several of his most experienced commanders to conduct an all-out blitz in the Northwestern Approaches where, on the evening of March 6, four boats located westbound Convoy OB-293, which they attacked for 24 hours. At dusk on the 7th, Prien in *U-47*, seeking to increase his bag of some 160,000 tons, attempted to penetrate the screen under the cover of a rain squall. H.M.S. *Wolverine* spotted Prien's submarine through the gloom and dispatched the killer of the *Royal Oak* with a barrage of depth charges. Eight days later the remainder of the group located HX-112. Although Schepke in the *U-100* promptly sank a 10,000-ton tanker, the U-boats achieved no further sinkings until the night of the 16th when the *U-99's* commander, Otto Kretschmer, slipped through the screen and, racing up and down the columns, torpedoed four tankers and two freighters before disappearing astern of the main body. At midnight the escort commander, Commander Donald Macintyre in H.M.S. *Walker*, detected *U-100* approaching on the surface. Crash diving, Schepke escaped, but a determined joint attack by two destroyers forced him to the surface where he was fatally rammed by H.M.S. *Vanoc*. Minutes later the *Walker* blasted *U-99* to the surface with an accurate pattern of depth charges. Most of the crew, including Kretschmer, were subsequently rescued by Macintyre. Thus the British captured the *U-Waffe's* most brilliant tactician, whose score of 266,629 tons sunk was unequalled during the war.

The loss of their three outstanding aces within little more than a week produced profound depression at BdU headquarters at Lorient. With other losses, the Germans were suddenly confronted with an attrition rate of nearly 20 per cent in the Northwestern Approaches. As foul weather continued to frustrate *Luftwaffe* reconnaissance over the North Channel, between Ireland and Scotland, Dönitz reluctantly shifted his wolf pack operations some 200 miles to the west, beyond the range of Coastal Command bombers based on Northern Ireland. This move provided the first indication of his "tonnage warfare," the strategic corollary of wolf-pack tactics. Tonnage warfare was founded on the concept of concentrating U-boat activity in areas where the most Allied merchant tonnage might be sunk at least cost to the *U-Waffe*. Thus, when defenses became strong in one area, Dönitz would shift his boats to another in order to capitalize on remaining "soft spots," even though vital Allied cargoes might meanwhile be delivered to crucial areas. As a result, during several critical periods in the war the North Atlantic was almost completely uncontested.

On April 1, 1941, the British Admiralty received operational control of Coastal Command aircraft and hence was able to integrate air activities directly with convoy movements. Beginning in April, long-range aircraft were based on Iceland, whence they were able to cut drastically the size of the Black Pit, which now came to be known as the Greenland Air Gap. With these changes came increased fuel capacity in the newer escorts, which enabled escort to be provided as far as 35° W. The increasing strength of the Royal Canadian Navy permitted the Canadians to undertake escort in the western Atlantic and to establish a link with the British. On May 27, 1941, there sailed from Halifax Convoy HX-129, the first North Atlantic convoy to be escorted all the way across the ocean.

This sailing marked the end of the second phase of the Battle of the Atlantic. Since the beginning of the war, the U-boats had sunk some 650 ships, yet only ten per cent of these had been lost from escorted convoys, and none had been sunk when air escort supplemented surface escorts. On the other hand, 60 per cent of all U-boats lost had been sunk while attacking convoys. Now, the Germans would be obliged to attack convoys, accepting an increased loss rate of U-boats if they were to maintain their rate of sinkings.

## Phase III: "All Aid to Britain Short of War"

From the earliest days of the war the United States had watched the events in Europe apprehensively, and most Americans desired to remain on the sidelines. The U.S. Navy had studied the Battle of the Atlantic, but America's primary naval efforts were directed at keeping the belligerents out of the Western Hemisphere. On September 5, 1939, in an effort to avoid involvement, President Roosevelt had established a Neutrality Patrol. Early in October, the Pan-American republics had announced a neutrality zone extending some 300 miles out into the Atlantic. Both of these measures were designed to keep the war localized. Strong anti-war sentiment had resulted in the American Neutrality Act of 1937, which abandoned many of the neutral rights the United States had fought for in World War I and established the "cash-and-carry" principle that belligerents could trade with the United States only if they bought goods with cash and carried them in their own ships. The Act prohibited trade in munitions, but rising pro-Allied sentiment in November 1939 brought about a change to permit munitions to be sold on the same basis. Although by language the cash-and-carry policy was strictly neutral, actually it favored the British, for their blockade allowed no German shipping in the North Atlantic.

The end of the period of "Phony War" awakened the American Congress to the threat from abroad. Swiftly it passed legislation providing for a two-ocean navy and for the first peacetime draft in United States history. Events however were moving faster than legislation. Great Britain's desperate need for destroyers grew more evident every day. On the other hand, considerable doubt existed, in Washington as elsewhere, that Britain could survive the German onslaught. The prospect that the Royal Navy might be turned over to Germany made it necessary for the United States to conserve ships and to build new ones as rapidly as possible. Accordingly, President Roosevelt sought assurance from Churchill that the British fleet would never be surrendered to Germany. Churchill refused to make an unequivocal promise. The most he would say was that *he* would never do it; in the event of a British defeat, his government might be turned out of office and another group might use the fleet as bargaining chips at the surrender table.

Although this assurance was somewhat less than satisfactory, Roosevelt decided to take a calculated risk and transfer 50 American destroyers to the British flag. There was of course a danger that Germany would declare war on the United States, but Hitler had no desire to involve himself with America until the situation in Europe was settled.

Lord Lothian, British Ambassador to the United States, concluded arrangements in late July 1940 for a deal whereby the United States would give 50 "obsolete" destroyers to Great Britain in return for 99-year leases on a series of bases running from Newfoundland to Trinidad. Final agreement was signed in September. By mid-April of the following year, the 50 destroyers had been delivered, as well as ten *Lake*-class Coast Guard cutters well equipped for antisubmarine duty.

The American destroyers alone were not enough to solve Britain's problems of supply. In response to the destroyers-bases deal, Hitler on September 6, 1940 removed the last restrictions on U-boat warfare against British ships and accepted the possibility that some American ships might accidentally be sunk. He even toyed with the idea of seizing some of the Atlantic islands, but Raeder warned him that the German navy was in no position to mount such operations.

In an effort to give further assistance to Great Britain in her struggle against Nazi Germany, President Roosevelt in December 1940 proposed the idea of Lend-Lease. British ships would still have to pick up the goods; only the "cash" part of the "cash-and-carry" policy was to be changed. This proposal, unlike the destroyers-bases deal, required Congressional approval, which took place in March 1941 after extended hearings. Once again Hitler did not declare war.

The change from the Neutrality Act to Lend-Lease was another step in the President's "all aid short of war" policy. In order to see how America's efforts could best be directed to the common cause, Roosevelt sent military representatives to England in August 1940 for "exploratory talks." These discussions led to plans for cooperation in the Atlantic war in the event of American participation. This conference was followed by another in Washington in late January 1941, which resulted in the "ABC-1 Staff Agreement," which spelled out, first, America's "short of war" contribution and, second, the action to be taken by the United States in the event she was forced into the war. Fundamental to this doctrine was the basic concept that in event of war with Japan, Britain and the United States would devote their primary effort to defeating Germany first. Germany was considered the more dangerous because of her industrial development, the achievements of her scientists, her proximity to Britain and Russia, and her military achievements thus far. This strategic decision was never changed during the war, even though it later became possible to take the offensive in both oceans at the same time. The United States agreed that in the near future the U.S. Navy would assist in escorting convoys in the North Atlantic.

To prepare for these new responsibilities, the Navy Department reorganized the Neutrality Patrol and gave it the more appropriate title of United States Atlantic Fleet. On February 1, 1941 Admiral Ernest J. King hoisted his flag as its commander. By mid-June plans for American escort of transatlantic convoys were made whereby the U.S. Navy was to concentrate on the segment from Argentia, Newfoundland to Iceland, where British escorts would take over. The acquisition of terminal bases for these operations posed a difficult problem, one whose solution was suggested early in March when Hitler publicly extended his U-boats' war zone right up to Greenland's three-mile limit. Under strong British persuasion, the government of Iceland on July 7 permitted an American naval force to land the First Marine Brigade at Reykjavik as an advance element in the relief of Britain's garrison already there. Within two months, United States naval patrol squadrons were flying convoy coverage from Reykjavik, while surface escorts refueled at nearby Hvalfjordur.

While the Atlantic Fleet's short-of-war operations provided badly needed protection for Allied and neutral shipping that joined American-escorted convoys, these operations were, for political reasons, initially declared to be independent of the North Atlantic convoy pattern that Britain had developed between Nova Scotia and the British Isles. By July the Anglo-Canadian system had achieved at least minimum anti-submarine surface escort for both slow (6½-knot) and fast (9-knot) convoys all the way across the North Atlantic. Canadian escorts normally shepherded these "Halifax" convoys as far east as a Mid-Ocean Meeting Point (MOMP) at the 35th meridian, where British warships based in Iceland took charge, proceeding with little air cover to the EASTOMP, about the 18th meridian, before turning the convoy over to Western Approaches forces for the final run to the North Channel. A heavy attack on Convoy HX-126, which lost nine ships off Cape Farewell, Greenland, during May, underscored the pressing need for continuous air escort for North Atlantic convoys, but two grim years lay ahead before such coverage could be extended to the Greenland Air Gap.

Three events of May 1941 brought about a further bold American step despite dangers of involvement in the war. First was the sinking by a U-boat of the neutral Egyptian ship *Zamzam* carrying about 150 American passengers. The second was the sinking in late May of the South Africa-bound American freighter *Robin Moor* by a U-boat which left without making any provisions for the safety of the crew. The third was the appearance of the *Bismarck*, which shocked American as well as British public opinion by her sinking of the *Hood*. On May 27, the very day the *Bismarck* was sunk, President Roosevelt declared an Unlimited National Emergency and announced to the country that more vigorous steps would be taken to keep the Germans from American waters.

The United States Navy found itself as ill-prepared for antisubmarine war as the British had been in 1939. The obvious need was for an escort vessel smaller than a destroyer and especially designed for convoy work, a vessel which could be built more rapidly than a destroyer and at lower cost. While in many ways a destroyer is an ideal escort ship, her high speed and versatile offensive power are largely wasted in escort-of-convoy work. The answer was found in the destroyer escort, a smaller version of the destroyer, slower, and especially designed for antisubmarine operations. The British and Canadian navies began building steam versions of these vesels at the rate of about eight a month, and in July 1941 American shipyards started construction of them for the British at the rate of ten a month. American models included both steam and diesel-electric types.

The German invasion of Russia in June 1941 added considerably to the problems of supply, for the Russians were also afforded Lend-Lease aid and had few ships in which to transport the goods. To discuss this problem and others, Churchill and Roosevelt met at Argentia, Newfoundland in August. This meeting enabled the Chiefs of Staff of the two countries to discuss plans for American escort of convoys, and it produced the Atlantic Charter, a statement of the war aims of England and the United States.

For a considerable period American warships on Atlantic patrol had broadcast to the British the location of U-boats detected, although the Americans had refrained from attacking. After Admiral King had described such U-boats as "potentially hostile," there was some doubt as to what action an American naval vessel should take if it should encounter a U-boat in the American zone of responsibility. That question was answered by the affair of the *Greer*. This U.S. destroyer was about 200 miles southwest of Iceland when on September 4, 1941 she received a signal from a British plane that a U-boat was about ten miles ahead of her. The *Greer* made sound contact with *U-652*, keeping the contact for over three hours, but not attacking. At length, the U-boat fired a torpedo at the *Greer*, which evaded, and then counterattacked with depth charges. Thus the first shots were exchanged in the undeclared war between German and American naval forces. President Roosevelt issued a statement declaring, "From now on, if German or Italian vessels of war enter the waters, the protection of which is necessary for American defense, they do so at their own risk."

By this time Dönitz had an increased and rapidly growing number of U-boats and was responding to Allied end-to-end convoys by strong wolf pack attacks. The *U-Waffe* however had been frustrated by fog and inadequate air reconnaissance, claiming only 377,339 tons of shipping during the third quarter of 1941. In mid-October BdU succeeded in staging a major attack against North Atlantic convoys. On that occasion, American escorts dispatched to the relief of Convoy SC-48 learned a number of hard lessons, including the futility of indiscriminate depth charging and the need for aggressive night patrolling. Assaulted some 400 miles south of Iceland, this 50-ship convoy had already lost three vessels when five U.S. destroyers and two British escorts reached the scene. Their close screening tactics failed to prevent the U-boats from sinking six more ships with relative impunity, and shortly thereafter they torpedoed but failed to sink the American destroyer *Kearny* as she was silhouetted by one of the burning freighters. The Atlantic Fleet had scarcely digested the lessons of this encounter when it sustained its first loss, U.S.S. *Reuben James,* on October 31 as she and four other American destroyers were escorting HX-156 some 600 miles west of Ireland.

Notwithstanding these early disasters, British naval officials keenly appreciated the growing United States commitment in the North Atlantic, and by mid-October 1941, following American agreement to extend convoy coverage east to within 400 miles of Ireland, the Commander in Chief, Western Approaches (Cincwa) found it possible to shift three escort groups from the Northwestern Approaches to supplement the escorts of hard-pressed convoys bound for Gibraltar and West African ports. This strategic redeployment proved highly opportune for the Admiralty, now confronted with reports of U-boat activity in several new maritime theaters. Heavy weather weakened Dönitz' North Atlantic campaign during the last quarter of 1941, a period in which U-boats sank only 342,820 tons of Allied shipping, yet these same months saw increasing concentrations of U-boats all the way from North Cape to the African Gold Coast. Long-range 1,100-ton (Type IX-B) U-boats had launched operations off Freetown, West Africa in May 1941, highlighted by the record success of *U-107,* which sank some 87,000 tons of shipping in a single patrol and obliged the Admiralty to divert convoys well west of the Canaries. German plans for a mid-winter blitz off Capetown were temporarily frustrated by British success in sinking two German supply ships, but it was evident that South African antisubmarine defenses would soon be strained to the utmost.

In spite of Allied air bases in Iceland, there still remained the Greenland Air Gap, where U-boats ranged freely in the continued absence of aircraft and where convoys still sailed with inadequate numbers of surface escorts. To assign fleet carriers to the convoys for air protection was out of the question, for the fleet had too few for its other needs. Yet something had to be done not only to afford protection in the Greenland Air Gap but also to protect ships from *Luftwaffe* attacks, which had accounted for 44 ships of 94,551 tons in the months of June, July, and August. Because early experiments with catapult-equipped merchant ships flying off expendable aircraft had been obviously makeshift, the Admiralty had been experimenting with inexpensive, easily constructed carriers especially designed for operating with convoys. At first the British con-

verted merchant ships or naval auxiliaries; later they designed escort
carriers from the keel up. The first to see action, H.M.S. *Audacity*, a converted German prize, proved herself in her short career. The *Audacity*
accompanied Convoy HG-76 of 32 ships, whose escort of 12 corvettes,
sloops, and destroyers, was under command of Captain Frederick John
Walker, one of the Royal Navy's ablest antisubmarine tacticians.

The initial U-boat onslaught on December 17 was disrupted by several
of the *Audacity*'s planes, which sighted *U-131* some 20 miles ahead,
homed in five escorts, and assisted them in sinking the contact keeper.
Another stalker, *U-434*, was sunk by destroyers on the 18th, and although
*U-574* managed to blow up H.M. destroyer *Stanley* during a midnight
melee that also claimed a merchantman, H.M. sloop *Stork* finished off
the U-boat by ramming. On December 21, after the *Audacity*'s airmen
had destroyed four German Kondor aircraft, several U-boats finally succeeded in penetrating the screen at night, sinking one ship. The *Audacity*,
steaming alone, ten miles from the convoy screen, fell a victim to *U-751*
some 500 miles west of Cape Finisterre. Counterattacking with disci-
plined coordination, Walker's escorts flushed *U-567*, sending her veteran
crew to the bottom. Concurrently the convoy came within range of
United Kingdom-based air escorts. The combined effect broke the back
of the pack's running assault and induced BdU to break off this costly
attack. Upon reviewing this nine-day operation, Dönitz recognized that
the aggressive British escort tactics and particularly the use of the escort
carrier, which had cost him five boats, raised serious doubts about the
future of wolf pack operations in the eastern Atlantic. Renewed opportunity for successful tonnage warfare now beckoned from the west however, and by the close of 1941 the BdU was eagerly planning his first
campaign in North American waters.

### Phase IV: The U-Boat Offensive in American Waters

After the Japanese attack on Pearl Harbor on December 7, 1941 had
brought the United States officially into the war against the Axis powers,
Churchill and his Chiefs of Staff visited Washington to work out with
Roosevelt and the American Chiefs of Staff the strategic direction of the
war. Churchill recognized that American aid to Britain would necessarily
be cut back for the time being as the United States began to grapple
with her new responsibilities in the war. He recognized however the
potential power of the New World and was confident of victory.

Top military direction of the war was organized at the Washington
meeting. The British representatives—Admiral Sir Dudley Pound, the
First Sea Lord; Air Chief Marshal Sir Charles Portal, the Chief of the
Air Staff; and Field Marshal Sir John Dill, the former Chief of the Im-

perial General Staff—sat down with General George C. Marshall, U.S. Army Chief of Staff; General Henry H. Arnold, Chief of Staff of the U.S. Army Air Corps; and the newly appointed Chief of Naval Operations, Admiral Ernest J. King. These men, or their successors on the British side, and with the addition of Admiral William D. Leahy, Chief of Staff to the President, constituted the Combined Chiefs of Staff. On their shoulders rested the burden of the responsibility for global war.

Direction of the American effort in the war fell to the Joint Chiefs of Staff—the four top American military men, Leahy, Marshall, Arnold, and King. To King in particular the earliest burden fell, since it was at sea that America could first challenge the Axis and first was challenged.

To meet these new threats, the United States Navy was extensively reorganized in the early months of the war. King had relieved Admiral Harold R. Stark as Chief of Naval Operations (CNO) in December 1941. Admiral Chester W. Nimitz relieved Admiral Husband E. Kimmel as Commander in Chief of the Pacific Fleet (Cincpac) in the same month. King's old job as Commander in Chief of the Atlantic Fleet (Cinclant) was taken over by Admiral Royal E. Ingersoll. In March 1942, because of confusion as to the division of function of the offices of the Chief of Naval Operations and that of the Commander in Chief, U.S. Fleet (Cominch), the two offices were vested in Admiral King, who became the first and only man ever to hold both titles. Also, because the Naval District organizations were primarily administrative commands, King found it advisable to set up operational commands known as Sea Frontiers which would conduct operations in the waters they included. These commands were the Eastern Sea Frontier in the Atlantic, the Caribbean Sea Frontier, the Gulf Sea Frontier, the Panama Sea Frontier at the approaches to the Canal, and the Western, Northwestern, and Hawaiian Sea Frontiers in the Pacific.

Japan's attack on Pearl Harbor had proved a complete surprise to Germany. Hence, although Germany and Italy declared war on the United States on December 11, over a month elapsed before the U-boats could launch an attack on vulnerable American shipping. To the chagrin of Dönitz, eager for a spectacular blow, the SKL insisted on retaining a large proportion of some 64 Atlantic boats in the Mediterranean and in the heavily patrolled approaches to Gibraltar. As a result, BdU was initially able to allocate only five 1,100-ton U-boats for the impending attack on shipping between Cape Hatteras and the Gulf of the St. Lawrence. This opening thrust, designated Operation PAUKENSCHLAG, was designed to paralyze offshore traffic, thus reducing the flow of oil and other raw materials to the American East Coast industrial areas. By a gradual extension into the Gulf of Mexico and the Caribbean, BdU hoped to stretch Allied escort strength to the breaking point. Broadly speaking,

Dönitz calculated that seaborne trade in the Western Atlantic, weakly protected by inexperienced forces, might yet provide a key to tonnage victory. According to BdU estimates at this time, a sustained monthly merchant ship attrition of 700,000 tons was necessary to achieve this objective. Even if Britain could not be completely strangled, she might yet be driven to accept a negotiated peace.

The U-boat assault in North American waters temporarily stunned both United States and Canadian defense forces. Hard-hitting Group *Paukenschlag* of five boats had been closely followed across the Atlantic by six 740-ton boats which unleashed a concurrent attack in the waters off Newfoundland. Group *Paukenschlag* swiftly ambushed a score of independents between Hatteras and Cape Breton Island. From the outset, these U-boats found particularly happy hunting off the Carolina Capes, discovering many merchantmen unarmed and some still burning their running lights. In the absence of convoys *Rudeltaktik* was unnecessary. Operating individually, the Germans lay submerged offshore until dusk, then moved in with decks awash and dispatched their victims with gunfire or torpedoes. Worldwide merchant tonnage losses were greatly inflated by this mounting slaughter. From December's toll of 124,070 tons lost to U-boats, the totals climbed in January to 327,357 tons, 467,451 tons in February, and 537,980 tons in March. During March, 28 vessels aggregating 159,340 tons were sunk in the Eastern Sea Frontier alone, over half of these ships being tankers.

Against this onslaught, American shipping defense measures proved inadequate, notwithstanding the remarkable fact that Dönitz never had more than a dozen boats in the Western Atlantic. Because of demands from the Pacific and a continuing commitment of other available destroyers to North Atlantic convoys, Commander Eastern Sea Frontier, Vice Admiral Adolphus Andrews, possessed negligible surface forces and only nine patrol aircraft at the close of 1941. Although 170 army and navy aircraft were committed to offshore patrol by late March 1942, Andrews regarded his hundred-odd destroyers, Coast Guard cutters, converted yachts, and armed trawlers as insufficient for coastal convoys. Convinced that a "convoy without adequate protection is worse than none," a dictum contrary to British wartime experience, the Eastern Sea Frontier resorted to a series of emergency measures, including hunter groups, "offensive" patrols, and U-boat decoy vessels ("Q-ships") with concealed guns. The slight value of these measures can be seen not only in the destruction of 23 ships in the Eastern Sea Frontier during April, but also in the fact that not a single U-boat had been sunk in this area during the first three months of the East Coast blitz. It is small wonder that the U-boat crews referred to this period as the "Second Happy Time."

Drastic measures were required to avert a shipping catastrophe, for in March total Allied merchant ship losses had soared to over 800,000 tons for the first time in World War II. In February the British had given the United States 24 trawlers and ten corvettes, all provided with the latest asdic equipment. The first step toward providing coastal convoys was taken by the establishment of "Bucket Brigades," small convoys that ran escorted during daylight hours and put into protected anchorages at night. In mid-April the Admiralty decreased the frequency of its convoy sailings from Halifax from five to seven days, enlarging the convoys and releasing two desperately needed escort groups for service in American waters. Increasing the size of convoys cut the ratio of escorts to the ships protected, for the number of ships which can be protected depends on the *area* of the circle enclosing them, while the number of escorts depends on the *circumference* of a larger concentric circle.

It took another month to establish a convoy system on the East Coast of the United States. "Escort is not just one way of handling the submarine menace," wrote Admiral King, "it is the only way that gives any promise of success. The so-called hunting and patrol operations have time and again proved futile." That King was right can be seen from the results. U-boats had sunk 87 ships of 514,366 tons during their first four months off the East Coast, yet Dönitz promptly began shifting his boats southward on the appearance of convoys, making no effort to contest them by wolf pack tactics. The Germans found profitable hunting in the Gulf of Mexico and Caribbean where no convoy system existed, and sank 41 vessels of 219,867 tons during May, nearly half being tankers torpedoed off the Passes of the Mississippi. This onslaught was checked by the establishment of an Interlocking Convoy System which enabled ships to transfer at sea from one convoy to another. This system required extremely careful planning of convoy movements and rendezvous, but it offered the necessary flexibility for the complicated pattern of Caribbean and Gulf shipping.

Moving once again in search of unprotected ships, U-boats fell upon independent traffic off Trinidad, Rio de Janeiro, and Capetown, exploiting the logistic versatility of a handful of new 1,700-ton supply U-boats or "milch cows." Thus supported, U-boat commanders managed to double the length of their patrols off the Panama Canal and along the Guianas coast, with devastating results. In the Western Atlantic, U-boats claimed 26 merchant ships in May and averaged over 20 victims in the four ensuing months, notwithstanding the extension of convoys to Port of Spain in July. Round-the-clock air cover, as distinct from air escort, failed to deter these U-boats because they evaded radar detection by conforming to convoy course and speed during their furtive assaults. Allied escort forces succeeded in destroying three U-boats in these waters in the fall

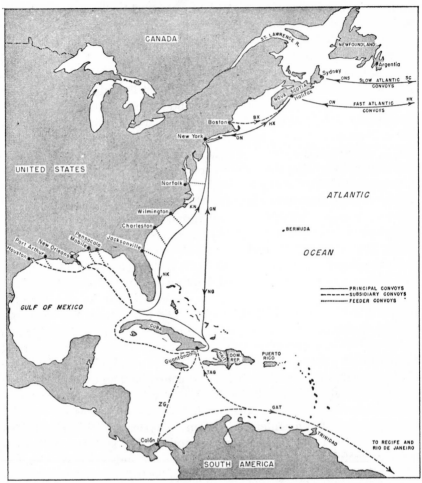

THE WESTERN ATLANTIC, SHOWING THE INTERLOCKING CONVOY
SYSTEM AS DEVELOPED IN 1942

of 1942, yet the Germans continued to exploit the Trinidad approaches
with profit to the end of the year since many independent ships continued
to use these waters.

Caribbean operations accounted for but a fraction of the 1,505,888
tons of Allied shipping lost to U-boats in the third quarter of 1942. In
mid-August ten U-boats moved into Brazilian waters for a blitz against
coastal and transatlantic shipping. Five Brazilian freighters were torpedoed by *U-507* off Bahia, provoking Brazil to declare war on Germany
and emphasizing the urgency of extending the coastal convoy system
southeast of Trinidad. Escort shortages delayed creation of this final link,
but Vice Admiral Jonas H. Ingram, commanding the U.S. South Atlantic

Fleet, scraped together sufficient forces to frustrate German hopes of reaping yet another windfall of shipping. Although dissatisfied with the meager results of this attack, Dönitz dispatched a second wave of U-boats to the Cape San Roque area during November and December. His U-boats claimed over 20 ships before the establishment of regular convoy between Trinidad and Bahia, and the destruction of *U-164* and *U-507* by Catalinas broke the back of this distant offensive.

### Phase V: Return to the Mid-Atlantic

Following the adoption of convoys with air as well as surface escort in American waters, Dönitz decided to shift the burden of his attack back to the mid-Atlantic, where the U-boats would be free to attack convoys without air escort. Yet immediately he was called upon to divert a significant portion of his strength to attacking Allied convoys on the "Murmansk Run" to North Russia.

British convoys to North Russia, begun in August 1941, had suffered negligible losses to U-boat and air attack during the first three months of 1942, but with a northward shift of German surface strength, the situation changed rapidly. The new battleship *Tirpitz*, sister of the *Bismarck*, now in service, moved to Norwegian bases, as did the *Scheer, Lützow,* and *Hipper.* The next few convoys met increasingly severe air and U-boat attack. At this time, because of the Madagascar operation, American units reinforced the Home Fleet at Scapa Flow and were available for operations to protect the convoys bound for North Russia.

These convoys both Roosevelt and Churchill held to be political necessities for keeping Russia in the war. Yet increasingly severe attacks on ships making this passage led professional opinion to consider these convoys little better than suicide. Convoy PQ-16 in May lost seven out of 34 merchant ships, and casualties to the accompanying warships were heavy. The SKL planned an all-out attempt, Operation RÖSSELSPRUNG, to annihilate the next convoy to Russia, employing the *Luftwaffe,* U-boats, and heavy and light surface forces.

Fully aware of the grave risks, the Admiralty provided PQ-17 with 21 escorts and a covering force of three destroyers and four cruisers, while dispatching a distant support force of two battleships, H.M.S. *Duke of York* and U.S.S. *Washington,* three cruisers, 13 destroyers, and H.M. aircraft carrier *Victorious.* The convoy left Hvalfjordur, Iceland on June 27, 1942 with 33 merchant ships, three rescue vessels, and a fleet oiler. Routed well north of Bear Island, where the midnight sun provided continuous daylight for air attack, the convoy was subjected to three days of intensive onslaught reaching a climax on July 4. Throughout, the convoy maintained taut discipline, thereby minimizing casualties and destroying several German planes. After thwarting these attacks with the loss of only four ships, one a cripple that eventually reached port, the convoy's confidence was high. Then came a stunning series of messages from the Admiralty:

> 9:11 P.M. Most Immediate. Cruiser Force withdraw to westward at high speed.
> 9:23 P.M. Immediate. Owing to threat of surface ships, convoy is to disperse and proceed to Russian ports.
> 9:36 P.M. Most Immediate. Convoy is to scatter.

Behind this extraordinary series of messages lay the Admiralty's conviction that the *Tirpitz* would be able to engage the convoy and the cruiser force. Reconnaissance planes had lost contact with her, but the British knew that she might be in position to intercept any time after 0200 July 5. The support force of battleships and the *Victorious* was too far west to interfere, for it was protecting westbound QP-13, which was beyond Jan Mayen and thus out of serious danger. The First Sea Lord had based his decision on negative intelligence and interfered with operations 1,500 miles away where he could not know the situation. In view of the urgent tone of the Admiralty messages, Rear Admiral L. H. K. Hamilton, commanding the cruiser force, expected to see the *Tirpitz* at any moment and felt he had no alternative but to comply. The destroyers with the escort also detached themselves to support the cruisers in their anticipated desperate battle with the *Tirpitz*.

Ironically, though the *Tirpitz, Scheer,* and *Hipper* did begin to carry out Operation RÖSSELSPRUNG, as a result of confused aerial reconnaissance and of Hitler's no-risk policy, they returned to port after ten hours at sea. The British Admiralty had no way of knowing that the Germans would not attack, but they did know from past experience that German surface ships were reluctant to engage strongly escorted convoys and consistently refused action with escorts of even cruiser strength.

As a result of the order to scatter, PQ-17 lost 21 more ships. Of the 13 that reached port, 11 had joined rump convoys. Two ships were lost from the rump convoys, but 19 independents were sunk. Thus, the subsequent fate of PQ-17 indicates that even under the most difficult circumstances, convoy integrity provides the greatest chance of survival of merchant ships.

Significant consequences flowed from this operation, most notably the British decision to suspend convoy sailings to North Russia until the fall of 1942. American disappointment over the futile employment of the *Washington* and her consorts led to Admiral King's rapid transfer of these ships to the Pacific. Henceforth King viewed combined U.S.-British naval operations with disfavor. German forces in Norway had meanwhile been thoroughly roused by the success of RÖSSELSPRUNG, making a resumption of Allied convoys to North Russia additionally perilous.

When powerfully protected PQ-18 of 40 merchant ships sailed in

September, it included in its escort the British escort carrier *Avenger*, whose planes, together with the convoy's antiaircraft guns, destroyed some 40 German planes. The surface escort sank three U-boats. Although the convoy lost 13 ships, only three were sunk by U-boats. Instead of scattering, the convoy remained together, vindicating once against the wisdom of convoy integrity. For the next few months, because of the impending landings in North Africa, the British were unable to send convoys to Russia. By means of Operation TRICKLE, the dispatch of small "flights" of unescorted merchant ships in company, they managed to "pray through" only five of the 13 ships they sent, losing over 60 per cent.

In the south too U-boats became active. In mid-October, Group *Eisbaer* passed through the Atlantic narrows, and after waylaying isolated shipping, including the ill-fated British transport *Laconia*,* prepared to unleash an offensive off Capetown. One of these raiders, the *U-179*, was promptly sunk, but the remaining boats proceeded to devastate shipping east of the Cape, claiming in October and November 31 ships off Capetown and in Mozambique Channel before beginning the long return passage.

Dönitz recognized that a decisive victory could be obtained only in the mid-Atlantic. U-boat production had by July 1942 reached the rate of 30 boats a month, and this increase in strength enabled him to accept increased risks in making attacks on convoys. The risks were constantly mounting, for most Allied air and surface escorts were now equipped with radar. In addition, the availability of larger numbers of escorts permitted the Allies to form Antisubmarine Support Groups of six to eight destroyers, frigates, and corvettes. Later, escort carriers operated with the surface ships. These Support Groups, manned by highly experienced personnel, had no regular escort duties, but were available to come to the aid of convoys undergoing heavy U-boat attack.

Keenly conscious of the added danger of air escorts, Dönitz concentrated his attack in the Black Pit area. He stationed picket lines on both sides so that convoys moving in either direction could be attacked throughout its entire width while the U-boats enjoyed virtual immunity from air attack. The loss figures mounted, reaching a peak of 807,754

---

* The *Laconia* was sunk on September 12 northeast of Ascension Island by *U-156*, which discovered that the transport carried 1,800 Italian prisoners of war as well as 811 British servicemen. On orders from BdU, other *Eisbaer* boats moved to the rescue, while *U-156* broadcast a plain language appeal for assistance. The U-boats had several hundred survivors under tow on the afternoon of the 16th when an American B-24, flying from Ascension, circled and finally attacked *U-156*, even though she displayed a Red Cross flag on her bow. On receiving a report on these proceedings Dönitz forbade all attempts to rescue merchant ship survivors. During the Nuremberg Trial, Allied prosecutors attempted to prove that this "*Laconia* order" had actually constituted a veiled attempt to encourage deliberate slaughter of survivors. A full examination of relevant facts, including known cases of atrocities, destroyed this contention.

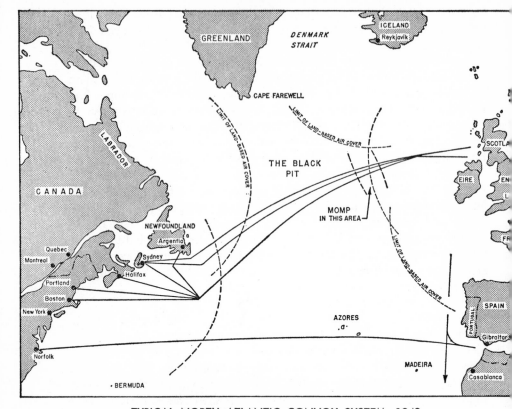

## TYPICAL NORTH ATLANTIC CONVOY SYSTEM, 1942

Allied convoys were designated by a combination of letters and numbers indicating the port of origin, destination, and the particular convoy number. Principal ocean convoy routes and their destinations were: Halifax-United Kingdom, HX; United Kingdom-Halifax, ON; Sydney, Nova Scotia-United Kingdom, SC; United Kingdom-Sydney, ONS; Boston-Halifax, BX; United Kingdom-Gibraltar, OG; Gibraltar-United Kingdom, HG; United Kingdom-North Russia, PQ (later JW); United States-Gibraltar, UGS; Gibraltar-United States, GUS.

G.R.T. in November 1942, at which time Dönitz was forced to weaken the attack in a belated effort to disrupt the North African landings. Nonetheless, U-boats continued their efforts in the Black Pit area, rising to a crescendo in March 1943.

By Christmas 1942 the Allies recognized that they must devise some methods of countering the flexibility of strategic deployment enjoyed by the highly centralized U-boat command. Hence when the Allied heads of state met with the Combined Chiefs of Staff at Casablanca in January 1943, they agreed that "the defeat of the U-boat must remain a first charge on the resources of the United Nations" and ordered a staff conference to reorganize Atlantic convoy control. The consequent Washington Convoy Conference rejected politically explosive proposals for a unified Allied antisubmarine command and on March 1 adopted Admiral King's formula whereby the British and Canadians retained control of North Atlantic convoys, while the United States assumed responsibility for Central Atlantic convoys (to the Mediterranean and to the south from ports south of Halifax) as well as for the Interlocking Convoy System.

In Britain, Admiralty Operations Research scientists in analytical studies of the convoy battles of 1941–42 discovered that the number of ships sunk from convoys was completely independent of convoy size. Instead sinkings depended only on numbers of attacking U-boats and, when no air escort was present, on the number of surface escorts. Thus if the average size of convoys could be increased from 32 to 54 ships, the number of escorts would increase from six to nine, while convoy losses would be reduced 56 per cent by the enlargement of the convoy and 25 per cent by the increase in number of escorts. If air escort was present only during an average of eight hours a day, losses could be reduced 64 per cent from those obtaining during the period of 1941–42. Increasing the size of convoys would reduce their frequency, enabling the strengthened surface and air escorts to be provided without any increase in the escort forces. Also the same number of merchant ships then being employed could actually provide an increase in deliveries.

Although Allied shipping losses declined to 344,680 tons in April 1943, BdU clearly regarded this as a temporary slump, inevitably following the intensive operations of March. To offset the decreasing effectiveness of individual boats resulting from the marked improvement of Allied countermeasures, Dönitz prepared to build a new concentration of unprecedented magnitude in the North Atlantic. The showdown in the North Atlantic came on April 28, when westbound Convoy ONS-5 was intercepted by a U-boat picket line off Iceland, losing one merchantman and escaping a general attack only by heading into a fog bank. Although badly scattered by a gale off Cape Farewell, this 42-ship convoy was brilliantly rounded up by its escort commander, Commander Peter W. Gretton RN, and headed south into what proved to be a concentration of 51 U-boats. Newfoundland-based Catalina aircraft claimed the *U-630* on May 4, but by nightfall U-boat Group *Fink* was moving in from all quarters, catching the freighters sharply etched against the northern lights. Eleven U-boats nearly swamped ONS-5's escort and sent seven ships to the bottom before dawn, adding four more victims the next morning from among the stragglers. The corvette *Pink* succeeded in depth charging *U-192* fatally, but by dusk, as some 15 U-boats moved in, the battered convoy faced annihilation. Then the tactical situation changed completely. Nosing into another fog bank late on the evening of May 5, ONS-5 sustained no fewer than 25 separate attacks without losing a single ship. Dönitz' boats, lacking radar, were repeatedly driven off by the seven escorts. The aggressive attacks of two freshly-arrived Antisubmarine Support Groups, taking maximum advantage of radar and H/F D/F, completed the Germans' frustration and helped send four more boats to the bottom between midnight and dawn.

This action proved to be the climax of the Battle of the Atlantic. The U-Waffe never recovered from this unexpected reverse off Newfoundland. German wolf packs had decimated their last Halifax convoy. The intervention of Antisubmarine Support Groups, escort carriers, and long-range aircraft had provided the key to Allied success. In the three weeks following the ordeal of ONS-5, twelve convoys crossed the Black Pit, losing a total of only five ships, while air and surface escorts sank 13 U-boats. Against Dönitz' large and relatively blind wolf packs, the British tactics of bait and kill now came to fruition, forcing the U-boats to abandon the North Atlantic in May and search for less dangerous hunting grounds. Confronted by the enormous loss of 41 submarines in "Black May," Dönitz resorted once again to tonnage warfare strategy, ordering his boats south in hopes of saving the U-Waffe from annihilation until technological developments permitted a return to the North Atlantic. This decision permitted relatively unimpeded passage of Allied convoys in the twelve months before the invasion of Normandy. Thus, under combined pressure of vastly improved Allied antisubmarine measures and a great increase in American shipbuilding, the strategy of tonnage warfare collapsed. In July monthly Allied ship production at last exceeded worldwide shipping losses from Axis action, and by the end of the year the Atlantic Allies achieved an annual production rate of 14.4 million tons of merchant shipping, exceeding German estimates by 40 per cent.

The devastating antisubmarine offensive undertaken by Anglo-American forces late in the spring of 1943 was the product not simply of mounting warship and aircraft production but also of extensive reorganization, systematic indoctrination of personnel, and decisive advances in the science of undersea warfare. The creation of the U.S. Tenth Fleet, invested with broad supervisory control of American antisubmarine development, proved of fundamental importance in stimulating effective training, supplying scientific methods to the perfection of weapons and tactics, and coordinating operational intelligence. Established on May 1, under the personal command of Admiral King, with Rear Admiral Francis S. Low as chief of staff, this secret administrative organization provided comprehensive support for operations of the Atlantic Fleet, whose newly-activated Hunter-Killer Groups of escort carriers and destroyers or destroyer escorts were soon to distinguish themselves in the Central Atlantic.

## Phase VI: The Central Atlantic and Biscay Offensives

Dönitz' decision late in May 1943 to shift pack operations southwest of the Azores presented Commander U.S. Atlantic Fleet, Admiral Ingersoll, with a long-awaited opportunity to employ his new Hunter-Killer Groups. For rapidity of tactical innovation, operations during the next three months by groups centered on the escort carriers *Bogue, Card, Core,* and *Santee* in support of Central Atlantic convoys are virtually unsurpassed in naval history. Airmen from the *Bogue,* pioneering Wildcat-Avenger team tactics, located Group *Trutz* on June 3 while escorting Convoy GUS-7A, sinking *U-217* and the milch cow *U-118* and damaging several other boats. Subsequent efforts by this 17-boat pack to locate Central Atlantic convoys were frustrated south of the Azores in mid-July by the widely-roving *Core* and *Santee* groups, which destroyed four more boats, including two supply submarines, while introducing "Fido," the U.S. Navy's new antisubmarine homing torpedo.

Driven to desperation by these aerial tactics, remaining German submariners fought back on the surface, enabling the *Bogue, Santee,* and *Core* groups in mid-summer to claim five more victims. Meanwhile the *Card's* air group, commanded by Captain Arnold J. Isbell, had sent four more submarines, including two milch cows, to the bottom. In less than three months, Ingersoll's Hunter-Killer Groups had sunk 15 U-boats, eight operating as supply boats, with the loss of only three aircraft. This attrition of U-tankers, sharply contrasting with the sinking of one convoyed merchantman, effectively disrupted German efforts to concentrate on Central Atlantic convoys and greatly reduced the impact of U-boat operations in the Caribbean and in the South Atlantic and Indian Oceans.

Severe as were the *U-Waffe's* losses in mid-Atlantic, they were of less concern to BdU than the concurrent slaughter of U-boats in the Bay of Biscay, where since the spring of 1942 the R.A.F. Coastal Command had been attempting a sustained offensive. Employing radar, the British aircraft had enjoyed a limited success in detecting U-boats in this transit area. This advantage disappeared when Dönitz began fitting his U-boats with a radar receiver called *Metox,* which could pick up the radar search signal at a far greater range than the reflected signal could be detected by the search receiver. Early in 1943 however planes suddenly resumed attacking surfaced U-boats while *Metox* was giving no indications. BdU interpreted this phenomenon to mean that *Metox* was emitting a signal detectable on passive radar and accordingly ordered commanders to discontinue its use. Actually the British had developed a new ultra-high-frequency radar of ten centimeter wavelength, which *Metox* could not detect. The attacks continued, aided by the aircraft Leigh Light, an 80-million candlepower attack searchlight, employed in conjunction with radar in sudden blinding night attacks from the air. Throughout March and April many of these attacks were limited in success because of the U-boats' regular practice of crash diving when attacked. While German scientists worked desperately and fruitlessly to improve *Metox,* Dönitz added antiaircraft armament to his U-boats and, reversing his previous

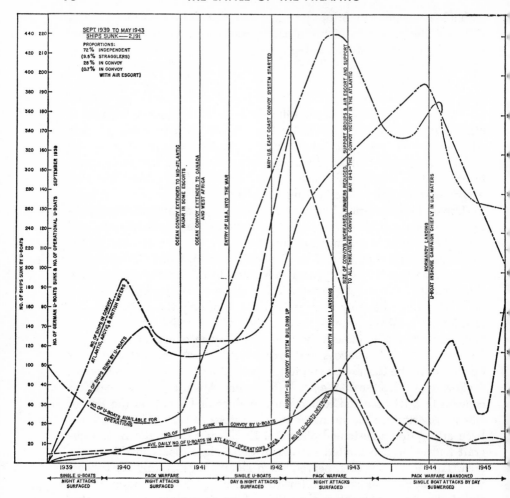

## THE EFFECT OF THE CONVOY SYSTEM

instructions, ordered all Biscay transients to proceed submerged at night and surface to charge batteries only in daylight. Most significantly of all, BdU advised all commanders to fight back on the surface whenever their aerial attackers were too close to permit crash diving.

Although British bombers destroyed six submarines in the Bay of Biscay during the first three weeks of July, the "Big Bay Slaughter" did not get underway until the 28th. In the next week, American and British aircraft and the British Second Support Group sank nine U-boats. Under such relentless pressure BdU not only discontinued its group transit policy but early in August suspended all departures from Biscay bases. Thus the Bay offensive culminated in a virtual blockade of Dönitz' West France flotillas. Later BdU managed to resume sailings, routing its

U-boats along the northern coast of Spain, where they enjoyed virtual immunity from radar detection. Altogether during the campaign 28 U-boats were sunk in attempting passage of the Bay of Biscay.

## Phase VII: The Final Struggle for the North Atlantic

After some three months of comparatively fruitless exploitation of tonnage warfare, Dönitz on September 19, 1943 gave orders to strike once again at the main Allied North Atlantic convoy routes. He was now prepared to employ a new weapon, the *Zaunkönig*, or acoustic torpedo, which would "home" on a ship's screws. Designed to be employed against the escorts, it was supposed to blast a hole in the screen to permit attacks on the merchant ships with conventional torpedoes. In September Group *Leuthen* struck at westbound Convoys ON-202 and ONS-18, sinking three escorts, damaging one, and sending six merchant ships to the bottom. To counter the *Zaunkönig*, British and American warships began using a noisemaking countermeasure called "Foxer," which when trailed astern drew the acoustic torpedoes harmlessly into it.

Ultimately however the German offensive in the North Atlantic was smothered by systematic day-and-night close air escort of all threatened convoys—in the old Black Pit as well as elsewhere. In this escort work, land-based planes coordinated with aircraft flying from escort carriers, which operated either with the convoys or with British Antisubmarine Surface Support Groups. The Surface Support Groups were now also able to join the land-based planes in providing night as well as day escort of convoys. These Allied countermeasures proved so effective that Dönitz withdrew his boats from the Black Pit and in October attempted a concentration south of Iceland, only to lose three U-boats to land-based aircraft. Although Dönitz recognized the extreme peril of attacking convoys in the North Atlantic, he persisted in doing so until February 1944, enduring heavy losses while inflicting only slight damage to Allied shipping. The combination of close surface escort, land-based air escort, and Antisubmarine Support Groups with escort carriers for local air support had made the North Atlantic convoys virtually immune to attack.

In mid-October the Portuguese granted the British permission to operate Coastal Command aircraft from the Azores. This acquisition of a mid-Atlantic base, combined with night air escort of threatened convoys, proved the final blow to Dönitz' hopes of organizing a renewed campaign against convoys in the North and Central Atlantic. Renewed Allied successes in the Bay of Biscay, regular air patrols from the Azores, and the relentless probing of British and American Hunter-Killer Groups in the Outer Bay effectively broke the back of this last wolf pack effort. Pending the activation of the high-speed Type XXI U-boat, whose production was beginning to suffer under Allied bombing raids, Dönitz candidly stated, "In the present phase of the campaign it is not victory but the survival of boats and their crews that must take priority."

## Phase VIII: The Final Campaign

For several significant reasons, including the Anglo-American invasion of France, U-boat losses, which had totaled 237 during 1943, increased during the following year, while the production of the much-vaunted hydrogen-peroxide Walter U-boat continued to be delayed. Dönitz, now commander in chief of the German navy, was obliged to expend his *U-Waffe* in operations far from the vital North Atlantic.

The Royal Navy's escort carrier groups came fully into their own with the Murmansk convoys, which became the sole focus of wolf pack activity during 1944. The Admiralty, twice obliged to suspend sailings to Murmansk through the necessity of using all escorts elsewhere, had been able to reopen the North Russian route late in 1943. Northbound Convoy JW-58 provided an example of an antisubmarine task force convoy, being escorted by two escort carriers, two antiaircraft cruisers, and a close screen of nine warships, and enjoying the close cover of two Antisubmarine Support Groups. Captain F. J. Walker RN, who had commanded the *Audacity* group in December 1942, was in command of the escort. His group claimed the first shadower, *U-961*, on March 29, after which aircraft from H.M.S. *Tracker* and *Activity* teamed up with the close escort to dispose of three more boats, while the convoy proceeded without loss to Murmansk. Operating continuously within sight of the convoy, British escort carriers imposed an intolerable rate of exchange on the U-boats. Altogether British escort carriers destroyed 13 U-boats in northern waters during 1944, a period in which Murmansk convoys suffered the loss of only six ships. Increasingly heavy *Luftwaffe* attacks on subsequent convoys proved futile. Thus ended the grimly dramatic history of the North Russian convoys.

During 1944 American Hunter-Killer Groups, assigned the task of affording distant protection to North Africa- and Mediterranean-bound convoys, fulfilled their purpose chiefly by attacking U-boats refueling near the Cape Verde Islands en route to major offensives off Capetown and in the Indian Ocean. Late in February *U-709* blundered into a Hunter-Killer Group built around the escort carrier *Block Island* and was promptly finished off by two destroyer escorts, the *Bronstein* and *Thomas*. Shortly after midnight on the 29th the *Bronstein*'s captain, Lieutenant Sheldon H. Kinney, detected *U-603* moving toward the *Block Island*, drove the German down, and shortly thereafter applied the *coup de grâce*. After a brief respite the group headed southwest toward an apparent concentration of U-boats off the Cape Verdes, being rewarded on

March 17 when the *Corry* and *Bronstein*, following up a series of aerial attacks, sent the *U-801* to the bottom. Two days later the *Block Island's* aircraft spotted and destroyed *U-1059*, thus concluding a highly successful cruise for this new Hunter-Killer Group.

Disturbed by growing evidence of Hunter-Killer activity, Dönitz moved his main fueling rendezvous some 700 miles farther west in mid-April, only to discover that these waters too were infested with carrier aircraft. The impossibility of continuing U-tanker operations was grimly revealed to Dönitz by the report of *U-66*, which radioed on May 5, "Mid-Atlantic worse than Bay of Biscay." Scarcely had the German completed this transmission when he was located by a plane from the *Block Island*. Lacking bombs or depth charges, the pilot homed in the destroyer escort *Buckley*, which at 0320, May 6 succeeded in closing the range to 2,100 yards before scoring a hit forward of the submarine's conning tower. During the ensuing quarter-hour engagement, the *Buckley* evaded a torpedo and then rammed the German directly across her foredeck. As the Germans hastily abandoned ship, several boarded the *Buckley* to escape drowning. The Americans, misinterpreting their intention, at first beat them off with everything from machine guns to coffee cups. Later, in a search that lasted till after sunrise, the *Buckley* rescued 36 German survivors.

German transients henceforth exercised extreme caution in surfacing off the Cape Verdes, keeping a sharp lookout for escort carriers. Late in May, *U-549* escaped several attacks by aircraft from the *Block Island* and, penetrating the screen, on the night of the 29th, sent two torpedoes into her. Amid the confusion of rescue operations and depth charge barrages, the U-boat succeeded in blowing the stern off the destroyer escort *Barr* with a *Zaunkönig*, only to be destroyed by three patterns of hedgehogs, ahead-thrown antisubmarine weapons. The *Block Island's* loss was avenged early in June when a group built around escort carrier *Guadalcanal*, Captain Daniel V. Gallery, achieved a spectacular success. On June 4, 1944 the destroyer escort *Chatelain* blasted *U-505* to the surface with assistance from the carrier's Avengers. As the Germans hurriedly abandoned ship, a boarding party from the destroyer escort *Pillsbury* plunged down the conning tower hatch, disconnected the scuttling charges, and checked the flooding. Skillfully brought in under tow by the *Guadalcanal*, the *U-505* proved an exceptionally valuable capture, for with her code books and cipher machine, naval authorities were henceforth able to decipher operational orders from BdU. She was not however the only submarine captured during the war. The Germans took two British boats; the British seized three Italian and two German submarines.

The Indian Ocean venture, though providing the *U-Waffe* with its

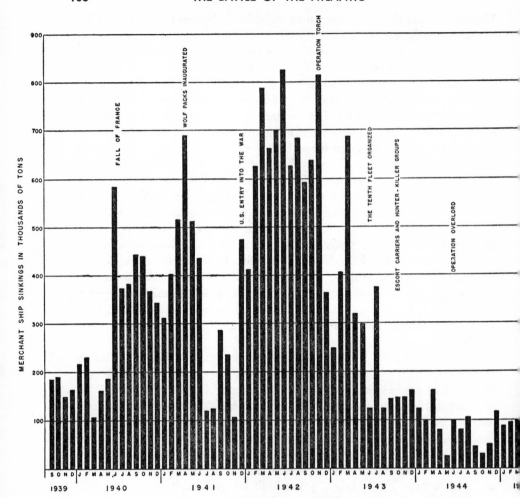

**BATTLE OF THE ATLANTIC: MERCHANT VESSEL LOSSES TO U-BOATS**

single area of feasible operations during 1944, tended, like patrols in the Mediterranean, to be a one-way proposition. Of the some 45 U-boats dispatched to those waters, 34 were sunk, many en route.

Belated German adoption of the snorkel (*schnorchel*), an air intake and exhaust trunk that permits a submarine to recharge batteries without fully surfacing, provided Germany with a slender hope of preserving the remnants of its *U-Waffe* long enough for the Walter boat to become operational. During the summer and fall of 1944, following the failure of his sizable anti-invasion flotilla to disrupt the Normandy landings, Dönitz dispatched several snorkel boats to the waters east of the Grand Banks with orders to operate as weather reporters. Hunter-Killer operations against these furtive boats proved relatively unrewarding, partly because the boats made no serious attempt to molest North Atlantic convoys. Amazingly enough, German submariners had sunk only half a dozen merchant ships en route from North America to the British Isles during the twelve months before Operation OVERLORD, the Normandy invasion, and their performance during the last year of the war was no more impressive. Nevertheless they managed to achieve minor success in British and American coastal waters, often lying on the bottom for hours to evade sonar detection and then cautiously launching torpedoes at their victims by means of sound bearings. These tactics were briefly effective in the Irish Sea early in 1945, but for the most part snorkel boats were as ineffective offensively as they were difficult to locate. Allied shipping losses to submarine action in the Atlantic rose from a monthly average of 30,580 tons in 1944 to some 63,270 tons during the first four months of 1945, but the pattern revealed by these sinkings indicated inshore nuisance activity rather than a threat to transatlantic convoys.

Axis U-boats destroyed 2,775 Allied merchant ships, but only some 28 per cent of these were sailing in convoy. Of over-all losses from all causes of 23,351,000 tons, U-boats accounted for 14,573,000 tons, or 62.4 per cent. All told, the Germans committed 1,175 U-boats to the war and lost 781, American forces accounting for 191. The Italians lost 85 submarines, 21 in the Atlantic. Against these figures, it can be noted that Allied merchant ships successfully completed over 300,000 voyages across the Atlantic, while hundreds of thousands more voyages were safely undertaken in the coastal waters of Britain. When Allied shipbuilding capacity reached its peak, the U-boats had no hope of winning. They lost because they dared not maintain the attack on the North Atlantic convoys which brought the material of victory to Britain. Convoy escorts proved to be a decisive task force for offensive action against attacking U-boats.

# 4

# The Allied Offensive against
# North Africa

Seldom in the history of coalition warfare has there been more complete trust and loyal cooperation between allies than there was between Britain and the United States in World War II. In part this was the result of the close community of interests of the two nations, dating back half a century. In part it was the result of the intimate friendship of the two heads of government, Prime Minister Churchill and President Roosevelt. In part it was the work of General Eisenhower, who made it his special business as commander in chief to attain close concord, and who would stand for no bickering among his subordinates. In part it arose out of the willingness of all the chief officers of both nations to give and take in a friendly spirit and to drive wholeheartedly toward common objectives. Yet, despite the operational harmony that prevailed, the military and political leaders of the two allies were repeatedly at loggerheads concerning strategy.

Most of the disagreements between the British and American leaders concerned where and when to get at the enemy. In simplest terms, the Americans favored the direct approach—a drive at the heart of Germany as soon as possible. The British favored an indirect or peripheral approach, encircling and wearing down the enemy before risking a drive at his heart. Possibly the greatest British contribution to World War II strategy was keeping themselves and the Americans out of western Europe until the Germans were sufficiently weakened and the Allies were sufficiently strong to assure a quick and not-too-costly Allied victory. Perhaps the greatest strategic contribution of the Americans was at last persuading the British to join them in invading western Europe in mid-1944, before the Germans could get their new and deadly rocket warfare into high gear.

The basis for Britain's reluctance was at least partly historical, grow-

ing out of more than two centuries of British military theory and experience. In the Seven Years' War (1756–63), William Pitt the Elder brought
into focus with his famous War Plan the strategy toward which England
had been groping since the Spanish Armada. In so doing he laid the
foundations of the British Empire. Pitt's Plan was to get at France and
her Spanish ally not by placing a major army on the Continent but by
lending all possible material support to Britain's continental allies, while
using British naval power to seal the enemy off from the seas, to support
operations around the enemy's continental position, to capture the
enemy's overseas trade, and to strike at the enemy's colonies beyond
the seas. Thus with the use of minimum military force, Britain succeeded
in containing France and Spain in Europe while establishing British
claims to India, to Canada, and to the future United States as far west
as the Mississippi.

In the Napoleonic Wars (1793–1815), Britain employed variations of
Pitt's Plan through three coalitions, supporting allies on the Continent
while using her sea power to seal off the enemy from most of the world,
to blockade and destroy his fleets, and to probe for and exploit weak
spots about his periphery. Thus the French, while not defeated, found
themselves constantly frustrated, always threatened, and brought to the
verge of bankruptcy. At length in the fourth and final coalition, Britain
put a large army on the Continent and drove into France, not directly
but from the south, via the Iberian Peninsula, with Portuguese and Spanish help. At the same time, the Russians, the Prussians, and the Austrians
drove in from the east. Between them, these combined forces at long last
crushed the Napoleonic empire.

On the eve of World War I (1914–18) a British school of peripheral
strategists proposed returning to the essential features of Pitt's Plan and
the first three coalitions of the Napoleonic Wars. Warfare in the main
continental theaters, said this school, should be left to the armies of Belgium, France, and Russia, and any other powers that could be attracted
into the war against Germany. These Britain would support by subsidy,
partly financed by capture of German trade, and by any other means
short of actually providing large numbers of troops at the main front.

Opposing the peripheralists was a vocal school of British continental
strategists who drew their inspiration from the fourth anti-Napoleonic
coalition. The Kaiser, like Napoleon, was surrounded. He had no choice
but to fight a two-front war. Britain's best contribution, said the continental strategists, was to place her main army on the Continent. The
British continental school had of course the full support of French military leaders, and French arguments were persuasive. At the outbreak of
World War I in August 1914, Britain at once threw an army on the
Continent. At the First Battle of the Marne, fought in early September
on Paris's doorstep, a hundred thousand British regulars held the Allied

left flank and helped drive a wedge between two separated German armies. The invaders were pressed back, and Paris was saved.

After the German repulse, the Western Front settled down to a four-year stalemate. Continental strategy at length won the war for the Allies, but only with American intervention and at a terrible cost in lives and treasure. The British Empire alone lost nearly a million men. To outflank the static Western Front, Winston Churchill, then First Lord of the Admiralty, had advocated peripheral strategy in the form of a campaign to seize Constantinople. The outflanking attempt failed both within the Dardanelles and among the rugged crags of Gallipoli, but in the years following World War I military analysts had concluded that Churchill's plan was strategically sound—that it failed through poor Allied planning, through a series of avoidable Allied errors, and as a result of the foresight and initiative of Liman von Sanders, German commander of the Turkish defense forces.

At the beginning of World War II, Britain again placed an army in France. Again the war in the West began with a German drive aimed at the quick defeat of France. This time the Germans succeeded. France was knocked out of the war, and the British Expeditionary Force was thrust off the Continent. Churchill, the advocate of peripheral strategy in World War I, returned to the same concept as Prime Minister and Minister of Defense in World War II. After the fall of France and the evacuation of the British army, he had no stomach for a return to western Europe—at least until Germany had been greatly weakened. And in fact Britain without allies had insufficient troops to man a new Western Front. On the other hand, Britain possessed sufficient naval power. In the circumstances, Churchill and the British Chiefs of Staff limited their offensive against the Axis powers to air attacks on German industries and communications, to attacks on German and Italian naval forces, to operations aimed at restoring British communications in the Mediterranean, to the Egyptian campaign, to distant attacks at Dakar and Madagascar, and to operations in Greece and Crete and probes at St. Nazaire and Dieppe. When Hitler invaded the Soviet Union, Churchill announced: "We shall give whatever help we can to Russia and the Russian people." Thus Britain was reviving two of the main features of Pitt's Plan: lending all possible material support to allies on the Continent, while using her naval power to support operations around the enemy's continental periphery and beyond the seas.

Soviet leaders, from the moment they found themselves in the war on the side of Britain, opposed the concept of peripheral strategy, demanding a "Second Front Now." When the United States entered the war, the American Joint Chiefs of Staff, General Marshall in particular, also insisted on an early return of Allied forces to France. What Marshall proposed was to seize a beachhead in France in the late summer of 1942,

Operation SLEDGEHAMMER. This was to be followed in 1943 by a major invasion, Operation ROUNDUP, a drive into Germany, involving a double envelopment of the Ruhr—as was actually carried out in 1944–45. In preparation for SLEDGEHAMMER and ROUNDUP, the Joint Chiefs gave top priority to the production of landing and beaching craft and began sending troops to Britain.

The British Chiefs tentatively accepted SLEDGEHAMMER, but only as an "emergency" or "opportunity" operation—in the event either the Russians or the Germans appeared on the verge of defeat—despite President Roosevelt's urging that SLEDGEHAMMER "be pushed with the utmost vigor" and without qualification. Roosevelt insisted that "it is of the highest importance that U.S. ground troops be brought into action against the enemy in 1942," but the British War Cabinet and the British Chiefs of Staff flatly refused to agree to an early invasion of the Continent on the President's terms.

Yet something had to be done in 1942. The Germans on the Russian front reconquered the territory lost during the winter and thrust toward Stalingrad on the Volga. There they could disrupt the flow of oil from the Caucasus and block American and British supplies to Russia via the Persian Gulf route. In North Africa, Rommel's tanks, forging ahead toward the Egyptian delta, appeared to have the momentum that would carry them through to Cairo and the Suez Canal.

Churchill proposed an invasion of western North Africa. There was much to commend in the proposal. Tunisia, Algeria, Morocco, and French West Africa, though loyal to the Vichy French government, were not occupied by the Germans. If the area were brought over to the Allies, Rommel could be trapped between the invading forces and the British Eighth Army, Malta could be relieved, and the Mediterranean could be reopened to Allied shipping, with a consequent saving of crucially short merchant tonnage. Moreover, bases would be secured for attacks on Italy and elsewhere in southern Europe, a French army might be mustered for action against the Axis, and phosphates and other resources would be denied the enemy.

President Roosevelt at first opposed the move into North Africa. He wished to see American forces in Europe as soon as possible—to boost the morale of the American public, to fulfill promises to Russia, and to bring a quick end to the war. The Joint Chiefs of Staff opposed the African invasion because they saw it as a strategically eccentric move that would draw more and more Allied forces away from the strategic center in western Europe and delay the invasion of France at least two years. Prime Minister Churchill insisted however that the invasion of North Africa was the best possible preparation for the invasion of France, since threatening the periphery of the Axis empire would draw German forces away from the invasion areas on the French coast.

Churchill at length convinced Roosevelt that if the Anglo-American forces were to see action against the Axis that year, there was really no alternative to his African plan. For once Roosevelt overruled his military advisers in a matter of strategy. On July 25, 1942, the Combined Chiefs of Staff committed themselves to the North African invasion, which was given the code name Operation TORCH.

## Strategic and Political Plans and Preparations

The immediate objectives of the landings were three major North African ports outside the operational radius of the *Luftwaffe:* Algiers and Oran on the Mediterranean shore, and Casablanca on the Atlantic. Bizerte and Tunis, in Tunisia, and Bone, in Algeria, were rejected as too close to enemy airfields in Sicily; while Dakar, in West Africa, was too far south to be useful. The choice also reflected a compromise between American Army planners, who wished to forestall possible German counteraction through Spain, and British planners, who expected the major enemy opposition to come through Tunisia. Once the immediate target cities were secured, part of the Allied forces would have to race the Germans for occupation of the ports in Tunisia while others rushed from Casablanca to the frontier of Spanish Morocco to guard the vital communications through the Straits of Gibraltar.

Best utilization of available ships and manpower determined the various assault force assignments. American Task Force 34, called the Western Naval Task Force, was to transport 35,000 troops directly from the United States to seize the Casablanca area. A Center Naval Task Force carrying 39,000 American troops with British naval support, all staging in Britain, would invade Oran. A third contingent, the Eastern Naval Task Force, would embark from Britain 23,000 British and 10,000 American troops assigned to seize Algiers. After the ports were taken, follow-up convoys would pour in reinforcements and supplies until the conquest was complete. Because intelligence reports indicated that defending Vichy forces would resist American troops less vigorously than British, all ground commanders in the initial assaults were American. Lieutenant General Dwight D. Eisenhower USA was named Commander in Chief Allied Force, while Admiral of the Fleet Sir Andrew B. Cunningham RN assumed over-all naval command. D-day was set for November 8, 1942, the last date that year on which landings were deemed feasible across beaches exposed to the heavy ground swell usually prevalent on the Atlantic coast of North Africa during the winter season.

The venture was risky enough to satisfy the boldest. Much necessarily depended on the unpredictable reaction of the North African French. Because of the British attacks on French naval forces at Mers-el-Kebir and Dakar in 1940, the Germans had permitted the French to assemble

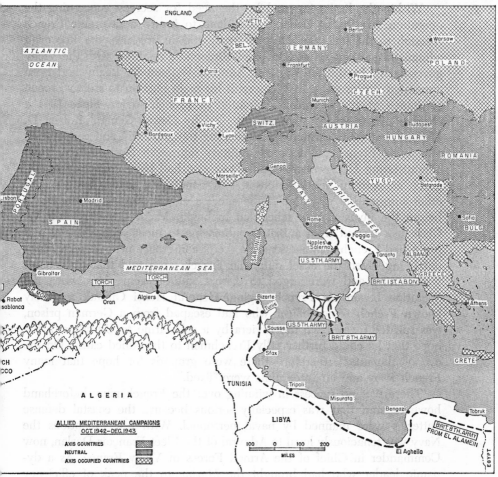

ALLIED CAMPAIGNS IN THE MEDITERRANEAN THEATER, 1942–1943

and equip a defense force of 120,000 men, 350 planes of fair quality, more than 200 tanks, a sizable amount of light artillery and mortars, and naval units which included the modern battleship *Richelieu* and a cruiser-destroyer force at Dakar. Another cruiser, the unfinished battleship *Jean Bart*, and numerous destroyers and submarines were in ports elsewhere along the coastline. If all these forces fought with determination, and if the Germans moved into Spanish and French bases to assist them, cutting the Allied supply route at Gibraltar, it appeared to many Allied staff officers that the invasion might be defeated. But it seemed more probable that the Franco government would resist a German entry into Spain, and that many of the defending French units, if they fought at all, would put up only a token resistance. Success however hinged as much on political as on military and naval factors.

Within the limits imposed by the need for secrecy concerning the operation, everything possible was done to insure a favorable French reaction to the landings. Despite strong public pressure, the Roosevelt administration had refused to break diplomatic relations with the Vichy government. In the fall of 1940, Admiral William D. Leahy had been appointed Ambassador to Vichy with his main mission to stiffen French resistance to any German domination of French Africa. Since 1941 a corps of American consular officials, led by Consul-General Robert D. Murphy, had been assiduously cultivating the good will and cooperation of leading French political and military figures in North Africa while administering U.S. economic aid. They also had been collecting intelligence concerning beach defenses, surf conditions, roads, bridges, and other information essential to the success of the landings. Two weeks before the invasion was scheduled to begin, Major General Mark W. Clark USA landed from a British submarine to meet with Murphy and pro-Allied French commanders in a secret conference near Algiers. Without being given the exact date, the French were told that the assault was coming and were urged to disrupt anti-invasion plans when the operation began. At French urging, General Henri Giraud, a widely known French senior officer who had escaped from a German prison, was spirited away from the Riviera by a submarine to Gibraltar in the hope that he could further rally Frenchmen to the Allied cause. On the eve of the attack therefore there were grounds for hope that many French army and air force units were "fixed."

There was no success in winning over the French navy beforehand however, and that was especially serious because the coastal defense batteries were manned by naval personnel. With few exceptions the Navy was tenaciously loyal to Admiral of the Fleet François Darlan, now Commander in Chief of the Armed Forces of Vichy France. As a dynamic leader who had brought the *Marine* to the peak of efficiency between wars, Darlan could both legally and morally command the allegiance of all French forces in North Africa with an authority second only to that of Pétain himself. A few weeks before the landings, Darlan sent feelers to American officials in North Africa suggesting negotiations. Murphy favored negotiating with the Admiral, but the U.S. State Department, deeply distrusting the Vichy government, feared that such contacts would lead to leaks concerning the forthcoming operation that would impel the Germans to rush troops and planes into Africa and thereby frustrate the entire scheme. Only three days before D-day however, Darlan flew to Algiers to be at the bedside of his sick son. Thus purely by chance he was well placed to exercise an immediate influence on the course of events. This totally unexpected development was to prove fortunate for the Allies.

## Tactical Plans and Preparations

Because the war against the European Axis was primarily an army responsibility, it was from beginning to end commanded on the highest military level by an army officer, and naval forces were assigned to the Army as needed. As a result the Army dominated joint operations,* and the Navy deferred to the Army's desires, even in amphibious assaults. This situation contrasted with that in the Pacific Ocean Areas, where the top command was naval, and army units were assigned to the Navy as needed. As a result amphibious operations developed along somewhat different lines in the two theaters.

Planning and preparation for Operation TORCH were complicated by division of command and shortage of time. From his London headquarters General Eisenhower and his British-American staff directed the detailed planning for the assaults on Algiers and Oran. But because the forces for Morocco were to stage from the United States, plans and preparations for this phase of TORCH were left to the Joint Chiefs of Staff. General Marshall delegated the planning for the landing force to the War Department, which delegated the detailed planning to Major General George S. Patton Jr., Commander Western Task Force. Admiral King delegated the fleet-level planning for the participating naval forces to Admiral Royal E. Ingersoll, Commander in Chief Atlantic Fleet, who delegated the detailed planning to Rear Admiral Kent Hewitt, the prospective commander of the Western Naval Task Force (Task Force 34). In the preparatory phase the army and navy commanders were independent, with no common superior below the President. The command structure was thus in the tradition of joint operations from Quebec in the Seven Years' War to Norway in World War II.

In practice, planning and preparation for the Moroccan attack were closely integrated, as indeed they had to be for so organic an operation as an amphibious assault. General Patton and Admiral Hewitt conferred frequently. To coordinate naval plans with those for the landing force, Hewitt's war plans officer spent several weeks in Patton's office in Washington. Then, to achieve final coordination, Patton's planning staff moved to Hewitt's headquarters at Ocean View, near Norfolk, Virginia. Because Hewitt, prior to assuming command of the Western Naval Task Force, was Commander Amphibious Force Atlantic Fleet (Comphiblant), the amphibious training for the Moroccan landing force was directed from his headquarters.

On October 13, 1942 the Joint Chiefs issued to all commands con-

* In American terminology a *joint operation* is one carried out by elements of more than one armed service of the same nationality; a *combined operation* is one carried out by forces of two or more nations. The British use the term *combined* for both sorts of operations.

cerned with the Moroccan operation their own high-level plan, titled "Joint Army-Navy Plan for Participation in Operation Torch." It provided that, once the expedition got under way, there should in each phase be a single commander at both the theater and the local level. For the first time in modern history a large-scale joint operation was to be under unified command throughout. Command relations were set forth as follows:

(a) The Commander in Chief, Allied Force [Eisenhower], will command all forces assigned to Operation TORCH, under the principle of unity of command.

(b) The Western Naval Task Force will pass to the command of the Commander in Chief, Allied Force, upon crossing the meridian of 40° West Longitude. This command may be exercised either directly by the Commander in Chief [Eisenhower] or through the Naval Commander, Allied Force [Cunningham]. (Prior to that time these forces will remain under the command of the Commander in Chief, United States Atlantic Fleet [Ingersoll], who will arrange their movements so that they will meet the schedule of the Commander in Chief, Allied Force.)

(c) Command relations of the Subordinate Task Forces are initially set up as given in subparagraphs (d), (e), (f), and (g). They are subject to change as found necessary by the Commander in Chief, Allied Force.

(d) The command of units of the Western Task Force which are embarked in the Western Naval Task Force, will vest in the Commander, Western Naval Task Force [Hewitt], until such time as the Commanding General, Western Task Force [Patton], has established his headquarters on shore and states he is ready to assume command.

(e) When the Commanding General, Western Task Force, assumes command on shore, the naval forces designated to give further support to the occupation of FRENCH MOROCCO will pass to his control, acting through the Commander, Western Naval Task Force.

(f) Following the assault operations and when and as released by Commander in Chief, Allied Force, the United States naval forces assigned thereto will revert to the command of Commander in Chief, United States Atlantic Fleet.

(g) The United States naval forces assigned for the operation of ports and for naval local and sea frontier defenses—Sea Frontier Forces, Western Task Force, and the Naval Operating Base, Center Task Force—will be under the command of the respective commanding generals of those task forces, under the principle of unity of command.

(h) The Commander in Chief, United States Atlantic Fleet, will exercise command over all forces employed for the cover and ocean escort in the ATLANTIC of follow-up convoys between the UNITED STATES and NORTH AFRICA.

Particularly to be noted in this Joint Plan is the break with the traditional system in amphibious operations, whereby the general commanding the landing force and the admiral commanding the naval support force remained independent and coequal throughout the operation. In the Moroccan invasion, first Admiral Hewitt and then General Patton would be in over-all command. And there would be at any given time only a single chain of command, via Admiral Ingersoll until the expedition reached mid-ocean, via General Eisenhower thereafter. Though the provision for unified local command was written only into the directive for the Western Task Force, it became the model for subsequent directives in the European theater of operations.

Plans for the three main landings, at Algiers, at Oran, and in the Casablanca area, while differing in such details as command relations, were otherwise similar in purpose and outline. The objective of the attacks was to enable the Allies to hurl a large army and air force into a prolonged campaign against a well-equipped foe, for even if the French put up no resistance, German and Italian reinforcements were sure to be rushed to Africa. Since nothing like the huge volume of supplies required to sustain the invasion forces, 600–700 tons daily per division, could be handled across beaches, it was essential to seize well-developed ports with ample berthing, unloading, and stowage facilities. But because direct assault inside harbors in the teeth of harbor defenses was infeasible without prohibitive losses, plans called for units to be landed on open beaches near the coastal cities so that their harbors could be taken from the flanks and rear. The troops would be carried to positions off the beaches in combat-loaded assault transports, and then transferred with their equipment to landing craft to be put ashore in surprise night landings. Gunnery ships and naval aircraft would support the flanking drives of the troops, while landing craft shuttled in reinforcements and supplies until the ports were secured and readied for use. Since the best chance for the enemy to defeat the onslaught was to deny the ports, and consequently the supplies, needed to build up large forces, it was vital to take the harbors as quickly and with as little damage as possible. Preventing the defenders from scuttling blockships or demolishing quays was considered so important that special units were assigned to dash in at the start of the attacks and seize port facilities at all three objectives. Simple in concept, complex in detail, the hastily drawn plans served as a model for organizing further assaults in the European theater.

The training of the assault forces was beset by myriad difficulties. Few of the land, sea, or air forces assigned to the operation were completely ready when the attack was ordered, nor did it seem likely in the scant five months until D-day that they could be properly trained. Responsible officers realized this, but they also knew that to delay until all participants were fully trained might permit the Germans to move in first, thereby making an Allied landing in Northwest Africa out of the question.

Fortunately for the Allies, the U.S. Marine Corps and U.S. Navy entered the war with a developed amphibious doctrine and training program. And though the amphibiously trained U.S. marines were committed to the Pacific, the U.S. Army had commenced training based in part on their doctrine. During 1941 and early 1942 three American infantry divisions trained with the marines in the United States. Other infantry divisions, dispatched to Great Britain, trained amphibiously with British forces in Scotland and Northern Ireland. In the time available however, it was not possible to train sufficient U.S. Army units to undertake all three North African landings. In view of the French attitude it would have been desirable to make the invasion an all-American show, but British troops had to make up the major part of the easternmost force, operating against Algiers.

By later standards the training both for the initial landings and for subsequent combat fell far short of what was desirable, but it had to suffice. Amphibious training of crews for transports and landing craft was especially deficient. Again, there was simply not enough time. Only half its assigned transports had reached the Western Naval Task Force by August 1, 1942, fourteen weeks before D-day. There was not enough time left even for adequate indoctrination. Moreover nearly all the ships required a good deal of work on communications equipment, and they needed alterations to their interior arrangements before they could participate in exercises. Landing craft were crucial items, for until the Army could seize and ready the ports, these little vessels would comprise the sole means of bringing in ammunition and supplies. Because of a failure to enlist small craft sailors, as such, when the war began, the Navy hastily assembled some 3,000 recruits, who commenced small craft training in June 1942. While the men worked hard and enthusiastically, for all practical purposes they had only two months to train specifically for the North African venture. It was soon apparent that the techniques of amphibious assault cannot be learned in so brief a time.

German U-boat activity worsened matters by forcing the landing exercises for the Western Task Force into the sheltered waters of Chesapeake Bay at Solomons Island. As a result the landing craft crews were unable to gain needed experience in handling their craft in a heavy surf. Crews who trained in Great Britain, the majority Royal Navy, were able to practice under more realistic but still far from satisfactory conditions. The Army's historian of the North African campaign concludes: "Training for the amphibious operations in French North Africa . . . fell short of what was desired and perhaps below the requirements for victory over a well-armed and determined foe." The massive assault forces that got under way from Britain and the United States knew that the French were not particularly well armed. They had yet to find out if they were determined.

## Morocco: The Approach

The Western Naval Task Force, commanded by Admiral Hewitt in the heavy cruiser *Augusta,* comprised 102 warships, transports, and auxiliaries which, when united at sea, covered more than 500 square miles of ocean. To mislead the enemy, the Northern and Southern Attack Groups sortied from Hampton Roads on October 23 and took a southerly course. The next day the Center Attack Group left Hampton Roads and took a northeasterly course as if headed for Britain. These groups later united and were joined on the 27th by a Covering Group sailing from Casco Bay, Maine; this group included the new fast battleship *Massachusetts* and two heavy cruisers. An Air Group dispatched ahead to Bermuda, comprising the aircraft carrier *Ranger,* four escort carriers newly converted from tankers, and a screen of a light cruiser and nine destroyers, joined the force on the 28th in mid-ocean.

After steering evasive courses to avoid or deceive known enemy submarine concentrations, the Western Naval Task Force neared the African coast in a strong northwest wind that raised heavy seas. Predictions from Washington were that surf on the Moroccan beaches would be too high for the landings on D-day, November 8, but Admiral Hewitt trusted the verdict of his aerological officer that the landings would be possible on the 8th but not for many days thereafter. He therefore proceeded according to plan. If impossible conditions developed, he could postpone the landings by radio and, if absolutely necessary, execute an alternate plan for landing inside the Mediterranean. As the task force approached Morocco, the men were cheered by the news that the British Eighth Army was pressing back Rommel's forces in Egypt after the great British victory at El Alamein on November 5.

On November 7 the Western Naval Task Force split apart. The Southern Attack Group turned south toward the small phosphate port of Safi, where it was to land 6,500 troops and 90 medium and light tanks to march on Casablanca from the south. The Center Attack Group headed for the small port of Fedala to land 19,500 troops and 79 light tanks to advance on Casablanca from the north. The Northern Attack Group shaped course for the coastal village of Mehdia to land 9,000 troops and 65 light tanks to capture the airfield at nearby Port Lyautey. The landings at Safi and Mehdia were expected also to tie down French units that might otherwise close in on the main landing at Fedala. The Covering Group moved toward Casablanca itself to take under fire any naval forces that tried to leave the harbor. The Air Group divided in order to support all three landings: one escort carrier to Safi, two escort carriers to Mehdia, the *Ranger* and one escort carrier to Fedala and Casablanca, only 15 miles apart.

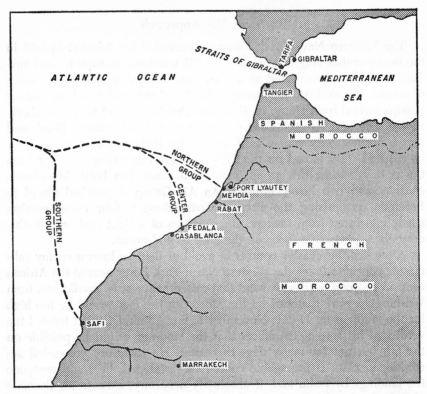

AMERICAN LANDINGS IN FRENCH MOROCCO, NOVEMBER 8, 1942

The Army had insisted upon night landings—both to achieve surprise and because army officers were not yet convinced that naval gunfire could provide adequate support for a daylight landing. But surprise would be lost if the attack groups were sighted from the Moroccan coast in the evening of November 7. To allow time for the approach, for loading of landing craft, and for the ship-to-shore movement, all in total darkness, H-hour was set at 0400, two hours before dawn.

The Army also required what the Navy regarded as an excessive amount of equipment to be carried in with the assault waves. This requirement put a strain on the supply of landing craft, which for this operation ranged from 36-foot plywood, gasoline-powered "Higgins boats" to 50-foot steel, diesel-powered LCM's (Landing Craft, Mechanized) capable of transporting a light tank. In subsequent assaults enough landing craft for army requirements would be brought to the beachhead area by LST's (Landing Ships, Tank), but for the North African invasion they were limited to the number that could be brought in by the transports.

Major General Jonathan Anderson, commanding the troops that were to land at Fedala, further complicated the landing craft situation for the Center Attack Group by a last-minute decision to increase the strength of the initial landing force by about 50 per cent. As a result, to provide enough landing craft for the assault waves, the Navy had to work out a complicated boat plan that would have been difficult for experienced coxswains to carry out on schedule even in daylight.

## Morocco: The Main Assault

The assault plan for Fedala required the 15 transports of the Center Attack Group to anchor at midnight in four columns six to eight miles north of the landing beaches. The four transports of the inshore line each carried a battalion landing team.* These four landing teams, comprising altogether 6,000 men, were to make the initial, pre-dawn assault. Because no transport carried enough landing craft to boat a whole team, the transports of the second, third, and fourth lines were directed to send forward additional craft to specific transports of the first line. As the craft were loaded with men and tanks, they were to advance to one of four control destroyers positioned in the rendezvous area a thousand yards nearer shore. Here they were to form "waves" of six to eight boats. When each of the loaded landing craft, numbering more than 200, had reported to its designated control destroyer, the destroyers would conduct them forward to the line of departure 4,000 yards from shore. Meanwhile four beach-marking scout boats would have advanced and anchored, each off one of the four segments of beach—designated Beaches Red 2, Red 3, Blue, and Blue 2—assigned to one of the four battalion landing teams. At 0335, the scout boats were to begin flashing flashlights seaward. At 0350, they were to ignite colored flares. At H-hour, 0400, the landing craft, on signal from the control destroyers, would head for their assigned beaches, accompanied by support boats armed with machine guns and guided by the flares in the scout boats. After putting the troops ashore, the landing craft were to retract and hurry back to the transport area for the follow-up troops. As we have seen, this elaborate and tightly scheduled plan had to be carried out in almost complete darkness.

As the Center Group transports, accompanied by the cruisers *Augusta* and *Brooklyn* and ten destroyers, headed in toward their anchorage, the Fedala assault plan began to come apart. An unexpected current carried the Center Group off course, necessitating a series of emergency turns. The first line of transports, those carrying the initial assault forces, reached the anchorage shortly before midnight, but by then the rest of the transports were straggling badly and out of position. As a result the landing craft from these vessels were late in reaching their assigned

---

* For an explanation of *battalion landing team* see the footnote on page 305.

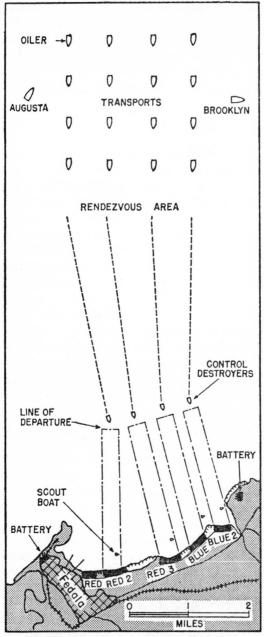

INITIAL LANDING PLAN FOR FEDALA

transports or never found them at all. The schedule was further retarded by the troops, who, overloaded with 60-pound packs, debarked very slowly down the landing nets into the pitching boats. As a result of these delays, only about half the scheduled waves of boats had reached the rendezvous area by 0400. The control destroyers however could wait no longer and began conducting their waves to the line of departure, which they reached in about 50 minutes. The beach-marking scout boats, uninformed of the delays, had for some time been showing their lights, but this only caused confusion, for two of the scout boats were out of position, one by more than two miles. At 0500, an hour late, the first waves of boats headed for the beach, followed at five to ten minute intervals by the second and third waves. The noise of the landing craft, now operating at full throttle, finally attracted the attention of shore batteries, which turned on searchlights, at first upward to look for aircraft, and then down on the water. When the support boats opened fire with machine guns, the lights went out abruptly. Meanwhile the inexperience of the coxswains was taking its toll as landing craft collided,

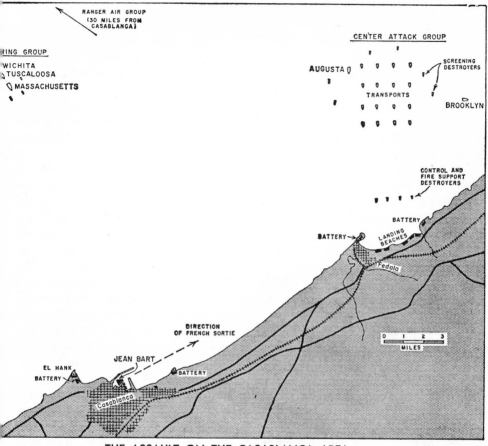

THE ASSAULT ON THE CASABLANCA AREA

crashed into rocks and reefs adjoining the designated beaches, or were caught in the surf, spun about, and broached on the beach. Some troops were spilled into the sea where they were pulled down by their heavy packs and drowned. Of the landing craft that safely made shore, many were left stranded by the receding tide and could not retract. Yet the naval crews who lost their craft were the exceptions. Most, despite their brief training, the darkness, and the difficult sea conditions, brought their troops safely ashore with their equipment and quickly returned to the transports. By dawn 3,500 troops had been landed, and the first echelons advanced and seized control of the town of Fedala. The batteries flanking the beach however were still in French hands.

Would the French fight, or would they welcome the invaders? As first light grayed the morning sky, the eyes of the fleet were on the French batteries, which would provide the answer. Friendly officers in Morocco had been tipped off that the invasion was taking place but not just where or in what strength. They had been working through the night trying to arrange for a bloodless landing. But the key French commanders, Resident General Noguès and Vice Admiral Michelier, remained unconvinced that there was a powerful American force offshore. They would not be party to a mere raid or temporary invasion. Were they to do so, Axis forces would also invade Northwest Africa, and unless the Americans had sufficient power to make good their foothold against the Axis, France would suffer reprisals without gaining offsetting advantages. Michelier therefore refused to rescind his order to the batteries to defend the coast.

Had the landing been made after dawn, as the Navy wished, or had the French batteries held their fire until the morning mists had lifted and revealed the magnitude of the American force, it is possible that General Noguès would have agreed to parley. But just as day began to break, shortly after 0600, the batteries flanking the Fedala roadstead opened fire on the landing forces and on the control destroyers. The destroyers quickly returned the fire, and were soon joined by the guns of the *Brooklyn* and the *Augusta*. The *Ranger's* aircraft, over Casablanca, now came under attack by French fighters; in a brief dogfight seven French and four American planes were shot down. Spotting planes from the Covering Group were soon being attacked by antiaircraft fire and fighter planes. At 0700 the *Massachusetts* and her consorts, the *Tuscaloosa* and the *Wichita*, turned their 5-inch batteries on the French aircraft, shooting one down. Immediately afterward the battleship *Jean Bart* in Casablanca harbor and the powerful battery at nearby Point El Hank opened fire on the Covering Group, which replied at once. The battle was on. To Admiral Michelier, putting up a fight was no longer just a matter of policy or of carrying out orders from above; it had become a requirement of honor. When later in the day a deputation from General Patton drove to Casablanca with an American flag and a flag of truce to arrange a ceasefire, they were let in through the lines and cheered in the streets, but Michelier refused even to receive them. As one of the American officers began to argue with the Admiral's aide, he was interrupted by a salvo from the El Hank battery that shook the windows of the Admiralty. Said the aide, *"Voilà votre réponse!"*

The *Jean Bart*, though uncompleted and temporarily immobilized, had an operational turret of four 15-inch guns that made her a formidable floating battery. In Casablanca harbor also were eleven submarines, eight sloops, eleven minesweepers, two super-destroyers, seven smaller destroyers, and the light cruiser *Primauguet*. The principal task of the American Covering Group was to prevent a sortie of these vessels against the Center Attack Group and the landing forces 15 miles away at Fedala. The carrying out of this task was hampered by the guns of the *Jean Bart* and by steady and accurate fire from El Hank's eight well-protected

5.3-inch and 7.6-inch guns, which had straddled the *Massachusetts* at 20,000 yards with their first salvo. The *Massachusetts* concentrated the fire of her nine 16-inch guns on the *Jean Bart.* Her fifth salvo struck the barbette of the functional turret, jamming it in train. For 45 minutes more the ships shot it out with the El Hank battery, driving the gunners temporarily to cover but not demolishing the guns. Not a ship in the Covering Group had yet been hit.

The second phase of the Naval Battle of Casablanca was initiated by Admiral Michelier, who, observing that the Covering Group had maneuvered westward, away from the transports off Fedala, seized the opportunity to send seven of his destroyers to attack the Center Group. Eight submarines also sortied. This was Michelier's best chance to break up the landing. Steaming close inshore and making expert use of smoke, the French destroyers approached the American transports and had hit one landing craft when they were intercepted and driven back by the *Augusta,* the *Brooklyn,* and two of the Center Group destroyers, which had been deployed to screen the transports against just such an attack. The cruiser *Primauguet* now sortied and led the French destroyers in a new advance. Hewitt had already summoned the Covering Group to return to the area. For two and a half hours the French ships dodged in and out of their smoke screen, exchanging salvos with the vessels of the Center and Covering Groups. Planes from the *Ranger* meanwhile made several strafing and bombing runs on the enemy force. Three of the French submarines had already been sunk in Casablanca harbor, but the remaining eight sortied and entered the confused battle. Their torpedo spreads narrowly missed several American vessels.

In the face of the immense American superiority of force, the gallant French attack, however skillfully conducted, could hardly have ended other than in disaster for the attackers. When the engagement ended just before noon, none of the American vessels had received damage of consequence. Of the French ships however, all but one had been severely damaged. Two had sunk, two others were in a sinking condition, one was dead in the water, and one had been beached to avoid sinking. Only one of the submarines returned to Casablanca harbor, and two made Dakar. Of the rest, attacked by American planes or destroyers, one was beached, one was scuttled at Cadiz, and the rest sank.

Early in the afternoon of November 8, the undamaged French destroyer and two sloops emerged from Casablanca to pick up survivors. Admiral Hewitt, taking this sortie for another attempt to attack his transports, ordered action resumed. The three French vessels made it back to the harbor under a smoke screen, but aircraft from the *Ranger* wrecked the *Primauguet.* At the end of the day the El Hank battery was still active, and workmen had completed repairs on the *Jean Bart's* damaged turret.

At Fedala the defending troops, chiefly Senegalese, quickly surrendered, and even the navy-manned shore batteries were in American hands before noon. French fighter aircraft made a few strafing runs over the beach, but bombers were chased off by aircraft from the *Ranger*. General Anderson organized his troops to meet counterattacks and prepared for the advance on Casablanca. He was severely hampered however by the increasingly behind-schedule landings of troops and supplies. There were not enough landing craft left to do the job properly, and the performance of the boat crews, exhausted after having worked all night, did not improve with the coming of daylight. Collisions and broachings continued. The numerous boats stranded and abandoned on the beach were banged together and shattered by the incoming tide and rising surf. By nightfall on D-day nearly half the 347 landing craft of the Center Attack Group had been destroyed, and only 40 per cent of the 19,500 troops embarked in the transports had been brought ashore. Unloading of supplies was even further behind schedule. It was apparent that the transports would have to remain off Fedala for several days. As they were brought in closer to the shore, a minelayer sowed a protective mine field to eastward, and the destroyers patrolled in screening areas north and west of the transport area.

## Morocco: The Southern Assault

Meanwhile, 150 miles by sea southwest of Casablanca, the Southern Attack Group had scored a spectacular success at Safi. In the blackness before H-hour, despite debarking troubles caused by a heavy ground swell and the inevitable errors of inexperienced personnel, the crucial phase of the assault was conducted according to plan. First, a scout boat located the turning buoy marking the entrance to Safi's small, breakwater-protected harbor. Next, guided by a light blinking seaward from the scout boat, came two old four-stack destroyers of World War I vintage, razeed to reduce silhouette. These, carrying about 200 assault troops each, led landing craft directly into the harbor. The French had been alerted and there was a lively exchange of fire as the first "four-piper," the *Bernadou*, slowly steamed in and drove the French gunners to cover with her guns. Her consort, the *Cole*, was able to come directly alongside the quay without a single casualty. While the old battleship *New York* and the light cruiser *Philadelphia* were silencing the coastal batteries, American troops took over key positions in the town. That afternoon, after the ex-train ferry U.S.S. *Lakehurst* had brought in her load of medium tanks, all objectives of the assault were attained. Aircraft from the escort carrier supporting the Southern Group destroyed most French planes in the area on the ground. Naval gunfire stopped a half-hearted French attempt at counterattack. The entire operation had been carried out with dispatch. Though supporting landings were made on beaches flanking the harbor, only one landing craft was lost. All ships were completely unloaded in three days. By the time resistance officially ceased, an American tank force was on its way by road from Safi to Casablanca accompanied along the coast by the *Philadelphia,* several destroyers, and six gasoline-carrying landing craft.

## Morocco: The Northern Assault

The primary objective of the Northern Attack Group was the Port Lyautey airfield, the only airport in Morocco with concrete, all-weather runways. Troops were to be landed on both sides of the Sebou, a narrow and winding but navigable river that connects Port Lyautey with the Atlantic. The initial attack was intended to overwhelm the seaside village of Mehdia and its ancient fortress, the Kasba, which guarded the mouth of the river. The invaders would then thrust inland to seize the airfield by double envelopment and to occupy Port Lyautey. U.S.S. *Dallas,* another razeed fourpiper, was to proceed upriver after a boom blocking access had been cut, and land a force to assist in the capture of the airfield. After the airfield was secured, an army fighter group catapulted from one of the escort carriers was to operate from the field, providing fighter cover for further operations by bombers flown in from Gibraltar.

The Northern Attack Group's assault plan was a smaller version of the one used at Fedala, except that the five landing beaches were much farther apart. Hence to the delays of debarking was added mounting confusion. Few of the troops reached the right beach. Badly scattered, they missed an early opportunity to seize the Kasba and the shore batteries near it, and were soon obliged to meet counterattacks by French colonial troops closing in from Port Lyautey. Efforts of a boat party to cut the boom blocking the river, and later efforts by the *Dallas* to ram it, failed completely under a hail of fire from the Kasba. The initial loss of landing craft was not great, but deteriorating weather and a rapidly rising surf made the build-up of supplies perilously slow. By the end of the second day only half the troops had been landed. Brigadier General Lucian K. Truscott, Jr., who commanded the landing force in this assault, did not at first make much use of naval gunfire. The light cruiser *Savannah* kept down the fire from the Kasba with her 6-inch shells, but the 14-inch shells of the old battleship *Texas,* which could have smashed the fort, were considered too dangerous to be fired at targets near where American troops were operating. Scout planes from both the cruiser and battleship however made a potent contribution in breaking up enemy tank columns by means of a novel but effective technique—dropping antisubmarine depth charges equipped with impact fuses.

On November 10, the situation took a turn for the better. In an early

morning attack, the invaders broke through to the airfield against French
defending troops who, expecting an early armistice, no longer offered
strenuous resistance. By that time a boat party had at last cut the main
cable of the river boom, enabling the *Dallas* to crash through and scrape
her way up the shallow Sebou to land her troops near the airdrome.
Shortly afterward the army planes from one of the escort carriers were
flown in and began operating from the field. Bombers from the other
escort carrier attacked the Kasba, which promptly surrendered to an
American infantry team. French armored forces coming up the coast road
from Rabat, the Moroccan capital, were turned back by destroyer and
cruiser fire. When a column of troop-laden trucks was spotted advancing
on Port Lyautey from the interior, the *Texas* reached more than eight
miles inland and cratered the road with her big shells, whereupon the
column quickly dispersed. That afternoon the French general in command of the area called for a cease-fire, which was granted at once. The
attack had attained its main object, capturing the airfield—but too late
to support the battle for Casablanca.

## Morocco Secured

General Anderson's troops and armor meanwhile had advanced from
Fedala to the outskirts of Casablanca. Two French corvettes, advancing
at 1000 on November 10 to fire on the American troops, were chased
back into Casablanca harbor by the *Augusta*. Then the *Augusta* took to
her heels as shells from the repaired turret of the *Jean Bart* began to
fall around her. Hewitt called for air support, and the *Ranger* sent in
dive bombers that scored two hits with 1,000-pound bombs and left the
French battleship settling in the harbor mud with her decks awash.

At the end of the 10th, the Americans had Casablanca surrounded.
They planned an all-out attack from land, sea, and air for the next morning. Fortunately, before the attack could be launched, Admiral Michelier
received orders to cease resistance, and a conference later on the 11th
ended the fighting. At the conference Admiral Hewitt held out his hand
to Admiral Michelier and expressed regret at having had to fire on French
ships. "I had my orders and did my duty," said Michelier, taking the
proffered hand, "you had yours and did your duty; now that is over,
we are ready to cooperate." Soon the French and the Americans were
working together to restore the port as a major rear base for supplying
the prospective campaign into Tunisia.

The Axis got into the Moroccan campaign after all, causing the
Americans far greater material losses than the French did. U-boats that
the American task force had evaded in the Atlantic were now converging on the Casablanca area. The transports of the Center Attack Group,
with no troops aboard but still unloading cargo, were obliged to remain

off Fedala because a new convoy approaching from the United States would occupy all available space in Casablanca's protected harbor. In the early evening of November 11, *U-173* slipped into the unloading area and sank a transport and damaged a destroyer and an oiler with torpedoes. The following afternoon, *U-130* got into the area and sank three more transports. *U-130* got away safely, but *U-173*, after heavily damaging an American cargo ship off Fedala on the 15th, was sunk the next day by three American destroyers.

## Algeria: Algiers

When the Allied forces staging from England steamed through the Straits of Gibraltar into the Mediterranean, the fact that some major move was under way could no longer be concealed from the Axis powers. The Italian naval command correctly guessed that Algeria must be the Allied target, but they were overruled by the Germans, who first estimated that the convoys were going to southern France, and then that they were headed for Crete, for Tripoli, or possibly for the relief of Malta. Axis forces—submarine, surface, and air—concentrated in the straits of Sicily, leaving the Allied transports largely unmolested. One American transport was torpedoed by a German aircraft off the African coast, but most of its personnel arrived safely, if tardily, at their destination after a long voyage in landing craft and an escort vessel. Otherwise the Eastern Naval Task Force arrived off Algiers without incident.

A massive array of naval strength supported the Mediterranean landings. The Royal Navy's Force H, based at Gibraltar, acted as a covering force. Consisting at this time of three battleships, a battle cruiser, two fleet aircraft carriers, and lighter vessels, Force H was to guard the amphibious forces from intervention by the Italian navy or by the Vichy French fleet based at Toulon. The Support Force of the Eastern Naval Attack Force consisted of three light cruisers, two escort carriers, three antiaircraft cruisers, a monitor, 13 destroyers, and 17 smaller warships. Directed from a British "headquarters ship," prototype of the later American amphibious command ship (AGC), the Support Force had the tasks of protecting the amphibious forces from air and submarine attack and from shore bombardment, and of providing tactical support for Allied troops while landing and ashore. Only 10,000 troops of the 33,000-man landing force were American, but because of the known French bias against the British, the major ground units were placed under American commanders so that the invasion would appear to be primarily American.

The plan for the capture of Algiers, capital of Algeria and best port on the Barbary Coast, called for simultaneous landings on three flanking beach areas and, as at Safi, a raid by two destroyers to seize port facilities and shipping in the harbor. In a relatively quiet and almost tideless sea, troops began to transfer to landing craft scheduled to hit the beaches at about 0100, November 8. Luckily for the invaders, there was no immediate opposition, for the troops and naval personnel assigned to this assault had had little opportunity for training in amphibious techniques. Hence the ship-to-shore movement to some of the Algerian beaches was even more confused and behind schedule than at any of the Moroccan landings. In one sector battalions were intermingled and scattered for miles along the coast. Nevertheless the landing forces managed to form up and push rapidly inland toward their objectives. Thanks to the activities of pro-Allied officers, many French troops, including the garrisons of two important airfields, surrendered without resistance. The swift Allied advance soon turned the operation into more of an occupation than a campaign, for only the coastal forts east of Algiers offered serious opposition.

Meanwhile two British destroyers had failed in their attempt to seize the port to prevent sabotage of facilities. Confused by darkness and strange waters in the early hours of November 8, the *Broke* and *Malcolm* missed the narrow harbor entrance on their first try. In their second, the *Malcolm* was so severely holed by shore batteries that she was forced to retire. The *Broke* however crashed through the boom, reached a quay, and landed her troops, who were quickly pinned down by small arms fire and captured. The *Broke* managed to escape, but she was so badly damaged that she later sank under tow.

Luckily for the Allies an early cease-fire at Algiers yielded them the port intact. Radio orders to stop resisting issued in the name of General Giraud had produced no effect. During the day however Robert Murphy succeeded in persuading Admiral Darlan to authorize the French commanding general to negotiate a truce. An oral armistice was reached at 1840, November 8, and an hour and 20 minutes later the Americans formally took over control of Algiers. Two days later Darlan, with Marshal Pétain's secret concurrence, ordered a cease-fire for all French units in Africa.*

It was well for the Anglo-Americans that the French were ready to quit. As D-day progressed, the weather worsened so rapidly that by 1800 all further support landings had to be canceled. By that time also, poor boat handling had cost the Eastern Naval Task Force 90 per cent of its landing craft. So few reinforcements and so little material had been unloaded that the situation ashore might have become desperate had French resistance continued. But Murphy's diplomatic triumph permitted the completion of the unloading of troops and supplies in the port of Algiers itself and paved the way for the launching of the Allied drive into Tunisia.

* The Marshal sent his approval by secret code. Officially and publicly however he was obliged to order French forces in Africa to continue resistance.

## Algeria: Oran

The most powerful of the Allied attacks was that made at Oran by the Center Task Force. Because French feeling had been inflamed there by the British attack on the French fleet at nearby Mers-el-Kebir in July 1940, the planners allotted to this assault the best-trained American units available, the 1st Infantry Division and half of the 1st Armored Division, the latter including two armored combat teams with light and medium tanks and tank destroyers. For the same reason no British ground troops were assigned to the operation, although units of the Royal Navy screened and escorted the transports. The Center Naval Task Force included a battleship, a large carrier, two escort carriers, an antiaircraft cruiser, 13 destroyers, more than a score of smaller warships, and transports carrying a landing force of 39,000 troops, nearly all American. The plan was almost identical to that for Algiers. Simultaneous landings were to be made at two beaches west of the city, and—the major effort—on a stretch of coast east of the city adjoining and including the small port of Arzew. Two converted United States Coast Guard cutters, given to Great Britain earlier in the war, would carry raiders into the port of Oran to seize harbor facilities and prevent sabotage. Airfields behind the city were to be quickly seized so that planes could be flown in from the airstrip at Gibraltar.

At Oran the transports debarked the troops smoothly and with little confusion into their landing craft shortly before midnight of November 7–8. Coming ashore between 0100 and 0130, the troops were much less scattered than in the other landings. They moved out quickly toward their assigned objectives. Sporadic and ineffective resistance was offered at Arzew, where infantry and a naval raiding party were able to seize intact four small ships and 13 French seaplanes fueled and loaded with torpedoes. The landings west of Oran were unopposed. Three shallow-draft tankers fitted to discharge tanks on the beach, prototypes of the LST, performed brilliantly, setting ashore armored units that rushed ahead of the main attack to seize an important airfield and vital road junctions on the plateau behind the city.

Satisfaction over the success of the Oran landings was tempered by the disaster that had overtaken the ex-United States Coast Guard cutters filled with raiders attempting to enter Oran harbor. At higher command levels there had been a serious dispute over the feasibility and timing of this strike scheduled for H-hour plus two. Objectors had pointed out that the defenses were very strong and that the long, narrow harbor was a trap. The only possible hope for success was either to effect complete surprise simultaneously with the landings on the beaches, or to wait until army troops had already entered the city before closing in on the docks. By entering the harbor two hours after the first attack on the beaches, the raiders had encountered alert defenses and forfeited support from other Allied units. The *Walney*, in the lead, bulled her way through a boom blocking the harbor entrance, only to be raked by point-blank fire from two French destroyers and a torpedo boat. Staggering to the head of the harbor, she blew up and sank with 75 per cent casualties among her sailors and troops. The *Hartland* gallantly followed her sister craft with no better luck. As she attempted to round a quay, she was taken under fire at 100-foot range by a French destroyer. Losing power, the cutter drifted away, shattered and burning. Half her personnel were mowed down when, forced topside by fires raging in every deck, they were exposed to machine gun fire from all quarters. The ship was abandoned and all survivors were captured. When the city was seized by advancing army troops, they found the harbor clogged with sunken merchant shipping and small warships, the result of French demolitions. Again the French navy had offered strong resistance, upholding its honor with a tragic loss of lives and ships. The ill-fated raiding force, as at Algiers, had gallantly but totally failed in its mission. Valor could not overcome the disadvantages of a faulty plan.

Although cut off from all support, the French garrison in Oran hung on for another day. But it was unable to check the American infantry and armored units from crashing into the heart of the city on the morning of November 10. When Admiral Darlan gave orders during the afternoon for all French troops to cease fighting, organized resistance at Oran had already ended. In marked contrast to the other landings, the landing craft here had been better handled with lower losses. With the help of the port of Arzew, the supply buildup was ample to sustain the fighting. Reflecting their better training, the soldiers had shown more skill and dash than in the other African attacks.

## Tunisia

With Morocco and Algeria secure, the Allies had valuable rear base areas, but Tunisia, separated from Europe by the 90-mile-wide Sicilian Channel, was their real strategic goal. The Germans moved swiftly to keep Tunisia out of Allied hands. By 1130 on D-day, November 8, the Nazis had forced the Vichy cabinet to accept their offer of air support from Sicily and Sardinia. "This caitiff decision," as Churchill branded it, "enabled the Germans to take the quick decisive action of occupying airfields in Tunisia, with all its costly consequences on our campaign." Then the Germans took over unoccupied France and attempted to gain possession of the Toulon fleet. Meanwhile Admiral Darlan, now fully committed to the Allies, was doing all he could to bring French forces and territory over from Vichy allegiance. He ordered the Toulon fleet to sortie to North Africa with the aid of British warships that stood by to offer help, but Admiral Laborde, the Vichy commander at Toulon, preferred neutrality, trusting a Hitler promise that Germany would never try to seize the ships. When the Nazis violated their word and broke into Toulon, Admiral Laborde settled the issue by scuttling his fleet.

Darlan sent orders to Admiral Estéva, senior French officer in Tunisia, for his forces to rally to the Allies, but German planes were already landing on Tunisian airfields. Except for an army contingent under General Barré that withdrew into the hills, French Tunisian forces that might have joined the Allies were quickly rounded up and disarmed. British troops joined the pro-Allied French troops on the Algeria-Tunisia border on November 12, but several thousand German paratroops landing in Tunisia the following day made it apparent that the Allies could look forward to no easy victory. There was consolation however in the information that Dakar and French West Africa had joined the Allied cause on November 23 and that Rommel was fleeing westward with the British Eighth Army in close pursuit.

Hitler's decision to hold what he could of North Africa proved foolish in the long run, for the six-month campaign that followed was far more costly to the Germans than to the Allies. But at the end of the year, heavy rains in Tunisia had mired the Allies so badly that they pulled their forces back to better defensive positions, while out in the desert the advance of Montgomery's Eighth Army was delayed until supplies could catch up with him. Despite temporary setbacks, caused largely by inexperienced personnel—the Army's counterpart of the Navy's landing craft troubles—General Eisenhower was able to get the offensive rolling again in the spring, even though by then nearly 200,000 German and Italian reinforcements and great quantities of Axis supplies had reached Africa. While the Allied forces out of Algeria drove east, with General Patton's armored divisions distinguishing themselves, the British Eighth Army fought its way north through the fortified Mareth Line. Rommel, broken in health, was ordered home by Hitler. On April 7, 1943 Eighth Army and American patrols met, having crossed 2,000 miles of Africa between them, and by May 13 the Tunisian campaign was over. Some 275,000 Axis prisoners of war were taken. Allied air, surface, and submarine forces had sunk 433,000 tons of Axis shipping. Only a few Axis troops escaped across the straits to Sicily. The first British trans-Mediterranean convoy since 1941 left Gibraltar on May 17 and reached Alexandria on May 26 without loss. Reeling back from the Russian offensive at Stalingrad and driven out of Africa, the Nazis had an early foretaste of ultimate disaster.

## The Casablanca Conference

Though at the end of 1942 it was not clear that the Axis had lost its capability of retrieving the initiative, strategic planning could not wait for the military situation to clarify. It was imperative that the Allied leaders get together and coordinate plans. Stalin could not leave Russia just as the Stalingrad campaign was reaching a climax, but Roosevelt and Churchill with their chiefs of staff met at Casablanca from January 14 to 23, 1943 to review the entire strategy of the war.

The main question before the Casablanca Conference was: What next? Since there had been no firm combined planning beyond the decision to seize the North African coastline, the British and Americans had to decide what further moves, if any, should be made in the Mediterranean theater once Tunis was secured.

General Marshall and the other United States Chiefs of Staff still hoped soon to direct all resources into a single, all-out cross-Channel attack somewhere in France, preferably in Normandy. If logistic difficulties made this impossible in 1943, as many American staff planners had at length concluded, then Marshall hoped that the Allies might pin down German troops by seizing the Brittany peninsula in western France. Against this view the British planners, armed with a host of statistics, were able to put up a convincing argument. They pointed out that the Germans could have 44 divisions in France by mid-1943 to oppose an Anglo-American landing, which by that time could muster no more than 25 divisions. Until the odds could be significantly bettered in favor of the Allies, the British believed that an assault on the coast of France could lead only to defeat in that area, and another costly, humiliating ejection from the Continent.

The British were willing to invade France—but only after the German forces there had been considerably weakened. For the time being, the British planners insisted, the best way of achieving that goal, and also of assisting the Russians, was through a continuation of peripheral strategy. Diversionary attacks from the Mediterranean into Southern Europe, said they, would draw so many German units from France and from the Eastern Front that in those areas Hitler would be 55 divisions short of the total needed to defend his empire.

Continued peripheral operations in the Mediterranean theater, the planners continued, could knock Italy out of the war and possibly bring in the Turks. If all this occurred, Hitler would face defeat—even without a cross-Channel attack. But assuming that such an attack was to be carried out, the landing in France would have a far greater chance for success if the Germans were first weakened in the West by attacks elsewhere.

Though the American Joint Chiefs were not entirely convinced by the British logic, they could find no valid counter argument. They disliked seeing more Allied forces sucked into the Mediterranean, which they considered strategically eccentric to the main objective. However, one fact stood out—the British were unwilling to risk returning to France in 1943, and without full British concurrence and cooperation there could be no cross-Channel attack. After much discussion, during which Admiral

King was able to present the case for stepping up the war with Japan by a series of limited offensives, the two Allies struck a bargain. The British desired to see the war in the Pacific limited to a holding operation until Germany was defeated; then all available Allied force would be turned against Japan. They abandoned that position and consented to allocate more men and materials to the Pacific, thereby enabling the Americans to retain the initiative they had won in that theater. The Americans, for their part, consented to postpone the cross-Channel attack till 1944. Meanwhile enemy strength in Europe would be diverted and pressure maintained by means of a Mediterranean offensive in the summer of 1943. Air attacks against the heart of Germany and the *Luftwaffe* would be stepped up. Everyone agreed that the Allies must give top priority to the antisubmarine war. Otherwise no offensives anywhere could succeed.

The remainder of the conference was devoted to finding an appropriate place to strike in the Mediterranean. In the end the planners considered two possibilities, the islands of Sicily and Sardinia. Sardinia was the more weakly defended of the two and would provide bomber bases for raids on the industrial centers of northern Italy, but the island lacked a harbor adequate to mount a major amphibious assault. On the other hand, capture of Sicily, although much more difficult, would more directly threaten Italy, possibly forcing her out of the war, would definitely secure the Sicilian Channel, and would offer the prospect of destroying more enemy forces. Sicily was therefore named the target, D-day being fixed for an appropriate time in July 1943. On this note of resolve and harmony the Casablanca Conference ended.

The day following the close of the Casablanca Conference, President Roosevelt startled statesmen and military leaders around the world by announcing to the press a policy that he himself had formulated, with the concurrence of Prime Minister Churchill. This was the decision that the United States and Britain would accept nothing short of "unconditional surrender" of Germany, Italy, and Japan. Terms would neither be offered nor considered. Not even Napoleon at the height of his conquests ever so completely closed the door to negotiation. To adopt such an inflexible policy was bad enough; to announce it publicly was worse.

The policy of Unconditional Surrender ran counter to the earlier insistence of British and American leaders that they were fighting not the people but the leaders who had misled them. The policy was the sort of mistake that statesmen of the 17th and 18th centuries never made. They understood better than some of their successors that today's enemy might be needed as tomorrow's ally. And a war pushed to the point of complete victory might ruin victor as well as vanquished.

# 5

# Operations against Sicily and Italy

Following the successful landings in French Morocco and Algeria, United States warships withdrew from the Mediterranean, leaving Allied operations in those waters to the Royal Navy. Vice Admiral Hewitt returned to the United States to resume his regular duty as Commander Amphibious Force Atlantic Fleet (Comphiblant). The U.S. Navy remained responsible in North Africa only for the Moroccan Sea Frontier, including the port of Casablanca and the air base at Port Lyautey, and the port of Oran, including Mers-el-Kebir.

With the Allied decision to invade Sicily it became necessary for United States naval forces, personnel, and material to return to the North African theater of operations. In February 1943 Admiral Hewitt was relieved as Comphiblant by Rear Admiral Alan G. Kirk and proceeded to North Africa to assume command of all U.S. naval forces and operations in that area as Commander United States Naval Forces Northwest African Waters. In mid-March Hewitt's command was designated U.S. Eighth Fleet. For the rest of the war the Eighth Fleet included all United States naval forces in the Mediterranean. Operationally it was subordinate to Lieutenant General Dwight D. Eisenhower, the Supreme Allied Commander, through Admiral of the Fleet Sir Andrew B. Cunningham, Commander in Chief Mediterranean. Administratively, it was directly under Admiral King as Commander in Chief U.S. Fleet. In other words, Hewitt received his military orders from Eisenhower but drew his ships, men, and material from King. It was the immediate responsibility of Hewitt and his staff to carry out the naval planning for the American phase of the invasion of Sicily.

Code-named Operation Husky, the Sicilian invasion was planned and executed as an operation in itself, a limited objective. The Allied chiefs proposed to invade Sicily and then see what happened before assigning further Mediterranean targets. Several benefits were expected to result, stated by Churchill as: (1) making Mediterranean communications more secure, (2) diverting German pressure from the Russian front, and (3) intensifying the pressure on Italy.

Churchill and the British Chiefs of Staff hoped that the fall of Sicily would lead to the collapse of the Mussolini government and the withdrawal of Italy from the war, thus opening the way to the Allies for further Mediterranean ventures. They also anticipated that the ensuing disaster to Axis arms might cause the Turks to abandon neutrality and enter the conflict against the Axis. Though the American Joint Chiefs of Staff were less enthusiastic, they admitted that Allied forces assigned to the European theater could not be kept idle until an invasion of France became possible in 1944, and that Sicily was the obvious target. All Allied leaders agreed that seizing a foothold on national territory of the Axis would bring a tremendous morale boost to the western Allies.

The military leaders who successfully concluded the Tunisian campaign continued in command of the Sicilian expedition. Eisenhower received four-star rank to assume over-all command of Operation HUSKY. His deputy, General Sir Harold R. Alexander, controlled all ground troops; naval forces again served under Fleet Admiral Cunningham; and Air Chief Marshal Sir Arthur W. Tedder commanded the Allied air forces. Ground forces assigned to the assault included the American Seventh Army (Lieutenant General Patton) and the British Eighth Army (Lieutenant General Montgomery). The naval assault forces were the Western Naval Task Force (Vice Admiral Hewitt) and the Eastern Naval Task Force (Vice Admiral Sir Bertram Ramsay). Under Vice Admiral Sir Algernon V. Willis, an all-British Covering Force of 6 battleships, 2 fleet carriers, 6 light cruisers, and 24 destroyers would protect both landing forces against possible incursions of the Italian fleet.

## Sicily: Planning and Preparations

Planning the Sicilian landings proved a long and complicated process. There was little opportunity for Eisenhower's top commanders to confer in order to iron out snarls. Headquarters of the commands were scattered across North Africa, far distant from each other. Moreover Alexander, Patton, Montgomery, and other senior officers were preoccupied with concluding the Tunisian campaign and could at first give Sicily scant attention.

Reconciling the strategic and tactical requirements of the various service arms vexed planning even worse. Everybody agreed that the ultimate tactical object was to seize the Straits of Messina as soon as possible. The main enemy supply artery would then be cut and Italo-German forces trapped before they could withdraw to the Italian mainland. But simply sailing in to land within the Straits was not considered feasible, because beaches therein lay beyond the range of effective Allied fighter cover. The only landing sites where adequate land-based air support could be provided lay in the southeast corner of Sicily between the cities of Licata and Syracuse. In this area Allied fighters from Malta, Gozo, Pantelleria, and the Cape Bon peninsula could effectively break up Axis air attacks. Yet this conclusion far from settled the matter. In the Licata-Syracuse region there were but three ports, of which only Syracuse had any considerable tonnage capacity. Both army and navy planners feared that the quantity of supplies that might be handled through these ports and across the beaches could not sustain the number of divisions necessary to defeat the enemy's garrison in Sicily. The best compromise appeared to be to seize beachheads in the part of Sicily that could be covered by fighters, developing airfields to extend fighter cover, and then to land a few days later on beaches near the major ports of Palermo and Catania.

No one really liked this complicated plan of successive assaults. Generals Alexander and Montgomery flatly rejected it on the ground that enemy reinforcements might penetrate between the widely dispersed Allied armies. Army commanders demanded a single, massed assault in the region of Sicily that could be covered by Allied fighters, a requirement that naval commanders considered impossible to fulfill logistically.

In the nick of time two developments in amphibious technology broke the deadlock in planning. With the arrival of numerous newly built LST's and hundreds of DUKW's (amphibious cargo-carrying trucks, known also as ducks or amtrucks), naval staff planners concluded that the army attack could just barely be supplied across the southeast Sicilian beaches with the help of the few available ports. Early in May General Eisenhower approved the new plan for a mass assault.

D-day was set for July 10, 1943, H-hour at 0245. The date and hour were selected to provide moonlight for paratroop drops, with the moon setting in time for the assault waves to close the beaches in total darkness. Because the selected H-hour exposed the fleet to a moonlight approach, navy planners suggested a later approach with landings after dawn, preceded by naval gunfire to neutralize beach defenses. The army planners discarded the suggestion, holding that ship-to-shore movement in darkness was necessary for surprise and insisting that naval gunfire would be ineffective because it was "not designed for land bombardment."

Admiral Hewitt's Western Naval Task Force, organized into three components codenamed *Joss, Dime,* and *Cent,* was to seize a beachhead incorporating the small ports of Licata and Gela and the fishing village of Scoglitti, along a 37-mile front on the Gulf of Gela. Subdividing into four groups, Admiral Ramsay's Eastern Naval Task Force was to seize the Pachino peninsula and an area along the Gulf of Noto just outside the coastal defenses of Syracuse. The landing front was tremendously wide, nearly 100 miles—the most extensive landing of any in World War

II. In numbers also the actual assault phase was the most powerful of the war, not equaled even by the assault on Normandy a year later. More than 470,000 troops, about half American and half British, were assigned to the initial landings. Staging through every available North African port from Bizerte westward, American forces embarked in a vast armada of 580 ships and beaching craft, carrying 1,124 landing craft. Staging from the Eastern Mediterranean and Tunisia, the British used 818 ships and beaching craft, including the vessels of the Covering Force, and 715 landing craft.

A serious defect in the preparations resulted from lack of cooperation of the Allied Air Forces because of a then irreconcilable difference of opinion regarding the employment of tactical air power. The Air Forces were addicted to their doctrine of "sealing off the beachhead" by blasting enemy communications so that there could be little or no movement into or out of the beachhead areas. Meanwhile attacks would be made on enemy airfields to ensure that air interference with the landings would be slight. The Air Forces believed that their technique would obviate the necessity of close tactical support available on call from ground observers on ships or shore. Hence they did not participate in the joint planning and forbade pilots to answer calls for support from ship-based or ground stations other than those approved by Air Force Headquarters in North Africa.

The Allied armies and navies mistrusted the effectiveness of this air doctrine. They wanted the kind of support that had been furnished off Casablanca by U.S. aircraft carrier *Ranger* and that was to become routine in Pacific operations. But Air Marshal Tedder had his way. Although a tactical air force was assigned to support the landings, it was to be controlled from North Africa with no assurance of priority to army-navy requests for aid. To fill the gap General Patton wanted aircraft carriers assigned to the assault forces to fly immediate strikes on call. But Admiral Hewitt felt that this could not really be justified in view of the great demand for carriers elsewhere and the presence of abundant land-based Allied air power from bases within easy range of the beachheads. The attack therefore proceeded without a firm air plan known to all the commanders. At best, air support would be slow; at worst, nonexistent.

Since no one wished to risk repeating the disasters that followed the attacks within the ports of Oran and Algiers, no forces were earmarked to land directly within enemy harbors. But British Commandos and American Rangers were to neutralize key enemy installations, and elements of two divisions of paratroops were to land before H-hour to seize vital airfields and bridges.

Because Sicily was such an obvious Allied objective, extensive efforts were made to convince the enemy that the main attack would come in Greece, with a secondary assault on Sardinia. The most dramatic was the dropping of a carefully prepared corpse into the sea off the Spanish coast to wash ashore near Cadiz. "Major William Martin," as the corpse was called, had a briefcase filled with choice misinformation that quickly fell into the hands of German agents. Local German and Italian commanders were not fooled, but Hitler and the German High Command were, with the result that German armored divisions and Axis mine and torpedo craft were moved to both Sardinia and Greece, where they contributed nothing to the defenses of Sicily. Slow Italian minelayers, left to mine Sicilian waters, did not lay enough mines to prove any serious obstacle.

Training for the Sicilian campaign was much more thorough than had been possible for the North African operation. As the new LST's, LCT's, and LCI's arrived in the theater, they were rushed into training maneuvers in virtually all ports, large and small, on the North African coastline.* While troops exercised with the crews of the new LCVP's in landing through the surf, shore parties practiced forwarding supplies, evacuating wounded, directing gunfire, and the myriad other tasks that are part of an amphibious assault. Most of the assault divisions managed to stage reasonably realistic rehearsals with their task forces on a divisional or near-divisional scale. While possibly no commander thought his particular unit had received enough training, by prior standards Hewitt's and Ramsay's task forces were well prepared.

A combination of beach gradient and surf in the tideless Mediterranean had caused the formation along the coasts of Sicily and elsewhere of "false beaches," sand bars a hundred yards or so offshore over which water shoaled too much to permit the passage of such large beaching craft as LST's.

The landing craft and bases command, under Rear Admiral Richard L. Conolly USN, resolved this problem during training in Africa by developing pontoon causeways, standard pontoon units shackled together to form a bridge to shore. It also proved feasible to "marry" LCT's to the larger LST's so that a sort of ferry service could be run between the LST's anchored offshore and the beach. Both methods worked; both were vital to the successful supplying of the Seventh and Eighth armies after the initial landings.

While the Allied forces prepared, so did the Axis. The Italian fleet remained the best weapon against the landings, for if it could evade the powerful British Covering Force it might play havoc with the assault convoys. But since Axis commanders could not know where or when the Allied blow would fall, their chance of achieving the necessary surprise

---

* The LST (Landing Ship, Tank), the LCT (Landing Craft, Tank), and the LCI (Landing Craft, Infantry) were *beaching craft*, permitting a shore-to-shore expedition by transporting men, vehicles, and supplies from one beach to another. The LCVP (Landing Craft, Vehicle and Personnel) and the LCM (Landing Craft, Mechanized) were smaller *landing craft*, generally carried aboard transports to make ship-to-shore landings.

for a successful naval counterattack was slight. Moreover the Italian *Supermarina*, citing lack of adequate fighter cover, forbade fleet operations within easy Allied air attack range in the waters around Sicily. The defending Axis commanders accordingly pinned their hopes on a successful ground and air defense. Air attacks and resistance by seven Italian coastal divisions were expected to pin the Allies to the beaches, while counterattacks by four Italian and two German mobile divisions were supposed to fling the attackers into the sea. Unwisely Mussolini refused Hitler's offer of three more German divisions. While coastal defenses around all the major ports were strengthened, anti-invasion exercises were held at Gela, for here both the Germans and the Italians expected an Allied landing. Mobile forces were billeted in strategic locations, and some 350,000 troops, including more than 50,000 Germans, awaited attack by the 470,000 Allied invaders.

To participants in the concurrent Pacific war, the odds, considering numbers only, would have appeared to favor the defenders overwhelmingly. In the New Georgia campaign, which roughly coincided with the Sicilian campaign, nearly 34,000 Americans spent six weeks wresting a small corner of New Georgia Island from about 8,000 Japanese defenders. In the Pacific, the Allies rarely undertook an assault without at least a 3-to-1 numerical superiority, and often the odds were far in excess of that. Yet, though air and surface support for Allied assaults against defended positions in the Pacific theater became increasingly powerful, the invaders could generally expect stout resistance. The Japanese would retreat only from an utterly hopeless situation. Few would surrender. If the retreat were cut off, they usually fought to the last man. To military men acquainted with that sort of war, the Allied plan to invade Sicily with only a slight numerical advantage over the defenders would have seemed an invitation to disaster.

But Sicily was a hollow shell. Poor deployment of defense forces, with little provision for defense in depth, was one reason. The main reason however lay in the attitude of the Italians. The Sicilian reservists, to whom Mussolini had entrusted the defense of their homeland, detested the Germans and were far from being ardent Fascists. The Sicilians, together with most of their compatriots on the Italian mainland, saw clearly that the war into which their government had led them was not likely to serve Italian interests. They regarded their military situation as hopeless and rather welcomed an Allied invasion that would take them out of the war and the hated Germans out of Italy.

As D-day approached, Air Chief Marshal Tedder's Mediterranean Allied Air Forces launched a series of raids that put all but a few airfields in Sicily out of operation and forced the Germans and Italians to base their remaining planes on the Italian mainland. And, though Tedder's planes failed to win complete control of the air over the target area, they badly disrupted the Sicilian transport system, and further reduced the already low morale of the Italian forces.

To the last, Mussolini and Field Marshal Albert Kesselring, the German army commander in Italy, remained confident that the invaders would be destroyed "at the water's edge," but General Guzzoni, the Italian commander in Sicily, knew his men and was less optimistic.

## Sicily: Assault and Follow-Up

On July 8, 1943, the jam-packed North African harbors emptied as the huge Allied invasion fleet stood out to sea. Routed so as to make it appear that Greece and Sardinia rather than Sicily were the targets, the convoys passed safely through the extensive Allied mine fields, and in due course turned toward their departure points off Malta.

The weather was calm, and there had been no enemy air attacks. By the morning of July 9 however, the confidence that reigned in the Malta headquarters of General Eisenhower and Admiral Cunningham changed to anxiety as the seas made up steeply in a howling wind. Soon the beaching craft were plunging heavily through rough seas, and even the large transports were taking green water over their bows. Trusting to the aerologist's reports that the wind would die down by the morning of D-day, Admirals Hewitt and Ramsay decided to let their task forces continue. After painful reflection, the commanders at Malta decided not to interfere. Navigation became intensely difficult as lighter craft, especially the LCT's, were slowed by the storm. Nevertheless the general pattern of the approach was maintained. Remarkably close to schedule the assault ships closed their assigned beaches, marked by British beacon submarines that blinked signals seaward.

Admiral Hewitt's Western Task Force concentrated its attacks on three groups of beaches in the Gulf of Gela. The western flank at Licata was assigned to the *Joss* force, the center at Gela to the *Dime* force, and the eastern flank at Scoglitti to the *Cent* force. All was quiet as the transports and the troop-carrying LST's anchored in position. Ashore, fires blazed here and there from Allied bombings, and occasional distant gunfire marked areas where paratroops, dropped earlier in the night, were harassing the enemy. Scout boats stealthily closed the shore, some putting men on the beach to determine exact landing points for the infantry. This proved no easy matter, for the smoke-shrouded hills looming in the darkness offered poor landmarks. Yet it was crucially important to place the troops on the right beaches lest the entire pattern of the attack be disrupted.

On the transports, organized confusion reigned as the ships rolled heavily in the aftermath of the storm. Rail loading the LCVP's that were to carry in the first assault waves was difficult, even impossible for some

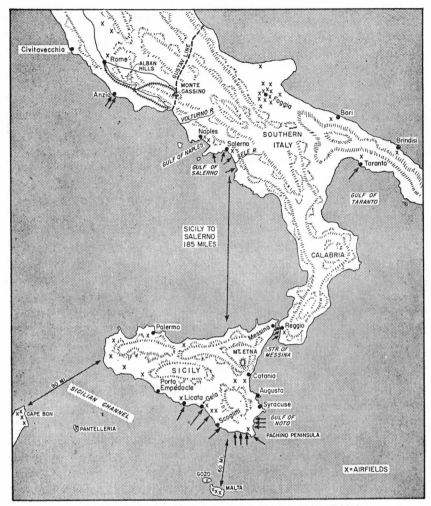

**ALLIED OPERATIONS AGAINST SICILY AND ITALY**

transports, so that for the most part the troops were obliged to clamber down the spray-drenched nets into the pitching small craft. Rocket-firing support boats suffered heavily; many were too damaged in launching to be able to participate. At Scoglitti, to which *Cent* force was lifted entirely in large transports that had steamed from Chesapeake Bay, the rolling of the ships so delayed launching that H-hour had to be postponed an hour. But from the *Joss* and *Dime* forces, waves of LCVP's circled until all their numbers had joined up and then, guided by minesweepers and submarine chasers, moved to the line of departure about 2,000 yards offshore.

Quiet still reigned as the first waves, on signal and guided by blinking lights from the scout boats, began the run from the line of departure to the shore. Admiral Hewitt, supporting the suggestion of the navy planners, had pleaded with the army to be allowed to deliver a dawn pre-invasion bombardment before the infantry hit the beach. But the army commanders, hoping to slip the men ashore in darkness before the enemy realized what was happening, refused. The best Hewitt could get was permission for supporting destroyers, gunboats, and rocket-firing craft to open fire if reaction from the shore indicated that the assault waves had been discovered.

It soon became obvious that tactical surprise was lost. Searchlights flashed across the water from the dark shore, picking up the LCVP's. With a distant crackle enemy machine guns opened up. When artillery shells began to raise geysers in the water, the supporting craft at last opened fire. Meanwhile the infantrymen, tense, seasick in the pitching assault boats, awaited the end of their seagoing ordeal. As the boats touched down and the bow ramps fell, they hesitated momentarily, then rushed ashore, forgetting nausea, scurrying inland to locate and consolidate their assigned positions.

Enemy fire was heaviest at Licata. Here a group of LCI's, scheduled to land behind a first wave of LCVP's that were to clear the beach defenses ahead of them, instead found themselves the lead wave. In the darkness, the smaller craft had headed for another part of the beach. The LCI's, pressing in despite fierce enemy fire from automatic weapons, established fire ascendancy with their own guns and landed their troops.

Enemy fire gradually lessened on all beaches as the invaders rapidly overran enemy pill boxes and gun emplacements, or as supporting destroyers and gunboats blasted hostile positions one by one. For several hours enemy shells fell sporadically on the various American landing areas, but by 0800 most enemy artillery was silent. The Americans climbed the hills toward their D-day initial lines well ahead of schedule. United States Rangers rushed into Licata and Gela—too late at the latter to prevent the dynamiting of an important pier earmarked for unloading. Except for some delays and scattering of troops on the wrong beaches as a result of difficulties of night navigation in landing craft, the landing had proceeded smoothly and more or less according to plan. Ground resistance was light, the Italians defenders happily surrendering at every opportunity.

With the initial beachhead secured, air attacks and unloading problems became Admiral Hewitt's principal worries. Of these, the air attacks proved the easier to deal with. A heavy volume of antiaircraft fire greeted the numerous flights that the Axis air forces placed over the ships, forcing the aviators to bomb inaccurately and indiscriminately. Use for the first time in the theater of proximity-fused (VT) antiaircraft shells greatly increased the effectiveness of defensive fire. Hewitt's ship losses were a destroyer, an LST loaded with badly needed anti-tank artillery, and an ammunition ship in a follow-up convoy.

The false beaches badly hampered off-loading supplies on D-day, preventing LST's from landing vehicles directly on shore. Pontoon causeways proved hard to rig in the heavy weather, and the number of available components was scanty. Clearing of supplies from smaller craft, LCT's, LCVP's, and LCM's, while more efficiently done than in North Africa, remained a troublesome bottleneck at Gela and Scoglitti. Poor beach exits through soft sand and the inefficiency of the army shore engineers caused material to pile up at the water's edge. Loaded landing craft frequently had to return to their ships.

Fortunately for the invaders, the use of DUKW's mitigated D-day supply difficulties. Launched from LST's or transports, these ingenious vehicles could carry ashore the army's standard 105 mm. artillery piece or three tons of other supplies. Several hundred DUKW's expedited unloading and rushed supplies inland to army dumps. But the DUKW could not carry a tank or heavy truck. Getting these ashore continued to plague landing officers until sufficient causeways and LCT's were available to clear transports and LST's of heavy equipment. After D-day, matters vastly improved as Hewitt's forces shifted unloading to better beaches—those at Scoglitti were abandoned altogether—and the ports of Gela and Licata finally became available for the use of LST's.

The temporary shortage of tanks, anti-tank guns, and tank destroyers on D-day and the morning following enabled the navy to make its most spectacular contribution to the success of the Sicilian operations—and incidentally to convince some skeptical army commanders of the value of naval gunfire against shore targets. General Guzzoni, as soon as he received news of the Allied landings, ordered counterattacks on Gela by armored forces. These attacks proved the most serious threat the Seventh Army encountered in Sicily. Patton, and the army in general, now learned in dramatic fashion the value of coordinated, carefully directed naval gunfire. At about 0900 on D-day U.S. cruiser *Boise* and two destroyers, aided by seaplane spotting, checked and turned back a group of Italian tanks closing in on Gela. The next day the *Boise* gave a front-row repeat performance for General Patton. Going ashore that morning, Patton found the beachhead menaced by an advance of about 60 tanks spearheading the German section of Guzzoni's attack. From the top of a building in Gela, Patton could clearly see the 30-ton Panther tanks advancing across the flat plain, with no anti-tank artillery between them and the beaches. A young naval ensign nearby with a walkie-talkie radio inquired of Patton if he could help, and received an emphatic "Sure!" whereupon the ensign radioed *Boise* the location of the enemy. The resulting shower of 38 six-inch shells, together with fire from newly-arrived divisional artillery, halted the German advance. Throughout the rest of the day, Hewitt's ships continued to batter retreating enemy tanks, infantry, and targets of opportunity.

Naval gunfire might have been even more effective had it been possible to have better air spotting. As the fighting progressed, ground observers were sometimes blinded by smoke from burning wheatfields and buildings and were always limited in their fields of observation. SOC float planes from the cruisers, sitting ducks for Messerschmitt fighters that the Nazis sent over the beachhead, were all too quickly shot down, though while they lasted they performed well in spotting targets. Fast fighters of the type used by Tedder's air forces, though clearly needed, were not available in Sicily.

The failure of the Air Forces to participate in joint planning now resulted in the most publicized disaster of the campaign. American paratroops had dropped behind Gela before the landings. Another drop from 144 transport planes was scheduled for the night of July 11–12. No one in the Western Task Force learned of this in time to get the flight routed away from the ships or to notify all antiaircraft crews. When the planes came over, their arrival coincided with the tail end of an enemy air raid. Through faulty identification, 23 of the Allied transports were shot down by antiaircraft guns on shore and in the task force. Two nights later another flight of transports was similarly handled over the British task force when eleven planes were downed by friendly fire.

Admiral Ramsay's Eastern Task Force, landing British troops on the Pachino Peninsula and in the Gulf of Noto in order to capture Syracuse, experienced conditions similar to those at the American landings. Rough seas hampered the swinging out and launching of assault boats. And although the British were somewhat more protected from the gale than the Americans, the problems of boat handling at the eastern beaches were formidable, and the waves of landing craft were mostly behind schedule. Fortunately for the invaders, enemy fire here was light, and in one area surprise, on which the Allied armies placed such high value, was so complete that Montgomery's troops caught the crew of an Italian fieldpiece fast asleep. Such batteries as opened fire were quickly silenced by Allied warships or by the rapidly advancing assault forces. Large numbers of Italian coastal troops actually stampeded in their eagerness to surrender. By the end of D-day the Eighth Army had not only made up lost time but was well ahead of schedule.

The British, because they were closer to enemy airfields in southern Italy than the Americans, suffered more severely from air attack. But the relatively new technique of ground-based fighter-director control of covering aircraft proved itself in this area, helping break up numerous raids. Admiral Cunningham, vividly recalling the savage bombing of his fleet at Crete two years earlier, found it little short of incredible that Allied naval forces could now remain off the enemy coast with near impunity.

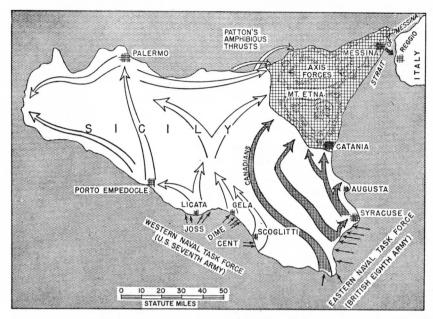

ALLIED INVASION AND AXIS EVACUATION OF SICILY

The most spectacular success of the Eighth Army attack was the speedy capture of Syracuse. A company of Montgomery's paratroopers jumped to seize a key bridge by which the port is approached from the south, and held it against everything the defenders could send against them during D-day. That evening the 19 survivors of the heroic 73 who held the bridge were relieved by the vanguard of Montgomery's army coming up from the south. That night the British occupied Syracuse without a struggle. When nearby Augusta fell a few days later, the Allies possessed two of Sicily's best ports. Though many beaching craft were still employed in running supply shuttles from Africa, they of course found it much easier to discharge in captured ports. In Sicily, more than in most places, the worst port proved better for bringing in supplies than the best beach.

## Sicily: The Axis Evacuation

The Allies hoped to capture most of the Axis forces in Sicily by entrapping them somewhere west of Mt. Etna in a great pincers movement. While Patton's Seventh Army swept northward across the interior of the island and then advanced eastward along the north coast, Montgomery's Eighth Army was to drive north along the east coast to capture Messina and cut the escape route to Italy across the Straits of Messina.

The Seventh Army carried out its part of the double envelopment

with breathtaking speed. Two regiments advanced west along the southern coast and on July 16 captured Porto Empédocle, thereby acquiring
a good port for supplying an advance to the north. In the Empédocle
area the Americans at last found Italians who would fight, but nevertheless captured 6,000 of them. Advancing north across Sicily, elements of
the Seventh Army in four days marched more than a hundred miles by
road to enter Palermo on the north coast on July 22. Here they were
greeted by crowds shouting "Down with Mussolini!" and "Long live
America!" By the 24th all western Sicily was in American hands, and
Patton was advancing along the north coast toward Messina, accompanied
by U.S. light cruisers *Savannah, Philadelphia,* and *Boise* and several destroyers to provide gunfire support and by beaching and landing craft to
bring forward supplies.

Meanwhile the other arm of the pincers, Montgomery's Eighth Army,
was stalled short of Catania on the east coast. To avoid having to make
a costly frontal assault on this enemy strong point, Montgomery decided
to leave the coast and strike inland, around west of Mt. Etna. Redeploy-
ing his forces for this change of front took until August 1. When the
Eighth Army again began moving, it made slow progress in the rugged
terrain at the base of the mountain, where minor defense forces could
harass and delay much stronger attacking columns. Patton's Seventh
Army, advancing in the interior and along the north coast, had by this
time also lost momentum. The Allied armies were now in fact in line
abreast on a front stretching from the north coast across the northeast
tip of Sicily to Catania on the east coast. Patton three times employed
his accompanying naval forces to land troops behind the enemy lines.
No enemy troops were entrapped by these amphibious thrusts, but the
first two, each in battalion strength, expedited the Axis withdrawal. The
third, in regimental strength, fell short of the now rapidly retreating
enemy. Admiral Cunningham, in a complimentary message to Admiral
Hewitt, characterized the naval support that Patton had received as "a
model of the effective application of sea power in the support of land
operations."

On the other hand, Cunningham complained that "No use was made
by the Eighth Army of amphibious opportunities." Certainly Montgomery
failed in his assigned task of cutting off the Axis at Messina. Patton
actually got there ahead of him, but not in time. On July 17 the Axis
forces in Sicily had received orders to fight a delaying action and then
to evacuate the island. Because the Eighth Army was nearer Messina
than the Seventh, elite Axis units, mostly German, had been sent to the
Etna area to hold Montgomery, while the rest of the Axis forces in Sicily
headed north and east for the Straits of Messina, rotating clockwise like
a swinging door with its hinge on Mt. Etna. The Seventh Army's early
advance, for all its speed, was not so swift as the Axis withdrawal. By

August 3 the German and Italian forces were in the northeast tip of Sicily holding back the Allied attack, and the Axis evacuation across the Straits of Messina had begun.

High level bombing by the Allied Air Force did little damage to the ferries, motor rafts, motor barges, and other Axis craft crossing and re-crossing the three-mile-wide Straits loaded with troops and equipment. Dive bombing was suicidal in the face of massed Axis antiaircraft fire. A few British motor torpedo boats penetrated the Straits but achieved little. The Allies were unwilling to risk larger naval craft against the formidable shore batteries that the enemy had assembled. By August 17 about 45,000 German and more than 60,000 Italian troops had made good their escape with most of their equipment.

## Sicily: Conclusions

Some postwar military commentators, particularly among the Germans, have expressed the opinion that an initial assault in or near the Straits of Messina would have been feasible. A successful landing here, while the defenders were deployed to contest a landing elsewhere, would have bottled up Axis forces in Sicily as they had been bottled up in Tunisia. But after the landings in Northwest Africa, Allied commanders in the European theater made it a set policy never to stage an amphibious assault beyond the radius of land-based fighter support—a wise decision, as experience proved. Carrier air, which in the Pacific proved fully able to fill the gap, was not in sufficient quantity in the Mediterranean. American fleet carriers were all in the Pacific. Escort carriers, still in short supply, were busy in the Atlantic combating the U-boat. There were never enough British fleet carriers, and these carried so few planes and of such inferior quality that they could do little more than provide air cover for the naval forces to which they were attached.

Despite the successful Axis evacuation, the Sicilian campaign was a major triumph for the Allies. Even before the campaign was over, the Axis coalition had begun to fall apart. In Italy the discouraging news from Sicily, climaxed by a 560-plane raid on Rome itself, finally prompted the King to make the popular move of deposing Mussolini and taking him into "protective custody." Marshal Pietro Badoglio, the new head of government, announced that he would continue the war against the Allies, a pronouncement that nobody took very seriously. Hitler considered rushing in enough German troops from Russia to seize Italy with an immediate *coup d'état*, but conditions on the Russian front forbade it. The most he could do for the time being was to accept the change of government, while moving additional German divisions into Italy from France and Germany.

With less than five per cent Allied casualties (7,800 killed, 14,000 wounded), Operation HUSKY in just over a month's time had achieved most of the objectives set forth at the Casablanca Conference. Allied Mediterranean communications were now completely secure. Italy seemed certain to collapse. Italian troops, no longer reliable, would have to be replaced in Italy, France, Yugoslavia, Greece, and elsewhere by German troops. On the Russian front, German pressure, especially from the *Luftwaffe,* was somewhat relieved. The way was laid open for further Allied attacks against which the Nazis had to prepare by further deploying their forces. British hopes that Turkey would enter the conflict were not realized, for the Turks insisted that they were not yet ready. But the Sicilian success greatly reinforced the Allied position in the eyes of neutral nations. Soon Germany would be fighting alone against heavy odds.

## Italy: Planning and Preparations

In May 1943, just as the Tunisian campaign was ending, Roosevelt and Churchill and the Combined Chiefs of Staff had met again, this time in Washington. Here they once more threshed over differences of opinion regarding the proper strategy for defeating Germany. The British advocated the invasion of Italy as the inevitable next step after Sicily. Their planners estimated that an Allied cross-Channel attack could succeed only if German forces in France were reduced to no more than 12 divisions. The surest way of attaining such a reduction, they argued, was to eliminate Italy from the war, for then the Nazis would have to send their own troops to replace 24 Italian divisions in the Balkans. An invasion of Italy moreover would enable the Allies to seize the complex of airfields about Foggia to strengthen the coming bombing offensive against Germany.

The Americans acknowledged the cogency of the British argument but reaffirmed their opinion that Germany could be defeated only by an invasion of western Europe. A campaign in Italy, they pointed out, would tie up Allied as well as German forces and thus might further delay the cross-Channel attack. General Sir Alan Brooke, Chief of the Imperial General Staff, then expressed the opinion that the invasion of France in any event would not be feasible before 1945 or 1946. If so, replied General Marshall, the Allies ought to stop planning for an operation that was continually being postponed, and the Americans should shift their main force to the Pacific, where it could be used at once.

Evidently, if the Allies were to adhere to their plan of putting the primary emphasis upon defeating Germany, they would have to reach another compromise. Being reasonable men, they succeeded—though the details were not all spelled out until some time after the actual conference had ended. The Americans agreed to the invasion of Italy provided only the forces already in the Mediterranean were used, plus a portion of the assault shipping earlier assigned to operations against Burma. Seven divisions however were to be withdrawn from the Mediterranean to the United Kingdom to form a nucleus for building up the Cross-Channel attack force. The British, for their part, committed themselves definitely to an invasion of France, with May 1, 1944 as the target date. They agreed that the general conduct of the war in the Pacific should be left to the American Joint Chiefs of Staff. They also accepted in principle the Joint Chiefs' "Strategic Plan for the Defeat of Japan," a remarkable document which we shall consider in a later chapter. They insisted however that the "Strategic Plan" be carried out with forces already assigned to the Pacific theater. Thus Allied operations against both Italy and Japan were to be limited in order to build up forces in the United Kingdom to 29 divisions for operations against Western Europe.

Since the team of Eisenhower, Alexander, Cunningham, and Tedder was to be retained, it fell upon their staffs to begin planning the invasion of Italy on the eve of the Sicilian assault. Despite pressure from Churchill, Eisenhower refused to make a firm commitment regarding the Italian operation until he had tasted the strength of the enemy in Sicily. However, within a week after the launching of Operation Husky, Allied prospects were sufficiently bright for Eisenhower's planners to begin considering when and where Italy should be invaded.

The success of Husky shocked Kesselring and other German continental strategists out of their conviction that the Mediterranean was a moat to their fortress. Viewing it now as a highway open to Allied exploitation by the use of sea power, they fully anticipated an early Allied invasion of Italy. Some German planners estimated that the Anglo-American forces might land as far north as Rome, possibly even at Leghorn or Spezia. In anticipation of a northern landing, the Germans made provisions to withdraw their forces rapidly beyond the Apennines to avoid having them trapped in the Italian boot.

But the Allied military leaders had no intention of invading beyond the range of their land-based fighter support. Original plans called only for an invasion via the toe of the boot. The final plan, authorized July 26, was for Montgomery's Eighth Army to cross the Messina Strait to Reggio as soon as feasible after the end of the Sicilian campaign. The invasion of the Italian toe was however to be now considered chiefly a diversionary attack, to draw the Germans away from the main assault. This was to be in the Gulf of Salerno, at the extreme attack radius of Sicily-based Spitfire fighters equipped with extra, droppable fuel tanks. Landing at Salerno on September 9, 1943, the newly formed Fifth Army under Lieutenant General Mark W. Clark USA was to drive for Naples 35 miles away.

What the Badoglio government wanted was merely to shift sides, to join Britain and the United States in an alliance against Germany without the humiliation of a formal surrender. But Roosevelt and Churchill, recalling the disapproving public reaction in their countries to the "Darlan deal" in North Africa, did not care to treat the Italians like returning prodigals. Besides, the President and the Prime Minister were inhibited by their own formula of "unconditional surrender." After lengthy and melodramatic secret negotiations reminiscent of spy fiction, a bargain was struck. Italy would surrender and get out of the war, the effective date to coincide with the landing at Salerno. From that date Italian troops who followed the Badoglio government would fight the Germans rather than the Allies. The Italian Fleet and Air Force were to proceed to designated points and place themselves under Allied control. Thus a major purpose of the Salerno and Reggio landings was fulfilled before the attacks began.

Because German troops continued to pour into Italy, Badoglio requested that the main Allied landing be made north of Rome, with an airborne division to be dropped on Rome itself. He promised to have Italian troops in place to join the Allied forces both near the beachhead and near Rome. Eisenhower favored the Badoglio plan, but uncertainty, shortage of forces, and lack of trust between the negotiating parties brought the project to nought. The Allies continued with their plan to land at Salerno, and did not risk informing an erstwhile enemy where the landing was to be. Hence the Italians were unable to assist the invaders in any way.

Meanwhile preparations for the Salerno operation were proceeding under circumstances even more trying than those for Sicily. For this assault Admiral Hewitt was to command all the Allied amphibious forces. These were divided into a primarily British Northern Attack Force carrying two divisions, and an American Southern Attack Force of equal strength. Two more divisions in floating reserve would follow up. Twenty-six transports, 120 LST's, and 90 LCT's prepared to land troops on two groups of beaches about eight miles apart in the Gulf of Salerno. The landings were to be supported by seven cruisers (including three American), two monitors, and 35 destroyers and a Support Carrier Force of five escort carriers and ten destroyers. The Royal Navy provided a Covering Force of four battleships, the fleet carriers *Illustrious* and *Formidable*, and 20 destroyers. The Covering Force, in addition to fending off surface attack, was assigned the task of providing combat air patrol for the Support Carrier Force.

The immediate targets were the port and town of Salerno, the Montecorvino airfield, and the passes through the hills leading to Naples. These objectives were assigned to British forces and to United States Rangers. American forces, to the south, would cover their flank, add depth and body to the beachhead, and link up with Montgomery's Eighth Army coming up from Reggio. The chances of the Eighth Army's being able to join hands with the Salerno beachhead were considerably lessened however by Montgomery's demands for massive artillery support to cover his crossing of the Straits of Messina. Fulfilling his demands took until September 3, and then the Eighth Army finally crossed virtually unopposed.

As the landing site, Salerno had both good and bad features. Readily identifiable mountain peaks behind the beaches offered excellent guides to the assault forces, but the mountains also provided superb sites for observation, defensive gun emplacements, and staging areas for counterattacks. The beaches, with better gradients and fewer offshore bars than those at Sicily, were suitable in some places for LST's to beach directly at the shore. On the other hand, the Gulf of Salerno was readily mined, and Allied intelligence learned belatedly that mines were sown there in abundance. Hence extensive minesweeping would have to precede the ship-to-shore movement. That meant that the transports were obliged initially to put their troops into landing craft nine to twelve miles from the beaches, and it required a complete rescheduling of the intricate landing plan.

Arrangements for air support over Salerno were superior to those for Sicily. The presence of the escort carriers in direct support would prove an immense advantage. Moreover Eisenhower demanded that the air forces cooperate more closely with the army and the navy. Admiral Hewitt now had his flag in the *Ancon*, an amphibious command ship (AGC), converted from a passenger-cargo vessel and equipped with elaborate radio and radar gear. Aboard the *Ancon* an air force general headed a fighter-director team, and there were two standby fighter-director ships. Air spotting for naval gunfire support was improved by the use of high performance army P-51's flown by pilots trained by naval aviators.

In other respects the planning for Salerno was less efficient than that for Sicily. Because the planners had great difficulty getting from the high command firm commitments for men and material, changes were being made on the landing plan even after the departure for the beachhead. Such apparent indecision was exasperating to the force commanders, who could not know that an important reason was the highly-secret peace negotiations, of which no more than a dozen men were informed. There were other reasons for last-minute changes. Priority for certain equipment had to be given to the Eighth Army, slowly working its way up the toe of the Italian boot. And while the Salerno task force was en route, several gunfire support cruisers, including U.S.S. *Boise*, were detached to join a force under Admiral Cunningham that would occupy the great naval base at Taranto when the Italian fleet steamed out to surrender under the terms of the armistice.

Again, as before HUSKY, the Army insisted that the landing be made in darkness and without pre-landing naval bombardment. Admiral Hewitt once more argued in vain against this plan. Complete surprise, he contended, was impossible, and in darkness confusion was inevitable. The *Luftwaffe* had already twice raided Bizerte, and these were no mere blind stabs, for Bizerte was the chief assembly point for beaching craft. Enemy reconnaissance planes would undoubtedly detect the assault forces en route to the beachhead. In any event, the Axis high command must have noted Salerno as a likely invasion point, for it was the key to Naples, Italy's finest port, and it was just within extreme operational radius of fighter planes based on Sicily. The army commanders remained unmoved, arguing that though the enemy might suspect Salerno, a little surprise was better than no surprise at all. A bombardment, they said, would be a dead giveaway, attracting additional German forces to the beachhead without achieving important destruction of enemy defenses. As a result of the Army's decision, there was no gunfire preparation at Salerno, and, in the American sector, not even any supporting fire as the assault waves closed the beach.

The Germans were in fact already at Salerno in division strength. As we have seen, when the German high command suspected that the Badoglio government was negotiating with the Allies, they lost no time dispatching divisions to take over Italy. By the time of the Salerno assault there were eight German divisions in northern Italy under Field Marshal Erwin Rommel, and eight in central and southern Italy under Field Marshal Albert Kesselring. Kesselring had organized southern Italy for defense against Allied landings. Lacking the strength to check Montgomery's advance from Reggio, he settled for a delaying action by two of his divisions, distributing the rest to protect Rome and the Naples area. Suspecting that the Allies would land at Salerno, for the reasons adduced by Hewitt, he ordered thither the bulk of the 16th Panzer Division and a regiment of paratroops to dig in at and behind the landing areas. The Germans arrived at Salerno in time to mine and wire the beaches, to mine the Gulf, to emplace guns in positions from the hills right down to the water, and to deploy tanks for counterattack. Kesselring also drew up plans for moving other German divisions rapidly to Salerno. Everything possible was done to make the region a hornet's nest for the Allied invaders. There was a real possibility that the Germans might be able to throw the Allied forces into the sea at the outset, or at least that they might reinforce their troops more rapidly than the Allies and thus be able to counterattack effectively a few days later.

Only one serious flaw marred Kesselring's preparations. His superiors declined to commit additional forces near Naples. Influenced by Rommel, Hitler originally intended to withdraw German forces north of Rome. It was only through Kesselring's persuasion that he agreed to make any stand at all in the south. Rommel, who understood sea warfare better than most of Hitler's generals, saw clearly enough that the Mediterranean was no barrier to naval power. The Italian coasts were standing invitations to the Allies to outflank and cut off any German forces in the Italian boot. The Apennines, on the contrary, as they swing across northern Italy from the Adriatic Sea to the Gulf of Genoa, form a barrier where relatively few defenders can hold the line against strong attacking forces. Hitler, taking the advice of both Rommel and Kesselring, but the full advice of neither, straddled the issue. He ordered Kesselring to make a stand in southern Italy but gave him insufficient troops to defend Salerno and Naples.

Various elements of the Salerno assault forces departed Oran, Algiers, Bizerte, and Tripoli between September 3 and 6. These joined other elements from Palermo and Termini north of Sicily, and on September 8 (D minus 1) shaped course for the Gulf of Salerno. During the approach, the task force came under attack by German aircraft that sank an LCT and damaged several other vessels.

At 1830 on September 8, as the Allied attack forces were approaching the Gulf, General Eisenhower broadcast a radio announcement of the Italian armistice. Badoglio confirmed the news in a broadcast from Rome. Then he and the King fled to Brindisi, leaving no one in authority in the capital. To the Germans the announcement was the signal to execute their carefully planned Operation ACHSE for disarming the Italians and taking over control of all Italian administration and communications. This they speedily accomplished against weak resistance. Only the Italian fleet and some of the air force units were able to escape. Most of the disarmed Italian troops simply vanished, blending into the civilian population. Mussolini, rescued by the Germans, was put at the head of a puppet government in northern Italy.

The Salerno-bound Fifth Army greeted Eisenhower's announcement with jubilation—and the conviction that the war was over. Senior officers found it difficult to convince the troops that, although the Italians had quit fighting, there were plenty of Germans to offer resistance.

## Salerno: Assault and Follow-Up

For once the approaching Allied assault forces were enjoying perfect weather. There would be no problems of heavy surf at Salerno. Aboard the transports and beaching craft the troops stirred restlessly in the heat, but lulled by the erroneous belief that only surrendering Italians would greet them, they displayed little of the anxiety that had been prevalent at Sicily.

At midnight the transports carrying American forces were in position off the southern sector of the Gulf of Salerno, and minesweepers advanced to clear channels to the shore. Scout boats, using radar fixes from extinct volcanoes looming dimly in the distance, closed the shore, located their assigned beaches, and blinked signals seaward. Rail-loaded LCVP's

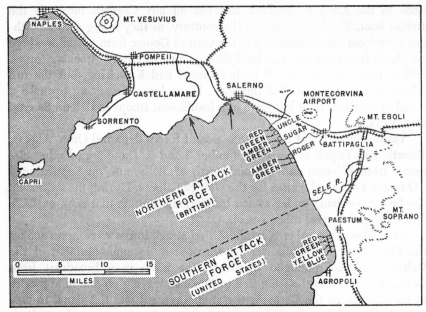

INVASION OF ITALY (SALERNO), SEPTEMBER 9, 1943

splashed into the water, then cast off to begin seemingly interminable circling until their waves had joined. That completed, they opened throttles and raced through darkness to the line of departure 6,000 yards offshore. From here, on signal, they headed for the beach. Tension grew as seasickness overcame many of the troops. Crews in the scout boats heard clanking and clattering and saw headlights ashore as German motorized troops moved to the water's edge to contest the landing. In this sector however the defenders chose to withhold their fire. Suddenly at H-hour, 0330, as the first wave of landing craft neared the beach, a loudspeaker ashore blared in English, "Come on in and give up! We have you covered!"

Despite the shock of realizing that they had a fight on their hands, the assault troops rushed resolutely ashore as, just at first light, the ramps of the landing craft slammed down. At that moment the quiet was succeeded by pandemonium. The German defenders at last opened up with rifle, machine gun, mortar, cannon, and tank fire, and German aircraft came sweeping over the beaches bombing and strafing. The troops of the first assault waves by-passed enemy strong points to gather in prearranged assembly areas. Then came DUKW's bringing ashore howitzers and ammunition. Thus armed, the invaders dueled German tanks and infantry at point-blank ranges. Landing and beaching craft pressed through heavy fire to land reinforcements. Sailors, struggling with pontoons, managed to rig causeways for landing tanks while shells slapped the water around them. By afternoon, though some individual beaches were completely interdicted by enemy fire, the Americans had seized a precarious hold on their sector of the beachhead.

In the British sector, to the north, the Germans inadvertently did the invaders a favor by opening fire on LST's before they could anchor in position to launch their LCVP's. That automatically canceled the Army's restriction against pre-landing naval fire support. Rear Admiral Richard L. Conolly usn, commanding an amphibious group in this sector, had forehandedly prepared for such an opportunity by ordering three destroyers into position a mile off the beach. These now opened fire against shore installations. Rocket-firing beaching craft supported the first assault wave as it headed for the beach. Despite this support, the first wave, landing precisely at 0330, met strong resistance, and beaching craft advancing to land ammunition and equipment suffered heavy damage from shell hits. Except on the extreme left flank, where American Rangers and British Commandos landed against little or no opposition and quickly pushed to the defiles in the hills, the pattern of combat was much the same in the northern sector as in the southern. Though by the end of D-day the Fifth Army had occupied all the designated beaches, the beachhead area in both sectors was still dangerously thin.

The beachhead, such as it was, had been saved by supporting warships. On call from shore fire control parties or using spotting aircraft, the light cruisers *Philadelphia* and *Savannah*, a British monitor, and four destroyers off the American beaches repeatedly silenced mobile enemy batteries, knocked out machine gun positions, and dispersed concentrations of enemy infantry and tanks. Three British cruisers and a monitor off the northern beaches, unable to establish dependable communication with their shore fire control parties, achieved little on D-day; but six destroyers and three beaching craft successfully took over the whole support role in this area, at times approaching so close to the shore as to come under enemy rifle fire. By the end of the day, Hewitt's ships had expended many hundreds of rounds on dozens of call-fire missions, and not a few rounds without benefit of ground or air spot.

As soon as the Germans realized the crucial role played by the supporting warships, they shifted the weight of their air attack to these vessels. Although their sorties were fewer than at Sicily, they were more effective. High altitude bombers introduced a radio-controlled glide bomb, released from great heights when German fighter-bombers had drawn down the Allied air cover. On September 11 one of the glide bombs ripped through the *Savannah*, blowing out a section of her bottom and forcing her to retire for repairs. Two days later the British cruiser *Uganda* suffered a similar fate. But U.S.S. *Boise*, having completed her part in the Taranto operation, was en route to Salerno, and Admiral Cunningham ordered two more British light cruisers up from Malta.

Meanwhile the *Philadelphia* was proving not only the most effective but the luckiest gunnery ship in Hewitt's force. Repeatedly near-missed by both conventional and glide bombs, sometimes by a matter of feet, she escaped severe damage and expended almost all of her ammunition on shore targets. The best defense against the glide bomb proved to be smoke. Even a fairly light smoke haze over the roadstead served to confuse the German radio operators who controlled the bombs.

By September 12 Clark's Fifth Army had somewhat enlarged its beachhead, but at the center it had not yet reached its assigned D-day line. On the 12th the supporting escort carriers were forced to retire to Palermo for refueling, first sending their aircraft ashore—not to the Montecorvino airport, which though in Allied hands was still under enemy fire, but to emergency airstrips hastily constructed within the beachhead. By now elements of five German divisions had reached the Salerno area and had massed 600 tanks and mobile guns for an all-out attack down the Sele River, the dividing line between the Allied sectors. The German strategy was to split the Fifth Army, concentrating first on one sector and then on the other.

This crisis came on September 13–14. As the German attack gained momentum, the Allied situation became so critical that General Clark asked Admiral Hewitt to prepare plans for evacuating either the northern or the southern Allied force and relanding it with the other. At Clark's request a division of paratroops was flown up from Sicily and dropped at Salerno at night. To avoid a repetition of the tragedy over Sicily, when paratroops were shot down by friendly fire, all antiaircraft guns in the Allied fleet and army were silenced. Meanwhile General Eisenhower ordered Marshal Tedder to support the Fifth Army with every available plane.

The German attempt to break through to the beach was defeated primarily by naval gunfire support, but also by the Fifth Army's hard fighting, by improved Allied air support, and by two faulty German decisions—one tactical, the other strategic. In the afternoon of the 13th, the local German commander ordered his main body of tanks to drive down the Sele toward a fork in the river and gain access to the beach across a bridge shown on German maps. But the bridge had already been destroyed, and the road that led to it was flanked by drainage ditches that prevented the tanks from deploying. When the absence of the bridge stopped the German tank column, the Americans, having noted the German movement, were ready with infantry and two battalions of well-sited artillery. The tank force, trapped in the narrow road, was destroyed. This setback ended the most promising attack the Germans were able to make. The fact was that Kesselring lacked the means to match the Allied rate of reinforcement. Two more German divisions during the first week of the invasion might well have thrown the Allies into the sea. But

Rommel, regarding the southern campaign as useless, refused to release any troops from northern Italy.

As Kesselring's forces renewed their attack on the 14th, the Allied cruisers and destroyers closed in to hammer tank columns and assembly points. The *Philadelphia* and *Boise* each expended several hundred rounds of 6-inch shell on all types of targets. As other ships, including the British battleships *Valiant* and *Warspite,* rushed to the Salerno area to assist, it became apparent that the tide had turned—though the venerable *Warspite* soon became the third victim of German glide bombs and had to be towed away.

On September 16, advance elements of the Eighth Army at last made contact with the Fifth Army. That same day Kesselring, concluding that his attempt to recapture the beachhead was proving too costly, decided to abandon Salerno and Naples and withdraw to a prepared defense line behind the Volturno River. "On 16 September," he afterward wrote, "in order to evade the effective shelling from warships I authorized a disengagement from the coastal front. . . ."

As the Nazis withdrew, they demolished the harbor of Naples and did what they could to wreck the city—not only to delay the Allies and add to their logistic problems but also to wreak vengeance on the turn-coat Italians. But the Allied navies, by opening the port of Salerno and performing near-miracles in supplying the army across the Salerno beaches, enabled Clark's Fifth Army to enter Naples on October 1, 1943. That concluded the Salerno operation, which had cost the Allies 2,100 killed, 4,100 missing, and 7,400 wounded.

Montgomery's Eighth Army meanwhile had occupied the Foggia airdrome near the Adriatic coast and pushed on to the northwest. On October 6 the two Allied armies abreast reached the Volturno. There the new battle line formed while both sides brought up reinforcements for the next round. The Navy's salvage experts, who had cleared the wreckage from harbors in North Africa and Sicily, had already set to work to restore Naples as the principal Allied port in Italy. Despite the German demolitions, Naples was soon receiving tonnage in excess of its peacetime capacity.

Most of the Italian fleet was now in Allied hands. On September 9 three new battleships, six cruisers, and ten destroyers had fled from Genoa and Spezia to give themselves up, as required by the terms of the armistice. Pounced upon off Sardinia by German bombers, the battleship *Roma,* fleet flagship, was sunk by a glide bomb with the loss of 1,400 lives. The rest of the force, and the older battleships from Taranto, proceeded to their destinations without being further molested. On September 11 Admiral Cunningham signaled the British Admiralty, "Be pleased to inform Their Lordships that the Italian Battle Fleet now lies under the guns of the fortress of Malta."

## Stalemate at Anzio

The invasion of the Italian mainland yielded disappointingly small dividends to the British and Americans. A few extra German divisions were tied down, and the Allies had gained additional combat experience, but even the value of the bomber base at Foggia proved to be largely negated by the barrier of the Alps. The Allies found themselves engaged in a major land campaign of minor strategic importance in a secondary theater of operations. Further advances would have to be conducted through terrain and weather that heavily favored the defense.

For the Germans the Volturno line was only a temporary stand, to be held while they prepared still stronger defenses farther up the Italian boot. Through October and the first two weeks of November, they fought rear-guard actions as they backed off to their Winter Line, 40 miles northwest of Naples. This line, a system of carefully prepared defense positions on the mountain slopes, they intended to hold as long as possible. Northern and central Italy were now securely under Nazi domination, and Marshal Kesselring, left in command of all German forces in Italy by Rommel's departure for France, could count on 19 German divisions to hold the 14 that the Allied Fifth and Eighth Armies assembled for an all-out attack on the Winter Line.

In seeking a means of breaking the Nazi defense barrier, Generals Eisenhower, Alexander, and Clark had already initiated planning for an end-run landing behind the Winter Line in the vicinity of Rome. Their purpose was to cut the enemy's main lines of communication and to threaten his rear. Much the best beaches for attaining the first of these objectives were at Anzio. Anzio was 37 miles southeast of Rome and 20 miles south of the Alban Hills (*Colli Laziali*), which dominated roads and railroads leading from Rome down to the German defense line.

But beaching craft and landing craft were now leaving the Mediterranean for Britain in such numbers that only a single-division assault on the Italian coast could be mounted. Hence the Anzio assault was planned to follow the opening of the drive against the main German defenses. Only if this drive were sufficiently successful for the Fifth Army and the landing force to be mutually supporting would the landing be undertaken. Eisenhower in fact stipulated that the Allied armies advancing up the boot must have reached a position where they could expect to join the Anzio amphibious force within 48 hours after the landing, for with the shipping now at his disposal he could not be certain of supplying the beachhead much beyond that length of time.

Montgomery's Eighth Army began its advance against the Winter Line on November 28, 1943. Clark's Fifth Army started two days later. Both quickly bogged down in the face of stiff German resistance and almost continual rain that sapped the strength of the invaders and turned dirt roads into quagmires. Three weeks after the opening of the drive, the Allied armies had not advanced ten miles, and the right flank of the new German Gustav Line was firmly anchored on Monte Cassino, nearly 75 miles from Anzio. The end-run project was clearly infeasible. On December 22, Alexander, on Clark's recommendation and with Eisenhower's concurrence, canceled the Anzio operation.

At this point Churchill intervened personally. Meeting with the leading Allied commanders at Tunis on Christmas Day 1943, the Prime Minister insisted that the Anzio project be revived. The end-run must be made moreover without waiting to see if a renewed attack on the German line would succeed. Whether or not the Anzio attack was successful in cutting the German supply lines, it could not fail, said Churchill, to divert strength from the Gustav Line. He conceded however that in the circumstances a one-division assault would be too risky. But cancellation of a planned operation against the Andaman Islands in the Bay of Bengal had released 15 LSI's (Landing Ships, Infantry) for use in the Mediterranean. And at Churchill's request President Roosevelt permitted 56 LST's to remain a little longer in the Mediterranean, with two important provisos: that the cross-Channel attack remain the paramount operation, and that Churchill drop his insistence upon further peripheral operations to be directed against Rhodes and the Aegean Islands.* Enough beaching craft and their associated landing craft were thus made available for a two-division assault on Anzio. That was enough for Churchill. He brushed aside objections by Eisenhower and others that even two divisions were insufficient for what would amount to an independent attack. Eisenhower in any event was about to leave the theater to prepare for the cross-Channel assault, which he was to command. His successor as Supreme Allied Commander Mediterranean, Sir Henry Maitland Wilson, accepted the risk of a two-division landing at Anzio. So did General Alexander. D-day was set at January 20, 1944. Drawn from the Fifth Army and earmarked for the assault were the United States 3rd Division, the British 1st Infantry Division, three battalions of Rangers, two battalions of Commandos, and a regiment of paratroops.

Ground forces for the Anzio attack were to be commanded by Major General John P. Lucas USA, naval forces by Rear Admiral Frank J. Lowry USN, Commander VIII Amphibious Force, U.S. Eighth Fleet. To meet

---

* At the Teheran Conference the preceding November Churchill had stated that a major purpose of the operations he proposed against the German-held islands in the Aegean area was to open up a shorter, more easily defensible supply line to Russia—the main objective, be it noted, of his Dardanelles-Gallipoli campaign of World War I. Another purpose, said he, was to provide Turkey with air support as a further inducement to enter the war on the Allied side. Churchill hoped that the Turks might be influenced to attack German forces in the Balkans. If not, the Allies would at least be able to operate from airfields in Turkey, whence, among other targets, they could strike at the Ploesti oil fields in Romania, on which the Germans were heavily dependent.

the early invasion date, army and naval staffs immediately went to work and by all-out effort had plans completed and approved by January 12, ten days before D-day, which at General Lucas's request had been postponed to January 22. Meanwhile the Eighth Army prepared to apply pressure on its sector of the Gustav Line in order to keep the Germans from transferring any of the defending troops elsewhere, and on January 17 the Fifth Army renewed its attack on Cassino both in order to attract German reserves that might be used against Anzio and in the hope of breaking the Gustav Line loose from its anchor. The Allied Air Forces began "sealing off the beachhead" by means of intensive raids on roads, railroads, bridges, and enemy airfields, and on January 19 reported that they had succeeded in their mission.

With misgivings about the strength of the coming assault heightened by a dismayingly poor landing rehearsal in the Gulf of Salerno, the Anzio forces left Naples on January 21, advancing by a roundabout 110-mile route to deceive the enemy. LST's, LCI's and LCT's formed the bulk of the troop lift, with numerous LCVP's aboard to boat the first assault waves. Careful reconnaissance revealed that only weak enemy forces manned the beach defenses. Rocket-firing beaching craft were to lay down a barrage a few minutes before the LCVP's touched down, primarily to detonate the mines on the beaches.

In contrast to the disorderly rehearsal, there followed one of the smoothest landings of the entire war. Lowry's forces hit the beaches exactly at H-hour, 0200, and quickly solved the problems caused by enemy mines and the confusion inevitable in night landings. Enemy resistance at the beach was slight. For once Allied assault forces had attained real surprise, and a night landing without preparatory naval fire had paid off. For three nights before the assault, Kesselring, vaguely aware that something was afoot, had ordered an alert against enemy landings at any of several points, including Anzio. But on the night of January 21–22 he had let his staff persuade him to discontinue the alert in order to rest the men. Once aware of his error, he rushed mobile guns and numerous battalions of troops toward Anzio over roads, railroads, and bridges that had been quickly repaired following the Allied air attack. The beachhead had not been "sealed off" after all. Nor had the Fifth Army attack on Cassino succeeded; there the Germans still held. Nevertheless the end of D-day saw 36,000 Allied troops ashore at Anzio, with fewer than 150 casualties. Despite a severe storm on D-day plus 4, nearly 70,000 men, more than 25,000 tons of supplies, 500 guns, and 237 tanks crossed the beaches in the first week of the attack. Lucas and Lowry's task was to keep them there; Kesselring's was to contain them and push them out.

General Lucas had two choices: to advance before consolidating, or to consolidate before advancing. If he advanced at once to the Alban Hills, his guns could block traffic to the Gustav Line before the Germans could bring up their forces in strength. Such a move would carry out the main intent of the original Anzio plan, but it would invite a German counterthrust that might cut Lucas's communications with the coast. General Clark, recognizing this danger, had ordered General Lucas only to seize and secure a beachhead and to "advance on" the Alban Hills, deliberately ambiguous phrasing that left Lucas considerable freedom of action. Interpreting his orders conservatively, Lucas chose to pause and consolidate his beachhead, throwing up strong defenses before pressing inland.

The Anzio landings had thrown the Germans into panic, causing them temporarily to evacuate Rome. But Lucas's cautious course enabled them to re-estimate the situation, and allowed Kesselring time to augment the German defenses. The delayed Allied attack failed to break through to the Alban Hills, but the German counterattack stalled in the face of Allied defenses, reinforcements, and naval gunfire. The end result was a stalemate. "I had hoped," said Churchill, "that we were hurling a wildcat onto the shore, but all we got was a stranded whale." The initial assault, as Eisenhower and other officers had foreseen, was too weak to carry out its mission, and the reinforcements came too late to do anything but save the beachhead. Lucas cannot be blamed for making the choice he did. The basic cause of failure was shortage of beaching and landing craft.

The saving of the beachhead was in itself something of a miracle. With naval forces and shipping at first considered barely adequate to lift, supply, and support the original two divisions, Admiral Lowry managed to evacuate most of the civilian population and ultimately to keep seven divisions supplied. The solution to the supply problem was the introduction of a system first worked out by the U.S. Seventh Fleet in the Pacific. Trucks and DUKW's were preloaded in Naples, driven aboard LST's, carried overnight to Anzio, and there driven directly to supply dumps. Through this means an LST that usually required a full day to unload could be emptied in an hour. By early February a regular ferry service had been established. Each day a convoy of six LST's left Naples carrying 1,500 tons of supplies preloaded in 300 trucks. Each week 15 LCT's made the run from Naples to Anzio. Every ten days four Liberty ships arrived at the beachhead with supplies from Naples or North Africa. Meanwhile the fleet, despite bad weather, fire from heavy German guns that rimmed the beachhead, enemy dive and glide bombs, and U-boat attacks, continued to support the forces ashore and to maintain their overwater line of supply. In the process it suffered its roughest handling up to that time in the Mediterranean. The British lost two cruisers, three destroyers, four beaching craft, and a hospital ship; the Americans, a minesweeper, a minecraft, six beaching craft, and two Liberty ships. Damage to vessels, particularly from aircraft, was widespread.

The miserable Italian stalemate lasted until mid-May 1944. Nothing much was accomplished by either opponent on either front. It soon became clear that the Fifth Army, instead of achieving a double envelopment of the enemy, had merely split into two segments, while the Germans, enjoying the advantages of the interior position, were able to shift forces rapidly as needed between the Anzio beachhead and the Gustav Line. In March 90,200 Americans and 35,500 British were packed into a beachhead surrounded by 135,000 Germans with well-sited guns up to 280 mm. that were able to reach every part of the beachhead and the roadstead. German shelling, sporadic by day, was stepped up after dark. During the night the invaders could also expect from one to half a dozen air raids. Allied headquarters at Anzio were established underground in a wine cellar. Wherever possible the troops also sought underground shelter, but the continual rains so raised the ground water level that most foxholes and dugouts soon filled. Hundreds of thousands of sandbags were used to build crude shelters on the surface. In such conditions the men passed week after week, constant targets for enemy fire. It is not surprising that of the 59,000 casualties suffered by the Allied forces at Anzio, nearly a third were from disease, exhaustion, and neuroses. Of the rest, 5,000 were killed in action and 17,000 wounded.

As the rains ceased and the roads hardened with the advance of spring, the Allies prepared to infuse new vigor into their attacks on the Gustav Line. By May they had 27 divisions in action in Italy—seven at Anzio, the rest opposite the main German line. To oppose these, Kesselring now had 25 divisions. On May 11, the Allies began an all-out offensive against the German defense barrier. On the 19th, a French corps of the Fifth Army at last broke the German hold on Monte Cassino and Allied troops surged up the Italian peninsula. On the 25th, an advance patrol coming up from the south made contact with a patrol out of Anzio. On the night of June 2–3, the Germans broke off contact all along the front and hastily withdrew to the north. On June 4, the triumphant Allies made an unopposed entry into Rome, where they were joyfully received by the inhabitants. On June 6, Allied forces in England crossed the Channel and invaded Normandy, thereby reducing the Italian front to a mere backwater of the European war.

# 6

# The Defeat of Germany

**F**ollowing the Casablanca Conference in January 1943, Lieutenant General Sir Frederick Morgan of the British Army had been directed to set up a Combined Planning Staff to prepare for the coming Allied invasion of western Europe. Shortening his title, Chief of Staff to the Supreme Allied Commander (designate) to Cossac, General Morgan built up a large and efficient organization that surveyed possible landing beaches from Norway to Portugal, with special attention to those on the English Channel, for the Channel beaches offered the shortest routes across water and hence the quickest turnabout of Allied shipping in the assault. The Cossac staff considered and dealt with problems as diverse as the tactical control of the Strategic Air Command in Britain and the availability of landing craft. On the solid foundation of General Morgan's work rested a great deal of the success of Operation OVERLORD, as the cross-Channel invasion came ultimately to be called.

By the time of the Teheran Conference in November 1943, Cossac had done all he could pending the appointment of the actual commander. At Teheran, Roosevelt, Churchill, and Stalin all agreed to the target date for OVERLORD of May 1, 1944, yet the supreme commander had still not been selected. When the cross-Channel attack was tentatively being planned for 1942 or 1943, the Combined Chiefs of Staff had reached an understanding that the commander of any large operation would be of the same nationality as the majority of the troops. Since at the earlier date British forces would necessarily predominate, Churchill had promised the command to Field Marshal Sir Alan Brooke; but as it became obvious that by May 1944 American troops would outnumber the British, Roosevelt and Churchill agreed that the supreme commander should be an American. At first the President planned to give the command to General Marshall, but Admiral King and others protested this selection, insisting that Marshall could not be spared from the Joint and Combined

Chiefs of Staff. In early December 1943 Roosevelt at last made his decision, appointing General Eisenhower to command Operation OVERLORD. The officers appointed to head the naval, ground, and air forces under Eisenhower were all British: Admiral Sir Bertram H. Ramsay, General Sir Bernard Montgomery, and Air Chief Marshal Sir Trafford Leigh-Mallory.

For his task Eisenhower was given the broadest of directives:

> You will enter the Continent of Europe, and, in conjunction with the other United Nations, undertake operations aimed at the heart of Germany and the destruction of her armed forces. The date for entering the Continent is the month of May, 1944. After adequate channel ports have been secured, exploitation will be directed towards securing an area that will facilitate both ground and air operations against the enemy.

The significant thing about this directive is that it provided for nothing less than ending the war. All previous British and American operations in Europe had had more limited objectives, for Allied commanders realized that decisive results could be attained only by means of a drive on Germany from the west. Operation OVERLORD however was conceived on a scale that would permit attaining the ultimate objective. Unlike the landings in Sicily, where the assault forces included most of the combat troops available, the divisions that were to seize a beachhead in western Europe were merely an advance force. Plans called for pouring in more than 50 divisions before the coming of winter.

Planning for OVERLORD was perhaps the most complex problem in the history of warfare. The problem had to be attacked from both ends at once, from the standpoint of strategic desirability and from the standpoint of logistic feasibility. Under the first consideration the planners of Supreme Headquarters, Allied Expeditionary Force (called Shaef for short) had to consider when and where to invade; under the latter, whether supplies, equipment, and personnel could be provided and transported to attain specific aims.

The choice of the landing area was a basic consideration. General Morgan had recommended a stretch of Normandy coast between the mouth of the Orne River and the Cotentin (Cherbourg) Peninsula, a selection accepted by Shaef and the Combined Chiefs. As Shaef planners recognized from the beginning, the chosen landing area was not ideal. An assault directly across the Strait of Dover to the Pas-de-Calais area offered the shortest sea route and hence the quickest turnabout of assault shipping. The Pas-de-Calais also offered the best natural beach conditions and was closest to the Dutch and Belgian ports and to the Ruhr, the industrial center of Germany. But it was obvious to Allied intelligence officers that the Germans expected the landing to come in that area and had made elaborate preparations to throw it back into the sea. Moreover the Pas-de-Calais beach area that could be quickly exploited was too narrow to support operations on the scale planned after the initial assault phase.

The Normandy coast had good beach conditions for part of its length, was somewhat sheltered by the natural breakwater of the Cotentin Peninsula, and was within operational radius of fighter planes based on England. And though the terrain behind the beaches offered special difficulties, it provided good possibilities for a breakout on both flanks. A thrust to the sea on the right flank would isolate German forces in the Brittany (Brest) Peninsula; a wheeling movement on the left flank would provide opportunity for capture of important French ports, notably Le Havre. (See map page 179.) Recognizing that capturing ports from the rear would take time and that the Germans would destroy the port facilities before abandoning them, the Allies decided to construct artificial harbors off the beachhead to expedite unloading of the deluge of supplies that would be required.

General Morgan had recommended a diversionary attack on the southern coast of France, to be carried out simultaneously with the Normandy landings. This proposal the Combined Chiefs of Staff at first accepted, seeing in an invasion of France from the Mediterranean not only a diversion but a means of cutting off German troops in Southwestern France and of securing the port of Marseille for supplying and reinforcing the southern flank of the Allied advance into Germany. The southern project was initially given the code name ANVIL.

General Morgan also recommended that if the necessary landing and beaching craft could be made available the Normandy assault should be broadened to include landings on the east coast of the Cotentin Peninsula. Landings here would permit the early isolation and capture of the port of Cherbourg at the tip of the Peninsula. One of Eisenhower's earliest official acts in assuming command of OVERLORD was to accept Morgan's concept of a broadened front in Normandy and to send Montgomery ahead to London to demand that the strength of the initial cross-Channel assault be increased from three to five divisions. Since the only place the landing and beaching craft for a broadened OVERLORD could come from was ANVIL, Operation ANVIL had to be postponed until the middle of August so that craft assigned to it could first be used in OVERLORD. This expedient together with the reallocation of one month's production intended for the Pacific brought the number of beaching craft for OVERLORD to the just-acceptable minimum. So short was the supply that the loss of three LST's to German motor torpedo boats during an invasion rehearsal brought the reserve force of LST's down to zero. Landing and beaching craft, given top priority by the American Joint Chiefs in anticipation of a 1942 or 1943 cross-Channel attack, had been cut back both to step up construction of antisubmarine craft for the

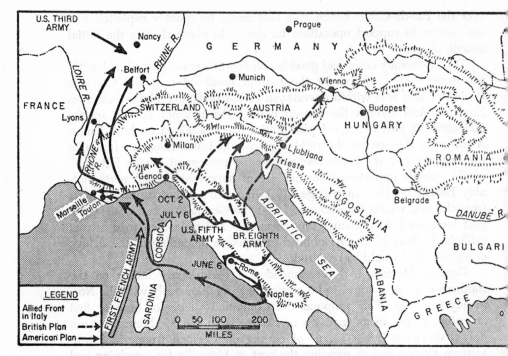

**AMERICAN AND BRITISH STRATEGIES IN THE MEDITERRANEAN,
SUMMER 1944**

Battle of the Atlantic and as a consequence of uncertainty as to when,
if ever, the Americans would overcome British reluctance to go ahead
with the invasion of western Europe. The postponement of ANVIL meant
of course that it could not serve as a diversion for OVERLORD, but to
Eisenhower the advantage of securing a major Mediterranean port on his
right flank made the southern invasion nevertheless eminently desirable.

Because troops for southern France would have to come from Italy,
Operation ANVIL was nearly canceled when the Allied drive stalled at
Anzio and before the German Gustav Line. Even after the Fifth and
Eighth Armies broke the German line in the spring of 1944 and then
went surging up the Italian boot, Churchill and the British generals insisted that ANVIL should be canceled. They wanted to exploit the momentum of the advance in Italy with a landing at Trieste on the Adriatic,
followed by a drive through the Ljubljana Gap to Austria. The Ljubljana
project was aimed as much at political as at military objectives, but it is
questionable whether Allied forces attempting to penetrate the rugged
Gap with its narrow, winding road could have overcome resistance by
the 25 German divisions in the area in time to reach the Danube ahead
of the Russians. Eisenhower kept insisting on ANVIL, which for security

reasons was renamed Operation DRAGOON. Backed by Roosevelt, who regarded the Ljubljana project as militarily eccentric, Eisenhower finally had his way.

As plans for Operation OVERLORD finally crystallized, they called for three paratroop divisions to be dropped the night before D-day. Then after sunrise on D-day, two American and three British divisions would make nearly simultaneous assaults from the sea. Five beach areas were selected: Utah and Omaha for the American assault; Gold, Juno, and Sword for the British. Preceding the landings, the beaches and their defenses would be subjected to heavy aerial and naval bombardment. By now not even the most skeptical Allied army officer opposed daylight landings and naval gunfire support.

Even though OVERLORD, including the follow-up forces, was the largest amphibious assault ever mounted, it was only part of the overall strategy against Germany in the spring of 1944. The Fifth and Eighth Army had 25 German divisions tied down in Italy, making them unavailable for use elsewhere. On the Eastern Front, where the beaten German armies were being driven back toward the Fatherland, 212 divisions faced the Soviets. Although Allied forces in Italy and Russia far outnumbered those that would be used in the invasion of western France, they had the strategic effect of a holding force as far as OVERLORD was concerned, enabling the invaders at Normandy to exert their full power against a fraction of the total German strength.

## German Defense Plans

Estimating that the Allies would at length attempt to re-enter the Continent from the west, Hitler ordered his western armies to prepare to throw the invaders into the sea. He also directed their commander in chief, Marshal Gerd von Rundstedt, to build an "Atlantic Wall" of casemated artillery to sweep every possible landing beach from Spain to Norway. But Hitler, his attention focused on Russia, could give only sporadic thought to the situation in the west. The Atlantic front remained the stepchild of the *Wehrmacht*.

Though the Germans agreed that the Allied assault on western Europe would come not later than the spring of 1944, they were not at all agreed as to *where* it would come. The army identified the Pas-de-Calais as the most probable target, both because it was nearest England and because here installations were being built for launching Hitler's V-weapons—pilotless aircraft and long-range rockets. As soon as the Allies detected these installations and recognized the peril they posed for England, they would doubtless drive at all costs for the launching sites. German army intelligence argued further that the Allies would avoid the Normandy beaches because these were backed by terrain that favored the defense—the difficult *bocage* country of small fields separated by earthen walls topped by trees and thick hedgerows. German naval intelligence officers however reached quite different conclusions. Studying the pattern of Allied bombing, minesweeping, and minelaying, and noting the degree of activity in various British ports, they concluded that the landings would come west of the Pas-de-Calais. And Hitler, in one of his intuitive insights, pointed out the Cotentin and Brittany peninsulas as likely Allied targets. As a result of these varying estimates, though the Pas-de-Calais beaches were the most strongly defended, the Normandy beaches were by no means neglected.

Rundstedt meanwhile had come to distrust the Atlantic Wall concept of static defense. Studying the Salerno assault, he reached the conclusion that his armies had little chance of defeating the invaders at the water's edge in the face of naval gunfire support. Hence he came more and more to rely on mobile infantry and armored divisions placed in strategic positions well inland, whence they could be rushed to the coast to prevent the Allies from exploiting any beachhead they might succeed in seizing.

In early 1944 Hitler placed Field Marshal Rommel under Rundstedt's command with the specific responsibility of defending the Atlantic coast from the Scheldt to the Loire, using the German Seventh and Fifteenth Armies. This appointment led to confusion and divided objectives, for Rommel, basing his estimate on his experiences in North Africa, concluded that Allied air power would prevent Rundstedt's mobile reserves from reaching the coast in time to achieve decisive results. He insisted that the armored defense forces must be placed within five miles of the coast. The decision, he argued, would have to be reached on the beach, and unless the invaders were thrown back into the sea within 24 hours, Germany faced defeat. Hitler, called upon to resolve the conflict between the theories of Rommel and Rundstedt, straddled the issue. He placed some of the armored forces under the former, but not enough to carry out Rommel's plan. The bulk of the reserves Rundstedt retained in the hinterland.

Denied the forces he believed he needed, Rommel concentrated upon static defense. He even neglected training, using his troops as laborers. He energetically set about strengthening the Atlantic Wall, with emphasis upon concrete casemates. He set great store by mines, both sea and land, and planned to sow them thickly on all the beaches and in the beach approaches, but German factories could supply only four per cent of the hundred million mines he wanted. He planned several rows of beach obstacles on which landing craft would impale themselves. Fortunately for the Allies, the two rows that would have been effective at low tide were not installed in time. All the obstacles were intended to be mined, but the mining was far from complete at D-day. As a

**DISTRIBUTION OF GERMAN DIVISIONS, JUNE 6, 1944**

second line of defense, behind the coastal gun sites, Rommel had the lowlands flooded wherever possible. For obstacles against paratroop and glider landings, he had stakes set close together into the ground ("Rommel's asparagus") in likely stretches of open country. For lack of mines, he planned to install specially rigged artillery shells atop the stakes and join the detonators together with barbed wire that would set off explosions on contact. This plan was largely foiled because the shells arrived too late to be installed.

Rommel, the master of mobility and maneuver, did not rely entirely on static defense. He did what he could to provide for the swift movement of his infantry forces and of the panzer divisions that Rundstedt retained in the rear area. But he lacked sufficient motorized vehicles and, as a result of Allied air supremacy and of previous bombing and sabotage of railroads and bridges, what he had were all but useless for transporting troops at the time of the landings. It is ironic that the inventors of the Blitzkrieg were obliged to proceed to the battle area largely on foot and on bicycles.

## Selecting D-Day and H-Hour

The target date for the invasion of France had been set for May 1, 1944, with the understanding that the actual date would be determined by the physical conditions of tide, visibility, weather, and availability of equipment. In order to get an additional month's production of landing and beaching craft, General Eisenhower, with the concurrence of the Combined Chiefs of Staff, postponed the target date to June 1. This was about as late as the invasion could well take place, for the Allies needed all the summer campaigning weather they could get in order to consolidate their conquest of France. With the June 1 target date in mind, the Shaef staff began to look for the combination of natural conditions most favorable for the landing. They desired a moonlit night preceding D-day so that the airborne divisions would be able to organize and reach their assigned objectives before sunrise. They wanted the naval forces and convoys to cross the English Channel during the hours of darkness and to have 30 to 90 minutes of daylight before the landings so that preparatory bombing and naval bombardment of defenses would be effective. The crucial requirement, to which the others would have to be geared, was the tide. It must be rising at the time of the initial landings so that the landing craft could unload and retract without danger of stranding. Reefs and foul ground off the British objectives made a landing at low tide infeasible. Yet the tide had to be low enough that underwater obstacles could be exposed for demolition parties. The final choice was one hour after low tide for the initial landings. Follow-up waves would then have less and less beach to cross as the tide came in. All the required conditions could be met over a three-day period once each month. A fortnight after the three-day period they would be met again except for the moon, which would then be in its new phase. The earliest date after June 1 when the conditions would be fulfilled was June 5, with June 6 and June 7 also suitable. Eisenhower accordingly selected June 5 for D-day, with H-hours ranging from 0630 to 0755 to meet the varying tidal conditions at the five assault beaches.

## The Naval Plan

The naval forces, predominantly British, bore large responsibilities for the Normandy invasion. They had to transport the assault troops to the beaches and land them with their equipment. They had to provide shipping to handle the enormous flow of supplies across the Channel—600 to 700 tons a day per division, in addition to mechanized equipment. They had to act as floating artillery until the guns could be put ashore. They had to provide for the orderly and timely arrival of reinforcement troops and their supplies and equipment, and they had to make provision for the evacuation of casualties. They had to keep German naval forces out of the Channel. They had to sweep lanes through the mine fields and clear the beaches of obstacles that would impede the landing and deployment of troops ashore.

Under Admiral Ramsay's over-all command, the 2,700 vessels (including beaching craft) of the Normandy attack force were divided into the mainly American Western Naval Task Force under the command of Rear Admiral Alan G. Kirk usn and the mainly British Eastern Naval Task Force under Rear Admiral Sir Philip Vian. The Western Naval Attack Force was further subdivided into Task Forces U and O to support Utah and Omaha Beaches respectively, and the Eastern Naval Task Force comprised Task Forces G, J, and S, which held the responsibility for Gold, Juno, and Sword Beaches. The Navy participated in training activities beginning in December 1943 and culminating in April and May, 1944 with full-scale rehearsals by each of the lettered task forces, including realistic landings on the south coast of England. These exercises simulated Operation NEPTUNE, as the naval phase of OVERLORD was called, in every respect except actually crossing the Channel. Even so, when the real NEPTUNE got under way, the meshing of the various task forces had to be extemporized from operational plans which until then existed only on paper. This was no small achievement, for the vessels came from points as widely separated as the Thames Estuary and Northern Ireland. Intricate timing was required to bring all the component parts of the invasion to the beaches on schedule; any disruption could prove disastrous.

## Bombing the Railroads

The Combined Chiefs of Staff at the Casablanca Conference of January 1943 had ordered American and British strategic air forces based on Britain to join in a combined bomber offensive for the "progressive disruption of the German military, industrial and economic systems, and the undermining of the morale of the German people to the point where their capacity for armed resistance is fatally weakened." The Allied air forces in short were to make an all-out attempt to defeat Germany by air attack alone. The combined air forces selected as their primary targets submarine construction yards, followed by the aircraft industry, transportation, oil plants, and other war industry, in descending order of priority. The Americans attacked by day in order to attain precision bombing; the British, regarding daylight bombing as too hazardous, preferred night area bombing that laid waste to industrial and military centers.

Whether this "strategic bombing" could actually force a determined foe to surrender was never really put to the test. The requirements of the Mediterranean theater delayed the offensive until the late spring of 1943. By then the *Luftwaffe* had acquired enough fighter aircraft to make the strategic bombing plan too costly. The drive to burn out German industry quickly shifted into a battle for air supremacy as the Allies concentrated their attacks on enemy planes, aircraft storage parks, and aircraft repair depots and on German aircraft and associated industries. Menwhile the Germans were busily shifting their key manufacturing facilities to the southeast, beyond effective attack from the Britain-based bombers. At the end of 1943, when Allied victory in the air appeared to be in sight, photographic reconnaissance detected the V-weapon launching sites in the Pas-de-Calais area and elsewhere—all pointed ominously at England. Destruction of these was then given overriding priority.

General Eisenhower, on assuming command of the Allied Expeditionary Force, was determined to avert the lack of cooperation that had marked Allied air force operations in the Mediterranean theater. Hence he demanded and obtained control of the U.S. Army Strategic Air Force and the British Bomber Command, both based on the United Kingdom. On attaining control, he shocked the strategic air command by adopting Air Chief Marshal Leigh-Mallory's plan for diverting a portion of the Allied air power to the destruction of railroads in France and Belgium. No one denied the necessity of disrupting and delaying German ground movements by any means whatever, because for OVERLORD to succeed, the Allies would have to follow up their relatively light assault with reinforcements at a much faster rate than the enemy could move defense forces to the invasion area. But the strategic air command believed that bombing the railroads would have little lasting effect, that the attempt would be a waste of bombs and bombers that could be used more profitably on other missions. The air command's objections were backed by Churchill and the British War Cabinet, who feared that too many French and Belgian civilians would be killed; having burned their fingers at Mers-el-Kebir and at Dakar, they had no desire again to risk turning potential allies into potential foes.

Despite resistance and counter-arguments, Eisenhower put Leigh-Mallory's "transportation plan" into effect in mid-April 1944. The Allied bombers first systematically worked over the railroad marshaling yards.

Early in May they also began hitting bridges, with such success that before the end of the month not a single bridge spanned the Seine between Paris and the English Channel. On May 21, which the air forces called "Chattanooga Day," fighter-bombers began bombing and strafing tracks, rail facilities, and trains, putting more than a hundred locomotives out of commission the first day. The French and Belgians, far from resenting these Allied attacks on their own soil, recognized their value and gleefully entered into the spirit of the thing with wholesale sabotage. Many a piece of rolling equipment was found useless because some essential part had vanished or a wheel had been mysteriously cracked. Missing railroad spikes caused numerous wrecks.

The Leigh-Mallory plan proved more effective than its stanchest adherents had anticipated. By D-day rail traffic that could have served the German defenses in the invasion zone had declined by about 50 per cent. German attempts to make good the shortage by greater use of road transportation were largely defeated by lack of sufficient trucks or enough gasoline. The preponderance of the Allied build-up in their Normandy bridgehead was assured, particularly since the Allied air forces, despite the diversion of many of their planes, had by D-day won nearly complete command of the air.

## On the Brink

Weeks before D-day the entire southern part of England became an armed camp, sealed off from the rest of the country. No one was allowed to cross the line in either direction without a special pass. Stores of all kinds crowded the depots, offering tempting targets to German bombers that never came. As early as May 30, troops began to embark in the transports and beaching craft that would carry them across the Channel. The next day the movement toward France began as 54 blockships, to be sunk as breakwaters off the beaches, left western Scotland. A hundred and fifty minesweepers next advanced into the Channel to begin sweeping a clear passage for the convoys. By Saturday, June 3, all troops were embarked, the fire support ships had put to sea from Scapa Flow, Belfast, and the Clyde, and the convoys were beginning to form off the ports of southern England. NEPTUNE-OVERLORD, the most complex and most minutely planned military operation in history, was under way. Nothing that could be anticipated had been left to chance. There was nevertheless one element of uncertainty—the weather, and on that everything else depended.

Beginning on June 1, at Admiral Ramsay's headquarters in a country mansion near Portsmouth, General Eisenhower met twice daily with the top army and navy commanders of NEPTUNE-OVERLORD to hear the weather forecasts. On the morning of the 3rd the forecasts began to be

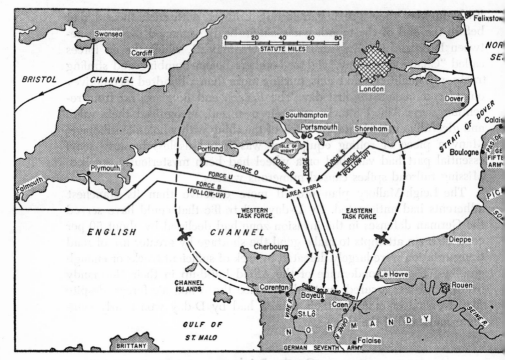

## ROUTES OF THE INVASION CONVOYS, OPERATION OVERLORD, JUNE 6, 1944

discouraging, and grew more alarming through the day. At a special meeting at 0400 on Sunday, June 4, the meteorologists reported hopeless prospects for the 5th. High winds, low clouds, and high waves would combine in the target area. Air support would be impossible, landing of troops most hazardous, and naval gunfire undependable as a result of the storm conditions. When Eisenhower had considered all factors, he made the decision to postpone the invasion 24 hours.

A mighty coiled spring already unwinding had to be stopped, wound up again, and readied for release the next day. That this was done without serious consequence is a tribute to the skill and adaptability of everyone who played a part in the operation. Sunday evening, as the wind howled outside and the rain came down in squalls, the commanders met again at Ramsay's headquarters. Faces were gloomy. It seemed inconceivable that the weather could clear by the morning of Tuesday, June 6, the new D-day. If there had to be another postponement, it would have to be for at least two weeks. June 7 was out, for some of the warships and convoys that had been marking time at sea were running low in fuel. In two weeks security would be lost, morale would suffer severely, the whole world would know that something had gone wrong.

To the relief of the commanders, the weather experts now reported prospects for a break in the weather. On this slender hope, Eisenhower set the invasion forces again into operation, but at Leigh-Mallory's request he called another meeting to be held a few hours later for the final decision. When Eisenhower left his mobile trailer camp headquarters to attend the last weather conference, it was still blowing and raining, but by the time the commanders had again assembled, the night sky had begun to clear. The meteorologists now brought in the word that the clearing weather would last at least until the afternoon of the 6th. On the basis of this report Eisenhower at 0415 made his irrevocable decision: "O.K. We'll go."

Across the Channel later that morning, Marshal Rommel left his headquarters in his command car and headed for his home in Germany, where he planned to spend June 6, his wife's birthday. He and the other top German commanders in the West had been warned by their intelligence organization that the Allied invasion was about to be launched, but the commanders had received so many false alarms that they failed to take the accurate warning seriously.* At any rate, they considered a landing unlikely under the weather conditions then prevailing. For lack of meteorological stations west of Europe they had no intimation of the clearing weather on the way.

Once Eisenhower had made his decision, Operation NEPTUNE gathered momentum. From all ports along the south coast of England, from ports on the east and west coasts, from Northern Ireland, from Scotland, and from the Orkneys elements of the armada put to sea. Most headed for Area Zebra, the assembly area southeast of the Isle of Wight. Remarkably enough, despite blowing weather, the thousands of ships involved came together at Area Zebra and moved across the Channel in darkness on almost perfect schedule. Halfway across, each of the swept lanes divided into two—one for fast, the other for slow convoys. While fighter aircraft provided a protective umbrella overhead, minesweepers led the way for the advancing forces, marking the swept lanes with lighted dan buoys. Because Allied bombers had destroyed most of the German coastal radar stations, and Allied jamming made the rest ineffective, the Germans did not detect the assault convoys during the crossing. The Allied fire support ships reached their assigned anchorages off Normandy around 0200, June 6. The attack transport *Bayfield,* head-

---

* German agents had penetrated Resistance groups on the Continent and learned the signal by which the underground would be alerted by BBC from London. It consisted of the first two lines of Verlaine's *Chanson d'Automne.* The first line, *"Les sanglots longs des violons de l'automne,"* was broadcast on June 1; the second, *"Blessent coeur d'une langueur monotone,"* was broadcast in the evening of June 5. German radio monitors heard and recorded both signals, but the practical-minded German commanders scoffed at the notion that the Allies would alert the underground by means of lines of romantic poetry inserted into a public broadcast.

quarters ship for Task Force U, dropped anchor off Utah Beach at 0230. The amphibious command ship *Ancon*, flagship of Task Force O, anchored off Omaha Beach 20 minutes later.

## The Normandy Landings

The first troops to land in Normandy were the three airborne divisions, which were dropped about 0130 in the morning of June 6. The British 6th Airborne Division landed between Caen and Cabourg with the mission of seizing bridges over the Orne River and the adjacent Caen canal in order to prevent German reinforcements from moving in from the northeast. (See map page 170.) The American 82nd and 101st Airborne Divisions landed behind Utah Beach. Their assignment was to seize control of the causeways leading inland from the beaches over meadows that the Germans had flooded, and to capture bridges in the vicinity of Sainte Mère-Eglise and Carenten. The paratroops at first met only limited resistance because the Germans, convinced that the main assault would be directed against the Pas-de-Calais area, regarded the Normandy drops as a mere diversion. By dawn, the 6th and 101st Airborne Divisions were approaching their objectives, and the 2nd was containing a German infantry division near Sainte Mère-Eglise.

Off the Normandy beaches, the Allied transports had begun lowering landing craft promptly after dropping anchor, and at 0400 they began debarking the assault troops. These were to advance in a series of waves along boat lanes to the line of departure, where the landing craft were to circle until signaled to advance to the beach. Between the transport area and the beach the fire support vessels were at anchor flanking the boat lanes—the battleships and cruisers 11,000 yards offshore, the destroyers 5,000 yards. Fire support for the American beaches was furnished by the old U.S. battleships *Texas, Nevada,* and *Arkansas,* which were to engage the heavy defenses with their 12- and 14-inch guns, while U.S. heavy cruisers *Tuscaloosa, Quincy,* and *Augusta,* five British and two French light cruisers, a Dutch gunboat, and 22 destroyers took on the lighter beach targets. In the British sector H.M. battleships *Warspite, Nelson,* and *Ramillies* provided the big guns, and were assisted by five British cruisers and numerous destroyers to blast smaller targets. As the leading boat waves headed in from the line of departure, they were to be accompanied by gunboats and rocket-equipped LCT's, which were to blanket the beaches with fire just before the troops stepped ashore.

A little after 0300 a German search radar station had at long last detected and reported "large craft" off the Normandy coast. The shore batteries thereupon were manned in full strength and readied for action. A little past 0500, when first light dimly outlined the silhouettes of the nearer fire support vessels, the batteries opened fire. A few of the vessels replied at once, and by 0600 the pre-landing naval bombardment of the beaches was under way in full fury.

At Utah Beach the support ships checked fire as 276 B-26 medium bombers from England swept over the beaches and dropped 4,400 bombs. Bombing visually through an overcast, many of the B-26's dropped their bombs harmlessly into the water. Nevertheless the American 4th Infantry Division went ashore at Utah in 26 waves against little opposition, the first wave hitting the beach right on schedule at 0630. Here lack of reference points ashore and a southerly tidal set caused the landing to be made three quarters of a mile south of the intended beaches. As it turned out, this accident proved fortunate for the Americans, because the beach obstacles were lighter in the actual landing area than in that designated in the NEPTUNE plan. Beaches in the Utah sector moreover were not protected by formidable obstacles, and here the coastal defense troops were from a "static" division of green reservists and foreign conscripts who were not inclined to fight past hope. By the end of D-day 21,300 troops, 1,700 vehicles, and 1,700 tons of supplies had been landed at Utah beach, and the invaders had suffered fewer than 200 casualties. The 4th Division had established a beachhead six miles deep and six miles wide, had made contact with the 101st Airborne Division, and was ready to press across the base of the peninsula and to link up with the V Corps in the vicinity of the Vire Estuary. As it turned out, the Americans took their heaviest material losses of the day in the waters off the beach, where undetected mines sank a destroyer, two LCI's, and three LCT's.

In sharp contrast to Utah, Omaha proved the most heavily armed and fortified beach that the Americans or their allies were to assault during the entire war.* Rommel had given this area special attention, and the defenders had armed the coast here to a strength approaching that of the Pas-de-Calais beaches. The Omaha defenses began 300 feet inshore of the low-water line with a row of 7-by-10-foot steel frames planted upright like gates. Behind these were sharpened, half-buried stakes pointed seaward. Next came a row of "hedgehogs," each composed of three six-foot iron bars crossed at right angles. Many of these obstacles were connected by wires and mined. Just inshore of the high-water line was a sea wall, partly concrete and partly piling, backed by a heavy coil of barbed wire. Behind this was a level shelf from 100 to 300 yards wide, thickly mined and crisscrossed by anti-tank ditches. On the far side of the shelf rose a line of bluffs, too steep even for tracked vehicles. Four deep ravines, breaks in the bluffs through each of which ran a narrow road, gave access to the interior. Guns were everywhere, some mobile, some

---

* This does not mean that Omaha Beach was necessarily the most formidably defended, for not even the hard-fighting Germans ever fought virtually to the last man, as the Japanese did on many an island in the Pacific.

casemated. Abandoned stone and brick villas at the foot of the bluffs had been converted into strong points. Trenches for riflemen ran along the top of the bluffs, and here also were machine-gun emplacements, artillery up to 88-mm. caliber, and mortars up to 90-mm. Other gun emplacements were dug into the bluffs so as to enfilade the beach and dominate the four exit ravines. Some of the defenses were manned by soldiers from a static division, such as guarded Utah Beach, but most of the defenders were first-line German troops of the 352nd Division. These had been moved from the interior to the coast at Rommel's insistence the preceding March.

At Omaha Beach shore batteries opened fire on the *Arkansas* at 0530. Some gunnery vessels replied at once, and at 0550 all began the scheduled bombardment of assigned targets. This beach was supposed to be bombed from high altitude by 480 B-24 heavy bombers. But the B-24's, obliged to bomb by instrument because of cloud cover, delayed releasing several seconds to avoid hitting ships or boats. As a result they scattered their 1,285 tons of bombs as much as three miles inland. At Omaha not a single bomb hit the beach or coastal defenses, and indeed the invasion forces did not know that the B-24's had passed overhead. But though bombers contributed little in breaching the Atlantic Wall, Allied fighter planes were entirely successful in keeping the *Luftwaffe* away from the American beaches throughout D-day.

The preparatory naval bombardment of Omaha Beach lasted only 35 minutes. Then all ships lifted fire as the first wave of landing craft headed in from the line of departure. The time allowed was obviously too brief, particularly since numerous targets had not been spotted in advance by aerial reconnaissance, and a good many of the known targets were invisible to spotter planes circling over the beaches. Despite the handicaps however, the ships had knocked out about half the enemy's guns.

The first infantry assault wave was preceded by LCT's carrying standard tanks and by amphibious tanks, some boated, some going in under their own power. Most of the non-boated amphibious tanks were swamped by the choppy sea and went down. The tanks that reached the beach came under heavy shelling, and several were stopped and set afire. LCVP's, coming in next, began taking hits while still 500 yards off shore. By the time they dropped ramps, at 0630 or thereabouts, the fire from the bluffs was intense. Through a hail of bullets and shells, the troops had to wade some 75 yards to the beach and then work their way 250 yards more through the obstacles to the dubious protection of the sea wall. A great many failed to make it.

While the first wave of assault troops huddled against the sea wall, 16 underwater demolition teams landed and proceeded to blast channels through the beach obstacles so that later waves could be brought in ever closer to the sea wall on the rising tide. The teams succeeded in blasting five broad channels, at the cost of more than half their number killed or wounded. Waves of infantry, coming in at ten-minute intervals after 0700, at first merely fed men into the growing mass of prone figures carpeting the beach behind the sea wall. A little after 0800 LCI's, LCM's, and DUKW's headed for the beach with artillery. Nearly all of the DUKW's were swamped or turned back by the choppy seas, and three of the LCI's were hit by shells, set afire, and sunk. Little artillery in fact reached Omaha Beach on D-day. But army engineers managed to blow gaps in the barbed wire behind the sea wall, machine guns were set up, and under the leadership of surviving officers, small groups of men began rushing across the shelf and scaling the bluffs. By noon the Americans had begun to penetrate inland.

What enabled the invaders, with almost no artillery, to advance against the fearsome defenses of Omaha Beach? Sheer courage played its part and tanks helped, but the principal answer is naval gunfire. The *Texas*, the *Arkansas*, and two British and two French cruisers, using air spot by Spitfires based on England, sealed off the beachhead with a ring of fire, preventing the Germans from either reinforcing or shifting their defense forces. But the direct support that cleared the way for the assault forces was provided by nine American and three British destroyers. Closing the shore to within 1,000 yards, actually scraping bottom, these delivered call fire as requested by shore fire control parties or fired at targets of opportunity. The bluffs, which proved an obstacle to vehicles, were a shooting gallery for the destroyers, which could supplement call fire by means of visual observation of enemy positions in the rising ground. During D-day U.S.S. *Carmick* alone expended 1,127 rounds of 5-inch shell, and other destroyers fired almost as many. Thus supported, by nightfall on June 6 some 34,000 troops, nearly five regiments of the 1st and 29th U.S. Divisions, had gone ashore at Omaha. Here they had overrun the bluffs, seized the exit ravines, and established a line more than a mile inland. The price had been high: casualties among the invaders amounted to about 2,000 killed, wounded, and missing.

The landings on the British beaches were easy compared to those at Omaha. In the British sector obstructions were less formidable and less thickly sown, and here the coast defenses were manned by troops of a static division including numerous Poles and Ukrainians. Here too the beaches got a far more extended preparatory naval bombardment than at either Utah or Omaha, for the British landings had to be delayed from an hour to an hour and a half to allow the rising tide to cover the reefs and foul ground in this area. By the end of D-day the 50th British, the 3rd Canadian, and the 3rd British Division, which had landed respectively at Gold, Juno, and Sword Beaches, had penetrated four miles inland, and the 3rd British Division had made contact with the 6th Airborne

Division. Though the British D-day penetration was much deeper than that attained by the Americans at Omaha, it fell short of plans, which included the occupation of Caen. The British were in fact to enter Caen only after weeks of hard fighting.

The Allied invasion could hardly have caught the Germans more off guard. Because of the bad weather preceding D-day, the German Seventh Army, defending Normandy and Brittany, had been taken off alert. Rommel, muttering, "How stupid of me! How stupid of me!" hastened back to France, reaching his headquarters on the 6th a little before midnight. After he had heard the reports of the day's fighting, he said to his aide, "If I were commander of the Allied forces right now, I could finish off the war in 14 days."

Hitler's headquarters, still convinced that the Normandy landings were a diversion and that the main Allied attack would come against the Pas-de-Calais, retained the bulk of the German Fifteenth Army in Flanders, holding back two panzer divisions that might have been rushed to the beachhead early on June 6. It was one of these divisions, belatedly committed, that initially kept the British out of Caen. Hitler now saw that an Allied drive south from Caen would isolate his Seventh Army from his Fifteenth, which continued to guard the Pas-de-Calais. He therefore ordered Rommel and Rundstedt to pour their available reserve strength into the Caen area, making it their focal point for the defense of the Continent. Hitler thus played neatly into Marshal Montgomery's hands. For it was Montgomery's plan to contain as many Germans as possible at Caen, while the Americans first captured the port of Cherbourg in order to assure an adequate inflow of supplies and then thrust south and east in the vicinity of St. Lô. The Allied forces would thus pivot on their left, using Caen as the hinge, and face east on a strong front—both to defend the lodgment area and for an advance toward Germany.

In the evening of June 6 perhaps the strangest fleet ever to sail from any harbor anywhere had got under way from British ports. Included were tired old merchant ships (code name: Gooseberries) on their last voyage, huge concrete caissons (Phoenixes), enormous cruciform steel floats (Bombardons) with their heads visible above the surface, and quantities of tugs and other auxiliaries. This was Operation MULBERRY, which was to provide harbors where none existed—one off Omaha Beach, the other off Gold Beach.

Mulberry A arrived off Omaha Beach at dawn on the 7th after a 5-knot crossing. Construction began that afternoon with the sinking of a line of Gooseberries off shore. To extend the line of Gooseberries, Phoenixes next were sunk with their flat upper surfaces protruding above the water. Outside the artificial harbor, or Mulberry, thus formed was moored a row of Bombardons to act as a floating breakwater. Inside, extending

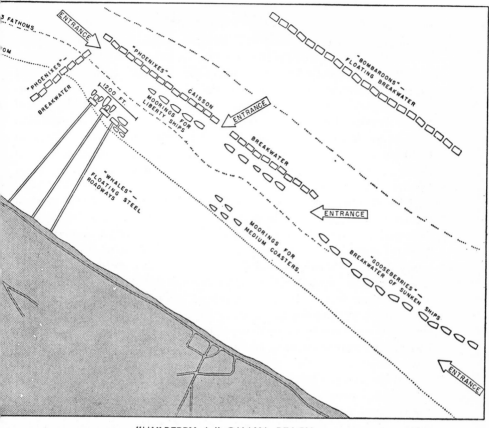

## "MULBERRY A," OMAHA BEACH

from the beach, were pontoon piers ending in pierheads constructed to
rise and fall with the tide.

By June 17 Mulberry A was ready to receive ships. Here and at Mulberry B in the British sector, which was ready at about the same time,
unloading proceeded rapidly. Two days later the worst storm in the English Channel in half a century roared down from the northeast, so battering Mulberry A that it had to be abandoned. Mulberry B, somewhat
protected by reefs and better sheltered under the lee of the cape north
of Le Havre, survived the storm with comparatively minor damage.
Before the invasion, many would have predicted that the loss of one of
the artificial harbors would have meant disaster for the Allies. But while
awaiting their construction the Navy had found it possible to beach LST's
shortly after high tide and unload them when the tide receded. By such
means unloading after the destruction of Mulberry A was actually
stepped up. At the end of June, 15,000 tons of supplies and 15,000 troops
were being landed daily over Omaha Beach alone.

## The Battle of Normandy

By June 18 a corps of the U.S. First Army had driven across to the Gulf of St. Malo, thereby sealing off the Cotentin Peninsula. The Americans then wheeled to the right and by the 24th had pushed the 40,000 German defenders to the northern tip of the peninsula and had surrounded Cherbourg. The Army now called upon the Navy to knock out the heavy coastal batteries guarding the waterfront and flanking the city. These batteries, up to 280-mm. (11-inch) caliber, and with a range up to 40,000 yards, were for the most part heavily casemated. Some were in revolving steel turrets capable of being trained inland as well as to sea. For naval vessels to attack such ordnance was contrary to established doctrine that warships should not expose themselves to coastal guns of caliber approaching their own. Nevertheless a naval force under Rear Admiral Morton L. Deyo usn complied with the Army's request. From 1200 till after 1500 on June 25, the *Nevada, Texas,* and *Arkansas,* U.S. heavy cruisers *Tuscaloosa* and *Quincy,* two British cruisers, and eleven destroyers stood up to the shore guns, pounding them from the sea while the American troops stormed Cherbourg from the landward side. The ships, directing their fire chiefly by means of shore fire control parties and spotter aircraft, did much to weaken the city's defenses. By use of smoke and violent maneuver, most of the vessels avoided anything worse than near misses. Two of the destroyers were hit however, and the *Texas* had her bridge wrecked by a 280-mm. shell. The next day the attacking troops received the surrender of the German defending general, and by July 1 the entire peninsula was in American hands. The Germans as usual had done their best to render the port unusable, but the destruction had been carried out so inexpertly that British and American salvage engineers had the harbor in partial use within two weeks.

During the drive for Cherbourg, the Allied forces in Normandy had established a continuous front and had attained an 18-mile southward penetration at the center. Aircraft based on England virtually isolated this beachhead area from the rest of France. German troops advancing from the interior had to move by night and in small formations. Highways leading to the Allied lodgment, under repeated attack from the air, became choked with dead men, dead horses, and shattered equipment. Meanwhile in the first 30 days 929,000 men, 586,000 tons of supplies, 177,000 vehicles, and vast quantities of armament poured into the beachhead from the Channel. The invaders thus attained over the enemy a two-to-one local superiority in manpower and a three-to-one superiority in tanks and guns. The time had come for the long-planned breakout on the western flank.

The British, continuing their pressure on Caen, opposite the eastern flank, entered the city on July 8, after it had been pulverized by artillery

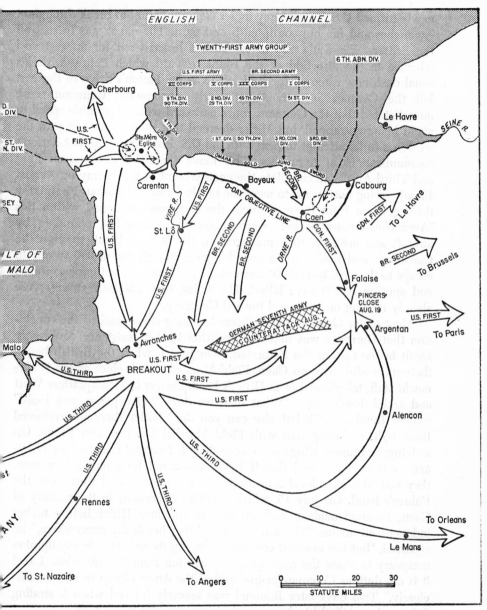

**INVASION AND BATTLE OF NORMANDY**

and 2,500 tons of aerial bombs. German-held St. Lô, after receiving a similar treatment, was occupied by the U.S. First Army on the 18th. The First Army then pressed southward, flanked on the left by elements of the British Second Army, and worked its way around the western flank of the German Seventh Army. This pressure on the Germans enabled the newly formed U.S. Third Army under General Patton to break through at Avranches and fan out south, east, and west. The effect was to seal off the Brittany Peninsula and to establish a broad front for an eastward advance in the direction of the Rhine, toward which Patton with his usual dash now directed the bulk of his army. Patton's drive to the east left the German Seventh Army nearly surrounded. Common sense now dictated that the Germans retire eastward with all possible speed to avoid being entrapped, but Hitler decreed that they should drive to the west in a futile attempt to penetrate the U.S. First Army and cut Patton's communications at Avranches. This move enabled the American First and Third Armies to complete the encirclement of the enemy on August 19, advancing northward to meet the newly formed Canadian First Army driving down from Caen. Though the Germans entrapped within this "Avranches-Falaise pocket" were subjected to merciless pounding by aircraft and artillery, they managed on the 20th to break through the Canadians and hold open a corridor long enough for 40,000 troops to escape to the east. But 50,000 Germans that did not get out were captured and another 10,000 were killed. The Allies, now 1,500,000 strong, were already moving on Paris and toward Germany.

Most senior German army officers had long since reached the conclusion that Germany was defeated and that further resistance could only result in the ruin of the Fatherland. On July 1, when the British began their successful drive on Caen, Field Marshal Keitel, chief of the *Wehrmacht* staff, telephoned from Hitler's headquarters to Headquarters West and asked despairingly, "What shall we do?" "Make peace, you fools!" replied Rundstedt. "What else can you do?" Hitler thereupon relieved Rundstedt, replacing him with Field Marshal Gunther von Kluge. On arriving in France, Kluge soon agreed with Rommel that further resistance was hopeless, and that if Hitler could not be brought to reason, they should seek a local armistice with Eisenhower and thus force the Führer's hand. On July 15, while directing operations in the vicinity of Caen, Rommel made a final attempt to convince Hitler before taking independent action. "The armies are fighting heroically everywhere," he reported, "but the unequal combat is nearing its end. It is in my opinion necessary to draw the appropriate conclusion from the situation. I feel it is my duty as Commander-in-Chief of the Army Group to express this clearly." Two days later Rommel was severely injured when a strafing fighter plane killed his driver, and his car crashed into a tree.

Meanwhile, officers nearer German headquarters, noting that Hitler seemed determined to pull Germany down in the ashes of his own funeral pyre, had decided that the Führer must be assassinated. On July 20 the attempt was made. A time bomb in a brief case was placed under a table at which Hitler was standing studying maps with his staff. The bomb exploded, killing four officers, but Hitler himself was only slightly hurt.

In reprisal nearly 5,000 people, in all walks of life, innocent or guilty, paid with their lives. The network of conspiracy and retaliation at length involved the "defeatists" in the general blood-letting. Hitler replaced Kluge and ordered him back to Germany. Fearing the worst, Kluge killed himself en route. To Rommel, the national hero, then recuperating at home, Hitler gave the choice of secretly taking poison or standing public trial and involving his family and his staff in his disgrace and destruction. When Rommel had poisoned himself, Hitler decreed national mourning and had him buried with full military honors. Rundstedt was required to read a prepared funeral oration.

By September 1, 1944, when Eisenhower established headquarters in France and took over the command of the Allied ground forces, the Allies had liberated Paris and crossed the Seine, the Somme, and the Meuse. Under Eisenhower, General Omar Bradley now commanded the 12th Army Group (U.S. First and Third Armies) on the right flank, and Marshal Montgomery commanded the 21st Army Group (Canadian First and British Second Armies) on the left flank. The need for a speedy advance by Montgomery through Northern France and Belgium had now become acute, for from these areas in mid-June the first of the German V-weapons had begun streaking toward London. This was the pilotless, winged, jet-propelled V-1. No sooner had the British learned to cope with the V-1, mainly by the use of VT-fused shells, than the Germans shifted to the more deadly V-2. Because these rockets sped faster than sound, the explosion was usually the first indication that the V-2 had been on the way. Against it there was next to no defense. The V-2's were in fact capable of destroying London, particularly if, as the Allies feared, the Germans were on the verge of producing an atomic warhead for them. Capture of the coastal V-2 launching bases was therefore given top priority.

## Operation Dragoon—The Invasion of Southern France

Not long after the Allied occupation of Rome, which, it will be recalled, nearly coincided with the invasion of Normandy, three American and two French divisions were withdrawn from the Italian front to provide a landing force for Operation DRAGOON, the invasion of southern France. Following the Normandy landings, beaching craft in large numbers left the English Channel for the Mediterranean. With the fall of Cherbourg at the end of June 1944, fire support ships headed south, until the Eighth Fleet had at its disposal to support the new invasion five battleships, U.S.S. *Arkansas, Nevada,* and *Texas,* H.M.S. *Ramillies,* and French *Lorraine,* and more than a score of cruisers, besides numerous destroyers. These were incorporated into Vice Admiral Kent Hewitt's Western Naval Task Force, which was to carry out the assault. The

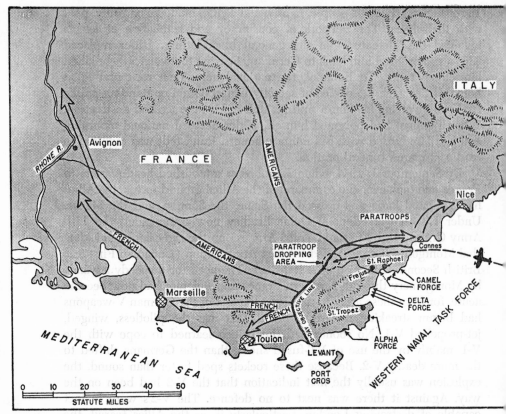

INVASION OF SOUTHERN FRANCE, AUGUST 15, 1944

initial landing force, commanded by Major General Lucian K. Truscott USA, comprised two regimental combat teams of each of the three American divisions, with the third team of each serving as reserve. The two French divisions would provide early follow-up. D-day was set at August 15.

The selected landing area was a 30-mile stretch of coast between Toulon and Cannes. The immediate objective was to establish a bridgehead for invasion and to capture the neighboring ports, with special emphasis upon the capacious harbor of Marseille. Then, as the landing force was reinforced, ultimately to 21 divisions, it was to drive up the Rhone Valley to make contact with General Patton's U.S. Third Army in the vicinity of Dijon and take over the right flank of the Allied invasion of Germany.

DRAGOON was a far easier invasion than OVERLORD. For one thing the beach situation in southern France was much more favorable for the invaders than at Normandy. A comparatively steep gradient and small tidal range made placement of underwater obstacles difficult, the beach areas were more sheltered from the action of the sea than in the north, and the time of year augured for good weather in the Mediterranean. Though the beaches were thickly mined and backed by powerful batteries, manpower requirements elsewhere had left the defenses lightly manned, partly by Czech conscripts and Polish prisoners of war who readily surrendered. Nevertheless DRAGOON stands out as one of the best executed assaults of the war, partly because the commanding officers, with accumulated amphibious experience behind them, worked in close harmony and anticipated nearly every difficulty. Planning began in Algiers in early spring of 1944. During the final planning, training, and rehearsal phase, Vice Admiral Hewitt, Lieutenant General Alexander Patch, whose U.S. Seventh Army included the assault force, Major General Truscott, Brigadier General Gordon P. Saville, who commanded the land-based air support, and their staffs occupied adjacent headquarters in Naples, where they were in constant consultation. The Western Naval Task Force trained the landing force, which thereby attained perfect timing and close coordination with the fleet.

When in mid-August the Western Naval Task Force approached its objective, it was heading for a coast that had been pounded with 12,500 tons of aerial bombs since the preceding April. During the night before D-day, raiders landed on Levant and Port Cros Islands to seize batteries that could be trained on the more westerly invasion beaches. Other raiders landed on the flanks of the invasion area to set up roadblocks. Those on the right were repulsed, but those on the left made a successful landing and blocked the roads leading from Toulon. Before dawn more than 5,000 British and American paratroops landed behind the beaches to block any approach of German reinforcements from the north or northwest.

In this invasion Admiral Hewitt at last had his way: H-hour for the main assault was set at 0800. Selection of this hour enabled the Task Force to approach the beachhead entirely in darkness, it avoided the inevitable confusion of a night assault, it provided more than two hours of daylight for pre-invasion bombing and bombardment, and it allowed ample time for the troops to secure a lodgment before nightfall. At dawn on August 15, the Western Naval Task Force stood off the invasion beaches. It was divided into three attack forces, named from left to right *Alpha, Delta,* and *Camel.* Each attack force carried one American division, the assault forces in LST's together with their landing craft, the reserves in transports.

The main assault began shortly before 0600 as the first squadrons of 1,300 bombers, flying from Italy, Sardinia, and Corsica, swept over the beaches escorted by fighters. The aerial bombing was almost continuous till 0730, when it stopped to allow full play to the naval bombardment.

The ships had already been pounding the shore for more than half an hour, whenever they could fire without danger to the bombers. Using cruiser aircraft spotting, they pinpointed their fire at specific targets that had already been detected by aerial reconnaissance. As the landing craft headed for shore, the battleships and cruisers checked fire, the destroyers advanced their fire inland, giving the area behind the beaches a drenching, and LCI's leading in the first wave fired rockets into the beaches themselves to explode land mines. The assault troops stepped ashore at seven selected beaches on the 30-mile front. All these landings were on time, and none met any serious resistance.

The one difficult beach was Camel Red in the Golfe de Fréjus. But difficulty had been anticipated here; hence the landing at this point had been deferred till 1400 to allow the forces landed at Camel Beach Green, farther eastward, to take out the defenses. But as the deferred H-hour approached, enemy fire continued so heavy that minesweepers could not operate inside the gulf. Rear Admiral Spencer Lewis, commanding the Camel Force, tried to get into radio contact with the divisional commander, Major General Dahlquist, who was already ashore. When he failed to do so, Lewis took the responsibility of ordering the landing shifted to Camel Green, a decision of which Dahlquist heartily approved when he learned of it. In earlier invasions such an unscheduled shift would have produced a first-class logistic headache. That it could be carried out across a beach over which supplies were flowing to forces already ashore demonstrates the remarkable efficiency with which Operation DRAGOON was planned and executed.

Throughout the operation a force including seven British and two American escort carriers stood off the coast sending in planes to spot for the gunfire support vessels and to range inland to disrupt enemy communications and to break up enemy troop concentrations. Though the *Luftwaffe* succeeded in making one effective raid on the invasion forces and actually sank an LST off Camel Beach Green, the Allied carrier pilots neither on D-day nor for three days thereafter saw a single enemy plane. The few they encountered thereafter they promptly shot down.

The French divisions, landing after the initial assault, promptly advanced westward toward Toulon and Marseille, while the paratroops moved in the opposite direction toward the lesser ports of Cannes and Nice. At the same time the main body of the Seventh Army began its drive to the Rhône. The capture of both Toulon and Marseille required several days of combined land and air assault supported by naval guns. The harbors of both cities were defended by powerful batteries that proved difficult to silence. The hardest to deal with was a 340-mm. battery which the French had installed before the war as a result of Mussolini's sword rattling and the building of the Italian navy up to parity with the French *Marine*. At last on August 28 the Germans in both major ports capitulated. Meanwhile, also with naval support, the paratroops were achieving their objectives; on August 24 they entered Cannes and on the 30th they occupied Nice.

By this time the main body of the invasion forces had advanced far to the north, pursuing rapidly retiring Germans. Seven French divisions formed the nucleus of a newly-formed French First Army, commanded by Générale de l'Armée Jean de Lattre de Tassigny. Follow-up American forces were incorporated with the assault troops in Lieutenant General Patch's U.S. Seventh Army. The French and the American army together comprised the Sixth Army Group under Lieutenant General Jacob L. Devers. On September 11 Devers' Army Group made contact near Dijon with elements of Patton's Third Army from Normandy. Thus the two great thrusts combined, sealing off all German forces in southwestern France. The Sixth Army Group next wheeled to the east and drew up in a line along the German frontier from the Swiss border for a distance of about 80 miles where their left flank was in contact with the right flank of the U.S. Third Army.

## The German Collapse

In the fall of 1944, after a breathtaking sweep across France and Belgium, the Allied armies under General Eisenhower reached the German frontier, stood on the Rhine near Strasbourg, and penetrated into Germany at Aachen. Then stiffening German resistance, worsening weather, and mounting problems of supply brought the advance in the west almost to a standstill. In Italy, the Allied Fifth and Eighth Armies, after pushing north of Florence, came virtually to a halt against the German Gothic Line. On the Eastern Front, the Russians continued to press forward in the north and south but came to a stop at the center just short of Warsaw.

In mid-December, Rundstedt, restored as Commander in Chief West, launched his last offensive. Taking advantage of bad weather that hampered Allied air operations, he committed Germany's last strategic reserves in a massive drive at the Allied center in the Ardennes. In what is popularly called the Battle of the Bulge, Rundstedt penetrated 50 miles westward, but there was never any real danger of his achieving his objective of splitting the Anglo-American armies apart. In fact, Eisenhower, who was aware of the existence of the German reserves, was glad of the opportunity of dealing with them early in the open rather than later behind their own fortifications. Improving flying weather and prompt Allied counterattacks soon obliged Rundstedt to pull back under threat of having his entire salient pinched off and surrounded. He had suffered greater losses than he had inflicted.

The Russians, resuming their offensive in mid-January 1945, advanced 250 miles to the Oder River in 30 days and directly threatened Berlin,

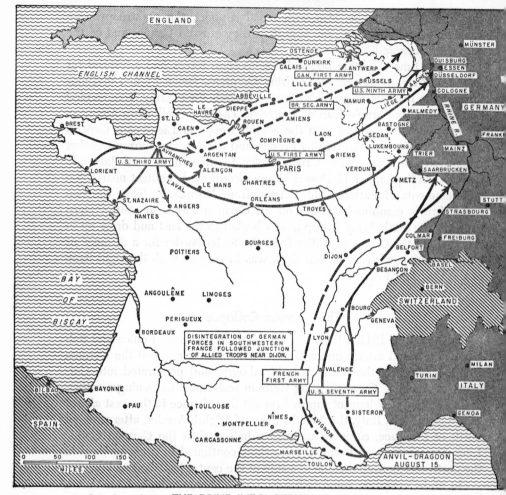

**THE DRIVE INTO GERMANY, 1944**

which Hitler refused to leave. In the south, the Russian advance past Budapest obliged the Germans to withdraw hastily from Greece and the Balkans to avoid being cut off from Germany.

By March 1945 Eisenhower's armies were lined up along the Rhine, which because of its swift current and steep banks was a formidable barrier. General Bradley, correctly assuming that the retreating Germans would try to destroy every bridge over the river, had months before turned to the Navy for help in getting across. Admiral Stark had readily provided Bradley's Army Group with landing craft, 96 LCVP's and 45 LCM's, together with crews, and the boats had been hauled to the front by army trucks and trailers. As luck would have it, the Germans failed to destroy the bridge at Remagen ahead of the fast-moving U.S. First Army, and on March 7 Bradley rushed five divisions across the Rhine to establish a shallow beachhead on the east bank. When the Remagen bridge collapsed under German bombardment ten days later, the naval landing craft were already at work on the river. Before the end of March they had ferried 14,000 troops and 400 vehicles of the First Army across the Rhine and assisted Army Engineers in constructing pontoon and Treadway bridges. As General Patton's U.S. Third Army had been the most spectacular in its sweep across France and into Germany, its employment of landing craft for crossing the Rhine was also the most striking. Using the boats for a quick build-up at four points on the east bank between Mainz and Koblenz while bridges were being constructed, Patton was able to strike into the heart of Germany with scarcely a pause.

By the end of March all the Anglo-American armies in the west had crossed the Rhine. The Canadian First and the British Second Armies on the left flank raced for the German North Sea Ports. The U.S. Ninth and First Armies carried out Eisenhower's long-planned double envelopment of the Ruhr, cutting off this industrial region from the rest of Germany and entrapping 325,000 troops, including 30 general officers. The Third Army kept on right across Germany, entering Czechoslovakia and advancing down the Danube to meet the Russians, who had just captured Vienna. While the French First Army covered its flank, General Patch's U.S. Seventh Army swept through southern Germany, capturing Munich and advancing through the Brenner Pass back into Italy.

In April 1945 the Allied Fifth and Eighth Armies in Italy at length pierced the Gothic Line. Fanning out, they shattered the German Army Group in Northern Italy and joined hands on the Riviera with French troops advancing eastward from Nice and in the Alps with their erstwhile comrades-in-arms of the Italian campaign advancing southward through the Brenner Pass.

As the war in Europe drew to its thundering conclusion, three of the major national leaders died within a few days of each other. On April 12 President Roosevelt died at Warm Springs, Georgia of a cerebral hemorrhage. On April 28, Benito Mussolini was overtaken and killed by anti-Fascists while fleeing toward the Swiss border. His body, brought back to Milan, was exposed to public execration by the Italians whom he had led into a disastrous war. On May 1, with the Russians surrounding Berlin and fighting in the streets, Adolf Hitler, hiding in a bunker at his Chancellery, put a pistol into his mouth and shot himself.

The German armies, reduced to mobs of terrified fugitives, now began to surrender to the British and the Americans. In the early hours of May 7, Marshal Alfred Jodl at General Eisenhower's headquarters at Reims placed his signature on the general surrender document: "We, the undersigned, acting by authority of the German High Command, hereby surrender unconditionally to the Supreme Commander, Allied Expeditionary Force, and simultaneously to the Soviet High Command, all forces on land, sea, and in the air who are at this date under German control."

At 2301 May 8, 1945, World War II officially ended in Europe.

# 7

# The Period of Japanese Expansion

Japan started down the road to World War II with her conquest of Manchuria in the last four months of 1931. Although the United
States refused to recognize changes brought about by force and sternly
reminded Japan of her treaty obligations, the failure of the European
powers to support the American position made it evident that Japan
might pursue her course of aggression with impunity. The only danger
was that of interference by Russia, which also had ambitions in Asia, and
against that the Japanese provided by signing an anti-Comintern pact
with Germany in November 1936. By this time military extremists were
gaining control of Japan, removing by assassination those moderate state-
men who opposed their policy. When in the summer of 1937 the Army
was ready, Japan embarked on the conquest of China proper.

## Oil and Appeasement

In order not to deprive China of war supplies, President Roosevelt
refused to invoke the 1937 Neutrality Act in this undeclared war. But
the Japanese also benefited, for they were dependent on American steel
scrap and Western Hemisphere oil.

In July 1939 U.S. Secretary of State Cordell Hull gave the Japanese
the required six months' notice for the abrogation of the commercial
treaty of 1911, thereby clearing the way for an embargo on munitions.
This move and the announcement the next month of the Russo-German
non-aggression pact had a temporarily sobering effect upon the Japanese.
Moreover, Japan was rapidly bogging down in the Chinese hinterland,
and her resources were under severe strain.

But the outbreak of the European war eased Japan's difficulties and
presented new opportunities. The fall of France and of the Netherlands
in the spring of 1940 left Indo-China and the Netherlands East Indies

orphaned colonies and so weakened Britain's position that she acceded to
Japanese demands to close the Burma Road, China's last connection with
the sea. The Imperial Japanese Navy, which had never favored the army's
mainland adventure, now saw an opportunity for expansion into the East
Indies to obtain oil, tin, rubber, and quinine. Japan had already worked
her way south along the China coast and early in 1939 had occupied
Hainan. Shortly after the fall of France the Vichy-controlled government
of Indo-China permitted Japanese occupation of the northern part of the
country. In September 1940 Japan concluded with the Axis powers an
alliance that was an obvious warning to the United States not to interfere
in either Europe or Asia.

With the termination in January 1940 of the treaty of commerce, the
United States was free to embargo shipment of strategic materials to
Japan. But the Roosevelt administration, warned by Ambassador Grew
in Japan that an abrupt cessation of trade with the United States might
cause the Japanese to invade the East Indies, delayed action in the vain
hope that supplying the materials for aggression would somehow prevent
aggression. In July 1940 Congress passed an act which provided for the
licensing of exports. This stopped the sale of aircraft and aviation gasoline to Japan, but the export of iron and steel was not cut off till autumn,
and the State Department continued to license the export of oil until July
1941.

## Planning for War

As it became apparent that Japan was preparing to move south, the
United States attempted to concert plans with potential allies. The
ABC-1 Conference held in Washington early in 1941, besides establishing
the European theater as primary, designated the Pacific theater as the
responsibility of the United States in event of war with Japan. A conference at Singapore in April proved ineffectual, producing only a recommendation for mutual support against aggression.

The Japanese advance in Indo-China was, in American eyes, the
crucial issue. When in July 1941 the Japanese announced that the Vichy
government had agreed to a "joint protectorate" of Indo-China, the United
States countered by freezing all Japanese assets in the United States, thus
at long last shutting off the supply of oil. This move precipitated the final
crisis. Japan had to have oil or see her military machine grind to a halt.
In October the Konoye government fell, and a military government
headed by General Tojo took over. In November a special Japanese envoy
arrived in the United States to assist Ambassador Nomura in negotiations
looking toward a resumption of the flow of oil. The failure of these negotiations led directly to Pearl Harbor.

## United States Preparations

The approach of war in the Pacific found the United States preparing but still unprepared. In 1938, in accordance with a directive of Congress, the Hepburn Board had recommended an extensive program for development of Pacific bases. Except for the fortification of Guam, most of the board's recommendations were adopted, and work was under way when war broke out.

The greater part of the United States Fleet had long been based on the West Coast, but in the spring of 1940 President Roosevelt, in the hope of deterring Japan from further aggression, directed that it be based at Pearl Harbor. Here it lay somewhat exposed while, after the outbreak of war in Europe, much of the new construction went to the Atlantic. In the spring of 1941, because of the necessity for convoying Lend-Lease goods, Admiral Harold R. Stark, Chief of Naval Operations, transferred from the Pacific to the Atlantic three battleships, the carrier *Yorktown*, four light cruisers, and two squadrons of destroyers. American plane production went chiefly to the Atlantic theater.

At the beginning of February 1941 the Atlantic Squadron, as we have seen, was made the Atlantic Fleet, while the fleet at Pearl Harbor became the Pacific Fleet. The small American force in the Far East, commanded by Admiral Thomas C. Hart, was for prestige purposes designated the United States Asiatic Fleet. It was provided that one of these three fleet commanders should also act as Commander in Chief United States Fleet. At the time of the attack on Pearl Harbor, Admiral Husband E. Kimmel was Commander in Chief both of the Pacific Fleet and of the United States Fleet.

In the Atlantic the Axis powers had not a single operational carrier, and the greater part of the British fleet was concentrated against the comparatively small German navy. In the Pacific the United States faced the formidable Japanese navy practically alone. Yet at the time of the Pearl Harbor attack the United States Fleet was fairly evenly divided between the two oceans, with nine battleships in the Pacific and eight in the Atlantic, three carriers in the Pacific and four in the Atlantic. True, the Atlantic Fleet lacked sufficient patrol craft and convoy escorts, but in the Pacific, even before the losses of Pearl Harbor, the fleet was inferior to the Japanese in every category. Most ominous, the three American carriers faced ten Japanese.

The British had undertaken to reinforce Singapore, but the crisis in the Far East coincided with a desperate situation in the Mediterranean, where they had suffered severe losses. After considerable hesitation the Admiralty consented to send the new battleship *Prince of Wales* to join the battle cruiser *Repulse* at Singapore with the hope that the presence of two capital ships would have an additional deterrent effect upon the Japanese. The new aircraft carrier *Indomitable* was to have joined these two vessels, but during her shakedown cruise in the West Indies she was damaged by grounding. The Admiralty felt that no other carrier could be spared from the European theater. The Dutch had nothing heavier than light cruisers in the East. America's allies, it was clear, could do little to redress the unfavorable balance of power in the Pacific.

American naval forces in the Pacific seriously lacked fleet auxiliaries. Planes were few and largely obsolete. Antiaircraft armament was short in quantity and quality. The American 1.1-inch gun proved so unsatisfactory that the Navy had to turn to the foreign-designed Bofors and Oerlikon guns.

In the Far East the situation was even more grave. With Japanese on Formosa less than 300 miles to the north, on Hainan and in Indo-China to the west, and in the Marianas and the Carolines to the east, the Philippines were almost surrounded. In July 1941 Douglas Mac-Arthur, then Field Marshal of the Philippine Army, was made Commanding General of the United States Army Forces Far East. Thereafter there was a rapid build-up in the Philippines both of air and of ground forces, designed to enable the islands to defend themselves by the spring of 1942.

In event of war with Japan, it had long been planned for the tiny U.S. Asiatic Fleet to fall back to the Malay Barrier, for it could hardly be expected to offer any significant opposition. But the increase of U.S. Army air strength in the Philippines gave hope that before long Luzon might be sufficiently secure to permit the fleet to continue operations from Manila.

## Final Negotiations

The negotiations between the United States and Japan were foredoomed, for neither government would retreat an inch. They bargained only for time. The United States had the advantage of being able to read the Japanese diplomatic correspondence, for American cryptanalysts had succeeded in constructing machines for deciphering the Japanese diplomatic code. Hence Washington knew that the Japanese Foreign Office had set the latter part of November as a deadline for the conclusion of the talks, after which "things are automatically going to happen." Washington knew also that the Japanese were receiving information regarding the movements of the vessels of the Pacific Fleet and their berthing in Pearl Harbor, and that Japan was calling for more specific and more frequent reports.

On November 26 the United States handed the Japanese a note which demanded that Japan evacuate China and support the regime of Chiang Kai-shek. There was no expectation that Japan would accept such demands, and deciphered Japanese messages at once indicated that the Japanese regarded the note as ending the conversations. The ambassadors however were to continue the pretense of negotiating "to prevent the United States from becoming unduly suspicious." On November 27 the U.S. Navy Department sent to Pearl Harbor a "war warning" indicating that the Department expected a Japanese move against the Philippines, Malaya, or Borneo. Apparently American officials were so hypnotized by Japan's obvious preparations to move southward that they overlooked or rejected her capability of striking in another direction as well.

By December 6 it was known in Washington that the Japanese were sending to their Washington embassy a message for the U.S. State Department breaking off diplomatic relations, the sort of message that in times past had been followed up with a surprise attack on the opposing fleet. It was known too that Japanese diplomats in London, Hong Kong, Singapore, Batavia, Manila, and Washington were burning their secret documents and codes—usually done only when war is imminent.

Thus by Saturday afternoon there was every reason to believe that war with Japan was only hours away. Then between 0400 and 0600 on Sunday, December 7, the U.S. Navy Department deciphered instructions to the Japanese ambassadors to deliver their message at 1 PM. One o'clock in the afternoon in Washington would be 7:30 AM at Pearl Harbor.

## The Attack on Pearl Harbor

Admiral Isoroku Yamamoto, Commander in Chief of the Japanese Combined Fleet, had early in 1941 proposed an attack on Pearl Harbor to make it impossible for the United States to attack Japan's flank while she was engaged in the conquest of the "Southern Resources Area." Details had been worked out in the early fall, and the final decision to go to war was made at an Imperial Conference on December 1.

Essentially the decision was a gamble on an Axis victory in Europe. In the fall of 1941 Rommel was threatening Egypt and the German armies were near Moscow. It seemed likely that the United States would be forced to let the Pacific go more or less by default while it faced the greater danger of an Axis triumph in Europe. In the meantime the Japanese would overrun Southeast Asia and the Southern Resources Area, and would protect them and Japan by a defensive perimeter of island air and submarine bases so strong that the United States would have to accept the *fait accompli*.

The attacking force, already at sea when the Imperial Council made its decision, consisted of six carriers—the *Akagi, Kaga, Soryu, Hiryu, Shokaku,* and *Zuikaku*—escorted by two battleships, three cruisers, and nine destroyers. Its course lay well to the north, both to avoid American

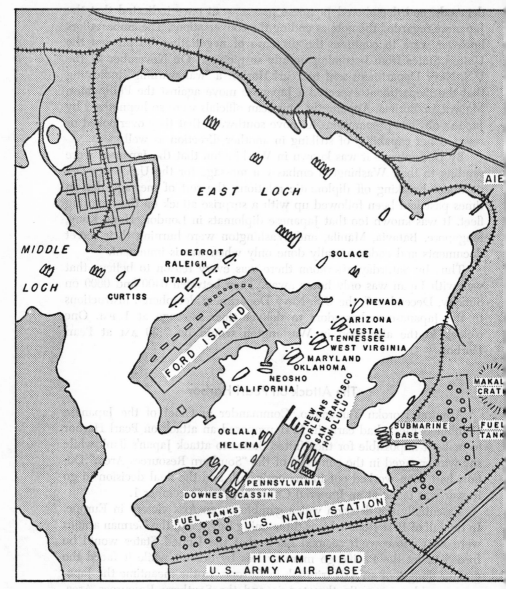

PEARL HARBOR, 0755, DECEMBER 7, 1941

air patrols and to decrease the chance of meeting merchant shipping. Twenty-seven submarines, of which eleven carried planes and five carried midget submarines to penetrate Pearl Harbor, had gone ahead earlier.

On December 6, the Japanese carriers received last minute information about the ships in Pearl Harbor. The *Enterprise* and *Lexington* were at sea, much to the regret of the Japanese Air Operations Officer, who said he would rather sink the two carriers than all eight battleships, but Vice Admiral Chuichi Nagumo, the task force commander, decided to launch the attack as planned. At 0615 on December 7 from a position 230 miles north of Oahu, Nagumo began launching his first wave of 183 attack planes.

At Pearl Harbor there was no premonition of the impending disaster. The warning of November 27 had indicated only that Washington expected Japan to make an aggressive move to the south, that is, toward the Philippines or Malaya. Accordingly Lieutenant General Walter C. Short, Commanding General Hawaiian Department, had taken precautions only against sabotage and had so reported to Washington. Admiral Kimmel had been given no information which would justify interrupting a very urgent training program.

The Sunday morning calm was slightly disturbed at 0645 when a destroyer sank a midget submarine outside Pearl Harbor, but the report did not lead to a general alert. It was hardly a matter to concern the ships in the security of the harbor. Many officers were having breakfast, and preparations were being made to change the watch when the first Japanese planes appeared. Their hostile character was not appreciated until the first bombs fell at 0755.

The battleships moored east of Ford Island were the principal target. Despite the surprise, American sailors took station with an alacrity that impressed the Japanese pilots but did not seriously disrupt their plans. A torpedo attack on the battleships was followed closely by high-level and dive bombing. The greater part of the damage resulted from this first attack, which was over by about 0830. Then after a brief lull came a second wave of 170 fighters and bombers, which concentrated on the ships that appeared least damaged. By this time however the Americans were thoroughly alerted, so that the second wave suffered the greater part of the Japanese casualties.

By the end of the attack the *Arizona* was a total loss. Moored inboard of the repair ship *Vestal*, which was too small to offer her much protection, she had taken several torpedo and bomb hits early in the action. One bomb exploded in a forward magazine. Surrounded by burning oil, the battleship sank quickly, taking with her more than a thousand men.

Of the ships moored in pairs, the outboard vessels suffered severely from torpedoes. The *Oklahoma,* moored outboard of the *Maryland,* received three torpedo hits in the first moments of the attack and at once began to capsize. She too was a complete loss and was later raised only to clear the harbor. The *West Virginia,* outboard of the *Tennessee,* was also torpedoed early in the action, but prompt counterflooding prevented her from capsizing, and her crew continued to fight as she settled to the bottom with only a moderate list. Their inboard partners fared much

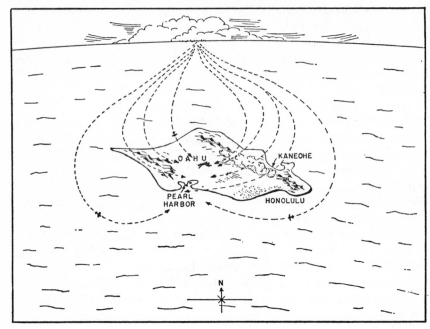

JAPANESE AIR RAID ON PEARL HARBOR, DECEMBER 7, 1941

better. The *Tennessee* took two bomb hits and was threatened by burning oil from the *Arizona*, but suffered only moderate damage. The *Maryland* escaped with only a couple of bomb hits.

The *California* was moored singly. Hit by two torpedoes and a bomb, she later settled into the Pearl Harbor mud in an upright position. The *Nevada*, moored alone at the opposite end of "Battleship Row," was the only vessel to get under way. Although hit by a torpedo forward, she was able to sortie under a rain of bombs and finally beached herself to avoid the danger of being sunk in the channel. The *Pennsylvania*, flagship of the Pacific Fleet, was in drydock, where she was safe from torpedoes, and she put up such an effective fire that she suffered only a single bomb hit.

While the fleet had been the primary objective of the Japanese, they had also attacked the airfields in the area. There the Americans hastily improvised defenses, but they nevertheless took heavy losses in aircraft, which had been parked in compact rows as a precaution against sabotage. The Navy lost 80 planes; and of the Army's 231, only 79 were usable after the attack. The Japanese lost only 29 aircraft over the target, but several others crashed in landing on their carriers.

American personnel casualties totaled 3,681, the Navy and Marine Corps losing 2,112 killed and 981 wounded; the Army, 222 killed and 360 wounded. These losses in particular had the effect of uniting the people of the United States in a vigorous prosecution of the war that had been forced upon them.

From the American point of view, the disaster was less severe than it first appeared, and considerably less than it might have been. The old battleships sunk at Pearl Harbor were too slow either to fight Japan's newer battleships or to accompany the fast American carriers. Their chief use came for shore bombardment in the last two years of the war, after all but the *Arizona* and the *Oklahoma* had been raised and renovated. Their temporary loss freed trained personnel, of which there was a great shortage, for use in carrier and amphibious forces, and it compelled the United States to adopt the carrier tactics that in the long run proved decisive.

In concentrating on ships, the Japanese had neglected the machine shops, leaving repair facilities substantially intact. They had overlooked the 4,500,000 barrels of oil exposed in tank farms near the harbor. This slowly accumulated fuel reserve was almost irreplaceable in view of America's European commitments. Without it, fleets could not have operated from Pearl Harbor for months. The greatest good fortune for the Americans was that their carriers had escaped. The *Saratoga* was on the West Coast, the *Lexington* was delivering planes to Midway, and the *Enterprise* was returning from having delivered planes to Wake. Moreover, very few cruisers or destroyers had been hit. Thus the ships for fast carrier striking forces, the most effective naval weapon of World War II, were left intact.

### Guam and Wake

Before the end of the day on December 7, Admiral Kimmel received word that both Guam and Wake had been attacked by Japanese planes. Guam, in the southern Marianas, well over 3,000 miles from Hawaii and 1,500 from Manila, was flanked by Japanese bases and practically defenseless. Five thousand Japanese put ashore on December 10 easily overwhelmed it. Wake however was a different matter. Although it was within bomber range of the Japanese Marshalls to the south, only about 2,000 miles of open sea lay between it and Pearl Harbor. More than a thousand construction workers were engaged in building an air and submarine base on the little atoll. About 450 marines equipped with a dozen 3-inch antiaircraft guns and a half-dozen old 5-inch guns constituted the defense. On December 4, twelve F4F Wildcat fighter planes had been flown in from the *Enterprise*.

After the island had been "softened up" by bombers from Kwajalein in the Marshalls, a Japanese force of three light cruisers and six destroyers, escorting several transports appeared at dawn on December 11. Commander Winfield S. Cunningham, the island commander, ordered the marines to hold their fire until the bombarding vessels were well within range. Then they opened up with their 5-inch guns, and the Wildcats took to the air. After the marines had succeeded in sinking two destroyers and damaging two cruisers and two more destroyers, the Japanese limped away without having put a man ashore.

Meanwhile Admiral Kimmel had made plans and issued orders for the relief of Wake. The *Saratoga* under Rear Admiral Frank Jack Fletcher was to cover the relief force directly while the other two carriers gave indirect support. But there were too many delays. The *Saratoga*, just arriving at Pearl Harbor from the West Coast, could not complete fueling and get under way till noon on the 16th. By the 21st she was only 600 miles from Wake, but she then paused for two days to refuel the destroyers of her group. There was hesitation at Pearl Harbor, where Admiral Kimmel's relief had not yet arrived.

The Japanese, quickly recovering from their initial repulse, sent against Wake on December 23 a new and stronger force covered by three heavy cruisers. Meanwhile Nagumo, returning from his attack on Pearl Harbor, had detached two of his carriers, the *Hiryu* and *Soryu*, to give air support to the landing. Planes from these carriers on the mornings of the 21st and 22nd destroyed the last planes on the island. Before light on the 23rd the Japanese landing craft came ashore, chiefly at points where the marines' artillery could not be brought to bear, while the bombarding cruisers remained outside the range of the 5-inch guns. After a struggle against hopeless odds, the defenders were forced to surrender.

On Wake and at other American bases, civilian construction workers had been exposed to enemy attack without having either the training or the legal right to defend themselves. To remedy this situation, the Navy early authorized the creation of Construction Battalions—the famous "Seabees." Men of various construction trades were enlisted with appropriate ratings and were given military training. Often going ashore with the assault waves, these men performed vital functions in the Pacific war, from building bases and airfields to repairing equipment. In their hands the bulldozer became one of the instruments of victory.

## Command and Strategy

The United States replied to the Japanese attack by declaring war on December 8, whereupon Japan's allies, Germany and Italy, declared war upon the United States. The new situation led to several command and administrative changes in the Navy. In mid-December Admiral Chester W. Nimitz was appointed Commander in Chief Pacific Fleet (Cincpac). The following April he was also made Commander in Chief Pacific Ocean Areas (Cincpoa), which gave him authority over the entire Pacific theater except for General MacArthur's Southwest Pacific Area and the inactive Southeast Pacific. Nimitz was a tow-haired, blue-eyed Texan, of the Naval Academy class of 1905. Tactful and modest, sound in his judgment of men and events, he was to prove a thoroughly fortunate choice.

Admiral King's first instructions to Nimitz, on December 30, defined his tasks as:

> (1) Covering and holding the Hawaii-Midway line and maintaining communications with the west coast.
>
> (2) Maintaining communications between the west coast and Australia, chiefly by covering, securing, and holding the Hawaii-Samoa line, which should be extended to include Fiji at the earliest practical date.

In broader terms, American strategy was to hold against any further Japanese encroachment a line running from Dutch Harbor through Midway to Samoa; thence to New Caledonia and to Port Moresby, New Guinea. To gain time for establishing this line Admiral Hart's Asiatic Fleet was to be sacrificed in a delaying action in the Netherlands East Indies.

## Beginning the Allied Retreat

The U.S. Asiatic Fleet was in fact only a modest task force. Its flagship and most powerful vessel was the heavy cruiser *Houston*. She was seconded by the 17-year-old light cruiser *Marblehead*. When the light cruiser *Boise* arrived at Manila with a convoy early in December she also was "impressed" into the fleet. These cruisers were supported by 13 flush deck, four-stack destroyers of the 1917–18 class. Twenty-nine submarines contributed a strong defensive element. It had been fully expected that the Japanese would attack the Philippines, and Admiral Hart had dispersed his fleet accordingly. The *Marblehead* with eight destroyers and a tender had been sent south to Borneo in November. The *Houston* and the *Boise* were in the relatively safe waters of the central Philippines.

News of the attack on Pearl Harbor reached Manila at 0300 on December 8, east longitude date. On orders from Admiral Hart, Rear Admiral William A. Glassford at once gathered several ships around the *Houston* and *Boise* and started south. Lacking dependable intelligence of enemy targets, the Army's 33 B-17's, of which only half had been transferred from Luzon to the comparative safety of Mindanao, were not sent to attack Formosa, as the Japanese feared they might. The Army fully expected a dawn air raid, and American planes took to the air on an early alert. But bad weather over Formosa delayed the Japanese take-off, and when the pilots finally arrived over Luzon about noon they

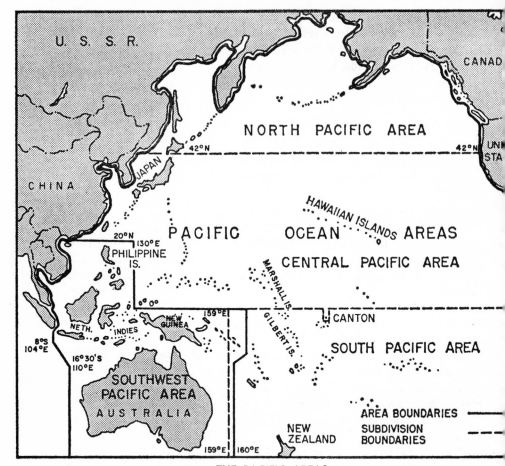

THE PACIFIC AREAS

Broken Vertical Line Shows South Pacific-Southwest Pacific Boundary
as Altered August 1, 1942

found the American planes on their fields in neat rows. As in Hawaii, the
aircraft were largely destroyed on the ground. With this loss there
vanished any real hope of repelling a Japanese invasion.

The attack on the Philippines was only one of several simultaneous
Japanese moves in the Far East. Imperial Army troops that had been
poised in Indo-China at once overran Thailand, where there was little
resistance. On December 8 and 9 forces from Hainan landed at Kota
Bharu on the Malay Peninsula and began a rapid advance toward
Singapore. The report of the landing at Kota Bharu caused Admiral
Tom Phillips RN to take the battleship *Prince of Wales* and the battle
cruiser *Repulse* north, escorted by four destroyers. Although the hard-
pressed Royal Air Force warned that it could provide no land-based

cover, Phillips, feeling that the Royal Navy could not stand idly by in the hour of crisis, made the gallant decision to go ahead. He arrived too late to catch the Japanese transports. Then acting upon a false report of a Japanese landing farther south, he stayed too long within range of Japanese planes based in Indo-China. He had been shadowed for some time when the main attack came in a little before noon on December 10. Both the *Prince of Wales* and the *Repulse* took several hits, capsized, and sank. Admiral Phillips was among those lost.

The sinking of these two capital ships—the first ever sunk by aerial bombing while under way at sea—eliminated the possibility of serious naval opposition to the Japanese advancing on Singapore. By December 19 the invaders had reached the Straits of Malacca.

On the same day that the Japanese sank the *Prince of Wales* and the *Repulse*, they made on the Cavite Naval Yard near Manila a heavy air attack that substantially destroyed the base. This attack also coincided with the first Japanese landings on Luzon, designed to secure airfields to support an advance on Manila. At Aparri on the north coast the Japanese, harassed by bad weather and by the remnants of the U.S. Army air force, put their men ashore hastily and departed without unloading their heavy equipment. A similar combination of bad weather, air opposition, and local resistance delayed for a day an attempt to land on the northwest coast near Vigan.

As General MacArthur expected, the main Japanese landing came at Lingayen Gulf, on the west side of Luzon above Manila. Japanese transports from Formosa entered the Gulf on December 21. American submarines, hampered by shoal water, had little success in intercepting. A few army planes and navy PBY's annoyed the convoy, but despite bad management the Japanese got their men ashore and with the help of the Vigan detachment, which had marched south to help, overcame resistance. On Christmas Eve the Japanese put another force ashore on the east coast opposite Manila.

MacArthur, already withdrawing from Manila, declared it an open city and moved his forces in a wheeling movement toward Bataan, while the Navy hastily moved from the city such material as it could. Rear Admiral Francis W. Rockwell, Commandant of the 16th Naval District, moved into the fortified island of Corregidor, and on the 26th Admiral Hart left by submarine to join his fleet in the south. Five days later the last of the American submarines left Manila. On January 2 the Japanese entered the city unopposed.

The stubborn defense of Bataan and Corregidor was important morally at a time when quick and easy enemy successes were all too frequent, and it had the important practical effect of denying Manila Bay to the Japanese, but it did not delay their advance toward the Indies. As early as December 17 they had landed on Borneo to begin seizure of its oil fields, and three days later in the Philippines they had landed at Davao Gulf, Mindanao, which became an important base for further thrusts to the south.

## The Japanese Advance into the Netherlands East Indies

Thus in little more than two weeks from the outbreak of war the Japanese had moved into and past the Philippines. The pattern of their multi-pronged advance was becoming clear. One line followed the Asiatic coast from Indo-China to Malaya and Singapore. A second thrust followed the west coast of Borneo south toward Sumatra. From Davao the Japanese advanced through both Makassar and Molucca Straits, taking important points along the way. Their ultimate objective was Java, richest and most highly developed of the Indies, with a population as great as that of England.

The Japanese moved by a series of amphibious landings on islands that had almost no interior communications, so that control of the sea and air was decisive. Their method was to seize a key point where they could take over or develop an airfield that would provide air support for the next move. Allied defenses were spread so thin that the Japanese had little difficulty in building up local superiority. For the most part they employed only modest forces and seldom required carrier support.

By early January 1942 the U.S. Asiatic Fleet had fallen back to the Netherlands East Indies. On the 10th British General Sir Archibald P. Wavell arrived in Java to take supreme command of the American, British, Dutch, and Australian (ABDA) forces in the area. Admiral Hart was given the naval command, while the air and army commands went to the British and Dutch respectively. But the ABDA command, facing insuperable difficulties, was never able to function effectively, nor was it able to work out a unified strategy.

As the Japanese advanced in a vast pincers movement on Java via the waters east and west of Borneo, it appeared that the ABDA forces might be able to exploit their interior position by striking first at one and then the other of the divided Japanese forces. But throughout January Allied naval vessels were so much in demand for convoying that it was impossible to form a striking force. Consequently Admiral Hart had available only a few United States vessels when in late January reconnaissance reported a Japanese convoy approaching the Borneo oil port of Balikpapan. On the night of the 23rd these ships steamed up Makassar Strait. En route the *Boise* struck an uncharted pinnacle rock, which put her out of the campaign, while the *Marblehead* developed turbine trouble. Proceeding without cruiser support, four destroyers in a surprise attack sank a patrol craft and four of the dozen transports present, be-

## THE NETHERLANDS EAST INDIES AREA, 1942

1. Action off Balikpapan, January 24
2. Madoera Strait, February 4
3. Banka Island, February 13–14
4. Badoeng Strait, February 19–20
5. Java Sea, February 27–28

sides damaging several others. This daring night raid was the only successful surface action fought by Allied forces during the entire Netherlands East Indies campaign.

After this, Japanese control of the air prevented adequate Allied reconnaissance while it assured the Japanese complete knowledge of all ABDA movements. As a result, ABDA forces were swung between the two arms of the Japanese advance without being able to strike effectively at either, and were often turned back short of their objective by Japanese planes. While Dutch ships were drawn to the west by a mistaken report, a Japanese force supported by carriers *Soryu* and *Hiryu* and two battleships took Amboina, anchor of the Dutch east flank. Soon afterward the Japanese occupied Kendari, in southeastern Celebes, and planes from the two carriers for a time based there. These planes on February 3 bombed Surabaya, the principal Allied naval base in Java, and destroyed most of the Dutch fighter aircraft in the vicinity.

By this time the task of reinforcing Singapore had been completed and an ABDA striking force had been formed of vessels released from convoy duty. In it initially were the United States cruisers *Houston* and *Marblehead* and four American destroyers, the Dutch light cruisers *De Ruyter* and *Tromp*, and three Dutch destroyers. Command was given to Dutch Rear Admiral Karel Doorman. These vessels escaped damage in the attack on Surabaya, but next morning as Doorman led them forth to attack a Japanese force reported reassembling at Balikpapan, they were discovered by Japanese planes. In a prolonged attack in Madoera Strait, the *Houston* received a hit that put her after turret out of commission for the rest of the campaign, while the *Marblehead* was so badly battered that she had to return to the United States.

Doorman next had to turn his attention to the Japanese western force. With five cruisers and ten destroyers he rushed to the relief of the great oil port of Palembang in eastern Sumatra, but when he arrived off nearby Banka Island on the night of February 13 he was met with repeated air attacks. Although no ship of his force was hit, several were shaken by near misses, and he retired without accomplishing anything.

In mid-February Admiral Hart relinquished command of the ABDA naval forces to Dutch Vice Admiral Conrad Helfrich and returned to the United States, leaving Admiral Glassford senior United States naval officer in the area. Singapore surrendered on February 15. After that, the Japanese were ready to close the pincers on Java, which they had started softening up by daily bombings.

Doorman had just returned from Banka Island when word came that the Japanese were landing on the island of Bali at the opposite end of Java. Doorman determined at least to hit the Japanese transports before they could withdraw, but because his ships were now divided between Surabaya and Tjilatjap he decided to attack in three successive waves.

For once the ABDA vessels outnumbered the Japanese warships, but the lack of concentration nullified this advantage. In the attack on the night of February 19, a Dutch destroyer was sunk and the cruiser *Tromp* badly damaged without inflicting damage on the Japanese.

By now Java was nearly isolated, and the Japanese set about cutting her last links with Australia. They first seized Timor, through which the Allies had been staging fighter planes from Australia to Java. Then on February 19 Admiral Nagumo's carriers raided Darwin, principal port of northern Australia. The Japanese planes sank a dozen ships in the harbor, including the United States destroyer *Peary*, and virtually destroyed the docks and warehouses. The battered city was evacuated before nightfall, and the port of Darwin was abandoned as a naval base.

## The Battle of the Java Sea

General Wavell, convinced of the futility of attempting any further defense of Java, left on the 25th, thus dissolving the ABDA command and leaving the Dutch to coordinate the continuing defense as best they could. By this time the Japanese were poised for the final attack. To the northwest Rear Admiral Jisaburo Ozawa was waiting near the Anambas Islands with 56 transports and cargo vessels and their escorts. To the northeast Rear Admiral Shoji Nishimura was waiting in Makassar Strait with 41 transports and a cruiser-destroyer covering force.

Doorman, after two days of patrolling along the north coast of Java to intercept any landing attempt, on the morning of February 27 was returning to Surabaya with his striking force for rest and refueling when a report came of Japanese transports west of Bawean Island. Although his crews were near exhaustion, there was nothing to do but put about for the ultimate battle.

Doorman's cruisers were in column, the flagship *De Ruyter* in the lead, followed by the British *Exeter*, the American *Houston*, the Australian *Perth*, and the Dutch *Java*. Three British destroyers screened the van, two Dutch destroyers were on the port flank, and four American destroyers brought up the rear. Half an hour after leaving Surabaya, Doorman sighted the enemy in two groups on his starboard bow, moving SW as if to cross his course. One group consisted of a light cruiser leading ten destroyers, the other of two heavy cruisers and one light, with a squadron of destroyers. Fire was opened at 28,000 yards, beyond the range of the light cruisers. Although the Japanese enjoyed the advantage of air spotting, for some time they scored no hits. Then an 8-inch shell struck the *Exeter*, slowing her and forcing her to turn out of column. The following vessels, assuming that Doorman had ordered a turn, also swung to port, throwing the Allied formation into confusion and presenting their broadsides to Japanese torpedoes. By good luck or maneu-

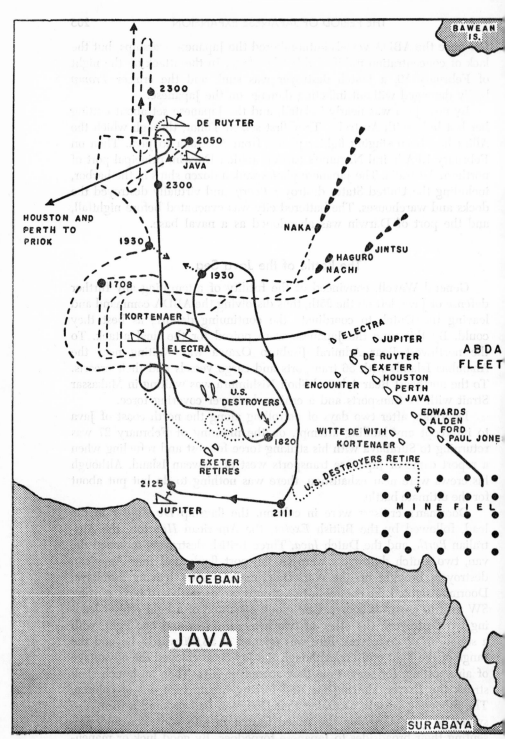

BATTLE OF THE JAVA SEA, FEBRUARY 27–28, 1942

vering all escaped except one of the Dutch destroyers, which took a torpedo, broke in two, and sank. When the Japanese closed in for the kill, a British destroyer was sunk by gunfire as she covered the damaged *Exeter*. The other cruisers withdrew and re-formed under cover of a torpedo attack by the American destroyers.

After a futile thrust toward the Japanese transports in the growing darkness, the striking force again approached Surabaya about 2100. At that point the American destroyers, their torpedoes expended and low in fuel, returned to port. There they found the *Exeter*, accompanied by the surviving Dutch destroyer.

As the remainder of the striking force steamed west along the Java coast, one of the British destroyers blew up and sank—probably the victim of a Dutch mine field laid that afternoon without Doorman's knowledge. Turning north, Doorman passed through the area where the Dutch destroyer had been sunk and detached his last destroyer to pick up survivors. Then with his four remaining cruisers he continued his thrust to the north and at 2300 again encountered the Japanese covering force. After 20 minutes of firing, the Japanese launched torpedoes that caught both the *De Ruyter* and the *Java*. As his flagship sank, Doorman signaled the *Houston* and the *Perth*, all that remained of his striking force, to retire to Tandjong Priok (the harbor of Batavia), which they reached safely a little after noon the next day.

## The Retreat from Java

The Allied vessels surviving the battle were now divided between Surabaya and Tandjong Priok, with strong Japanese forces between. The problem was how to withdraw from the Java Sea, for the enemy now controlled all the exits. Only the four American destroyers escaped. Leaving Surabaya on the night of the 28th, they slipped through Bali Strait and after a brief skirmish with Japanese destroyers made their way to Australia. Because the *Exeter*'s draft was too great to permit her to follow the same route, she was sent west to Sunda Strait, but on the way she and two escorting destroyers were intercepted and sunk. The *Houston*, the *Perth*, and a Dutch destroyer left Priok on the evening of the 28th. They had almost reached Sunda Strait when, an hour before midnight, they encountered a Japanese landing force. The Allied cruisers sank or forced the beaching of four transports before the enemy covering force closed in and overwhelmed them.

The few Allied vessels based at Tjilatjap, on the south coast of Java, were authorized by Admiral Helfrich to withdraw on March 1. Nagumo's carrier-battleship force operating south of Java intercepted a few, including two United States destroyers and a gunboat, but most reached Australia.

The Japanese had begun landing on Java on the night of February 28. Batavia and Surabaya fell quickly, and by March 9 the Japanese were in possession of the entire island. The ABDA forces had been expended to gain time, and they had bought little enough of that. But it is adversity that brings out the true quality of men and of navies. There is nothing finer in United States naval history than the performance of the Asiatic Fleet in the face of overwhelming odds.

## Holding the Line in the Pacific

While the ABDA fleet was buying time at the price of its own extinction, Allied forces elsewhere were stiffening the line that the United States was determined if possible to hold. This required reinforcing the essential bases on the route between the United States and Australia and then a build-up of forces in Australia itself. Vice Admiral Herbert F. Leary USN had arrived in Australia early in February to take command of an Anzac (Australian-New Zealand) Force, created on the recommendation of the Combined Chiefs of Staff after it became apparent that the ABDA forces were doomed. On March 17 MacArthur arrived at Darwin, designated at the request of the Australian government to take command of the Southwest Pacific Area, for which the United States had assumed responsibility. Already he was planning on a return to the Philippines, but for the moment he was a general without an army.

Although the United States was on the defensive, American strategy was far from passive. As Admiral King put it, American policy was "hold what you've got and hit them when you can." For the time being the hitting was to be done by the submarines and the carriers. Immediately after the Pearl Harbor disaster, the *Yorktown* had been ordered from the Atlantic to the Pacific. Her arrival brought the American carrier strength in the Pacific up to four, but on January 11 the *Saratoga* was torpedoed by a Japanese submarine 500 miles southwest of Oahu. She was able to make port, but repairs kept her out of the war for five critical months.

Fortunately for the Allies, the Japanese did not make the most effective use of their carriers during that interval. Upon Nagumo's return from Pearl Harbor his force was sent to support operations in the South. To cover the left flank of their advance the Japanese had already occupied the British Gilbert Islands in early December 1941, and in the latter part of January they sent their carriers for an unnecessary softening up of Rabaul, at the northern end of New Britain, in preparation for a landing on the 23rd.

Meanwhile there was considerable apprehension at Pearl Harbor that the Japanese might move from the Marshalls and Gilberts against Samoa. Accordingly reinforcements were dispatched to that group, and two carrier forces were sent to hit the Japanese bases. While Rear Admiral

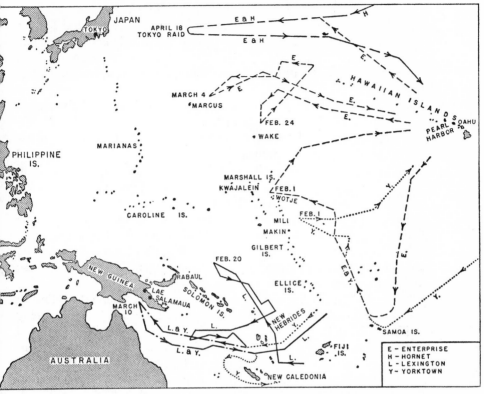

**EARLY RAIDS BY UNITED STATES CARRIER FORCES**

Fletcher's *Yorktown* group on February 1 raided Makin in the northern Gilberts and Jaluit and Mili in the southern Marshalls, Vice Admiral William F. Halsey's *Enterprise* group penetrated farther into the Marshalls to attack Wotje, Malœlap, and Kwajalein. Admiral Nagumo's carriers had just returned from Rabaul to Truk, the major Japanese base in the Carolines, when news of the attacks sent them on a futile chase after the Americans. Damage done by the American raids, particularly that on Kwajalein, was severe enough to make the Japanese concerned for the safety of Japan itself. Accordingly they detached the *Shokaku* and *Zuikaku* from Nagumo's group for a defensive patrol of Japanese waters, thus immobilizing one third of their most effective striking force.

At the time of the fall of Singapore in mid-February both the United States and Australian governments were apprehensive that the Japanese might advance from Rabaul to attack New Caledonia and the New Hebrides. Consequently Vice Admiral Wilson Brown's *Lexington* group was temporarily assigned to Leary's Anzac force and undertook an attack on Rabaul. But on his approach on February 20 the force was attacked by Japanese planes. With surprise lost, Brown abandoned the strike.

The critical situation in the Southwest Pacific was responsible for an attempt to divert the Japanese by an attack on Wake. Admiral Halsey, whose ready courage in undertaking such risky missions endeared him to Nimitz, struck Wake with planes of the *Enterprise* group on February 24, then pressed on to attack Marcus Island, less than a thousand miles from Tokyo.

By the time of the raid on Marcus, Allied naval forces had abandoned Java. Japanese bombing of points in New Guinea, including Port Moresby, and of Tulagi in the lower Solomons seemed to portend a further advance to the south or southeast. To check any such move, Admiral Brown was given a force built around the *Lexington* and *Yorktown* to make another attempt against Rabaul, which the Japanese were rapidly developing into a major base. But a report of Japanese landings on March 8 at Lae and Salamaua on the northern side of the New Guinea tail caused Brown to shift his attack to those points. Launching from south of Papua, he achieved surprise by sending his planes over the Owen Stanley Mountains and scored some successes against the few Japanese vessels still present.

While the United States and Anzac forces were thus attempting to check Japanese expansion to the south and east, the British were facing a similar problem in the west. In mid-January the Japanese had advanced from Thailand to begin their invasion of Burma. By early March Rangoon, the capital and key to lower Burma, had fallen, leaving the British the difficult task of withdrawing from upper Burma into India. In the latter part of March the Japanese protected the left flank of their advance by occupying the Andaman Islands, which put them in a position to threaten India. (See map page 432.) Then to render their sea route to Burma doubly secure they sent Nagumo's force to hit the British in the Indian Ocean.

When Vice Admiral Sir James Somerville, the former commander of Force H at Gibraltar, arrived in Ceylon at the end of March to replace Admiral Phillips, he had at his disposal the carriers *Indomitable, Formidable,* and *Hermes,* five battleships, and a number of cruisers and destroyers. On paper this was a respectable force, but the carriers were of limited capacity and the battleships old and slow. Shortly after his arrival, Somerville received a warning that the Japanese would attack Ceylon about April 1. He at once concentrated his force to the south of Ceylon, searched for three days, and then on April 2 retired to a secret base in the Maldive Islands.

Meanwhile Nagumo had entered the Indian Ocean with virtually the same carrier force that had raided Pearl Harbor. On Easter Sunday, April 5, his aircraft raided the British base at Colombo, Ceylon and shortly afterward sank H.M. heavy cruisers *Dorsetshire* and *Cornwall,* which had sailed the day before to join Somerville. Four days later

Nagumo raided Trincomalee, Britain's other base in Ceylon, and that same afternoon sank at sea the carrier *Hermes* and an accompanying destroyer. At both places the Japanese easily overwhelmed the weak British air opposition with negligible losses to themselves.

Vice Admiral Takeo Kurita had in the meantime entered the Bay of Bengal with six heavy cruisers and a light carrier and pounced upon merchant shipping. In the first nine days of April 1942, Japanese air, surface, and submarine forces sank four British warships and 135,000 tons of merchant shipping.

After this disaster Britain practically abandoned the Indian Ocean. Somerville sent his four slowest battleships to east Africa, while with the *Warspite* and his two remaining carriers he covered sea communications between India and the Persian Gulf. But there was serious apprehension that his base at Bombay might not long remain secure, for it appeared that a Japanese invasion of Ceylon and India might be imminent. Churchill asked that the United States Navy undertake some action that might force the Japanese to draw their carriers back into the Pacific, and arrangements were made for American vessels to join the British Home Fleet so that reinforcements might be sent to India.

It was only coincidence that the British plea for a diversion in the Pacific was followed by the most daring of the series of United States carrier raids, the Halsey-Doolittle raid on Tokyo on April 18. The plan was for the newly-arrived carrier *Hornet*, accompanied by the *Enterprise* and a cruiser-destroyer screen, under the over-all command of Admiral Halsey, to carry 16 Army B-25's to within 500 miles of Japan. The planes, manned by volunteers, were to hit targets in Tokyo, Nagoya, Osaka, and Kobe, cross Japan, and land on friendly airfields in China. But while the carriers were still 650 miles from Japan they encountered Japanese picket boats that reported their presence. Rather than abandon the raid, Colonel James H. Doolittle usa decided to launch at that distance. Waves were breaking over the *Hornet*'s bows and the carrier was pitching badly when Doolittle led his planes off. Not one of the pilots had ever taken off from a carrier deck before; yet somehow every one succeeded in getting his big, heavily-loaded plane into the air.

There was only scattered opposition, and none of the American aircraft was lost over Japan, but on arriving over China in the dark, 15 of the planes were lost in crash landings or when their crews abandoned them by parachute. The only plane to land safely was impounded by the Russians at Vladivostok. Of the 80 men who left the carrier, 71 survived the raid.

The physical effect of the raid on Tokyo was slight. Few of the Japanese public even knew that the city had been bombed, but Japan's rulers knew and were disturbed. The raid was to have an important effect on strategic developments.

None of the early raids inflicted really significant damage, but their moral effect on both sides was important. They seriously alarmed the Japanese rulers, while for the Americans they did much to dispel the gloom and defeatism engendered by the Pearl Harbor attack and to create a feeling that the United States was fighting back.

## Japanese Strategic Decisions

The conquest of the Philippines, the Netherlands East Indies, Burma, and Malaya, completed by the spring of 1942, had required only about half the time the Japanese had anticipated and had cost them only a few thousand casualties. In the entire campaign they had lost no naval vessel larger than a destroyer.

The rapidity with which the Japanese had achieved their main objectives left them without a decision as to their further strategy. Apart from consolidation of conquests to date, the three possibilities were to move westward against Ceylon and India, to move southward against Australia, or to move eastward against Hawaii. The first two were advocated by elements of the Naval General Staff, while Yamamoto and his Combined Fleet Staff espoused the third course. But the Japanese army, with its eyes upon the continent and Russia, objected to committing the large number of troops necessary for either of the first two. Hence the Naval General Staff worked out a more modest plan for isolating Australia by moving from Rabaul into Eastern New Guinea and down the Solomons and the New Hebrides to New Caledonia, the Fijis, and Samoa.

The first steps of this new Naval General Staff plan had already been taken with the landings at Lae and Salamaua in early March, and preparations for the capture of Port Moresby and Tulagi were under way by April. But Yamamoto and his staff, arguing that the destruction of the United States carriers was essential to Japanese security in the Pacific, insisted on early operations against Midway and the Aleutians that would be sure to draw out American naval forces. In early April they secured the reluctant consent of the Naval General Staff. The date and other details of the Midway operation were still in dispute however when the Doolittle raid seemed to prove the soundness of Yamamoto's argument. On the recommendation of the Naval General Staff the Imperial General Staff on May 5 ordered the Midway operation for early June.

Thus through compromise the Japanese had adopted two concurrent strategies which were destined to over-extend their forces. The first, the Naval General Staff's campaign to isolate Australia, was to lead to the Battle of the Coral Sea and eventually bring American marines to Guadalcanal, while Yamamoto's thrust toward Hawaii was to result in the Battle of Midway.

## The Battle of the Coral Sea

The occupation of Port Moresby and Tulagi had originally been planned for March, but the appearance of United States carrier forces in the southwest Pacific had caused the Japanese to delay the operation till early May so that the Fourth Fleet might be reinforced by the heavy carriers *Shokaku* and *Zuikaku* from Nagumo's force and the light carrier *Shoho* from the Combined Fleet.

The Japanese wanted Port Moresby in order to safeguard Rabaul and their positions in New Guinea, to provide a base for neutralizing airfields in northern Australia, and in order to secure the flank of their projected advance toward New Caledonia, Fiji, and Samoa. They wanted Tulagi, across the sound from Guadalcanal in the lower Solomons, to use as a seaplane base both to cover the flank of the Port Moresby operation and to support the subsequent advance to the southeast. To the Allies the retention of Port Moresby was essential not only for the security of Australia but also as a springboard for future offensives.

In the Japanese plan a Covering Force built around the 12,000-ton carrier *Shoho* was first to cover the landing on Tulagi, then turn back west in time to protect the Port Moresby Invasion Force, which was to come down from Rabaul and around the tail of New Guinea through Jomard Passage. There were close support forces for both landings, and in addition a Striking Force centered on the *Shokaku* and *Zuikaku* was to come down from Truk to deal with any United States forces that might attempt to interfere with the operation. Land-based aircraft were counted on for scouting and support. Altogether there were six separate naval forces engaged in this dual operation. Such complex division of forces was typical of Japanese strategy throughout most of the war. So far, against a weak and disorganized enemy, it had worked well, and it was not inconsistent with concentration so long as the forces were properly coordinated and sufficiently close together to render mutual support. But when the Japanese disregarded these two important conditions they met with disaster.

In the Coral Sea, Japanese coordination was to be provided by a unified command. Vice Admiral Shigeyoshi Inouye, Commander Fourth Fleet, was to direct all forces, including land-based air, from Rabaul. The Allied command was not so well integrated. The battle was to be fought in General MacArthur's Southwest Pacific Theater, but it was understood that any fleet action would remain under Admiral Nimitz' strategic control. The result was that Allied land-based air and naval forces were under separate commands without effective coordination.

Since the Pearl Harbor attack, the United States had broken the Japanese naval code and thus possessed the enormous advantage of ac-

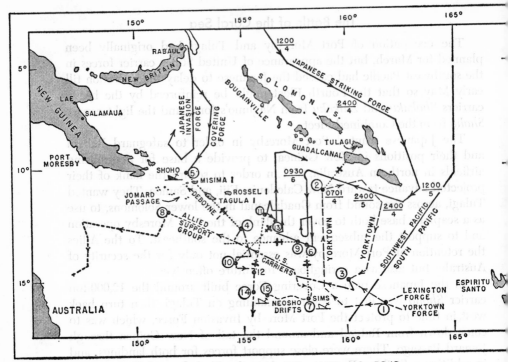

BATTLE OF THE CORAL SEA, MAY 4-8, 1942

1. May  1, 0623: *Yorktown* and *Lexington* meet.
2. May  4, 0701: *Yorktown* launches attack on Tulagi.
3. May  5, 0846: *Yorktown* rejoins *Lexington*.
4. May  7, 1000: Attack group launched.
5. May  7, 1150: *Shoho* sunk.
6. May  7, 0815: Japanese launch attack on *Neosho* and *Sims*.
7. May  7, 1230: *Sims* sunk.
8. May  7, 1425: Japanese planes attack Support Force.
9. May  7, 1615: Japanese launch night attack group.
10. May  8, 0900: U.S. carriers launch attack.
11. May  8, 0915: Japanese carriers launch attack.
12. May  8, 1118: U.S. carriers under attack.
13. May  8, 1058: Japanese carriers under attack.
14. May  8, 1956: *Lexington* sinks.
15. May 11, 1550: *Neosho* sunk by *Henley*.

curate and rather detailed intelligence concerning the enemy's plans. Even so, it was no easy matter to gather sufficient forces to meet the threat to Port Moresby. The *Saratoga* was still in Puget Sound undergoing repairs for the torpedo damage sustained in January. The *Enterprise* and *Hornet* did not return to Pearl Harbor from the Tokyo raid till April 25. Although they were hurried on their way as soon as possible, there was little likelihood that they could reach the Coral Sea in time to play a part. The only carriers immediately available were Admiral Fletcher's *Yorktown* force, which had been in the South Pacific for some time, and Rear Admiral Aubrey W. Fitch's *Lexington* group, fresh from Pearl Harbor. From Noumea, New Caledonia came the *Chicago*, while Rear Admiral J. C. Crace RN brought H.M.A. cruisers *Australia* and *Hobart* from Australia. The Japanese, overconfident from their long series of easy successes, assumed that a single carrier division was sufficient to support their new advance.

The two American carrier groups, which had been ordered to join under Fletcher's command, made contact in the southeast Coral Sea on May 1. Two days later Fletcher received a report of the Japanese landing on Tulagi. Leaving the *Lexington* group to complete fueling, he headed north with the *Yorktown* group, and during the 4th made a series of air attacks on the Tulagi area that sank a few minor Japanese naval craft. He then turned back south and formally merged his two groups on May 6. The two carriers were to operate within a single circular screen of cruisers and destroyers. Admiral Fitch, because of his long experience with carriers, was to exercise tactical command during air operations.

Fletcher's uniting of his forces was luckily timed, for the *Shokaku* and *Zuikaku* with their escorts, having swung around the southeastern end of the Solomons, had just entered the Coral Sea. The Japanese Striking Force was commanded by Vice Admiral Takeo Takagi, with Rear Admiral Tadaichi Hara commanding the carriers. Takagi, in coming around the Solomons, hoped to catch the American carriers in a sort of pincer movement. He almost succeeded, for on the evening of the 6th he was rapidly overhauling the American force, then refueling, and was actually within 70 miles of the Americans when he turned north.

At dawn on May 7, the American task force was cruising on a northwesterly course south of the Louisiades, which form an extension of the New Guinea tail. A little before 0700, Fletcher detached three cruisers and three destroyers under Admiral Crace and ordered them to push on to the northwest while the carriers turned north. The detached vessels were to prevent the Port Moresby Invasion Force from coming through Jomard Passage, regardless of the fate of the American carriers, which Fletcher expected would come under attack during the day. In sending Crace forward however, Fletcher was depriving a part of his force of carrier air cover and at the same time further weakening his already weak carrier antiaircraft screen.

Thus far neither Takagi nor Fletcher was sure that the other was in the area, though Fletcher had information that three Japanese carriers were involved in the operation. Takagi was depending on land-based searches which actually sighted the American carrier force but failed to get word through. Fletcher's air searches were defeated by bad weather to the northeast, where the two Japanese heavy carriers were operating. To the northwest however the weather was clear, and early on the

7th reports began to come in from American scout planes searching in this direction. At 0815 a pilot reported "two carriers and four heavy cruisers" not far north of Misima Island, whereupon Fletcher ordered attack groups launched from both his carriers. The 93 planes were well on their way before the scout returned and it was discovered that the report was an error due to improper coding—that the scout had meant to report two cruisers and two destroyers.

Fletcher made the courageous decision to let the attack proceed, probably thinking that with the Japanese Invasion Force nearby there must be some profitable targets. His boldness was rewarded at 1022 by a report which placed an enemy carrier with several other vessels only 35 miles southeast of the point toward which the strike had been sent. The attack group had to alter course only slightly for the new target.

The Americans came upon the *Shoho* about 1100 and, in the first attack ever made by American pilots on an enemy carrier, smothered her with 13 bomb and seven torpedo hits, which sent her down within a few minutes. Upon their return, Fletcher decided to withhold a second strike until the other two enemy carriers were located. Moreover, he suspected that the enemy knew his position, and it seemed likely that he would soon come under attack.

The Japanese failed to attack Fletcher on the 7th only because of a series of errors which by evening reached the fantastic. Before 0900 on the 7th, Inouye, directing the Japanese operation from Rabaul, had reports of two American carrier forces. One was Fletcher's; the other, some 45 miles to the west, was in fact Crace's cruiser-destroyer force. Then came a report from Takagi of a third American carrier in the eastern Coral Sea. This last was actually the oiler *Neosho*, which had been detached from Fletcher's force the evening before and was proceeding with the destroyer *Sims* toward a rendezvous.

At 0950 Japanese navy planes took off from Rabaul to attack the westernmost of the United States forces. The Japanese pilots returned with reports that they had sunk a battleship and a cruiser. Actually Crace's force survived without damage both this attack and another by B-26's from Australia, which mistook his vessels for Japanese.

The identification of the *Neosho* as a carrier had a serious effect on Japanese operations, for Hara at once launched a full attack upon the hapless oiler and her escort. The *Sims* with three hits went down with most of her crew. The *Neosho* took seven but remained afloat until her crew was taken off four days later.

This erroneous attack left Tagaki and Hara facing a critical situation. As night approached, the weather closed in, but Hara was determined to destroy the American carriers before they could further damage the Invasion Force. Selecting 27 pilots best qualified in night operations, he sent them out at 1615 in the direction in which he estimated the American carriers lay.

It was not a bad gamble, for in the foul weather and poor visibility the Japanese actually passed near Fletcher's force. The American combat air patrol, vectored out by radar, intercepted the Japanese planes and shot down nine. An hour later several of the returning Japanese, mistaking the American carriers for their own, actually attempted to join the *Yorktown's* landing circle until American gunners shot down one and drove off the others. The *Lexington's* radar showed planes circling as if for a landing about 30 miles to the east, which seemed to indicate that the Japanese carriers were very close indeed. Of the Japanese striking group, ten had been shot down, and eleven others went into the water in attempting night landings on their carriers. Hara recovered only six of his 27.

The pilots of these planes reported the American carriers only 50 to 60 miles away. Thus each of the opposing commanders was aware of the proximity of the other. Both seriously considered a night surface attack, and both abandoned the idea because they hesitated to weaken their screens with an enemy near. Thus the main action of the Battle of the Coral Sea was postponed another day.

Actually the distance between the two forces was greater than either commander imagined, for postwar plots show that they were nearly a hundred miles apart.

## The Battle of May 8

Thus far the antagonists had been together in the Coral Sea for two days, and had twice come within a hundred miles of each other without exchanging blows. On the evening of May 7 each of the opposing commanders felt that the enemy was uncomfortably close. There was every likelihood that a decision would be reached the next day. During the night Fletcher withdrew to the south and west, while Takagi moved north. For both commanders everything depended on locating the enemy as promptly as possible on the morning of the 8th. Both launched searches a little before dawn, and the scouts of each reported the other almost simultaneously a little after 0800.

The contest of May 8 started on curiously even terms. Each force contained two carriers. Fitch had available 121 planes, Hara 122. The Americans were stronger in bombers, while the Japanese enjoyed a preponderance in fighter and torpedo planes. The Japanese pilots had more combat experience, and their torpedoes were better. In another respect the Japanese enjoyed a significant advantage. By moving south through the night Fletcher had run out of the bad weather area in which he had been operating, and on the 8th his force lay exposed under clear skies, while the Japanese remained within the frontal area, under the protection of clouds and rain squalls.

Essentially the battle consisted of a simultaneous exchange of strikes by the two carrier forces. Between 0900 and 0925 both American carriers launched their attack groups. That of the *Yorktown*, consisting of 24 bombers with two fighters, and nine torpedo planes with four fighters, departed first. About 1030 the dive bombers found the Japanese carriers with their escorts in loose formation. While the pilots took cloud cover to await the arrival of the torpedo planes, the *Zuikaku* disappeared into a rain squall. Hence the attack fell only on the *Shokaku*.

When the torpedo planes approached, the SBD's began their dives. Although the attack was well coordinated, it was only moderately successful. The slow American torpedoes were easily avoided, but the dive bombers succeeded in planting two bombs on the *Shokaku*. Of the *Lexington* group, which departed about ten minutes later than the *Yorktown*'s, the 22 dive bombers failed to find the target. Only the eleven torpedo planes and the four scout bombers found the enemy. Again American torpedoes were ineffective, but the bombers succeeded in adding another hit to the two already sustained by the *Shokaku*. These three hits put the *Shokaku* out of action for the time being; because the damage to her flight deck prevented her recovering planes, Takagi detached her, ordering her to proceed to Truk.

The Japanese had sent off their group of 70 attack planes and 20 fighters at about the same time as the American launching. Although the American radar picked them up at 70 miles away, only three fighters succeeded in intercepting them before the attack. At a distance of 20 miles, still having met no interference by American fighters, the Japanese planes divided into three groups, two of torpedo planes and one of bombers.

The two American carriers were together in the center of their circle of screening vessels, but evasive maneuvers gradually drew them apart. The screen divided fairly evenly, but this breaking of the circle undoubtedly contributed to the Japanese success.

The *Yorktown*, which came first under attack, successfully evaded the torpedoes launched at her and took only a single bomb hit, which did not significantly impair her fighting effectiveness. But the *Lexington*, larger and less maneuverable, fell victim to an "anvil" attack on both bows simultaneously and took two torpedoes on the port side, which flooded three boiler rooms. Two bomb hits, received at almost the same time, inflicted only minor damage. The list caused by the torpedo hits was quickly corrected by shifting oil. Her engines were unharmed, and her speed did not fall below 24 knots. To her pilots returning from their strike she appeared undamaged.

As the American force began to recover its planes it appeared to have won the battle. Both carriers were operational with combat effectiveness essentially unimpaired. On the other hand, the *Shokaku* had been put out of action and was already withdrawing. Because the *Zuikaku* had been unable to take on all the Japanese planes, many had to be jettisoned. Admiral Hara had only nine aircraft fit for further operations, while Fitch could still put into the air 37 attack planes and twelve fighters.

Even had Fletcher and Fitch been aware of their advantage they could not have seized it, for at 1247 there was an explosion deep inside the *Lexington,* caused apparently by vapor from ruptured gasoline lines touched off by a spark from a generator. At first the full danger was not apparent, and the *Lexington* continued landing her planes. But at 1445 there was a more severe explosion. Fires passed rapidly out of control and the carrier was forced to call for assistance. The *Yorktown* took aboard the *Lexington* planes that were in the air, but there was no opportunity to transfer those already on the *Lexington.* With the ship burning furiously and shaken by frequent explosions there was no choice but to "get the men off." Abandonment was orderly, and after it was completed a destroyer was detailed to sink the carrier. She fired five torpedoes to send the *Lexington* down at 1956.

The Japanese pilots who returned from the attack reported sinking both American carriers, and Hara was sufficiently sanguine to forward that estimate to his superiors. This comfortable belief undoubtedly influenced both Takagi's decision to detach the damaged *Shokaku* and Inouye's decision to withdraw the entire Striking Force. But even though he imagined both American carriers had been destroyed, Inouye still deemed it necessary to postpone the Port Moresby invasion, apparently because he felt unable to protect the landing force against Allied land-based planes.

Admiral Yamamoto, Commander in Chief Combined Fleet, did not acquiesce in the Japanese retirement. At 2400 he countermanded Inouye's order and directed the Striking Force to advance and annihilate the remaining American forces. Takagi thereupon put about and searched to south and east. But Fletcher was by this time safely out of reach.

## Results

Thus the first carrier battle of the war, the first naval battle in history in which the opposing ships never came within sight of each other, closed with the Japanese holding the field and the Americans in retreat. Tactically the Coral Sea was by a slight margin a victory for the Japanese, for although they lost substantially more planes than the Americans and suffered twice as many casualties, the loss of the 30,000-ton *Lexing-*

*ton* far outweighed the sinking of the 12,000-ton *Shoho,* and the Japanese destroyer and small craft sunk at Tulagi scarcely balanced the loss of the *Neosho* and *Sims.* Strategically however the United States had won. For the first time since war began, Japanese expansion had been checked. The Port Moresby Invasion Force had been obliged to withdraw without reaching its objective.

The battle had other important consequences. The strategic success helped the United States morally by taking some of the sting out of the surrender of Corregidor, which came on May 6, during the battle. More important, the damage to the *Shokaku* and the necessity for reforming the battered air groups of the *Zuikaku* kept those two carriers out of the Battle of Midway, where their presence might well have been decisive.

# 8

# Midway and the Aleutians

On May 5, 1942, Japanese Imperial Headquarters, as we have seen, ordered the Midway operation for some time in June. This strategy bore no relation to the Battle of the Coral Sea, though the *Yorktown* had raided Tulagi the day before the issuing of the order. Nor did the outcome of the carrier battle of May 8 cause any modification of Japanese plans. Although Yamamoto's staff cautiously estimated that there might be two or three American carriers in the Midway area, it seemed more likely that there would be none, for the Japanese believed they had sunk both the *Yorktown* and the *Lexington,* and several days after the battle they sighted Halsey's *Enterprise* and *Hornet* in the South Pacific. The absence of American carriers from the Central Pacific would facilitate the capture of Midway but would partially frustrate the other Japanese objective, the destruction of the remaining United States naval forces.

## Japanese Plans

There was nothing petty in Japanese planning. The entire Combined Fleet, under the personal command of Admiral Yamamoto, was to be employed in a vast operation covering the Northern and Central Pacific. A carrier task force would strike in the Aleutians on June 3, after which occupation forces would land on Adak, Attu, and Kiska. This attack, to take place a day before that on Midway, was intended partially as a diversion. There would hardly be time for American forces actually to be pulled out of position, but the attack would at least confuse the American command.

At dawn on June 4 a second and larger carrier force, coming from the northwest, would bomb Midway Atoll, destroy the planes based there, and soften it up in preparation for the landing. Then on the night of June 5 the occupation forces, approaching from the southwest, would put

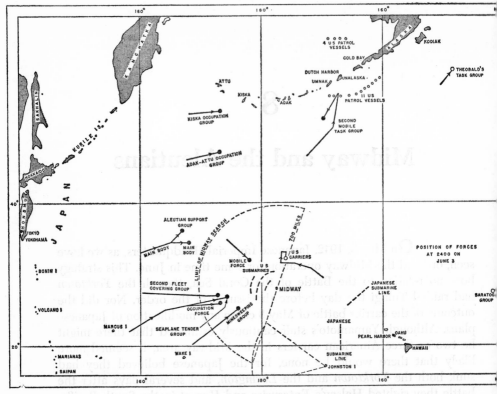

**BATTLE OF MIDWAY, THE APPROACH**

some 5,000 troops ashore to take the island and convert it into a Japanese base.

The Americans, the Japanese believed, lacked the will to fight but would be forced either to defend Midway or to attempt to retake it. When the United States fleet sortied from Pearl Harbor it would cross one or the other of two lines of submarines that the Japanese had placed to the west and north of that base. (See diagram above.) These would inflict some losses on the American fleet and would give Yamamoto ample warning. The Japanese carrier force would then attack the Americans and might well maneuver to get between them and Pearl Harbor. At that point Yamamoto's heavy surface ships of the Main Body, hitherto kept safely back to the northwest, would close in for the kill. The work of December 7 would be completed and the United States fleet destroyed before it could be reinforced by new construction. The Japanese had no immediate plan for the occupation of Pearl Harbor. When the American fleet had been eliminated there would be ample time to think of that.

The fixed pattern of Japanese strategic thinking is evident when this plan is compared with that for the Coral Sea. Again there was a dual objective, again a multiplicity of forces, and again the Japanese were obsessed with the notion of pincer movements and envelopments.

The multiplicity of forces is even more striking when one examines the Japanese organization in detail. Vice Admiral Hosogaya's Northern Area Force, destined for the Aleutians, contained three principal groups besides the command-supply group: Rear Admiral Kakuta's Second Mobile Group consisted of the carriers *Ryujo* and *Junyo*, two heavy cruisers, three destroyers, and an oiler; the Adak-Attu Occupation Group was separate from that destined for Kiska and operated independently.

Vice Admiral Nagumo's carrier force that had raided Pearl Harbor, Darwin, and Ceylon, reappeared in the Midway operation as the Mobile Force. Present were carriers *Akagi*, *Kaga*, *Hiryu*, and *Soryu*, screened by 2 fast battleships, 3 cruisers, and 11 destroyers and accompanied by their own oilers. Conspicuously absent were carriers *Shokaku* and *Zuikaku*, left behind in Japan, the one because of damage and both because of shortage of planes and pilots resulting from the Coral Sea battle.

A little to the south and west of the Mobile Force was the Main Body. It was composed of 7 battleships, including the *Yamato*,* flagship of Admiral Yamamoto, one light aircraft carrier, the *Hosho*, 2 seaplane carriers carrying midget submarines, 3 light cruisers, and 20 destroyers. But even this force was divided. On June 3 the greater part, including 4 battleships and 2 cruisers, turned north to become the "Aleutian Support Group." It was supposed to take a position about halfway between the Aleutian and Midway forces, presumably to be able to give support in either area.

The Midway Occupation Force was commanded by Vice Admiral Nobutake Kondo, who as Commander in Chief of the Second Fleet had participated in the conquest of the Philippines and Indies. It consisted of five groups. Its 12 transports were screened by a cruiser, 10 destroyers, and 3 patrol boats. The Close Support Group of 4 heavy cruisers and 2 destroyers was to cover the transports and support the landing. A powerful Second Fleet Covering Group, which Kondo retained under his direct command, was to assist in the same mission. It comprised 2 battleships, the light carrier *Zuiho*, 4 heavy cruisers, and 7 destroyers.

---

* The *Yamato* and her sister ship the *Musashi*, each 64,000 tons, were the largest battleships ever built. Their main batteries consisted of nine 18.1-inch guns, firing a 3,200-pound projectile, which was almost 50 per cent heavier than a 16-inch projectile. One of the triple-mounted turrets weighed as much as a large destroyer, and the ships' side armor was more than 16 inches thick. A third vessel of the class was laid down at Yokosuka early in 1940, but after the Battle of Midway the hull was converted into aircraft carrier *Shinano*. Construction was abandoned on a fourth unit of the class. The *Yamato* was completed in December 1941 and the *Musashi* eight months later.

A Seaplane Tender Group was intended to set up a base on Kure, to the northwest of Midway. A Minesweeper Group would clear the way for the landings. These forces operated more or less independently. The Second Fleet Group was usually more than 50 miles to the north or northwest of the transports, while the Close Support Group was usually some 75 miles to the northeast.

The Japanese as usual sent an "Advance Expeditionary Force" of submarines to scout ahead of the Combined Fleet. One boat went ahead to scout Midway, while four took positions off the Aleutians and two stationed themselves off Seattle. Most important of the submarine dispositions were two patrol lines designed to cover Pearl Harbor. One line of four submarines lay about 500 miles west of Oahu, while another of seven boats ran athwart the route between Pearl and Midway. These boats were to be on station by June 1.

Why did such a vast armada fail to accomplish its mission? There is no doubt that American intelligence of Japanese plans was a decisive factor. Even with ample warning Nimitz was barely able to get three carriers onto the scene in time. It is difficult to believe that without that warning he either could or would have done so. So one may say that the most obvious reason for the miscarriage of the plans of the Japanese was their failure to achieve the surprise on which they counted.

Surprise is extremely important in naval and military operations and ought to be exploited whenever possible. Very often the weaker force has no alternative to reliance on surprise to achieve its ends. But the Japanese made the mistake of planning a major operation so that it depended on surprise when there was no necessity for their doing so. Even with the most complete warning, it is inconceivable that the three United States carriers could by any combination of luck and skill have defeated and turned back the 8 carriers, 11 battleships, and immense number of supporting vessels which the Japanese committed to this action *had the Japanese fleet been concentrated.* As it was, June 3, the day of the attack on Dutch Harbor and of the first contact in the Midway area, found the Japanese surface ships in no fewer than ten groups scattered all over the North and Central Pacific. (See chart page 222.)

Concentration does not require the massing of forces in a single group. In what, then, did the Japanese fail? First of all, they failed to pursue a single objective. The two carriers sent to the Aleutians might well have supplied the decisive margin in the Central Pacific. Had the Midway operation succeeded, the Japanese could have taken the Aleutians at their leisure. Without success at Midway the Aleutian operation lost its meaning.

In the Midway area itself the Japanese had some of the elements of concentration. Their forces were grouped concentrically about Midway, which they assumed was the strategic center. They had a unified command under Yamamoto, who could bring about coordinated action. But when the crisis developed Yamamoto found that his forces were too widely separated for mutual support. He found after a vain attempt that he could not bring the scattered groups together in time to retrieve the situation.

Fault may also be found with the more detailed arrangements of the Japanese. The carriers of the Mobile Force were inadequately screened. The vessels scattered elsewhere might profitably have been used to give them better protection. The Main Body after the departure of the Northern Support Group was for all its surface strength an ill-balanced, useless force. The Occupation Force, which approached Midway from the southwest under clear skies, was dangerously exposed. It did not have adequate air protection and might well have become a principal target for American forces. Bringing the Occupation Force forward before the United States fleet had been accounted for bespeaks the callousness of the Japanese command, which was more careful of its battleships than of its transports.

One of the most serious mistakes of the Japanese was in their handling of their submarines. On the assumption that the Americans were not likely to sortie from Pearl before the attack on Midway, Japanese submarines did not take station until June 1. By that date the American carriers had actually crossed their patrol line between Pearl Harbor and Midway, the *Hornet* and *Enterprise* on May 29, the *Yorktown* on the night of May 31. Had the Japanese submarines been on station in time, there would have been no surprise at Midway and again the result might have been quite different.

## United States Preparations

Since the United States was intercepting and reading Japanese coded messages, American intelligence of the enemy's plans was remarkably complete. Nimitz' information indicated the Japanese objectives, the approximate composition of the enemy forces, the direction of approach, and the approximate date of attack. It was this knowledge that made the American victory possible, but in view of the meager forces available to meet the threat it must have seemed to the United States command very much like foreknowledge of an inevitable disaster.

The first decision confronting Nimitz was whether to let the Aleutians go by default or to reinforce them at the expense of the Central Pacific. He chose the latter course and sent to the Aleutians a force of 5 cruisers, 14 destroyers, and 6 submarines. These were under Rear Admiral Robert A. Theobald, who was also to command land-based air.

As for the Central Pacific, Midway itself was too small to support sufficient forces to repel an attack of the proportions of that impending.

Lying at the northwest end of the Hawaiian chain about 1,100 miles from Pearl Harbor, the little atoll consists of two islands surrounded by a reef. Sand Island, the larger of the two, is only about two miles long, while Eastern Island, on which the runways were situated, is little more than half as large. However, everything possible was done to strengthen Midway's defenses. The beaches and surrounding waters were mined. The marine garrison was reinforced and given additional antiaircraft guns. Finally, air strength was increased to the limit of the island's facilities. For search there were some 30 PBY's. There was between Midway and Oahu a constant interchange of B-17's that left 17 on Midway on June 3. The marine squadrons were equipped with planes cast off by the carriers, which had acquired more modern equipment. For defense they had 26 fighters operational on the day of the attack, mostly old Brewster Buffaloes. For attack there were 34 scout bombers, divided between Douglas Dauntlesses and Vought-Sikorsky Vindicators. Most of the pilots for these planes had been rushed out from flight school and had not yet practiced dive bombing. There were four Army B-26's, jury-rigged for a torpedo attack for which they were unsuited. The only really effective planes on the island were six TBF's, the first to reach the Pacific. This motley collection of planes was the best an unprepared country could provide for defense of a vital point.

The marines would undoubtedly have given the Japanese a warm reception had they come in for a landing, but it was clear that the fate of Midway depended ultimately on naval support. What could Nimitz assemble for the purpose? The *Lexington* had of course been sunk in the Coral Sea. The *Saratoga's* repairs had been completed and she was training on the West Coast, but there was delay in forming an escort for her, so that she left San Diego only on June 1 and did not reach Pearl till June 6, too late for the battle. The *Hornet-Enterprise* force had been hurriedly recalled from the South Pacific and arrived at Pearl Harbor on May 26. There illness compelled Halsey to relinquish command, and his place was taken by Rear Admiral Raymond A. Spruance, who had commanded the cruisers of the task force. Thoughtful, cautious, and modest, Spruance was in personality a striking contrast to the impetuous, colorful Halsey. But his unassuming manner concealed a brilliant mind and sound judgment, as the battle was to prove. The two carriers with a screen of five heavy cruisers, one light cruiser, and nine destroyers put to sea on May 28.

Fletcher's damaged *Yorktown* had also come back posthaste from the South Pacific. Repairs which would ordinarily have taken three months were compressed into three days, so that on the morning of May 30 she was able to put to sea with a screen of two heavy cruisers and five destroyers. The two carrier forces met northeast of Midway on June 2, and Fletcher, as senior, assumed local tactical command.

These three carriers and their escorts were all that could be assembled. The United States had some old battleships on the West Coast, but they were too slow to accompany the carriers, there were no destroyers available to screen them, and they scarcely fitted the "attrition tactics" Nimitz had decided to employ.

To backstop the carriers 19 submarines were assigned positions to cover the approaches to Midway. The *Cuttlefish* was stationed 700 miles west of Midway, where it was thought the Japanese might rendezvous. Three boats patrolled 200 miles to the west of the atoll. Six more 150 miles from the island patrolled an arc stretching from southwest to north, while two more were only 50 miles northwest of Midway. Others were stationed to support the carriers and to cover Oahu. Nimitz retained at Pearl Harbor the over-all command so that he could if necessary coordinate the movements of the submarines, the carriers, and the Midway planes.

The task that faced Fletcher and Spruance was appalling. Nimitz' instructions were: "You will be governed by the principle of calculated risk, which you shall interpret to mean the avoidance of exposure of your force to attack by superior enemy forces without good prospect of inflicting, as a result of such exposure, greater damage on the enemy." To fight cautiously, to meet a superior enemy force without unduly exposing one's own is difficult in the highest degree. That Fletcher and Spruance were able to carry out these orders successfully was due primarily to their skillful exploitation of intelligence, which enabled them to turn the element of surprise against the Japanese. The American command perceived that air power was the key to the situation and correctly concentrated on the Japanese carriers. The position northeast of Midway was well chosen, since it placed the United States carriers on the flank of the Mobile Force, which the Japanese were unable to succor in time because of the wide dispersion of their forces.

## The Attack on the Aleutians

Admiral Theobald, like a good many other officers, suspected that the information on which American intelligence estimates were based had been "planted" by the Japanese. He was particularly concerned that the threat of an attack on the western Aleutians might be designed to draw him away from the more important Dutch Harbor-Cold Bay area; hence he decided to concentrate his forces for the defense of the latter. Inasmuch as his surface vessels were completely dependent for air cover on land or harbor-based planes, the most westerly base for which was the secret field at Otter Point on Umnak, he could scarcely have done otherwise, but this decision meant that his task force was destined never to make contact with the enemy.

Theobald directed his main force of 5 cruisers and 4 destroyers to rendezvous 400 miles south of Kodiak. The last ships did not arrive till the morning of June 3, a few hours after the Japanese had struck Dutch Harbor. At Makushin Bay, Unalaska, he stationed a striking force of 9 destroyers to break up any landing the Japanese might attempt in the Dutch Harbor area.

Since the surface vessels could be used only if a favorable opportunity arose, the primary burden of defense fell upon the planes, and they were all too few. The Navy had 20 PBY's for search. The Army had about 65 pursuit planes, but little more than half of these were at Cold Bay and Umnak, where they were needed. The principal striking power lay in the 20 army bombers, chiefly B-26's, based at Kodiak, Cold Bay, and Umnak.

To provide early warning of the Japanese approach Theobald stationed his 6 submarines in likely positions for interceptions and placed 20 small vessels at a radius of 200 miles from Dutch Harbor, both to the south and in the Bering Sea. PBY's patrolled all the approaches, but their search was limited to 400 miles because of the scarcity of radar-equipped planes.

Somehow Kakuta's two carriers, approaching from the south-southwest, eluded submarines, picket boats, and planes. Although it was only an hour after midnight of June 2–3, there was already a foggy half-light in Alaskan latitudes when the Japanese admiral launched 36 planes from a position about 165 miles south of Dutch Harbor. But the bad weather that had enabled him to escape detection now favored the Americans. The *Junyo's* planes wandered in the fog and returned to the carrier without finding the target. The *Ryujo's* group, emerging into locally clear weather over Dutch Harbor, scored almost complete surprise however and were able to inflict considerable damage with the loss of only two of their number.

On their return the Japanese sighted five destroyers of Theobald's force in Makushin Bay. Kakuta at once launched another strike at these targets, but worsening weather prevented the group from joining up. American P-40's from Otter Point shot down two, and none reached Makushin Bay.

After the attack on Dutch Harbor, American patrol planes made strenuous efforts to discover the Japanese carrier force, but without success. Their failure was in part due to a belief that the attack had come from the Bering Sea, in part to the fact that Kakuta had retired to the southwest after his attempted strike on Makushin Bay. His orders were to attack Adak, but unfavorable weather in that direction forced him to abandon the project and return for a second attack on Dutch Harbor.

Kakuta had already started toward Dutch Harbor when at 0450 on the 4th a PBY reported his position. Thereafter American aircraft maintained intermittent contact and subsequently made a series of sporadic attacks, but none of the planes—PBY's rigged with torpedoes, B-26's, and B-17's—were really suited for operating against ships. Although the pilots attacked with great gallantry, they achieved nothing better than a few near misses at the cost of three planes, one of each type.

Before the American attacks began, Kakuta had launched a striking group, which arrived over Dutch Harbor at about 1600. During the next half hour it bombed and set fire to the new fuel oil tanks with some 22,000 barrels of fuel, the old station ship *Northwestern,* which had to be beached, a warehouse, and an empty aircraft hangar. Afterward the *Junyo's* planes, making rendezvous over the western end of Unalaska, discovered the Army's secret airfield at Otter Point when American pursuit planes rose to shoot down four of them.

Meanwhile there were indications that the Japanese operations around Midway were going less well than in the Aleutians. Soon after launching his strike, Kakuta had received from Yamamoto the order to join the Mobile Force immediately, and at about the same time he was informed that the occupation of Midway and the Aleutians had been postponed. Kakuta waited till he recovered his planes more than two hours later before setting course to the south to join Nagumo. By that time Yamamoto, at the urging of his staff, had changed his mind about the Aleutian landings and authorized the occupation forces to proceed according to plan. However, Hosogaya, Commander of the Northern Force, made one modification. He canceled the landing on Adak. Apparently he considered it too risky to land only 350 miles from the newly discovered American airfield at Otter Point.

Soon after noon on June 6, about 1,250 men of a Special Naval Landing Force went ashore on Kiska, where they took prisoner the personnel of a small United States weather station. In the early hours of the following morning 1,200 Japanese troops landed on Attu, "capturing" 39 Aleuts and an American missionary and his wife. It was not till June 10 that American patrol planes discovered the Japanese on the two islands.

## Midway Area—First Contacts, June 3

The PBY's based on Midway departed before dawn each morning to search the western sector to 700 miles. That distance was calculated to prevent any force which might be just out of range from reaching a launching position before the next day's search. During the last days of May and the first days of June coverage was excellent except in the critical area beyond 350 miles to the northwest, where the weather was bad.

The first contact of the battle was made on the morning of June 3 when a patrol plane reported "six large ships in column" about 700 miles to the southwest. American commanders both on Midway and in the carriers surmised correctly that this was part of the Japanese Occupation Force. Since the main attack was expected from the northwest, the American carriers kept their position some 300 miles north-northeast of Midway, and the island forces for a while held their attack. Finally, a little after noon, when no new contacts had been made, nine B-17's with bomb-bay fuel tanks took off from Midway. Their attack, delivered about 1630, was ineffective. First blood of the battle was to be drawn by four radar-equipped PBY's which took off that night with torpedoes and hit and slightly damaged a Japanese oiler. Before these planes returned, Midway was under attack.

## The Attack on Midway, June 4

As the American commanders expected, the Japanese carriers were approaching from the northwest under cover of the weather front. At 0430 on the 4th, half an hour before sunrise, at a distance of 240 miles from Midway, Nagumo sent off an attack group of 108 aircraft, made up of equal numbers of fighters, bombers, and torpedo planes. Weather was clear with scattered clouds and good visibility, and a southeast wind permitted him to hold his course while launching.

At Midway in the meantime patrol planes had as usual taken off at 0415, followed by the B-17's, which were put into the air to prevent their being surprised on the ground. At 0545 a PBY pilot reported in plain English, "Many planes heading Midway, bearing 320, distance 150." Five minutes later the Midway radar picked up the approaching planes at a distance of 93 miles. But where were the Japanese carriers? The answer for which American commanders both on Midway and in the carriers were waiting came just two minutes later when a PBY pilot reported two carriers and their escorts, bearing 320° from Midway, distance 180 miles. This report placed the Japanese about 40 miles southeast of their true position, an error which was to cause difficulty for the American carrier planes. The B-17's, then in the air, were at once directed to the enemy carriers, while the marine attack planes, the

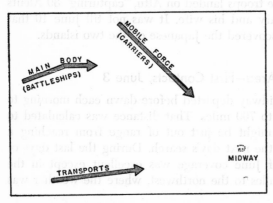

JAPANESE APPROACH TO MIDWAY, JUNE 3

four B-26's, and the six TBF's, already warmed up and manned, took off to attack the same targets.

By this time the Japanese planes were approaching Midway. The marine fighters met them 30 miles out. "Each pilot made only one or two passes at the bombers and then spent the remainder of the time trying to shake from one to five Jap fighters off his tail," for the Zeke easily outperformed the American fighters.* Midway antiaircraft opened up as the Japanese formation came within range. The first bomb fell at 0630. Within the next half hour almost everything above ground was damaged; the power house was hit, the fuel tanks set afire, a hangar destroyed. Only the runways escaped injury. When it was all over, the marine fighters were told to land. "Pitifully few" responded. Of the 26 planes, 16 were missing, and only two of the survivors were fit for further combat. Only half a dozen of the Japanese planes failed to return to their carriers.

## Midway Strikes Back, June 4

Midway's attack on the Japanese carriers was executed with high courage, but it was piecemeal, uncoordinated, and ineffective. It did however serve a useful purpose, for it distracted the Japanese at a critical moment, prevented their launching, and thus helped make possible the success of the American carriers.

The B-26's and TBF's attacked at low altitude separately but simultaneously just after 0700. The Japanese ships made smoke, maneuvered radically, and threw up a heavy antiaircraft fire, while Zekes intercepted. The American planes scored no hits. Five of the six TBF's and two of the four B-26's were shot down, while the three planes that returned were too badly damaged for further use.

Almost an hour later Major Lofton R. Henderson's marine scout bombing squadron attacked the enemy force. Since the pilots were fresh from flight school, untrained in dive bombing, they were forced to make a more dangerous glide bombing attack. They scored no hits on their target, the carrier *Hiryu*, and only eight of the 16 planes returned to Midway. Six of these were badly shot up.

About 15 minutes later fifteen B-17's arrived. Bombing from 20,000 feet, the Fortresses suffered no casualties and inflicted none. They were just departing when the second marine group arrived. Making a high speed approach at low level, the marines encountered such heavy antiaircraft and fighter opposition that they were unable to reach a carrier

---

* The famous Japanese fighter was called Zero until 1943. Thereafter Zeros with rounded wingtips were called Zekes and those with square wingtips were called Haps. Zeke however was the general term applied to all Zeros after 1943.

but dropped at a battleship instead. Again they scored no hits, and two planes made water landings before reaching Midway.

The first round of the Battle of Midway had clearly gone to the Japanese. They had pretty thoroughly smashed Midway. The island had sacrificed half its planes without damaging any enemy vessels in return. As Nimitz observed, "Most of Midway's fighters, torpedo planes, and dive bombers—the only types capable of making a high percentage of hits on ships—were gone." It was at this point that the United States carriers entered the battle.

### The United States Carriers Intervene

When the Midway scout first reported the Japanese carriers at 0552 the American striking force was approximately 200 miles E by N of the Mobile Force. Fletcher immediately sent the *Hornet* and *Enterprise* toward the contact with orders to "attack enemy carriers when definitely located," while the *Yorktown* continued on an easterly course in order to land the planes of her morning search.

Spruance in the *Enterprise* decided to close the range for an hour before launching in order to bring the enemy more safely within the 175-mile combat radius of his torpedo planes. It was well he did so, for the distance was actually 25 miles greater than the report indicated. Finally, about 0700, when he estimated that he was 150 miles from the enemy and when there seemed a good chance of catching the Japanese refueling the planes which had struck Midway, he ordered launching.

In preparation for action the two carriers had separated, dividing the screening vessels between them. This was to avoid the error of the Coral Sea, where the *Lexington* and *Yorktown* had drawn apart under attack and had split the screening formation. The *Enterprise* put into the air 33 dive bombers, 14 torpedo planes, and 10 fighters. The *Hornet* group consisted of 35 bombers, 15 torpedo planes, and 10 fighters. To expedite the attack Spruance ordered the *Enterprise* bombers to proceed before the torpedo squadron was fully launched, and the *Hornet* bombers and torpedo planes, flying at different altitudes, became separated. Thus the attack force soon after its departure at approximately 0800 fell into four separate groups.

The *Yorktown* meanwhile had completed recovery of her search planes at about 0630 and turned to follow the *Enterprise* and *Hornet*. Because Fletcher had expected four or five carriers in the enemy force and only two had thus far been reported he hesitated to commit the *Yorktown*'s air group until the other enemy carriers had been accounted for. Finally, a little after 0830, in the absence of any further reports, he decided to launch half the *Yorktown*'s planes. In the next half hour the

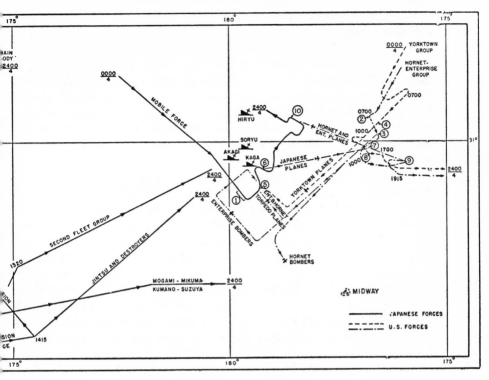

## BATTLE OF MIDWAY, JUNE 4

1. 0705-0830: Midway planes and Nautilus attack Japanese carriers.
2. 0705: Enterprise and Hornet begin launching attack groups.
3. 0806: Enterprise and Hornet planes depart.
4. 0838: Yorktown begins launching.
5. 0920-1025: U. S. carrier planes attack Japanese carriers.

6. 1115: Hiryu attack group departs.
7. 1208: Japanese dive bombers attack Yorktown.
8. 1500: Yorktown abandoned.
9. 1530-1615: Enterprise and Hornet launch attack group.
10. 1701: Hiryu bombed.

carrier launched 17 dive bombers, 12 torpedo planes, and 6 fighters. Then, still concerned about the two or three enemy carriers that had not yet been sighted, Fletcher launched a search to the north and west a little after 1100.

Nagumo had up to this time been acting with admirable caution. Although his intelligence led him to expect no naval opposition, he had sent only about half his available planes against Midway and had kept the rest on deck, armed with torpedoes, ready for action should any American vessels appear. Then, after his planes had departed for Midway, he had ordered his cruisers to catapult seven planes for a search to the east and south. These had departed at intervals through the next half hour, with the *Tone*'s plane last to take to the air.

At 0700 Nagumo's strike commander, then returning from Midway, reported that another strike at the island was necessary. Midway's torpedo attack, which came in almost immediately afterward, seemed to emphasize the point. By that time Nagumo's cruiser search planes had been gone for from 2 to 2½ hours and should have reached a radius of at least 200 miles. It seemed safe now to relax his precautions. At any rate, the planes from the Midway strike would soon be landing and would require servicing.

Therefore at 0715 Nagumo issued the fateful order, "Planes in second wave stand by to carry out attack today. Re-equip yourselves with bombs." It was just 13 minutes later that the *Tone*'s scout reported ten American ships about 200 miles to the northeast. It is easy to imagine how different the Battle of Midway might have been had the *Tone*'s plane been launched promptly so that this report might have come in half an hour earlier. Surface vessels 200 miles away did not constitute an urgent problem, but at 0745 Nagumo sent his carriers the order, "Prepare to carry out attacks on enemy fleet units. Leave torpedoes on the attack planes which have not yet changed to bombs." It was not till 0820 that the *Tone* scout reported that one of the American ships appeared to be a carrier.

Nagumo was undoubtedly aware of the desirability of striking first, even though a single United States carrier against his four did not seem particularly dangerous. But he could not launch immediately because of the necessity of re-arming his planes. Moreover he was under attack by Midway planes from 0705 to 0830, taking evasive action which would have interfered with launching. Another distraction was provided by submarine *Nautilus,* which had intercepted the Midway scout's first report of the Japanese carriers and had headed toward them. Between attacks by Midway planes she stuck up her periscope in the midst of the Mobile Force and fired two torpedoes to set off a grand confusion of circling destroyers and exploding depth charges. This turmoil had scarcely subsided before Nagumo had to recover the planes of his Midway strike, which began to arrive about 0830. After the last of these had been taken aboard at 0918, he withdrew to the north to reorganize his force while he struck them below and brought up fresh planes for an attack on the American naval vessels. By that time it was too late, for the United States carrier planes were upon him.

The *Enterprise-Hornet* planes had broken into four groups, while the *Yorktown*'s made a fifth, so that whatever coordination was achieved in the ensuing attack was entirely accidental. The *Enterprise* fighters, which were supposed to protect their carrier's torpedo squadron, had by mistake joined the *Hornet's* instead. Climbing to 20,000 feet en route, these fighters were above the Japanese force when both the *Hornet* and the *Enterprise* torpedo planes made their ill-starred attacks; but, not receiving the pre-arranged signal for help, they circled until their fuel ran low, then returned to the carrier without having engaged in the battle.

Because of the scout's error in reporting the Japanese position, aggravated by Nagumo's change of course to the north, the Mobile Force was not where the American pilots expected to find it. The *Hornet's* dive bombers, flying at high altitude, failed to sight the Japanese and continued on to the southwest. However, "Torpedo 8," beneath the clouds, sighted the enemy carriers to the northwest at 0920 and immediately began its approach. Japanese fighters, which had been brought down to lower levels to counter the attacks by Midway planes, met them well out, and the veteran Japanese pilots easily overwhelmed the slow and clumsy torpedo planes. All 15 were shot down before they were able to drop their torpedoes. Only one pilot survived. He escaped strafing or capture by hiding under a floating seat cushion till dark. The *Hornet's* dive bombers continued to the southwest until their fuel ran low. Then 21 returned to the carrier, while the remaining 14 headed for Midway, where three crashed. All the accompanying fighters, which had shorter ranges, landed in the sea when their fuel was exhausted.

The *Enterprise* torpedo squadron arrived 10 or 15 minutes after the *Hornet's.* Like Torpedo 8, it was without fighter protection, and it fared little better. The squadron split in an attempt to make an attack on both bows of the Japanese carriers, but the carriers turned to keep the planes on their quarter and to prolong their approach. Zekes swarmed over them and shot down ten of the 14. Again there were no hits. But the sacrifice of the torpedo squadrons was not in vain, for their attacks drew the Zekes down to low altitudes, and in their preoccupation with the torpedo planes the Japanese forgot to look up.

The *Enterprise* dive bombers, like the *Hornet's,* failed to find the enemy in the position expected, but Lieutenant Commander Clarence McClusky, Jr., the Air Group Commander, making "one of the most important decisions of the battle," turned north to fly the first leg of an expanding square. A little after 1000, setting his course by a straggling Japanese destroyer, he was rewarded by a view of the Mobile Force. The four carriers were in a sort of diamond formation with the *Hiryu* somewhat off to the north. McClusky divided his attack between the two carriers in the southwest portion of the formation, which happened to be the *Akagi* and *Kaga.* Just as Spruance had hoped, their decks were covered with planes which they had been refueling and which they were now endeavoring to launch. Into the midst of these the American pilots dropped their bombs. There was no fighter

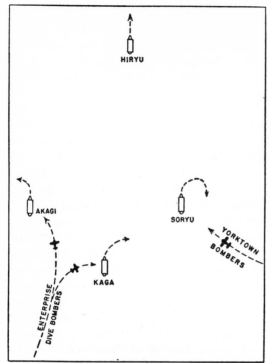

DISPOSITION OF JAPANESE CARRIERS AT
TIME OF BOMBING ATTACK BY ENTERPRISE
AND YORKTOWN PLANES, 1020, JUNE 4

opposition until after they pulled out of their dives. By that time both carriers were burning. Off to the east the *Soryu* was also on fire, for the *Yorktown* planes had made a simultaneous attack.

The *Yorktown* air group had been launched more than an hour later than those of the *Enterprise* and *Hornet*, but rapidly clearing weather aided it both in joining up en route and in finding the enemy. Consequently its attack, without either group's being aware of it, coincided with that of the *Enterprise* dive bombers. Coming in from the east, the *Yorktown* planes concentrated on the nearest carrier, which was the *Soryu*. The torpedo squadron was slightly ahead. Despite the efforts of the six accompanying fighters, only five of the dozen planes survived to reach a dropping point, and only two returned to the carrier. They scored no hits. But the bombers, diving in from the sun, encountered no fighter and little antiaircraft opposition. By the time the first 13 had completed their dives the *Soryu* was so completely aflame that the four remaining planes turned to other targets.

It was indeed fortunate for the Americans that they had caught the Japanese carriers refueling their planes, for the few hits they made would scarcely have been fatal had the Japanese been in a less vulnerable condition.

## Attacks on the *Yorktown,* June 4

Three of the four Japanese carriers had been put out of action, but the fourth, the *Hiryu,* standing off to the north, had escaped unscathed. A little after 1000 she started launching an attack group of 18 bombers and six fighters, followed an hour later by ten torpedo planes and six fighters. That seemed adequate to take care of the one American carrier which had thus far been reported to the Japanese command. In the meantime Nagumo had with difficulty been persuaded to transfer from the flaming *Akagi* to a cruiser, while Kondo was bringing his powerful Second Fleet Group from the transports, which did not seem to be threatened, to reinforce the screen of the Mobile Force.

The *Yorktown* had just completed launching her search planes and was refueling fighters of her combat air patrol and preparing to recover her striking group when about noon her radar picked up the *Hiryu's* planes at a distance of less than 50 miles. Refueling was hastily abandoned, planes on the flight deck were quickly launched with orders to clear the area, and returning bombers were waved away. The carrier's screen was in the standard circular disposition with a cruiser on either bow as the attack came in.

The combat air patrols of the *Enterprise* and *Hornet* had joined that of the *Yorktown* to make a total of 28 fighters. So effective was their interception that the Japanese attackers were split into small groups, and only about eight bombers succeeded in reaching the *Yorktown*. These scored three hits. One bomb holed the flight deck, while another exploded on the fourth deck and forced flooding of the magazines in the vicinity. A third hit ruptured the uptakes, disabled two boilers, and extinguished the fires in all but one.

Repairs did not take long. Fires were quickly brought under control, the hole in the flight deck was covered, and boilers were relighted. The carrier was steaming at 20 knots and again refueling fighters when at about 1430 her radar picked up the *Hiryu's* torpedo group only 40 miles away. Once more refueling was suspended and the combat air patrol vectored out, but the *Yorktown* was still launching fighters when the attack developed.

The American fighters shot down a few of the Japanese before they came within range of the ships' guns. The *Yorktown's* screen, which after the first attack had been reinforced by two cruisers and two destroyers from Spruance's force, threw up a formidable barrage, but a few planes succeeded in penetrating it. The carrier avoided two torpedoes by maneuvering, but two more caught her amidships on the port side. Three fire rooms were flooded, and white smoke issued from her stacks as she slowed to a stop with a heavy list to port.

There was no power for shifting fuel or for counter-flooding, and as the list increased to 26 degrees there seemed to be imminent danger of the ship's capsizing. So at 1500 her captain ordered Abandon Ship, and destroyers took off the crew. That evening the screening vessels departed, leaving only the destroyer *Hughes* standing by to sink the carrier, if necessary to prevent her capture.

## Elimination of the *Hiryu*

Just as the attack on the *Yorktown* was drawing to a close, one of her scouts launched three hours earlier reported the *Hiryu* force approximately a hundred miles WNW. Spruance thereupon ordered a strike, and the *Enterprise* at once began launching an attack group of 24 bombers, of which ten were *Yorktown* refugees, while the *Hornet* launched 16. Both groups departed about 1600. There was no fighter escort, because Spruance felt that all fighters were needed for protection of the carriers.

The *Enterprise* group sighted the *Hiryu* at 1700. Off to the south three columns of smoke marked the other three Japanese carriers. There were a few Zekes in the air, and they shot down three of the bombers, but the others succeeded in planting four hits on the carrier. By the time the *Hornet* planes arrived half an hour later, the *Hiryu* was burning so fiercely that she was no longer a profitable target; so they attacked the escorting vessels instead.

Spruance meanwhile had reported the attack on the *Hiryu* to Fletcher, who had transferred from the *Yorktown* to heavy cruiser *Astoria*. He added: "Have you any instructions for further operations?" "Negative," replied Fletcher. "Will conform to your movements." He thus transferred the tactical command of both forces to Spruance. This was a wise decision, for carrier operations can best be controlled from a carrier, where the admiral can immediately question his returning aviators. Spruance, with an experienced staff and with his flagship *Enterprise* undamaged, was fully prepared to take control.

On the bridge of the Japanese flagship *Yamato* news of the disabling of the *Akagi, Kaga,* and *Soryu* had caused consternation, but Yamamoto saw no reason to abandon his plans, for he believed that the attack had been made at least in part by land-based planes. He still supposed that there was only one American carrier present, and the *Hiryu* was dealing with that. Consequently he decided to proceed with the occupation of Midway, with only a few changes in the disposition of his fleet. Kondo's Second Fleet, which was already on the way, would reinforce the Mobile Force. Midway transports were to retire to the northwest till the situation became clearer. The Aleutian Support Group was to rejoin the Main Body.

It was not till 1300 that Yamamoto learned that the American force contained three carriers. He had just received a report that the *Hiryu*'s planes had left one of these burning, but that still left two against the single *Hiryu*. It was on the receipt of this news that Yamamoto temporarily canceled both the Midway and Aleutian landings and recalled Kakuta's Second Mobile Force from Alaskan waters. With his forces united he would have three fleet carriers to deal with the two remaining American carriers.

The *Hiryu* was meanwhile preparing to get off an evening strike with all her remaining planes—five bombers, five torpedo planes, and ten fighters. She had turned into the wind and was just commencing to launch when the *Enterprise* bombers attacked at 1701. Half an hour later Yamamoto learned that his fourth carrier was burning.

By this time there was little hope of saving any of the other three. The American submarine *Nautilus*, which had doggedly trailed the Mobile Force most of the day, at about 1030 sighted on the horizon three columns of smoke from the burning carriers. In the early afternoon she closed the *Kaga* and fired three torpedoes. Two missed and the third was a dud. But the *Kaga* was doomed nevertheless; she went down at 1925 as a result of internal explosions. The *Soryu* sank about the same time. The *Akagi* and *Hiryu* remained afloat till next morning, when Japanese destroyers sank the burning hulks with torpedoes.

## Midway, Night of June 4

The *Yorktown* had been abandoned, and all the American air groups had suffered severely. The torpedo squadrons had been wiped out, and losses of both bombers and fighters had been heavy. Yet there were no enemy planes left to dispute the control of the air, and with it the control of the sea, now exercised by the weary aviators of the *Enterprise* and *Hornet*. The action of June 4 had decided the Battle of Midway. But this was not immediately evident to most of the principals of the action, and indeed, had Spruance shown a little less judgment the battle might yet have moved on to a new climax and to another dramatic reversal of fortune.

On Midway itself the defenders awaited developments with considerable apprehension through the afternoon and evening of the 4th. They had received no clear reports of the success of the American carriers and knew only that the Midway planes had been so badly shot up that it was doubtful that they had inflicted any significant damage. Through the afternoon B-17's were dispatched, in small groups as they became available, to attack elements of the Mobile Force, but they scored no hits. On the report of a burning carrier 200 miles to the northwest, the eleven surviving marine dive bombers took off about 1900. They encountered rain squalls and failed to find the target. Eleven PT boats that left about the same time on a similar mission had the same experience. Meanwhile refueling of planes by hand and preparations for repelling a landing continued through the night. When a Japanese submarine shelled Mid-way about 0130 it looked as if zero hour might be drawing close.

## Yamamoto Tries to Retrieve the Battle

Aboard the Japanese flagship Yamamoto clung doggedly to his plans of conquest. At 1915 he sent a message to his commanders: "1. The enemy fleet, which has practically been destroyed, is retiring to the east. 2. Combined Fleet units in the vicinity are preparing to pursue the remnants and at the same time occupy Midway. . . . The Mobile Force, Second Fleet, and Submarine Force will immediately contact and attack the enemy." Yamamoto may have been confused as to the real situation, or he may have been whistling in the dark to sustain Japanese courage, but it was evident that he was determined to carry on the fight. An hour later he ordered the submarine *I-168* to shell Midway till 0200, when it would be relieved by a cruiser division from the Occupation Force.

Nagumo did not share his chief's offensive frame of mind. While things had been going well he had shown high competence, but since the bombing of his flagship he had revealed signs of shock and failing judgment. Now at 2130 he reported to Yamamoto: "The total strength of the enemy is 5 carriers, 6 cruisers, and 15 destroyers. These are steaming westward. . . . We are offering protection to the *Hiryu* and are retiring to the northwest at 18 knots. . . ." Obviously Nagumo intended to continue his retreat. After a second communication in the same vein Yamamoto replied with the order: "Commander in Chief Second Fleet Kondo will take command of the Mobile Force excepting the *Hiryu, Akagi,* and the ships escorting them." Kondo, who had shown both good judgment and initiative in the crisis, was even then well on his way toward joining the remnant of the Mobile Force. He at once sent out orders for concentrating his force for a night surface action. For this he would have 4 battleships, 9 cruisers, and 19 destroyers.

But this engagement, by which Yamamoto might yet have restored his situation, was not destined to take place. Spruance, now in tactical command of the American naval forces, had decided to set course to the east for the night. As he subsequently explained, "I did not feel justified in risking a night encounter with possibly superior enemy forces, but on the other hand, I did not want to be too far away from Midway in the morning. I wished to have a position from which either to follow up retreating enemy forces or to break up a landing attack on Midway. At this time the possibility of the enemy having a fifth CV somewhere in the area, possibly with his occupation force or else to the northwestward, still existed."

By midnight Yamamoto had to face the facts. There were at least two American carriers still operational. They were retiring to the east, so that there was very little likelihood of their being forced into a surface action. Rather, his own vessels, if they persisted on their present courses, would almost certainly be caught by air strikes at dawn. Consequently at 0015 Yamamoto ordered Kondo's striking force, which had not yet united, to rendezvous with the Main Body. At 0255 he reluctantly canceled the Midway operation and ordered a general withdrawal to the west.

## Pursuit on June 5

So it was that the submarine's shelling of Midway was the Japanese swan song and not the prelude to invasion. But an incident of the early morning of June 5 delayed American recognition of the fact and contributed to making the 5th a day of fruitless pursuit, a blank day in the midst of the battle.

Spruance had not believed that the enemy would attempt a landing after losing his four carriers, but the possibility could not be disregarded. At 0215 the submarine *Tambor* reported "many unidentified ships" about 90 miles west of Midway. "This looked like a landing," as Spruance reported, "so we took a course somewhat to the north of Midway at 25 knots." Back at Pearl Harbor Rear Admiral Robert H. English, Commander Submarines Pacific Fleet, came to the same conclusion and pulled his boats in to a five-mile radius from Midway. Thus American forces were moving in the wrong direction for pursuit.

The *Tambor*'s "unidentified ships" were four cruisers and two destroyers which had been ordered to relieve the *I-168* in shelling Midway. Not long after the *Tambor*'s report they received Yamamoto's retirement order and put about. It was after this turn that a Japanese lookout sighted the *Tambor*. In maneuvering to avoid the submarine the heavy cruisers *Mogami* and *Mikuma* collided. The *Mogami*'s bow was damaged, and one of the *Mikuma*'s fuel tanks was ruptured so that she streamed oil. Before dawn the cruisers *Kumano* and *Suzuya* retired to the northwest, leaving the slower, damaged vessels escorted by two destroyers on a westerly course.

Not till dawn could the American commanders be certain that the Japanese were in retreat. About 0600 the *Tambor* identified the vessels she was trailing as two *Mogami*-class cruisers and reported their westerly course. Between 0630 and 0800 Midway planes reported the few Japanese vessels within range, all on retirement courses. Besides the two damaged cruisers, mis-identified as "battleships" and now 125 miles to the west, they found the *Kumano* and *Suzuya* 175 miles to the northwest, and finally several ships to the northwest, including a burning carrier about 250 miles distant. This was the *Hiryu*, which sank shortly afterward, momentarily in the company of elements of Kondo's striking force, now hurrying to join Yamamoto to the west.

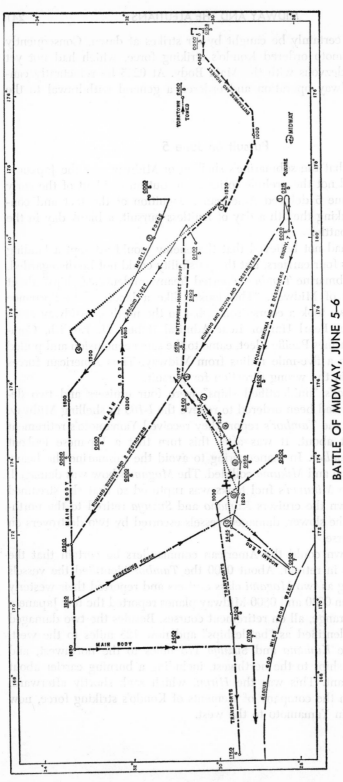

## BATTLE OF MIDWAY, JUNE 5-6

### JUNE 5

1. 0215: Tambor sights Crudiv. 7; Mogami and Mikuma collide.
2. 0719: Midway patrol planes report burning carrier (Hiryu), two battleships, cruisers and destroyers in this position.
3. 1500-1530: Enterprise and Hornet launch search-attack groups.
4. 1830: Enterprise-Hornet groups attack destroyer Tanikaze.

### JUNE 6

5. 0757: Hornet launches attack group.
6. 0950: Hornet group attacks Mogami, Mikuma, and two destroyers.
7. 1045: Enterprise launches attack group.
8. 1250: Enterprise group attacks.
9. 1330: Hornet launches attack group.
10. 1445: Hornet group attacks.

At the first report of the "battleships" to the west, the twelve remaining marine dive bombers took off from Midway. Following the clearly visible oil slick, they found the two crusiers about 0800 and attacked at once. They made no hits, but Captain Richard E. Fleming USMC, commanding one of the two sections, dove his flaming plane into the after turret of the *Mikuma*, causing considerable damage. The Japanese were so engrossed in repelling this attack that they failed to notice a group of high-flying B-17's until their bombs began to burst around the vessels. Even so, the bombers scored no hits.

In the early afternoon twelve B-17's took off from Midway to attack the burning carrier to the northwest. It had of course gone down hours before. All the bombers found was a "cruiser"—actually the destroyer *Tanikaze*, which had been sent to ascertain whether the *Hiryu* had sunk and was now scurrying back to Yamamoto. In two attacks the Fortresses dropped eighty 500-pound bombs with nothing better than a few near misses.

Dawn of the 5th found the two American carriers about 130 miles northeast of Midway. As it became clear that the Japanese were in retreat, Spruance had to select his targets from the ships reported by Midway patrol planes. He chose the group to the northwest, which, although it was farther away, reportedly contained two battleships and a carrier. Knowing that the attack would have to be made at extreme range, Spruance ordered the bombers armed with only a single 500-pound bomb each in order to enable them to carry maximum fuel, and held the strike till about 1500 in order to close the distance as much as possible. Delaying the launching till that hour meant that the planes could not return before dark and that the carriers would have to illuminate to receive them, but Spruance, believing that he was in pursuit of the fourth Japanese carrier, accepted the risk.

All that the carrier planes found was the little *Tanikaze*, which they attacked with no more success than had the army B-17's. When they returned, the *Enterprise* turned on both deck and search lights, and the *Hornet* followed suit. Although there was a possibility that an enemy submarine might be lurking in the area, Spruance was considerably more concerned about the recovery of his pilots, most of whom had never before landed on a carrier at night. All came in safely however except for one plane, the crew of which was rescued by a destroyer.

Spruance had ascertained that there were no Japanese forces for more than 250 miles ahead, and the carriers were approaching the bad weather area, into which it was futile to follow. Consequently he altered course to the west for the night and slowed to 15 knots to save fuel for his destroyers and to avoid overtaking any enemy battleships in the dark.

## Last Contacts, June 6

June 6 dawned clear with a smooth sea and good visibility. *Enterprise* planes flying a dawn search to the west soon discovered the *Mogami* and *Mikuma* approximately 130 miles southwest of the American force. A southwest breeze facilitated launching and recovery as the carriers moved toward the contact.

In three successive attacks American planes made repeated hits on the two cruisers and put one bomb on the stern of each of the two accompanying destroyers. By the time of the third strike the carriers had closed to 90 miles, so that pilots could see both forces simultaneously. Despite a terrific battering the *Mogami* was able to stagger off to Truk, but she was out of the war for more than a year. The *Mikuma* went down a few hours after the last attack, taking a thousand men with her.

On the evening of the 6th Spruance abandoned the pursuit. He had detached destroyers as their fuel ran low, so that he now had only four left. That was too few for safety in waters in which Japanese submarines had been reported. His aviators were exhausted from three days of continuous operations. Finally, it seemed unwise to come within air range of Wake, where he believed the Japanese had concentrated planes to be transferred to Midway. Consequently he turned back to the northeast toward a rendezvous for the first refueling of his force since May 31.

Again Spruance's caution was the highest wisdom, for Yamamoto, fleeing to the west with his scattered forces, had not yet given up hope of salvaging something from the operation. The attacks on the *Tanikaze* on the 5th and on the *Mogami* and *Mikuma* on the 6th told him he was being pursued and gave him some indication of the movements of the American force. At about noon on the 6th he dispatched a force of seven cruisers and eight destroyers to the south with the dual object of protecting the *Mogami* and *Mikuma* and of destroying the American carrier force. The commander of this "Screening Force" made preparations for an engagement during the night of the 6th, and the chart shows that he would probably have had it if Spruance had continued west. Meanwhile Yamamoto's Main Body was also moving south to join in the engagement, and planes were coming north from the Marshalls to reinforce Wake's striking power. Everyone was there except the victim.

## End of the *Yorktown,* June 7

After the abandonment of the *Yorktown* on the afternoon of June 4, her screening vessels withdrew, leaving only the *Hughes* to stand guard over the carrier, which was then stable with a list of about 24 degrees. On the morning of the 5th the firing of a machine gun from the port side of the *Yorktown* caught the attention of a lookout on the *Hughes.*

An investigating party rescued two wounded men and discovered three secret coding devices that had been overlooked in the hasty abandonment of the vessel. But no one that morning noticed somewhere in the distance a Japanese cruiser-type plane, one of two that the fleeing Nagumo had that morning sent out for a search to the east. It reported the position of the abandoned carrier.

About noon the minesweeper *Vireo* arrived from Pearl and Hermes Reef, where she had been on patrol when Nimitz ordered her to go to the assistance of the *Yorktown*. She soon had the carrier under tow toward Pearl Harbor at about three knots, but that was more than the little vessel could maintain, and by morning of the 6th she was scarcely making steerageway. In the meantime five more destroyers had joined, and at daylight on the 6th the *Hammann* went alongside the carrier to put aboard a salvage party of *Yorktown* officers and men.

During the day the party made considerable progress. They reduced the list by two degrees and were lowering the water level in some of the flooded compartments. The *Hammann* was secured forward along the *Yorktown*'s starboard side to supply foamite for fighting fires and power for the pumps. The other destroyers were circling the carrier as a precaution against submarines.

At 1335 the wakes of four torpedoes were sighted to starboard. These had been fired by the *I-168*, which after shelling Midway on the early morning of the 5th had received orders to go after the carrier reported by Nagumo's plane. After searching for a day and a half she had just found the *Yorktown*. There was no time for the *Hammann* to pull clear. One torpedo broke her back, while the other two passed under her to explode against the carrier. The *Hammann* went down at once, and underwater explosions killed many of her crew in the water. Some of the destroyers picked up survivors while others went after the submarine. They succeeded only in damaging the boat, which later limped back to Kure for repairs.

The *Yorktown* remained afloat for some time, riding low in the water but with her list partially corrected. In the early morning of June 7 she rolled over to port and went down.

## Conclusion

Midway was essentially a victory of intelligence. In attempting surprise, the Japanese were themselves surprised. But in addition they made serious errors which the American command skillfully exploited while making few of its own. Like the Coral Sea, the battle was entirely a contest of air power. The Japanese were given no opportunity to employ their immense superiority in surface ships.

The American performance, while not without faults, showed a more professional touch than at the Coral Sea. Better tracking by scouts and more rapid communications would have paid handsome dividends. The pursuit phase of the battle could have been immensely more profitable had there been an earlier realization that the Japanese were in retreat. Prompter and more determined damage control might have saved the *Yorktown*. The poor performance of American torpedoes and the inferiority of American planes were again demonstrated.

For the Japanese it was the first major defeat since that at the hands of the Korean Yi Sun Sin at the end of the 16th century. Against the *Yorktown* and *Hammann* they had to list four carriers and a heavy cruiser sunk. The United States lost 150 planes, but the Japanese carriers took down with them their entire complement, bringing Japanese aircraft losses to 322. While 307 Americans died in the battle, 3,500 of the Emperor's subjects, including a hundred first-line pilots, lost their lives. This loss of experienced pilots was not the least important consequence of the battle, for it began a process of attrition that was eventually to prove fatal to Japan.

The battle marks a turning point in the war. It removed the margin of superiority that had enabled the Japanese to take the offensive at will. For the United States it ended the purely defensive phase of the war and introduced a period in which American arms could take some initiative.

The Japanese concealed their defeat not only from their public but even from officials in responsible positions. They deleted mention of it from war diaries and reports, but they could not undo its effects.

# 9

# Guadalcanal

The Battle of Midway jarred the Japanese out of their faith in their own invincibility. A week after the battle, Imperial General Headquarters canceled the bold plan for the invasion of New Caledonia, Fiji, and Samoa, originally scheduled for July 1942. The immediate and imperative task was strengthening the defense perimeter.

To the Bismarcks came Vice Admiral Gunichi Mikawa with a force of cruisers and destroyers. More planes and equipment arrived to buttress airdromes in New Guinea, the Bismarcks, and the Upper Solomons. Yet there still remained the Allied base at Port Moresby. The Imperial Navy had signally failed to eliminate that threat. Now the army would have a try, striking from the north coast of Papua across the Owen Stanley Mountains. To cover the flank of this operation, work was begun on a bomber strip on Guadalcanal, 20 miles south of the Japanese seaplane base already operating at Tulagi.

To the Allies the results of Midway spelled opportunity. Now that the enemy was off balance, with his preponderance of strength cut down, the time had come to seize the initiative and block his expansion by an offensive-defensive move—*tactically* offensive because the move would require seizing points not already held; *strategically* defensive because the immediate purpose was to thwart an enemy effort.

Where to strike depended upon probable future enemy thrusts. As early as February 1942, Admiral King had pointed out the growing Japanese base at Rabaul as a likely springboard for the next enemy advance. To counter any move from this quarter and also to provide a jumping off place for an Allied drive through the Solomons and the Bismarcks, he ordered a base constructed on Efate in the New Hebrides. He then set up a separate command in the South Pacific, subordinate to Admiral Nimitz' Pacific Ocean Areas, and appointed Vice Admiral Robert L. Ghormley Commander South Pacific Force and Area. Ghormley

## SCENE OF EARLY OPERATIONS IN THE SOUTH AND SOUTHWEST PACIFIC THEATERS

established headquarters at Auckland, New Zealand and promptly began work on a second New Hebrides base on Espiritu Santo.

The Navy's plan called for a carrier-supported initial landing in the southeast Solomons by the amphibiously trained 1st Marine Division. Here the Americans would construct airfields to provide land-based air cover for capture of islands farther up the chain. On these islands they would build additional airdromes to advance their bomber line still closer to the main target. Thus in a series of steps, each new landing covered by land-based air, they would at length bring Rabaul itself under intensive air attack. Each step would have to be less than 300 miles, the extreme operational radius of American fighter planes in 1942, because fighters would be needed over the target to protect both the bombers and the expeditionary force from enemy aircraft.

After Midway, both Admiral Nimitz and General MacArthur were of the opinion that the counteroffensive should be launched as quickly as possible, but there were difficulties. Nimitz, as Commander in Chief Pacific Fleet and Pacific Ocean Areas, controlled the marines, the transports to carry them to the beachhead, and the carriers and gunnery vessels needed to support them. The Solomons however were all within General MacArthur's Southwest Pacific Area. Accordingly, Nimitz and MacArthur each, with some reason, insisted that the entire campaign should be under his command. The latter moreover had his own idea about how to attain the objective. Give him the fleet and its carriers and the 1st Marine Division, said MacArthur, and he would go in and recapture Rabaul in a single uninterrupted operation.

There is much to be said for MacArthur's bold strategy. Rabaul was growing steadily more formidable. With each month of delay it would be harder to capture. Once it was in Allied hands, the Japanese in the Solomons and on Papua would be hopelessly cut off, the threat to Australia and United States-Australia sea communications would be entirely removed, and the way would be open for an Allied advance on the Philippines. But the Navy was unalterably opposed to sending scarce carriers and its single division of amphibious troops across the reef-strewn, virtually uncharted Solomon Sea into the teeth of a complex of enemy air bases. Later on, with more carriers and more amphibious troops at their disposal—and more experience in using them—naval strategists could afford to be more daring. They would in fact stage amphibious assaults on the most strongly defended enemy positions using air support from carriers only. But in the present circumstances they favored the step-by-step approach as the more likely to achieve success and avoid disaster. They insisted moreover that Pacific Fleet forces should remain under naval control.

Here was an impasse that could be settled only in Washington, for Nimitz and MacArthur was each supreme in his own area. Here also was another of the many difficulties resulting from divided command within a single theater. Should the entire Pacific have been put under a single officer? There were convincing arguments for such a move. There were equally strong arguments that with a military front extending from the Aleutians to Australia, the strategic problems of the various areas were on too large a scale for one officer to grasp. Proponents of the latter view decried uncritical adherence to the principle of unified command. These advocated unified command only within a geographic entity that gives coherence to operations. Their opinion prevailed, and for better or worse, MacArthur's Southwest Pacific Area and Nimitz' Pacific Ocean Areas remained separate and independent commands, responsible only to the Joint Chiefs of Staff.

It was within the Joint Chiefs that the differences were resolved. In a series of conferences, General Marshall and Admiral King reached agreement and on July 2, 1942 issued a directive that substantially followed the Navy's proposals. The opening operations, seizure and occupation of the Santa Cruz Islands, Tulagi, and adjacent positions, would be under the strategic control of Admiral Nimitz. To facilitate command problems in this first step, the boundary between the South Pacific and the Southwest Pacific Areas was shifted westward to 159° East Longitude, just west of Guadalcanal. As soon as a suitable base had been secured in the Tulagi area, the strategic command would pass to General MacArthur, who would coordinate a move up the Solomons with a second thrust—up the Papuan Peninsula to Salamaua and Lae. The two Allied advances would then converge on Rabaul. Target date for the initial invasions, called Operation WATCHTOWER, was set for August 1.

## Planning "Operation Shoestring"

Admiral Nimitz, anticipating the Joint Chiefs' directive, had almost completed basic planning for Operation WATCHTOWER by the first week in July. Vice Admiral Ghormley, as Nimitz' deputy in the South Pacific Area, would exercise strategic control, with Vice Admiral Frank Jack Fletcher, of Coral Sea and Midway fame, in tactical command of the Expeditionary Force. From King's staff, where he had headed the War Plans Division, came Rear Admiral Richmond Kelly Turner to command the Amphibious Force. The 1st Marine Division, which would make the assault, was to be commanded by Major General Alexander A. Vandegrift, who had learned the business of fighting in the jungles of Nicaragua and the theory of amphibious warfare on the staff of the Fleet Marine Force.

A month was of course an uncomfortably brief period in which to assemble forces, work out details, and complete training and rehearsals for so complex an operation as an amphibious assault. Moreover, adequate reinforcements and proper air and surface support were hard to come by. The invasion of North Africa, planned for November, had top priority for everything. MacArthur's three divisions, assigned to the protection of Australia, could not be touched. South Pacific bases would have to be stripped of part of their defense forces to provide garrison troops to follow up the marines. Little wonder the somewhat baffled participants in Operation WATCHTOWER soon began calling it "Operation Shoestring."

While Fletcher and Turner were conferring with Nimitz at Pearl Harbor, there came the startling news that an American patrol plane had sighted an airstrip under construction on Guadalcanal. This information put a more urgent complexion on the WATCHTOWER project. Obviously Guadalcanal would have to be included in the Tulagi-Santa Cruz plan, but King and Nimitz would allow no more than one additional week to prepare for the expanded operation. D-day was set definitely for August 7. The airfield had to be captured before the Japanese could complete it. Whoever first put it into operation might well be the victor.

In the latter part of July the situation took another turn when a Japanese convoy landed 1,800 troops near Buna, on the Papuan Peninsula directly opposite Port Moresby. This invasion was a source of grave concern to MacArthur, particularly as the Southwest Pacific Forces had been on the point of occupying the Buna area themselves. But in the South Pacific the news was received with a certain measure of relief. Japanese attention was focused on the old target of Port Moresby, not upon the end of the Solomons chain. Rabaul was looking southwest instead of southeast. Surprise was possible.

## The Allied Invasion

Steaming from points as widely separated as Wellington, Sydney, Noumea, San Diego, and Pearl Harbor, the various components of the Watchtower Expeditionary Force, some 80 vessels in all, met at sea on July 26 south of the Fijis. Here Admiral Fletcher held council aboard his flagship, the carrier *Saratoga*. Admiral Ghormley, then shifting his headquarters to Noumea, could not be present. He at no time saw the fleet over which he exercised a distant control or met all his top commanders to discuss operation plans. After a less than satisfactory landing rehearsal in the Fijis, the fleet steamed westward. In the Coral Sea it shaped course due north and headed for Guadalcanal through rain squalls that grounded all aircraft, including Japanese search patrols.

Guadalcanal, part of the drowned volcanic mountain range forming the Solomons, rises steeply in the south from a narrow coastal flat. Only on the north side of the island are there plains broad enough to provide level ground for airfields. Here on Lunga Plain, mostly rain forest traversed by numerous creeks and small rivers and broken here and there by coconut plantations and grassy fields, the Japanese had landed and begun their airdrome. This was the main Allied objective. The secondary objective was the Japanese seaplane base in the Tulagi area, 20 miles to the north.

Under a clearing sky in the dark early hours of August 7, the *Saratoga*, *Enterprise*, and *Wasp* carrier groups moved into position south of Guadalcanal while Turner's Amphibious Force slipped up the west coast, split into two groups around little Savo Island, and entered the body of water later named Ironbottom Sound—in honor of the many vessels sunk there in the next few months. This first Allied invasion in the Pacific theater resembled the last in the European theater—after the Army, in top command there, had learned to accept the Navy's advice about the timing and support of amphibious operations. Thus the approach to Guadalcanal, by navy decision, was made in darkness, and the landings were made in daylight and were preceded by a naval bombardment and an air strike. When the marines headed for the beach at sunrise, there was little of the confusion that was to afflict the North African night landings three months later. Moreover the surprise of the Japanese was complete, and the initial landings were unopposed.

By nightfall 10,000 marines were on Guadalcanal, and the beach was cluttered with supplies. One combat team had advanced west along the shoreline, while a second was penetrating the jungle in a southwesterly direction. Most of the 2,000 or so Japanese on the island, chiefly construction workers, had fled westward during the bombardment, but a few determined warriors had remained behind to snipe and to man machine guns. These the marines encountered and destroyed on the second day of their advance. In mid-afternoon of the 8th, one marine team had entered the main Japanese base, taking possession of machine shops, electric power plants, and considerable stores of provisions, firearms, and ammunition. A little later the other team occupied the airstrip, the future Henderson Field.

On the north side of Ironbottom Sound, operations did not proceed so smoothly. Here the objectives were three small islands lying inside a bight of the larger Florida Island: Tulagi, a two-mile-long ridge rising abruptly from the Sound, and Tanambogo-Gavutu, a pair of islets joined by a narrow causeway. In this area, despite naval bombardment and bombing and strafing by carrier aircraft, which quickly knocked out all the enemy seaplanes, the marines ran into trouble.

On Tulagi, by picking an unlikely beachhead, the invaders got ashore easily enough. It was only when they reached high ground that they found an enemy so well dug in that they had to dislodge him with machine guns, mortars, and grenades. Gavutu had to be taken by amphibious assault in the face of heavy small-arms fire, for this island, rising sheer out of a broad coral shelf, could be invaded only by way of the seaplane ramp. An attempt to take Tanambogo on August 7 was thrown back. Before these three little islands could be secured on the 8th, Vandegrift had to double the 1,500 marines he had originally sent against the 780 defenders. This used up all his reserves and meant that the Santa Cruz

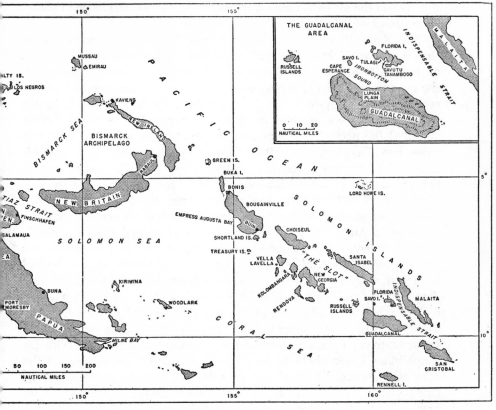

THE APPROACHES TO RABAUL

phase of Operation WATCHTOWER would be postponed and eventually abandoned.

A few hours after the first landing, enemy bombers and fighters from Rabaul appeared over Ironbottom Sound. Alerted by a coastwatcher,* the American carriers sent in a strong combat patrol of fighter aircraft which soon decimated and routed the intruders. Warned the following morning of approaching torpedo planes, Turner had his transports and screening vessels in cruising formation and maneuvering at top speed when they arrived. Caught between the devastating fire of more than 50

---

* The Australian coastwatchers manned a network of small radio stations along the coasts of the Bismarcks and the Solomons. Established before the war and incorporated into the Australian navy in 1939, some remained after the Japanese invasion; others returned later. Operating in concealment usually with portable radio equipment and assisted by loyal natives, they were of inestimable value in warning Allied commands of enemy ship, troop, and plane movements. A similar New Zealand network operated in the Gilberts, the Ellices, the Fijis, and the more easterly islands. Many coastwatchers were captured or killed by the advancing Japanese.

vessels and the air patrol sweeping down from above, the torpedo planes were almost wiped out.

The Expeditionary Force came through the air attacks rather better than many would have ventured to predict—18 carrier aircraft lost from all causes, two destroyers damaged, a transport set fatally ablaze. But the long absence of the cargo vessels from their anchorages had utterly confused an already critical logistics problem. By the evening of August 8 some of the vessels were no more than 25 per cent unloaded, so Turner accepted the necessity of remaining in Ironbottom Sound at least two more days. Then came two bits of information that abruptly changed his mind. The first was news that Admiral Fletcher, citing heavy loss of fighter planes and a need for refueling, had requested permission from Ghormley to withdraw the carrier force from the Guadalcanal area.* The second piece of news came from MacArthur's headquarters. That morning an Australian pilot on air patrol had sighted Japanese vessels heading to enter the passage—later known as "the Slot"—between the major Solomons. Instead of immediately sounding a radio alert, as he had been instructed to do, he spent several hours finishing his patrol and then returned to base before making a contact report. Not sure what he had seen, he identified two of the vessels as probably "seaplane tenders." Turner, accepting this identification, concluded that the enemy force was en route to set up a seaplane base in the Central Solomons. With his Amphibious Force about to be stripped of carrier support and at the same time menaced by probable new dangers from the air, he decided that he had no choice but to withdraw the following day. He therefore sent for General Vandegrift and Rear Admiral V. A. C. Crutchley RN, the screen commander, to come to his flagship to hear his decision and help him make plans.

Crutchley, speeding to the rendezvous in the cruiser *Australia,* had drawn up no battle plan for countering a surface attack and had designated no one to the over-all command of the cruisers and destroyers in his absence. These vessels, in second condition of readiness, were divided several ways, in groups too far apart for quick mutual support. Light screens of destroyers and minesweepers covered the Guadalcanal and Tulagi beachheads, where the transports were anchored. One cruiser-destroyer group patrolled the passage between Savo and Florida Islands, another patrolled the passage between Savo and Guadalcanal, while a third patrolled the east channels. Just northwest of Savo was a radar

* Fletcher, having already lost two carriers since the outbreak of war, was understandably loath to risk further losses, but opinion is divided as to whether his situation off Guadalcanal was as critical as he implied, for he still had 83 fighter planes. Nimitz, calling Fletcher's withdrawal "most unfortunate," suggested that he might have solved his fuel problem by sending the carrier groups southward one at a time for refueling.

patrol of two destroyers. There were no picket vessels patrolling the outer approaches to Ironbottom Sound.

## The Battle of Savo Island

The Japanese force sighted by the Australian plane in the morning of August 8 was composed of five heavy and two light cruisers and a destroyer, commanded by Admiral Mikawa. Mikawa's objective was Ironbottom Sound; his mission, to smash the Allied transports and break up the invasion by a night attack.

For years the Japanese navy had been training to offset superior opposition by making use of foul weather and darkness. Many of its major fleet exercises had been carried out in the stormy North Pacific, where day and night it trained under conditions of such extreme severity that many men were killed in each exercise. For night work the Japanese developed superior binoculars, highly dependable starshells and parachute flares, and the most lethal torpedo in the world—the 24-inch Long Lance, which could carry a thousand pounds of explosive eleven miles at 49 knots, or 20 miles at 36 knots.* Because limited resources made Japan a weak base for naval operations, the Japanese counted on surprise coupled with adverse forces of nature to give them the advantage over better-based adversaries.

After he had been sighted from the air, Mikawa entered the Slot and headed directly for Guadalcanal. Late in the evening two of his cruisers launched float planes, which proceeded ahead to report the location of ships in Ironbottom Sound and to provide illumination when needed. Some Allied vessels saw the aircraft and tried to warn the flagship but were defeated by static; others assumed, since no general alarm had been sounded, that the planes must be friendly. A few minutes after 0100, when Mikawa's force was heading for the passage between Savo and Cape Esperance, Japanese lookouts dimly made out the hulls of the picket destroyer *Blue*. Promptly the entire force prepared for action, training all guns. But there was no reaction from the picket, which steamed tranquilly away, having observed nothing. Mikawa, puzzled, suspecting trickery, detached his destroyer to watch the *Blue* and engage her if she should attempt to follow him. Then he entered the Sound.

Not since the Pearl Harbor attack had American or Allied forces been taken so unaware. As the Japanese planes overhead eerily illuminated the area with parachute flares, Mikawa's cruisers dashed past the South

---

* The contemporary American torpedo was 21 inches in diameter and carried a 780-pound charge three miles at 45 knots, 7.5 miles at 26.5 knots. Through the first two years of the war the exploder and depth regulating mechanisms remained notoriously undependable, particularly when the torpedoes were launched from submarines.

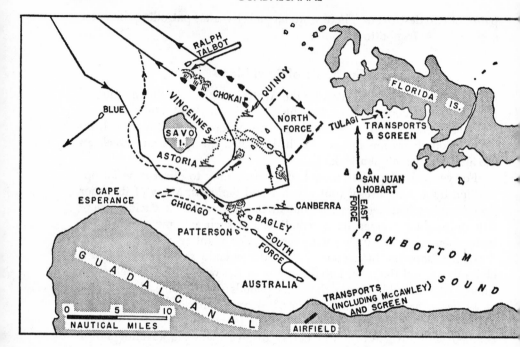

**THE BATTLE OF SAVO ISLAND, AUGUST 9, 1942**

Patrol Force firing torpedoes and shells. The destroyer *Patterson* had sounded the alarm by voice radio: "Warning! Warning! Strange ships entering harbor!" but it was too late. Before the Allied vessels could bring their guns to bear or the surprised torpedomen could insert firing primers, Japanese torpedoes had blown a chunk out of the bow of the American heavy cruiser *Chicago* and crushed in the side of the Australian heavy *Canberra*, which lost way and began to blaze under a hail of enemy shells. Still unscratched, the attacking column split into two divisions and wheeled north, three cruisers passing across the van of the North Patrol Force and four steaming across the rear, searchlights open, guns blazing. In a matter of minutes all three cruisers of the North Force, the American heavies *Vincennes*, *Astoria*, and *Quincy*, were afire and listing. The *Quincy* managed to get a couple of shells into the Japanese flagship *Chokai*, smashing the staff chart room and killing 34 men. Hits made by the other American cruisers did only trifling damage. At 0220 Mikawa ordered "All ships withdraw," and his attack force headed back up the Slot. North of Savo Island one of his cruiser divisions encountered the second picket destroyer, the *Ralph Talbot*, and concentrated upon her a massed fire that left her superstructure a shambles.

Mikawa, mindful that he had not completed his mission, considered returning to Ironbottom Sound to blast the transports. He rejected the idea because he was sure that Fletcher's carriers were already pursuing him and that they would attack at first light. The farther he could get to the northwest, the better the chances would be for a successful counter-attack by aircraft out of Rabaul. But there was neither attack nor counter-attack. Fletcher had received his permission to withdraw and was moving in the opposite direction. By dawn the carriers were far to the southeast. The Japanese attack force retired up the Slot unmolested.

In the waters off Guadalcanal the *Quincy* and the *Vincennes* had gone down shortly after the battle. The *Canberra*, helpless, unable to leave the Sound, was sunk by an American destroyer at 0800 the next morning. The *Astoria* lingered until noon before she plunged. The attack had cost the Allies four desperately needed heavy cruisers and a thousand lives. It had vindicated the confidence of the Japanese in their night-fighting techniques.

## The Lull

The roar of battle had scarcely died away before the American sailors and marines resumed unloading cargo. After dawn, alarms of air raids that never materialized twice sent all ships into the open Sound for evasive maneuvers. Hence when the transports and cargo vessels weighed anchor that afternoon, they carried away more than half the supplies they had brought. The last ship of Turner's Amphibious Force cleared Ironbottom Sound just before dark. The 16,000 marines left behind on Guadalcanal and Tulagi would be limited to two daily meals of B and C rations eked out with captured rice.

For several days the Japanese limited their offensive against the new American positions to light aerial bombings and to bombardments by surfaced submarines. During this relative lull, marine engineers, using hand shovels and captured steam rollers and trucks, got the airstrip in good enough shape to receive light planes. On August 15 four American destroyer-transports darted into Ironbottom Sound bringing aviation gasoline, bombs, ammunition, and ground crews. On the 20th an escort carrier approached Guadalcanal from the southeast and flew in twelve dive-bombers and 19 fighters. Fletcher's carrier force meanwhile patrolled the waters between the Solomons and Espiritu Santo, guarding the sea communications.

Despite their apparent inactivity, the Japanese were not idle. They were gathering forces to recapture Guadalcanal and also to reinforce their campaign in Papua. By mid-August, the whole Combined Fleet had moved to Truk, and 17,000 troops had arrived in the area or were on the way. Because the Japanese, through a monumental misestimate, believed that no more than 2,000 Americans had landed in the Solomons,

11,000 of the new arrivals were promptly dispatched to Papua. The rest were assigned to the first of four attacks aimed at regaining Guadalcanal and its airfield.

## The August Attack

Because most of the Japanese transports in the South Pacific were assigned to reinforcing the campaign against Port Moresby, only a few hundred troops at a time could be sent to Guadalcanal. Even the first Reinforcement Group, commanded by Rear Admiral Raizo Tanaka, split into two sections. One section, comprising six destroyers, left Truk at dawn on August 16, proceeded to Guadalcanal at 22 knots, and landed 900 troops two nights later west of Henderson Field. The second section, which left Truk shortly after the first, could make only 8½ knots because its 1,300 troops were carried in three slow transports. Escorting the transports was the light cruiser *Jintsu*, Tanaka's flagship, and four patrol boats.

While Tanaka was still at sea with his slow convoy, he and Japanese headquarters received three reports that changed the whole strategic picture. The first report, on August 20, was that Fletcher's carrier task force was cruising southeast of Guadalcanal. The second, also on the 20th, was that American planes were operating from Henderson Field. The third, on August 21, was that the 900 troops put ashore on Guadalcanal had attacked prematurely and had been wiped out almost to a man. The Japanese would have been even more shocked had they known that this action, known as the Battle of the Tenaru River, had cost the marines only 25 lives.

As a result of the first of these reports, Rabaul radioed Tanaka orders to reverse course. The following evening he was told to resume his advance toward Guadalcanal. Vice Admiral Nobutaka Kondo was bringing down the Combined Fleet to support his landing and, if possible, to destroy Fletcher's task force. This decision led to the second naval battle of the campaign, the Battle of the Eastern Solomons. Dawn on August 24 saw the Japanese sea forces emerging on a southerly course from an overcast that had con-

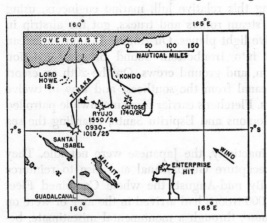

**BATTLE OF THE EASTERN SOLOMONS,**
**AUGUST 24–25, 1942**

cealed their advance—Tanaka 250 miles north of Guadalcanal, with Kondo, his main air strength concentrated in the sister-carriers *Shokaku* and *Zuikaku,* 40 miles to the east covering his flank. Far in advance was a third group centered about the light carrier *Ryujo,* whose aircraft were assigned the task of neutralizing Henderson Field.

When Fletcher, cruising 150 miles east of Guadalcanal, learned from patrol planes of the presence of the *Ryujo,* he was taken aback. Not anticipating fleet action, he had sent the *Wasp* group southward to refuel. Though this left him only two carriers to oppose to an enemy of undetermined strength, he decided to seize the initiative. Retaining his entire combat air patrol of 53 F4F Wildcat fighters to defend his fleet from attack, in the early afternoon he sent 30 bombers and eight torpedo planes against the *Ryujo.* These found the little carrier shortly after she had launched the bulk of her aircraft against Henderson Field and in a well-coordinated attack sent her down.

When American patrol planes located the big Japanese carriers to the north, Fletcher promptly made preparations for an attack from that quarter. He turned fighter-plane direction over to Rear Admiral Thomas Kinkaid's *Enterprise* group and, hoping to divide the enemy, withdrew with the *Saratoga* group ten miles to the southeast. When radar detected aircraft approaching from the north, he ordered the remaining bombers and torpedo planes of both American carriers to take to the air and seek out the hostile fleet, while the fighters stacked themselves over the American groups and on the line of approach of the enemy planes. Kinkaid's Wildcats quickly broke the enemy formations and shot down half a dozen bombers before they could begin their dives. The rest, ignoring the distant *Saratoga,* swooped down upon the *Enterprise* group, where they ran into blistering antiaircraft fire which no torpedo planes and few bombers penetrated.

Three determined bomber pilots however bored through the fire and made direct hits in quick succession on the flight deck of the *Enterprise,* killing 74 men, knocking out two elevators, wrecking compartments, and blasting holes in her side. Six minutes after the first attack on the carrier, the battle was over, and a small remnant of the attacking squadrons was fleeing northward with the Wildcats in hot pursuit. The Americans had lost only 15 planes. Within an hour damage control parties aboard the *Enterprise* had corrected her slight list and she was steaming south at 24 knots landing aircraft. The American air attack squadrons meanwhile had missed the main enemy carrier force and instead struck a detached group, sending the seaplane carrier *Chitose* flaming out of action.

At midnight Kondo, having lost a carrier and 90 planes, withdrew toward Truk. But Tanaka's Reinforcement Group, accompanied by destroyers, steamed doggedly southward through the night to become the morning target of Henderson Field bombers, which severely damaged

the *Jintsu* and sank a transport. Not long afterward B-17's from Espiritu
Santo struck the Reinforcement Group and sank a destroyer. Rabaul
thereupon acknowledged the failure of this first attempt to recapture
Guadalcanal by recalling Tanaka and canceling the operation.

## The September Attack

Tanaka, though shaken by his experiences in the Battle of the Eastern
Solomons, had scarcely reached the naval staging base in the Shortland
Islands before he was busy with his inadequate transport facilities pushing more troops into Guadalcanal. In a sunset attack on August 28,
Henderson Field bombers sank a troop-carrying destroyer and damaged
two others. Thereafter the Japanese timed their approaches more cautiously. Hovering up the Slot until dark, destroyers and small transports
darted into Ironbottom Sound by night so regularly that the marines
began to refer to them as the "Tokyo Express." After putting men and
supplies ashore they would lob a few rounds of shell at the airstrip and
be back up the Slot out of reach of marine bombers before light. Allied
vessels, after the night sinkings of two destroyer-transports by Japanese
destroyers, shunned the Sound after nightfall as conscientiously as the
enemy shunned it after dawn. Thus the Americans, under protection of
Henderson Field aircraft, commanded the waters around Guadalcanal by
day, and the Japanese commanded these waters by night. Every surface
action in Ironbottom Sound resulted from contacts made when Allied
warships outstayed the sun or ventured into the waters north of Guadalcanal after dark.

By September 10, the Japanese had 6,000 troops on Guadalcanal,
divided between positions east and west of the American perimeter. The
time had come for a second drive to recapture the airfield. The Imperial
Army commander ashore, accepting the official underestimate of American forces, reported that he had sufficient strength for an attack. Thereupon Kondo's Combined Fleet again departed Truk to lend support
and to fly planes in to the airstrip as soon as it was captured. The
Japanese troops, after chopping a trail through the jungle, at nightfall
on September 12 struck with their main force along the high ground,
subsequently known as Bloody Ridge, that led from the south directly to
Henderson Field. But their move had been anticipated, and marines
were waiting for them with mortars and machine guns backed by 105-
mm. howitzers. The American lines held through the night and the
next day. When darkness came on the 13th, the marines opened and
maintained a continuous barrage of shells which the Japanese for lack of
artillery could not counter. Just before midnight, Imperial Army troops
launched a final attack that carried them perilously close to the airfield

before collapsing under withering massed fire. By first light the Japanese were in disorderly retreat. Planes taking off from Henderson Field peppered the jungle with strafing fire, helping to bring enemy losses to 1,500. American casualties were 40 dead and 103 wounded.

Once more Kondo's fleet retired on Truk. The second attack had failed.

In the Coral Sea however, where Fletcher's carriers continued to patrol, Japanese submarines were taking a grievous toll of American naval strength. On the last day of August, a submarine had fired a torpedo into the *Saratoga,* putting her out of action for the three crucial months to follow. Two weeks later, the *Wasp,* the new battleship *North Carolina,* and the destroyer *O'Brien* were all torpedoed within a quarter of an hour. The two torpedoes that struck the *Wasp* ignited open fuel lines and at the same time broke her water mains so that effective fire fighting was impossible. Captain Forrest P. Sherman, her commanding officer, after vainly attempting to confine the flames by turning her undamaged stern into the wind, at length ordered Abandon Ship, and a destroyer sent her down with torpedoes. The *North Carolina,* with a 32-foot underwater rip in her hull, made Pearl Harbor for repairs, but the *O'Brien* broke up and sank before she could reach drydock.

That day's series of calamities left the Allies with only one operational fleet carrier, the *Hornet,* and one undamaged new battleship, the *Washington,* in the whole Pacific. Luckily, the convoy that the *Wasp* and the *Hornet* had been supporting reached Guadalcanal safely. Aboard were 4,200 troops, Turner's last marine reserves, which he had withdrawn from the defense of Samoa.

## The October Attack

The crushing defeat of the Imperial Army forces in the Battle of Bloody Ridge had a profound effect upon Japanese strategy. It shocked Tokyo into realizing that the Americans were on Guadalcanal in considerable force and that Japan was likely to lose the island for good unless stronger measures were taken to recapture it.

Over in Papua, the troops based on Buna had penetrated a 6,500-foot-high pass in the Owen Stanley Mountains, descended the southern slope, and come almost within sight of Port Moresby in spite of courageous resistance by MacArthur's Australians. On September 18 Imperial General Headquarters ordered the Japanese troops to cease their advance and withdraw back across the mountains to Buna, where they were to take a strong defensive position and hold it until Guadalcanal had been recaptured. Everything was now to be subordinated to that objective. In line with the new emphasis, the Tokyo Express stepped up operations, until by October 1 it was transporting as many as 900 troops a night down the Slot. Meanwhile a fresh Japanese division moved to the Shortlands for transfer to Guadalcanal.

In an attempt to counter this formidable enemy buildup, Admiral Ghormley stripped his New Caledonia garrison of 3,000 United States Army troops and embarked them to reinforce Vandegrift's marines. Task forces built around the *Hornet* and the *Washington* cleared the way for the convoy, and a force of four cruisers and five destroyers under Rear Admiral Norman Scott advanced to derail the Tokyo Express.

In preparation for their October offensive, the Japanese planned a series of naval bombardments of Guadalcanal which, together with intensified air attacks, were calculated to put Henderson Field out of operation. The first bombardment group, three cruisers and two destroyers from Rabaul, came to grief when it blundered head-on into Scott's cruiser-destroyer force just north of Cape Esperance toward midnight on October 11. For once Japanese cat eyes had not penetrated the darkness, and the American force was almost equally blind because Scott had chosen as his flagship the *San Francisco*, which was not equipped with the new SG surface-search radar. But good fortune was with the American cruisers. They had just reversed course by column movement. This is a dubious maneuver in disputed waters because it masks one's batteries and provides the enemy with a stationary point of aim, but as luck would have it, the move carried the American cruiser column on a T-capping course directly across the head of the oncoming Japanese column.

At length becoming aware of the enemy, the Americans opened fire, sinking a cruiser and a destroyer and setting another cruiser ablaze. In the subsequent pursuit of the surviving Japanese vessels, Scott's force battered the previously undamaged enemy cruiser with shellfire, but one of his own cruisers was put out of action and another was damaged by two hits. The American van destroyers had no luck at all. The initial countermarch, led by the cruisers, threw them out of line. As they raced to regain the head of the column, they were caught between the opposing forces. One of the destroyers was holed by two American shells; another, furiously battered by friend and foe, caught fire and sank.

This action, known as the Battle of Cape Esperance, temporarily lifted flagging Allied spirits in the South Pacific, particularly as the Americans greatly overestimated the damage they had done the enemy. The situation looked still brighter on the 13th when the convoy from New Caledonia reached Guadalcanal, discharged soldiers and cargo, and got safely away. But that night two Japanese battleships entered Ironbottom Sound and systematically pounded the Henderson Field area for an hour and a half with hundreds of high-capacity shells, churning up the landing strips and destroying half the aircraft on the island. Two air raids the next day and a bombardment by heavy cruisers the following night

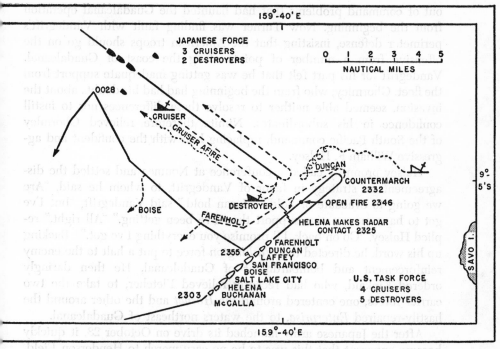

BATTLE OF CAPE ESPERANCE, OCTOBER 11–12, 1942

added to the destruction. Only a few planes were left to oppose a convoy of six transports which in the early hours of October 15 brought in some 4,500 Japanese soldiers. The new arrivals raised the enemy garrison to 22,000, the majority fresh troops, to oppose 23,000 Americans, mostly battle-worn, malaria-ridden marines.* As the Imperial Army forces confidently prepared for what they regarded as the inevitable recapture of the airdrome, Admiral Kondo brought down from Truk the most powerful battleship-carrier fleet assembled since the Battle of Midway.

In the face of these vast enemy preparations, morale in the South Pacific took a new plunge. Part of the general lack of confidence grew

* The following table gives approximate troop strengths on Guadalcanal on important dates:

|         | AMERICAN | JAPANESE |
|---------|----------|----------|
| Aug. 7  | 10,000   | 2,200    |
| Aug. 20 | 10,000   | 3,600    |
| Sept. 12| 11,000   | 6,000    |
| Oct. 23 | 23,000   | 22,000   |
| Nov. 12 | 29,000   | 30,000   |
| Dec. 9  | 40,000   | 25,000   |
| Feb. 1  | 50,000   | 12,000   |

On August 7 there were also 780 Japanese in the Tulagi-Tanambogo-Gavutu area. Some 6,000 United States marines landed on these islands, and a garrison of around 5,000 Americans was maintained in this area throughout the campaign.

out of command problems that had haunted the Guadalcanal operation from the beginning. Now Turner was finding fault with Vandegrift's perimeter defense, insisting that the American troops should go on the offensive from a number of points along the coast of Guadalcanal. Vandegrift for his part felt that he was getting inadequate support from the fleet. Ghormley, who from the beginning had had his doubts about the invasion, seemed able neither to resolve these differences nor to instill confidence in his subordinates. Nimitz therefore relieved Ghormley of the South Pacific command, replacing him with the confident and aggressive William F. Halsey.

Halsey promptly called a conference at Noumea and settled the disagreement on strategy in favor of Vandegrift, to whom he said, "Are we going to evacuate or hold?" "I can hold," said Vandegrift, "but I've got to have more active support than I've been getting." "All right," replied Halsey. "Go on back. I'll promise you everything I've got."* Backing up his word, he directed the *Washington* force to put a halt to the enemy reinforcement and bombardment of Guadalcanal. He then daringly ordered Kinkaid, who had recently relieved Fletcher, to take the two carrier forces, one centered around the *Hornet* and the other around the hastily-repaired *Enterprise,* to the waters northeast of Guadalcanal.

After the Japanese army launched its drive on October 23, it quickly became apparent that this was to be no easy march to Henderson Field. The well-entrenched Americans refused to give ground. The three lines of the Japanese advance got out of phase. After the army command had thrice notified Kondo's carriers that they might approach and send in planes, and each time postponed the hour, Admiral Yamamoto, at Truk, lost patience. He warned the army that the fleet was running out of fuel and would have to retire unless Henderson Field were soon captured.

In the early hours of the 26th, PBY's from Espiritu Santo reported that Kondo was heading northward, away from the Guadalcanal area. Kinkaid's two carrier forces had by this time reached the vicinity of the Santa Cruz Islands, within striking range of the Japanese fleet. Admiral Halsey noted all this on his operations chart at Noumea and just before dawn flashed the electrifying order: "Attack—Repeat—Attack." Search planes promptly left the deck of the *Enterprise* and began the day auspiciously by locating the major enemy carrier group and with a pair of 500-pound bombs blasting a hole in the flight deck of the light carrier *Zuiho.*

Thereafter events worked increasingly to American tactical disadvantage. Kinkaid, whose experience prior to Operation WATCHTOWER had been with battleships and cruisers, adopted Fletcher's plan of control-

* From William F. Halsey and J. Bryan III, *Admiral Halsey's Story* (New York: McGraw-Hill Book Company, Inc., 1947), 117. Copyright, 1947, by William F. Halsey. Copyright, 1947, by The Curtis Publishing Company.

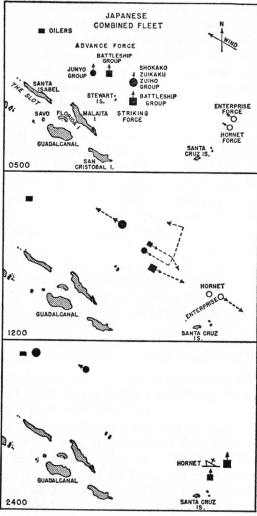

**BATTLE OF THE SANTA CRUZ ISLANDS, OCTOBER 26, 1942**

ling all fighter-direction from the *Enterprise,* but with less precision and certainly with less luck. Because the Japanese got the jump on him by putting a strike in the air 20 minutes before the Americans launched, Kinkaid had to accept battle over his own decks before his fighters attained altitude; and as ill fortune would have it, the enemy concentrated on the *Hornet* force while the *Enterprise* was ten miles away. Five bombs struck the *Hornet's* flight deck, some penetrating deep into the hull before detonating. Two torpedoes exploded in her engine spaces, severing electric cables and water mains and flooding fire rooms. Listing, ablaze, without power or communications, the carrier went dead in the water. Meanwhile, far to the northwest, the *Hornet's* bombers were exacting vengeance by fighting their way through strong Japanese air patrols to cripple the heavy cruiser *Chikuma* and put the carrier *Shokaku* out of the war for several months.

An hour later a second Japanese air strike found the *Enterprise* force unready and in a state of some confusion because a submarine had just torpedoed the destroyer *Porter.* Accuracy and volume of antiaircraft fire, especially from the new battleship *South Dakota,* limited damage this time to three bomb hits on the flight deck of the *Enterprise.* After a third morning attack had damaged two more of his ships, Kinkaid ordered the *Porter* scuttled, and the *Enterprise* force retreated to the southeast.

Left thus without fighter cover, the *Hornet* became the target of repeated afternoon air attacks. When another torpedo and two more bomb hits made her blaze afresh and heel over dangerously, the force commander ordered the carrier abandoned. He then withdrew, leaving two destroyers behind to sink her. These expended all their torpedoes and more than 400 shells without producing any effect except to start new fires. After dark, when the American destroyers had departed, ships of Kondo's fleet approached the burning derelict. Unable to take her in tow, they sent her down with four Long Lances.

Though tactically the Americans had got the worse of this action, known as the Battle of the Santa Cruz Islands, in the long run it worked to their strategic advantage. Kondo had lost 100 planes; Kinkaid, 74. This disparity was more one-sided than the bare numbers indicate, for the Japanese were to be quickly outmatched by the upsurging American pilot training and aircraft construction programs.

Though the fleet at a heavy price had won important long-term gains, it was the American soldiers and marines on Guadalcanal who saved the immediate situation. They held firm while the enemy attack rose to a crescendo and finally died out on the 26th. Henderson Field remained in American hands, and Japanese casualties were roughly ten times the American losses. Enemy ground forces would no longer pose a serious threat.

## The November Attack

Convinced that they had barely missed recapturing Guadalcanal, the Japanese in early November duplicated their October preparations, but at a swifter pace. The night-running Tokyo Express sped up operations until Imperial Army forces on Guadalcanal outnumbered the Americans by several thousands. These piecemeal reinforcements however were merely a preliminary to the 13,500 troops which the persistent Admiral Tanaka was about to bring down from the Shortland Islands in a Rein-forcement Group of 11 transports escorted by 11 destroyers. Exactly as in October, a battleship group and a cruiser group would bombard Hender-son Field on successive nights, and bombers would raid by day. To provide some air cover for Tanaka's transports, Kondo's carriers would maneuver north of the Solomons, but they were under orders to avoid a fleet engagement.

Arrival of fresh troops from New Zealand and the United States enabled Halsey to strip the remainder of his island garrisons and rush 6,000 soldiers and marines to Guadalcanal escorted by Turner's surface forces. By direct intervention of President Roosevelt, additional cruisers, destroyers, and submarines were ordered to the South Pacific; bombers and fighter planes were flown in from Hawaii and Australia. Finally, as the November showdown became imminent, Admiral Kinkaid set out from Noumea with the *Enterprise* force, now including the *Washington* as well as the *South Dakota*, taking along a tender so that repair to the damaged carrier could continue at sea. The Battle of the Santa Cruz Islands had taught Halsey caution also, for he directed Kinkaid under no circumstances to take the *Enterprise* into the waters north of the Solomons.

Though Turner beat Tanaka to Guadalcanal, he did not arrive undetected by the enemy. Bombers struck repeatedly at the American troop convoy in Ironbottom Sound. On November 12, a Japanese pilot crashed his burning plane into the *San Francisco*, knocking out a gun director and a fire control radar and killing or injuring 50 men. Some of the bombers were from the carriers, for Kondo had already brought his fleet down from Truk to a position north of Santa Isabel Island. Thence he dispatched Vice Admiral Hiroaki Abe southward with the first Bombardment Group. Tanaka's Reinforcement Group was on the point of departing the Shortlands for its dash down the Slot.

Notified by scout planes of the approaching Bombardment Group, Turner at sunset withdrew his convoy to the southeast. To break up the impending night attack on Henderson Field, he detached five cruisers and eight destroyers from his convoy escort and sent them back to Ironbottom Sound under the command of Rear Admiral Daniel J. Callaghan. He thereby set the stage for the opening action of the three-day Naval Battle of Guadalcanal.

Callaghan's force was a David sent against a Goliath, for Abe, besides a cruiser and 14 destroyers, was bringing down the battleships *Hiei* and *Kirishima*. Fortunately for the Americans, the Japanese 14-inch guns were provided with bombardment rather than armor-piercing shells; otherwise the United States force could hardly have avoided annihilation. In any event, it was little prepared for the sort of battle it was about to fight. Callaghan neither issued a battle plan nor provided for any means of scouting ahead. In imitation of Scott in the Battle of Cape Esperance, he disposed his vessels in a single column, cruisers in the center, destroyers divided between van and rear. Also like Scott, he chose for his flagship the *San Francisco* with her inferior radar. Scott, now second in command, led the cruisers in the *Atlanta*, which also lacked SG radar.

Under a moonless but starry sky, Callaghan's force passed back through the eastern channel and re-entered Ironbottom Sound. His vessels had almost reached the waters north of Lunga Point, when Abe's Bombardment Group, without radar, entered the sound through the passage south of Savo with a pair of detached destroyers scouting out ahead. The two forces were thus speeding toward each other almost on a collision course when the cruiser *Helena* detected the enemy 14 miles away and warned the flagship by voice radio. Callaghan thereupon ordered two successive column movements to the right, which put him on course due north. He apparently hoped by this maneuver to reproduce

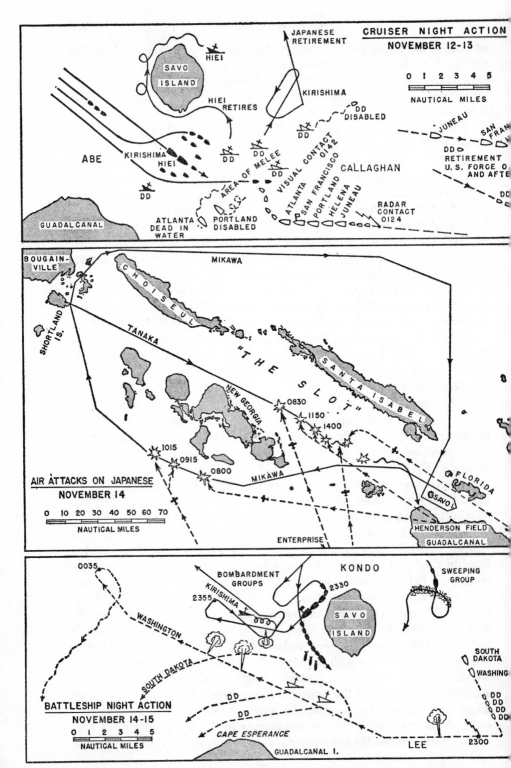

NAVAL BATTLE OF GUADALCANAL, NOVEMBER 12–15, 1942

Scott's capping position of the month before. But the leading destroyer *Cushing*, suddenly espying enemy scout destroyers dead ahead, swung out of line and threw the van into disorder. Callaghan's cruisers then wheeled left to avoid their own destroyers, and Japanese and American ships intermingled.

There followed a half-hour melee which for confusion and fury is scarcely paralleled in naval history. All formations broke and the engagement became a series of individual ship duels with each side at one time or another firing on its own vessels. From this midnight brawl the contending forces at length managed to extricate themselves, but both had been desperately hurt. Dawn revealed the extent of their injuries. The Japanese had lost two destroyers; and Abe's flagship *Hiei*, riddled by more than 50 shells, was helpless north of Savo, where aircraft from Henderson Field struck her again and again until she sank. Admirals Callaghan and Scott and most of the members of their staffs had been killed. Four American destroyers had been lost. The cruiser *Portland* and a destroyer were unnavigable; the *Atlanta*, flame-gutted, and shelled by friend and foe, had to be sunk. All but one of the other American vessels were damaged. The cruiser *Juneau*, while retiring from battle with a weakened keel, was torpedoed by a submarine and went down, carrying nearly 700 of her crew. Yet the Americans, despite overwhelming odds, had by sheer valor carried out their mission. Abe's battleships had been turned back; Tanaka's transports returned to base.

The frustration of their intended battleship bombardment interrupted the Japanese schedule scarcely at all. Down came Mikawa from the Shortlands with his Cruiser Bombardment Group, and in the early hours of the 14th he carried out his bombardment of Henderson Field, achieving considerably less damage than Abe might have done with his 14-inch guns. The fortunes of war were turning against the Japanese however, for Kinkaid's *Enterprise* force had at last arrived within flight range of the Solomons.

Daybreak on November 14 disclosed two Japanese forces to American search planes—Mikawa's Cruiser Bombardment Group south of New Georgia Island on a westerly retirement course and Tanaka's Reinforcement Group once more in the Slot approaching Guadalcanal. Bombers from Henderson Field and from the *Enterprise* first struck Mikawa, sinking one cruiser and damaging three others. Then, joined by B-17's from Espiritu Santo, they struck repeatedly at Tanaka's lightly-protected transports. By evening seven of them, carrying about 1,000 troops each, were sunk or sinking.

The complicated Japanese scheme was now becoming absurd as well as tragic. The transports were the heart of their whole November offensive, yet they had come down the Slot shielded by a mere handful of destroyers and a meager cover of fighter planes operating at near extreme range out of the Upper Solomons and from the decks of Kondo's carriers maneuvering far to the north. In his extremity Tanaka now rose to a sort of magnificence. With remarkable if perhaps foolhardy tenacity he pushed on toward Guadalcanal with four damaged transports, all he had left of his convoy. Meanwhile, Kondo himself with the *Kirishima,* four cruisers, and nine destroyers was heading down from the north to redeem Abe's failure of two nights before by blasting Henderson Field with a really effective bombardment.

At the same time up from the south came the *Washington,* the *South Dakota,* and four destroyers, detached from the *Enterprise* group with orders from Halsey to protect the field. The American force, under command of Rear Admiral Willis A. Lee in the *Washington,* reached Guadalcanal first, and late in the evening under a setting moon passed into Ironbottom Sound through the passage north of Savo. Though Lee had detected nothing, Kondo had seen Lee and divided his force into three groups, two to attack and the third to keep the Americans under observation. (See diagram page 268.)

As Lee's force, in column with the destroyers leading, turned west toward Cape Esperance, the battleships made radar contact with the Japanese sweeping group and chased it away with a series of salvos. But one of the attack groups, a light cruiser leading several destroyers, had passed west around Savo so that it could not be detected by American radar. This group now attacked Lee's van with shells and torpedoes, sinking two of his destroyers and putting the other two out of action. To avoid colliding with the disabled vessels the *Washington* shifted to port and the *South Dakota* swung to starboard, toward the enemy. This accidental separation of the American battleships occurred at a critical moment, for Kondo was about to strike again. His main attack group, the *Kirishima,* two heavy cruisers, and two destroyers, which had been maneuvering northwest of Savo, emerged from behind the island and took the nearby *South Dakota* under fire, so wrecking her superstructure that she was obliged to retire.

The *Washington* was thus left to face the entire Japanese force. Lee, with the advantage of radar fire control, at which he was expert, accepted the challenge and quickly evened the score. With his 5- and 16-inch guns, he concentrated on the *Kirishima.* Seven minutes and 50 shell hits later the Japanese battleship was helpless and turning in circles. Lee continued for a while to the northwest to attract the enemy away from his cripples and then withdrew to the south.

Kondo now gave up, ordered the *Kirishima* and a disabled destroyer scuttled, and left the area. But "Tenacious Tanaka," who had steamed unflinchingly through the embattled waters, continued on to Guadalcanal, where he beached his four remaining transports. After dawn

American planes and ship and shore artillery quickly smashed them to pieces—but not before the surviving troops had landed.

Japan's final attempt to recapture Guadalcanal had ended in failure like all the rest. Thereafter Yamamoto risked no more capital ships in the Solomons campaign.

## The Battle of Tassafaronga

Following the collapse of their November attack the Japanese went entirely on the defensive, maintaining their garrison on Guadalcanal merely as a holding force to keep the Americans occupied while they prepared a new defense line by constructing a pair of airfields on Kolombangara and New Georgia in the Central Solomons. In the meantime Admiral Tanaka contrived a streamlined Tokyo Express of fast destroyers to keep the garrison precariously alive by dropping floating drums of food and medical supplies offshore and then darting back up the Slot before daylight. To derail this new express Halsey assigned to Admiral Kinkaid a force of cruisers and destroyers.

Kinkaid, an able tactician with surface forces, prepared a detailed battle plan designed to secure him from the errors his predecessors had made. Not for him was the blind approach or the single unbroken column. In night engagements he would use float planes for early warning and for parachute flare illumination when needed. His destroyers were to speed ahead to make a surprise torpedo attack and then turn away. His cruisers, holding off at 12,000 yards, out of visual range of the enemy, were to open with their guns the moment the torpedoes hit. But Kinkaid was detached for duty elsewhere and it fell to his successor, newly-arrived Rear Admiral Carleton Wright, to execute this plan.

Warned that Tanaka was about to begin operations, Wright approached Guadalcanal on November 30 and that evening took his force through the east channel—four destroyers in the van, followed by five cruisers. Two additional destroyers, which joined too late for briefing, were stationed at the rear of the column. Forming line of bearing inside Ironbottom Sound, the cruisers swept westward with the destroyers on their flanks. Meanwhile Tanaka with eight destroyers had entered the Sound from the opposite direction; but of this Wright was unaware, for the float planes that were to give him warning had been unable to rise from the water because of the dead calm.

At 2306 Wright's flagship made radar contact with the Japanese, whereupon the cruisers promptly resumed column formation and wheeled to parallel the enemy. Now was the moment to release the van destroyers, but Wright hesitated because he could get no clear radar data; Tanaka's force, speeding past on an opposite course, merged with the nearby

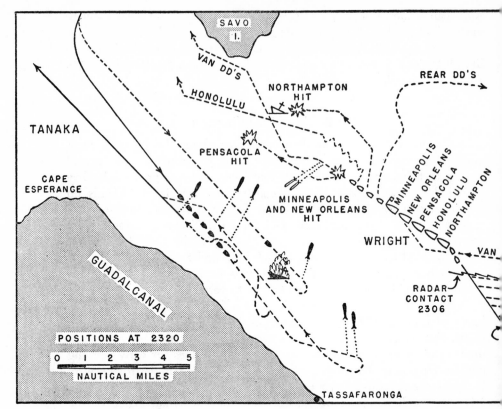

BATTLE OF TASSAFARONGA, NOVEMBER 30, 1942

shoreline. When at last Wright ordered his van destroyers to launch torpedoes, the moment of opportunity had passed. The range was opening rapidly and none of the torpedoes found a target. The cruisers however opened fire on a destroyer somewhat nearer than the others, and sent her down in flames.

The other Japanese destroyers had now reversed course by divisions. Since the Americans had no flashless powder, their gun flashes provided Japanese torpedo directors with a point of reference. Tanaka's well-drilled team released a score of deadly Long Lances at the extended American track. Because they were well aimed and ran true, and Wright's cruisers maintained course and speed, the torpedoes inevitably found their targets. Every one of the cruisers except the *Honolulu* took one or more hits. The *Minneapolis* and the *New Orleans* had their bows ripped away. The *Pensacola,* her after engine room flooded, three of her turrets knocked out, was quickly wreathed in oil fires. Worst hit of all was the *Northampton;* as water poured into her gashed-in side and blazing oil drenched her decks, the crew abandoned ship and she heeled over and sank. By that time Tanaka's seven surviving destroyers, virtually undamaged, were far up the Slot. This brief battle, which besides vitally needed cruisers cost the Americans 400 lives, provided a sort of textbook, later well studied, on how not to combat the powerful and accurate Japanese torpedo.

Wright's battered force was obliged to withdraw from the Guadalcanal area. Its retirement seemed to open the way for Tanaka's Express, which was scheduled to come down the Slot at four-day intervals, covered until dark by Zekes from the Shortlands. The Americans however found ways to complicate Tanaka's problem. As his ten destroyers started down the Slot on December 3, aircraft from Henderson Field flew out to meet them. They damaged one destroyer slightly, shot down three Zekes, and lost two of their own planes. Tanaka's force nevertheless pressed on and dumped 1,500 drums of supplies off Tassafaronga. Such was the exhausted and weakened state of the Japanese garrison however that the troops succeeded in hauling only 310 of these ashore by dawn. American fighter planes then sank the rest of the drums with machine gun fire.

The Tokyo Express in its December 7 approach came under a more severe air attack that left one Japanese destroyer so damaged that she had to be towed back to base under escort. Hence only a portion of the Express reached Ironbottom Sound, and here they were met by torpedoes and machine gun fire from eight PT boats out of Tulagi. None of the torpedoes found a target and one PT boat was heavily damaged, but the Express was constrained to retire without delivering any supplies. Tanaka led the December 11 Express in person, flying his flag in Japan's newest and best destroyer, the 2,500-ton *Teruzuki*. His force passed unscathed through the usual sunset air attack and dropped 1,200 drums off Cape Esperance. As the destroyers were withdrawing however, the American PT boats found them and put a torpedo into the *Teruzuki*, which caught fire. Her after powder magazine blew up, and Tanaka was among the wounded. Two other Japanese destroyers stood by to remove survivors from the sinking vessel. They rescued Tanaka and a few others, but before they could complete their task they were driven away by the arrival of more PT boats. Following this repulse, Tokyo at last concluded that Guadalcanal would have to be abandoned.

## Guadalcanal Secured

In December the malaria-ridden veterans of the 1st Marine Division together with their commander, General Vandegrift, were evacuated to Australia, and Major General Alexander M. Patch USA took command of the Guadalcanal garrison, which was soon raised to corps strength by the arrival of an additional army division directly from the United

States. In January 1943 Patch had 50,000 soldiers and marines (of the 2nd Marine Division) under his command. Unaware that the enemy had already conceded defeat, he began an all-out offensive in mid-January, driving westward from the American defense perimeter toward the area where all the enemy were now concentrated.

The Japanese, using cleverly sited artillery, gave ground stubbornly, fighting for time to carry out their evacuation. This they achieved by means of a neatly-timed stratagem. While transports and destroyers assembled at Rabaul and in the Upper Solomons, Admiral Kondo brought the Combined Fleet once more to the waters north of Guadalcanal. As the Japanese had expected, all this activity caught Halsey's attention. What did it portend? Was the enemy, after failing four times, about to make a fifth attempt to recapture the island? If so, the South Pacific at long last had power aplenty to turn him back. Halsey promptly dispatched to Guadalcanal an additional troop convoy supported by five task forces, including two fleet and two escort carriers and three battleships. But no fleet action ensued, for Kondo had brought his ships down not to do battle but merely to create a diversion. Instead, the Japanese struck from the air. At night, using parachute flares and floating lights, torpedo planes from the recently-constructed airfield on New Georgia succeeded in sinking the cruiser *Chicago*. Evidently the enemy had developed yet another technique for turning the night to his advantage.

As the main body of Patch's troops advanced westward along the north coast of Guadalcanal, a battalion was ferried around to a new beachhead west of Cape Esperance. The newly-landed troops then advanced eastward to meet the approaching main body in order to nip off the enemy's communications with the coast and seal him up in the jungle for annihilation. But when the American forces made contact on February 9, they found that the quarry had slipped through their fingers. While American attention had been diverted elsewhere, a score of destroyers in three high-speed night runs down the Slot had carried away the 12,000 half-starved survivors of the Imperial Army garrison. Thus on a note of mingled frustration and triumph for both sides, the Guadalcanal campaign came to an end.

Of about 60,000 American soldiers and marines who fought on Guadalcanal, 1,600 were killed and 4,200 wounded. Of more than 36,000 Japanese on Guadalcanal, about 15,000 were killed or missing, 9,000 died of disease, and 1,000 were captured.

## Papua Secured

While the Americans were tightening their grip on Guadalcanal, Allied forces a thousand miles to the west were with equal difficulty and equal success wrestling from the Japanese the peninsula of Papua. As

Australian troops pursued the retreating enemy via the direct route across the Owen Stanley Mountains, American and Australian forces crossed the mountains by a roundabout trail or were flown to airfields on the north coast in areas not held by the enemy. All Allied forces then converged on the Buna area and in mid-November 1942 began a coordinated offensive to capture it from the Japanese defenders.

The Allied situation on Papua was now the reverse of that on Guadalcanal, for on Papua it was the Allies who were assaulting a well fortified perimeter defense—fighting along matted jungle trails, across fields of man-high kunai grass, and through dense mangrove swamps. The Papuan campaign however, unlike that on Guadalcanal, never involved major fleet elements. A strong naval force might quickly have turned the tide either way by repeated bombardment and by supporting rapid waterborne supply and reinforcement. But neither side ventured major ships into this area of uncharted waters and hostile airfields. The sea however did play an important part in the campaign. The Japanese tried first to reinforce and then to evacuate the Buna area by means of nightrunning barges, but American PT boats made such attempts too costly. And although airdrop and later airlift were an important means of Allied supply, more than three quarters of the material brought in to the investing forces came by luggers and small commercial steamers.

Though MacArthur at length committed nearly 30,000 troops, half Australian and half American, to dislodge some 12,000 enemy from Papua, the Japanese held their bit of coastline until late January 1943. Then at last their defenses collapsed, as much from starvation and disease as from outside pressure. In recapturing Papua, 3,095 Allied troops had lost their lives, nearly twice as many as were killed on Guadalcanal.

The long and critical preliminaries were over. South Pacific and Southwest Pacific forces had each captured a base that the Japanese had intended to use as a springboard for further aggression. For the Allies two roads to Rabaul were now open.

## Conclusion

Until the Battle of Midway the Japanese had been superior in the Pacific, but at the time of the invasion of Guadalcanal the opposing forces, all elements considered, were roughly equal. Guadalcanal moreover lay exactly equidistant from Rabaul, the nearest Japanese base, 560 miles to the northwest, and Espiritu Santo, the nearest Allied base, 560 miles to the southeast. What, then, enabled the Allies to win the victory?

In the first place, before August 7, 1942 the Japanese had held the island too lightly. With a whole division of crack troops and the advantage of surprise, the Americans easily wrested Guadalcanal from the few hundred combatants defending it. Thereafter the situation favored the Americans, for it is enormously more difficult to capture a strongly defended position than to hold it.

The retirement of Fletcher and Turner on August 9 left the Japanese in potential command of the sea around and the air over Guadalcanal, but they were not prepared to make their control permanent by seeking out and destroying the Allied fleet in the Coral Sea. Their experience at Midway made them wary of this classic means of isolating the target. Instead they chose to begin by putting troops ashore by one means or another to defeat the American occupation force and recapture the airfield. As the plan gradually evolved, carriers would then approach and send in planes to operate from the captured airfield and seize command of the air over the island. Under cover of this air power, now land based, fleet units could move in to take command of the waters around Guadalcanal.

This plan of reconquest was destined to failure because the Japanese, grossly underestimating the number of Americans on Guadalcanal, for two months directed their main strength against Papua. When they learned the truth, it was too late. In the reinforcement race they could never get a sufficient preponderance of manpower on the island, with the necessary artillery, ammunition, and supplies, to wrest the airfield from the entrenched Americans. By November the Japanese situation was hopeless because superior Allied training and construction programs were beginning to make themselves felt, particularly in the vital areas of manpower and airpower. True, the Japanese at that time had three heavy carriers, the *Zuikaku, Junyo,* and *Hiyo,* to oppose damaged U.S.S. *Enterprise,* but that bald statement fails to take into account the severe losses in aircraft they had suffered in the Battles of the Eastern Solomons and the Santa Cruz Islands, their inability to replace these losses quickly, and the growing power of the Henderson Field airdrome. The Japanese moreover were coming to realize that they had achieved maneuverability in the air at high cost. Their fragile planes quickly disintegrated in the face of massed American antiaircraft fire. Yamamoto was well advised not to expose his carriers to close support of the November attack. Japanese carriers did not in fact go into action again until the middle of 1944.

One of the greatest weaknesses of the Japanese counterattack lay in the field of command. The Imperial Army and Navy, which were supposed to be cooperating in the Guadalcanal campaign, not only failed to coordinate planning but worked together, if at all, with ill-concealed hostility. Even within the services, commands overlapped and were at odds with one another. The result was a kind of grudging, improvised collaboration that looked to the Allies like a single grandiose, inflexible plan of operation repeated four times. On the Allied side also there was some lack of coordination, particularly between the Southwest Pacific and South Pacific commands. But there was never any doubt that General MacArthur was in full command in the Southwest Pacific; and after Admiral Halsey arrived in Noumea, there was no question of who was running the show in the South Pacific.

The one real and continuing advantage the Japanese had over the Americans in the Guadalcanal campaign was superiority in night surface tactics. This was of course a Japanese specialty, emphasized to make fullest use of the superb Long Lance torpedo. The new SG radar, then being installed in American vessels, could have offset enemy binoculars and night training had more American commanders understood its capabilities. But the fact was that the Americans were not well prepared for night surface action; that was not the sort of warfare they had anticipated. The dreadful example of the Battle of Savo Island, together with the scratch teams and impromptu commands that characterized all Allied surface action in 1942, constrained commanders to adopt a single-column, defensive formation in which destroyers, attached to the van and rear, could not scout ahead, readily use their torpedoes, or reach the enemy with their 5-inch guns. Admiral Kinkaid's battle plan pointed the way toward better night tactics, but his ideas would not reach fruition until late 1943, with the development of the Combat Information Center and the establishing of surface forces with some permanence of composition and command.

# 10

# The Limited Offensive

Following the Allied capture of Guadalcanal and of Buna, there was a pause in military operations in the Pacific theater. This was a period of planning and preparation for both the Japanese and the Allies.

As noted in chapter 4, the Combined Chiefs of Staff at the Casablanca Conference of January 1943 had allocated a greater percentage of men and material to the Pacific in order to keep the offensive rolling in that theater. At the Washington Conference of the following May they assigned the general conduct of the war in the Pacific to the American Joint Chiefs of Staff. They also accepted in principle the Joint Chiefs' "Strategic Plan for the Defeat of Japan." This plan assumed that the Japanese were to be defeated (1) by blockade, especially through cutting off Japan's access to the oil of the East Indies; (2) by sustained aerial bombing of Japanese cities; and (3) possibly by actual invasion of the Japanese home islands. To provide a base for carrying out these operations, all major lines of Allied advance were to converge on Hong Kong and the China coast. The British army, with Chinese and American help, was to invade Burma and reopen the Burma Road in order to supply the Chinese army, which would drive in from the west. Even if the Chinese did not reach Hong Kong, they would at least draw Japanese forces from the coast, making Allied invasion from the sea less hazardous. The British fleet was to penetrate the Straits of Malacca and advance to the Celebes Sea. Here it would be joined by MacArthur's Southwest Pacific forces, advancing from the east, and together they would recapture the Philippines and seize Hong Kong by amphibious assault. Meanwhile, Nimitz' Central Pacific forces would have advanced westward across the center from Pearl Harbor via the Marshalls and the Carolines and reached Hong Kong by way of Formosa.

This complex program had to be drastically curtailed because the British found that they could not disengage enough forces from the

Mediterranean campaign to carry out their part of the plan and because the Japanese launched an offensive in China that eliminated the possibility of Chinese participation. The drive on Japan would have to be carried out by the Americans, aided only by such limited forces as Canada, New Zealand, and Australia could provide. The program actually put into effect included intensified submarine attacks on Japanese sea power and three ground-air-surface offensives:

1. North Pacific forces to eject the Japanese from the Aleutians.
2. Central Pacific forces to advance westward from Pearl Harbor.
3. South Pacific and Southwest Pacific forces to cooperate in a drive on Rabaul. Southwest Pacific forces then to press on westward along the north coast of New Guinea.

Because No. 2, the Central Pacific drive, was given priority in men and materials, No. 1 and the first phase of No. 3, with which this chapter deals, were necessarily limited offensives. The best in new naval construction, especially carriers, battleships, and attack transports, was deliberately hoarded at Pearl Harbor for the drive across the center, which was to begin as soon as the build-up permitted. The Japanese, noting this growing concentration of power, also held back their capital ships. But they recklessly expended their naval aircraft without setting up an adequate training program for replacement of pilots. That, as we shall see, proved their undoing.

In March 1943, Admiral King had clarified naval organization by inaugurating a numbered fleet system whereby United States fleets operating in the Atlantic and Mediterranean would bear even numbers, and those in the Pacific would bear odd numbers. Under this plan, the principal naval forces in the Pacific were designated as follows:

CENTRAL PACIFIC. The Central Pacific Force, based at Pearl Harbor, would become the U.S. Fifth Fleet.

SOUTH PACIFIC. Halsey's South Pacific Force became the U.S. Third Fleet, with Halsey in direct command; and Turner's amphibious team became the Third Amphibious Force.

SOUTHWEST PACIFIC. MacArthur's miniature Naval Forces Southwest Pacific became the U.S. Seventh Fleet, under Vice Admiral Arthur S. Carpender (later succeeded by Vice Admiral Kinkaid), with amphibious craft and support designated as Seventh Amphibious Force, under Rear Admiral Daniel E. Barbey. Unlike the Third and Fifth fleets, the Seventh Fleet and its components were not part of the U.S. Pacific Fleet and hence were not subject to control by Admiral Nimitz.*

---

* The fleets would be divided into task forces, task groups, and task units as operations required. Thus TU 31.2.3 would be a component of TG 31.2, which would be a component of TF 31, which would be a component of the Third Fleet. For logistic purposes, ships of the same type requiring the same sort of equipment and services continued to be organized (on paper at least) into squadrons and divisions.

## The Reconquest of Attu and Kiska

For nearly a year following the Japanese occupation of Attu and Kiska, Allied operations in the Aleutians were limited to harassing and isolating the enemy-held islands by air and submarine action. In August 1942, an American cruiser-destroyer force finally penetrated the Aleutian fog to give Kiska its first pounding from the sea. For several months thereafter the job of harassment was left in the hands of Canadian and U.S. Army air forces, which raided the islands whenever the weather permitted. During the winter of 1942-43, the Americans occupied Adak and Amchitka, the latter only 65 miles east of Kiska. On these islands they constructed airfields in record time so that fighters could escort bombers in stepped-up attacks which soon cut off Kiska from all surface contact with Japan.

In order to isolate the more westerly Attu, Rear Admiral Charles H. McMorris in mid-February 1943 bombarded the island, and then led his cruiser-destroyer group to the southwest to patrol the enemy supply line. Here he had the satisfaction of sinking an ammunition ship en route to Attu and sending two accompanying transports fleeing back to the Japanese base at Paramushiro in the northern Kurils. Vice Admiral Boshiro Hosogaya, realizing that the last Japanese surface supply line to the Aleutians could not much longer be maintained, early in March rushed to Attu a convoy escorted by his entire North Area Force, unloaded, and got safely back to Paramushiro. Later the same month he tried it again, but this time McMorris's group of two cruisers and four destroyers was patrolling in an intercepting position south of the Russian Komandorski Islands. Contact between the two forces resulted in the Battle of the Komandorskis, last of the classic daytime surface actions.

An hour before sunrise on March 26, the American task group made radar contact with the Japanese convoy to the north, and McMorris promptly gave chase, little guessing that he was in pursuit of a force considerably stronger than his own. As Hosogaya made out the approaching American vessels in the first light of dawn, he ordered his two transports to retire to the northwest and hastened to put his four cruisers and four destroyers between the Americans and their Aleutian bases. The pursuer now became the pursued. The three-hour westerly chase that followed is chiefly remarkable for how little the Japanese accomplished with superior speed and firepower. They lost their speed advantage by zigzagging in order to use their after turrets, which would be masked in a bows-on approach; and the Americans avoided serious damage by making smoke and by expert salvo chasing, i.e., heading for the last shell splashes so as to avoid being struck when the enemy guns corrected their aim. At length however the cruiser *Salt Lake City* took a hit that flooded an engine room. Her engineers, in attempting to correct a resulting list, inadvertently let sea water into a fuel line, thereby extinguishing her burners and bringing her temporarily to a standstill. In this desperate situation, McMorris retained one destroyer to make smoke around the stalled cruiser and ordered the other three to delay the enemy with a suicide torpedo attack. The latter reversed course at once and steamed boldly into the blazing guns of the Japanese cruisers, only to observe that the enemy was breaking off action. Hosogaya, unable to see the motionless *Salt Lake City* through the smoke, felt that he had stretched his luck far enough. His fuel was running low, and American bombers could be expected at any moment from Adak and Amchitka. So he took his entire convoy back to Paramushiro, where his displeased seniors relieved him of his command. Thereafter only submarines attempted to get supplies through to Attu and Kiska.

In thus isolating the enemy, the Allied North Pacific forces had done well enough. A few thousand starving Japanese on ice in the Aleutians could hardly have any influence on the outcome of the war. But the American public remained uneasy at the thought of United States territory, however worthless, in enemy hands, and the Combined Chiefs wanted the Aleutians cleared for use as a route for staging aircraft into Siberia—if and when the Soviet Union joined the war against Japan.* Kinkaid, still a rear admiral when he took over the Aleutian command in January 1943, regarded the reconquest of the lost islands as his special responsibility and kept pressing for an early assault on Kiska. Informed that he could not for several months have all the ships and men he needed, Kinkaid took another look at the reconnaissance reports and decided that he could temporarily by-pass Kiska and with a much smaller force seize the more distant Attu. His estimate was correct, for the 2,600 defenders of Attu were fewer than half the number on Kiska, their airstrip was unfinished, and they had no coast defense and few antiaircraft guns.

When the Joint Chiefs accepted the substitution, Admiral Nimitz ordered three old battleships north for extra gunfire support and set May 7 as target date. Designated as the landing force, the 7th U.S. Infantry Division, which had been training in the Nevada desert, moved to the California coast for amphibious exercises. In late April the division sailed away to the Aleutians and a kind of warfare for which it had had little realistic preparation. After two postponements because of heavy surf, an assault force of 3 battleships, 6 cruisers, 19 destroyers, 5 transports, and an escort carrier under Rear Admiral Francis W. Rockwell on May 11 landed 1,000 troops without opposition near Holtz Bay on the north coast of Attu and 2,000 more at Massacre Bay on the south coast.

* Soviet vessels carried lend-lease goods from the west coast of the United States to Vladivostok throughout the war. The Japanese, anxious to avoid trouble with the Soviet Union, were careful not to interfere.

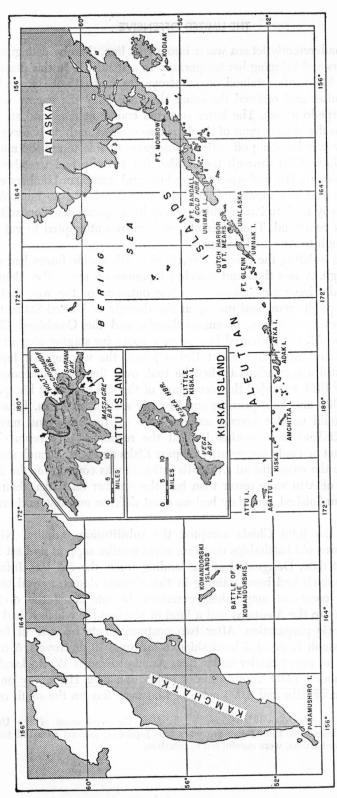

THE ALEUTIAN THEATER OF OPERATIONS

The northern and southern invasion forces were to advance and meet in the mountainous interior and then drive the Japanese into the eastern tip of the island, where fleet guns and planes from the escort carrier could pound and strafe them into submission. But the Japanese, instead of retreating eastward, holed up in the mountain passes and by use of concealed artillery prevented the juncture of the American forces until 11,000 soldiers, including the entire reserve, had been put ashore. Kinkaid, impatient at the numerous delays, relieved the general in command of the ground forces. At least part of the fault however lay with the supporting battleships, which stood six to eight miles offshore delivering a neutralizing fire that drove the enemy temporarily to cover but left his positions largely intact.

By the end of May the remnant of Japanese defenders on Attu had been forced into the highlands near the north shore, where fleet guns proved more effective against them. When the Japanese had used up their store of shells and most of their small arms ammunition, they threw away their lives in a massive banzai charge. Before dawn on the 29th, a thousand Imperial Army troops, many armed only with knives or bayonets, came silently down from the hills. At first light they hurled themselves through a gap in the American lines, overran two command posts, and broke into a medical station, where they butchered the sick and wounded. At last brought to bay, some 500 of the attackers committed suicide with hand grenades. Surviving Japanese made further attacks that day and the next morning until all the defending garrison except 28 captives had killed themselves or been killed. American losses by that time amounted to about 600 killed and 1,200 wounded. Nearly 1,500 more had been put out of action during the campaign because their shoes and clothing, not to speak of their training, had been ill-suited to the cold, damp climate of the Aleutians.

The only attempt of the Japanese to support their troops on Attu was by submarines, which made no hits, and by aircraft from Paramushiro, which were generally defeated by fog. The Combined Fleet never intervened because the Commander in Chief was at Tokyo looking three ways at once. Worried over Allied offensive preparations at Pearl Harbor and in the New Guinea-Solomons area, he could not bring himself to commit major naval forces to the Aleutians.

In preparing for the assault on Kiska, set for mid-August 1943, the North Pacific command put to good use the hard lessons learned at Attu. In six weeks Eleventh Air Force planes dropped 1,200 tons of bombs on the island. Battleships, cruisers, and destroyers bombarded the main camp and harbor. At Adak 29,000 United States and 5,300 Canadian troops under Major General Charles H. Corlett usa, equipped to a man with tested arctic gear, practiced landings and maneuvered across the muskeg. This huge force, carried in numerous transports and supported by nearly a hundred men-of-war, left Adak August 13. Before dawn on the 15th, gunnery support vessels were off Kiska thundering away at enemy positions. At first light, LST's, LCI's, and LCT's moved to the beach and disgorged their troops. There followed the greatest anticlimax of the war. The Japanese escape artists had carried out another evacuation. Three weeks before, while fog covered the area and the American blockading force had temporarily withdrawn to refuel, cruisers and destroyers had slipped in and carried away the entire Kiska garrison.

Some officers now urged using the recovered islands as jumping off points for an advance on Japan via the Kurils, but the Combined Chiefs never took such suggestions very seriously. The cold, fog, and foul weather of the North Pacific forbade proper logistic support for such a drive, and even if it had been logistically feasible, it was strategically unsound because it would leave intact Japan's principal external source of strength, the oil-rubber-rice shipping line from the East Indies, which Japan had gone to war with the United States to establish. The North Pacific forces lapsed back into their former patrol functions, and Kinkaid, promoted to vice admiral, went south to assume command of the U.S. Seventh Fleet under MacArthur.

## Preliminaries to the Dual Advance on Rabaul

With the expulsion of the Japanese from Guadalcanal and Papua early in 1943, the Allies completed Task One of their campaign against Rabaul. During the pause in the Allied offensive that preceded Task Two, the coordinated advance via the Solomons and via New Guinea, both the Japanese and the Allies set out to strengthen their own positions and to weaken the enemy.

The Japanese drew in the defenses of Rabaul to a line running from their new airfield at Munda Point on New Georgia to Salamaua in New Guinea. The Imperial Navy, with assistance from army infantry, assumed the responsibility of guarding the Central Solomons; the Imperial Army, with the assistance of naval ships and aircraft, would defend the Northern Solomons and New Guinea. In command of the defense forces were Vice Admiral Jinichi Kusaka and General Hotishi Imamura. There was no unified joint command nearer than Tokyo.

The night-running Tokyo Express again went into high gear, pouring troops into the Central Solomons. Reinforcing the Lae-Salamaua area in New Guinea was more risky, for this involved passage over open seas partly by daylight. Early in March a convoy of eight Japanese transports escorted by eight destroyers met disaster while carrying 7,000 troops from Rabaul to Lae. Medium and light bombers out of Papua attacked it persistently almost at masthead level, using slow-fused bombs that permitted the aircraft to pull out of range of the explosions. The Battle of the Bismarck Sea continued for three days, until all of the transports and four of the destroyers had been sunk and about 25 planes of the Japanese combat air patrol had been shot down by Allied fighters. Some of the surviving troops made their way to New Guinea in boats and on rafts, but at least 3,600 were lost. After additional sinkings of Japanese vessels in the next few days, Imperial General Headquarters forbade sending more convoys to New Guinea. Any further reinforcements or supplies would have to go by submarine or barge.

Alarmed by the deteriorating situation, Yamamoto himself came to Rabaul to direct an all-out air offensive which he counted on to snarl up Allied plans. By stripping some 200 planes from the Imperial Third (Carrier) Fleet and adding them to his 100 land-based naval aircraft, he built up the most powerful Japanese air armada of the war and sent it first against the shipping in Ironbottom Sound and then against targets in Papua. Its achievements were by no means negligible: a destroyer, a corvette, a tanker, and two transports sunk, 25 Allied planes destroyed. But these results had been attained at the cost of 40 aircraft and a heavy loss of first-line carrier aviators which rendered the Japanese carrier force considerably less battleworthy than before.

In preparation for further aerial offensives, Yamamoto set out with his staff on an air tour of the Upper Solomons to inspect installations and raise morale. Unfortunately for the Japanese, the Americans had decrypted radio messages from which they inferred that Yamamoto would arrive by air at a certain time in southern Bougainville. Counting on his known passion for punctuality, a squadron of long-range P-38's took off from Henderson Field and shot him down precisely on schedule as his plane was coming in for a landing. To the Japanese navy the loss of its most able and colorful commander was the equivalent of a major defeat.

Yamamoto's successor, Admiral Mineichi Koga, directed frequent air raids against Guadalcanal but with steadily diminishing success, for the Imperial Navy had expended its best flyers. The ineptitude of the new, hastily-trained aviators was spectacularly demonstrated in mid-June, when 24 Japanese bombers and 70 Zekes struck at transports in Iron- bottom Sound. All but one of the attacking planes were shot down, at a cost of six Allied fighters.

While the Japanese were in general weakening themselves in their attempts to shore up their defenses, the Allies were emphasizing prepara- tions for their coming offensive. Because General MacArthur proposed to advance along the northern New Guinea coast by a series of waterborne leaps, the Southwest Pacific command set out to build up the tiny Seventh Fleet into a respectable force. The South Pacific meanwhile

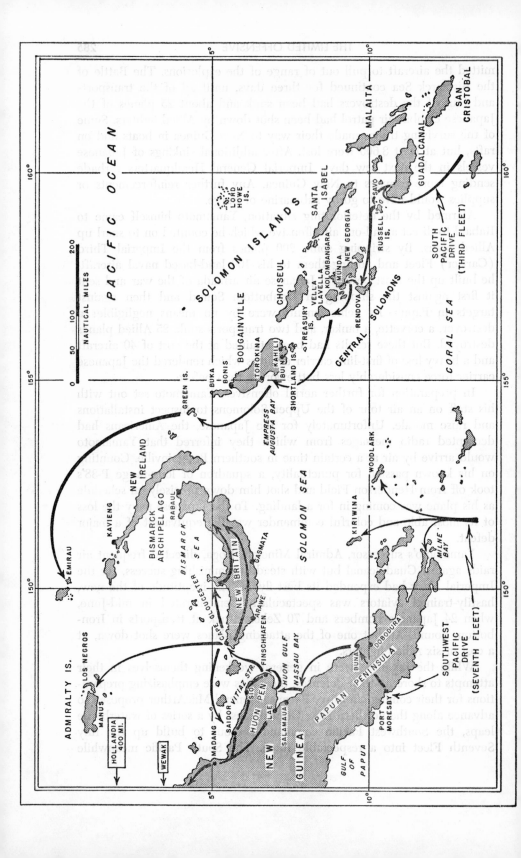

was training the 43rd Infantry Division to operate amphibiously while the 1st and 2nd Marine Divisions were undergoing rest and rehabilitation from the rigors of the Guadalcanal campaign.

Henderson Field was expanded into a complete bomber base surrounded by three fighter strips. Five miles to the east, Carney Field, a bomber base bigger than Henderson, went into operation on April 1, 1943. By this time there were on Guadalcanal more than 300 aircraft of every variety. Operating together were bombers and fighters of the Royal New Zealand Air Force and of the United States Army, Navy, and Marine Corps. To this heterogeneous but closely-integrated force, known as Air Command Solomons—Airsols for short—was to fall the major burden of knocking out Rabaul. Equally powerful were the mutually supporting Allied army airfields on New Guinea—at Dobodura near Buna, at Milne Bay, and at Port Moresby. From these fields operated General George C. Kenney's U.S. Fifth Air Force, to which Royal Australian Air Force squadrons were attached. Airsols and the Fifth Air Force were destined within a few months to win command of the air over the whole Eastern New Guinea-Solomons-Bismarcks area.

Meanwhile the pair of Japanese airfields in the Central Solomons, on Munda Point and at the mouth of the Vila River on nearby Kolombangara Island, proved a continuing nuisance and threat to Guadalcanal. As a step preliminary to seizing or neutralizing these fields, Admiral Turner's Third Amphibious Force put troops and Seabees ashore in the Russell Islands, 65 miles northwest of Henderson Field. Here small craft bases were established, and a pair of airstrips was constructed to extend the reach of Airsols bombers a little farther up the Slot. Before and after the Russell Islands occupation, Allied ships and aircraft mined the waters around New Georgia and southern Bougainville, Airsols bombed the Munda and Vila fields by day and by night, and a pair of cruiser-destroyer task forces under Rear Admirals Stanton Merrill and Walden L. Ainsworth took turns making night runs to subject the airstrips to prolonged naval bombardment.

Merrill's and Ainsworth's task forces were a far cry from the usually ill-prepared, often hastily assembled scratch teams that had fought in Ironbottom Sound during the Guadalcanal campaign. Naval forces operating in the Solomons in 1943 were better equipped and much better organized to meet the night-fighting Japanese. Dependable radar had now become generally available on Allied vessels, and fleet personnel had learned to use it effectively. The scopes were housed in a special compartment known as Radar Plot, where contacts were plotted and analyzed. Gradually other information, from radio and lookouts, began to be correlated here, and Radar Plot became the Combat Information Center (CIC). Possession of the CIC gave the Allies an enormous advantage over the Japanese, whose radar, still primitive by American and British standards, had at this time been installed in only their largest vessels. Equally important to the improvement of Allied night fighting tactics was the comparative permanence of the new surface task groups and task forces. Operating regularly together, commanders and crews developed the skills and the confidence that eventually enabled them to expel the Japanese night fighters and their Long Lances from the Solomons. In this exacting school of tactics, three names stand out: Commanders Frederick Moosbrugger and Arleigh Burke and Rear Admiral Merrill, who were to fight three of the most skillfully conducted battles of the war.

At the end of March 1943, the Joint Chiefs of Staff issued a directive covering Task Two of the campaign against Rabaul. MacArthur's assignment was to control the Huon Gulf and Peninsula and to invade New Britain. Halsey's was to invade Bougainville Island and there establish airfields whence fighter-escorted bombers could strike regularly at Rabaul. Before either commander could move upon his assigned objective however, he would have to seize intermediate positions. MacArthur would occupy Kiriwina and Woodlark Islands; simultaneously Halsey would invade the Central Solomons. The purpose of this intermediate step was to deny these positions to the enemy, to extend the Allied bomber and fighter radius to cover the final step, and to afford air staging and mutual support between the two Allied lines of advance.

Since the dividing line between Halsey's and MacArthur's areas of command lay just west of Guadalcanal, Task Two would see South Pacific forces penetrating the Southwest Pacific Area. This led to a curious command situation, with Halsey planning the details of his own operations but looking to MacArthur for general strategic directives and to Nimitz for ships, troops, and aircraft to carry them out.

## The Central Solomons Campaign

Getting at Munda airfield, the South Pacific's first major objective in Task Two, presented a tricky problem, for the only New Georgia beaches in the vicinity were within easy artillery range of Rendova Island, five miles to the south. But the Japanese, failing to appreciate their advantage, had no artillery and only 120 troops there. So on June 30, 1943 Turner's Third Amphibious Force put ashore on Rendova 6,000 soldiers and marines who wiped out the enemy garrison and turned American guns on Munda. Then, under artillery cover, they began ferrying troops over to New Georgia for the drive on the Japanese airfield. Airsols fighters chased enemy aircraft away whenever they appeared. Only one Allied vessel, Turner's flagship *McCawley*, was seriously damaged. Put out of action by a Japanese airborne torpedo, she was subsequently sunk by an American PT boat that mistook her in the darkness for an enemy.

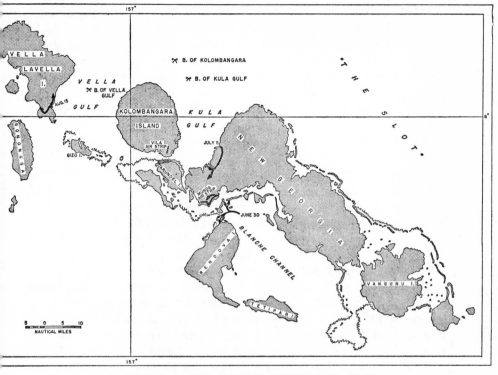

OPERATIONS IN THE CENTRAL SOLOMONS, 1943

So far the operation had gone according to schedule, but once the assault forces entered the New Georgia jungle, the optimistic picture changed abruptly. Some 4,500 Japanese, well-entrenched behind a strong defensive perimeter and sporadically reinforced, held off the attackers for a month. The Americans once more faced the problem of seizing a well defended position from a determined enemy under difficult natural conditions. As at Buna and on Attu, there was a shake-up in the U.S. Army command, and all available reserves had to be committed—32,000 soldiers and 1,700 marines. Even after the airfield had been captured, the invaders had to spend several more weeks dislodging and pursuing enemy defense forces, who, when counterattack proved hopeless, generally succeeded in working their vanishing act, slipping away by water to nearby Kolombangara.

Halsey's original plan had called for a continuation of the "island hopping" campaign, which would bring Allied forces next against Kolombangara and Vila airfield. Admiral Kusaka, who suspected and indeed hoped that this would be the next Allied target, had been reinforcing Kolombangara for weeks, making an assault on that island an increasingly unattractive prospect. Halsey, noting the build-up of enemy strength, decided not to play Kusaka's game. He would by-pass Kolombangara and invade lightly-held Vella Lavella beyond. Such a move would be distasteful to an army general engaged in continental warfare, for it would leave an enemy force in position to intercept his supplies and attack his rear. But, as Kinkaid had recently demonstrated in going past Kiska to take Attu, the naval commander can sometimes outflank the enemy with impunity provided that in doing so he can isolate him, cut his communications, and leave him to "wither on the vine."

On August 15 the Third Amphibious Force, now headed by Rear Admiral Theodore S. Wilkinson, began putting some 6,000 Americans ashore on Vella Lavella under cover of Airsols fighters operating from the newly captured strip at Munda. Despite persistent enemy air attacks, the assault forces suffered only a few casualties and slight material damage. Wilkinson avoided the high costs and delays of the Munda drive by invading the southern tip of the island, where there were no enemy forces. Here the invaders established a defense perimeter within which Seabees began constructing a new airstrip. When it became apparent that there was to be no counterattack on the American position, troops moved out of the perimeter in both directions along the coast to entrap or destroy the small enemy garrison, which Rabaul made no attempt to reinforce. In September, New Zealanders relieved the Americans and soon pocketed about 600 Japanese in the northwest corner of the island.

With the Allied landings on Vella Lavella, Kusaka's defense in depth collapsed. When the Japanese had foreseen the necessity of evacuating Guadalcanal, they had held on there until they could complete and fortify Munda airfield. The campaign against Munda gave them time to build up forces on Kolombangara, and these were counted on to delay the Allied advance while Bougainville was strengthened. Now by his end-run Wilkinson had rendered Kolombangara impotent and was directly threatening Bougainville. A last-ditch fight for Vella Lavella was out of the question, for Imperial Headquarters refused to commit any more troops to the Solomons. To reinforce Bougainville, Kusaka would have to evacuate both Kolombangara and Vella Lavella. This brings us to the problem of sea communications and the operations of American and Japanese surface forces.

Besides bringing invasion forces to the beachheads, transporting supplies and reinforcements, and bombarding enemy positions, the U.S. Third Fleet had the responsibility along with Airsols of cutting the enemy's communications with his rearward bases. Interception of the Tokyo Express was assigned to Ainsworth's and Merrill's cruiser-destroyer forces. Merrill made no contact with Japanese surface forces during the Central Solomons campaign, but while the Americans were driving on Munda, Ainsworth twice met the enemy in the same waters a little after midnight and fought the almost identical night battles of Kula Gulf

(July 6) and Kolombangara (July 13) with similar tactics and similar results. Allied achievements and shortcomings in these battles demonstrate how far American night-fighting tactics had progressed since 1942 —and how far they yet had to evolve to offset Japanese training and skill.

Ainsworth entered both battles in the favored nighttime formation, a single column with cruisers in the center and destroyers in the van and rear. In both, his cruisers closed the enemy, fired with almost machine-gun rapidity for five minutes, and then reversed course together to avoid enemy torpedoes. This was sound doctrine, but there were two flaws in the performance. First, the radar operators selected only the largest or nearest target instead of providing for effective distribution of fire; as a result, the Allied force, though much the stronger in both battles, sank only one vessel in each—a destroyer in one and a light cruiser in the other. Secondly, Ainsworth came in too close to the enemy, making himself an easy visual target, and he waited too long to open fire, thereby permitting the enemy to take careful aim and release torpedoes that reached his position just as he reversed course. In each battle therefore one of his cruisers was torpedoed on the turnaway—U.S.S. *Helena*, sunk in the first battle; H.M.N.Z.S. *Leander*, put out of action in the second. In both battles, Japanese destroyers withdrew temporarily to reload their torpedo tubes, a capability that Ainsworth did not suspect, and came back to fight again. In the first battle, the rearmed destroyers fired torpedoes at American vessels engaged in picking up survivors of the *Helena* but misssed; in the second, the returning Japanese torpedoed two cruisers and a destroyer. The cruisers were not severely damaged, but the destroyer could not be saved. In the Battle of Kolombangara, Ainsworth, in addition to turning away after opening fire, released his van destroyers for a torpedo attack, and it was these that sank the Japanese cruiser, *Jintsu*, already put out of action by shellfire. In short, the Americans at this stage showed considerable advance in tactical doctrine over the preceding year but still fell short in battle efficiency and in intelligence of enemy capabilities.

Convinced that Ainsworth's force was smashed, Rear Admiral Shoji Nishimura came steaming down the Slot a few nights after the Battle of Kolombangara with a strong cruiser-destroyer force looking for Merrill. Merrill's ships were not out that night, but a PBY "Black Cat" picked up Nishimura by radar and flashed the word back to Guadalcanal, whence came bombers that sank two of his destroyers, damaged a cruiser, and sent the rest of his force reeling back to the Shortlands. The Japanese, after this sample of the new American aerial night-fighting techniques, steered clear of the Kula Gulf route to their base at Vila, choosing rather to thread the ticklish passage south of Kolombangara. Here American PT boats sank one enemy barge and battered several others but proved no barrier to the Tokyo Express of heavier types.

Admiral Wilkinson decided early in August to put larger craft on the new enemy reinforcement route. Because Merrill's force was too far away and Ainsworth's was depleted by the July battles, he ordered to the area what he had available—Commander Burke's division of six destroyers. Burke, most vocal proponent of independent action for destroyers, had worked out for just such a mission an ingenious plan using two mutually supporting columns. This concept Burke derived from his study of the Punic Wars. "The tactics of Scipio Africanus particularly interested me as being sound, simple of execution, and adaptable to naval employment," said he. "The plan was based on hitting the enemy with one sudden surprise after another. This was accomplished by putting two destroyer divisions in parallel columns. One division would slip in close, under cover of darkness, launch torpedoes and duck back out. When the torpedoes hit, and the enemy started shooting at the retiring first division, the second half of the team would suddenly open up from another direction. When the rattled enemy turned toward this new and unexpected attack, the first division would slam back in again. Of course, the Solomon Islands area was ideally suited to this type of tactic, with the many islands helping prevent radar detection of the second column."

On the eve of battle Burke was detached to assume a higher command. Luckily, his successor was Commander Moosbrugger, who adopted the essential features of Burke's plan and carried them out with such skill and sense of timing that in the Battle of Vella Gulf he achieved a little classic of naval warfare.

Warned by a search plane that the Express was en route, Moosbrugger's destroyers entered Vella Gulf from the south at 2200, August 6, two columns in line of bearing, and advanced northward, hugging the coast to avoid radar or visual detection. A little before midnight, four enemy destroyers, three of them crowded with troops for Vila, entered the Gulf from the north and soon registered themselves on American radar scopes. Moosbrugger's first division thereupon raced past the enemy column on a parallel and opposite course, launched torpedoes, and then promptly turned away together. The other division meanwhile came about on a T-capping course across the van of the enemy column. Just as the torpedoes struck their targets, both American divisions opened up with gunfire. Under this neatly-timed triple blow, the three troop-carrying destroyers exploded, hurling 1,800 soldiers and sailors into the water and creating such a pyrotechnical display that PT boatmen 30 miles away in Kula Gulf thought a volcano had erupted on Kolombangara. The escorting enemy destroyer escaped only because the torpedoes that slid under her hull failed to detonate. None of the American vessels were damaged. The Battle of Vella Gulf provides a perfect example of tactical concentration achieved by divided but mutually supporting forces. Americans at last had outperformed the Japanese at their own specialty.

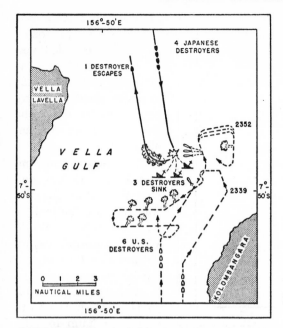

**BATTLE OF VELLA GULF, AUGUST 6–7, 1943**

As usual, the Japanese proved more adept at evacuation than at reinforcement. After the American invasion of Vella Lavella, they waited until late September and the dark of the moon before sending destroyers, submarines, and swift barges to evacuate Kolombangara. American destroyers sent out to intercept succeeded in damaging a destroyer and sinking a submarine and about a third of the barges. Nevertheless three quarters of the garrison of 12,400 got safely away. Obviously the Allies, though they had by-passed Kolombangara, had not truly isolated it.

After the Battle of Vella Gulf, the Japanese had generally avoided surface action, but during their evacuation of Vella Lavella, which closely followed that of Kolombangara, a force of Japanese destroyers found themselves at such a numerical advantage that they disdained to turn tail and run from the Americans. The resulting Battle of Vella Lavella brought little tactical credit to destroyermen on either side.

Warned by search planes of the approach of six Japanese destroyers escorting small craft, Captain Frank R. Walker took the destroyers *Selfridge, Chevalier,* and *O'Bannon* into the waters northwest of Vella Lavella to intercept. As Walker advanced to attack, the nearer Japanese division of four destroyers missed a chance to cross his T and then masked its own fire by approaching in line of bearing. The Americans fired 14 torpedoes and a hail of shells at the nearest enemy vessel, which burst into flames and presently blew up. By this time the Japanese had turned away under a smoke screen. Walker might properly have turned away also to avoid the inevitable Japanese torpedo attack. Instead, he chose to maintain course in order to keep his guns bearing. As a result, the *Chevalier* and the *Selfridge* both had their bows blown off by torpedoes, and in the confusion the *O'Bannon* rammed the *Chevalier*. The timely arrival of three more Third Fleet destroyers obliged the enemy

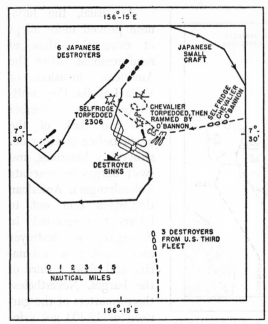

**BATTLE OF VELLA LAVELLA, OCTOBER 6–7, 1943**

to retire, but while the Americans were looking after their crippled vessels and sinking the helpless *Chevalier*, the Japanese small craft proceeded to Vella Lavella and carried out still another evacuation.

The Japanese had completed their mission and won the battle, but this was the last battle they were to win in World War II. And their victory did not alter the fact that the Allies now held the Central Solomons, with air fields close enough to support a jump to Bougainville.

## The Bougainville Campaign

The scheduled Allied invasion of fiddle-shaped Bougainville, northernmost and largest of the major Solomons, would permit construction of bomber and fighter strips from which Airsols could bring Rabaul under continuous attack. On and near Bougainville there were 33,000 Japanese—mostly in the south, at Kahili and Buin and in the nearby Shortland Islands, and in the north, at Buka and Bonis. Profiting by lessons learned at Munda and on Vella Lavella, Admiral Halsey planned to by-pass the concentration of Japanese strength in the southern bases and invade half way up the weakly defended west coast at Cape Torokina in Empress Augusta Bay. Here the Allies would establish a powerful perimeter, lay out their airstrips, and let the Japanese come to them, over rough mountains and primitive jungle trails.

For so formidable an operation, Halsey had barely enough troops— some 34,000, including the 3rd Marine Division, the 37th Infantry Division, and a brigade group of New Zealanders, which together made up the I Marine Amphibious Corps, commanded by General Vandegrift. Naval forces were even more scarce because of the concurrent Mediterranean campaign and because Nimitz was about to unleash the U.S. Fifth Fleet in the Central Pacific. Wilkinson would have to cram his first echelon landing force into a dozen transports,

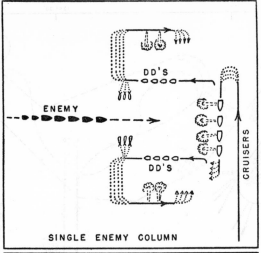

SINGLE ENEMY COLUMN

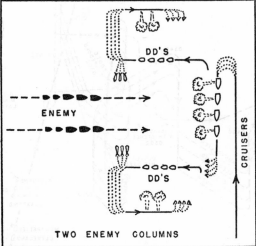

TWO ENEMY COLUMNS

MERRILL'S BATTLE PLAN FOR NIGHT ATTACK

escorted by eleven destroyers. Support would be provided by Task Force 39 (Merrill's cruiser-destroyer force) and by Rear Admiral Frederick C. Sherman's carrier task group, including the *Saratoga* and the light carrier *Princeton,* on loan from the Fifth Fleet.

In preparation for the new assault, the Fifth Air Force began a series of massive raids on Rabaul, while Airsols bombed out Japanese airfields on Bougainville. On October 27, 6,000 New Zealanders seized the Treasury Islands for a small-craft staging base, and that night 725 marines landed on Choiseul to attract Japanese attention away from the main Allied invasion area. A little after midnight on D-day, November 1, Merrill's TF 39 provided further diversion by bombarding Buka and Bonis airfields; then while Merrill raced back south to bombard the Shortlands at first light, Sherman's carriers sent in planes to continue the pounding of Buka and Bonis.

While Japanese attention was thus diverted in several directions, Wilkinson's amphibians entered Empress Augusta Bay at dawn on the 1st. Despite determined resistance from about 300 Japanese at the beachhead and an air attack from Rabaul, which Airsols fighters soon scattered, the invasion progressed rapidly. By nightfall the Third Amphibious Force had put ashore 14,000 troops and 6,000 tons of supplies. In the early evening the transports pulled out, and four minelayers began laying a mine field off the beachhead.

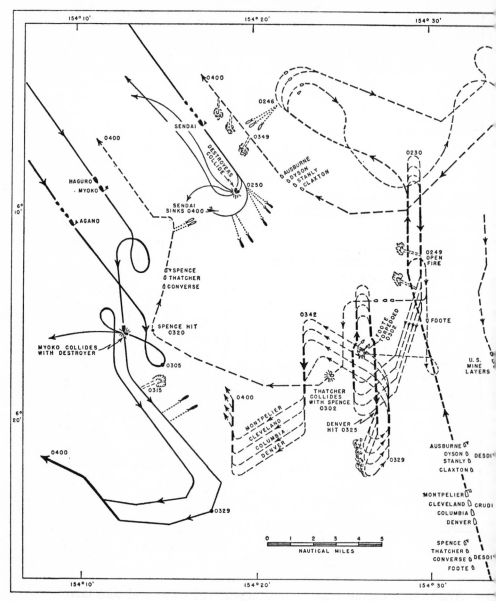

BATTLE OF EMPRESS AUGUSTA BAY, NOVEMBER 2, 1943

   The Imperial Eighth Fleet reacted to the new landing much as it
had 15 months before when the marines had landed on Guadalcanal.
Down from Rabaul came a hastily organized cruiser-destroyer force
under Rear Admiral Sentaro Omori to smash the American transports.
This attack force was early spotted by Airsols patrol planes, which

promptly and accurately reported their find to South Pacific headquarters and continued tracking. By 0200, November 2, Omori in intense darkness under a rain squall, was approaching the Torokina beachhead, his two heavy cruisers *Myoko* and *Haguro* flanked to starboard and port by light cruisers *Agano* and *Sendai*, each leading three destroyers.

The only force available to stop Omori was TF 39. Though the crews were exhausted after having carried out two bombardments in the past 16 hours, Admiral Halsey had no choice but to order them to Empress Augusta Bay. Caution was imposed on Merrill by the fact that TF 39 was now the principal Allied surface force in the whole South Pacific. Instead of risking scarce cruisers in a battle of annihilation, he would have to limit himself to repulsing the attackers from the beachhead. In accordance with an oft-rehearsed plan, he intended to release his destroyer divisions for torpedo attacks on the flanks of the enemy. With his four light cruisers he would block the entrance to the bay and, by continuous fire from his six-inch guns and a series of simultaneous reversals of course, gradually force the enemy out to sea. Merrill was fortunate in having Arleigh Burke, now Captain Burke, as commander of his Destroyer Division 45, for the two had operated together and saw eye-to-eye in tactical matters. But Desdiv 46, his other four-destroyer division, would be at a disadvantage, for it was so new as a unit that Commander Bernard Austin had not yet had an opportunity to exercise his vessels in formation.

At 0227, as TF 39 neared Empress Augusta Bay on course 345° with the three divisions in line of bearing north to south, the flagship *Montpelier* detected the enemy 18 miles away, coming down from northwest. Merrill thereupon shifted to course due north, which brought his divisions into the usual American single column formation for night action. As soon as the enemy appeared on his radar scopes, Burke, in the van, swung left and led Desdiv 45 toward the flank of the northern enemy group. The American cruisers then reversed course together, and Merrill detached Desdiv 46 to strike the southern enemy group.

At 5,600 yards on the *Sendai's* port bow, Desdiv 45 fired half salvos of torpedoes and turned away together. None of the torpedoes found targets, for the Japanese had changed course. The *Sendai* had seen the American cruisers and launched torpedoes, warning Omori, who ordered his divisions to wheel south to form a line of battle.

"My guppies are swimming!" Burke had reported at the moment he launched. Merrill then began to count off the six minutes it would take the torpedoes to complete their run, but when his CIC reported the enemy change of course, he at once ordered his cruisers to open fire. Forty-eight guns promptly began to roar, taking as their target the nearby northern group, which replied with shells that fell forward and short. Two of the Japanese destroyers collided while maneuvering to avoid the concentrated 6-inch American fire, and the *Sendai* began to blaze and fell out of line with a jammed rudder. The Americans had handily won the first round, but Desdiv 45 had become separated on the turnaway. It would take Burke an hour to locate and reassemble his vessels and bring them back into the battle.

Because of Omori's change of course, the TF 39 cruisers at 0251 turned together to course 200° in order to close the range. It now appeared that Austin's destroyers had been released prematurely, for Merrill's advance to the southwest brought them within the cruisers' line of fire. Moreover, the destroyer *Foote* had become separated. When Desdiv 46 had countermarched to conform to the cruisers, she had turned at once instead of following around in column. In racing west to rejoin, the *Foote* cut across the path of the oncoming cruisers so that the *Denver* had to sheer left to avoid a collision.

To clear Desdiv 46 and close on the *Sendai* group, the cruisers at 0302 turned north. Almost at once they had to swing right to avoid hitting a vessel dead in the water. It was the *Foote* again. Still heading west she had been struck by one of the *Sendai's* torpedoes, which had demolished her stern.

At 0310 Merrill turned south once more, thus completing the first loop of a huge figure eight. The waters of the South Pacific were now witnessing a new high in ship handling. Barking his orders by TBS through the roar of gunfire, Merrill kept his cruisers in perfect order— zigzagging and swinging back and forth across the enemy's line of fire to present him constantly changing problems in range and deflection. Through 30 minutes of rapid maneuver Merrill managed always to be somewhere else when the enemy's shells or torpedoes arrived.

To take advantage of his 8-inch guns, Omori, like Merrill, wanted to fight at long range, but he was having difficulty locating the Americans. So he began a complete loop, thereby sadly confusing the *Agano* group, which vaguely tried to conform. Then as he steadied again on a southerly course, American 6-inch shells began to fall all around him. One of the *Agano* destroyers, while dodging, collided with the *Myoko* and had a piece of her bow sheared off. Then six shells, including four duds, hit the *Haguro*. By this time Japanese planes arriving over the American cruisers were dropping red and white parachute flares. These, reflecting off the low cloud ceiling, combined with star shells to turn the night into an eerie twilight and thereby rob Merrill of some of his radar advantage.

Now at last Omori saw Merrill and advanced southeast to close the range a little. The *Myoko* and the *Haguro* launched torpedoes and fired salvos of shells. Three shells hit the *Denver*, whereupon Merrill turned away, making smoke. Omori, under the illusion that he had sunk several heavy cruisers, also turned away and presently ordered a general retirement. In so doing he abandoned his assigned mission of sinking the American transports. But, greatly overestimating the force opposing him, he thought he had done well enough, and he wanted to be out of easy range of Airsols by dawn.

While Merrill and Omori were dueling it out, Austin's division was suffering one unlucky break after another. The *Foote*, as we have seen, was early put out of action. Then, while the other three destroyers were maneuvering frantically to avoid being silhouetted by starshell and to clear the line of fire of their own cruisers, the *Spence* sideswiped the *Thatcher*. Though both vessels suffered heavy topside damage, Desdiv 46 proceeded westward at high speed until it was 6,000 yards on the port bow of the enemy center group, in perfect position to carry out a torpedo attack against the Japanese heavy cruisers. At that moment the *Spence* was temporarily slowed down by a shell hit at the water line. Immediately afterward, the CIC evaluator became disoriented and reported to Austin that the *Myoko* and *Haguro* were American ships. With no time to check, Austin turned north to go after the *Sendai*, which was turning in circles but still firing. A couple of his destroyers launched torpedoes and apparently made hits, but the cruiser was still afloat as he headed northwest in pursuit of her two collision-damaged destroyers.

Burke, after having cruised far and wide to reassemble his scattered division, now sped in from the east and sent the *Sendai* down at last in a hail of shells. Then, because radar recognition was working badly that night, he set out in hot pursuit of Austin. Presently Austin's division opened fire on the Japanese destroyers, one of which caught Burke's attention. "We have a target smoking badly at 7,000 yards, and we are going to open up," Burke warned by TBS. "Oh-oh, don't do it," replied Austin, "that's us." And so the two Japanese destroyers got away, and Burke turned his fire on the *Spence*. "Hope you are not shooting at us," said Austin. "Sorry," Burke responded, "but you'll have to excuse the next four salvos. They are already on their way." After such loss of opportunity and near disaster the two division commanders at length located each other and with special satisfaction joined forces in sending down the last of the Japanese cripples in the area, the destroyer whose bow had been ripped off by the *Myoko*. Except for the lost *Sendai* the remainder of Omori's force was making best speed for Rabaul.

Because dawn was breaking, Merrill ordered his divisions to leave off the chase and to rendezvous for better defense against the inevitable air attack. Leaving three destroyers behind to salvage the torpedoed *Foote*, he headed south with the rest of TF 39. At 0800 the Japanese struck with a hundred carrier bombers and fighters from Rabaul. By a combination of accurate antiaircraft fire and deft ship handling, the Americans shot down 17 attacking planes and avoided all but two rather inconsequential bomb hits. Before the enemy planes could come in for a second strike, Airsols fighters arrived and chased them away, shooting down eight more.

The American performance in the Battle of Empress Augusta Bay was not without flaws, particularly in the accuracy and distribution of radar-controlled gunfire, but Merrill had brilliantly carried out his mission of repulsing the enemy from the beachhead. His night victory demonstrated the soundness of the tactical doctrine and practice that his predecessors had been groping for.

Incensed at Omori's poor showing, Admiral Koga promptly relieved him of his command. He then ordered Vice Admiral Takeo Kurita south from Truk with a stronger, better integrated cruiser-destroyer force to redeem Omori's failure. To bolster the air defense of the Bismarcks, he once more stripped his carriers, sending down 173 fleet aircraft.

On November 4, Airsols planes sighted Kurita approaching Rabaul to refuel and flashed a timely warning. Kurita's force was too strong for Merrill, even if Merrill's cruisers and destroyers had been within reach and his crews fresh. In this desperate emergency Halsey did what the Navy had recoiled from doing 16 months before when MacArthur had suggested it. He sent Sherman's carrier group into the Solomon Sea for an attack on the ships at Rabaul. At the same time he directed Airsols to lend Sherman every bit of help it could.

Halsey's perilous resort succeeded beyond the most sanguine hopes of anybody in the South Pacific command. On the morning of November 5, as Sherman maneuvered under a concealing cloud cover 60 miles southwest of Empress Augusta Bay, Airsols fighters from Vella Lavella arrived and took over combat air patrol. The carriers were thus able to send nearly a hundred planes against the target. Striking from clear skies over Rabaul, Sherman's bombers bored in through a steel curtain of antiaircraft fire. Their objective was Kurita's force, which had anchored in Rabaul's Simpson Harbor just two hours before. At a cost of ten aircraft, the American dive bombers and torpedo planes put Kurita out of business, damaging two destroyers and six cruisers, including the heavy cruiser *Mogami*, newly repaired from her battering at Midway. There would be no surface attack on the amphibious shipping in Empress Augusta Bay.

Elated at the success of his experiment, Halsey tried it again on a larger scale. From the Fifth Fleet he borrowed an additional carrier group, including the *Essex*, the *Bunker Hill*, and the *Independence*, under Rear Admiral Alfred E. Montgomery. On November 11 he sent both Sherman and Montgomery against Rabaul. Sherman attacked first from the waters north of Bougainville but was thwarted by foul weather. Montgomery had better luck. Striking from south of Bougainville under Airsols fighter cover, his carriers launched 185 planes, which thrust aside defending Zekes to hit shipping once more in Simpson Harbor.

Kurita had prudently departed, but there were other targets. The Americans sank a destroyer, torpedoed another, sheered off the stern of a light cruiser, and played havoc among transports and cargo vessels.

This time Admiral Kusaka located the source of his attackers and struck back. In the afternoon, 120 Japanese planes swooped down from the north and headed for Montgomery's carriers. Their raid cost them 35 aircraft without damaging a single ship. American losses in both attack and defense were limited to eleven planes. The opposition of carrier fighters plus land-based combat patrol plus intense VT-fused antiaircraft fire was simply too formidable for the hastily trained Japanese aviators who now replaced the veterans expended in the defense of the Solomons.

Sherman's and Montgomery's carrier groups now steamed away to participate with the Fifth Fleet in opening the drive across the Central Pacific. Their contribution to the campaign against Rabaul, though potent, was not the most lasting of their achievements. They had settled once and for all the long-debated question as to whether carriers could be risked against powerful enemy bases. Moreover they had paralyzed the Combined Fleet at a crucial stage in the war. The Central Pacific forces would meet no fleet opposition at the outset of their offensive, for Koga was obliged to send his carriers to Japan to train new flyers to replace his losses.

With the departure of Sherman's and Montgomery's carriers, the conduct of the Solomons campaign once more devolved upon local forces. In the afternoon of November 24, Captain Burke, then heading for Bougainville with a squadron of five destroyers, received a message from Admiral Halsey's headquarters: "Thirty-One-Knot Burke, get athwart the Buka-Rabaul evacuation line. . . . If enemy contacted, you know what to do."*

The Japanese Army command at Rabaul, believing that the Americans were about to assault Buka, had requested the Navy to rush more soldiers to the area and bring away the airmen. A Tokyo Express of two destroyers and three destroyer-transports was told off to do the job. This was the movement that Halsey wanted stopped, and Burke knew very well what to do. Here at last was an opportunity to make personal use of his destroyer battle plan.

The Battle of Cape St. George, which occurred that night, was in essence a duplication of the Battle of Vella Gulf, followed by a chase. Reaching the interception point a little before 0100, Burke made radar

---

* By this message Halsey's operations officer, Captain Harry R. Thurber, conferred upon "31-knot Burke" the nickname that soon became known around the world. The prefix, from an old destroyer shipmate, was a gentle gibe at Burke's repeated reports that he was "making 31 knots" with a force previously considered to be capable of no more than 30 knots sustained speed.

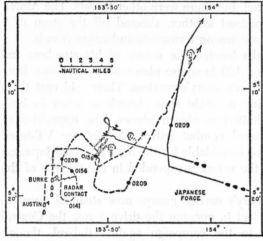

**BATTLE OF CAPE ST. GEORGE,
NOVEMBER 25, 1943**

contact with the two vessels of the enemy screen. Then while Commander Austin with two destroyers maneuvered to take them under fire at the appropriate moment, Burke led his other three toward the enemy's flank, launched 15 torpedoes at his extended track, and turned away. The Japanese destroyers, having seen nothing, plowed unsuspectingly ahead. Both blew up as Burke's torpedoes reached them at the calculated point. Austin thereupon opened fire and swung in to finish them off. By that time Burke was away after the loaded transports. He sank one with shellfire and chased the other two to within 60 miles of Rabaul before turning away to clear the area while it was still dark.

Meanwhile Vandegrift's soldiers and marines on Bougainville had moved steadily forward despite increasing opposition from Japanese forces filtering through the jungles. Airsols lent close, effective air support and, together with the Third Fleet, kept the Tokyo Express from resuming operations. The Third Amphibious Force, despite vicious and damaging air attacks out of Rabaul, in two weeks brought 34,000 men and 23,000 tons of supplies to the expanding perimeter. The I Marine Amphibious Corps in another month of hard fighting pushed the defense line inland and laterally along the coast until it enclosed 22 square miles. Within this area Seabees and a New Zealand engineering brigade constructed a fighter and a bomber strip by the end of 1943. These airfields, just 220 miles from Rabaul, extended Halsey's bomber line to include the Bismarcks. The South Pacific forces had completed their assignment in Task Two.

## The New Guinea Campaign

We now have to backtrack a few months and follow the operations of Southwest Pacific forces. It will be recalled that MacArthur's assignment in Task Two of the campaign against Rabaul was to control the Huon Gulf and Peninsula and to invade New Britain. But, like Halsey, he was obliged first to seize positions nearer his established airfields.

On June 30, 1943, timed to coincide with South Pacific landings on Rendova and New Georgia, Southwest Pacific forces began putting troops ashore without opposition on Kiriwina and Woodlark Islands off the Papuan Peninsula and at Nassau Bay 17 miles southeast of Japanese-held Salamaua. Admiral Barbey's Seventh Amphibious Force staged the island invasions, proceeding from Townsville and Milne Bay with destroyers, transports, and beaching craft. But because no one was yet ready to risk such valuable vessels in the inner reaches of the Solomon Sea, the Nassau Bay operation was a mere 40-mile run up the coast with elements of the 41st U.S. Infantry Division carried in PT's and landing craft. Four such night runs established a beachhead.

The main purpose of the Nassau Bay operation was to secure a coastal position to ease the problem of supplying the 3rd Australian Division in the Bulolo Valley. Here at the site of a small pre-war airstrip just 30 miles southwest of Salamaua, Australian troops had been isolated since the Japanese invasion of New Guinea. Meagerly supplied and reinforced by air, they had successfully held off all enemy attacks for more than a year. Once the Bulolo Valley veterans had joined hands with the newly-arrived Americans however, MacArthur had a special assignment for the combined forces. He ordered them to make a diversionary attack on Salamaua, which he was about to by-pass by sea and by air. In preparation for the by-pass, surveys of the dangerous offshore reefs went on apace, and General Kenney's Fifth Air Force planes ranged as far west as Madang and Wewak destroying enemy aircraft. The diversionary attack, which thrust back the defenders of Salamaua to within six miles of the town, put the Japanese in the Huon Gulf area into a quandary. Cut off from Rabaul by Allied aircraft and barge-hunting PT boats, they were obliged to reinforce threatened Salamaua by drawing troops from Lae—exactly what MacArthur hoped they would do.

In the night of September 3–4, Barbey's Amphibious Force at last penetrated the Solomon Sea, moved across the Huon Gulf past Salamaua, and after dawn put nearly 8,000 Australians ashore east of Lae in the face of an enemy air attack, which the Fifth Air Force quickly dispersed. The next day, army transport planes from Port Moresby, escorted by fighters from a new airfield at Marilinan, flew over the jungle and dropped 1,700 American paratroops, who quickly seized a Japanese airstrip west of Lae. The 7th Australian Division was then flown in to the captured field and began advancing on Lae from one side to meet their seaborne compatriots moving in from the other. The Japanese thereupon abandoned Salamaua and attempted to take a stand at Lae, which however soon became untenable under the pounding of American destroyer guns. So, as the pincers closed, the Imperial Army evacuated Lae also. The 7,500 defenders took to the jungle and began a starving month-long march northward across the Huon Peninsula to the coastal town of Sio. (See map page 286.)

From captured Lae, Barbey in late September carried a brigade group of Australians by sea 82 miles around the tip of the peninsula for pre-dawn landings north of Finschhafen. This invasion took the enemy completely by surprise. Expecting the Allied forces to march overland, they had deployed most of their troops south and west of the town. Only a handful of Japanese guarded the northern approaches. These the Australians quickly pushed aside and, after a series of skirmishes, took possession of Finschhafen on October 2. The local defenders thereupon pulled out to a nearby mountain range to await a Japanese division coming overland from Madang. But the Australians, using water transportation, could be supplied and reinforced more rapidly than their antagonists. They shattered a Japanese counterattack in mid-December and by early December were pushing 7,000 enemy survivors along the coastal road toward Sio. Meanwhile, the 7th Australian Division had outflanked Sio by way of the river valleys and was advancing on Madang from the interior.

In a series of quick strokes MacArthur had conquered all of the Huon Peninsula except the Sio area. He thereby completed his conquest of the northeast coast of New Guinea from Milne Bay to Vitiaz Strait. The quick acceleration of the Southwest Pacific advance, in such striking contrast to the painful march on Buna, resulted in part from a touch of sea power in the form of Barbey's makeshift amphibious force. It was also made possible by the diversion of Japanese strength in the vain attempt to stop Halsey's march up the Solomons.

Admiral King had early in the year questioned the wisdom of expending time and lives to capture Fortress Rabaul. At far less cost, once airfields were operational on Bougainville, Rabaul could be bombed into impotence while Southwest Pacific forces broke through the barrier of Bismarck-based air and sea power and captured the Admiralty Islands on the far side. In the Admiralties was ample level ground for airfields and base installations, and here also was Seeadler Harbor, a finer anchorage than Rabaul's Simpson Harbor. In August the Combined Chiefs, then meeting at Quebec, concurred with King in deciding that Rabaul was to be neutralized and by-passed rather than captured.

Nevertheless, MacArthur decided to go ahead with the invasion of New Britain. Before advancing westward through Vitiaz Strait, he wanted both shores in Allied hands to secure his sea communications from air or surface attack. By late December the stepped-up Fifth Air Force and Airsols offensives had brought the whole Bismarck defense system to the verge of collapse. But MacArthur, not realizing that the door to the west stood open before him, went ahead with his original plan and ordered the 1st Marine Division into New Britain. An Army invasion at Arawe on the south coast in mid-December provided a small-craft staging base that was never used. Then on December 26 the Guadal-canal veterans, supported by Seventh Fleet guns and Fifth Air Force planes, stormed ashore near Cape Gloucester on the north coast. Fighting through swamps in the monsoon rain, the marines captured the nearby enemy airfield in less than a week. Then they shattered the local defense forces and chased the 17th Imperial Division back to Rabaul.

Meanwhile, Barbey on January 2 had used his Cape Gloucester task force to rush an American regimental combat team of 7,000 troops* to a landing at lightly-held Saidor, a village on the New Guinea north coast. Meeting only slight resistance, the soldiers quickly took possession of a prewar airfield nearby. The sorely reduced Imperial Army Air Force did not react until mid-afternoon, after all Allied vessels had got clean away. Subsequent echelons of troops and engineers soon turned Saidor into an important Allied naval and air staging base.

The occupation of Saidor became something of a model for subse-quent Southwest Pacific amphibious operations. It by-passed the 12,000 fugitives from Lae and Finschhafen now at Sio, cutting them off from the rest of the Japanese Eighteenth Army at Madang and Wewak. It provided an excellent base for covering Vitiaz Strait and for supporting the concurrent Cape Gloucester operation, the scheduled assault on the Admiralties, and the planned westward advance along the New Guinea coast. Moreover it was a classic example of what Admiral Wilkinson, in baseball parlance, had called "hitting 'em where they ain't."

The Japanese at Sio, cut off from supply by land and sea and too weak to attack the growing Allied garrison at Saidor, abandoned Sio to the Australians on January 15, turned inland, and set out on foot for Madang by way of the jungle. Two thousand of them, starved and diseased, died on the way. Hardly had the survivors arrived when the 7th Australian Division, attacking from the interior, obliged the whole Madang garrison to fall back to Wewak.

---

* A *regimental combat team* (abbreviated RCT), or simply *combat team*, was defined as follows in the Army Field Manual in use at this time: "The infantry regiment may be grouped with a battalion of light artillery and units of other arms in suitable proportion. Such tactical groupings are called *combat teams*, and their composition may be prescribed in standard operating procedure." For amphibious operations the combat team was subdivided into (usually three) *battalion landing teams*, or simply *landing teams*.

The combat team system was the ground forces' counterpart to the Navy's task force system. For administration and training, the army or marine corps division segregated its elements by type. A typical division would be administratively or-ganized into three regiments of infantry, each comprising three battalions, an artillery regiment, an engineer regiment, and battalions of special and service troops (tank, special weapons, transport, medical, and so on). For specific tasks such as am-phibious assaults, the division (usually reinforced) was divided into combat teams of size and composition suitable to the task. The troops were carried to the combat area in teams so that the sinking of a single transport would not mean the loss of all the division's artillery, tanks, or other element.

## Neutralizing Rabaul

Though Rabaul had been stunned by the Allied air offensive in the fall of 1943, it remained far too powerful either to be invaded or entirely by-passed. The 90,000 Japanese there began to go underground, scooping out subterranean barracks, shops, and hangars. Though the fleet had left, Kusaka retained some small craft and more than a thousand seagoing barges. All carrier planes had been withdrawn, but as late as mid-December there were at Rabaul and at other Japanese bases in the Bismarcks nearly 300 serviceable aircraft. This was more striking power than either MacArthur or Nimitz cared to have athwart his communications as his forces advanced westward.

So with the completion of the new Airsols fighter strip on Bougainville in mid-December, Halsey launched an all-out air offensive to pound the Bismarcks into final impotence. Then and later, enemy aircraft were to be the principal targets. In January, when the bigger fields at Torokina became operational, Airsols bombers operating directly from Bougainville stepped up the raids to one or more a day. A month later they were averaging a thousand sorties a week. For a while Admiral Koga kept rushing additional planes to Rabaul. But in mid-February the U.S. Fifth Fleet, advancing rapidly across the Central Pacific, made a devastating raid on Truk. Koga thereupon abandoned Rabaul as indefensible and began pulling aircraft out of the Bismarcks to areas where they could be used more profitably. U.S. Third Fleet destroyer squadrons now moved freely along the coasts of New Britain and New Ireland, demonstrating Allied control of the sea and air by bombarding Japanese shore installations.

Fortress Rabaul had been knocked out. But to make sure that the Japanese should not again make use of their extensive facilities in the Bismarck Archipelago, Halsey and MacArthur completed their ring of steel around the enemy stronghold.

In February 1944, Wilkinson's Third Amphibious Force placed nearly 6,000 New Zealand and American troops ashore in the Green Islands 115 miles due east of Rabaul. After the invaders had destroyed the small Japanese garrison, Seabees built a fighter strip on the main island, thereby bringing the entire Archipelago within the radius of fighter-escorted Airsols bombers.

At the end of February, MacArthur ordered a thousand-man American reconnaissance-in-force on Los Negros, easternmost of the Admiralties. Though there were 4,300 Japanese on the islands, Allied fleet guns and air support enabled the invaders to turn the reconnaissance into a regular invasion. They seized part of the airdrome and drew around it a tight perimeter into which poured fresh echelons of troops with artillery and

Seabees with bulldozers. These quickly expanded the beachhead and made the airstrip operational.

In mid-March, the Third Fleet put the 4th Marine Regiment ashore on Emirau, 70 miles northwest of Kavieng. Soon 18,000 men had gone ashore on this island which the Japanese had never occupied, and work was underway on a PT base and another airstrip.

The boxing in of Rabaul was complete, but this time there was scarcely a pause in Allied offensive operations. As the marines occupied Emirau, MacArthur's soldiers were invading Manus, main island of the Admiralty group. By the end of March 3,300 Japanese had been killed or captured in the Admiralties, as against 300 Americans killed, and work on the naval and air base was under way—not merely to help keep Rabaul neutralized but to support further operations westward.

Development of the base facilities in the Admiralty Islands (or simply Manus, as they came collectively to be called) was the last cooperative effort of the South and Southwest Pacific commands. The South Pacific Area, left far behind by the war, was being gradually reduced to garrison status. Its army forces, plus a few warships, were allotted to MacArthur; its marine and most of its naval forces went to Nimitz. MacArthur had hoped to enlist Halsey to command his Seventh Fleet, but Admiral King had other plans. Halsey was ordered to Pearl Harbor for a seagoing command under Nimitz.*

For MacArthur, the capture of Manus marked the end of one campaign and the beginning of another. Even before the Admiralties were secured, he was planning a tremendous 400-mile leap westward to Hollandia, a movement not inappropriately named Operation RECKLESS. Beyond Hollandia he would leap forward again and again until at length he reached the Philippines, in fulfillment of his promise: "I shall return."

## Conclusion

As noted at the beginning of the chapter, 1943 saw Allied offensives underway in the North, Central, and South Pacific. The table on page 308 shows concurrent Allied operations from early 1943 to the end of the campaign against Rabaul in March 1944.

Operations in the North Pacific were not only of little importance in themselves; they had little influence on events elsewhere. The 20-month campaign against Rabaul, on the contrary, was of enormous significance. Among the numerous advantages accruing to the Allies from this cam-

---

* The plan that brought Halsey and MacArthur into close cooperation during the advance on Rabaul was given the code name ELKTON, after the small Maryland town famous for quick marriages. At the same time, the tentative plan for operations westward after the reduction of Rabaul was prophetically named RENO.

| | NORTH | CENTER* | South Pacific | Southwest Pacific |
|---|---|---|---|---|
| **1943**<br>March | 26—Battle of the Komandorskis | | | 2-5—Battle of the Bismarck Sea |
| April | | | 18—Death of Yamamoto | |
| May | 11—Assault on Attu | 30—First of new carriers joins U.S. Pacific Fleet | | |
| June | | | *The Dual Advance on Rabaul* | |
| June | | | 30—Invasion of New Georgia Group | 30—Invasion of Kiriwina, Woodlark, and Nassau Bay |
| July | | | 6—Battle of Kula Gulf<br>13—Battle of Kolombangara | |
| Aug. | 15—Occupation of Kiska | | 6-7—Battle of Vella Gulf<br>15—Invasion of Vella Lavella | |
| Sept. | | 1—Raid on Marcus I.<br>18-19—Raid on Gilberts | | 16—Capture of Lae |
| Oct. | | 5-6—Raid on Wake I. | 6-7—Battle of Vella Lavella | 2—Capture of Finschhafen |
| Nov. | | 20—Assault on the Gilberts | 1—Invasion of Bougainville<br>2—Battle of Empress Augusta Bay<br>5 & 11—Carrier Strikes on Rabaul<br>25—Battle of Cape St. George | |
| Dec. | | | | 26—Assault on Cape Gloucester |
| **1944**<br>Jan. | | | | 2—Occupation of Saidor<br>15—Capture of Sio |
| Feb. | | 1—Assault on the Marshalls<br>17—Assault on Eniwetok<br>17-18—Raid on Truk<br>22—Raid on the Marianas | 15—Occupation of the Green Is. | 29—Assault on the Admiralties |
| March | | | 20—Occupation of Emirau | |

* Operations in the Central Pacific are covered in Chapter 11.

paign, five stand out: (1) it enabled MacArthur to break through the Bismarcks barrier of enemy air and sea power and advance toward the Philippines, (2) it by-passed and put out of the war more than 125,000 Japanese troops, (3) it reduced Japanese air power to the point where it was no longer a serious threat, (4) it forced the Japanese to withdraw their carriers from the Pacific, and (5) it gained for the United States time to provide ships, weapons, and trained manpower for a swift advance across the Central Pacific in 1944.

Japan lost nearly 1,000 naval aircraft trying to recapture Guadalcanal and about 1,500 more defending the Upper Solomons and Rabaul. Exact figures for Japanese army aircraft lost in the defense of New Guinea are unavailable, but they must have been almost as great. When Airsols, the Fifth Air Force, and U.S. Pacific Fleet carriers combined efforts in support of the Bougainville invasion, they very nearly wiped out the Japanese carrier planes committed to the defense of Rabaul. With the Combined Fleet stripped of half its fighters, 85 per cent of its dive bombers, and 90 per cent of its torpedo planes, Admiral Koga had no choice but to send his carriers back to the home islands to train new flyers. This fruitless draining away of Japanese air power left Japan's defenses vulnerable everywhere. It enormously facilitated Nimitz' drive across the center, and this in turn allowed the Japanese at most six months to train new fleet aviators before they were forced into battle against American flyers with generally two years' training and a minimum of 300 hours flying time.

Task Two and subsequent joint operations against the Bismarcks are best referred to as the "Dual Advance on Rabaul"—to avoid confusion with the far more powerful Dual Advance on the Philippines, with which it eventually merged. Advancing simultaneously along more than one line toward an objective undeniably risks defeat in detail, but a dual or multiple drive also confers the advantages of exterior position: it can keep the enemy off balance and under continuous pressure, it obliges him to divide his own forces and leaves him in doubt where the next attack will come, and it is a means of achieving strategic concentration by bringing one's main strength against part of the enemy forces while the enemy is held at other points.

No one has adversely criticized the concept of the Dual Advance on Rabaul. True, the Japanese gained some of the advantages of interior position in that they, at least theoretically, could strike with the same forces from New Britain against either line of Allied advance, but the great merit of the Allied plan was that the South Pacific and the Southwest Pacific offensives were mutually supporting. For the Allies to have advanced exclusively via the Solomons or exclusively via New Guinea would have meant leaving a flank uncovered.

# 11

# Beginning the Central Pacific Drive

From the beginning of Operation WATCHTOWER in 1942, General MacArthur had in mind a fairly complete strategic plan for defeating the Japanese. Early in 1943 he spelled it out and laid it before the Joint Chiefs of Staff. He proposed that, once Rabaul had been captured or neutralized, the transpacific advance on Japan should be via New Guinea and the Philippines by forces under his command. This drive, along what he called the New Guinea-Mindanao Axis, would be mainly an army offensive, with troops carried forward by naval forces in a series of coastal leaps and landed under cover of army aircraft. The Navy, besides transport and convoy, would carry out such supporting functions as shore bombardment, guarding communications, and securing the flank of the Army's advance by neutralizing enemy-held offshore islands.

MacArthur argued that his proposed line of advance made use of bases already established in the South Pacific and Southwest Pacific Areas, that it would maintain a defensive shield between Australia and the enemy-occupied Central Pacific islands, that it was the only feasible route along which land-based air support could be provided all the way, and that the large land masses in the southwestern and western Pacific would enable Allied forces to by-pass enemy strong points and seize relatively unopposed beachheads.

Opponents of the New Guinea-Mindanao Axis argued that it was a roundabout approach to Japan, uneconomical of force and requiring long and vulnerable communication lines; that it was a slow means of approach, with each successive advance limited to the attack radius of fighter aircraft and of fighter-escorted bombers; that, once begun, it was obvious and predictable, permitting the enemy to mass his strength in the path of the oncoming Allied forces; that it exposed troops to malaria and other diseases of the tropical jungles; that it was by way of close and mutually supporting enemy strong points; and that the successive beachheads of this line of advance would be subject to attack by troops moving overland, and its flank, rear, and communication lines, to attack from the Japanese-held islands of the Central Pacific.

The United States Navy, faced since 1898 with the problem of defense or recovery of the Philippines, had long ago concluded that the best line of advance was directly across the Central Pacific. Here there were no large land masses, only hundreds of small islands and atolls, providing a choice of numerous targets. An Allied advance in the Central Pacific would be construed by the enemy as a potential threat to his whole island empire, obliging him to fragmentize his strength all over the Pacific to defend each position. Allied forces coming against such tiny points of land would of course have to assault defended beachheads, but only so many troops could occupy any one small island or group of islands. Because of the vast distances between the island groups, they could not in general be mutually supporting and, once isolated by America's growing carrier air power, they could not be reinforced. The advance across the center, through an area where the climate was healthful and the communication lines short, would be economical of troops and shipping. It would cut Japan's communications to the South Pacific and establish shorter Allied lines to the same theater. It would speedily bring the war into Japanese waters and force out the enemy fleet for a decision that presumably would leave Japan itself open to attack.

In anticipation of the eventual opening of a Central Pacific Axis, the United States Navy, just before and after the declaration of war, had ordered 22 new fleet carriers, and these were becoming available in 1943. Used in support of the New Guinea-Mindanao Axis they would be largely wasted, but freed from a merely auxiliary role they could be used continuously to win command of the sea over ever-increasing areas. Central Pacific forces, spearheaded by these mobile airfields, could eventually dispense with land-based air support and make tremendous leaps, invading any point to which reasonably secure communication lines could be established.

The Joint Chiefs of Staff and their subcommittees, after carefully weighing all the arguments, reached a compromise that largely favored the Navy's plan. Over MacArthur's vigorous protests, they decided to open a Central Pacific Axis as the main line of advance against Japan. In deference to Australian fears however and because Allied forces in the south were already in contact with a retreating enemy, the chiefs did not propose to reorient the fighting front entirely but to continue along the New Guinea-Mindanao Axis as a supporting operation for the Central Pacific Axis.

Admiral King had tentatively brought up the idea of a new line of advance at the Casablanca Conference in January 1943. The startled British Chiefs protested that thus broadening the offensive against Japan

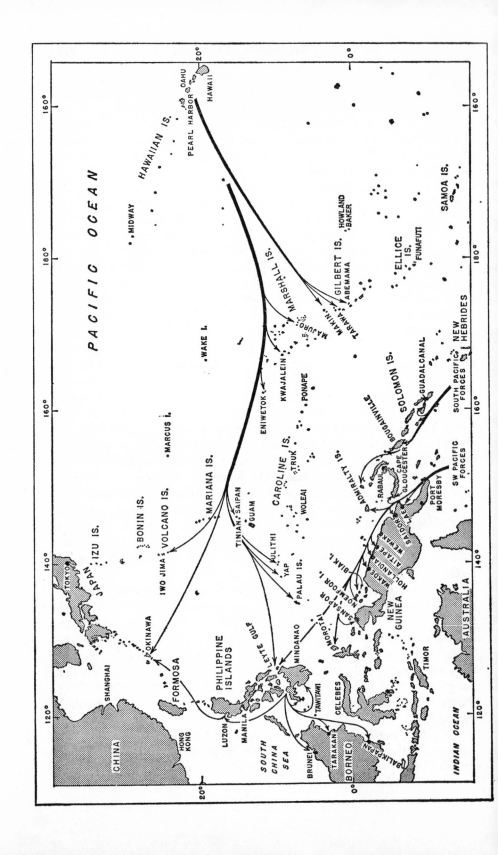

might reduce the scale of operations in Europe, which was and remained the primary theater. General Marshall won British assent however with assurances that the new drive could be carried out with resources already assigned to the Pacific. The Joint Chiefs thereupon developed their "Strategic Plan for the Defeat of Japan," which the Combined Chiefs endorsed at the Washington Conference in May. This plan, it will be remembered, called also for early participation of British and Chinese forces. When these were not forthcoming, the final strategic plan for 1943–44 provided only for the following ground-air-surface offensives:

1. North Pacific forces to eject the Japanese from the Aleutians.
2. Central Pacific forces to advance westward from Pearl Harbor.
3. South Pacific and Southwest Pacific forces to cooperate in a drive on Rabaul. Southwest Pacific forces then to press on westward along the north coast of New Guinea.

No. 1 and the first phase of No. 3 were covered in the preceding chapter. This chapter deals with the opening of Offensive No. 2.

The combination of Nos. 2 and 3 would form another dual advance, on a much larger scale than the Dual Advance on Rabaul. The proposed Allied westward drive along two parallel lines again gave the Japanese an interior position, but the Joint Chiefs counted on the power and mobility of America's new carrier power to offset this advantage. On the other hand, a dual advance would protect the New Guinea-Mindanao Axis from attacks on its flanks and communications and at the same time oblige the Japanese to divide their strength. Because of the many possibilities, the Joint Chiefs kept the plan flexible by not settling details far in advance. Opportunities as they arose would determine how the strategy would be executed.

Because a dual drive must be closely coordinated in order to attain maximum effectiveness and mutual support, certain naval officers suggested that it had at last become mandatory for the entire Pacific theater to be placed under Admiral Nimitz. This proposal was well founded, for the Joint Chiefs had clearly stipulated that the Southwest Pacific forces were to operate in support of the Central Pacific Axis, which, as we have seen, was to be the main line of advance. But the proposal was not followed for a variety of reasons, not the least of which were the military reputation and towering stature of MacArthur himself, for MacArthur had captured the imagination of the world by his defense of the Philippines and his promise to return. On the other hand, the Joint Chiefs would not give the over-all command to MacArthur, at least at this stage, because they did not agree with his strategy. Thus the two offensives rolled forward with no common command closer than the Joint Chiefs themselves in Washington. As it turned out, instant worldwide radio communications overcame most of the disadvantages of such an arrangement—at any rate until the two offensives came into actual contact.

## Power for the New Drive

The Central Pacific drive was unique in the history of warfare. Nothing in the past gave any sure clue as to how armed forces could advance in great leaps across an ocean studded with hostile island air bases. Carrying out the new offensive required new methods of training, new techniques of combat, support, supply, and maintenance, and a whole arsenal of new weapons. Yet when the drive began in the autumn of 1943, less than two years after the attack on Pearl Harbor, the means were at hand. That perhaps was the most remarkable achievement of World War II.

The main combat arm of the Central Pacific forces was the U.S. Fifth Fleet, a complex of men, ships, and aircraft organized for the purpose of projecting power at a distance.* It began to take form with the arrival at Pearl Harbor of the first of the new 27,000-ton, 32-knot *Essex* class of heavy carriers in the spring of 1943. The first of the equally swift new 11,000-ton *Independence* class of light carriers soon followed. By autumn there were in the Fifth Fleet six heavy and five light carriers, eight escort carriers, five new and seven old battleships, nine heavy and five light cruisers, 56 destroyers, 29 transports and cargo vessels, and large numbers of landing and beaching craft. Commanding this considerable and growing fleet was Vice Admiral Raymond A. Spruance, a man of outstanding intellect and an austere and exacting officer. His work on the staff of the Naval War College had won him a reputation as a strategist. The Battle of Midway had demonstrated his brilliance as a tactician. Since then, as Admiral Nimitz' chief of staff, he had assisted in planning the operations he was to lead.

Spearheading the Fifth Fleet was the Fast Carrier Task Force, whose specific task was to support amphibious operations—by distant strikes to isolate the beachhead, by pre-invasion raids on the target area, by tactical support of the assault troops, and by interception of air and surface threats to the amphibious forces. The Fast Carrier Task Force operated normally in four task groups, each of which at full strength typically contained two heavy and two light carriers surrounded by an escort of one or two fast battleships, three or four cruisers, and 12 to 15 destroyers. While the group was cruising, the destroyers formed an outer screen for submarine detection, but when air attack was imminent they joined the inner circle of battleships and cruisers. Highly flexible, the carrier groups could operate together or independently, and they could detach vessels to form surface striking forces or to carry out special missions. Such was the floating air base that was to lead the way across the Pacific to the

---

* The Central Pacific Fleet did not officially assume the title Fifth Fleet until early in 1944, but for simplicity this narrative follows the informal practice of calling it the Fifth Fleet from the beginning of operations in 1943.

shores of Japan. The Fast Carrier Task Force commanded by Rear Admiral Charles A. Pownall in 1943 was however only a miniature version of the armada that later wiped out Japanese air power and shattered the Combined Fleet.

The amphibious component of the Fifth Fleet was the Fifth Amphibious Force, organized and commanded by Rear Admiral Richmond Kelly Turner. In an invasion this force controlled transports, cargo vessels, landing and beaching craft, and LSD's (landing ships, dock), and also the destroyers, escort carriers, cruisers, and old battleships assigned for close support. The Amphibious Force was normally split into two or more Attack Forces, and it often detached elements for special missions. Some fast gunnery vessels operated either with the carrier groups or with the amphibious groups as the tactical situation required. With growing experience and specialization, a Support Force of escort carriers and gunnery vessels of the Amphibious Force tended to take over tactical support of the troops, leaving the fast carriers and their escorts as a Covering Force for interceptions.

Troops assigned to the Fifth Amphibious Force, both army and marine, were designated V Amphibious Corps. Commanding the Corps was Major General Holland M. Smith USMC, whose typical reaction to an inept or slovenly performance had won him the nickname "Howling Mad Smith." Though "Howling Mad Smith" was as stubborn and outspoken as "Terrible Turner," the two made an effective team, for both were amphibious experts and each recognized and appreciated the special qualifications of the other.

Finally, the Fifth Fleet had its own land-based air force, composed of army, navy, and marine corps planes under the operational control of Rear Admiral John H. Hoover. At first, Hoover's Defense Force and Shore-based Air supplemented the carriers by pre-invasion photographic reconnaissance and by raids on or about the target. But as the Fast Carrier Task Force and the Fifth Amphibious Force acquired power and experience to support invasions unsupplemented by shore-based air, Hoover's command changed its title to Forward Area Central Pacific, with the responsibilities of air reconnaissance, neutralization of enemy bases, and defense of newly-acquired Allied bases.

To thrust rapidly across the Central Pacific, seizing command of the sea as it went, the Fifth Fleet had to have mobility and strategic momentum to an unprecedented degree. It could not, like fleets of the preceding hundred years, be closely tied to rearward bases for supply, refueling, and upkeep. The Fast Carrier Task Force had to remain at sea or in the forward area in order to keep the enemy from attacking positions already won and to deal him blow after blow to pave the way for further assaults. The key to the endurance of the Fifth Fleet was quickly-established advanced bases—largely afloat, in the lagoons of atolls or in other protected anchorages. As the war progressed, the advanced bases were more and more supplemented by replenishment at sea.

Service Force's mobile service squadrons of tenders, repair ships, and floating drydocks made it possible to supply all ships in the forward area and to repair all but those so extensively damaged as to require the facilities of a completely equipped navy yard. Elements of the Fifth Fleet periodically visited the advanced bases, set up ashore and afloat by Service Force, for a few days of maintenance and repair for the ships and rest for the crews, before again picking up the burden of the war. As operations progressed westward, the mobile service squadrons would move to another suitable anchorage in order to establish a new advanced base nearer to the operating area.

Visits of the Fast Carrier Task Force to the advanced base were kept to a minimum by underway replenishment groups which delivered essential material to the ships at sea. Late in the war one carrier task group would leave the operating area each day for a rendezvous with an underway replenishment group, the other carrier groups continuing operations against the enemy. On meeting the replenishment group, the carrier group would refuel, take on replacement ammunition, food, stores, aircraft, and personnel, receive mail from home, and evacuate its serious casualties to a hospital ship. The carrier group would then return to the operating area to relieve another group, which would repeat the process the next day. The underway replenishment group, after servicing the whole carrier force, amalgamated cargoes and sent its empty ships back to the advanced base to fill up again, while freshly laden ships from the base replaced them. This whole elaborate bucket brigade system was only a facet of the planning, construction, procurement, training, transportation, and maintenance that brought together the integrated forces to strike the swift and powerful blows that carried decisive military power from Pear Harbor to the Philippines in less than a year.

## Plans and Preliminary Operations

Early plans provided for opening the Central Pacific drive with an invasion of the Marshall Islands. But the more the staff planners in Washington and at Pearl Harbor studied the strategic and logistic picture, the less enthusiastic they became about such a beginning.

Like most island groups in the Central Pacific, the Marshalls are an archipelago of atolls, each a perimeter of flat coral islets surrounded by a fringing reef and enclosing a lagoon. Included are some 35 atolls, most of which contain one or more islands large enough for an airfield. Within aircraft support radius are the Gilberts, the eastern Carolines, and Wake. The Marshalls, under Japanese mandate since World War I, had been closed to foreigners since 1935. In the years of privacy thus afforded,

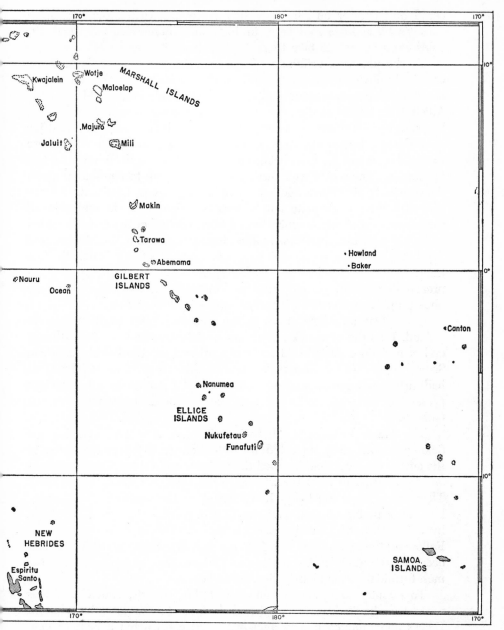

MARSHALLS-GILBERTS-ELLICES-SAMOA CHAIN

Japan had had ample opportunity to fortify and make them as impregnable as natural conditions permitted. Allied intelligence correctly estimated that they contained at least half a dozen air bases. But no one could be sure, for no Allied military force had visited the area since Halsey's hit-and-run raid early in 1942, and there were no Allied airfields close enough to take them under reconnaissance.

To the planners, weighing all the available evidence, it became increasingly obvious that the Central Pacific forces had neither the power nor the experience to go in and take the Marshalls in 1943. Most of the Allied troops then available in the Pacific were assigned to defending bases, to the Aleutians campaign, or to the South-Southwest Pacific drive on Rabaul. Though the U.S. Fifth Fleet was steadily growing more formidable, it was far from being up to planned strength. Besides, no one in mid-1943 knew how well carriers could stand up to land-based air in the proximity of fully developed enemy strong points. Lastly, the Americans still lacked adequate amphibious experience, for in mid-1943 all their invasions of any magnitude had been carried out over undefended or lightly defended beaches. In the circumstances, the Washington and Pearl Harbor staffs concluded that the conquest of the Marshalls, like the drive on Rabaul, had to be achieved by means of a step-by-step approach that would permit land-based Allied planes to make adequate photographic reconnaissance and to supplement carrier air.

There was an island route to the Marshalls, just as there was to Rabaul. Like the Bismarcks, the Marshall Islands stand at the northwest end of a chain of islands. At the southeast end are the British-American Samoa Islands. In between are the British Gilberts and Ellices. The Allies had airfields in Samoa, and on Canton Island, another British-American possession some 800 miles north of Samoa and 800 miles east of the Gilberts.

The Marshalls-Gilberts-Ellices-Samoa chain, roughly paralleling the Solomons, had early attracted the attention of the Japanese, who at the outbreak of war had invaded the Gilberts and set up a seaplane base on Makin Atoll to keep the islands to the southeast under observation. They correctly assessed the Halsey attack as the one-shot affair it was, but saw a prelude to full-scale invasion in a subsequent raid on Makin by a battalion of United States marines who arrived by submarine.* Following the marine raid, the Japanese quickly strengthened Makin and occupied the atolls of Abemama and Tarawa, turning the latter into the most formidable small bastion in the Pacific.

To counter the Japanese move into the Gilberts, American forces meanwhile had advanced up the chain from Samoa into the adjacent Ellices and dredged out an anchorage and constructed a bomber base at Funafuti Atoll, 700 miles from Tarawa. When the Japanese decided to make their initial advance against United States-Australia communications not via the Marshalls-Gilberts-Ellices-Samoa chain but via the Solomons and the New Hebrides, Funafuti fell into neglect while the

* Details of this raid are given in Chapter 14.

Americans rushed forces southward to join their allies in stopping the enemy at Guadalcanal and forcing him back on Rabaul.

On receiving orders after the Casablanca Conference to prepare for a Central Pacific drive, Nimitz reactivated Funafuti. In mid-June 1943 he received further orders from the Joint Chiefs of Staff to prepare for operations against the Gilberts. The following month, marines and Seabees occupied and began building bomber strips on Nukufetau and Nanumea in the upper Ellices. Early in September, an aviation engineer battalion landed on Baker Island, an American possession 480 miles east of the Gilberts, and constructed a fighter strip there to supplement the bomber base on Canton.

Into the anchorage at Funafuti moved the first of the mobile service squadrons to be formed, and into Funafuti, Nukufetau, Nanumea, Canton, and Baker moved Admiral Hoover's Defense Force and Shore-Based Air, its main striking power concentrated in 90 Seventh Army Air Force B-24 heavy bombers operating out of the Ellices. Meanwhile the 2nd Marine Division in New Zealand and the 27th Infantry Division in the Hawaiian Islands, alerted for the Gilberts operation, were undergoing amphibious exercises and training.

The new fast carriers *Essex, Yorktown, Lexington, Bunker Hill, Princeton, Belleau Wood, Cowpens, Monterey,* and *Independence* had by this time joined the veteran *Enterprise* and *Saratoga* in the Pacific, and with them came supporting vessels of all sorts fresh from shipyard and shakedown. As the new men-of-war arrived at Pearl Harbor, they had been formed into task groups and sent against live targets for warm-up and training. In early September a three-carrier group struck Marcus Island, doing great damage to installations and destroying several Japanese bombers. On September 18–19, another three-carrier group joined Seventh Air Force bombers from Canton and Funafuti in a raid on the Gilberts. The main purpose of this joint attack was to ease enemy pressure on the American air bases in the Ellices, which had been bombed by planes from Tarawa and Makin. This aim was more than fulfilled, for the Japanese immediately evacuated all air units from Tarawa and left at Makin only four amphibious planes for reconnaissance. Equally important, the defenders shot off a great deal of ammunition that they were unable to replenish, and the attackers succeeded in getting some excellent photographs of both Tarawa and Makin. Eighteen days later, a six-carrier force, the largest yet organized, staged a massive raid on Wake, so denuding the base of aircraft that the Japanese had to send up additional planes from the Marshalls. Lastly, in early November, as we have seen, carrier groups under Admirals Sherman and Montgomery assisted Halsey's Bougainville campaign by raiding Rabaul.

A major result of the considerable increase in carrier strength was the decision to abandon the practice of operating each carrier in a separate formation. Maneuvering several carriers within a single ring of escorts was not an easy technique and it sacrificed some flexibility, but these handicaps were more than offset by the defensive advantages of concentrated combat air patrols and massed VT-fused antiaircraft fire.

Alarmed by the carrier raids, Admiral Koga in September and again in October took the main strength of the Combined Fleet to the Marshalls, but failing to make contact with the American task forces, he returned each time to Truk. From here in early November he dispatched most of his carrier aircraft to the defense of Rabaul. While thus engaged, they came under attack by Airsols and by Sherman's and Montgomery's carrier groups, which destroyed two thirds of the planes and more than half the flight crews. During the same period, Koga lost the use of most of his cruisers, sunk or damaged at Rabaul or in the Battle of Empress Augusta Bay. Thus on the eve of the launching of the Central Pacific drive, Allied operations against Rabaul paralyzed the Combined Fleet, rendering it impotent to oppose the invasion of the Gilberts or, subsequently, of the Marshalls.

The Americans, unaware of the paralysis of the enemy fleet, took elaborate care to achieve surprise, in order to gain a foothold in the Gilberts before Koga could strike. So as not to disclose the target, Hoover's B-24's delayed regular raids on the invasion area until mid-November, when the Fifth Fleet was already at sea en route to the assault.

## Reconquest of the Gilbert Islands

The objectives of the U.S. Fifth Fleet were, from north to south, the atolls Makin, Tarawa, and Abemama. To assault Makin Atoll came a Northern Attack Force from Pearl Harbor, bringing a regimental combat team of the 27th Infantry Division. The rest of Admiral Turner's Fifth Amphibious Force, designated the Southern Attack Force, picked up the 2nd Marine Division at Wellington, New Zealand, rehearsed landing operations in the New Hebrides, and then headed for Tarawa Atoll. The submarine *Nautilus*, carrying a single company of marines, set out to scout lightly-held Abemama, which was to be invaded after Makin and Tarawa had fallen. The Gilberts invasion, like all operations against Japan in the Central Pacific until the final stages of the war, was carried out exclusively by United States forces.

At appropriate moments in the intricate pattern of approach, the four task groups of the Fast Carrier Task Force set out for their assigned supporting and covering positions—two from Pearl Harbor and the two from the South Pacific that had just completed their raids on Rabaul. While the carrier groups were pounding away at the Gilberts and nearby enemy strong points, the Northern and Southern Attack Forces made contact at sea and moved on parallel courses toward Makin and Tarawa, prepared to land troops simultaneously on the morning of November 20, 1943.

Though Tarawa was known to be the strong point of the Gilberts, both Admiral Turner and General Holland Smith gave their personal attention to the assault on Makin, for Makin lay only 190 miles from the nearest enemy base in the Marshalls—a hundred miles closer than Tarawa. Because of Makin's exposed position, a one-day conquest here was deemed essential so that the supporting fleet could be quickly withdrawn. Accordingly 6,500 assault troops were assigned to seize little Butaritari, main island and headquarters of the atoll, which was known to be lightly fortified and defended. The occupation forces on Butaritari in fact amounted to no more than 800 men, comprising 284 naval infantry commanded by a junior grade lieutenant and an assortment of non-combatants, including ground crewmen of the recently departed seaplanes, Japanese construction troops, and Korean laborers.

Division plans called for an initial landing on the head of hammer-

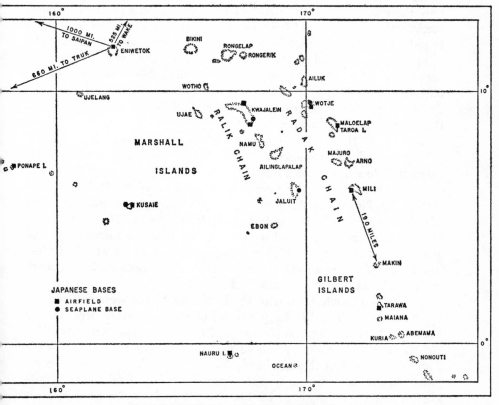

THE MARSHALLS AND THE GILBERTS

shaped Butaritari to draw the Japanese out of their main defensive area about a third of the way down the narrow handle. This was to be followed two hours later by a second landing, against the stronghold itself, in order to put the enemy between two fires. Unfortunately for the success of this plan, the Japanese generally remained in their defenses and let the Americans come to them. Fleet guns and carrier aircraft prepared the way so well that the scheduled landings were made against only minor opposition. Once ashore however, the invaders aroused the wrath of Holland Smith by losing momentum and bogging down. Instead of clearing the island in a single day, they spent two days dislodging the enemy from his main defenses and nearly two more pushing him the full length of the handle.

Responsibility for the slowdown has been attributed to poor leadership and faulty indoctrination of the 27th Division, which after long garrison duty in Hawaii was seeing combat for the first time. Over-age officers had unrealistically trained the division in the continental-style warfare typical of World War I, a combat method whereby troops advance deliberately and methodically under a barrage and do not proceed until the enemy's fighting potential has been shattered by artillery. Such tactics are out of place in island warfare where a quick victory is essential in order to release the fleet from support. Moreover, when the area to be conquered is small and the dangers of physical exhaustion and outrunning supply are not excessive, speed is especially desirable to keep the enemy off balance, permitting him little opportunity to dig in. In such a tactical situation, isolated pockets of resistance should be by-passed and left to the rear echelons to clean up.

In view of their inexperience and inadequate training, it is not surprising that whole companies of the invading regiment were held up for hours by a few snipers or a machine gun or two, or that they gave away their positions at night by nervously firing at anything that moved or rustled. By November 23 however, sheer numbers had conquered the island at the cost of 64 American soldiers killed and 152 wounded. All of the defenders were wiped out except one Japanese infantryman and 104 construction troops and laborers taken prisoner. In view of the 23-to-1 superiority of American to Japanese combatants on Butaritari, the American casualty rate must be considered excessive.

By far the heaviest losses of the battle for Makin were suffered not by the troops ashore but by personnel of the supporting fleet. During the naval bombardment on November 20, a turret explosion aboard the old battleship *Mississippi* killed 43 men and wounded 19 more. On the 24th, when the fleet should already have been withdrawn from the exposed waters off Makin, a torpedo from a newly arrived Japanese submarine struck the escort carrier *Liscome Bay*, which simply blew apart as the blast set off her stored aircraft bombs. Of her crew of about 900, nearly 650 were killed by the explosion or in the flaming oil that spread out from her shattered hull. Nowhere has the Navy's insistence upon speed in amphibious assault been more sharply vindicated.

The demands of the defense of Rabaul had so drained Japanese aircraft from the Central Pacific that the American carriers were able to shield the Gilberts invasion forces from all effective air attacks. Not a single enemy plane appeared over Makin during the fighting there, and the two minor strikes against Tarawa were ineffective. The only important enemy air raid during the first six days was by 16 torpedo bombers out of the Marshalls, which in the evening of the 20th attacked Admiral Montgomery's Southern Carrier Group, then 30 miles west of Tarawa. Eleven of the attacking aircraft were shot down. One of them however succeeded in putting a torpedo into the light carrier *Independence*. With 17 killed and 43 wounded, her magazine, fireroom, and after engine room flooded, the *Independence* retired to Funafuti for temporary repairs that enabled her to proceed under her own steam to Pearl Harbor. In the evening of the 25th, aircraft reinforcements from Truk struck from the Marshalls at Admiral Turner's Northern Attack Force and at Rear Admiral Arthur W. Radford's Northern Carrier Group, both off Makin. Turner completely foiled the enemy by radical maneuvering. Radford's ships broke up the attack of the 25th with antiaircraft fire. In another attack the following evening, Radford's carrier group made history and threw the enemy into confusion by launching against him a newly organized, radar-equipped night combat patrol of three fighters. In none of the attacks of November 25–26 was a single American ship hit.

Meanwhile, a company of marines and a submarine were making history of another sort at tiny Abemama Atoll. The capture of Abemama was not expected to present much of a problem, but nobody foresaw that the atoll would fall into American hands without preparatory bombardment and even without a regular assault. When the marine scouts, put ashore from the *Nautilus,* found only 25 defenders, they called on the submarine for gunfire support and went ahead and captured Abemama themselves.

Interest in the Gilberts operation centers chiefly on Tarawa, where at the cost of heavy casualties the Americans learned the techniques that were to carry them across the powerfully defended beaches of the Central Pacific. The storming of Tarawa proved a bitter school for amphibious assault, completing the lessons of the Solomons and New Guinea operations and the prewar exercises of the Navy and the Fleet Marine Force.

The main target for Rear Admiral Harry Hill's Southern Attack Force was narrow, two-mile-long Betio, only fortified island in Tarawa Atoll and strong point and administrative center of the Japanese-held Gilberts.*
On Betio there were about 2,600 Japanese naval infantry, elite troops

* Pronunciations: TA-ra-wa, BAY-shio.

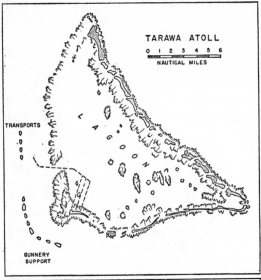

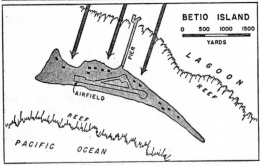

**THE ASSAULT ON TARAWA,
NOVEMBER 21, 1943**

corresponding somewhat to marines in other navies. There were also 1,000 Japanese construction troops (comparable to Seabees), and 1,200 Korean laborers. Since some of the construction troops were trained and equipped for combat, a fair estimate would place the combat effectives on the island at about 3,000. The American landing force was to be drawn from Major General Julian C. Smith's reinforced 2nd Marine Division, comprising some 16,000 men, mostly veterans of Guadalcanal. One regimental combat team was assigned to corps reserve, to be used on either Makin or Tarawa as needed. The other two combat teams were assigned to Tarawa. Of these, three battalion landing teams would make the assault landings. The remaining three would constitute the follow-up forces of the regimental and division reserves. Since the landing teams averaged only about 900 infantry each, the invaders were going in shorthanded, for it is a military axiom that assault troops should outnumber defenders by at least three to one.

For this assault the marines needed every advantage in numbers and support that could be made available to them, for Betio presented problems never faced before by any sea-borne invader. The strength of the island lay not only in the quality and number of its defenders but also in the difficulty of its approaches and the nature of its fixed defenses. It was surrounded by a wide shelf of coral, barely submerged at low tide. On this shelf the Japanese had laced together concrete, coral, and metal obstacles with barbed wire to force approaching craft into lanes covered by shore-based artillery. Along the beach at the high-water line ran a four-foot-high sea wall of tough, green coconut logs, almost impervious to anything but heavy caliber fire. Directly behind the wall and forming a part of the barrier was a series of gun emplacements, interconnected by trenches and protected by logs and sandbags and in some places by steel and concrete. From these positions antiboat guns and machine guns were sited to fire over the wall or through ports so as to command the beach and the seaward approaches. At points along the shore were pillboxes containing field guns, emplacements for antiaircraft guns, and a number of coast defense guns ranging up to 8 inches. Inside the sea wall, particularly in the area of the airstrip and taxiways, were half-submerged bombproof shelters built of double layers of green coconut logs braced together with angle irons and having six-foot-thick roofs of logs and corrugated iron piled high with sand so that they resembled igloos. Interspersed among these were steel-reinforced concrete blockhouses with six-foot-thick roofs and walls, to be used as command posts. Having thus thoroughly fortified his island, Rear Admiral Keiji Shibasaki, commanding the defense force, boasted that Betio could not be conquered by a million men in a hundred years.

Against a small island so strongly manned and defended, the possibility of an unopposed or even a lightly opposed landing was of course out of the question. Invading adjacent islets to set up supporting artillery was ruled out by the requirement of speed to release the fleet quickly. The marines would have to go in and seize a foothold by sheer frontal assault. Hence the planners gave careful consideration to the choice of a beachhead. Photographic reconnaissance had revealed no weak spots in Betio's defenses, but there was an option of difficulties. The slight concavity of the south shore permitted enfilade defense fire from the flanks. The west shore was considered too narrow for the initial assault. Both seaward beaches were somewhat more strongly defended and more heavily barricaded with underwater obstacles than those inside the lagoon. For the assault landings therefore the planners selected a 1,500-yard strip of beach on the lagoon side.

Essential for an amphibious assault is correct hydrographic intelligence, but the invaders had only conflicting information regarding the tidal conditions at Betio. At least four feet of water was needed to float standard landing craft, but the time chosen for the assault was a period of neap tides when even at best there might not be more than two or three feet of water over the reef. At the various American command levels, there was hope up to the last moment, but no certainty, that there would be enough water at Betio to float the LCM's and LCVP's up to the beach. In the circumstances, the Navy did what it could to obtain scarce amphibian tractors (LVT's—Landing Vehicles, Tracked), familiarly

known as amtracs, that operate as easily ashore as afloat. By D-day
however only 125 amtracs were available for Betio, not nearly enough
to carry all the assault waves across the reef.

The American commanders, studying reconnaissance photographs
concluded that to avoid prohibitive losses and achieve sustained momentum, the attacking forces would have to destroy most of Betio's defenses
before the landing took place. Experienced officers did not count heavily
on the effectiveness of a week of bombing by Hoover's B-24's or of raids
by the Fast Carrier Task Force immediately preceding D-day. They
pinned their hopes mainly on close-range pre-invasion gunfire from Hill's
three old battleships and five cruisers.

At 0400 on November 20, the Southern Attack Force was off Betio
with buglers sounding "Boats away!" Half an hour later, most of the
transport-carried landing craft were circling in the water or transferring
marines of the first waves to the amtracs, which had been brought to the
area by LST's. Shortly after 0500, shore batteries on Betio opened up,
whereupon Hill's gunnery vessels replied with counterbattery fire that
knocked out coastal guns, blew up ammunition dumps, and ignited
wooden barracks. At dawn the American guns checked fire to permit aircraft from Montgomery's Southern Carrier Group to take over, but no

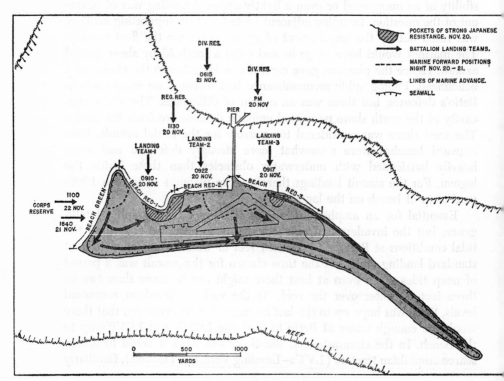

**THE BATTLE FOR BETIO**

planes appeared. For some reason, Hill had not been notified that the air strike had been postponed until 0610, sunrise, and he could not contact Montgomery because radio aboard Hill's flagship, the *Maryland*, had been temporarily knocked out by the jar of the ship's own first salvo. During the check fire, near misses by Japanese shells obliged the transports to haul farther out to sea. At sunrise the aircraft arrived on schedule, gave Betio seven minutes of scattered bombing, and then departed.

At 0620 the pre-invasion bombardment began. In two and a half hours, Hill's battleships and cruisers, using the best gunfire-support doctrine developed up to that time, poured nearly 3,000 tons of projectiles into little Betio. At ranges varying from 15,000 down to 2,000 yards, they worked methodically over the island for 75 minutes with destruction fire—intended to knock out the enemy's defenses and smash his emplacements, pillboxes, shelters, and blockhouses. Then the gunnery vessels shifted position to enfilade the beachhead and delivered 45 minutes of high-speed neutralization fire, to drive the enemy to cover and leave him dazed. Five minutes before the first wave landed, the gunners were to lift fire inland while fighter aircraft strafed the beaches. This treatment was supposed to render Betio virtually defenseless.

The massed bombardment was extraordinarily spectacular. The whole island appeared to be aflame and an enormous pall of dust and smoke billowed into the air. Betio was hurt, no question about that, but it was not hurt badly enough. A good many Japanese were killed; some of the coast-defense, antiaircraft, and antiboat guns were knocked out; most of the above-ground structures were destroyed; camouflage screens were burned off; and, most important, the network of telephone wires on which the Japanese depended for coordination was completely disrupted. On the other hand, few of the enemy's blockhouses, pillboxes, shelters, or protected gun emplacements were seriously damaged. The defenders were still prepared to sweep the beachhead and its approaches with light artillery, machine guns, and rifles.

Just as the naval bombardment was getting under way, two minesweepers advanced under a smoke screen and swept a channel into the lagoon. While one remained inside to mark the line of departure for the assault waves, the other turned back to escort in two destroyers, which took the beachhead under fire. One of the destroyers was hit by a pair of duds, but there were no other damages to the four vessels, which were soon joined by a dock landing ship (LSD) bringing tanks.

The landing craft, now making their way from the rendezvous area outside the lagoon to the line of departure inside, were so delayed by head winds, a choppy sea, a receding tide, and breakdowns among the amtracs that Admiral Hill was obliged to postpone H-hour, the scheduled landing time. Beginning at 0825 the first three assault waves, amtracs carrying troops, crossed the line of departure at three-minute intervals and headed for the beach some 6,000 yards away. The fourth, fifth, and sixth waves, LCM's and LCVP's carrying troops, tanks, and light artillery, soon followed. Each wave carried elements of three battalion landing teams, each assigned to a 500-yard stretch of beach designated from west to east Beach Red 1, Beach Red 2, and Beach Red 3.

Just as the first waves were leaving the line of departure, fighters from the carriers passed over the beach for the final strafing that should have immediately preceded the landing. Because the *Maryland's* radio was again inoperative, they had received no word of the postponement. Delays in the run to the beach, which for the first waves took more than three quarters of an hour, obliged Admiral Hill to postpone H-hour once more. At 0845, fearful of hitting the landing craft, which were invisible to the fleet through the dense smoke, he ordered all ships outside the lagoon to cease fire. The first wave was then still 15 minutes from the shore.

During this period of respite, the Japanese left their shelters and their emplacements on other beaches and massed behind the sea wall on the beach toward which the assault waves were moving. Apparently because of the threat of the gunnery ships off the west coast and the continued firing of destroyers and minesweepers inside the lagoon, the defenders bunched in two major pockets of resistance, leaving relatively undefended the extreme right and the left center of the beachhead. These "weak spots" were to prove the key to the conquest of Betio.

From the moment they left the line of departure, the amtracs came under scattered enemy fire. The reef, as many had feared, was under only two or three feet of water, but the tracked craft merely lumbered onto and across it. As they did so, they ran into a crescendo of machine gun, rifle, and antiboat fire that threw the waves into confusion. Worst hit during the approach across the reef were the troops of the battalion heading for Beach Red 1, for these had to enter a deep cove where they were raked by fire from the more westerly enemy pocket. Here many of the amtracs were hit and disabled while still in the water, and of those that reached the beach few were able to retire.

Far heavier casualties were suffered by troops of the fourth, fifth, and sixth waves, whose conventional landing craft grounded on the edge of the reef. Some of the troops jumped out into deep water and were pulled down by their heavy gear. Others were ferried in by returning amtracs of the first waves. Most got out into the shallow water and waded 600 yards to the beach through withering machine gun and rifle fire. A few Sherman tanks, discharged by LCM's onto the reef, made the shore; but LCVP's bringing in 37- and 75-mm. guns had no choice but to retract and wait for the tide to rise.

The low water that held up the landing craft proved a blessing in that it left a stretch of sandy beach on which the marines who reached the shore could assemble with some protection afforded by the sea wall. At the far right of Beach Red 1, marines quickly seized the northwest tip of the island. At the right center of Beach Red 3, there was a break in the wall some 200 yards east of a pier jutting out into the lagoon. Through this opening plunged two amtracs, carrying some 50 marines. Other marines followed and, despite heavy flanking fire, expanded their salient west and south. Along the more heavily defended stretches of beach, those adjacent to the two enemy strong points, casualties were extremely heavy. The marines in these areas could do little except huddle against the wall with their dead and wounded. Even to stand erect made one the target of deadly fire from several directions. Yet after the first shock, marines even here began climbing the wall and clearing out gun emplacements and rifle pits with charges of TNT.

While still boated, the assault commander, Colonel David M. Shoup, ordered his regimental reserve committed without delay. He then radioed General Julian Smith, in the *Maryland*, for immediate gunfire and air support. The division commander not only saw that Shoup got the support he requested but also committed half the division reserve to reinforce the decimated marine left flank. As further reports of the critical situation ashore reached him, Julian Smith radioed General Holland Smith, then off Makin, requesting and receiving permission to commit the corps reserve.

Nearly a third of the 5,000 Americans who reached Betio before dark on November 20 were casualties. At nightfall most of the marines who had been able to land near the strong enemy defense areas were either dead or still pinned to the beach, but nearly half of the western shore was in American hands to the depth of 150 yards, and at the base of the pier the marines had established a perimeter 300 yards deep and 500 yards wide. During the hours of darkness, the invaders maintained remarkable fire discipline—scarcely a shot was fired. The expected enemy counterattack never came, apparently because Admiral Shibasaki could establish communications with only a small portion of his troops. The principal nocturnal activity of the Japanese was by individuals who prepared for sniping the next day by concealing themselves in suitable positions ashore or by wading out to disabled amtracs and tanks on the reef. Through a peculiarity of the time and place, the tide continued too low to float in the landing craft stalled at the edge of the reef, but enough amtracs had survived the first day to bring some of the light artillery to the beach, whither additional tanks also made their way.

During the next day, D plus 1, call strikes from the carriers and call fire from the gunnery vessels developed steadily increasing accuracy. On the marine right flank, a naval gunfire spotter called destroyer fire so accurately on enemy positions that the invaders were able to advance with little opposition the whole length of Betio's western shore. Over this beach, designated Beach Green, poured a battalion of the regiment that had been released from corps reserve. By the end of the day, the marine perimeter at the base of the pier had also expanded across to the south shore.

On November 22, D plus 2, a second reserve battalion landed at Beach Green. As the assault phase came to an end, General Julian Smith came ashore and took command. His immediate objectives were to clean out the enemy pocket at the boundary between Red Beaches 1 and 2 and to begin an advance to the east. In both offensives the principal task was clearing out enemy-occupied pillboxes and shelters. Tanks and artillery were useful in this perilous business, but generally the job had to be completed by infantrymen with flamethrowers and hand-delivered charges of TNT.

During the night of November 22–23, the Japanese who had been squeezed into the narrowing tail of the island made three counterattacks. The attempts ended in such heavy losses for the attackers that the marines were able the next day to penetrate swiftly to the eastern end of the island. By that time the Japanese position between Red Beaches 1 and 2 had been eliminated by a steady drive from all directions, including a frontal infantry-artillery assault across the beach.

When Julian Smith announced the end of organized enemy resistance in the afternoon of the 23rd, the defenders had been practically wiped out. More than a hundred Korean laborers had been captured, but of the Japanese, only one officer and 16 enlisted men had surrendered as prisoners of war. Of the 18,300 Americans, marine and naval, ultimately committed to the capture of Tarawa, more than 3,000 were casualties. Of these, more than a thousand were killed or died of wounds.

A nation shocked by the cost in lives of the brief Gilberts campaign could not be expected to understand at once that here was a new kind of warfare, in which lasting control over a large area was purchased at the price of heavy losses compressed into a few days. The casualties suffered in the quick conquest of the Gilberts were not nearly so high as those incurred in the six-months campaign to capture Guadalcanal, yet the advantages gained were closely similar. Each of the captured bases safeguarded established and potential communication lines, and each provided airfields for bombing and photographing the next objective. The conquest of the Gilberts removed a menace to American communications with the South, Southwest, and Central Pacific, and it provided an essential base for air support of the forthcoming invasion of the Marshalls.

Equally important were the tactical lessons the Americans learned in the Gilberts—especially at Tarawa. It was discovered that a few hours of bombing and bombardment are not enough to knock out the numerous strong points of fortified positions like Betio. What was needed was precision bombing and accurately controlled gunfire delivered over a much greater period of time, with frequent checking of fire to permit smoke to subside in order to assess the progress of destruction. More plunging fire, using major-caliber armor-piercing shells, was needed to penetrate the overheads. Rapid shifting of fire, designed originally to confuse moving targets, was found merely to hamper fire control when directed against stationary targets. Armored amtracs were shown to be essential for carrying troops across reefs, and the need was demonstrated for close-range neutralizing fire against the beachhead right up to the moment of landing. Experiences at Tarawa again showed the need for special amphibious command ships like those already in use in the Mediterranean, with no responsibility for gunfire support, and for improved radio equipment ashore and afloat. Had these lessons not been learned at Tarawa, they would have had to be learned elsewhere, at similar or greater cost.

On the other hand, the conquest of the Gilberts provided some evidence that carrier planes could gain command of the air over enemy atolls and proved that the fleet could operate against such positions with acceptable losses, and that, with naval air and gunfire support, well trained, resolute troops could cross reefs under even the most adverse conditions and seize strongly fortified islands. There was a strong indication moreover that the Japanese fleet was not prepared to sortie and offer powerful resistance to thwart an invasion anywhere in Japan's island empire.

## Invasion of the Marshall Islands

Planning for the Marshalls invasion was well under way before the assault on the Gilberts. The first formal operation plan, issued by Admiral Nimitz in mid-October 1943, called for simultaneous assaults on Maloelap and Wotje Atolls, the two Marshallese bases nearest Pearl Harbor, and on Kwajalein Atoll, Japanese headquarters at the center of the archipelago.

After the shock of Tarawa, General Holland Smith recommended that the Marshalls plan be reconsidered, contending that not enough troops and support were available to capture three major bases at the same time. Admirals Spruance and Turner concurred. They favored a two-step operation: Maloelap and Wotje to be captured first and developed into American bases to support a later assault on Kwajalein. To their surprise and consternation, Nimitz proposed instead that Maloelap and Wotje be by-passed and that the forthcoming assault be carried out against Kwajalein alone.

Spruance, Turner, and Smith argued strongly against Nimitz' proposal, pointing out that Kwajalein in American hands would be subject to air attack from Japanese bases at Maloelap, Wotje, Mili, and Jaluit, which were also in position to intercept communications from Pearl Harbor or the Gilberts, while an air pipeline back to Japan through Eniwetok Atoll would be left intact. When Nimitz insisted upon by-passing the more easterly bases, Spruance requested and received permission to occupy undefended Majuro Atoll in the eastern Marshalls. Occupation of this atoll would provide a protected fleet anchorage in the area of operations, for use until Kwajalein was secured, and a base whence aircraft could cover communications between Kwajalein and the Gilberts. Included in the final plan also was a tentative proposal for the capture of Eniwetok, the date and the forces to be used contingent upon the success and speed of the Kwajalein operation.

The decision to go directly to the heart of the Marshalls took the Japanese as much by surprise as it did Nimitz' commanders. The chief question in the minds of the Imperial High Command was whether the next assault would come against Mili and Jaluit from the Gilberts or against Wotje, or possibly Maloelap, from Pearl Harbor. Accordingly, these outer atolls were given priority in defense materials and personnel. As Admiral Nimitz correctly estimated, the fortification of Kwajalein remained comparatively light, certainly nothing on the order of what the marines had found on Betio. Though the occupation forces on Kwajalein numbered in excess of 8,000, fewer than 2,200 of these were trained combat troops. The rest were technicians, mechanics, laborers (many Korean), grounded aviators, marooned sailors, and the miscellaneous spinners of red tape found at any military headquarters. How effective these non-combatants proved as defenders is difficult to assess. All of the Japanese were probably given arms of one sort or another, and most of them appeared determined to avoid capture and to sell their lives as dearly as possible.

The attack on the Marshalls was begun early in January 1944 by Admiral Hoover's land-based planes operating from the Ellices and from the new American airfields in the Gilberts. On January 29, an expanded Fast Carrier Task Force, now designated Task Force 58, arrived in the Marshalls under the command of Rear Admiral Marc A. Mitscher with 750 planes to step up the destruction. While Hoover's aircraft concentrated on neutralizing Jaluit and Mili, one carrier group attacked Maloelap, another hit Wotje, and the other two struck Kwajalein, destroying every plane on the atoll in a single raid. That night TF 58 gunnery vessels moved in and bombarded airfields to keep the Japanese from flying planes in from Eniwetok. At dawn on the 30th, one carrier group hit Eniwetok, destroying the aircraft banked up there. On the 30th also, two carrier groups worked over the defense installations on Kwajalein, and one kept both Maloelap and Wotje under attack. This series of strikes completely eliminated Japanese air power in the Kwajalein area and went far toward destroying the shore defenses in the Marshalls.

Meanwhile the attack forces of the Fifth Amphibious Force were on the way: nearly 300 vessels bringing 53,000 assault troops—of whom half were soldiers and half were marines—and 31,000 garrison personnel. As this armada approached the Marshalls, a Special Attack Group under Rear Admiral Hill was detached to occupy Majuro. Into Majuro's lagoon followed a mobile service squadron prepared to look after the needs of the naval forces. Thus was set up another of the series of temporary forward bases which freed the fleet from immediate dependence upon Pearl Harbor and extended its reach step by step across the Pacific.

On January 30 the Northern Attack Force, under Rear Admiral Richard L. Conolly, and the Southern Attack Force, under Admiral Turner's direct command, reached Kwajalein Atoll and added their guns and escort carrier planes to those of the fast carrier planes to step up the three-day intensive preparation. The Navy's meticulous study of the Tarawa assault now paid off. The primary invasion targets, Roi and Namur, a pair of islands connected by a causeway at the north end of Kwajalein lagoon, and Kwajalein Island, 44 miles to the south, were pounded with four times the weight of bombs and shells that had been hurled against Betio. Aircraft picked their targets and bombed precisely. Gunnery ships varied range and trajectory, and shifted from high-capacity to armor-piercing shells as the situation required.

On January 31, troops seized islets near Roi-Namur and near Kwajalein Island to permit entry of amphibious and close-support vessels through the narrow passes into the relatively calm lagoon and to site artillery to cover the main landing beaches. That day and the following night, newly organized underwater demolition teams of swimmers, protected by naval gunfire, reconnoitered the approaches to the beachheads. They found no offshore mines or obstructions and reported reef and surf conditions not too hazardous.

All through the night, destroyers wore down the resistance of the enemy troops with harassing fire. Then, shortly after dawn on February 1, the pre-invasion softening up began, climaxing the preceding two days of bombing and bombardment. Fleet guns blasted Roi-Namur and Kwajalein from close range,* artillery on the adjacent islands added enfilading fire; from above the trajectory of the shells, Gilberts-based B-24's dropped 1,000- and 2,000-pound bombs on Kwajalein Island. While the guns paused, carrier aircraft came in to dive-bomb and strafe. Coordinating all this destruction, and other phases of the assault as well, were new amphibious command ships (AGC's), carrying the force, corps, and division commanders and their staffs. Conolly ran the northern operation from the AGC *Appalachian* off Roi-Namur; Turner and Holland

* Confirming Admiral Conolly's nickname "Close-in-Conolly," earned for his close support of the assaults on Sicily and at Salerno.

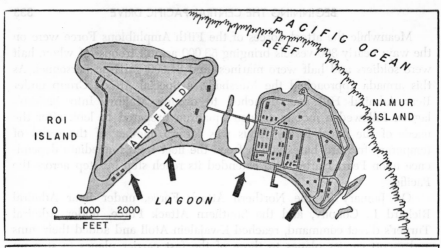

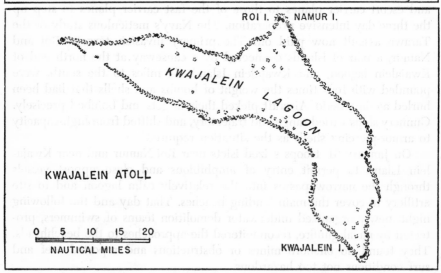

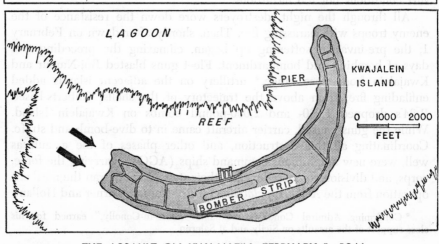

THE ASSAULT ON KWAJALEIN, FEBRUARY 1, 1944

Smith, the southern operation, from the AGC *Rocky Mount* off Kwajalein Island.

There were still not enough amtracs to carry all the assault waves over the reefs, but the amtracs available were all now armored, and armed with machine guns. In the Southern Attack Force moreover they were supplemented by the Army's equally versatile DUKW's, which would bring in supplies. The amtracs were to be carried to the line of departure by LST's, out of which they would crawl fully loaded under their own power. To accompany the first wave were armored amphibians* and shallow-draft LCI's converted into amphibious support vessels by the addition of rocket racks and 20- and 40-mm. guns. Air observers were prepared to drop parachute flares to signal the fleet when the leading waves were 500 yards from the beach. Such were the new amphibious weapons and techniques developed in response to the lessons of Tarawa.

Despite the thoroughness of the pre-invasion bombardment, which had knocked out most of the enemy's fixed defenses and killed more than half of the defenders, the assault on Roi and Namur was marred by disorder and poor timing. In part this was the result of the unexpected choppiness of the waters inside the lagoon, from which the northern assault was made. But the chief cause was inexperience, for the invasions in this area were carried out by green troops brought to the line of departure by inexperienced sailors.

The landing force was Major General Harry Schmidt's newly organized 4th Marine Division, untried in battle and lifted directly from the United States to the Marshalls with inadequate opportunity to practice landings. The confusion began on January 31, when one of the division's three regimental combat teams seized the islands adjacent to the main targets. The amtracs that had participated in these operations were supposed to return to their parent LST's, refuel, and take aboard troops of the combat team assigned to make the assault on Namur. At 0900 on February 1, few of the LST's involved had located all their amtracs and none of the beaching craft had reached the assembly area south of the line of departure. Even the fresh LST's, those bringing in the combat team assigned to Roi, failed to reach the area on time and, once there, they encountered unforeseen difficulties in bringing their amtracs down by elevator from the weather decks.

After repeated postponements, the control destroyer at the line of departure finally flagged in the first wave at 1112, though many amtracs

---

* So called by the Navy and the Marine Corps. The Army called them amphibian tanks. The official designation was LVT(A)(1). Each of these vehicles carried a turret-mounted 37-mm. gun and three .30-caliber machine guns, and some were equipped with flamethrowers. The armored amphibians should not be confused with the light and medium tanks, strictly land vehicles, that were brought to the beach in LCM's.

were still not accounted for, and others were milling about in the distance. Rocket-firing LCI's led the way, followed by a wave of armored amphibians, two waves of infantry in amtracs, and two waves of tanks in LCM's. After the battleships and cruisers outside the lagoon had lifted fire inland, nearby destroyers continued to pound the shore as long as they could do so without endangering the marines.

Remarkably enough, though the approach to the beach at Roi was marked by numerous collisions among the amtracs, the assault forces landed here in good order—two battalions abreast, as planned. During the approach, the defenders had fruitlessly fired a few shells in the general direction of the landing craft. As the troops set foot on shore, there was a burst of machine gun fire from the left. At the same time two Japanese soldiers armed only with bayonets rushed down to the water's edge, charging at the invaders in a brave but futile gesture. Without pausing, the marines pushed into the interior, advancing rapidly with considerable spirit but not much coordination and almost no fire discipline. Some troops even wounded each other in their anxiety to get a shot at one of the 300 or so Japanese left alive by the bombardment. Because Roi was mostly airfield, with little room for buildings or installations, the defenders had scarcely any opportunity to take cover or to put up an effective resistance. Before nightfall the island was in American hands.

Because only a fraction of the assault forces intended for Namur had arrived at the line of departure when the first waves were flagged in, the landings on this heavily built-up island were chaotic and piecemeal. Fortunately for the marines, there was no resistance or other impediment at the beach. In the interior however, the invaders were confronted with a wilderness of rubble, undergrowth, and shattered palms that held up tanks and troops and provided concealment for enemy snipers. To maintain momentum through this maze of destruction, the assault forces were obliged to leave behind a great many pockets of resistance for later echelons to clean out with demolition charges and flamethrowers. On this island, explosions of stored Japanese ammunition caused severe casualties. The heaviest explosion was unintentionally set off by the marines themselves when they mistook a blockhouse full of torpedo warheads for an enemy command post. As the blockhouse burst asunder, the island was instantly covered with a pall of acrid smoke, and for minutes afterwards chunks of concrete and metal rained down on invaders and defenders alike. After a night in which the assault troops were harassed as much by trigger-happy marines in the rear as by infiltrating Japanese in front, they pushed rapidly to the north shore. Namur was declared secured in the early afternoon of February 2.

American casualties on the northern islands of Kwajalein Atoll were 196 killed and about 550 wounded. Of the 345 Japanese troops and

3,200 other occupying personnel in the area at the beginning of the bombardment, all were killed except 40 captured Korean laborers and 51 Japanese taken as prisoners of war.

In the Kwajalein Island area, at the southern end of the lagoon, Major General Charles H. Corlett's 7th Infantry Division was carrying out an assault using a plan almost identical with that employed by the 4th Marine Division at the northern end. In the south, as in the north, two regimental combat teams captured the main target; the third, the adjoining islets. The principal difference was that Kwajalein Island was invaded end-on. An assault on Kwajalein's concave lagoon side was ruled out because it would have exposed the invaders to flank fire from the shore. A landing on the ocean side was equally unacceptable because of rough surf and heavy defenses. That left only the narrow western beach, where the two assigned combat teams necessarily went ashore in column of battalions rather than battalions abreast.

In contrast to the confused assault on Roi-Namur, the landings on Kwajalein Island were almost flawless. Mild seas in this area helped, but the efficiency of the operation was mainly the product of the rigorous training and rehearsals that Corlett had put his division through since it fumbled on Attu the preceding May. Taking station west of the line of departure, the LST's discharged their troop-loaded amtracs, and the LSD's launched LCM's carrying medium tanks. These landing craft circled in columns of waves until the transports had launched the LCVP's, which were to bring in the supporting waves. First to head toward the shore were three LCI gunboats that swept the landing beaches with 40-mm. fire and rocket salvos. Control vessels flanking the line of departure flagged the first waves across the line precisely on schedule at 0900. The leading wave, which included 16 amtracs, 16 armored amphibians, and two control craft to keep the line in order, was followed by three more waves at four-minute intervals. The whole parade then moved in at a steady five knots. As the landing craft neared the shore, the distant battleships and cruisers lifted fire inland, while four nearby destroyers continued to pound the beach until the last moment. When the first wave was 200 yards from the shore, the LCI's pulled over to the flanks and stood by to provide call fire. The first wave, still exactly on schedule, touched down at 0930. While the amtracs unloaded and circled back to bring in troops boated in LCVP's from the edge of the reef, the armored amphibians continued inland a hundred yards or so to cover the beachhead. Within twelve minutes, 1,200 troops had landed and begun to organize for advance. Though there was some small arms fire from the enemy on the island, there was not a single casualty among the assault forces. This was as near perfection as any such operation was ever likely to attain.

By the end of the day on February 1, some 11,000 soldiers were ashore on Kwajalein Island. Compared to the marines on the northern islands, they advanced very slowly. The reason for their slower rate appears to be three-fold: they had to defeat a larger defense force, their choice of landing beach obliged them to fight their way the whole length of the island while presenting a narrow front that could be resisted by a relatively small force, and they used infantry tactics inherited from the fairly static conditions of World War I. After three days of typically deliberate advance under a barrage of shells and aerial bombs, the soldiers squeezed a few hundred surviving defenders into Kwajalein's northern tip and began the final mopping up. By the afternoon of February 4, all effective resistance had ended.

American casualties on Kwajalein Island and the adjacent islets were 177 killed and about a thousand wounded. The enemy occupation force, originally comprising some 1,800 ground troops and about 3,200 other personnel, were all killed except 125 captured Korean laborers and 49 Japanese prisoners of war. Throughout the four-day conquest, the fleet had stood by in support. Except for a few minor hits from coast defense guns, not a ship was damaged.

Because he had not had to commit the 10,000 troops of the corps reserve, Admiral Spruance could push on without delay to the conquest of Eniwetok Atoll. Here he planned to set up another logistic base to support his next westward leap. But Eniwetok, largest of the western Marshalls, was in an exposed position, only 1,000 miles from the Marianas, less than 700 from Truk, less than 600 from Ponape. To prevent interference with the new operation, these Japanese bases had to be neutralized. That was quite an undertaking and might have been considered too risky before American carrier-air power had so brilliantly demonstrated its capabilities by isolating Kwajalein. Now Admiral Nimitz did not hesitate to order the new invasion and all the operations necessary to support it.

When the Japanese high command had been forced to concede that the Bismarcks, the Gilberts, and the Marshalls were no longer tenable, Tokyo had drawn in its defenses to a more restricted perimeter stretching south through the Marianas and the Palaus to western New Guinea. Garrison troops on the islands east of the new defense line were given the suicide mission of delaying and weakening American forces so as to allow Japan time to build up her depleted air power. With the fall of Kwajalein, Admiral Koga felt so exposed at Truk that he prudently withdrew the bulk of the Combined Fleet to the Palaus, leaving behind only two light cruisers and eight destroyers to defend local naval forces and cargo vessels at the base.

Meanwhile training of aviators went on apace in Japan. As soon as crews for land-based aircraft had attained enough skill to fly so far, they took their planes south along the new inner defense chain and to outposts, such as Truk, in the Carolines. In this manner the Japanese began building up power along the restricted perimeter to destroy any invading force that might approach. By mid-February 1944, there were 365 planes at Truk, and 200 more were ready to take off from Japan for the Marianas.

That was the situation when Marc Mitscher's TF 58 sortied from Majuro, and Harry Hill's Eniwetok Expeditionary Group left Kwajalein. Both headed for Eniwetok, and while one group of the Carrier Force remained in that area to support the assault, the other three shaped course southwest for Truk. Bombers of the Seventh Air Force were already reaching out 900 miles from Tarawa to take the fight out of Ponape with a series of sharp blows.

Truk, an archipelago of islands surrounded by a coral reef, provides one of the world's finest anchorages. Its reputation for impregnability while under Japanese mandate had earned it such names as "the Japanese Pearl Harbor" and "Gibraltar of the Pacific." Task Force 58 exploded that reputation and at the same time proved the ability of the carriers to neutralize enemy bases without any assistance from land-based air. While Mitscher's planes hit Truk repeatedly on February 17, Spruance led the 45,000-ton *Iowa* and *New Jersey*, with two heavy cruisers and four destroyers, in a sweep around the archipelago to sink any ships attempting to escape through passages in the perimeter reef. To catch any vessels that might elude Mitscher's planes and Spruance's guns, Nimitz had sent ten submarines to patrol the area. During the night of February 17–18, carrier aircraft, exploiting a newly-developed technique, bombed vessels in Truk lagoon by radar. At dawn the carriers, already beginning to withdraw, launched a final all-out attack. In the course of this two-day strike, the attackers destroyed about 200 enemy aircraft and damaged some 70 more. They sank 15 Japanese naval vessels, including Koga's two cruisers and four of his destroyers, and sent down 19 cargo vessels and five tankers. The cost to the Americans was 25 aircraft lost, and severe damage to the carrier *Intrepid*, which was hit by a night-flying torpedo plane in the only counterattack Truk was able to launch during the entire operation.

"Impregnable Truk" had been proved a myth. Japan's maritime investment during the 20 years of her mandate had gone into her fleet and not, as many had supposed, into building up an oceanic Maginot Line. By smashing the air power of Truk, TF 58 had both isolated Eniwetok and completed the neutralization of Rabaul. Airsols planes on February 18 encountered not a single enemy aircraft over the Bismarcks.

Following the successful raid on Truk, Admiral Mitscher with two groups of TF 58 set out for the Marianas Islands. Detected by a Japanese patrol plane in the afternoon of February 22, Mitscher's force was attacked by aircraft through the night. Rather than lose time by turning into the wind to launch fighters, the Americans defended themselves with gunfire alone. So effective were their radar-aimed, VT-fused anti-aircraft shells that not a ship was hit. The speedy approach paid off handsomely, catching the enemy awkwardly off balance. Vice Admiral Kakuji Kakuta, commanding the Marianas Air Base Force, had just moved about 150 torpedo-bombers in from Japan, ahead of the fighter squadrons. After sunrise on the 23rd, TF 58 planes struck at Guam, Tinian, and Saipan and wiped out the bombers before the fighters could arrive to protect them. As important to the Americans as this destruction of Marianas air power were aerial photographs taken of airfields and of beaches suitable for assault.

While Mitscher and Spruance were thus pounding distant enemy bases, Hill's force captured Eniwetok, using techniques similar to those employed at Kwajalein. But whereas the assault troops at Kwajalein had outnumbered the defenders nearly 6 to 1, the ratio at Eniwetok was less than 3 to 1. Hence the three occupied islands of Eniwetok Atoll had to be taken one at a time. The landing force here consisted of the 22nd Marines (a detached regimental combat team, nucleus of the future 6th Marine Division) and two battalion landing teams of the 27th Infantry Division, which had also provided the landing force for Makin. Originally assigned to corps reserve, none of these troops had been adequately rehearsed in making assault landings—and none thus far had had any battle experience. The 22nd Marines however had been superbly trained in jungle warfare during 18 months' garrison duty in Samoa, whereas the army troops were drawn from the division that earlier, in the Gilberts operation, had revealed lack of suitable training.

Predictably enough, the assaults at Eniwetok were marked by considerable confusion. Once ashore however, the marines advanced with the speed and precision of veterans, overruning the islands of Engebi and Parry each in a single day. But on Eniwetok Island, the soldiers got off to such a slow start that one of the marine landing teams had to be rushed in to take over the brunt of the fighting. Conquest of this island required three days, partly because the invasion force, discovering belatedly that it was defended, had given it too little bombardment, and partly because of the dissimilar tactics of the soldiers and the marines. Individuals of both services showed high courage and determination, but the superior training and leadership of the 22nd Marines gave them a cohesiveness and *esprit de corps* that, here as on Makin, was lacking in elements of the 27th Division.

By now the Americans, moving out from their lodgements on Roi-Namur and Kwajalein Island, had cleared the enemy from all his positions in the chain of islands surrounding Kwajalein lagoon. The invaders were soon moving into the rest of the Marshalls—all except strongly fortified, heavily occupied Wotje, Maloelap, Mili, and Jaluit. These enemy bases were kept neutralized by occasional air raids. Cut off from all supply and reinforcement except by submarine, they could create no serious problem in the rear of the American advance. On the contrary, they proved useful as live targets for newly arrived air reinforcements.

For their achievement in conquering the Marshalls, and in recognition of their increased responsibilities in an expanding fleet, Mitscher, Holland Smith, Turner, and Spruance were each awarded an additional star. In Admiral Mitscher, Nimitz had found a carrier force commander worthy to complete the Smith-Turner-Spruance team. Marc Mitscher, soft-spoken, often reticent, had little of the colorful command personality of Smith or Turner and few pretensions to the intellectual eminence of Spruance, but 30 years of intense devotion to naval aviation had fitted him uniquely to command the Navy's roving air bases of World War II.

# 12

# The Dual Advance to
# the Philippines

The Joint Chiefs of Staff early in March 1944 reaffirmed the concept of a dual advance across the Pacific and specified the next objectives for each of the two offensives. MacArthur's Southwest Pacific forces were to continue northwestward along the north coast of New Guinea and in mid-November invade the southern Philippine island of Mindanao. Nimitz' Central Pacific forces, beginning in mid-June, were to occupy the islands of Saipan, Tinian, and Guam in the Marianas. In mid-September they were to begin seizing bases in the Palaus. In November they would provide fleet support and cover for MacArthur's invasion of Mindanao. The dual advance was thus to be a converging movement. (See map page 312.)

The Marianas operation was expected to yield rich dividends. American occupation of islands in this group would cut the main air pipeline from Japan to the Carolines and New Guinea, provide bases for stepped-up submarine attrition of tankers and freighters plying between Japan and the East Indies, and furnish sites for airfields from which the Army Air Forces' new long-range B-29 bombers could strike directly against the Japanese home islands. An invasion so near Japan moreover would almost certainly force out the Japanese fleet for destruction—possibly removing it from the board prior to MacArthur's return to the Philippines.

While the Central Pacific command was planning the Marianas operation, General MacArthur's Southwest Pacific forces were completing their conquest of the Admiralties and preparing to advance westward by sea to Hollandia on the north coast of New Guinea. They would thus by-pass the Japanese Eighteenth Army at Wewak, some 20,000 combat effectives, including survivors of the march from the Huon Peninsula.

But the 400-mile leap to Hollandia would carry the Seventh Amphibious Force beyond the radius of efficient land-based air support and at the same time expose it to attack from western New Guinea and the Carolines. So the floating airfields of the Fifth Fleet were called upon to neutralize the Carolines, to lend support and cover to the new invasion, and to protect the amphibious shipping of the Seventh Fleet.

## Task Force 58 Supports MacArthur

Toward the end of March 1944 three groups of TF 58 departed Majuro and headed for the western Carolines to give the new Combined Fleet base in the Palau Islands the same treatment they had given Truk the preceding month. Detection of this westbound force by patrol aircraft stimulated the Japanese into extraordinary activity. When Admiral Koga had pulled back to the Marianas-Palaus-Western New Guinea line, he had declared that this was to be his last retreat—he would hold the new line at all costs. Estimating that the Americans were now about to attack his new defense perimeter, Koga summoned all available aircraft, including carrier planes, and ordered his surface fleet to sortie from the Palaus and stand by to the northward to await reinforcement and possible action. He then set out with his staff in three planes for new headquarters at Davao in Mindanao. En route they ran into bad weather and two of the planes crashed, including Koga's. The Combined Fleet was once more without a commander in chief.

All the Japanese hustle and bustle was to no avail. As March was turning into April, TF 58 struck the Palaus, destroying most of the defending aircraft and sinking practically all the ships that had not departed. Before the Combined Fleet could assemble for counterattack, TF 58 had also raided the nearby islands of Yap and Woleai and was well on its way back to the Marshalls. The western Carolines were at least temporarily neutralized; MacArthur's right flank was safe.

In mid-April the fast carriers and their escorts were again at sea, this time in direct support of the Hollandia landing. On the return passage, the carrier aircraft gave Truk another pounding which left it so helpless that bombers from Eniwetok and the Admiralties had no further trouble keeping it neutralized. Before returning to base, TF 58 detached cruisers to bombard the central Caroline island of Satawan, and Vice Admiral Willis A. Lee's battleships, formed into battle line, shelled Ponape in the eastern Carolines.

In the course of these two advances into enemy territory not a single American ship had been damaged, evidence of the decreasing effectiveness of Japanese air power and of the growing efficiency of American air defense measures.

## Hollandia and Westward

The Hollandia invasion, which included a subsidiary landing at Aitape to the southeast, was by far the largest amphibious operation undertaken up to then in the Southwest Pacific Area. Assigned to the operation were 84,000 troops, of whom 52,000 were to make the assault. These were carried to three beachheads by 113 ships and supported by the combined striking power of the Fifth and Seventh Fleets.

Admiral Barbey's Seventh Amphibious Force, divided into three attack groups, sortied from Manus supported by eight escort carriers on loan from the Fifth Fleet. After setting a course toward the Palaus to mislead the enemy, the groups split in the evening of April 21 and headed for their separate objectives. The Eastern Attack Group, with the escort carriers, proceeded to Aitape, 125 miles southeast of Hollandia, and put ashore a regiment of American soldiers. The small enemy garrison after negligible resistance fled into the jungle. Engineer battalions quickly began constructing an aircraft staging base, while the assault troops set about plugging the coastal road between Wewak and Hollandia in order to contain the Japanese Eighteenth Army. For the latter task the invaders were eventually reinforced to corps strength—and none too soon, for shortly afterward the enemy advanced from Wewak and attacked. While warfare raged in the jungle, Allied PT boats and aircraft kept the Japanese from using the coastal road or sending supplies by barge; and with the aid of Australian spotting planes, Seventh Fleet cruisers and destroyers bombarded the enemy's inland supply line. Thus deprived of food and ammunition, the initial Japanese counteroffensive at length collapsed with heavy losses. American (and subsequently Australian) forces based on Aitape nevertheless had their hands full until the end of the war. By that time the Eighteenth Army was very nearly wiped out, and the Allies had suffered 4,600 casualties, including 900 killed.

Simultaneously with the invasion at Aitape, Barbey's Central and Western attack groups landed two American infantry divisions 20 miles apart in the Hollandia area. Thanks to a series of massive bomber raids by General Kenney's Fifth Air Force, which had destroyed nearly 500 enemy planes at Hollandia, and to vigorous support by TF 58 and by Seventh Fleet gunnery vessels, these landings also were made virtually without opposition. The Allied objective here was three Japanese airfields south of the coastal Cyclops Mountains. Passing around the ends of the range, one invading division advanced from the west, the other from the east. They closed the pincers on April 26, having taken the fields by double envelopment. Of the 11,000 Japanese in the area, 650 were taken prisoner. Most of the rest fled into the jungle, where all but about a thousand died of starvation or disease before reaching the nearest Japa-

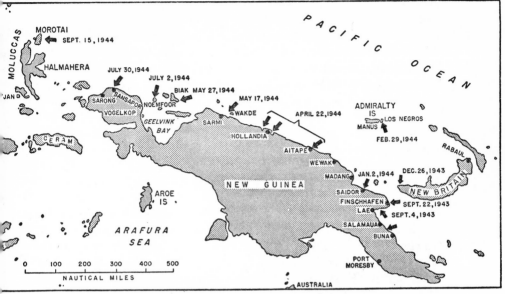

THE NEW GUINEA CAMPAIGN, 1943–1944

nese base at Sarmi, 145 miles to the northwest. The Americans suffered 1,200 casualties, including 160 killed.

General MacArthur was now launched upon his drive to capture Japanese airstrips and convert them to his own use, ever advancing his fighter-escorted bomber line until it could cover his invasion of Mindanao. Determined to maintain momentum, he issued his next invasion order only five days after the Hollandia landings. The new target was Wakde Island just off the New Guinea coast 130 miles northwest of Hollandia. His plan called also for occupation of the adjacent mainland, both to provide sites for artillery support of the assault on Wakde and to secure Wakde from enemy shellfire after it had been captured. This double operation, successfully carried out in mid-May by MacArthur's well-balanced infantry-navy-air force team, demonstrated the contrasting problems of coastal invasion and small island assault. The troops met little resistance on the mainland beach, but over a period of several months they had to defend their positions against repeated enemy counterattacks that eventually took 400 American lives. At Wakde, on the contrary, they had to fight their way ashore, yet they conquered the island once and for all in a little over two days by destroying the 800-man garrison, at a cost of 40 American lives. A week later army engineers had lengthened the Wakde airstrip for use by heavy bombers, just in time to support MacArthur's next westward leap.

This was the invasion of Biak, a large island in the mouth of Geelvink Bay, 190 miles northwest of Wakde. Here, through a misestimate of enemy strength and intentions, MacArthur's swift-moving advance nearly met disaster. The 12,000 American assault troops that landed on Biak on May 27 were expected to achieve a quick conquest, for the island was thought to be lightly held. In fact, however, the garrison numbered over 11,000, a good third of whom were trained combat troops. More ominous than the unexpected strength of Biak was the unforeseen reaction of the Japanese high command.

Early in May, Admiral Soemu Toyoda had assumed command of the Combined Fleet with orders from the Naval General Staff to put an end to the passive policy of Admiral Koga, his predecessor, and actively seek a decision at sea. Toyoda promptly issued a plan, designated Operation A-Go, calling for fleet action in the western Carolines area— on the assumption that the Allies were committed to a single line of advance, via New Guinea, and that TF 58 would continue in direct support of MacArthur. He then ordered his best combat vessels to Tawitawi, between the Philippines and Borneo. The force thus assembled was the First Mobile Fleet, newly organized around carriers in evident imitation of TF 58. Commanding this force was Vice Admiral Jisaburo Ozawa, Japan's top naval air officer. Because Operation A-Go called for use of land-based air to offset the inferiority of the Mobile Fleet, Biak suddenly assumed new importance in the eyes of the Imperial High Command. Allied or Japanese bombers from here could supplement the striking power of their own naval forces operating in the designated battle area. It was thus essential to the A-Go plan that the island be kept out of Allied hands. For this reason MacArthur's invasion spurred the Japanese into drastic action.

First, they drained their Central Pacific bases of much of their air power, rushing planes to New Guinea and Halmahera from Japan, from the Marianas, and from the Carolines. Seventh Fleet antiaircraft fire kept the new arrivals from achieving much on and around Biak, but the hostile planes considerably weakened Biak's air defense by damaging or destroying upwards of 60 Allied aircraft parked on Wakde. They might have done more had not the Japanese aviators from more healthful latitudes to the north quickly succumbed to malaria and jungle fever. Even those who survived were out of action through the crucial month of June.

The air attack was a mere preliminary. From Tawitawi Ozawa released surface units to reinforce the troops on Biak, somewhat in the manner of the Tokyo Express of the Solomons campaign. The first reinforcement group prudently turned back after being sighted by a submarine and by aircraft from Wakde. A second was chased away from the Biak area by a cruiser-destroyer force from the U.S. Seventh Fleet. To support the third attempt, and also in hopes of luring TF 58 into the designated combat area, Ozawa sent his superbattleships *Yamato* and *Musashi* and several cruisers and destroyers under Vice Admiral Matome Ugaki. This formidable force on June 11 assembled at Batjan in the Moluccas, just west of New Guinea, for a quick run to Biak. But the very day that Ugaki reached Batjan, the strategic picture abruptly changed for the Japanese. A thousand miles to the northeast the U.S. Fifth Fleet attacked the Marianas preparatory to invading Saipan. Toyoda at once suspended the Biak operation and activated a modified version of Operation *A-Go*. Ozawa sortied from Tawitawi to do battle, and Ugaki, leaving his transport units at Batjan, headed northeast to join the Main Body of the Mobile Fleet east of the Philippines.

Ozawa's defeat in the great sea-air Battle of the Philippine Sea (June 19–20, 1944) took the pressure off MacArthur. He could proceed unmolested with his conquest of Biak, an operation that required two months of hard fighting and cost the Americans 474 killed, 2,000 wounded, and several thousand incapacitated by disease. By the time Biak was secured, it was already in the rearward area of the Southwest Pacific drive. In early June a regimental combat team had invaded Noemfoor Island, 50 miles farther west. The naval bombardment supporting this landing was so thorough that the surviving Japanese defenders were too stunned to offer any organized resistance. At the end of July, Southwest Pacific forces went ashore at Cape Sansapor near the western end of New Guinea. Here the invaders encountered no enemy at the beachhead but later succeeded in ambushing a few hundred Japanese who were withdrawing westward in hopes of being evacuated.

In a little more than three months, General MacArthur's forces had advanced 550 miles from Hollandia to Cape Sansapor, seizing five enemy air bases en route. Only the Moluccas and the Talaud Islands now stood between MacArthur and Mindanao, 500 miles to the northwest.

We must now backtrack a little in time in order to follow the Central Pacific Axis of the dual Allied advance.

## Across the Center

June 1944 saw unleashed the most titanic military effort in history. Almost simultaneously, American forces in the Pacific and predominantly American forces in Europe cracked the inner defense lines of Japan and of Germany. In terms of sheer magnitude, including the follow-up forces, the cross-Channel invasion of France is without rival, but the assault on Saipan nine days later was scarcely less complex, for the Saipan operation required projecting overwhelming power more than three thousand miles westward from Pearl Harbor and a thousand miles from Eniwetok, the most westerly American anchorage in the Central Pacific. Yet whereas planning for the Normandy invasion had been under way for more than two years, Spruance, Turner, and Holland Smith and their staffs had

had only three months to plan and organize the expedition against the Marianas.

On June 6, Task Force 58, with Admiral Spruance in the *Indianapolis* and Vice Admiral Mitscher in the *Lexington,* left Majuro in the Marshalls and headed northwest, followed at a considerable distance by the amphibious forces, which included 535 ships, carrying more than 127,000 troops, two thirds of whom were marines. During the advance of the Fifth Fleet, army planes from the Marshalls and from the Southwest Pacific Area created a diversion and cut down Japanese air power by striking repeatedly at enemy bases in the Carolines. On June 11, when TF 58 had reached a point 200 miles east of Guam, Mitscher hurled his carrier air groups against the southern Marianas. (See map page 335.) Enemy plane losses were heavy and retaliation was light, partly because, as we have seen, most of the Japanese air power in the Central Pacific had been drained away southward in defense of Biak.

On June 13 Mitscher detached his seven battleships under Vice Admiral Lee to begin the bombardment of Saipan and nearby Tinian. On the 14th he detached two carrier task groups northward under Rear Admiral Joseph J. Clark to attack landing fields on Iwo Jima and Chichi Jima in order to cut air communications from Japan and thereby complete the isolation of the Marianas. The other two carrier groups steamed around to the west of the island chain to lend direct support to the invasion of Saipan.

## The Assault on Saipan

Mountainous, 14-mile-long Saipan could not be bombarded into impotence as the flat islets of Kwajalein Atoll had been. Yet the island had to be seized quickly from its 32,000 defenders because the Japanese were certain to react violently to an invasion so near their homeland. The proposed solution was to strike for a broad, deep beachhead from which the invaders could seize the main airfield and drive straight across the island.

On June 14 the old battleships and other fire support vessels of the amphibious force relieved Lee's battleships off Saipan and began a methodical bombardment. The same day underwater demolition teams reconnoitered the approaches to the beachhead, on the relatively flat southwest coast, and blasted passages through the coral reef. In the early hours of the 15th, transports and LST's bringing the 2nd and 4th Marine Divisions reached Saipan.

After a final two-hour naval bombardment, interrupted by a half hour of air strikes, eight battalions of marines in amtracs advanced toward the beach on a four-mile front. LCI gunboats led the way. Armored amphibians accompanied the first wave. Battleships, cruisers, and destroyers delivered support fire from so close inshore that the landing craft passed between them as they advanced from the line of departure to the beach.

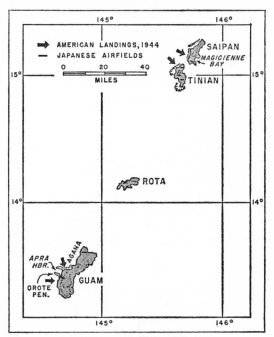

**THE SOUTHERN MARIANAS**

Though 8,000 marines reached shore in the first 20 minutes, it was soon evident that the bombardment had been too brief for a strongly defended island the size of Saipan. Moreover it had been too general, with insufficient fire directed at the immediate beachhead area. Still intact behind the beach and on the flanks were numerous mortar and machine gun nests backed by well-sited artillery in the hills. By nightfall the marines had penetrated inland only about half way to the D-day objective line. Of the 20,000 who had landed during the day, more than ten per cent had been killed or wounded.

The next morning, informed by submarine reports that a Japanese fleet was approaching, Admiral Spruance postponed the intended early invasion of Guam. Admiral Turner thereupon ordered ashore his reserve, the 27th Infantry Division, and directed the Guam Attack Force to stand by in the event even more troops should be needed on Saipan.

By June 17, the American offensive, now amply supported by tanks and artillery, had overcome fierce Japanese resistance and begun to roll. The next day the 4th Marine Division reached the east coast, and the 27th Division captured the main airfield. On the 19th, as the fleets joined battle in the Philippine Sea to westward, the two marine divisions began to pivot for a drive to the north.

## Spruance Covers the Beachhead

On June 14 the situation of the U.S. Fifth Fleet superficially but rather startlingly resembled that of the Japanese Combined Fleet two years earlier, when it had advanced on Midway with results so disastrous to itself. The Saipan Attack Force was heading in for the assault. The

Floating Reserve and the Guam Attack Force were maneuvering east of the Marianas awaiting the outcome of the Saipan invasion. Half of TF 58, including Mitscher's flagship, was steaming to a covering position west of Saipan; the other half, under Clark, was moving north for the strike at Iwo Jima and Chichi Jima, 500 miles away. The parallel would have been exact had the Japanese, with advance intelligence of American intentions, brought their whole carrier fleet undetected to the Marianas before the Americans arrived. Then, while the Fifth Fleet was divided several ways, the enemy carriers might conceivably have struck the two task groups west of Saipan before the rest of the Fifth Fleet could come to their support. The Japanese might thus have defeated the two American groups as decisively as the Americans defeated Nagumo's Mobile Force on June 4, 1942.

But the relative state of military intelligence in June 1944 was such that nothing of the sort occurred. The American attack on the Marianas took the enemy completely by surprise, and Spruance knew very well where the Japanese fleet was—at least until June 15. United States submarines were on station off Tawitawi and in the Philippine Sea keeping close watch on the Mobile Fleet and on all approaches to Saipan. The submarine *Redfin* observed and reported Ozawa's sortie from Tawitawi on the 13th. Coastwatchers kept Spruance informed by radio of the progress of the Japanese Main Body as it threaded its way through the Philippines. On the 15th, the submarine *Flying Fish* reported it debouching from San Bernardino Strait. Spruance knew then that battle was imminent. Calculating the enemy's rate of advance, he postponed the invasion of Guam, transferred eight cruisers and 21 destroyers from the Saipan Attack Force to TF 58, directed Turner's old battleships to operate 25 miles west of Saipan in order to cover the beachhead, and ordered Clark's two carrier groups to complete their strikes on the 16th

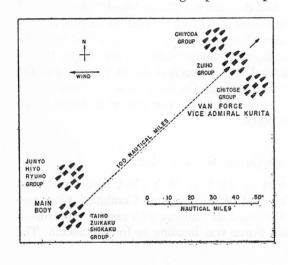

DISPOSITION OF
MOBILE FLEET,
JUNE 19

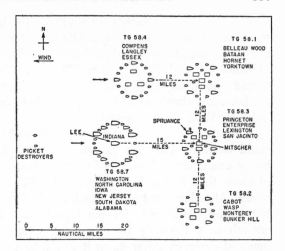

DISPOSITION OF
TF 58,
JUNE 19

and head back south to rejoin the other two groups. Then in the
*Indianapolis,* which had been off Saipan, he steamed back to resume his
place in the carrier force west of the Marianas. Though Spruance did
not take tactical control of TF 58, he told Mitscher that he would "issue
general directives when necessary," and he expected Mitscher to inform
him in advance of his intentions.

An hour after the *Flying Fish's* June 15 report, the submarine *Seahorse*
sighted Ugaki's battleship force on a northeasterly course in the Philippine Sea. The reports of these submarines established that the Japanese
fleet was in at least two widely separated divisions; and since the rendezvous of Ozawa and Ugaki on the 16th went unobserved, Spruance
remained uncertain whether the enemy had massed his forces or was
employing the tricky strategy of divided force which had characterized
most of his operations up to that time. Two contacts by the submarine
*Cavalla* on the 17th indicated that the Japanese were still advancing on
the Marianas, but because the *Cavalla* had sighted only part of the
Mobile Fleet, Spruance continued to suspect that not all Japanese forces
had been accounted for.

At noon on June 18, Clark's two carrier groups rejoined TF 58,
whereupon Mitscher ordered his seven fast battleships, plus four heavy
cruisers and 14 destroyers, detached from the carrier task groups to form
battle line under Lee, ready for a surface engagement should opportunity
offer. The five task groups thus formed, all in circular formation, then
deployed for safe maneuver with 12- to 15-mile intervals between groups.

During the period of expectant waiting, Mitscher, in compliance with
orders from Spruance, maintained a covering position near the Marianas
and the Saipan beachhead, advancing westward by day and retiring
eastward by night so as to prevent any enemy naval force from passing
him in the darkness. Through the daylight hours of the 18th, TF 58

shaped the usual westerly course toward the last enemy contact, feeling out ahead with search planes. The carrier aircraft found nothing.* At nightfall, having developed no further intelligence regarding the enemy, Mitscher ordered TF 58, then 270 miles WSW of Saipan, to reverse course and head back east. Two hours later he received from Pearl Harbor radio direction finder bearings that placed the Mobile Fleet 355 miles WSW of his own position.

The situation was not at all to Mitscher's liking. He knew that Ozawa could outreach him, for Japanese carrier planes unencumbered with heavy armor and self-sealing fuel tanks had an optimum striking radius of more than 300 miles, compared to 200 miles or less for American planes. Mitscher wanted to attack the Mobile Fleet early the next day, but if the direction-finder bearings were correct, he could be close enough to strike only by advancing westward during the remaining hours of darkness. After dawn it would be too late, for flight operations would then oblige his carriers to turn repeatedly into the steady easterly trade wind, thus backing off from the enemy. Mitscher was anxious also to put distance between himself and the Marianas. To remain near enemy airfields would invite simultaneous attacks by enemy land-based and carrier-based planes. It would also enable the Japanese carrier planes to shuttle-bomb him, that is, take off from their decks while the Mobile Fleet was well beyond American reach, attack TF 58, proceed to nearby Guam, there refuel and rearm, hit TF 58 again, and return to their carriers with fuel to spare. With these possibilities in mind, Mitscher proposed to Spruance by voice radio that TF 58 "come to a westerly course at 0130 in order to commence treatment of the enemy at 0500."

After an hour-long discussion with his staff, Spruance a little after midnight rejected Mitscher's proposal. He was just as eager as Mitscher to sink enemy carriers, but his overriding objective—the only one mentioned in his orders—was to "capture, occupy and defend Saipan, Tinian and Guam." Everything else had to be subordinated to this paramount purpose. In the circumstances TF 58 was primarily a Covering Force; its dominant mission at that moment was defensive, to shield the beachhead and the amphibious forces at Saipan. Recalling that the Japanese had used flanking forces in the battles of the Coral Sea and Midway and in the actions off Guadalcanal, Spruance sought a position where no enemy units could get behind his back to strike at the invasion forces. He discounted arguments that search planes could readily detect and bombers easily frustrate such an "end run." Up to that time, so far as he knew, American aircraft had utterly failed to locate the enemy. He

* Fighter aircraft, which had no radar but could elude or fight off Zekes, were used for daylight search. A PBM, operating from a tender off Saipan, made radar contact with the Mobile Fleet at 0115 on June 19 but could not get the word through by radio because of atmospheric conditions.

could not be sure that they would do any better the next day. He distrusted the direction-finder fix as possibly a decoy; this contact however proved nearly exact. On the other hand, a badly garbled transmission from the submarine *Stingray* had left him with the impression that the Mobile Fleet was much farther east than it actually was. Through the night therefore he continued to close the Marianas, accepting the risks of placing himself between enemy carriers and enemy airfields—and within range of each. Dawn on June 19 found TF 58 ninety miles SW of Saipan, 80 miles NW of Guam, still with no precise information regarding the location of the Mobile Fleet.

## The Advance of the Mobile Fleet

In 1944 Japanese naval leaders, with the tide of war turning ever more against them, became obsessed with a false parallel between the Russo-Japanese War of 1904–5 and World War II, and looked to a new Battle of Tshushima to extricate them from their difficulties. This was the spirit and intention of Operation *A-Go*, announced by Admiral Toyoda on assuming command of the Combined Fleet.

The selection of Tawitawi as base for the carrier-centered First Mobile Fleet was dictated chiefly by the chronic fuel shortage that hampered Japanese naval operations more and more with the steady attrition of tankers by American submarines. Tawitawi was within easy cruising range of the Western Carolines battle area designated in the original *A-Go* plan. It was also near the remarkable wells of Borneo, which produced pure but dangerously volatile oil that in a fuel emergency could be used by ships without processing.

But Tawitawi proved an unfortunate choice after all. When documents captured in New Guinea revealed to the Allies the existence and location of the new Japanese carrier fleet, American submarines converged upon the Celebes Sea and the Philippine Islands in such numbers that Ozawa dared not leave port for maneuvers. And since there was no suitable airdrome on or near Tawitawi, his aviators, who had been sent to the carriers with a minimum of basic training, ceased training altogether and merely loafed, losing their fighting edge.

When aircraft from TF 58 attacked the Marianas on June 11, Toyoda, as we have seen, immediately suspended operations for reinforcing Biak and ordered Ozawa and Ugaki to rendezvous in the Philippine Sea. Because there was not sufficient processed oil available for distant operations, oilers accompanying the two segments of the Mobile Fleet carried crude Borneo petroleum. At 1700 on June 16, Ozawa and Ugaki joined forces east of the Philippines and refueled with the dangerous crude. In the early afternoon of the 17th they resumed their advance, with radio orders from Toyoda to "attack the enemy in the Marianas area and annihilate the invasion force."

Ozawa, estimating correctly that TF 58 was nearly twice as strong as the Mobile Fleet on the surface and more than twice as strong in the air, was acutely aware of the inadequate training of his flyers.* But he counted on certain advantages—or supposed advantages. He and Ugaki had, for example, selected routes of advance beyond the range of air reconnaissance from Manus. The trade wind would give him the lee gage, permitting him to launch and recover aircraft while advancing on the enemy. Having appraised Spruance as a cautious man on the basis of his tactics at Midway, he rightly estimated that TF 58 would maintain a close covering position off the Saipan beachhead. That and the long striking radius of his planes gave him all the advantages that Mitscher feared. Ozawa expected aircraft based on Rota and Guam to attack first and achieve at least 33⅓ per cent attrition of TF 58 before the Mobile Fleet went into action. Then he intended to stand off beyond reach of the American carriers and make use of the Guam airfields to shuttle-bomb them into final defeat.

In the afternoon of June 18, planes from the Japanese carriers located TF 58 some 200 miles west of Saipan. Ozawa thereupon began to take disposition for an attack the next morning. Under Vice Admiral Takeo Kurita, a Van Force consisting of three circular groups, each centered on a single light carrier, advanced to a position 300 miles WSW of TF 58, just outside the extreme attack radius of the American planes. A hundred miles to the rear of the Van Force, that is, 100 miles farther from TF 58, was the Main Body under direct command of Admiral Ozawa. This consisted of two circular groups, each centered on three carriers—six carriers in all, five heavy and one light. Most of the heavy surface ships were in Kurita's Van, for this force with its concentration of antiaircraft fire was expected to absorb the first shock, should the aircraft of TF 58 manage to attack. Ozawa's disposition had a certain logic, but as in the Battle of Midway the Japanese divisions were too widely separated for mutual support, and the heavy carriers were poorly protected against possible submarine attack.

"The fate of the Empire depends on the issue of this battle; let every man do his utmost," Admiral Togo had announced to his fleet just before the Battle of Tshushima. And from Japan Admiral Toyoda had repeated Togo's exhortation to the Mobile Fleet, now going into action. As dawn grayed the skies over the Philippine Sea on the morning of June 19,

* Mobile Fleet: 9 carriers, 5 battleships, 13 cruisers, 28 destroyers, 430 carrier aircraft, 43 float planes. Task Force 58: 15 carriers, 7 battleships, 21 cruisers, 69 destroyers, 891 carrier aircraft, 65 float planes. The Japanese had gathered extensive intelligence about the U.S. Fifth Fleet from captured documents, from daring air reconnaissance over the Marshalls, and from interrogation of downed American aviators.

1944, more than 300 Japanese carrier planes prepared to take off against TF 58, in order to repeat by other means Togo's decisive victory of 39 years before.

### The Battle of the Philippine Sea, June 19–20, 1944

Had Ozawa realized that TF 58 had already reduced Japanese air power in the Marianas to no more than 30 operational planes, that Clark had destroyed aircraft reinforcements coming down from Japan, and that the aviators sent to the relief of Biak were in no condition to return, he might have been less sanguine about the approaching battle. Aircraft based on Guam attempted to attack TF 58 early on June 19, but Hellcats pounced on them as they were taking off, shot down a few, and then turned their attention to 19 reinforcements arriving from Truk. In this early morning skirmish, 33 Hellcats destroyed 30 fighters and five bombers. That ended the participation of land-based air in the Battle of the Philippine Sea.

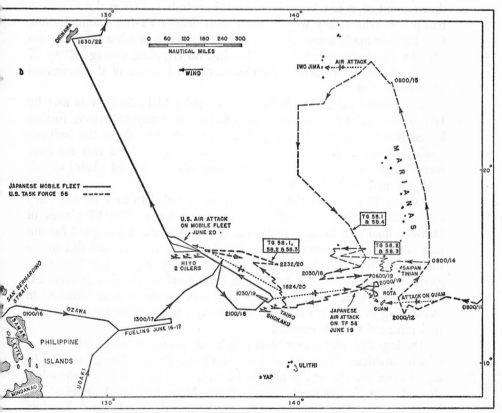

BATTLE OF THE PHILIPPINE SEA, JUNE 19–21, 1944

Having at last reversed direction at 0619, TF 58 steamed on a south-westerly course awaiting attack. Finally at 1000 American radars detected aircraft at 150 miles, approaching from the west. This raid, the first of four launched by the Mobile Fleet, consisted of 45 bombers, eight torpedo planes, and 16 Zekes from the three light carriers of Kurita's Van Force. Task Force 58 steamed steadily toward the contact for 20 minutes, then turned into the wind and launched every available fighter, numbering more than 450. Mitscher next ordered into the air all bombers and torpedo bombers. These remained clear of TF 58 while the carriers landed, rearmed, refueled, and again launched the Hellcats. Many of the bombers, at first on their own and later on orders from Mitscher, dropped their bombs on the airstrips on Guam, keeping them generally unusable by the would-be shuttle-bombers from the Mobile Fleet.

While the Japanese planes of the initial attack were regrouping 70 miles from TF 58, American fighter directors, operating with superb efficiency, vectored out the Hellcats and stacked them at high altitude, whence they swooped down on their ill-trained opponents and shot down about 25. A few Japanese aircraft penetrated as far as the American battle line, where they were blasted with deadly VT-fused ammunition. One bomber made a near miss on the *Minneapolis;* another hit the *South Dakota,* causing numerous casualties but no crippling damage. Only 27 Japanese planes returned to their carriers. All but one of the American planes returned.

The second raid, 128 planes from Ozawa's Main Body, was met by Hellcats 50 miles out and cut down to half size. Survivors took further losses over the battle line and one crashed into the side of the *Indiana,* Lee's flagship. A few reached the carrier groups, where two bombers started fires on the *Bunker Hill* with near misses. Only 31 planes of this raid returned to the Mobile Fleet.

Of the 47 planes of the third raid, most failed to find TF 58. They caused no damage and suffered only seven losses. The 82 planes of Ozawa's final raid became scattered. One group was intercepted far out and cut in half; another reached the American carriers and did minor damage with near misses, but was very nearly wiped out. The third group headed for Guam, jettisoning bombs. Here Hellcats intercepted them and shot down 30. Nineteen Japanese survivors were wrecked in attempting to land on the cratered runways. Only 11 planes of the final raid returned to their carriers.

During this eight-hour decimation of Japanese naval air power, which American flyers called the "Marianas Turkey Shoot," other disasters were overtaking the Mobile Fleet. Two American submarines had slipped through the weak screen of the Main Body and attacked the heavy carriers. The *Albacore* put a single torpedo into Ozawa's flagship, the new *Taiho.* Three hours later the *Cavalla* fired three torpedoes into the veteran *Shokaku*. From ruptured fuel tanks and bunkers, gasoline fumes and explosive vapors from the crude Borneo petroleum seeped through the vessels. Damage control parties worked valiantly, but they had developed no techniques adequate to deal with such a situation. In mid-afternoon both carriers blew up with tremendous loss of life. Among the survivors were Ozawa and his staff, who transferred from the sinking *Taiho* to a cruiser and thence to the carrier *Zuikaku*.

Ozawa ordered a general retirement to the northwest for refueling, intending to resume battle the next day, for he believed reports from his aviators that TF 58 was badly crippled. When the tally was in and he learned that his carrier planes had been reduced from 430 to an even hundred, his only reaction was to postpone the proposed attack till the 21st.

Night was approaching before TF 58, then 35 miles west of Rota, had recovered the last of the planes from the Turkey Shoot. Now that the enemy's wings were clipped, Spruance was ready to advance on the Mobile Fleet. Leaving one carrier group behind to keep Guam and Rota neutralized, Mitscher moved S by W through the night. The choice of course, based on a misestimate of the enemy's position, was unfortunate, for though the Americans were making five knots better speed than the Japanese, they closed the range only slightly. After a fruitless search to westward in the morning of the 20th, Mitscher at noon changed course to NW, but because he was obliged to turn into the easterly wind several times to launch and recover search planes, he ceased to gain on the enemy.

As the day wore on it appeared that the hoped-for counterstroke could not be delivered after all. Not a single American carrier plane had yet seen the Mobile Fleet. Mitscher had received no information on Ozawa's position since the *Cavalla* had reported her attack on the *Shokaku* at noon the preceding day. At last toward 1600 the long-awaited word came in. A search pilot had sighted the Mobile Fleet, which he reported on a westerly course 220 miles WNW of TF 58.

This was considerably beyond the optimum attack radius of American carrier planes. If Mitscher launched a strike so late in the day at such a distance, the flyers would have to return in darkness and make night landings, for which they were untrained. With feelings of almost paternal affection for his aviators, Mitscher had always sought to minimize the risks of their dangerous calling. Yet now, with the enemy at last within his reach, he felt he had no alternative but to attack. "Launch 'em," said he firmly.

The flyers were quickly briefed, with orders to concentrate on the Japanese carriers. Then they raced for their planes. The first deckload strike—85 fighters, 77 dive bombers, 54 torpedo bombers—was in the air by 1630. Thereupon TF 58, having turned into the wind for launching, resumed course toward the enemy in order to close the range for recovery of its returning aircraft. Then came a shock. The search pilot who had reported the location of the Mobile Fleet had made a mistake. His corrected report placed the enemy 60 miles farther away.* Mitscher considered recalling the planes already launched, then, after restudying the charts, decided against it—merely canceling the second deckload.

Shortly before sunset the aviators from TF 58 sighted the Japanese oilers. While a few planes attacked these, sinking two, the rest went after the enemy carrier groups, now scattering fanwise to the northwest. In a series of uncoordinated but otherwise neatly executed attacks, the American bombers ripped up the flight decks of and set fire to the carriers *Chiyoda* and *Zuikaku* and damaged a battleship and a cruiser. The only combat vessel actually sunk was the victim of torpedo planes. Avengers, dropping out of a cloud, succeeded in releasing their torpedoes at low altitude, one, possibly two, of which found their mark in the carrier *Hiyo*. Ablaze and racked by internal explosions, the *Hiyo* gradually settled at the bow and went down.

Ozawa managed to get 75 planes airborne, and these survivors of the Turkey Shoot gave a good account of themselves. Antiaircraft guns and swift-darting Zekes shot down 20 American planes, but Japanese losses were much heavier. When the sun set on June 20, the Mobile Fleet had left only 35 carrier aircraft.

The American air groups, their mission completed, headed back toward TF 58. Fuel gauges in a few of the bombers and torpedo planes were far below the half-full mark; some showed perilously close to empty. Pilots with badly damaged aircraft were among the first to go down. Those who had neglected fuel-conserving measures soon followed. Others wasted fuel in a vain attempt to outspeed nightfall. One group took a vote by radio to ditch together instead of each continuing until his fuel was exhausted. "O.K.," said the chairman, "here we go."

Mitscher had spread out his three carrier groups to allow more maneuvering room for recovery operations. As the minutes ticked past he prowled restlessly between Flag Plot and Flag Bridge. A little after 2000 Air Plot announced the approach of the first of the returning planes, whereupon the task force turned into the east wind to take them aboard. Mitscher went back into Flag Plot, took a seat, and puffed thoughtfully on a cigarette. If he lighted up the task force, he would save many a desperate pilot who otherwise must make a water landing, but he would also expose his fleet to possible submarine and aircraft attack. Still, he

---

* The *Lexington* received the correction at 1605, but radio traffic was then so heavy that by the time the communicators had copied, decoded, and rushed the corrected report to Mitscher, the strike was on its way. Because TF 58 had to turn east for launching while the Mobile Fleet continued west, the American air groups had to fly more than 300 miles to make their attack. Task Force 58, by heading at maximum speed toward the enemy fleet, considerably shortened the return flight.

knew what he had to do—not only for humanitarian reasons but because a carrier stripped of its planes is a liability rather than an asset. To his chief of staff, Captain Arleigh Burke, he said, "Turn on the lights."\* Then he went back to the bridge. On went running lights, truck lights, and glow lights to outline the flight decks, while 5-inch guns of the screen fired star shell, and searchlights pointed straight upward as homing beacons.

Landing signal officers, gesturing with fluorescent batons, waved in the first few planes smoothly enough, but as the newly-arrived aircraft swarmed into the landing circles, the officers were obliged to wave off far more than they landed. When planes exhausted their last drops of fuel and went down, destroyers moved busily through the fleet seeking survivors. Pilots, ordered to land wherever they could find a flight deck, shopped through the fleet for an uncrowded landing circle. One desperate pilot disregarded a wave-off from the *Lexington* and crashed into six newly-landed planes, killing two men and injuring half a dozen others. Two aircraft in quick succession disregarded signals and crash-landed on the *Bunker Hill*, killing two men and injuring four. Aboard the *Enterprise* a fighter and a bomber landed at the same time and incredibly did not crash, the fighter's tail hook catching the second cable and the bomber's, the fifth.

Since the battle over the Mobile Fleet, 80 American aircraft had ditched, or crashed on landing. After completing recovery of planes at 2232, TF 58 shaped course toward the scene of the twilight battle, proceeding at 16 knots through the night and the next day along the path of the returning flyers. By this means destroyers and float planes rescued all but 49 of the 209 aviators who had participated in the battle of June 20.

Spruance estimated that the two hours the American force had spent on an easterly course recovering planes plus the subsequent slow speed to facilitate rescues had permitted the fleeing enemy to get beyond reach of a second air strike. This opinion was confirmed early on the 21st when long-range Avengers found the Mobile Fleet making 20 knots on a NW course 360 miles away. All that day Hellcats searched fruitlessly for possible enemy cripples. An hour after sunset Spruance ordered the search abandoned, and TF 58 turned back east.

Since the submarines *Albacore* and *Cavalla* had not stayed to observe the results of their marksmanship on June 19, and reports from TF 58 aviators were conflicting, American evaluators could assume with confidence only that one Japanese heavy carrier had been sunk and two

---

\* Mitscher had ample precedent for his action in Spruance's daring illumination for night recovery in the Battle of Midway, when the U.S. Navy had no carriers to spare. (See page 243.) In that battle Mitscher commanded U.S. carrier *Hornet*. Arleigh ("31-knot") Burke, who had made his reputation with the destroyers in the Solomons campaign, had joined TF 58 just before the raid on the Palaus.

or three light carriers damaged. To many naval officers this was a disappointment, falling far short of the overwhelming victory they felt they had a right to expect. And though Admirals Nimitz and King both applauded Admiral Spruance's decision to remain close to Saipan until the enemy wing's had been clipped, Spruance himself regretted that his primary responsibility had kept him tethered to the beachhead. But if Mitscher had moved westward to attack the Mobile Fleet on June 19, his planes would have encountered the heavy antiaircraft fire of Kurita's Van Force while the Japanese heavy carriers were still a hundred miles away. By remaining on the defensive near the Marianas, TF 58 had all its fighter planes available for interception. These aircraft, with able assistance from Lee's battle line and the carrier groups, shot down most of the Japanese planes at or near the limit of their attack radius and destroyed the planes on Guam as well. Thus TF 58 on the 19th was at the optimum position to hurt the enemy. True, most of the Japanese carriers got away, but they had lost nearly all of their trained aviators.

## Conquest of the Southern Marianas

Until the Japanese Mobile Fleet had been defeated and repulsed, the U.S. Fifth Fleet was unable to give its full support to the assault on the Marianas. Saipan, as we have seen, received only two days of pre-assault bombardment, and during the Battle of the Philippine Sea all amphibious forces not absolutely essential to the operation retired from the area to await the outcome. The American naval victory at once altered this situation. Since there was no longer any serious danger from enemy naval forces, Fifth Fleet carrier aircraft and gunnery vessels could devote their full attention to supporting the American troops on Saipan and to preparing for the forthcoming assaults on Tinian and Guam.

As the two marine divisions on Saipan pivoted for their drive to the north, Holland Smith ordered the 27th Infantry Division to the center of the new front. But the tardy compliance and deliberate tactics that had slowed down elements of this division on Makin and on Eniwetok now brought it so nearly to a standstill that the inner flanks of the advancing marine divisions became more and more exposed. His patience exhausted, General Smith, with the concurrence of Turner and Spruance, summarily replaced the 27th Division's commanding general.

Thereafter, well supported by naval guns and aircraft, the Americans advanced together up the narrowing north peninsula, where the enemy was deeply entrenched in a network of fortified caves and underground defenses. At the end of the first week in July, some 3,000 Japanese, finding themselves being forced into an ever-diminishing perimeter, struck out in a desperate early morning banzai charge. They broke through a gap in the 27th Division front and surged forward more than a mile before the greater part of them were killed and the rest repulsed, at a cost of 400 American lives. Holland Smith now withdrew most of the army troops into reserve. Three more days of fighting carried the marines to the northeast tip of the island. That ended organized Japanese resistance on Saipan, but several thousand enemy troops in by-passed caves and ravines still remained to be captured or destroyed before Admiral Spruance could declare the island secured.

The capture of Saipan had cost 16,500 American casualties, including 3,400 killed—mostly during the first few days. The subsequent conquests of Tinian and Guam were much less costly, partly because these islands were more lightly garrisoned than Saipan but chiefly because they received more sustained and more systematic bombardment.

All through the Saipan campaign, naval bombers and guns had intermittently softened up nearby Tinian. As the campaign came to an end, most of the artillery on Saipan, nearly 200 field pieces, was placed hub to hub on the southwest shore to take over the bombardment of the northern half of Tinian, while the ships and aircraft continued working over the rest. Because Tinian's two best landing beaches, one in the southwest and one in the east, were heavily mined and fortified, Admiral Turner, after exchanging views with Generals Harry Schmidt and Holland Smith and Admirals Hill and Spruance, decided to invade over two very narrow beaches on the northwest coast. Achieving a secure landing through these restricted corridors required surprise, speed and new logistic techniques. On July 24, while the 2nd Marine Division staged a mock assault on the southern beach to bemuse the defenders, the 4th Marine Division was transported from Saipan to the area off Tinian's northwest beaches. From LST's amtracs carried the invaders ashore in 15 closely spaced waves, which quickly crossed the beaches and fanned out. This was, as it were, the Saipan invasion turned sidewise, making up in momentum what it lacked in breadth. Because the canefields of generally flat Tinian offered little opportunity for the Japanese to take protective cover, the marines abandoned their usual rushing tactics for a methodical advance behind artillery barrages. Now for the first time aircraft used the deadly napalm fire bomb to destroy pockets of enemy resistance. At the end of a week the 2nd and 4th Marine Divisions, late victors of Saipan, had reached the southern end of Tinian.

The conquest of Guam took longer because this island was considerably larger and more heavily garrisoned. Thirteen days of sustained, methodical bombardment however demoralized the defenders and knocked out most of their artillery. In the morning of July 21, Rear Admiral Conolly's Southern Attack Force arrived off the west coast of Guam bringing the new III Amphibious Corps, commanded by Major General Roy S. Geiger usmc. Advancing shoreward in amtracs under rolling naval barrages, the 3rd Marine Division landed north of Orote

Peninsula, and the 1st Provisional Marine Brigade,* followed by the 77th Infantry Division, landed south of Orote. From the two beachheads, the invaders forced their way to a meeting in the hilly interior, sealing off the Peninsula, which the Marine Brigade soon captured. The Americans were thus early enabled to use Orote airfield and nearby Apra Harbor. (See map page 349.) The 3rd and 77th Divisions then advanced together to the north, with the fleet providing call fire by day and harassing fire and star shell illumination by night. On August 10 Guam was declared secured, though as on Saipan and Tinian a great many Japanese troops were still at large.

The successful landings in the Marianas revealed the increasing efficiency of American amphibious techniques, and the invasion of Tinian provided a striking demonstration of their flexibility. Ship-to-shore movement as practiced by the Central Pacific forces had evidently reached maturity. At Guam American fleet support had attained similar efficiency. It should be noted however that the pre-assault bombardment that neutralized Guam was stretched over many days. Saipan after two days of bombardment was far from neutralized. Even a two-day bombardment was practical only for assault on an island or on a stretch of coast that could be completely isolated. In the European theater, as we have seen, the naval bombardment could never be extended beyond a couple of hours because in that area of developed overland communications it quickly attracted defending reinforcements to the beachhead area. With the weapons available in 1944, no means could be devised for softening up a strongly defended position quickly.

Conquest of the southern Marianas cost more than 5,000 American and nearly 60,000 Japanese lives. Japan had lost its direct air staging line to the Carolines. The United States had acquired logistic bases for further conquests westward, submarine bases for stepping up attacks on Japanese communications with the Southern Resources Area, and air bases from which the new long-range B-29's could blast the industrial concentration in and about Tokyo. The loss of the Marianas was the beginning of the end for Japan. Yet not all Allied officials saw it that way. The general refusal of Japanese troops to surrender even when hopelessly overpowered, and the wholesale suicide of Japanese civilian residents of Saipan in order to avoid capture led many to the chilling conclusion that Japan could be conquered only by direct invasion and the virtual extermination of her armed forces and population.

This assumption was incorrect. The Emperor and other high Japanese officials knew very well that they must soon capitulate. The Tojo government fell and was succeeded by a cabinet to whom the Emperor made known his desire for early peace negotiations. Yet so binding was the

---

* Including the 4th and 22nd Marine Regiments, a further step toward the formation of the 6th Marine Division. See page 340.

Japanese military code, so rigid the demands of Oriental "face," that for a whole year no official in Japan could bring himself to initiate steps for ending hostilities. On the Allied side, the goal of unconditional surrender set by Roosevelt and Churchill at Casablanca forbade the proffering of terms which might have served as bases for negotiation.

## Preliminaries to the Invasion of the Philippines

While the Spruance-Turner-Smith team was busy conquering the Marianas, Nimitz ordered Halsey up from the South Pacific to relieve Spruance in command of the Central Pacific Force and to plan for participation in the forthcoming invasion of the Philippines. As preliminary operations, beginning September 15, 1944, the forces under Halsey were to capture staging and support bases in the western Carolines—Peleliu and Angaur islands in the Palaus, and Ulithi Atoll and Yap Island between the Palaus and the Marianas. Halsey was also to support MacArthur's Southwest Pacific forces, which would invade Morotai, half way between New Guinea and Mindanao, on September 15; the Talaud Islands, half way between Morotai and Mindanao, on October 15; Mindanao, southernmost of the Philippines, on November 15; and Leyte, in the central Philippines, on December 20. The date for the contemplated invasion of Luzon, northernmost of the Philippines, was to be contingent upon the success and speed of the earlier invasions. (See map page 372.)

Such was the plan. But the Joint Chiefs of Staff, King in particular, had begun to question the desirability of approaching Japan by way of the Philippine archipelago. Such a step-by-step approach would be costly, and it would inevitably slow down the tempo of the war. It would mean more "island-hopping," the sort of warfare the Allies had abandoned since the Fifth Fleet had demonstrated its capacity for by-passing and isolating Japanese positions with thousand-mile leaps. After MacArthur had conquered a foothold on Mindanao, suggested the Joint Chiefs, let him establish air bases there to reduce enemy air power on Luzon; then let him join forces with Nimitz' Central Pacific command in an invasion of Formosa and the China coast. This by-passing strategy would give the Allies a base quite as good as Luzon for blockading Japanese communications with the East Indies, and it would in a single stroke provide a convenient staging area for invading Japan itself. Japan would thus be defeated sooner and the Filipinos liberated earlier, so ran the argument, than by means of a time-consuming campaign through the Philippines.

General MacArthur reacted strongly against the Joint Chiefs' suggestion. At a July 1944 conference in Honolulu, he pointed out to President Roosevelt that thousands of Filipino guerrillas were already harassing the Japanese occupation forces, that nearly the entire Filipino population could be counted on to join the American campaign of liberation, that to by-pass and seal off these friendly people and the American prisoners in the islands would expose them to frightful privations and to mistreatment at the hands of their Japanese captors, that for the United States to fail to honor its promise to liberate the Filipinos at the earliest possible moment would be construed in the Orient as a second American abandonment of the Philippines. The President found these arguments convincing, but a final decision had not been reached when the Combined Chiefs of Staff met with Roosevelt and Churchill at the second Quebec conference on September 11.

By this time, Spruance, Turner, and Smith had returned to Pearl Harbor to rest and to plan future operations. Their places in the Pacific Fleet command echelon were taken by Admiral Halsey, under whom the Central Pacific Force was designated U.S. Third Fleet; by Vice Admiral Theodore Wilkinson, Commander Third Amphibious Force; and by Major General Geiger, to whose III Amphibious Corps all the Central Pacific invasion troops were now assigned.* Vice Admiral Mitscher, by his own choice, remained in command of the Fast Carrier Task Force, now called Task Force 38. This change of titles accompanying successive changes of command incidentally led the Japanese to suppose that two mighty fleets, the Third and the Fifth, were alternately opposing them in the Central Pacific.

Just as the Combined Chiefs were assembling at Quebec, Halsey in his flagship *New Jersey* joined TF 38 and carried out air strikes against the central Philippines in strategic support of the impending invasions of Morotai and Peleliu. The results were startling. At the cost of eight planes and ten aviators, TF 38 destroyed about 200 enemy aircraft and sank a dozen freighters and a tanker. Convinced that the central Philippines were "a hollow shell with weak defenses and skimpy facilities," Halsey sent Nimitz an urgent radio dispatch recommending that the planned seizure of Yap and the Palaus be abandoned forthwith and that the ground forces for these operations be turned over to MacArthur for an invasion of Leyte at the earliest possible date. Nimitz, willing to by-pass Yap but insisting upon the capture of the Palaus, forwarded Halsey's suggestion to Quebec. The Joint Chiefs thereupon radioed for MacArthur's opinion. When MacArthur concurred in the speed-up plan, they canceled the proposed landings on Yap, the Talauds, and Mindanao, and ordered MacArthur and Nimitz to combine forces for an invasion of Leyte on October 20, 1944—two months ahead of schedule.

---

* Because General Geiger was detained too long by the Guam operation to participate fully in planning the western Carolines campaign, over-all command of the amphibious corps for the conquest of the Palaus, Ulithi, and Yap was assumed by Major General Julian C. Smith, of Tarawa fame.

Nimitz now ordered the Eastern Attack Force, then en route to Yap with the XXIV Army Corps, to shape course instead for Manus and report to General MacArthur's Southwest Pacific command. This transfer at sea of command of a mixed force from one theater commander to another is indicative of the flexibility of planning and of the cooperation of the theater commanders. The Western Attack Force continued on toward the Palaus with the warning that fire support vessels, escort carriers, transports, and escorts of this force also would report to Mac-Arthur as soon as they could be released from the Palau-Ulithi operation. The U.S. Third Fleet was thus to be stripped down virtually to TF 38. Practically everything else would be transferred to the Southwest Pacific forces in preparation for the assault on Leyte.* Meanwhile the four groups of TF 38 deployed to support the landings on Morotai and Peleliu.

These concurrent mid-September invasions by the Southwest Pacific and the Central Pacific forces provide a study in contrasts. Except for the hazard and inconvenience of natural beach obstacles, the capture of Morotai proved to be one of the easiest conquests of the war; while overcoming the intricate defenses of Peleliu cost the attackers the highest combat casualty rate (nearly 40 per cent) of any amphibious assault in American history.

By-passing heavily garrisoned Halmahera, the Seventh Amphibious Force, with 28,000 army troops aboard, took Morotai by surprise. While Third and Seventh Fleet carrier planes and Fifth Air Force planes from Biak and Noemfoor isolated the target, a two-hour naval bombardment sent the few hundred defenders scurrying to the hills. Despite delays caused by an almost impassable reef, mud flats into which troops sank to their hips, torrential rains, and absence of coral suitable for surfacing, engineers had two bomber fields and a fighter strip ready on Morotai in time to cover the left flank of the Philippines invasion.

The conquest of much-smaller Peleliu, 500 miles to the northeast, was a very different story. In this area, the attack force by-passed Babelthuap, largest of the Palaus with a 25,000-man garrison. But on four-mile-long Peleliu there were more than 10,000 Japanese, about half of whom were combat troops of the crack 14th Army Division. Moreover, the Peleliu garrison had diligently complied with a July directive from Imperial General Headquarters setting forth a new defense doctrine.

Formerly, orders issued to Japanese island commanders anticipating an amphibious attack by Allied forces had specified that the defenders were to "meet and annihilate the invaders at the beachhead." Against the

---

* The stripped-down Third Fleet also included TG 30.8 (At Sea Logistic Group Third Fleet), comprising oilers, escort carriers with replacement aircraft, fleet tugs, ammunition ships, and attached screening vessels (destroyers and destroyer escorts). Elements of TG 30.8 met, refueled, and replenished TF 38 at designated points.

power-packed American ship-to-shore movement and support, this doctrine had everywhere proved disastrous. The new Japanese plan employed a carefully calculated defense in depth. Expendable forces at the beach were intended merely to delay the invaders. The main line of resistance was to be far enough inland to escape the full power of the naval bombardment. This line would be backed by a defense fortress that took full advantage of irregularities in the terrain, made as impregnable as possible by every device that human ingenuity could contrive. Troops were to be held in reserve for counterattack when opportunity offered. There were to be no useless banzai charges; every defender was to sell his life dearly.

The three-day naval bombardment of Peleliu completely wiped out all visible defenses on the beach and on the plain behind it. When the 1st Marine Division headed for the shore, most of the casualties to their landing craft were caused by artillery fire from the reverse slopes of the "fortress," a system of ridges to the northeast. Despite continuing fire from these ridges and a series of counterattacks from the main Japanese defense line, the marines quickly made good their beachhead and captured the airfield. When they penetrated the northeast ridges however, they ran into a new sort of resistance. Here the Japanese had withdrawn into a labyrinth of more than 500 natural and artificial caves, mostly interconnected, some fitted with steel doors, all skillfully camouflaged or concealed by vegetation.

By this time, regiments of the 81st Infantry Division, which had been standing by as a floating reserve, had proceeded to invade nearby Angaur Island and distant Ulithi Atoll. Fortunately for the Americans, Angaur proved to be lightly defended and Ulithi not defended at all. General Geiger was able to detach one regiment from the Angaur operation and rush it across to Peleliu to join the hard-pressed marines. Bazookas, demolition charges, and tank-mounted long-range flamethrowers provided an eventual answer to the new Japanese defense techniques, but clearing the enemy off Peleliu was a slow, costly process lasting until February of the following year.

Long before then, American planes were operating from airfields on both Angaur and Peleliu, and Allied ships were using Kossol Passage at the northern end of the Palaus as an emergency anchorage. While it might be questioned whether these advantages offset the cost, 10,000 American casualties, including nearly 2,000 killed, there can be little doubt that the Palaus left entirely in Japanese hands would have been a real threat to MacArthur's advance to the Philippines. The advantages of the bloodless occupation of Ulithi are beyond question, for Ulithi provided the Pacific Fleet with an anchorage and logistic base of major importance, largely replacing Majuro, Kwajalein, and Eniwetok. Every subsequent operation of the Central Pacific forces was at least in part launched from here.

While the invasion forces were assembling at Manus and Hollandia, Allied air and sea power staged a campaign to isolate Leyte. From bases in the South and Central Pacific, aircraft attacked Japanese-held islands in the Marshalls and the Carolines. From western China, B-29's of the 20th Bomber Command and medium bombers of Major General Claire L. Chennault's Fourteenth Air Force operated against Formosa and the China coast. General Kenney's Far Eastern Air Forces, based on New Guinea, Biak, and Morotai, hit the southern flank, striking repeatedly at Japanese airfields in Mindanao and the East Indies.

The Third Fleet, assigned the mission of neutralizing the northern flank, struck Okinawa on October 10, attacked airfields on Luzon on the 11th, and on the 12th began a three-day campaign against bases on Formosa. Here the carrier planes destroyed shipping and airdrome installations and quickly shot down more than 200 fighter aircraft. When Japanese torpedo bombers from the home islands began reaching Formosa via the hastily repaired Okinawa airfields, they too took heavy losses. They succeeded however in torpedoing the cruisers Canberra and Houston,* which had to be taken in tow. The Japanese aviators, elated by this moderate success and supposing that they had achieved a great deal more, flashed word back home that they had sunk eleven carriers, two battleships, and three cruisers. They thereby set off victory celebrations in Japan, and Radio Tokyo broadcast the fictitious triumph to the world. Taking advantage of the enemy's delusion, Halsey set a trap. He temporarily withdrew the bulk of the Third Fleet from Formosan waters, leaving behind the damaged cruisers and a single task group to lure out the Japanese fleet and thus precipitate a sea battle.

Admiral Toyoda took Halsey's bait. He sent all his better trained carrier air squadrons to help the land-based torpedo bombers complete their supposed victory, and he ordered his Second Striking Force of cruisers and destroyers to sortie from Japan "to mop up remaining enemy elements." But long-range Japanese search planes, quartering the seas for a final check, at length found all the groups of the U.S. Third Fleet and reported none noticeably impaired. So Halsey's trap was exposed, and the Second Striking Force prudently retired to the Ryukyus. The Japanese aircraft got in the last lick however, firing another torpedo into the battered Houston. That ended the battle. Both damaged American cruisers, saved by efficient damage control, at length reached Ulithi under tow. The rest of the Third Fleet, having wiped out the greater portion of Japanese land-based air power and the only effective part of Japanese carrier air power, proceeded to station off Leyte to support the invasion of the Philippines. Between October 11 and 16, Halsey's carrier squadrons had destroyed about 350 aircraft and lost 89.

---

* The second cruisers in World War II so named. U.S.S. Canberra was the first American warship to be named for a foreign city.

## The Invasion of Leyte

The main elements of the Leyte attack forces sortied from Manus and Hollandia in several echelons between October 10 and 15. On the 17th and 18th the advance units put Rangers ashore on the islands guarding the entrance to Leyte Gulf in order to secure the flanks of the oncoming invasion forces. On the 18th minesweepers and underwater demolition teams began their important preparatory work off the Leyte beachheads, while fire support ships and escort carriers came in for a two-day pounding of Japanese coastal defenses.

In the early hours of October 20, the transports entered the Gulf and steamed to position for the assault—those of Admiral Barbey's Seventh Amphibious Force off Tacloban, capital of Leyte; those of Admiral Wilkinson's Third Amphibious Force off Dulag, 17 miles south of Tacloban. At the same time one regimental combat team was lifted down to Panaon Island to seize a base whence PT boats could patrol the southern entrance to Surigao Strait, gateway into Leyte Gulf from the south. After a final bombardment of the shoreline, troops headed for the marshy beaches in a variety of craft, including amtracs, which had been loaded in Third Amphibious Force LST's for the canceled invasion of reef-surrounded Yap.

Conforming to their new defense doctrine, most of the Japanese retreated to prepared positions in the hilly interior, leaving behind only enough troops to harass and delay the landings. The Japanese at the beachheads caused some casualties with rifle, machine gun, mortar, and artillery fire. A single torpedo plane, attacking in the late afternoon, heavily damaged the light cruiser *Honolulu*. Compared to most invasions in the Pacific however, the landings on Leyte were easy. By sunset on the 20th more than 60,000 assault troops and more than 100,000 tons of supplies and equipment were ashore, both Leyte beachheads had expanded more than a mile inland, and the Tacloban airstrip was in American hands.

A few hours after the first landings on Leyte, General MacArthur came ashore accompanied by Sergio Osmeña, President of the Philippines. Stepping up to a signal corps microphone, the General broadcast his speech of liberation for all Filipinos to hear: "This is the Voice of Freedom, General MacArthur speaking. People of the Philippines! I have returned. By the grace of Almighty God our forces stand again on Philippine soil—soil consecrated in the blood of our two peoples. . . . Rally to me. Let the indomitable spirit of Bataan and Corregidor lead on. As the lines of battle roll forward to bring you within the zone of operations, rise and strike. Strike at every favorable opportunity. For your homes and hearths, strike! For future generations of your sons and daughters, strike! In the name of your sacred dead, strike!"

## Conclusion

Operations in the Pacific theater during 1944 have been described in several ways. Some officers thought of the series of landings along the coast of New Guinea as the principal line of advance toward the Philippines and Japan. They regarded the conquests of Nimitz' Central Pacific forces as useful chiefly for clearing the right flank of the Southwest Pacific drive, and hence were critical of the leap from the Marshalls to the Marianas while the Carolines were left in Japanese hands. The drive across the Central Pacific was officially designated as the main line of advance, but in practice this designation was meaningless, for in the allocation of men, supplies, and weapons neither advance was favored over the other. Yet there were officers who considered MacArthur's operations as useful principally for clearing the left flank of the Central Pacific forces and for protecting Australia. The truth lies between these two extremes. The Allied advance to the Philippines was along two distinct but mutually supporting lines, enjoying the advantages and running the risks of the exterior position.

The campaign against Rabaul, by greatly weakening Japan's carrier air power, enabled the Fifth Fleet to seize the Gilberts and Marshalls without having to fight off any significant counterattack. The Fifth Fleet raid on the Palaus removed the Japanese fleet from MacArthur's path. MacArthur's invasion of Biak pulled out of the Central Pacific land-based aircraft that otherwise might have resisted the Fifth Fleet assault on Saipan. The Fifth Fleet, by invading the Marianas, drew Ugaki's battleships away from their intended attack on MacArthur's forces at Biak and attracted the Mobile Fleet into the Philippine Sea, where the "Marianas Turkey Shoot" stripped it of planes. The Third Fleet raids on Okinawa, Luzon, and Formosa so weakened Japan's air power that it could make no immediate resistance of any consequence to MacArthur's invasion of Leyte.

The two Allied forces advancing across the Pacific operated as a team, each relieving the other of a portion of its burden. The Allied forces attained strategic concentration by holding part of the enemy in one quarter while bringing their main attack against the enemy in another. Such concentration may be achieved, among other means, by either interior or exterior position (or interior or exterior lines of advance), but the exterior position, being more risky, is best avoided by the weaker power. Suppose for example Ozawa had had the strength to defeat Spruance in the Battle of the Philippine Sea. The Mobile Fleet might then have taken advantage of its interior position by turning south and advancing directly through the Japanese-held Carolines to smash MacArthur's forces at Biak before a weakened Fifth Fleet could come the long way around east of the Carolines to lend support.

Those who question the wisdom of opening the Central Pacific drive point to the high costs of capturing such positions as Saipan or the Palaus, each of which cost more casualties than MacArthur's entire advance from the Admiralties to the Philippines.* These critics however fall into the common fallacy of assuming that the Japanese would have acted as they did even had the Allies acted otherwise than as they did. Ukagi's advance from Tawitawi to Batjan and his subsequent shift from Batjan to the Philippine Sea is sufficient evidence that, had there not been a Central Pacific drive to attract and hold Japanese forces elsewhere, the Southwest Pacific forces would have met far greater resistance in the New Guinea area.

Spruance's controversial tactics in the Battle of the Philippine Sea have led some critics to assert that he failed to make best use of fleet mobility, that in fact he was using TF 58 as a fortress fleet. Such a criticism raises again the old question of whether the commander of armed forces should, in the Nelsonian or Clausewitzian tradition, regard the destruction of enemy armed forces as his primary objective, or whether he should make all tactical decisions in the light of ultimate and paramount objectives, strategic and national. It also raises the question whether at that time, and in the light of all that followed, it was more to the Allied advantage to destroy trained Japanese aviators and Japanese aircraft or to sink Japanese carriers. Certainly Spruance could not have destroyed both enemy planes and enemy carriers without risking heavy losses to his fleet and assault forces.

---

* Saipan: 3,426 killed in action, 13,099 wounded in action. Palaus: 1,950 killed in action, 8,515 wounded in action. Aitape, Hollandia, Wakde, Biak, Noemfoor, Sansapor, Morotai, and associated operations: 1,648 killed in action, 8,111 wounded in action. Figures given in the text are round figures.

# 13

# The Battle for Leyte Gulf

The Battle for Leyte Gulf, touched off by the American invasion of the Philippines, is for complexity and magnitude without parallel in naval history. Lasting four days, it was actually a series of battles and subsidiary actions hundreds of miles apart. The most important were the Battle of the Sibuyan Sea on October 24, and the Battle of Surigao Strait, the Battle off Cape Engaño, and the Battle off Samar on October 25, 1944. When the long-drawn-out conflict at length subsided, the Imperial Japanese Navy no longer existed as an effective fighting force, and the United States Navy commanded the Pacific.

## Activating Sho-Go

When the Americans broke Japan's inner defense perimeter by seizing the southern Marianas, the Imperial High Command readjusted its strategy in preparation for last-ditch defense. The home islands had of course to be defended, but almost equally vital to Japanese security were the Philippines, Formosa, and the Ryukyus. Behind the screen of these off-shore islands, the dwindling tanker fleet could still transport vital supplies of oil from the East Indies to Japan. Hence the new Japanese defense plan, called Sho-Go ("Victory Operation"), was worked out in four variations: Sho 1 for the Philippines; Sho 2 for Formosa, the Ryukyus, and southern Japan; Sho 3 for central Japan; and Sho 4 for northern Japan. Like the A-Go plan, which came to grief in the Philippine Sea, Sho-Go anticipated massing sea and air power against the next American assault, with land-based planes striking a first, devastating blow.

Whatever chance Sho-Go had of working was spoiled in advance of the Philippine invasion. The U.S. Third Fleet in its series of air attacks on the Philippines, the Ryukyus, and Formosa in September and October had reduced Japanese air power by more than 1,200 planes. American submarines, by giving high priority to the destruction of Japanese tankers

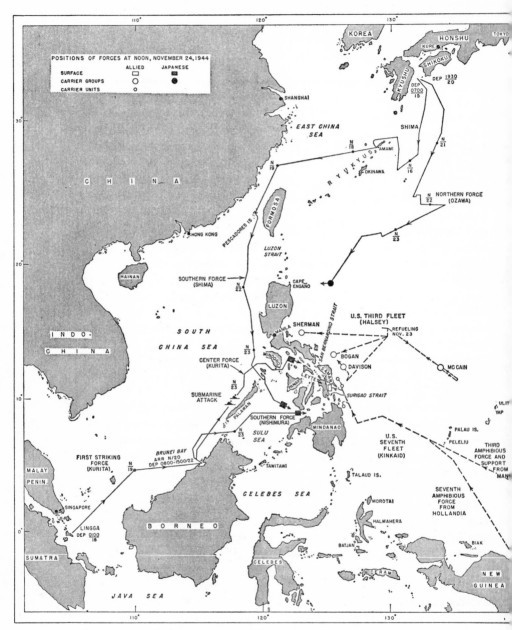

## APPROACH OF ALLIED AND JAPANESE NAVAL FORCES TO LEYTE GULF

Unless otherwise indicated, the daily positions are as of 1200 hours.

and thereby nearly shutting off the flow of oil to Japan, had rendered the Mobile Fleet incapable of operating as a unit out of home ports. In this critical situation Admiral Toyoda had no choice but to divide the fleet. Retaining his carriers in Japan for repairs and pilot training, he sent the bulk of his surface vessels to operate in the Singapore area, where fuel was plentiful.

On October 17, when the Rangers landed in Leyte Gulf, the Mobile Fleet was dispersed as follows: (1) A force of battleships, cruisers, and destroyers commanded by Vice Admiral Kurita was at Lingga Roads, near Singapore. (2) A force of cruisers and destroyers under Vice Admiral Kiyohide Shima was at Amami in the Ryukyus. This was the group that sortied from Japan on October 15 to mop up the "remnants" of Halsey's Third Fleet, and then hastily retired when the over-optimistic reports of the Japanese aviators proved false. (3) A force of carriers and screening vessels under Vice Admiral Ozawa was in the Inland Sea, between the Japanese home islands of Honshu and Shikoku.*

With the landing of the Rangers, Toyoda promptly activated the naval phase of *Sho* 1. Though he knew that his forces were vastly outnumbered on the sea and in the air, he had no thought of not putting up a fight. For if the Japanese lost the Philippines, they would lose everything. The lifeline between Japan and the East Indies would be severed, the Mobile Fleet would be permanently divided, and there would be no means of supplying Kurita's force with ammunition or Shima's and Ozawa's with fuel. The fleet could be defeated in detail and Japan blockaded.

Kurita's force departed Lingga in the early afternoon of October 18, with orders to head for Leyte Gulf—eluding the U.S. Third Fleet if possible, engaging and defeating the U.S. Seventh Fleet if necessary—in order to attack the American amphibious shipping off the beachhead. On October 20, just as MacArthur was gaining a foothold on Leyte, Kurita entered Brunei, Borneo, and began to refuel. Early on the 22nd, he led out the greater part of his force (the two superbattleships *Yamato* and *Musashi*, three older battleships, ten heavy cruisers, two light cruisers, and 15 destroyers) and shaped course for Palawan Passage. This segment became known to the Americans as the Center Force. With it Kurita planned to cross the Sibuyan Sea, south of Luzon, penetrate San Bernardino Strait, and enter Leyte Gulf from the north at dawn on the 25th.

Vice Admiral Shoji Nishimura sortied from Brunei in the afternoon of the 22nd with the rest of Kurita's force (two old battleships, the heavy

---

* The Japanese called the forces under Kurita, Shima, and Ozawa respectively the First Striking Force, the Second Striking Force, and the Mobile Force. That part of the Mobile Force which Ozawa led out of the Inland Sea was called the Main Body. The Americans, as they made contact with the various segments of the Mobile Fleet, called them the Center, Southern, and Northern forces.

cruiser *Mogami*, and four destroyers). This segment was to be the south-ern arm of a double envelopment. Nishimura, after a swing to the north to elude enemy submarines, headed via the Sulu and Mindanao Seas for Surigao Strait in order to strike at Leyte Gulf from the south in coor-dination with Kurita's attack from the north.

On receiving Toyoda's order activating *Sho* 1, Shima's force (two heavy cruisers, a light cruiser, and four destroyers) headed for the Pesca-dores, west of Formosa, and thence shaped course southward with orders to cooperate with Nishimura in the attack through Surigao Strait. Nishi-mura's and Shima's forces became known to the Americans as the South-ern Forces.

A few hours after Nishimura departed Brunei, Ozawa sortied from the Inland Sea with the Northern Force (the heavy carrier *Zuikaku*, flagship; the light carriers *Zuiho*, *Chitose*, and *Chiyoda*;* the *Hyuga* and the *Ise*, converted battleships with flight decks aft but never actually used as carriers; and a screen of three light cruisers and eight destroyers). This force was not expected to provide much direct assistance in the impending battle, for the loss of Japanese carrier pilots over Formosa had been so severe and the training of new pilots was so far from complete that there remained in the Imperial Navy few pilots with enough skill to land on flight decks. The mission of the Northern Force was to decoy the Third Fleet away from the vicinity of Leyte Gulf, leaving the transports open to attack by Kurita, Nishimura, and Shima. Toyoda, who had correctly guessed that Spruance would not let himself be drawn away from Saipan, now estimated that Halsey, presented with an opportunity to sink carriers, might well be lured away from Leyte. He assumed that the Northern Force, serving as bait, would be annihi-lated.

Thus at one time four separate Japanese forces were converging on Leyte Gulf. The success of so complex an operation depended upon teamwork and perfect timing. These in turn depended to a large extent upon good radio communication, but time and again during the battle the widely scattered segments of the Mobile Fleet failed to get crucial information through to the other segments.

### First Blood

Kurita's Center Force soon ran into trouble. An hour after dawn on October 23, it was attacked off Palawan by the *Darter* and the *Dace*, two of the American submarines assigned to patrol the approaches to the Philippines. Kurita's flagship, the heavy cruiser *Atago*, hit by four

* Ozawa sortied with enough carriers to make an attractive bait but left his less expendable carriers in Japan for future use. Left behind were four large new carriers, the *Shinano*, the *Amagi*, the *Unryu*, and the *Katsuragi*, and two older 28,000-ton carriers, the *Junyo* and the *Ryuho*.

torpedoes from the *Darter*, sank in 18 minutes. Two more torpedoes so severely crippled the heavy cruiser *Takao* that she was obliged to head back toward Brunei escorted by a pair of destroyers. Just after the *Atago* went down, the *Dace* put a spread of torpedoes into a third heavy cruiser, the *Maya*, whose exploding magazines blew her apart in a series of searing blasts.

From the *Atago* Kurita and his staff managed to escape to a destroyer and transferred thence to the *Yamato*, which became the new flagship. Early on the 24th the surviving vessels of the Center Force passed south of Mindoro Island into the Sibuyan Sea. Kurita, shaken by his experience of the day before, realized that the presence of his force was now known to the Americans and that he was coming within easy attack radius of Halsey's carriers east of the Philippines.

Nearly 200 miles to the south, in the Sulu Sea, Nishimura, with Shima trailing some 60 miles behind, was also coming within striking radius of Halsey's carrier planes. The main phase of the battle was about to begin.

## Disposition of the Allied Forces

During the first stages of the Leyte invasion, Allied naval forces, almost entirely American, were disposed in several layers off the beach-head.

Inside Leyte Gulf was the greater part of the enlarged Seventh Fleet, including the two amphibious forces of transports, cargo vessels, and amphibious craft, and also a Bombardment and Fire Support Group composed of six old battleships and of cruisers and destroyers, commanded by Rear Admiral Jesse B. Oldendorf. Here also were Commander Seventh Fleet Vice Admiral Kinkaid in the AGC *Wasatch* and General MacArthur in the cruiser *Nashville*. To the east, just outside Leyte Gulf, were three Seventh Fleet carrier task units commanded by Rear Admiral Thomas L. Sprague. These units, which initially included 18 escort carriers screened by destroyers and destroyer escorts, were on anti-submarine, antiaircraft, and ground support patrol.

East of Luzon were the combat vessels of Admiral Halsey's Third Fleet, temporarily stripped down to TF 38 in order to build up the Seventh Fleet for the Leyte invasion. The four task groups making up TF 38 were at this time commanded by Vice Admiral John S. McCain and Rear Admirals Gerald F. Bogan, Frederick C. Sherman, and Ralph E. Davison. These groups, though not uniform, averaged about 23 ships each—two heavy carriers, two light carriers, two new battleships, three cruisers, and 14 destroyers. Halsey, in the *New Jersey*, was with Bogan's group; Mitscher, in the *Lexington*, was with Sherman's. Because as a combat force Third Fleet and TF 38 were now identical, Halsey exercised direct tactical command.

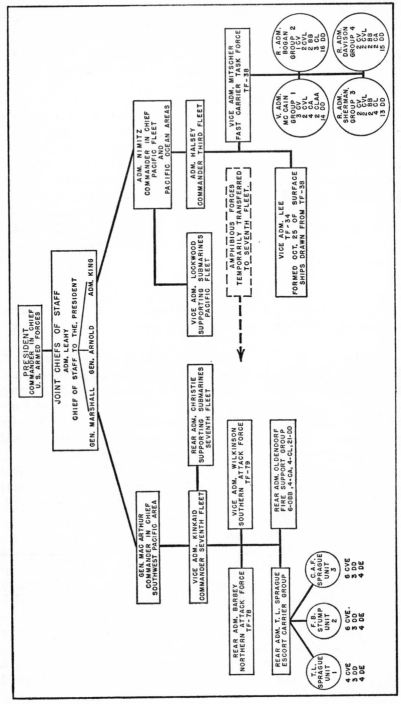

MAJOR U.S. NAVAL FORCES AND CHAINS OF COMMAND IN LEYTE OPERATION

When the landings on Leyte were carried out without hindrance from the Japanese fleet, Halsey seized the opportunity to refuel and rearm his ships and to give his tired crews a little rest. Intending to replenish one task group at a time, he had already dispatched McCain's group toward Ulithi when he received the *Darter's* report of Kurita's approach from the west. Evidently the Japanese fleet was about to strike after all. Halsey let McCain's group continue southeastward but at once ordered his other three groups to rendezvous with oilers for refueling and then to head in closer to the Philippines. Fanning out during the night, the groups by dawn on October 24 had reached positions 125 miles apart—Sherman's off Luzon, Bogan's off San Bernardino Strait, Davison's off Leyte Gulf. Before 0630 scout planes were away from all three groups, searching west, northwest, and southwest.

## The Battle of the Sibuyan Sea

A little after 0900 on the 24th, scout planes from Davison's group discovered Nishimura's force, van of the Southern Forces, in the Sulu Sea and attacked at once, slightly damaging the old battleship *Fuso* and a destroyer, without however cutting down the speed of either. Later in the morning a Fifth Air Force bomber sighted Shima's rear echelon, also in the Sulu Sea. Kinkaid, assuming that these two groups were divisions of a single force and correctly estimating that their destination was Leyte Gulf via Surigao Strait, prepared to strengthen Seventh Fleet defenses in that quarter.

Halsey's interest in these small Southern Forces was overshadowed by news of much bigger game farther north, for at 0810 one of Admiral Bogan's flyers had sighted Kurita's Center Force about to enter the Sibuyan Sea. Leaving the Southern Forces to Kinkaid and the Seventh Fleet, Halsey ordered Davison and Sherman to close at best speed on Bogan, at the center, and to concentrate their full air power upon stopping Kurita. At the same time he directed McCain to reverse course and to refuel at sea in order to be available for whatever might develop.

From the carrier decks of the Third Fleet task groups, five air strikes attacked Kurita on October 24 as, virtually without air cover, the Center Force doggedly plowed across the Sibuyan Sea toward San Bernardino Strait. By mid-afternoon four of Kurita's battleships had been hit, the heavy cruiser *Myoko* had been put out of action and was retiring westward, and the superbattleship *Musashi*, struck repeatedly by torpedoes and bombs, had fallen far astern of the formation. The final attack of the day concentrated on the *Musashi* which, after being hit by 19 torpedoes and 17 bombs, at length capsized, carrying down 1,100 men, half her complement.

Complaining bitterly by radio about the lack of air support that had

left him open to crippling attack, Kurita at length ordered his Center
Force to reverse course and head back west.

## Attacks on Sherman's Task Group

Kurita lacked air support because the Japanese air command on
Luzon had concluded that it could best assist the Center Force by
attacking the American carrier groups. The hastily-trained Japanese
pilots, it was believed, had a better chance of hitting the enemy's ships
than of hitting the enemy's planes over their own ships. Hence when a
searching Luzon-based pilot sighted and reported Sherman's task group
early on October 24, the Japanese launched against it every plane they
could muster.

Sherman's group detected the oncoming enemy aircraft just as the
carriers were about to launch a strike of their own against the Center
Force. Sherman postponed his strike, returned his bombers and torpedo
planes to the hangar decks, and scrambled (ordered into the air) every
fighter, while his task group retired under a rain squall. As in the
Marianas Turkey Shoot, the highly trained, experienced American pilots
decimated their inexperienced opponents. During the air battle not a
single Japanese aircraft got close enough to Sherman's carriers to attack.
A little after 0930 however, when the air had apparently been cleared
of hostile planes and the task group was emerging from the overcast to
take the fighters aboard, a lone bomber dived out of a cloud and bombed
the light carrier *Princeton*. Gasoline from shattered planes spread fires
through the hangar deck, where six torpedoes, loaded in Avengers for
the postponed strike, went off one at a time, blowing out both elevators
and ripping up much of the flight deck.

In the circumstances Sherman did not close on Bogan as Halsey had
directed. Instead he left several cruisers and destroyers standing by the
burning carrier and maneuvered the rest of his group within support
range. Late in the morning his three remaining carriers at last got off
their strike against Kurita.

Search planes from Ozawa's Northern Force, now maneuvering off
Cape Engaño, the northeast tip of Luzon, had by this time also located
Sherman. At 1145 Ozawa launched a strike of 76 planes, which included
most of the operational aircraft he had left. An hour later American
radar detected their approach, just as Sherman was about to launch a
second attack against the Center Force. This time he launched the
strike at once and then scrambled his fighters to ward off the new
attack. So successful were Sherman's Hellcats that the Japanese in this
raid achieved nothing at all. Of Ozawa's attacking aircraft, some 20 fled
to Luzon. The rest were lost.

Fire fighters aboard the *Princeton* meanwhile were apparently getting her fires under control. But in mid-afternoon one stubborn blaze reached the torpedo stowage, setting off a tremendous explosion that blasted off most of her stern and after flight deck. The *Birmingham,* then alongside, was swept by debris and chunks of steel which killed more than 200 of her crew and injured nearly twice as many others. Shortly afterward the captain of the *Princeton* ordered Abandon Ship.

## Halsey Uncovers the Beachhead

Though the Leyte invasion brought Central Pacific and Southwest Pacific forces together in a single operation, no provision was made for an over-all commander at the scene of action. Admiral Halsey, as Commander Third Fleet, was responsible to Admiral Nimitz at Pearl Harbor, and Admiral Nimitz was responsible to the Joint Chiefs of Staff in Washington. Admiral Kinkaid, as Commander Seventh Fleet, was responsible to General MacArthur in Leyte Gulf, and General MacArthur was responsible to the Joint Chiefs. Though Halsey and Kinkaid were thus operationally independent of each other, no serious difficulties were anticipated. Both were seasoned commanders and could be expected to cooperate and to coordinate their efforts. Yet seeds of trouble were present, for the two fleet commanders went into battle with differing conceptions regarding the specific mission of each.

It was clear that the Seventh Fleet, which had escorted the invasion forces to Leyte, was to furnish close support for the assault. But which fleet was to provide cover, that is, fend off hostile naval forces from the beachhead? Nimitz' Operation Plan directed Halsey to "cover and support forces of the Southwest Pacific," from which Kinkaid assumed that it was the business of the Third Fleet to protect Seventh Fleet amphibious shipping. The task of the Seventh Fleet, said he, ". . . was to land troops and keep them ashore. The ships were armed accordingly with a very low percentage of armor-piercing projectiles. The CVE's carried anti-personnel bombs instead of torpedoes and heavy bombs. We were not prepared to fight a naval action."

But Nimitz' Plan also directed: "In case opportunity for destruction of major portion of the enemy fleet offer or can be created, such destruction becomes the primary task." From this, Halsey concluded that the mission of the Third Fleet was offensive, not defensive. "It was not my job to protect the Seventh Fleet," he later wrote. "My job was offensive, to strike with the Third Fleet."

Kinkaid early on October 24 assumed the task of blocking Surigao Strait, adjacent to the beachhead area, against the approach of the Japanese Southern Forces. Halsey meanwhile massed all his available air strength against Kurita's formidable Center Force. In mid-afternoon, while Kurita was still boring steadily eastward evidently intent upon

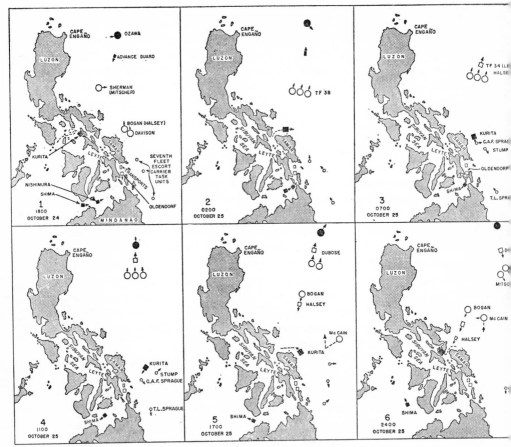

**FLEET MOVEMENTS, BATTLE FOR LEYTE GULF**

breaking through San Bernardino Strait, Halsey made provision for possible surface action. At 1512 he sent his subordinate commanders a radio message, headed "Battle Plan," in which he stated that four battleships, including the flagship *New Jersey*, three heavy cruisers, three light cruisers, and 14 destroyers from Bogan's and Davison's task groups "will be formed as Task Force 34" under Vice Admiral Lee. "This dispatch, which played a critical part in the next day's battle," said Halsey, "I intended merely as a warning to the ships concerned that if a surface engagement offered, I would detach them from TF 38, form them into TF 34, and send them ahead as a battle line."

Kinkaid, though not an addressee, intercepted Halsey's 1512 dispatch and read it with considerable satisfaction. Not intercepting further modifying messages, he assumed that Halsey had carried out his intention as expressed in the preparatory dispatch and that San Bernardino Strait was being guarded by a strong surface force. "It was inconceivable," said he, "that Halsey would have scrapped a perfect battle plan."

The movement of Kurita's force in the Sibuyan Sea and of Nishimura's and Shima's forces in the Sulu Sea suggested a pincer attack of surface forces on Leyte Gulf. But what about the Japanese carriers? Surely in a naval attack of such magnitude the enemy would use his carrier force. Since it was almost certain that the carriers had been in Japanese waters at the time of the Leyte invasion, it could be inferred that they were now at sea, coming down from the north to coordinate with the Japanese Southern and Center forces in their grand convergence on Leyte Gulf.

Ozawa's carrier force was indeed to northward, as we have seen. It was doing its utmost to attract American attention—making smoke, breaking radio silence on various frequencies, and even sending forward an advance guard of surface vessels in a fruitless attempt to contact and engage the Third Fleet. Through the morning and early afternoon Sherman, whose responsibility it had been to search to the north, had sent out no scout planes because he was preoccupied with warding off air attacks and with covering the burning *Princeton*. At last, late in the afternoon, his scout bombers found the Japanese carrier force only 190 miles away to the NNE and flashed back the word. Mitscher passed the information to Halsey, and Sherman sent in a cruiser to sink the derelict *Princeton* with torpedoes.

Now that Halsey had at last located all the pieces of the Japanese puzzle, the picture seemed to confirm his first impression—that the Southern Forces heading for Surigao Strait, the Center Force heading for San Bernardino Strait, and the Northern Force coming down from Japan were all moving toward a rendezvous in the vicinity of Leyte Gulf. This massing of hostile forces he was determined to thwart. He felt he could ignore the weak Southern Forces, leaving them to Kinkaid. According to his pilots, the Center Force had received so much damage to guns, fire-control instruments, and communications that it too could be left to Kinkaid. Moreover latest reports indicated that it had reversed course and was retreating to the west. That left the carrier-centered Northern Force, fresh and undamaged, with a combat radius hundreds of miles wider than the others. In the circumstances, Halsey selected destruction of the Northern Force as his primary objective. How best to meet this antagonist offered him a choice of alternatives.

He could guard San Bernardino Strait with his whole fleet and wait for the Northern Force to approach and strike. This he rejected because it left the Third Fleet between Japanese carriers and Japanese airfields, subject to attack from both and to shuttle-bombing by the carriers. In the Battle of the Philippine Sea, Mitscher's bombers had forestalled such attacks by keeping the airfields on Guam neutralized, but neutralizing all the enemy airfields in the Philippines was manifestly impossible.

He could guard San Bernardino Strait with TF 34 while striking the Northern Force with his carriers. This he rejected because, overestimating the enemy's land-based and carrier air power, he believed that together they might inflict far more damage on a divided fleet than on the Third Fleet intact. He wanted all his available antiaircraft fire to protect his carriers and all his carrier air cover to protect his surface vessels.

He could leave San Bernardino Strait unguarded and strike the Northern Force with his whole fleet. Although this alternative involved also leaving his covering position off the American beachhead, he accepted it for, as he said, "It preserved my Fleet's integrity, it left the initiative with me, and it promised the greatest possibility of surprise. Even if the Central Force meanwhile passed through San Bernardino and headed for Leyte Gulf, it could only hope to harry the landing operation. It could not consolidate any advantage, because of its reported damage. It could merely hit and run. I felt Kinkaid was amply strong to handle this situation if it should develop." His decision made, Halsey went into Flag Plot just before 2000, put his finger on the charted position of the Japanese Northern Force 300 miles away, and said to Rear Admiral Robert B. Carney, his chief of staff, "Here's where we're going. Mick, start them north."

Carney promptly sent off a series of radio messages: to McCain, ordering him to close the other Third Fleet carrier groups at best speed; to Davison and Bogan, to shape course due north; to Sherman, to join the Davison and Bogan groups at midnight as they dashed past; to Mitscher, to re-assume tactical command of TF 38 at that time and strike the Northern Force early on the 25th. To Kinkaid he radioed in Halsey's name: "Am proceeding north with three groups to attack enemy carrier force at dawn."[*]

Kinkaid, believing that TF 34 had been formed, interpreted this latest dispatch to mean that Halsey was sending three *carrier* groups north. Kinkaid had already sent most of the Seventh Fleet gunnery vessels south to block Surigao Strait and destroy the approaching Japanese Southern Forces. Though he felt safe in his assumption that TF 34 was blocking San Bernardino Strait, he took the routine precaution of ordering searches to the north, by night-flying PBY's after dark on the 24th and by his escort carrier aircraft at first light on the 25th. He did not order Seventh Fleet planes over the Sibuyan Sea to locate and trail Kurita lest they tangle in the darkness with Third Fleet planes presumably doing the same job. As it turned out, the one PBY that flew through San Bernardino Strait passed over the area a little too early to detect anything, and the escort carrier planes were launched a little too late.

Of his decision to attack the Japanese Northern Force, Admiral Halsey afterward wrote: "Given the same circumstances and the same information as I had then, I would do it again." Hostile carriers were, in Halsey's opinion and in the opinion of practically all naval commanders

[*] All dispatches are quoted verbatim from the appropriate message files.

at that time, the principal threat to any operation involving ships or shipping. Sherman's search planes had reported only a few enemy carriers to the north, but Halsey could not be sure that they had seen the entire Northern Force—and of course he had no way of knowing that Ozawa's carriers had come south as decoys or that Ozawa had already expended most of his aircraft. Weighing immediate objectives against the long-range objective of bringing Japan to defeat, Halsey had concluded that his best contribution to the war as a whole was to seize the opportunity, now apparently within his grasp, of destroying Japan's naval aviation capability. With this point of view his staff was in entire agreement.

Admiral Halsey believed that it was within Admiral Kinkaid's capacity to handle both the Japanese Southern Forces heading for Surigao Strait and also Kurita's damaged Center Force should it attempt to sortie from San Bernardino Strait to attack in Leyte Gulf.* Nevertheless Halsey was taking a risk and he knew it, but most of his military successes up to that time had been based upon calculated risks. Moreover, he interpreted that part of his orders specifying as his primary task "destruction of major part of the enemy fleet" as a mandate to do exactly what he was doing.

So convinced was Halsey that he was doing the right thing that he was undeterred by reports sent in by night-flying aircraft from the carrier *Independence* that Kurita's Center Force had turned back east and was heading again for San Bernardino Strait and that navigation lights in the Strait, long blacked out, had now been lighted. He was similarly undeterred by messages from Bogan and Lee implying doubt as to his course. He heard nothing from Mitscher, who vetoed a suggestion of his staff that he urge Halsey to turn back south with the battle line. "If he wants my advice, he'll ask for it," said Mitscher. Sherman's task group joined Bogan's and Davison's at 2345, October 24. An hour later the Japanese Center Force emerged from San Bernardino Strait into the Philippine Sea behind Halsey's back.

Kurita had turned back east shortly before sunset. His renewed advance toward the Strait was spurred on not long afterward by a peremptory order to the Mobile Fleet from Admiral Toyoda in Tokyo: "Trusting in Divine Assistance, all forces will advance to the attack." By this Toyoda meant that the raid on Leyte Gulf was to be carried out in spite of any obstacles and at any sacrifice.

On reaching the Pacific, Kurita fully expected to run into an ambush, but he found nothing there. The only vessels standing between him and

---

* Comparative strengths available for combat at sunset 24 October: Kurita, Nishimura, and Shima combined—4 new and 2 old battleships, 8 heavy cruisers, 3 light cruisers, 19 destroyers. Kinkaid—6 old battleships, 4 heavy cruisers, 4 light cruisers, 21 destroyers; also 39 PT boats and 16 escort carriers screened by 9 destroyers and 12 destroyer escorts.

the thin-skinned American transports and supply shipping were the small Seventh Fleet carrier task units operating eastward of Leyte Gulf. His sortie was not detected by the Third Fleet because the *Independence* night flyers had been recalled from tracking the Center Force in order to search ahead of TF 38 for the Northern Force.

Though Toyoda's decoy scheme had succeeded, Kurita did not know it then or later. Ozawa's dawn radio announcement that Halsey was hot on his trail was not received by the other commanders of the Mobile Fleet.

### The Battle of Surigao Strait

Since October 20, an antisubmarine picket of seven American destroyers had been patrolling the northern end of Surigao Strait, where it opened into Leyte Gulf. These had later been supplemented by PT boats that patrolled inside and at the southern end of the Strait. On October 24, after the approaching Japanese Southern Forces had been sighted, all available PT's in Leyte Gulf were sent south, bringing the total of patrolling torpedo boats to 39. In sections of three boats each, these took station at intervals from a little below the destroyer picket line to positions far out in the Mindanao Sea. At noon on the 24th, Admiral Kinkaid alerted the Seventh Fleet to prepare for a night attack by enemy surface forces, and three hours later he ordered Admiral Oldendorf to block the northern exit from Surigao Strait with gunnery vessels. Confident that Halsey's Third Fleet

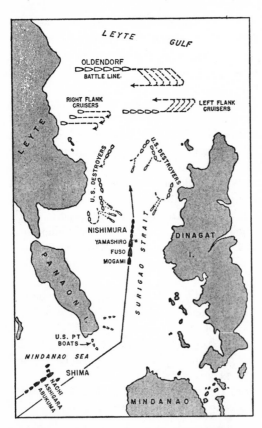

OLDENDORF'S TRAP, BATTLE OF SURIGAO
STRAIT, POSITIONS AT 0330,
OCTOBER 25, 1944

was guarding the approach from the north, Kinkaid assigned to the task the entire Seventh Fleet Bombardment and Fire Support Group, consisting of six old battleships, four heavy and four light cruisers, and 21 destroyers.

In view of his immense superiority of force, Oldendorf determined not merely to repulse but to destroy his antagonists. To that end, and also because he was somewhat short of armor-piercing projectiles, he planned for a short and decisive action at close ranges. His battleships, mostly veterans of the Pearl Harbor attack, he placed cruising back and forth across the upper end of the Strait a little north of the destroyer picket line. In this position he had ample sea room for maneuver, while any enemy approaching from the south would be restricted within the confines of the Strait; and from here, if necessary, he could quickly transfer his battle line to cover the eastern entrance to Leyte Gulf. He extended the flanks of the battle line with his cruisers, and stationed his destroyers also on or ahead of his flanks for high-speed torpedo runs on the enemy as he approached. Any hostile force entering Surigao Strait from the south would thus have to run a gantlet of torpedo fire, first from PT boats and then from destroyers, and at last come under T-capping shellfire from battleships and cruisers.

Across the Mindanao Sea toward this perfect ambush sped Nishimura's force, with Shima's force 40 miles behind. Though these two Japanese forces had been ordered to cooperate, the commanders at no time communicated with each other directly. Shima, unaware that he had been sighted by the army bomber, hoped through maintaining radio silence to surprise the Americans by bringing his reinforcement into Leyte Gulf unexpectedly. He avoided making radio contact with Nishimura moreover because Shima was the senior of the two. Had he notified Nishimura of his presence, the ironbound Japanese rules of seniority would have required him to assume tactical command of both forces. That, Shima felt, would only lead to confusion since he was a newcomer, unacquainted with the details of the battle plan. Nishimura, with ideas of his own on how to make the attack, was content to operate independently.

Late in the afternoon Nishimura was notified that the Center Force had been delayed in the Sibuyan Sea by air attacks and could not arrive in Leyte Gulf on schedule. He thereupon advanced his own time of arrival in order, apparently, to reach the Gulf under cover of darkness. From 2300 October 24 until after 0200 October 25, he ran the gantlet of American PT boats, hitting three with gunfire and so damaging another that it had to be beached. The PT's, long without experience in torpedo work, did no damage at all, but they performed an invaluable service in keeping Oldendorf advised of Nishimura's arrival and of his progress up the Strait.

The main action of the battle was opened at 0230 by five of the picket destroyers. Warning the PT's to stand aside, they went speeding down Surigao Strait in two divisions, fired 47 torpedoes from east and west, turned away making smoke, and cleared the area without sustaining damage despite heavy enemy fire. In this remarkable attack, the Americans hit both of Nishimura's battleships, sank a destroyer, and put two more destroyers out of action. The battleship *Fuso* sheered out of line and presently blew apart into two burning halves. Nishimura's flagship, the battleship *Yamashiro,* though struck by one torpedo, pressed on to the north accompanied by the heavy cruiser *Mogami* and the destroyer *Shigure.*

Now in quick succession Oldendorf struck first with his right flank destroyers and then with his left flank destroyers. These put three more torpedoes into the *Yamashiro* and sank one of the destroyers disabled by the pickets. Meanwhile, at 0351, as the remnant of Nishimura's force came within 23,000 yards of the American battle line, Oldendorf's cruisers opened up, followed a minute later by all of his battleships that could find a target. In 18 minutes they fired nearly 300 rounds of 14- and 16-inch and more than 4,000 rounds of 6- and 8-inch projectiles. Under this hail of shells the *Yamashiro* began to sink, the *Mogami* blazed up and came almost to a stop, and the *Shigure* sheered to the right, hit by a dud and further damaged by numerous near misses. At 0409 Oldendorf, informed that his retiring left flank destroyers were under fire, stopped the shelling. The destroyer *Albert W. Grant,* hit 19 times by friend and foe, had been put out of action with a loss of 34 of her crew. This was the sole damage suffered by the Americans during the battle.

Shima's force had by this time fought its way past the PT boats, which however put a torpedo into the light cruiser *Abukuma,* slowing her down to ten knots. To the north lay a dense pall of smoke through which Shima could discern arching tracers and the flash of gunfire. At 0410, as the firing ceased, he passed the burning halves of the *Fuso,* which he took to be both the *Fuso* and the *Yamashiro.* Ten minutes later he saw the burning *Mogami* ahead and to starboard, apparently dead in the water. Immediately afterward his radar detected targets ahead. Ordering his destroyers forward to attack, he at once turned his cruisers 90 degrees right so that they could fire torpedoes short of the *Mogami,* where they would not be silhouetted by her flames. On the new course, Shima's flagship, the heavy cruiser *Nachi,* collided with the *Mogami,* which was actually moving south at eight knots.

Shima now recalled his destroyers and withdrew down the Strait, accompanied by the crippled *Shigure* and the burning *Mogami.* Obviously Nishimura had run into a deadly trap. Shima saw no reason why he should offer his own ships for similar fruitless destruction. The last word he had from the Center Force was that it was retiring westward. He had no information at all from the Northern Force. In the circumstances, Shima decided that his best course was to retire also and await a better opportunity to close the pincers on Leyte Gulf in coordination with Kurita and Ozawa.

Oldendorf, having detected Shima's retiring force by radar, set out in pursuit with cruisers and destroyers. In the dim light of early dawn, he at length made visual contact with the enemy column, trailed by the *Mogami*. After shelling the damaged cruiser until she was once more ablaze, he temporarily turned away to evade enemy torpedoes. A little later a part of his force encountered and sank the last of Nishimura's disabled destroyers. The rest of the Japanese fugitives, four cruisers and five destroyers, fought their way back past the PT boats and regained the Mindanao Sea. Here planes from the southernmost of the Seventh Fleet escort carrier units attacked them, finally stopping the die-hard *Mogami*, which the Japanese themselves sank after removing her crew. Of Nishimura's force, only the battered destroyer *Shigure* was left, but Shima still had all his ships, and of these only the *Abukuma* was seriously damaged.

In the midst of the American mopping up operations, there came an electrifying report: Kurita's Center Force had penetrated San Bernardino Strait and was off Samar attacking the northernmost of the Seventh Fleet escort carrier units. Oldendorf at once called off his pursuit and hastened to reassemble his forces. The planes that had attacked the *Mogami* refueled at Tacloban and went after Kurita.

Admiral Kinkaid was in a quandary. He knew now that the whole Third Fleet was far to the north, unable for many hours to answer his calls for help. He knew that Shima had escaped and, given an opportunity, might return through Surigao Strait and attack the American shipping. Kinkaid's solution was to order Oldendorf to lead his force back into Leyte Gulf where it could cover both the southern and eastern entrances, then to divide the force into two equal groups and take one group some 25 miles eastward where it would be in position to sortie in support of the embattled escort carrier unit. This was a measure of desperation, for even if Oldendorf could reach the combat area in time to be of help, which was doubtful, his ships were now too low in armor-piercing ammunition to fight a running battle.

## The Battle off Cape Engaño

In the dark early hours of October 25, while Kurita was debouching from San Bernardino Strait and Nishimura and Shima were advancing into Surigao Strait, Halsey and Mitscher, with Bogan's, Davison's, and Sherman's task groups, were speeding north in pursuit of Ozawa. A little after 0200 *Independence* search planes scouting ahead of TF 38 made radar contact with two separate enemy surface groups. These were the advance guard and the main body of Ozawa's Northern Force, which the day before had split apart in the frustratingly difficult task of attracting American attention, and were now heading on converging courses for a 0600 rendezvous. On receiving word of this contact, Halsey at last formed TF 34, enlarged to include all six of the battleships attached to the Third Fleet. With this force he set out in advance of the carrier groups, intending to complete the work of Mitscher's planes by sinking cripples and stragglers and any other Japanese vessels he could overtake.

As dawn was breaking, search planes followed by a deckload strike of 180 aircraft took off from the American carriers. An hour later the TF 38 scouts regained contact with the Northern Force, now united and comprising one heavy and three light carriers, two carrier-battleships, three light cruisers, and eight destroyers. The American attack groups, quickly vectored in, arrived in sight of the enemy fleet a little after 0800. Hellcats shot down most of the dozen or so fighter aircraft that came out to meet them, while the American bombers and torpedo planes bored in through intense antiaircraft fire to drive home their strike. The attacking air groups promptly sank a destroyer, bombed the light carriers *Zuiho* and *Chitose,* and torpedoed the heavy carrier *Zuikaku.* The *Chitose,* holed below the waterline, soon went down. The *Zuikaku,* steering erratically, began to fall behind, obliging Admiral Ozawa to shift his flag to a cruiser in order to direct the defense of the main body. A second American air strike at 1000 found the Northern Force widely scattered. One group of bombers worked over the cruiser *Tama* and slowed her down to ten knots. Another group left the light carrier *Chiyoda* dead in the water, afire and listing.

By this time Admiral Halsey, forging ahead with TF 34, scanning the horizon for masts of Japanese stragglers, was having his attention diverted more and more from the impending surface action. At 0412 that morning Admiral Kinkaid had informed him by radio that Seventh Fleet surface forces were engaging enemy surface forces in Surigao Strait. Then, to reassure himself, he added a question: "Is TF 34 guarding San Bernardino Strait?" It is part of the bad radio communications bedeviling this whole battle that Halsey did not receive Kinkaid's message until 0648. He then promptly radioed back: "Negative. TF 34 is with carrier groups now engaging enemy carrier force"—a reply that dumfounded Kinkaid.

At 0800 Halsey received the much-delayed news that the enemy had been repulsed in Surigao Strait. From this he assumed that the Seventh Fleet was now free to give Leyte Gulf whatever cover it might need. Twenty minutes later he received a radio call for help, also delayed, from Rear Admiral Clifton A. F. Sprague, commanding one of the three small escort carrier task units off Leyte Gulf. Kurita's Center Force had suddenly appeared and was attacking Sprague's little carriers, then cruising near Samar Island. Halsey was not alarmed. "I figured," he said, "that the sixteen little carriers had enough planes to protect themselves until Oldendorf could bring up his heavy ships."*

On the heels of Sprague's call for help Halsey received a whole series of messages from Kinkaid, one in plain English, requesting air strikes and support by fast battleships. Kurita, listening in, was rattled by the plain language dispatch, concluding from it that powerful forces were close enough to lend Sprague prompt assistance. Halsey was exasperated. "It was not my job to protect the Seventh Fleet," said he. "My job was offensive, to strike with the Third Fleet, and we were even then rushing to intercept a force which gravely threatened not only Kinkaid and myself, but the whole Pacific strategy." In the circumstances, he took what he deemed to be the only appropriate action. He radioed McCain's task group, then fueling to the southeast, to go "at best possible speed" to the aid of Sprague and notified Kinkaid that he had done so. Then with TF 34 and three groups of TF 38 he pressed on to the north, away from Leyte Gulf.

At Pearl Harbor, Admiral Nimitz, who had been listening in on all radio communications and watching the progress of the battle on the operations chart, at length felt compelled to intervene. He sent Halsey a sharp and laconic message: "Where is, repeat where is, Task Force 34?" When Halsey received this dispatch a little after 1000, he was annoyed, for he recognized it as a prod. He was further displeased to note that Admiral King and Admiral Kinkaid had been cut in as information addressees. He was enraged when his eyes ran past the end of the message to the final padding, which he took to be part of the text. With padding included, the dispatch seemed to be couched in insulting language: "Where is, repeat where is, Task Force 34? The world wonders."†

* Two of the original 18 escort carriers had departed for Morotai the day before to bring back replacement aircraft.

† The ensign who encrypted the message at Pearl Harbor, following normal procedure, added random phrases ("padding") at both ends to increase difficulty of enemy cryptanalysis. He violated regulations by using end padding that could possibly be read as part of the text. On being queried later, he professed not to have recognized his mistake. "It was just something that popped into my head," said he.

In the *New Jersey* the communicators had orders that when an urgent operational dispatch came in they were not to take time to copy the message on a dispatch form but were to rush the decode tape directly from the decoding machine to Admiral Halsey or Admiral Carney—*after first tearing off the padding*. When Nimitz' message came off the machine, the padding was plainly separated from the text by double letters, as regulations prescribed. But the end padding was so plausible that the communicators decided not to remove it, on the chance that might be

The more Halsey thought about Nimitz' message and its curious ending, the angrier he became. At length, a little before 1100, he took a step he afterward regretted. He ordered TF 34 to change from course 000 to course 180—from due north to due south. "At that moment," says Halsey, "the Northern Force, with its two remaining carriers crippled and dead in the water, was exactly 42 miles from the muzzles of my 16-inch guns. . . . I turned my back on the opportunity I had dreamed of since my days as a cadet. For me, one of the biggest battles of the war was off, and what has been called the 'Battle of Bull's Run' was on. I notified Kinkaid. . . ."* At 1115 Task Force 34 came about and headed south. As it passed the still-northbound TF 38, Halsey picked up Bogan's carrier task group to provide air cover and detached four cruisers and ten destroyers under Rear Admiral Laurance T. DuBose to provide additional surface support for the carriers remaining under Mitscher.

Mitscher, with Sherman's and Davison's carrier groups and DuBose's surface group, continued to the north to launch further air attacks on the Northern Force. The third strike of the day, more than 200 planes, took off a little before noon with instructions to sink the enemy's two remaining operational carriers. The *Zuiho* was heavily damaged but managed to stay afloat. Three torpedoes finished off the *Zuikaku*, last survivor of the carrier attack on Pearl Harbor and veteran of every carrier battle of the Pacific war except Midway. The fourth air strike in mid-afternoon at last sank the die-hard *Zuiho*. The fifth and final attack, carried out by aviators who had been almost constantly at battle for two days, concentrated on the converted battleship *Ise* but achieved only a succession of near misses.

Around 1400 Mitscher, deciding that his carriers were getting too close to the enemy for safety, turned east with Sherman's and Davison's groups, and detached DuBose's cruisers and destroyers north to finish off the enemy cripples. This last was no casual mission, for Ozawa still had his two converted battleships—and Halsey had taken all six Third Fleet battleships south with him. DuBose's group, pausing to sink the derelict *Chiyoda*, last of Ozawa's bait carriers, was outsped by most of the retreating Northern Force. After dark however DuBose overtook a group of three destroyers and sank one in a running gunfire-torpedo

---

part of the message. The strip of paper handed Halsey read as follows: "FROM CINCPAC [Nimitz] ACTION COM THIRD FLEET [Halsey] INFO COMINCH [King] CTF SEVENTY SEVEN [Kinkaid] X WHERE IS RPT WHERE IS TASK FORCE THIRTY FOUR RR THE WORLD WONDERS."

Because the *repeat* (RPT) device was used by communicators to repeat important words that might be lost in garble as well as by senders for emphasis, it has been deleted in most official files, which record the message simply as "Where is Task Force 34?"

* Halsey was often referred to in the press (but not by his intimates) as "Bull" Halsey.

battle. Farther to the north, the cruiser *Tama*, limping home alone, was sunk by one of the numerous submarines that Vice Admiral Charles A. Lockwood, Commander Submarine Forces Pacific Fleet, had ordered to cover all likely escape routes.

Ozawa, minus his bait carriers but with ten of his 13 surface vessels, returned to Japan. His decoy mission had succeeded beyond his most hopeful expectations. He had not only saved Kurita from annihilation but extricated a good portion of his own suicide force as well. Yet the Japanese failed to attain the ultimate object of Ozawa's mission, for Ozawa was unable to establish radio communication with Kurita, who faltered when the amphibious shipping in Leyte Gulf was almost under his guns.

### The Battle off Samar

On arriving in the Pacific, a little before 0100 on October 25, Kurita's Center Force, by then reduced to four battleships, six heavy cruisers, two light cruisers, and eleven destroyers, went to General Quarters and steamed cautiously eastward in a night search disposition. At 0300 the

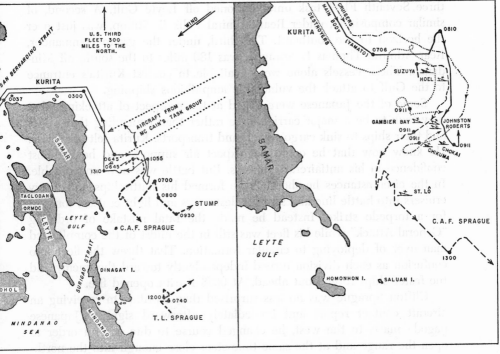

**BATTLE OFF SAMAR, OCTOBER 25, 1944**

force wheeled to starboard and proceeded southeast down the coast of Samar. On this course Kurita received Nishimura's final radio report, stating that he was under attack in Surigao Strait. An hour later, he received word from Shima that he was "retiring from the battle area." From these two messages Kurita correctly surmised that the southern Japanese attack had met with disaster. He heard nothing at all from Ozawa, to the north.

At sunrise Kurita began to deploy his force from search disposition, with ships in several columns, to circular antiaircraft formation. Hardly had he given the signal for deployment when a lookout in the crow's-nest of flagship *Yamato* reported masts looming over the horizon to the east. Presently the masts and then the hulls of carriers and escorting vessels became visible from the *Yamato's* bridge. The consensus of Kurita's staff was that they had come upon a task group of Halsey's Third Fleet, that the vessels dimly visible on the horizon were fleet carriers, cruisers, destroyers, and perhaps a battleship or two. Halsey however was then 300 miles to the north engaging Ozawa. What Kurita and his staff saw in the morning haze was the task unit of six little 18-knot escort carriers, three destroyers, and four destroyer escorts commanded by Rear Admiral Clifton A. F. Sprague. This was one of the three Seventh Fleet task units stationed off Leyte Gulf. A second, of similar composition, under Rear Admiral Felix B. Stump, was just over the horizon to the southeast. The third, under the group commander, Rear Admiral Thomas L. Sprague, was 130 miles to the south, off Mindanao. These vessels alone were available to contest Kurita's entrance to the Gulf to attack the vulnerable amphibious shipping.

Some of the Japanese were elated at the prospect of attacking what they took to be a major carrier force rather than expending themselves and their ships to sink cargo vessels and transports. Kurita felt otherwise. He knew now that he could not expect air support, and he had lost confidence in his antiaircraft gunners. But battle was now unavoidable. In the circumstances he should have formed his battleships and heavy cruisers into battle line and sent his destroyers and light cruisers forward for a torpedo strike. Instead he made the fatal mistake of ordering "General Attack" while his fleet was still in the midst of the complicated maneuver of deploying to circular formation. That threw the fleet into confusion as each division turned independently toward the enemy and the faster ships forged out ahead. At 0658 Kurita opened fire.

Clifton Sprague was no less surprised than Kurita. On receiving an aircraft contact report and immediately afterward sighting Japanese pagoda masts to the west, he changed course to due east in order to open the range and at the same time steer close enough into the northeast wind to launch aircraft. He next ordered his planes into the air, armed with whatever they had on board. Then, as 14-, 16-, and 18-inch shell splashes began walking up on his carriers, he directed all ships to make smoke and headed at flank speed for the cover of a nearby rain squall. In plain language he radioed for help, knowing well that his little carriers and his thin-hulled escort vessels were by no stretch of the imagination a match for the swift Japanese surface vessels. "It did not appear," said he, "that any of our ships could survive another five minutes of the heavy-caliber fire being received."

There followed one of the most extraordinary chases of naval history —climaxed by a surprise ending. Concealed by rain, Sprague's unit turned south and headed toward Leyte Gulf in the hope of meeting Seventh Fleet surface vessels which Sprague presumed would soon be on their way to assist him. Presently, the American force passed out of the squall and again became visible to the Japanese, but Kurita refrained from cutting across the angle and heading directly for his quarry. Instead he continued for some time on his original easterly pursuit course, intent upon getting ships to windward of the Americans so that the carriers could not turn into the wind for further air operations.

By 0800 Sprague had battleships and heavy cruisers overtaking him from astern, while more heavy cruisers crept up on his port flank, gradually forcing him around to course southwest and threatening to cut off his retreat. Toward 0900 a squadron of four destroyers and a light cruiser, which had been trailing the battleships, advanced on Sprague's starboard quarter. Evidently he was about to be boxed in.

Shortly after the battle opened, Sprague's three destroyers, later joined by three of his destroyer escorts, began making a series of suicidal attacks with shells and torpedoes on elements of the pursuing Japanese fleet. As the commander of one of the destroyer escorts announced to his crew upon heading for the enemy, this was "a fight against overwhelming odds from which survival could not be expected." Plowing forward under a hail of heavy-caliber fire, the little ships resolutely pressed home their attacks—chasing salvos, making smoke, and dodging into rain squalls.

In the first attack, the destroyer *Johnston* put the heavy cruiser *Kumano* out of action with a single torpedo. It is possible that others of the escort vessels then or later also torpedoed the heavy cruisers *Chokai* and *Chikuma*. The heavy cruiser *Suzuya*, already slowed to 20 knots by an aerial bomb, came alongside the *Kumano* to remove the division commander and his staff and never again caught up with the running battle. But, as events were to prove, the most important result of the first attack by Sprague's escorts was that the flagship *Yamato*, accompanied by another battleship, turned north to evade torpedoes and fell far behind in the chase. Kurita thus lost sight of the carriers and was not again able to get a clear picture of the tactical situation.

As the attacks on the Japanese fleet continued, the destroyer *Hoel,* hit more than 40 times, went dead in the water and was abandoned by her crew. Stationary, she became the target of every enemy ship within gun range. These pumped shells into her until she went down. A few minutes later, the destroyer escort *Samuel B. Roberts*, her side ripped open by 14-inch shells, rolled over and sank. The destroyer *Johnston*, badly damaged, her torpedoes expended, presently observed a squadron of four Japanese destroyers and a light cruiser coming in to attack the carriers. These were the vessels that threatened to complete the boxing in of the American force. The *Johnston* promptly advanced and took the whole squadron under such furious, close-range fire that the Japanese ships launched their torpedoes prematurely, too far short of the carriers to be effective. They then turned on the *Johnston* and circled her, firing into her until she went down. By this time two of the surviving vessels of Sprague's carrier screen had been damaged by shellfire. In the annals of naval warfare few men-of-war ever performed their duty more gallantly or against heavier odds than Sprague's little escorts.

The six American carriers, forced by Kurita's heavy cruisers to steam before the wind, could no longer be adequately covered with smoke. They began to take hits, at first from the heavy cruisers coming up on their port quarter and then from two battleships which soon plowed the cruisers' wake. That the carriers were not all sunk can be attributed to poor Japanese gunnery, expert American damage control, and the fact that the attackers were using armor-piercing shells that passed through the unarmored carriers without exploding. However, the carrier *Gambier Bay* at length took more hits than her engineers and damage control parties could handle. She lost power, began to list, and at 0907 capsized and sank.

The really decisive attack on the Center Force was carried out by aircraft. Torpedo planes, bombers, and bomb-carrying fighters from Clifton Sprague's and Felix Stump's task units were gradually reinforced over the Japanese fleet by aircraft from Leyte and from Thomas Sprague's unit, including those returning from the strike on the *Mogami*. The planes kept up an almost continuous attack. When they exhausted their ammunition, they made dry runs to divert the enemy, or they landed on Stump's nearby carriers or on the more distant Tacloban airstrip to rearm. Under this unremitting pressure, the heavy cruisers *Chokai*, *Chikuma*, and *Suzuya* were battered into sinking condition. The rest of the widely dispersed Center Force, following Japanese doctrine for each ship to maneuver independently under air attack, fell into increasing confusion. The Japanese commanders overestimated their rate of advance and were confirmed in their belief that they were chasing fast fleet carriers.

Kurita, who had lost touch both with Clifton Sprague's carriers and with most of his own force, concluded that his prey had escaped and that the time had come to bring order out of chaos. So at 0911 he headed north at 20 knots, summoning his ships by radio to converge on the *Yamato*. Thereupon the two Japanese heavy cruisers still in action reversed course—almost within point-blank range of the carriers. So did the two battleships that had been following the cruisers. The destroyer squadron that had advanced into the battle lingered a little longer to finish off the *Johnston* before retiring.

Sprague's task unit, bewildered by the sudden retreat of the enemy vessels, which a few minutes before seemed to have every advantage on their side, again shaped course for Leyte Gulf, 25 miles away.

## The Kamikazes Strike

With Kurita's turnaway, the Seventh Fleet escort carriers escaped annihilation by what at the time seemed a miracle, and remained until after the war a profound mystery to the Americans. The hazards of the day were by no means ended however, for on October 25 the Japanese also carried out the first successful operations of the newly-organized Kamikaze ("Divine Wind") Special Attack Corps, composed of suicidally-inclined aircraft pilots and taking its name from typhoons that in 1273 and 1279 saved Japan by scattering Kublai Khan's invasion fleets.

When word of Kurita's advance toward Leyte Gulf reached the Japanese air forces in the Philippines, Vice Admiral Takijiro Onishi, commanding the 1st Air Fleet, decided that the time had come for his aviators to take similarly desperate measures. Evidently, ill-trained flyers piloting bombers were not elusive enough to penetrate American air defense and turn back the Allied attack, but the inexperienced Japanese aviators might yet prove effective if they flew highly-maneuverable Zeke fighters armed with light bombs directly into their targets. Onishi personally put the proposition before his aviators at Clark Field on Luzon and received immediate and wholehearted acceptance. Thus at last, when it was too late, the Japanese began improvising a new and terrifying means of disputing America's growing command of the sea.

Following the invasion of Leyte, the Special Attack Corps sortied four successive days but because of bad weather, or out of sheer ineptitude, failed to find a target. On the 24th, the limited success of the conventional attack against Sherman's carrier task group off Luzon underlined the growing necessity for better methods and more certain results. Clearly, if the kamikazes had a better method, the time to demonstrate it had arrived. The next morning they staged their first successful attacks.

At dawn on October 25, six Special Attack planes took off from

Davao, Mindanao and, winging almost due north, discovered Thomas Sprague's carrier task unit. Out of an overcast at about 10,000 feet the Zekes dived directly, some almost vertically, at the escort carriers just as they were launching planes for a strike against Kurita's Center Force, then engaging Clifton Sprague's task unit to the north. The Zekes heading for the carriers *Petrof Bay* and *Sangamon* were deflected by antiaircraft fire, but the other two carriers in this unit, the *Suwannee* and the *Santee*, were both struck by aircraft whose exploding bombs tore gaping holes in their flight and hangar decks. In the midst of the ensuing confusion, the *Santee* was also torpedoed by an undetected Japanese submarine. Despite these attacks, the damaged carriers kept station in the formation and by means of quick emergency repairs resumed flight operations within a couple of hours.

Later in the morning, after Kurita had broken off action, kamikazes from Clark Field went after Clifton Sprague's battered carriers. One of the suicide pilots, diving at the *Kitkun Bay,* succeeded in striking her only a glancing blow, but his bomb exploded and did considerable damage. Two more kamikazes crashed into the *Kalinin Bay,* already scarred by 14 shell hits, and started fires. One rammed through the flight deck of the *St. Lô,* caught fire, and detonated bombs and torpedoes on the hangar deck. The resulting series of explosions nearly blew the *St. Lô* apart. She sank a little before noon.

Leaving his remaining escort vessels to pick up the *St. Lô*'s survivors, Clifton Sprague withdrew toward Manus with his carriers. "We had been through so much by then," said he, "that it didn't seem to matter whether we had escorts with us or not."

## Kurita's Retirement

Kurita meanwhile, having reassembled the remnant of his Center Force, was steaming off Samar on various courses trying to decide what to do next. Despite his losses, he thought he had done a good morning's work by sinking, as he supposed, three or four fleet carriers, two heavy cruisers, and several destroyers. Once he shaped course again for Leyte Gulf but presently thought better of it and turned away. By now, he reasoned, the transports and cargo vessels would surely have been unloaded, and with plenty of warning they must have withdrawn from the Gulf. On the other hand, radio intercepts left him with the impression that powerful air forces were assembling on Leyte and that Third Fleet carrier groups were converging on him from all directions. Though the horizon was empty, he felt surrounded. In the circumstances Leyte Gulf might easily prove a trap instead of an opportunity. At any rate, he definitely preferred fighting the next battle in the open sea.

Kurita's orders, like Halsey's, gave him the option of engaging enemy carrier forces if opportunity offered. From Manila that morning had come a radio report of American carriers to the northeast of Samar. After due consideration, Kurita and his staff concluded that these non-existent carriers were their most profitable objective. With the aid of planes from Luzon, the Center Force might yet win a decision—or at least go down gloriously, fighting capital ships. A little after 1300, as the American escort carrier aircraft came in for their final attack, Kurita headed north in search of enemy carriers.

Not long afterward came the first of several attacks by carrier planes coming in from the northeast. These were from McCain's group, which was speeding toward Samar in response to Halsey's summons. McCain's aircraft, because they had to strike from extreme range, were hampered by wing tanks and carried bombs instead of heavier torpedoes. They inflicted no important damage, but they did confirm Kurita in his decision to avoid Leyte Gulf.

At Kurita's request, nearly every operational plane on Luzon made rendezvous with his force in the late afternoon for a coordinated attack on the supposed American carrier group. This was the sort of support Kurita had been trying to get for two days, but now that he had it, no trace of enemy ships was to be found. By this time the Japanese destroyers were low in fuel, and Kurita and his staff were utterly exhausted after three days under attack from surface, subsurface, and air. In the circumstances Kurita saw retirement from the field of battle as his only alternative. Toward dusk the Center Force headed for San Bernardino Strait, which it entered at 2130. One vessel, the destroyer *Nowake*, having stopped to remove the crew of the doomed *Chikuma*, trailed far behind the others.

By this time the massed power that Halsey had assembled off Luzon the night before was split four ways. Mitscher's forces in the north were divided, with DuBose's cruiser-destroyer group advancing ahead of the carrier groups to pick off cripples and stragglers from Ozawa's Northern Force. In an attempt to beat Kurita to San Bernardino Strait, Halsey had further divided the Third Fleet by detaching from his southbound vessels his two fastest battleships, the *Iowa* and the *New Jersey*, together with three light cruisers and eight destroyers. With this detachment he raced ahead, but the race was futile, for when Halsey arrived off the Strait a little after midnight the only ship of the Center Force that had not already passed through was the *Nowake*. This lone vessel Halsey's cruisers and destroyers quickly sank with gunfire and torpedoes. The fast battleships of the Third Fleet had steamed 300 miles north and then 300 miles back south between the two major enemy forces without quite making contact with either.

Through the night the Japanese Center Force made best possible speed across the Sibuyan Sea. After dawn on the 26th it passed through Tablas Strait on the far side and shaped a southerly course west of Panay. Here it came under attack by planes from Bogan's and McCain's groups, which had made rendezvous off Luzon. The carrier planes sank the light cruiser *Noshiro* and further damaged the straggling heavy cruiser *Kumano*. That ended four days of attack on the much-battered Center Force. Kurita escaped with four battleships, two heavy cruisers, a light cruiser, and seven destroyers—not a powerful force for offensive action but a fleet-in-being that MacArthur and Kinkaid would have to take seriously into account in planning further operations in the Philippines.

## Conclusion

The main conditions affecting the Battle for Leyte Gulf were the greatly superior power of the United States Navy, supplemented by a few Allied combat vessels; the immense superiority of American air support; the division of the Japanese fleet, caused by Allied submarine attacks on the Japanese oil supply and augmented by Japanese dispersion tactics; and poor radio communications and generally inadequate exchange of information among the segments of both fleets. The American naval forces were undoubtedly hampered by lack of unified command in the theater of operations; but the Japanese fleet, despite unified command in the person of Admiral Toyoda, was even less successful than the Americans in achieving coordination and mutual support. Out of these conditions developed the most complex and far-flung naval battle in history, a battle notable on both sides for remarkable achievements as well as for lost opportunities.

The Japanese, without attaining their main objective of sinking the amphibious shipping in Leyte Gulf, lost 306,000 tons of combat ships— three battleships, four carriers, ten cruisers, and nine destroyers. The Americans not only saved their amphibious shipping but also destroyed the enemy's capacity to fight another fleet battle, at a cost of 37,000 tons of ships—one light and two escort carriers, two destroyers, and a destroyer escort. The Battle for Leyte Gulf was thus an overwhelming victory for the United States. Yet the Americans, as well as the Japanese, failed to employ their naval power with optimum efficiency.

Admiral Kurita, though under the most unremitting attack of any naval commander in history, fought his way without air support across the Sibuyan Sea and passed unobserved through San Bernadino Strait into the Pacific. Once there however he failed to recognize or to profit by his opportunities. He made a disorderly attack on a small American escort carrier unit, became confused, lost touch with the enemy and with his own ships, took heavier losses than he inflicted, and retreated back the way he had come. Admiral Nishimura, advancing ahead of schedule via Surigao Strait to cooperate with Kurita in Leyte Gulf, ran into an ambush and sacrificed his force in vain. Admiral Shima, for reasons he considered sufficient, failed to cooperate with Nishimura, but prudently withdrew from Surigao Strait when he perceived that Nishimura had met with disaster. Admiral Ozawa sacrificed his bait carriers, as he expected, but succeeded in decoying the U.S. Third Fleet away from Leyte Gulf and preserving most of his surface force as well. Though Ozawa saved Kurita from annihilation, he was unable to inform his colleagues of his own success and of Kurita's opportunity. Another Japanese success, limited but ominous for the future, was achieved by the new kamikaze suicide corps which on October 25 made the first of many attacks on Allied ships.

The individual segments of the American naval forces performed brilliantly, but the Third and Seventh fleets, misled by a series of unconfirmed assumptions, also failed to coordinate. Admiral Halsey concentrated upon and battered the Japanese Center Force into temporary retreat in the Sibuyan Sea; he then abandoned that target and uncovered San Bernardino Strait and the American beachhead on the assumption that the Seventh Fleet was prepared to cover the northern approach to Leyte Gulf. Admiral Oldendorf, in possibly the last line battle of naval history, overwhelmed the Japanese in Surigao Strait with a perfect ambush and an almost flawless attack. Oldendorf could hardly have failed to win a victory, for Admiral Kinkaid had given him nearly all the surface combat strength he had, assuming that the Third Fleet was covering the northern approach to Leyte Gulf. Admiral Mitscher, with his usual resolution and effective employment of air forces, worried the Japanese carriers to destruction; yet elements of both the Northern and Center Japanese forces were able to escape because Halsey carried the main American surface strength fruitlessly north and then south through the most crucial hours of the battle, leaving inferior forces to deal with the enemy in two areas. The most memorable achievement of the battle was the combination of American forces off Samar that turned back the Japanese Center Force within a few miles of Leyte Gulf. Here Admiral Clifton Sprague, backed by Admiral Stump and Admiral Thomas Sprague, squeezed every possible advantage from wind, rain, smoke, interior position, and air and surface attack to confuse and repulse an immensely superior enemy. Overhead, the escort carrier planes, untrained for attacking ships, performed like fast carrier aircraft at their best. On the surface, Clifton Sprague's little screening vessels, steaming boldly into battleship and cruiser fire, dodging through smoke and rain, chasing salvos, opposing 14- and 16-inch shells with 5-inch when they had expended their torpedoes, provided the slender margin that enabled the air attack to succeed and most of the escort carriers to escape. The history of the United States Navy records no more glorious two hours of resolution, sacrifice, and success.

# 14

# Submarines in the Pacific

There was a grim symbolism in the fact that on December 31, 1941 Admiral Nimitz took command of the Pacific Fleet on the deck of a submarine—the *Grayling*. Though the new Cincpac was an old submariner, the choice was not a matter of sentiment. The hard fact was that at this time the suitable surface combatant ships were on the bottom or en route to the West Coast for repairs. None but submarines were available for the brief and businesslike assumption-of-command ceremony.

Since the Pearl Harbor disaster none but submarines had been available to carry the attack to Japan. On December 7 the U.S. Chief of Naval Operations had ordered unrestricted submarine warfare against the Island Empire. The little-publicized, unremitting campaign of attrition by the "dolphin Navy"—though dogged by bad luck and faulty equipment in the early months—was to sever Japan's logistic jugulars, and virtually to starve Japan into submission. The American submarines were to be second to no other service branch in their contributions to victory.

The singular success of the U.S. submarines would derive not merely from exemplary command and crew performance, but also from a sound doctrine—always well-directed, but sufficiently flexible to be improved in the light of combat experience and the changing nature of the war. Japan's brave and well-trained submariners on the other hand would be largely wasted, hampered by a faulty doctrine and a myopic high command.

It is often forgotten that the attack on Pearl Harbor began, not with carrier planes, but with Japanese miniature submarines attempting to penetrate the harbor. As we have seen, one was sunk by an American destroyer 70 minutes before the first air strike. These midgets, five in all, had been carried to the scene on specially converted I-class submarines as a part of the force of 27 boats intended for reconnaissance, for intelligence information on the carrier force, and for attacks on ships escaping from the harbor. Although the midgets accomplished nothing, their abortive attack illustrates a key aspect of the Japanese submarine doctrine. In spite of the records of U-boats in World War I and in spite of the Allied losses in the Battle of the Atlantic in World War II, the Japanese persisted in discounting the value of the submarine as a commerce raider. Not only did they have no plans for employment of their submarines against Allied shipping; they had no plan for convoying their own merchant ships. Their primary submarine doctrine was to use their boats in support of fleet operations. The Japanese, moreover, so underestimated the potentialities of the American submarines that their striking force made no substantial attack on the U.S. Submarine Base at Pearl Harbor.

## The Japanese Drive into the Southern Resources Area

Simultaneously with the attack on Pearl Harbor, the Japanese forces, as we have seen, struck out for their real goal in the war—the rich resources of oil, rubber, tin, copper, and rice in the Netherlands East Indies, Borneo, Celebes, Halmahera, Malaya, and Indo-China. The American embargo of July 1941 had obliged the Japanese to begin expending their 6,450,000-ton oil reserve. Unless they could win the East Indies, they would be oil starved. Hence all else depended on the seizure of the Southern Resources Area oil fields, on their proper exploitation, and on the transport of their products to the home islands. The weak Allied forces in the Far East could do nothing to prevent Japan's attainment of the first two requirements, but submarines could and did strike at the third, the transport of oil and other strategic resources to Japan.

American submarines in the Pacific Theater were divided between the Asiatic Fleet Submarine Force, based at Cavite in Manila Bay, and the Pacific Fleet Submarine Force at Pearl Harbor. The Asiatic Force at this time consisted of six S-class boats, 23 larger fleet types, three tenders, and one rescue vessel. The old S-class boats were small and uncomfortable, with relatively short cruising radius. They were numbered, not named. As rapidly as replacements became available, they were withdrawn from combat service and assigned to training commands. The fleet boats, named for fish and other marine creatures, were much more battleworthy. The *Gato*, built in 1941, was the archetype. It displaced 1,500 tons on the surface, was 312 feet in length, had a cruising radius of 12,000 miles, and carried 24 torpedoes and ten tubes, six forward and four aft. A 3-inch gun and up to four light automatic weapons mounted topside completed the armament. The complement was approximately eight officers and 80 men. This was the type of boat that carried the war to Japan.

The first American submarines to engage the Japanese had the mission of helping protect the Philippines from invasion. They operated under instructions to proceed cautiously, feeling out the Japanese defense and antisubmarine measures. Forming a defensive cordon around Luzon, they watched and waited. Meanwhile the *Sealion*, undergoing refit at Cavite, was destroyed in the first Japanese air attack. She was the first of 52 American submarines to be lost during the war. At this time every single combat vessel counted importantly in the hopelessly outnumbered Allied fleet in Asiatic waters. The simultaneous loss of the *Prince of Wales* and the *Repulse* left a surface force with no vessel larger than a cruiser.

The submarines struck back, but in vain. During December the 28 boats made 31 determined attacks on warships and transports bringing the Japanese landing force to the Philippines. Expending 66 torpedoes, the submariners suffered the bitter disappointment of sinking only two Japanese vessels. From perfect attack positions the torpedoes missed or fired prematurely. The U.S. Navy had a defective torpedo design which caused the loss of priceless opportunities to destroy enemy shipping and to delay the Japanese campaign.

Because of equipment difficulties, no submarine guarded Lingayen Gulf in northern Luzon as the Japanese expeditionary force landed on December 21 to begin its march on Manila. The Japanese were heavily escorted and, once in the Gulf, they skillfully took advantage of shoal water and protective reefs to frustrate belated attempts of American submarines to disrupt the landing. Only the S-38, in a daring penetration, managed to sink a transport at its anchorage, while the *Seal* torpedoed a small freighter en route to the landing area.

The threat to their bases near Manila forced a retreat of the Allied naval forces. The Asiatic Fleet Submarine Force, under command of Captain John Wilkes, moved its base first to Darwin, and later to Fremantle, Australia. Only the tender *Canopus* remained in Manila Bay to service submarines there as long as possible.

While continuing their patrol missions, submarines began a series of evacuation runs, removing civilians, key military personnel, and treasure from besieged Bataan and Corregidor, and at the same time delivering food, medical stores, and ammunition to the ever-diminishing numbers of defenders. On the first of these runs, the *Seawolf* took in 37 tons of .50-caliber ammunition and brought out 25 army and navy aviators, a selection of submarine spare parts, and 16 torpedoes from the *Canopus*. The *Trout*, requesting 25 tons of ballast to replace the cargo brought in, received two tons of gold, 18 tons of silver, and five tons of U.S. mail and negotiable securities. On her way back, the *Trout*, not allowing her cargo to interfere with essentials, torpedoed a freighter and a submarine chaser.

Although no submarine sinkings occurred during the Java Sea campaign, Americans were establishing their patrol zones and improving their tactics. Early doctrine called for daylight submerged attack, with periscope observations kept brief and infrequent in order to avoid detection. Attack doctrine also limited the use of sonar equipment to its listening component, lest the pings of its echo-ranging feature reveal the presence of the attacking submarine. Since early periscopes lacked precise range-finding equipment, and since use of sonar solely as a hydrophone could give only the bearing of a target, skippers preferred to attack so that the torpedo would run either parallel to or at right angles to the track of the target, thereby canceling the range factor. In time, periscopes were equipped with stadimeter range finders. Commanding officers also learned that a single range-finding ping on the sonar was unlikely to alert the enemy. Thus, with accurate ranges, a submarine was able to employ any gyro angle with some assurance of hits. For a considerable while, despite German successes with night surfaced attacks, daylight submerged attack continued to be standard practice in the U.S. Navy. The solid black American hulls, so painted to conceal a submarine from air observation, offered poor camouflage to a submarine on the surface at night, and lack of a good night periscope precluded successful submerged attacks after dark. Later experiments proved that a light gray color on the sides gave good camouflage qualities at night, and the development of an effective night periscope made possible submerged night attack. But before the American submarines could become really flexible day-or-night weapons for combating Japanese ships, they had to be provided with a reliable torpedo data computer (TDC), more effective radar, and—above all—more reliable torpedoes.

As the Japanese extended their conquests, they exposed their shipping more and more to submarine attack. Nevertheless in the period between the Pearl Harbor raid and the Battle of the Coral Sea, they managed to keep their losses well within bounds. Allied submarines during this phase of the war sank only three surface warships, none larger than a destroyer, two submarines, and 35 merchantmen. But American submariners were beginning to learn Japanese traffic patterns, with fruitful results in the months to come.

Japanese use of submarines in support of fleet operations is well exemplified in the Battle of Midway, in which boats were sent out individually or positioned in cordons to scout and intercept American fleet movements. It will be recalled that the two cordons between Pearl Harbor and Midway took position too late to observe or intercept the American carriers. The only Japanese submarine that accomplished any positive results in this battle was the *I-168*, which sank the *Yorktown* and the destroyer *Hammann*.

American submarines, stationed on the western approaches to Midway, achieved even less. During the carrier battle, the *Nautilus* fired a harmless dud at the carrier *Kaga*, and thought she had sunk the *Soryu*. That night the heavy cruisers *Mogami* and *Mikuma* collided while maneuvering to avoid the submarine *Tambor*. Thus crippled and slowed, the *Mikuma* later became a victim to American carrier planes.

Between the Battle of Midway in June and the invasion of Guadalcanal on August 7, 1942, the chief American submarine operations were attacking Japanese merchant ships, sinking about 60,000 tons during the period. The Japanese during the same period concentrated a large measure of their submarine efforts in the Indian Ocean, sinking ships as far west as Mozambique Channel, between Madagascar and Africa. Other Japanese submarines operated around Australia, New Guinea, and Samoa. Total sinkings for this period amounted to some 30 Allied ships.

## The Makin Raid

Early in August 1942, the *Nautilus* and the *Argonaut*, two of the largest American submarines (more than 370 feet long and displacing 2,700 tons surfaced), operated together in one of the most unusual special missions of the war. At Pearl Harbor they took aboard Lieutenant Colonel Evans F. Carlson and two companies of marines for a commando raid on Makin in the Gilbert Islands. This was at the time of the Guadalcanal invasion, and the Makin operation was intended as a diversion— to attract Japanese forces away from the Solomons. The marines got ashore without opposition at dawn on August 16. Soon however they began to encounter Japanese troops arriving by foot, on bicycles, and by truck. On request from the marines, the *Nautilus* opened fire in the general direction of the fighting, but lacking spotters to pinpoint targets in this area, she shifted fire to the lagoon and sank a 3,500-ton merchant ship and a patrol boat.

Japanese aircraft forced both submarines to submerge several times during daylight hours, but on two successive nights they took aboard what were presumed to be all the surviving marines. Nine however were left behind. Captured by the Japanese, they were taken to Kwajalein, where they were beheaded.

The landing party had wiped out the small garrison on Butaritari Island, destroyed installations, and picked up useful intelligence material. Though this operation boosted Allied morale, from the strategic point of view it was a failure. Not only were the Japanese not diverted from Guadalcanal; they began to build up formidable defenses in the Gilberts, especially on Tarawa, which were to cost the lives of many Americans a little more than a year later.

## The Solomons Campaign

When the United States assumed the offensive-defensive with the landings on Guadalcanal, American S-boats from Brisbane were assigned by Rear Admiral Charles A. Lockwood, Commander Southwest Pacific Submarine Force, to regular patrol areas in the vicinity of the Bismarcks and New Guinea to attack Japanese ships. The S-boats were also to cover and, insofar as possible, blockade bases at Rabaul, Kavieng, Buin, Lae, and Salamaua, in order to keep the Japanese from reinforcing the lower Solomons. Meanwhile boats from Pearl Harbor established a close blockade on Truk, the so-called "Gibraltar of the Pacific." In addition to sinking 79 merchant ships for a total of 260,000 tons during the Guadalcanal campaign, American undersea craft sank the light cruiser *Tenryu*, an old destroyer, and one of the big I-class submarines. They also accounted for the heavy cruiser *Kako*, one of the victors of the Battle of Savo Island, fought on the night of August 9, 1942. Returning with her sisters in triumph to Rabaul the next morning, the *Kako* fell victim to four torpedoes from the *S-44*, which was patrolling the entrance to the harbor. This successful attack in some small measure compensated the Americans for their crushing defeat at Savo, and, more important, it caused the Japanese to adopt more cautious measures in employment of their surface ships for the Tokyo Express.

Japanese submarines too operated in support of the Solomons campaign. As usual, they made little effort to interfere with American logistic shipping but concentrated rather on warships. Their mere presence in the area however forced the Americans to take extensive antisubmarine measures, employing forces that might otherwise have been used elsewhere. On a run from Espiritu Santo to Guadalcanal, an American convoy, escorted by a close screen and supported by the *Wasp*, *Hornet*, and *North Carolina*, on September 14 ran into a group of Japanese submarines. It would not be correct to call these boats a wolf pack, for they were not making a concerted attack, nor were they under any sort of common tactical command. The *Wasp*, the *North Carolina*, and the escorting destroyer *O'Brien* were all heavily hit by torpedoes in the space of ten minutes. The battleship received very serious damage. The *Wasp*, afire, had to be abandoned and sunk. The *O'Brien* broke up and sank before she could reach drydock. The important point to remember about this attack however is that the Japanese made no effort to attack the convoy itself, for Japanese commanders believed that only warships were worthy targets for sea warriors. The loss of the *Wasp*, combined with heavy damage sustained by the *Saratoga* two weeks earlier, brought American carrier strength in the Pacific down to two, the *Hornet* and the *Enterprise*. In the remainder of the Solomons campaign, the Japanese submarine force sank only two more American warships, the destroyer *Porter* during the Battle of the Santa Cruz Islands, and the light cruiser *Juneau* following the Cruiser Night Action of the Naval Battle of Guadalcanal.

Participation by American submarines in the Solomons campaign took the form of strategic support. Submarines took up their patrol stations near the bases from which the Japanese ships operated against the Solomons—Truk, the Palaus, and Rabaul. In addition they covered the straits in and about the Bismarck Archipelago and gave support to MacArthur's drive up the Papuan Peninsula of New Guinea. These assignments kept the submarines well clear of the operating area and minimized the risk that American boats might be attacked by their own surface forces.* One exception to this practice took place when, during the October crisis on Guadalcanal, the *Amberjack* delivered a load of aviation gasoline to Tulagi, the only time during the war that an American submarine was employed as a tanker.

The most famous story of this period of operations concerns the *Growler*, which was patrolling near the Bismarcks in February 1943. At 0110 on the 7th she sighted an enemy ship and began a surface run. As the range closed, the target, a 2,500-ton Japanese gunboat, sighted the submarine, reversed course, and rushed at her. The *Growler's* radar operator below decks noted the enemy's change of course promptly, but her skipper, Commander Howard W. Gilmore, and the other six men on the bridge did not see the maneuver in the darkness. The command "Left full rudder!" came too late to avoid collision; the *Growler* plowed into the Japanese gunboat at 17 knots. All hands were knocked down by the impact. As the submarine, which had heeled far over, righted herself, the gunboat sprayed the bridge with machine gun bullets. The junior officer of the watch and one of the lookouts were instantly killed; Commander Gilmore was severely wounded. Clinging to the bridge frame, he made his voice heard: "Clear the bridge!" The four other living men scrambled through the hatch. Unable to follow, Commander Gilmore gave his last command: "Take her down!" For this "distinguished gallantry and valor," Commander Gilmore was posthumously awarded the Medal of Honor.

In January 1943 Rear Admiral Robert English, who had commanded the submarines of the Pacific Fleet under Admiral Nimitz, was lost in a plane crash. Admiral Lockwood was ordered to assume Admiral English's job, while Rear Admiral Ralph W. Christie took over Lockwood's Southwest Pacific submarine command. Lockwood immediately set about establishing a submarine base nearer than Pearl Harbor to the submarine patrol areas. At this time the logical forward base for American submarines was Midway Island, which was equipped with submarine tenders and with a minimum shore installation. This base saved a submarine 2,400 miles of travel on each patrol. The chief disadvantage was Midway's unpopularity with submariners. On the islands, submariners complained, were nothing "but sand and gooney birds." To sustain morale, Lockwood arranged schedules so that boats returned to Pearl Harbor periodically.

To give maximum rest and relaxation to submarine personnel, when a boat returned from patrol, its crew, officers and men alike, would be

---

* This was an important consideration: air and surface forces were inclined to shoot first and ask questions afterward. Because of failure or misunderstanding of recognition signals, no less than 28 U.S. submarines were strafed or bombed by U.S. aircraft. Five others were shelled by U.S. surface craft. The *Dorado* and the *Seawolf* were sunk with all hands by "friendly" forces. Nine others were more or less severely damaged.

removed to recuperation camps or hotels while a relief crew took over. Thus the sea-going crew would have no responsibility for their boat until she was ready to leave on her next assignment. Even the commanding officer would be temporarily relieved so that he had no legal responsibility during the time. Submarine squadron commanders, who had no regular combat assignments, supervised and executed this program. On completion of the upkeep period, the reassembled crew would take their boat out for a few days of refresher training and then depart on patrol. This system proved of great benefit to the morale of submariners, who were thus kept in top form for the performance of their primary duties.

## Torpedo Troubles

The blame for the malfunctioning of torpedoes which beset the U.S. Navy in World War II can be laid in some measure to imperfect design and a stubborn confidence in the magnetic exploder. Yet defects in design would have been more quickly revealed had sufficient funds been available for testing. With the limited funds provided, peacetime tests with live torpedoes were out of the question, since to explode a single live torpedo would cost a substantial fraction of the torpedo facility's annual budget. Hence tests were made with exercise heads and with the torpedoes set to pass under rather than to hit the target. These trials thus tested nothing but the gyro steering mechanism and the steam propulsion units. The critical warhead had to be taken on faith. And the faith was misplaced.

The Mark 6 exploder, highly secret before the war, contained a magnetic impulse device, activated by a sharp change in the earth's magnetic field, such as that caused by the steel hull of a ship. Doctrine called for torpedoes employing Mark 6 exploders to pass ten feet beneath the enemy ship so that the explosion would rupture her bottom tanks and perhaps break her back. In practice many torpedoes failed to explode, even though they passed directly beneath the target. Reports such as that from the *Sargo*, which suffered 13 misses out of 13 easy shots, caused Lockwood to conduct a series of tests. Eight shots fired through a fish net ran an average of 11 feet deeper than set. The Bureau of Ordnance finally conceded that the torpedoes with heavy warheads (750 pounds of TNT) *did* run 10 feet deeper than set. However, when set to allow for this error, another serious problem was introduced: the torpedo often ranged up and down in a kind of sinusoidal wave. If it happened to be at the top of its cycle when it passed under the target, it would go off; otherwise the change in the magnetic field was not great enough, and the torpedo passed harmlessly beneath.

Premature explosions, which often deceived the submariner into believing that he had obtained hits, now redoubled. Near the magnetic equator, the horizontal component of a ship's magnetic field is often stronger than the vertical component, with the result that the Mark 6 exploder frequently went off some 50 yards from the target. The resultant explosion, shower of water, and heel of the target led to many reports of hits which were in fact prematures. In view of these findings, Lockwood in June 1943 ordered the inactivation of the magnetic component in order to rely on the contact exploder built into the Mark 6 for use if the magnetic exploder failed.

An outbreak of duds followed. The contact device too was faulty, but its weaknesses had been concealed by the deep running and the premature firing of the torpedoes. The discovery of the defects of the contact feature of the Mark 6 came as a result of the frustrations of Lieutenant Commander L. R. Daspit, commanding the *Tinosa*, which encountered a mammoth 19,000-ton tanker west of Truk in late July 1943. The *Tinosa* had 16 torpedoes remaining and fired four at long range from an unfavorable track angle. Two torpedoes hit and went off near the stern, and the huge tanker stopped. Two more hits were scored on her port quarter. Daspit then worked the *Tinosa* into an ideal firing position on the target's beam and fired nine thoroughly checked torpedoes at her, deliberately, and in single shots. Nine hit and nine failed to explode. The exasperated but clear-thinking Daspit took his one remaining torpedo back to Pearl Harbor for examination.

This move resulted in the final cure. Lockwood ordered the contact feature of the mechanism to be thoroughly tested. The results indicated that the firing pin assembly was too weak to withstand a square hit. On a glancing hit, at an angle of 45° or less, the firing pin would function, but on the so-called "perfect hit," the delicate mechanism would jam and the torpedo would fail to go off. This bore out the *Tinosa*'s experience perfectly, for the four torpedoes which had exploded had all hit at the curve of the stern, while the nine duds had all hit from the perfect right-angle track. Corrective modifications were accomplished at Pearl Harbor, and American submarines finally had a reliable weapon. Thus at long last was overcome the effect of misguided "super secrecy" and insufficient testing of material before the war.

The electric torpedo began to appear soon after the steam torpedo had been brought to satisfactory performance. Its low speed (28 knots vs. 46 knots for the steam torpedo) made the electric torpedo tardy in winning acceptance, but its wakeless feature came to offset its slowness in the minds of submarine officers. At length the majority of torpedoes employed were electric.

## The Gilberts and Marshalls

For the invasion of the Gilbert Islands in November 1943, Admirals Nimitz, Spruance, and Lockwood worked together as a team. They decided that enemy surface opposition to the landings must emanate from Truk, that it would probably swing north to avoid land-based air searches from Guadalcanal, and that it would have to refuel in the Marshalls. So three submarines took station off Truk, three more patrolled the Marshalls, and two patrolled the line between. A ninth was stationed 300 miles west of Tarawa to send daily weather reports.

Because no Japanese surface forces went to the Gilberts, the submarines had little to do except attack whatever convoys or unescorted merchantmen came their way. Nevertheless two of the boats were lost. The *Corvina*, off Truk, was sunk on November 16 by a Japanese submarine—probably the only American submarine so destroyed during the war. The *Sculpin*, between Truk and the Marshalls, was detected on the 19th while closing in on a convoy. She underwent a depth charge attack from the convoy escorts, receiving damages that forced her to the surface, where her crew fought her deck guns as long as they could and then scuttled her. Thirteen officers and men rode the *Sculpin* down. Among these was Captain John P. Cromwell, whom Admiral Lockwood had sent to take command of a wolf pack, should one be formed. Because Cromwell possessed important information about war plans, he had elected to go down lest the Japanese extract his information through torture or "truth serums." For his decision he was posthumously awarded the Medal of Honor. Of the members of the *Sculpin*'s crew that abandoned ship, the Japanese picked up 42. One of these, badly wounded, was callously tossed back overboard by his captors. The rest were taken to Truk, where they were transferred to the escort carriers *Unyo* and *Chuyo* for transportation to Japan.

Now came one of the most tragic and ironic coincidences of the war. Approaching Japan was U.S. submarine *Sailfish*, on her tenth war patrol—her first under Lieutenant Commander Robert Ward. Her crew often referred to her as the *Squailfish* because she had formerly been the famous *Squalus*, which had gone down off Portsmouth, New Hampshire in 1939. It was the *Sculpin* that had then located her on the bottom, making possible the rescue of her crew and her subsequent raising. Now, four years later, Ward, in common with other American submarine commanders, was keenly aware that no large Japanese warship had been sunk by a submarine in 16 months. He was anxious for the *Sailfish* to break this run of bad luck. She did, but from the American point of view there was a tragic irony in her success.

Just before midnight on December 3 in typhoon weather, the *Sailfish* made radar contact with several large targets. Despite the gale and near zero visibility, Ward soon reached firing position and fired four tubes. One torpedo scored a hit on a carrier, which managed to limp away through heavy seas. Despite depth charge attacks that drove him down, Ward regained contact with his quarry and stalked her through the night. At dawn he fired three more torpedoes and made another hit, this time leaving the carrier dead in the water. At 0940 he fired a spread from his stern tubes and got a third hit. Eight minutes later the carrier went down, unobserved by the submarine, which had been driven deep by the Japanese escorts. The *Sailfish* had sunk the escort carrier *Chuyo*. The *Chuyo* had 21 *Sculpin* survivors aboard, all but one of whom were lost.

The deployment of submarines for the Gilberts operation impressed Admiral Spruance so favorably that he advocated the same pattern thereafter. Instead of having a scouting line at sea, he requested that the submarines be stationed in waters, particularly straits, through which the enemy was likely to pass in order to approach the scene of action.* Unlike the Japanese at Midway, he got his submarines to their stations early enough for them to be of value.

By this time submarine doctrine had come to include several distinct missions:

    1. Submarine concentration to cut the enemy's supply lines to the target areas.

    2. Submarine photographic reconnaissance of beachheads marked for amphibious landings and enemy military or naval installations marked for future reference.

    3. Submarine lifeguarding during air strikes.

    4. Submarine scouting duty in the target area and off enemy bases to report enemy movements and intercept and attack enemy forces which emerged to oppose the attacking United States forces.

    5. Submarines stationed to intercept and attack fugitive shipping attempting to flee the target area.†

For the Marshalls landings of January 1944 four submarines performed photo-reconnaissance. Again three submarines took station off the approaches to Truk, and this time two of the three sank destroyers. The deployment of the other available submarines for this operation was patterned on that of the Gilberts operation.

For the three big carrier strikes at Truk, Saipan, and the Palaus in early 1944, the pattern varied somewhat, since Spruance believed that his opposition would come not from surface units but from the enemy's land-based air, while the surface units and the merchant ships present would flee the areas. Consequently he requested submarines where they might intercept the fugitives. Off Truk the *Skate* sank the light cruiser *Agano*, and the *Tang* got a cargo ship. At Saipan the *Sunfish* sank two merchantmen; the *Tang*, four. Off Palau the *Tullibee* was sunk by her own circling torpedo, and apparently most of the Japanese ships escaped through the area assigned to her. It was on this occasion however that the *Tunny* put two torpedoes into the superbattleship *Musashi*.

---

* Submarines remained under operational command of the type commander. Joint plans were agreed on in conference between Admiral Lockwood and the fleet commander concerned.

† Theodore Roscoe, *United States Submarine Operations in World War II* (Annapolis, 1949), 361.

## The Marianas

Before the American invasion of the Marianas in June 1944 Admiral
Lockwood, of the Pacific Fleet, and Admiral Ralph Christie, of the
Seventh Fleet, both positioned their submarines at the request of Admiral
Spruance. Three boats scouted the Tawitawi area as the Japanese fleet
assembled at Tawitawi; others operated off the principal straits through
which it would have to pass to reach Saipan; four more patrolled the
Philippine Sea in 90° arcs inside and centered on the corners of a great
square. Still others were in motion, relieving patrollers or returning to
base after relief; two of these transients played major roles in the development of the battle. There was also a wolf pack on routine patrol—the
*Shark II*, the *Pilotfish*, and the *Pintado*—called Blair's Blasters after group
commander Captain L. N. Blair.

On May 31, 1944, the submarine *Silversides*, patrolling an adjacent
area, informed the Blasters that a convoy was coming their way, apparently heading from Honshu to Saipan. By the time the *Silversides* had
joined forces with the wolf pack, two more convoys had appeared in the
area. Early on June 1 the *Pintado* picked off a freighter from the first
of the three convoys. All that day and for several days thereafter the
wolf pack chased the third convoy, but the *Silversides*, her torpedoes
expended, had to withdraw. The *Shark* sank a cargo ship late on June 2
and another on the morning of June 4. On the evening of June 5 she
got two more, one a passenger-cargo vessel of 7,000 tons. That same
night the *Pintado* sank two ships. As a result of these sinkings, half a
division of Japanese reinforcement troops was drowned, and many other
soldiers reached the Marianas without guns or battle gear. The Japanese
commander on Saipan had to ration munitions. Blair's Blasters had greatly
lessened the opposition the American assault troops would have to overcome.

From June 6 through June 9 the submarine *Harder*, under Commander
Samuel D. Dealey, set a remarkable record in the vicinity of Sibutu
Passage, between the Sulu Archipelago and Borneo, sinking three destroyers and damaging at least two more. On the morning of June 10, as
the *Harder* was patrolling in the Sulu Sea off Tawitawi, she witnessed
the sortie of Admiral Ugaki's battleship force for the relief of Biak and
radioed a timely warning to Allied commands.

When planes from the U.S. Fifth Fleet began their preliminary
bombing of the Marianas on June 11, 1944, the Japanese high command
realized that an invasion of Japan's inner defenses was imminent. Admiral
Toyoda suspended the Biak operation and ordered the two segments of
the Mobile Fleet, under Admiral Ozawa and under Admiral Ugaki, to
rendezvous in the Philippine Sea and "attack the enemy in the Marianas
area."

As this movement got underway, Christie's and Lockwood's careful positioning of their submarines began to pay off. The submarine *Redfin* saw the carrier force, under Ozawa, sortie from Tawitawi on June 13 and flashed a warning. In the early evening of the 15th, the submarines *Flying Fish* and *Seahorse* sighted the two segments of the Mobile Fleet 300 miles apart in the Philippine Sea. Early on the 17th, the *Cavalla* made contact with an oiler convoy, and Admiral Lockwood ordered her to follow, on the chance that the oilers would lead her to the Japanese combat vessels. The *Cavalla* soon lost the oilers, but that evening she sighted the Mobile Fleet, now united and heading for the Marianas. As a result of these sightings, Admiral Spruance postponed the invasion of Guam and prepared for the Battle of the Philippine Sea. Admiral Lockwood now shifted the four submarines, patrolling from the corners of a square, southward a hundred miles. Now that the approximate location of the Japanese fleet was known, Lockwood gave his submarines permission to shoot first and transmit contact reports afterward. Thus it was that the *Albacore*, assigned to the southwest corner of the new square, found herself in the right place with the right orders to enable her to sink the carrier *Taiho*. Three hours later the ubiquitous *Cavalla* put three torpedoes into the carrier *Shokaku* and sent her down.

In contrast to the precision with which Christie and Lockwood had stationed their submarines, the Japanese had theirs all in the wrong place. MacArthur's landing on Biak had led them to expect that the next Fifth Fleet operations would be against the Palaus instead of the Marianas, for it was the Palaus that Spruance had hit in support of MacArthur's invasion of Hollandia. Confident that the Americans would come that way again, the Japanese sent submarines to operate north of the Admiralties. In setting up their screen they not only selected the wrong area; they also failed to allow for improvements in American antisubmarine warfare. By mid-1944 the war in the Atlantic against the U-boat had been won, and escorting vessels were bringing the weapons and experience of the Battle of the Atlantic to the Pacific. Of some 25 I-boats and RO-boats operating in connection with the Marianas campaign, 17 were sent to the bottom by American destroyers, destroyer escorts, and aircraft.

The exploits of U.S. destroyer escort *England* (Lieutenant Commander W. B. Pendleton) in May 1944 demonstrate the impotence of Japanese submarines against the new type of attack. Alerted by the news that an American destroyer division had sunk a submarine near the Green Islands, the destroyer escorts *England, Raby,* and *George* proceeded from Ironbottom Sound off Guadalcanal to the Bismarcks area. The next day the group made contact north of the Solomons with the *I-16* on a cargo-carrying mission out ahead of the main line of Japanese submarines. The *England* attacked with hedgehogs, ahead-thrown bombs that explode on contact with the submarine. She obtained five hits, whereupon she was rocked by a terrific explosion as the I-boat blew apart. Proceeding northwest, the group ran into the main defense line of seven RO-boats. Here on three successive days, May 22, 23, and 24, the *England* sank RO-boats *106, 104,* and *116.* Proceeding to Manus to take on more hedgehog ammunition, the group toward midnight on the 26th made radar contact with *RO-108.* The group commander gave the *Raby* first chance at this submarine, but she lost contact, and the *England* made another kill. Joined by a fourth destroyer escort bringing the needed ammunition, the *England's* group returned to the hunting grounds, where they were integrated into a hunter-killer group of destroyers and an escort carrier. When this combined group made contact with the *RO-105* in the early hours of May 31, the officer in tactical command deliberately ordered the *England* to stand aside in order to give the other ships an opportunity to score. When their attacks failed, in came the *England* once more and destroyed the boat with another hedgehog salvo. When the report of this action reached Washington, Admiral King signaled: "There'll always be an *England* in the United States Navy."

## The Palaus and the Philippines

Before the invasion of the Palaus in September 1944, the *Burrfish* made a combined photographic and landing-party reconnaissance of Peleliu and Yap. Because four of the men put ashore on Yap failed to return to the submarine, the landing-party reconnaissance mission, rarely employed by the United States Navy, was abolished.

Admiral Halsey's ideas for submarine deployment differed somewhat from those of Admiral Spruance. Though Halsey agreed that the narrow seas should be patrolled, he placed considerable reliance on use of a scouting line in the open ocean. Hence he requested that while four boats watched important straits, nine form a double scouting line between the Philippines and the Palaus. Two submarines from each of three wolf packs formed a first line of six, and the third boat of each pack formed a second line, in safety position. Because these submarines, called "Halsey's Zoo," made no important contacts during the operation, the submarine scouting line was not used again by the Americans during the war.

The story of submarine operations at the time of the Battle for Leyte Gulf has already been told in some detail. Southwest Pacific submarines *Darter* and *Dace,* it will be recalled, on October 23, 1944 gave the first warning of the approaching Japanese Center Force, and directly afterward sank two of Admiral Kurita's heavy cruisers and put a third out of action. During the same morning, the submarine *Bream* severely damaged the heavy cruiser *Aoba* off Manila Bay. On the morning of the 25th, while TF 38 was pursuing Ozawa's carrier group northward in the Battle off Cape Engaño, Lockwood ordered two wolf packs, Clarey's Crushers and Roach's Raiders, into an intercepting position. It was the *Jallao* of Clarey's Crushers that sank Ozawa's damaged light cruiser *Tama*.

## Other Operations Against the Japanese Navy

In operations less closely associated with the surface fleet, American submarines achieved several more successes against large warships. The most noteworthy were the sinkings of the battleship *Kongo* and the carrier *Shinano*.

The 31,000-ton *Kongo*, which went down in November 1944, was the only battleship sunk by an American submarine. On November 21, the *Sealion II* (Commander Eli T. Reich) encountered her victim 40 miles north of Formosa. The first radar contact showed the target so far distant that the officer of the deck mistook it for land, but when a further contact showed the target moving nearer, he called the captain. It was just past midnight, with the sky overcast but visibility fair. Identifying the contact as comprising at least two battleships, two cruisers, and several destroyers heading for Japan, Reich elected to make a surface approach, using radar. By the time he had gained the desired attack position and made visual contact with the enemy, the sea was rising, whipped by a night wind. At 0256 Reich fired six bow torpedoes at the leading battleship, at a range of 3,000 yards. Throwing the rudder hard right, he brought his stern tubes to bear on the second battleship and got away three more torpedoes at 0259. Then he took the *Sealion* away at flank speed. To his great disappointment, the task force continued on course at 18 knots. Taking water over the bridge and a good deal down the conning tower hatch, the *Sealion* gave chase. At 0450 the battleship at which the bow tubes had been fired slowed to twelve knots and dropped astern of the task force with two destroyers standing by. Shortly afterward this ship, the *Kongo*, went dead in the water. As the *Sealion* maneuvered into attack position, a flash of light, presumably from the explosion of the battleship's magazines, illuminated the entire area, and the *Kongo* sank. The *Sealion* immediately began to pursue the other battleship but was unable to overtake her in the now heavy seas. Only after the war did the *Sealion's* crew learn that one of its sterntube torpedoes fired at 0259, missing its intended battleship target, had sunk a destroyer.

Even this achievement was overshadowed about a week later when the *Archerfish* (Commander J. E. Enright) sank the *Shinano*. The *Shinano* was of 68,000 tons displacement, one of the largest warships in the world. Begun as a sister ship to the superbattleships *Yamato* and *Musashi*, she had been converted into an aircraft carrier. She was commissioned on November 18, 1944 and sunk ten days later. When the *Archerfish* found her 150 miles south of Tokyo, she was on her way to the Inland Sea for fitting out in comparative safety from air attack. The submarine made radar contact with the carrier and her four escorts at 2048. A stern chase ensued, which the *Archerfish* must inevitably have lost had the target not zigzagged. At 0300 a radical change in the Japanese base course put the submarine ahead of the carrier, and a zig at 0316 made the position perfect except for a rather large gyro angle. At 0317, with range 1,400 yards and a 70° starboard gyro angle, Enright fired a spread of six torpedoes, all of which probably hit and at least four of which certainly took effect.

The *Shinano* probably would not have sunk had the crew not been inexperienced and the ship unready for sea. Doors that should have been watertight had no gaskets; water poured through them and through unsealed conduits. Steam pumps had not yet been installed, and piping was incomplete. There were too few hand pumps. When the morale of the crew failed also and discipline broke down, the loss of the ship was inevitable. It is fitting that an American submarine should climax the undersea campaign against Japanese warships by sending down the new queen of the Imperial Navy before she had an opportunity to come into action. It is also ironic because Japan no longer had any use for such a vessel. She had freely expended four of her remaining fast carriers as mere decoys in the Battle for Leyte Gulf because she lacked trained pilots for carrier aircraft.

## The Lifeguard League

While American submarines were decimating the Japanese navy, they were simultaneously performing a mission of lifesaving. When planning was in progress for the Gilbert Islands invasion, Admiral Lockwood received the suggestion that submarines might well be employed to rescue downed fliers. He agreed at once, and thus was born the successful Lifeguard League, which rescued 504 airmen before the end of the war. Submarines were stationed in appropriate positions, and airmen were briefed on their locations. The pilot of a crippled plane would set it down as near the submarine as possible, and then he and the crew would take refuge aboard. Lifeguarders also performed notable service for army flyers, especially crews of B-29's shot down while engaged in operations against Japan from bases in the Marianas. These rescues were by no means always easy or free of danger. The *Harder,* for example, went into the shoals of Woleai Island and brought out a navy fighter pilot from the shore by means of a volunteer crew in a rubber boat, all the time under sniper fire. The most dramatic story however is that of the *Stingray,* under Lieutenant Commander S. C. Loomis, which in June 1944 received a report of a downed aviator near Guam. When the *Stingray* got to the position, she found the pilot in his rubber raft acting as involuntary target for a Japanese shore battery. Not daring to surface, Loomis raised both periscopes, one for observation, and the other for the pilot to employ as a cleat for a line from his raft. The pilot at first seemed not to understand, and the *Stingray* made three unsuccessful approaches in the midst of numerous shell splashes. At last on the fourth try, Loomis ran the periscope into the pilot, and he hung on. When the *Stingray* had towed him well out of range of the guns, she surfaced and took the aviator aboard. "We are on speaking terms now," Loomis noted, "but after the third approach I was ready to make him captain of the head."

## Further Japanese Submarine Operations

Like the Americans, the Japanese often sent their submarines on special missions, some of them peculiar to the Imperial Navy. Such was the practice of "piggy-backing" small attack devices into effective range. These included midget submarines, aircraft, and outsize torpedoes, called *Kaitens*, steered by a one-man suicide crew. Midgets carried out several attacks early in the war, achieving their most notable success by damaging H.M. battleship *Ramillies* at Madagascar. Thereafter the Japanese dropped them from use, replacing them later in the war with the newly-designed *Kaitens* as a kind of naval equivalent of the kamikazes. Unlike the kamikazes however, the *Kaitens* achieved nothing.

Submarine-launched aircraft carried out some successful photo-reconnaissance missions, and one of them dropped several incendiary bombs in the forests of Oregon. Difficulties of launching and recovery precluded widespread use of aircraft-carrying submarines. The war was ending when Japan began to commission the *I-400*-class of 3,500-ton monsters, each of which was intended to bring three planes to within range of the Panama Canal.

The Japanese sometimes used their submarines for nuisance raids of little strategic value. Occasionally the boats refueled seaplanes to extend their radius of attack. In 1942 submarines caused some alarm along the Pacific Coast of North America by sinking a few ships and shelling Vancouver Island, Astoria, and an oil installation near Santa Barbara. Several boats tried to establish liaison with Germany, but only the *I-8* made the round-trip successfully.

The poor showing of the Japanese submarines in contrast to the remarkable success of the American boats invites analysis. The small, obsolete Japanese RO-class was greatly inferior to the corresponding American S-boat, but the modern I-class was fairly comparable to the U.S. fleet boat. At the outbreak of war the Americans together with the Dutch had about as many submarines in the Pacific and Far Eastern waters as the Japanese had. But most of the American boats were S-class, while most of the Japanese were I-class, giving Japan a nearly 2-to-1 advantage in battleworthy craft. Moreover the Japanese torpedo, besides being more dependable than the American, had greater speed, longer range, and a more powerful warhead. Technical deficiencies of the Japanese boats themselves of course account to some extent for their comparative ineffectiveness. Until late in the war they had no radar, and their sound gear was extremely inefficient, leaving them far more vulnerable to countermeasures than German U-boats. The main trouble however was simply strategic blindness on the part of the Japanese high command. The Imperial Navy never used its submarines in a regular campaign against merchant shipping, apparently failing to realize the central place of logistics in modern war.

When the Germans pointed out the extraordinary effectiveness of the submarine as a weapon against cargo carriers and urged Japan to use her underwater fleet against Allied merchant ships, the Japanese invariably replied that they would risk their submarines only against warships. So while American submarines were wearing down Japan's fighting potential by unremitting attacks on her cargo ships, the Japanese disregarded the vulnerable tankers and freighters on which the Allied fleets depended, and sent their boats after well-screened fleet units.

With the inauguration of the Allied by-passing strategy, the desperate Japanese sidetracked even this objective. To supply their isolated garrisons, they began at the insistence of the army to use their submarines as cargo carriers. Gradually their best boats were pressed into such unsuitable service. Hence even while the Allied forces were operating at ever-increasing distances from their continental bases, and closer to Japanese bases, the effectiveness of the Japanese submarines steadily declined. Seldom in the long history of warfare has a primary weapon been used with less grasp of its true potential.

## The Assault on Japanese Merchant Shipping

While Japan's submarines were achieving less and less, American submarines, as we have seen, were sinking increasing numbers of Japanese warships. Even more significant in the outcome of the war was the achievement of American submarines against the cargo ships of Japan, which carried the life blood of her existence. Japan's shipping problem was complex, for having no industry in her resources areas and no resources in her industrial area, she had to bring all raw materials to Japan for manufacture and then distribute them to the ultimate consumers which, in war, were the forces in the field. Basically there were two main routes required by these circumstances: across the Sea of Japan or the Yellow Sea to Japan to bring iron and coal from Manchuria, and, more important, the route from the Southern Resources Area past

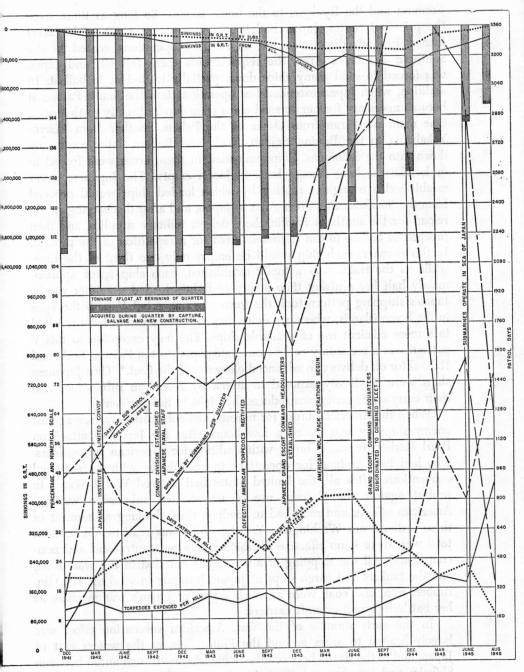

**ATTRITION OF JAPANESE SHIPPING IN WORLD WAR II**

Formosa and the Ryukyus to the home islands. So long as these were the principal routes, Japan had little difficulty, for ships could travel loaded in both directions. But as military operations ceased in the Southern Resources Area, the requirements there fell off, and Japan was forced to send many ships down partially loaded or in ballast. In addition, when Japan extended her operations into the South Pacific, it became necessary for her to send ships from Japan directly to that area. One main route ran from Osaka to the Palaus, another from Tokyo-Yokahama to the Bonins, Saipan, Truk, and Rabaul, later continuing down into the Solomons. Ships unloaded in these areas were forced to undertake the long voyage back to Japan empty. The Japanese never established a triangular routing by which loaded ships would proceed from the Southern Resources Area to Japan, and after discharging cargo, reload for the southern Pacific, there deliver military supplies, and then proceed in ballast to the Resources Area for a repetition of the process. In this manner, each ship would be empty only one third of the time, while as the traffic was actually established, each ship spent approximately half her cruising time empty or lightly loaded. In other words, Japan's shipping pattern took the form of an inverted V with the apex in the home islands, whereas a delta-shaped pattern would have resulted in a more efficient use of available ships. The only exception to this V pattern was a secondary route from Balikpapan to the Palaus, Truk, and Rabaul for oil delivery to advanced elements of the fleet.* Thus Japanese ships were needlessly exposed to attack by American submarines and their carrying capacity was reduced by eight to ten per cent.

When the American order for unrestricted submarine warfare against enemy shipping was issued a few hours after the Japanese attack on Pearl Harbor, it was a break with tradition for American submariners, who had been trained for operations in accordance with international conventions. After all, the United States had entered World War I in protest against the German use of unrestricted submarine warfare. American officers and men had to readjust their thinking as a result of these orders from Washington. Yet the order was realistic. In modern total war, there is no effective distinction between contraband and non-contraband. All the shipping of a country is enrolled in the war effort, and the tankers and cargo ships of Japan, bringing in vital oil, rice, tin, rubber, iron, and coal, were as much a part of Japan's war machine as her battleships and aircraft carriers.

In the early months of the war, American submarine effort was largely limited to areas around the Philippines, to the waters east of Japan, and to the straits between the home islands—Bungo Suido between Shikoku and Kyushu, and Kii Suido, between Shikoku and Honshu. A

* In addition to these major routes, minor ones connected the islands in the Resources Area and served as feeders to the principal convoys.

few boats attacked ships on the Manila-Formosa-home islands run. The British and Dutch had a limited number of submarines operating and achieved considerable success in the Straits of Malacca against ships sailing between Rangoon and Singapore, sinking in all 16 warships and 39 merchant vessels, totaling 30,000 and 110,000 tons respectively.

Until April 1942 Japanese shipping sailed independently, without benefit of convoy escort. Growing losses however caused the Japanese to establish limited convoys at that time and to organize the First Convoy Escort Fleet in July with headquarters on Formosa. This force had the responsibility for escort of convoys in the East China Sea, or between Formosa and Japan, although later the convoys were extended into the South China Sea, to Manila, Saigon, and Singapore. These Japanese convoys were small in comparison to those of the North Atlantic, consisting of only six to ten ships escorted by a single old destroyer or smaller vessel. The reasons for Japanese neglect of convoy were similar to those of the British in late 1916 and in the 1930's. First, the Japanese underestimated the potential threat of Allied submarines. Second, they looked on convoy escort as defensive, and both the army and navy were offensive-minded, having contempt for defensive operations. In contrast, the Allies had come to regard escort of convoy as both defensive and offensive, offering the best chance for killing submarines. So long as the Japanese believed that convoy work was defensive, their convoys received little support from Combined Fleet headquarters, which even refused to permit fleet destroyers on the way to operating areas to serve en route as convoy escorts. Such assignment, said Combined Fleet, would interfere with the warships' basic missions. And escort vessels in any case were in short supply.

As the Japanese ultimately established their convoy system, they sacrificed the advantages of a strong offensive screen around a large convoy in favor of retaining as much of the flexibility of independent shipping as possible. This compromise was efficient neither in protecting ships nor in killing the attacking submarines, which could readily avoid a single escort. If the Japanese had employed convoys of 30 to 50 ships with five or six escorts, they would have given their ships greater safety at no loss in carrying capacity and with no increase in the number of ships allocated to escort work. In addition, these multiple escorts would have been much more dangerous to the attacking submarines than a single one could be. When the Japanese in November 1943 established a Grand Escort Command Headquarters and adopted more sizable convoys, the Americans resorted to wolf-pack operations as a counter. Yet in spite of all the weaknesses of Japanese convoys, sinkings of independently routed ships were two and a half times as numerous as those of ships in convoy. Furthermore the U.S. Navy lost more submarines to convoy escorts than they lost to patrols, mines, aircraft, or any other single agency. The inference is clear: Japan might have severely curtailed the effectiveness of the American submarines, if she had employed convoys earlier and more efficiently.

By the end of 1943, most Japanese shipping was provided with some kind of escort protection. In view of the small size of Japanese convoys, American wolf packs rarely comprised more than three submarines, a practice that promoted close-knit cooperation. Initial wolf-pack tactics called for a boat on each flank of the convoy and a third behind to get stragglers. Such station keeping on a sharply maneuvering convoy proved so difficult however that doctrine gave way to improvisation on the spot, and American skippers made themselves virtuosos of undersea warfare. They made kills at all hours, from all depths and angles, including "down the throat" and "up the kilt"—difficult shots from dead ahead and dead astern. The curve of sinkings soared.

With the increasing destruction of Japanese shipping, especially of vital tankers, the efficiency of Japan's war machine declined even more sharply. On the eve of the Philippine Sea battle, it will be recalled, scarcity of oil in the home islands forced the Mobile Fleet to base at Tawitawi. After the battle Admiral Ozawa took his fleet to Japan for repairs and ammunition, but there he found an acute shortage of fuel. So the fleet had to be divided, and Admiral Kurita took most of the surface vessels back south where there was oil aplenty but where repair facilities and ammunition were lacking. The Imperial Fleet was thus caught in two widely separated parts when the Americans invaded the Philippines, precipitating the last great clash of fleets in the Battle for Leyte Gulf. Even then the Japanese might have achieved something had they been able to use their carriers as combatant ships rather than as mere decoys. But the carriers were powerless to strike because Japan, largely for lack of aviation fuel, could never train enough replacement pilots to offset the heavy losses which began with the Battle of Midway. Thus American submarines, patiently tracking and destroying oil-bearing ships from the East Indies, 110 in all, divided the enemy's sea power and rendered him incapable of maintaining his air power.

## Operation Barney—The Sea of Japan

By the spring of 1945, Japan was almost completely cut off from the Southern Resources Area, but she was still able to draw supplies from the mainland of Asia, especially Manchuria, across the Sea of Japan. Because all entrances to this sea were heavily mined, American submarines had not as a rule been able to operate in these waters. The *Wahoo* had made two daring penetrations into the Sea of Japan, but she had defective torpedoes on her first patrol and did not return from her second. Until some method could be found of avoiding the mines at the entrances, the Sea of Japan remained, as the submariners called it, "Hirohito's Lake," and the blockade of the islands could not be complete.

The answer came in a new electronic sonar device, FMS, which gave a visual presentation of objects in the water all around a submarine and which had sufficient powers of resolution to indicate mines as well as ships. Beset with growing pains, the device won slow acceptance by submariners, but eventually it proved the key to unlock the barred passageways into the Sea of Japan.

In possession of this device, Lockwood planned a penetration in force called Operation BARNEY. It involved nine submarines, *Sea Dog, Crevalle, Spadefish, Tinosa, Bonefish, Skate, Tunny, Flying Fish,* and *Bowfin,* which were to pass through Tsushima Strait in relays between June 3 and 6, and to commence operations against Japanese ships on the 9th. The *Sea Dog* leading the way, all boats got through successfully. Once in the Sea of Japan, all commanding officers had a hard time holding themselves in check until the official starting time, for the many Japanese ships they sighted were sailing on a peace-time basis singly, with no escort, and with running lights burning. As one cynical torpedoman put it, "The skipper almost couldn't wait to open his packages."

Operating in three wolf packs, but under such freedom as to be almost on individual patrols, the boats struck hard when the time came at last. They sank the submarine *I-122* and 28 merchant ships for a total of 55,000 tons. The *Bonefish* was lost, but the remaining eight submarines passed successfully out of La Perouse Strait north of Hokkaido on the night of June 24.*

## Conclusion

The story of the decline of the Japanese merchant marine is told graphically on page 419. Submarines sank 1,113 merchant vessels of over 500 tons, with an additional 65 "probables," for a total of 5,320,094 G.R.T. In addition they accounted for 201 sure and 13 probable naval ship kills, for a total of 577,626 displacement tons. This they achieved at a loss to themselves of 52 boats, all but seven in action against the Japanese. Before Japan could be invaded, before the atomic bombs were dropped, the Japanese were making surrender overtures, starved into defeat.

On 24 November 1945, Admiral Nimitz again stood on the narrow deck of a submarine in a change of command ceremony, this time to relinquish to Admiral Spruance the responsibilities of Cincpac and

---

* The successful completion of Operation BARNEY was the fulfillment of a naval tactician's dream. As far back as the Class of 1923 at the U.S. Naval War College, Newport, R.I., the students concluded that only when Japan was completely isolated from the Asiatic Mainland could Japan be forced to surrender. Operation BARNEY served that purpose. [Footnote by Admiral Nimitz.]

Cincpoa he had borne so long and so well. This time there perhaps was a concession to sentiment on the part of the commander of the greatest fleet in the world's history, for surely there were available plenty of more commodious decks than that of U.S.S. *Menhaden*. Every submariner in the fleet recognized the significance of the fact that a great commander deliberately carried out his last official duty in that command aboard a submarine. It was his salute to all of them for a job well done.

# 15

# The Defeat of Japan

As the war in the Pacific moved toward its inevitable conclusion, Allied leaders propounded various theories as to how Japan could most quickly and economically be made to surrender. Many submariners held the view that submarines could do the job alone, as U-boats had twice nearly defeated Britain. The scientists and military men involved in the Manhattan Project were convinced that once they produced the atomic bomb Japan could not long hold out—especially after the development of the B-29, capable of carrying the bomb, and the American conquest of the southern Marianas, providing airfields from which the target could be reached. Others pointed to the coming defeat of Germany or the promised invasion of Manchuria by the Russians as the final blow that would convince Japan that further resistance was futile. There was undoubted merit in all these views, yet the majority of Allied military leaders and statesmen adhered to one or a combination of three other theories. For convenience we may call these the Army Theory, the Navy Theory, and the Air Force Theory, provided we understand that none of the three was advocated exclusively by any one service or branch.

The Army Theory regarded the invasion of Japan as a necessary step in breaking the Japanese will to resist. Military history supported this view, for in the past nations generally had capitulated only after invaders had occupied a substantial portion of their territory, usually including the capital. The Army Theory gained wider acceptance after the American conquest of Saipan, for here even Japanese civilians had committed suicide in wholesale numbers rather than surrender. This sort of fanaticism convinced many officers that nothing short of physical seizure of their home islands could make the Japanese stop fighting.

The Navy Theory, as old as naval history, proposed defeating Japan by means of blockade. Like England, Japan was peculiarly vulnerable to attacks on her sea communications. An island nation, overpopulated and lacking internal resources for carrying on modern warfare, she was absolutely dependent upon imports. She had gambled all she had won in Asia by warring on the United States to obtain unimpeded access to the essential oil, rubber, and other products of the East Indies. With the recapture of the Philippines and the virtual destruction of Japanese sea and air power, Allied air, surface, and subsurface forces operating from Luzon would be able to interdict the flow of materials from the Southern Resources Area and thus gradually render Japan incapable of fighting.

The Air Force Theory was that Japan could be defeated by continuous bombing of her cities and industries until she lacked the will and means to make war. Though bombers from the Marianas could reach Tokyo, airfields still nearer Japan would have to be captured for such strategic bombing to achieve maximum effect.

In line with the American policy of "unremitting pressure" on Japanese military and naval power, the Joint Chiefs of Staff directed operations to put into effect all means of defeating the enemy—and all except actual invasion of the Japanese home islands were carried out.

## The Navy Finds New Objectives

The Battle for Leyte Gulf was the Trafalgar of World War II. Halsey and Kinkaid in 1944, like Nelson in 1805, had finally wiped out the Japanese fleet as an effective fighting force. There would be no more stand-up battles at sea in this war. Moreover the United States Navy in bringing the Army to the Philippines had apparently assured the success of the Navy's primary objective of cutting Japan's communications with the Southern Resources Area.

After Trafalgar the Royal Navy had been at loose ends, not quite knowing what to do with its fighting fleets. In consequence it had spent several years engaging in all sorts of eccentric operations before it found its true function. While continuing to control the sea, the Royal Navy put the Army on the Continent and kept it supplied and reinforced where it could come actively to grips with Napoleon.

After Leyte Gulf the United States Navy had no doubts regarding its further function. It had entered World War II with a well-established tradition of cooperating closely with the sister service. After the Navy had attained its own major objective in the fall of 1944, it continued to assist the Army and the Army Air Forces to attain theirs. The 21st Bomber Command, based on the Marianas, was hampered because fighter planes lacked sufficient range to support the B-29's in the long flight to Japan and back. So following the Battle for Leyte Gulf Admiral Halsey prepared to take the Third Fleet north for a joint raid on Tokyo.

He did not make the move however, for it soon appeared that the Sixth Army still required the support of the Third Fleet in the Philippines campaign.

## The Leyte Campaign

The Japanese High Command had correctly estimated that the two transpacific lines of Allied advance would converge on the Philippines, and the operations of the U.S. Third Fleet in the fall of 1944 convinced them that an invasion was imminent. From Manchuria in early October Imperial Headquarters transferred Japan's ablest army commander, General Tomoyuki Yamashita, conqueror of Singapore, to command the Japanese army in the Philippines. Uncertain where the impending invasion would come, Yamashita kept his 387,000 troops distributed through the islands. As a result, when the Americans landed on October 20, there were only 22,000 Japanese troops on Leyte. The High Command nevertheless decreed that here the decisive battle for the Philippines must be fought. Hence Yamashita began rushing reinforcements to Leyte, and the Mobile Fleet began converging on Leyte Gulf. The crushing defeat of the Imperial Navy in the battle of October 23–26 did not alter the basic Japanese plan.

Torrential rains brought by the monsoons soon turned Leyte into a quagmire that minimized the American superiority in numbers of troops and in motorized equipment. The invaders had found only one usable airstrip on the island, that at Tacloban. Efforts by U.S. Army Engineers to improve or construct others were for a long time defeated by a combination of continuing rain and unsuitable subsoil. At the same time the Japanese were staging in fresh planes from Formosa and the home islands and operating from the all-weather airfields of Luzon. A few days after the Battle for Leyte Gulf, General MacArthur directed the Army Air Force to relieve the Seventh Fleet escort carriers of responsibility for air operations in the Leyte area. When the little carriers departed however, the Air Force proved unable to take over. It did not have enough planes available, it did not have enough usable airfields, and its aviators were not trained to provide the sort of support that was needed at Leyte. As a result, the U.S. Third Fleet was obliged to return to Philippine waters. At the end of October, Admiral McCain assumed temporary command of TF 38 in order to give Admiral Mitscher a much-needed rest.

In late October and November 1944 Third Fleet aviators, striking chiefly at Luzon airfields and at enemy shipping in the Luzon area and en route to Leyte, destroyed about 700 planes and sank three cruisers, ten destroyers, and numerous transports and other auxiliaries. They sent one complete convoy to the bottom, drowning about 10,000 Japanese. Further to supplement his inadequate land-based air power, General MacArthur in November ordered marine air groups up from the Solomons to provide close air support for his troops and borrowed other marine groups from Peleliu to cope with the wily Japanese night bombers.

Despite all efforts the Americans could not regain command of the air in the Leyte area. Kamikazes struck repeatedly at the Third and Seventh Fleets. In Halsey's fleet they damaged six carriers. In Kinkaid's they hit two battleships, two cruisers, two attack transports, and seven destroyers, one of which, the *Abner Read*, sank. After a particularly severe suicide attack on TF 38 on November 25, the Third Fleet temporarily ceased operating in Philippine waters. It had been at sea and in combat almost continuously for three months.

The Japanese, in spite of severe losses, by mid-November had 70,000 troops on Leyte to resist the 100,000 Americans then on the island. Joining the campaign to cut down Japanese reinforcements, PT boats occasionally slipped around west of Leyte, where they sank a number of troop-carrying barges, two freighters, two small transports, and two patrol craft. After the departure of the Third Fleet, Kinkaid had minesweepers clear the passage between Leyte and Bohol. (See map page 391.) He then sent small groups of destroyers around for night sweeps, chiefly off Ormoc, the principal port on the west coast. The first destroyer sweep sank a surfaced submarine. The second sank a freighter. The third, sent to attack a Japanese convoy approaching Ormoc, was itself furiously attacked by aircraft and by a pair of destroyers. The Americans sank one of the Japanese destroyers, but the other succeeded in putting a torpedo into U.S. destroyer *Cooper*, which broke in two and went down in less than a minute.

By December 1 Japanese casualties were far exceeding reinforcements. By the same date the number of American troops on Leyte had increased to 183,000. Nevertheless American combat operations, supplied over muddy, primitive roads, had slowed down. The U.S. 1st Cavalry Division was making a hotly contested advance through the mountains toward Ormoc from the north. The U.S. 7th Infantry Division was making a similarly contested coastal drive toward Ormoc from the south. To accelerate operations and shorten the campaign, Lieutenant General Walter Krueger, Commander Sixth Army, decided to divide the enemy by landing troops between the Japanese fighting the U.S. 1st Division in the north and those fighting the U.S. 7th Division south of Ormoc. On December 6 two regimental combat teams of the 77th Infantry Division embarked in beaching craft and destroyer-transports and were escorted around to the western side of Leyte by twelve Seventh Fleet destroyers. At sunrise on the 7th they began landing three miles south of Ormoc. Because the Japanese defenders had been drawn away from the Ormoc area in an attempt to stop the simultaneous American advances down from the north and up from the south, the landing was virtually unopposed. Only after the troops were safely ashore did the Japanese react. Then the naval force, still off the beachhead, came under fierce attack by kamikazes that outnumbered the combat air patrol of U.S. Army fighters. Crashing suicide planes so damaged the destroyer *Mahan* and the destroyer-transport *Ward* that both had to be abandoned and sunk. A few days later kamikazes hit the second resupply convoy to the new beachhead, sinking the destroyer *Reid* and heavily damaging the destroyer *Caldwell*. The evident improvement in the techniques used by the suicide pilots boded increasing peril to Allied naval operations against the Japanese.

The American landing on the Leyte west coast proved decisive. The 77th Division promptly took Ormoc and then moved up Ormoc Valley, making contact on December 21 with the southward advancing 1st Division. Though destroying the Japanese survivors, most of whom were now sealed off in the northwest peninsula, was to require four more months, General MacArthur could declare on Christmas Day that all organized resistance on Leyte had ended. American troops and Filipino guerrillas had already liberated nearby, more lightly held Samar. On December 26 Lieutenant General Robert L. Eichelberger relieved General Krueger, taking over the command of the American troops in the Leyte area, who were now designated U.S. Eighth Army—a change of command and force designation similar to that of the U.S. Third-Fifth Fleet the preceding August. By the time the army under Eichelberger completed the conquest of Leyte, about a thousand Japanese had succeeded in escaping from the island, 400 had surrendered, and about 68,000 had been killed or died of starvation or disease. American casualties ashore for the entire campaign were 12,000 wounded and 3,500 killed.

## The Return to Luzon

Long before Leyte was secured, General MacArthur's staff had begun planning for the recapture of Manila. First however airfields would have to be secured nearer Luzon and on the western side of the Philippines, outside the monsoon rain belt. So on December 13 the Third Fleet, after two weeks' rest at Ulithi, again stood to east of the Philippines and began operations against Luzon airfields in preparation for an Allied landing on Mindoro Island, 300 miles northwest of Leyte. Meanwhile a Seventh Fleet invasion convoy, the Mindoro Attack Force, carrying 12,000 combat, 9,500 Air Force, and 6,000 service troops had set out for Mindoro via Surigao Strait and the Mindanao and Sulu seas. Admiral Kinkaid also sent along a covering force of six escort carriers, with battleships, cruisers, and destroyers in the screen. Further cover and support would be provided by the Fifth Air Force, operating from Leyte.

Detected by the Japanese during the approach, the Mindoro Attack Force became the target of numerous kamikazes, one of which hit the convoy flagship *Nashville*, killing 133 officers and men, wounding 190, and obliging the cruiser to return to Leyte. Another suicide plane severely damaged a destroyer, which also had to turn back. However, with tactical cover by planes from the escort carriers and from Leyte and strategic support from Halsey's fast carriers, the invaders went ashore on December 15 without opposition. Only after the assault troops were ashore did the kamikazes succeed in making a D-day strike, which cost the expeditionary force two LST's.

All the aircraft that attacked Mindoro and the Mindoro Attack Force between December 14 and 16 were from the Central Philippines. The Third Fleet was keeping the airfields on Luzon blanketed, maintaining an umbrella of fighters over them around the clock to prevent planes from taking off. In the process the Third Fleet planes destroyed nearly 200 enemy aircraft, mostly on the ground. This achievement was the result of one of several innovations that Admiral McCain had introduced into TF 38 to meet the threat of the kamikazes. He had cut the number of dive bombers aboard his heavy carriers to less than half, and more than doubled the number of fighters. The change actually increased the striking power of the carriers because the Hellcat and Corsair fighters had been modified to carry 2,000 pounds of bombs and thus became dual-purpose planes.

During the same period not a single enemy plane reached TF 38. McCain as a further countermeasure had reduced the number of task groups from four to three in order to concentrate his antiaircraft fire and combat air patrol. Moreover while strikes were in progress, radar picket destroyers were stationed 60 miles from the task force on the flanks of the target-bearing line to give early warning of approaching enemy planes. The pickets had their own combat air patrol, and American planes returning from a strike were required to make a turn around a specified picket so that the destroyer's air patrol could weed out any kamikazes that had joined the returning planes as a means of locating the carriers. Aircraft approaching the task force from a direction other than that of the designated picket destroyer were assumed to be enemy and were treated accordingly.

On December 17, TF 38 withdrew eastward to refuel, but worsening weather obliged Halsey to discontinue fueling a little after noon. On the morning of the 18th, a small, tight typhoon, which the aerologists had not detected, struck the task force in full fury. The commanding officers of the destroyers *Hull, Monaghan,* and *Spence,* hoping to take on much-needed fuel, waited too long to reballast their partly empty tanks with sea water. As a result all three destroyers capsized at the height of the storm and went down. Seven other ships were heavily damaged; 186 planes were jettisoned, blown overboard, or collided and burned; and nearly 800 officers and men were lost. The task force was as badly battered as if it had fought a major battle.

Because of the typhoon and the delay in fueling, TF 38 could not carry out strikes on Luzon scheduled for December 19–21. On the 21st the strikes still could not be carried out because the typhoon was then passing over Luzon. So the Third Fleet returned to Ulithi, where the crews got some much-needed rest, and Service Squadron 10 repaired the storm-damaged ships. During the short respite at Ulithi, Admiral McCain and his staff devised more means for increasing the Third Fleet's combat efficiency. Some of the carriers were assigned a still higher pro- portion of the dual-purpose fighters, including two squadrons of Marine Corsairs, the first marine planes to operate from carriers. A special duty task group, comprising the *Enterprise* and *Independence* with a screen of six destroyers, was organized in TF 38 to specialize in night opera- tions, including bombing, search, combat air patrol, and special missions. On December 30 the Third Fleet departed Ulithi to support the impend- ing invasion of Luzon with a strike at Formosa.

Meanwhile, Allied operations on Mindoro and on the Mindoro supply line continued under sporadic enemy attack. Kamikazes on December 21 struck the first resupply convoy, sinking two more LST's. On Christ- mas Eve a Japanese cruiser-destroyer force—the one that Admiral Shima had commanded in the Battle of Surigao Strait—departed Camranh Bay, Indo-China, and set out eastward across the South China Sea. Concealed by foul weather, this force was within 200 miles of Mindoro when it was sighted by a Leyte-based navy reconnaissance plane. There were at that time no Allied naval vessels in the area larger than PT boats. Arriving off Mindoro in the night of December 26–27, the Japanese ships briefly bombarded an airfield but were driven off by air attack. While they were retiring a PT boat sank one of the destroyers with a spread of torpedoes. At the end of the year a resupply convoy to Mindoro, attacked by Japanese aircraft, lost four ships, including an ammunition vessel that blew up and sank with her entire crew. In the same convoy, kamikazes damaged four more ships. Off Mindoro in the next few days three cargo vessels were bombed from the air, and a kamikaze rammed into an ammunition ship, which instantly exploded, killing another entire crew. The attacks on Mindoro then abruptly ended, for the Japanese shifted their attention to the Allied forces heading for Luzon. By that time there were on Mindoro three operational airfields. These proved invaluable in supporting the Luzon invasion.

The assault on Luzon was to be north of Manila inside Lingayen Gulf, where the Japanese had landed three years before. The expedi-

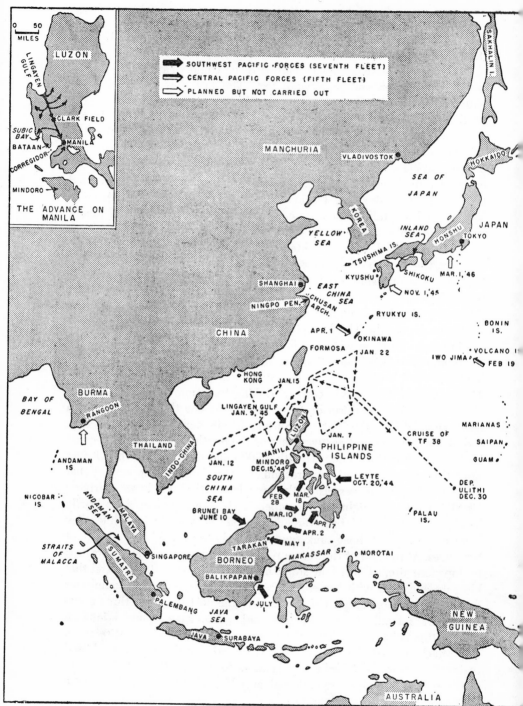

FINAL OPERATIONS OF THE WAR AGAINST JAPAN

tionary force, scheduled to make the assault on January 9, 1945, was about the same as for the invasion of Leyte: the Sixth Army and the Seventh Fleet supplemented by the Third Amphibious Force from the Pacific Fleet. The Army Air Force, operating from Morotai, Leyte, and Mindoro would cover the convoys and operate against airfields in southern Luzon. Further cover was to be provided by escort carriers accompanying the invasion forces. Halsey's Third Fleet, still stripped down to TF 38, would interdict airfields on Formosa and northern Luzon.

The Lingayan assault was spearheaded by a support force of 164 ships, including 6 old battleships, 12 escort carriers, 10 destroyer-transports carrying underwater demolition teams, and 63 minesweepers. This force, commanded by Vice Admiral Oldendorf, was to proceed to Lingayen Gulf to sweep mines, search the beach approaches, and give shore defenses three days of bombardment before the amphibious forces arrived. As it turned out, the principal contribution of the support force was to serve as bait for the kamikazes, which very nearly expended themselves on Oldendorf's advance echelon before the transports arrived.

In the late afternoon of January 2, as Oldendorf's leading group debouched from Surigao Strait, it was seen and reported by a Japanese lookout in a church steeple on high ground on the northeastern point of Mindanao. The next morning in the Mindanao Sea, a Japanese bomber made a suicide crash on an oiler in the group, doing little material damage but killing two men. This was the ominous beginning of a kamikaze campaign that, in proportion to numbers of planes committed, was the most effective of the war.

When Oldendorf's force reached the Sulu Sea, the Japanese, as we have seen, terminated operations against shipping at Mindoro and went after the new and fatter targets. In the afternoon of January 4, as the Lingayen support force was passing to westward of Panay, a two-engine bomber dived into the flight deck of the *Ommaney Bay*. The carrier, aflame and torn by internal explosions, had to be abandoned and sunk. The next day, as the force stood off Manila, 16 kamikazes succeeded in penetrating the combat air patrol. Suicide planes crashed into U.S. heavy cruiser *Louisville*, H.M.A. heavy cruiser *Australia*, U.S. escort carrier *Manila Bay*, a destroyer escort, and an LCI gunboat, and caused damage to four other vessels with near misses. It began to appear that the Special Attack Corps had indeed found the long-sought-for means of repelling Allied invasions.

On January 6, as the heavy ships were entering Lingayen Gulf preceded by the minesweepers, the kamikazes began a series of furious attacks that between 1145 and sunset damaged eleven ships and sank one. Suicide planes crashed into the battleships *New Mexico* and *California*, the cruiser *Columbia*, three destroyers, a destroyer-transport, a seaplane tender, and a minesweeper. The cruisers *Louisville* and *Australia* were each hit a second time. The minesweeper *Long*, hit twice, her back broken, capsized and went down. Since leaving Leyte Gulf Oldendorf's force had suffered 325 men killed and nearly 800 wounded by enemy aircraft. Nevertheless both minesweeping and shore bombardment proceeded on schedule.

The attacks on the Lingayen support force might have been even more severe if the Third Fleet, despite murky weather, had not hit Formosan airfields on January 4 and again on the 5th. As a result of these strikes, no reinforcements of aircraft reached Luzon from the north. Halsey's planes struck Luzon airfields on the 6th, according to schedule, but continuing foul weather made blanketing of the fields impossible. On the 7th, at Kinkaid's request, Halsey again struck Luzon, canceling a scheduled strike on Formosa. This time the combination of Third Fleet carrier, Seventh Fleet escort carrier, and Army Air Force planes very nearly put Luzon airfields out of operation. Only a few enemy planes appeared over Lingayen Gulf that day, and most of these were shot down. Two more minesweepers were sunk however, one by aerial bombs, the other by an airborne torpedo. The Japanese had now decided to evacuate what planes they could from the Philippines. After January 7 there were no more organized air attacks on the Allied forces, but individual pilots struck at the Allied shipping from time to time on their own initiative.

The amphibious forces, bringing elements of the Sixth Army from various points in the South and Southwest Pacific Areas, were now en route to Luzon. In Leyte Gulf General MacArthur, in the light cruiser *Boise*, joined Admiral Barbey's Seventh Amphibious Force (TF 78), which carried the I Corps (6th and 43rd Infantry Divisions); and Admiral Kinkaid, in the AGC *Wasatch*, joined Admiral Wilkinson's Third Amphibious Force (TF 79), which carried the XIV Corps (37th and 40th Infantry Divisions). Barbey's force then led the way toward Lingayen Gulf, using the same route that Oldendorf had taken. Use of the shorter route, via San Bernardino Strait was out of the question so long as the Japanese had airfields in southern Luzon.

As Admiral Barbey's force was passing via Mindoro Strait into the South China Sea early on January 7, it came under air attack, and a bomb narrowly missed the *Boise*. That afternoon a kamikaze penetrated intense antiaircraft fire and crashed into an LST. The next morning, as Barbey's force stood off Luzon, a bomb-carrying Japanese fighter dived into the escort carrier *Kadashan Bay*, putting her out of action. Shortly afterward another kamikaze crashed into a troop-filled transport. Wilkinson's force also came under attack on the 8th, a little before sunset. In this force the escort carrier *Kitkun Bay* was crashed by a suicide plane and extensively damaged. Inside the Gulf that day, the *Australia* was hit twice again, but refused Admiral Oldendorf's offer to relieve her of further duties.

Despite the air attacks, the amphibious forces arrived in Lingayen Gulf on schedule, and at sunrise on January 9 all transports were in position for a landing. A few minutes later three kamikazes appeared. One knocked down the mast of a destroyer escort; another crashed into the *Columbia,* already heavily damaged by her earlier hit. In the afternoon a kamikaze dived into the battleship *Mississippi,* causing heavy casualties, and the luckless *Australia* took her fifth hit.

Meanwhile the assault troops had made their landings with no opposition except from Japanese batteries in the hills on the north flank of the beachhead. Oldendorf's heavy and prolonged bombardment had not been necessary, for the Japanese were employing their new tactics of contesting the beaches, if at all, only with delaying forces. General Yamashita with the bulk of his army was already withdrawing northward to make a stand in the mountains. By sunset on the 9th the invaders had penetrated inland as deep as three miles.

That night, while the ships in Lingayen Gulf lay under a blanket of smoke to conceal them from air attack, some 70 plywood powerboats, manned by Japanese troops and carrying depth charges, headed for the fleet. Most were repelled by gunfire and nearly all were destroyed, but a few managed to release their explosives against the sides of Allied vessels and then speed away. In this manner an LCI was sunk, and a transport, an LCI, and four LST's were damaged.

On the night of January 9–10 also, Halsey boldly led the Third Fleet through Luzon Strait and penetrated deep into the South China Sea. In the absence of McCain's carrier planes to keep the northern Luzon airfields neutralized, individual kamikazes began to appear over Lingayen Gulf in greater numbers, striking at arriving and departing Allied convoys. The suicide planes damaged two ships on January 10, nine on the 12th, and three on the 13th. The kamikaze attacks on the Seventh Fleet then sputtered out. Since January 3, Japanese aircraft, mostly kamikazes, had damaged 43 Allied vessels, 18 seriously, and sunk 4; and they had killed 738 men of the Allied forces and wounded nearly 1,400.

Halsey had entered the South China Sea to safeguard the Mindoro-Lingayen supply line by attacking a Japanese fleet, including the battleships *Ise* and *Hyuga,* presumed to be in Camranh Bay. On January 12 McCain's carrier aircraft flew nearly 1,500 sorties over the Indo-China coast without finding any signs of the enemy fleet, which had prudently departed for Lingga Roads some time before. But there was shipping aplenty, and the TF 38 planes sank 44 ships, including a dozen tankers and the light cruiser *Kashii.* They also destroyed more than a hundred enemy aircraft. On the 15th the carrier squadrons hit Takao on the southwest coast of Formosa. Here they were hampered by low ceilings but managed to sink a destroyer and a transport, to disable a tanker, and to wreck 34 planes. The next day they struck the China coast, concentrating on the Hong Kong area, but again they were partially defeated by bad weather, and they lost 22 planes from intense antiaircraft fire. Their score in this attack was a freighter and a tanker sunk, four more ships heavily damaged, and 13 planes destroyed. On January 17 TF 38 began refueling from a fast fueling group that had followed it into the waters west of Luzon. Then while Radio Tokyo was announcing to the world that the U.S. Third Fleet was bottled up in the South China Sea, Halsey slipped back through Luzon Strait at night under an overcast and re-entered the Pacific.

Before returning to Ulithi to turn his fleet over to Spruance in accordance with the plan for alternating commands, Halsey struck again at Formosa, sinking five tankers and five freighters and destroying at least 60 planes on the ground. This time Japanese aircraft succeeded in striking back. A bomb hit the light carrier *Langley*, and suicide planes crashed into the heavy carrier *Ticonderoga* and the picket destroyer *Maddox*. The *Langley*, only moderately damaged, was able to continue operations, but the kamikaze victims had to retire to Ulithi under escort. The rest of TF 38 moved northeast for photo-reconnaissance of Okinawa in preparation for an impending American assault. On January 25 the Third Fleet steamed back into Ulithi Lagoon, having completed its mission of supporting MacArthur's Southwest Pacific forces in their invasion of the Philippines. Halsey was well satisfied. "I am so proud of you," said he in his farewell message to the Fleet, "that no words can express my feelings. . . . Superlatively well done!"

With the return of the Third Fleet to Ulithi, the lines of advance of the Central Pacific forces and of the Southwest Pacific forces diverged. Most of the ships on loan to the Seventh Fleet came again under Nimitz' command for operations northward, in the direction of Japan. At the same time, MacArthur was planning a drive southward for recovery of the rest of the Philippines and of the East Indies.

## The Liberation of the Philippines

While the I Corps contained Yamashita in the hills northeast of Lingayen Gulf, the XIV Corps advanced on Manila. On January 29, 1945, the Seventh Amphibious Force put 30,000 troops ashore without opposition on the Luzon west coast near Subig Bay, both to prevent the Japanese from withdrawing into Bataan Peninsula and to provide additional punch for the drive on Manila from the north. Two days later, 8,000 Americans landed south of Manila Bay for an advance on Manila from the southwest. The XIV Corps' final drive from the north was assisted and expedited by two Marine Air Groups that dispelled the skepticism of army commanders by successfully providing close air support for the ground forces. On February 4 the XIV Corps reached Manila, which was defended by 16,000 naval troops and 5,000 soldiers. There followed a solid month of fighting, street by street and house by house, until the last of the Japanese garrison had been killed or captured, and the city was a shambles.

Three weeks before Manila fell, operations were initiated to secure the bay and harbor. (See map page 432.) On February 15 a regimental combat team went ashore at the tip of Bataan Peninsula against negligible opposition. The next day the island fortress of Corregidor was assaulted by a regimental combat team of paratroops from the air and a battalion landing team of infantry from the sea. The conquest of Corregidor proved an unexpectedly costly and time-consuming operation, partly because Intelligence had estimated the enemy garrison at 850, whereas there were actually nearly six times as many Japanese on the island. The Rock was finally secured in early March. Conquest of the other islands at the mouth of the Bay extended into April. Commodore William A. Sullivan, who had played a major part in clearing the ports of Casablanca, Palermo, Naples, Cherbourg, and Le Havre, was by then busy directing operations to clear the harbor of Manila. This proved Sullivan's hardest task of the war, for here the Japanese had sunk hundreds of ships. By the time the port was in regular use, troops put ashore at Legaspi (see map page 203) had secured Luzon's southeast peninsula, thereby easing the problem of supplying the American forces on Luzon by opening San Bernardino Strait to Allied communications.

While General Krueger's Sixth Army was pursuing General Yamashita's 170,000 surviving troops into the mountains of Luzon, Admiral Kinkaid's Seventh Fleet, now stripped of the Third Amphibious Force, cooperated with General Eichelberger's Eighth Army in clearing the enemy out of the rest of the Philippines. This operation was contrary to the intention of the Joint Chiefs of Staff, who had expected the Filipinos to complete the job of liberation by themselves. But since the forces under General MacArthur were not immediately needed elsewhere, the Joint Chiefs raised no objections.

Between late February and mid-April 1945, Admiral Barbey's Seventh Amphibious Force staged no fewer than 38 landings in the Central and Southern Philippines. These were all minor operations compared to the assaults on Leyte and Luzon. Though some of the islands were fairly heavily garrisoned, the defenders had almost no aircraft; and no naval forces came to their aid, for Japan had written the Philippines off. Moreover, in accordance with current doctrine, the Japanese defenders never seriously opposed the landings. They held the cities as long as they could, wrecked them with demolition charges when forced out, and then withdrew to the mountains, where far more died from starvation and disease than as a result of military operations. Usually only a small fraction of the original garrison survived till the general surrender at the end of the war.

The first of the new series of landings were carried out on February 28 against Palawan Island and on March 10 against Zamboanga, the tip of the western tail of Mindanao. Allied aircraft operating from these positions could intercept enemy naval units approaching the Central Philippines from the Celebes and South China seas. The Americans then invaded Panay, Negros, Cebu, Bohol, and a number of smaller Central Philippine islands. At the same time they advanced southwest from Zamboanga, landing without opposition on the islands of Basilan, Tawi-tawi, and Jolo in the Sulu Archipelago. These islands, along with Palawan, provided airfields for close support of MacArthur's planned assault on Borneo. Lastly, the Americans staged a series of invasions of the mainland of Mindanao. Here the purpose was to complete the work of a 25,000-man guerrilla army that already controlled 95 per cent of the island and had confined the Japanese garrison of 42,000 to the cities and a few other strong points. From beachheads on the west, north, and south coasts, the invaders advanced, splitting the Japanese forces and preventing them from achieving a united front. The Americans then ousted the enemy from the cities into the countryside, where the Filipino guerrillas kept them under attack until the end of the war.

## The Royal Navy

After the surrender of the Italian fleet in September 1943, the Royal Navy was at last able to release some ships to the Indian Ocean. By the following January the British Eastern Fleet, commanded by Admiral Sir James Somerville, was again operating out of Ceylon. At British request, Admiral Nimitz loaned Admiral Somerville U.S. carrier *Saratoga* to teach the Eastern Fleet American methods of carrier operations. In the spring of 1944 Somerville's fleet with the *Saratoga* and H.M. carrier *Illustrious* raided Japanese bases on and around Sumatra and Java.

With the defeat of the U-boat and the successful invasions of France, the Royal Navy by the late summer of 1944 was virtually without employment in the Atlantic and Mediterranean theaters. The U.S. Joint Chiefs of Staff therefore pressed the British to employ their naval forces against Borneo, relieving the U.S. Seventh Fleet in support of Australian troops under General MacArthur. Recapture of Borneo would deprive the Japanese of their principal oil wells and refineries and at the same time provide British and American fleets in the Far East with a handy source of fuel at an enormous saving in tankers.

The British Chiefs of Staff agreed and began planning for a return to Borneo. When the Americans announced their intention of invading Japan in 1945 however, Prime Minister Churchill felt that the British should participate—as American forces had participated in the invasions of North Africa, Italy, and France. Accordingly he offered the British fleet for operations under American command in the Pacific Ocean, and President Roosevelt accepted the offer. Admirals King and Nimitz were at first dismayed over this decision. As they saw it, the British ships could be used to best advantage in the East Indies, while in the Pacific they were not needed. Second, British fleet carriers were neither constructed nor trained to support large-scale amphibious assaults. Lastly, the facilities of Nimitz' Service Force were already stretched to the limit in meeting the logistic needs of the U.S. Pacific Fleet. King insisted that if the Royal Navy joined the operations against Japan, it must provide its own service force, a stipulation to which the British agreed. In the end however most of the service vessels attached to the British Pacific Fleet had to be supplied by the United States, and the British carriers had to be provided with American planes since their own were too short-ranged for distant operations.

As a result of Churchill's offer and Roosevelt's acceptance, the reconquest of Borneo was left to the Australian army and the Seventh Fleet, under the over-all command of General MacArthur. The fastest and best ships of the Royal Navy proceeded via the Indian Ocean to join the forces under Admiral Nimitz. En route, during December 1944 and January 1945, the British Pacific Fleet made three carrier attacks on the oil refineries of Sumatra—both to cut down the supply of aviation fuel reaching Japanese air forces in Burma and to gain the sort of combat experience needed for the war against Japan. Left behind in the Indian Ocean were the older and slower British and allied ships, now called the East Indies Fleet.

The first task of the East Indies Fleet was to support the British campaign in Burma by covering the sea approaches and by staging an amphibious assault in early May 1945 on the port of Rangoon. But so rapidly was the situation ashore turning in favor of the British that the Japanese had evacuated Rangoon before the assault could be launched. A little later however five destroyers operating in support of the Burma campaign had their hour of glory. Pursuing a Japanese vessel reported damaged by an escort carrier plane, they overtook her in darkness off the Strait of Malacca and found they were confronting a heavy cruiser— actually the *Haguro*, which had fought with Kurita's Center Force in the Battle for Leyte Gulf. The destroyers nevertheless attacked, eluded the cruiser's superior fire, surrounded her, and sent her down with torpedoes.

## The Borneo Campaign

MacArthur's Borneo campaign opened with an assault on Tarakan Island off the east coast, with the objective of capturing oil fields and airstrips. Eschewing surprise, elements of the Seventh Amphibious Force spent several days sweeping mines and clearing obstacles off the beachhead. On April 30, 1945, troops went ashore on an adjoining island and emplaced artillery to support the main landing. At dawn on D-day, May 1, an attack group, including American and Australian cruisers and destroyers, under Rear Admiral Forrest B. Royal USN, arrived off Tarakan and began landing 18,000 troops, mostly Australian but including some American and Dutch. The 2,300 Japanese defenders, as usual at this stage of the war, offered no opposition at the beach, but in the interior they put up stubborn resistance, requiring the invaders to call for destroyer gunfire support for nearly a month. A small remnant of the Japanese garrison held out on Tarakan till the end of the war.

On June 10 Admiral Royal's task group took more Australian troops around to the opposite coast for a series of landings in the Brunei Bay area. All the invasions were monotonously similar—extensive minesweeping followed by unopposed landings, which in turn were generally followed by increasing resistance in the interior. The sole novelty was the appearance of a few Japanese planes which did no damage. North Borneo was declared secured on July 1.

On the same date a Seventh Fleet attack group, including three American escort carriers, eight cruisers (five American, two Australian, and one Dutch), and nine destroyers, commanded by Rear Admiral Albert Noble USN, put a reinforced division of Australian troops ashore near the oil-rich port of Balikpapan on Makassar Strait. This invasion was unique in several respects: it was carried out against the most formidable beach defenses that the Southwest Pacific Forces encountered during the entire war; it was preceded by 16 days of naval bombardment, the longest for any amphibious assault of the war; and it was the final invasion of the war.

Balikpapan's defensive strength was based on natural conditions similar to those at Omaha Beach on the Normandy coast—shallow approaches and hills behind the beaches. For many months the Allies themselves had been inadvertently contributing to Balikpapan's defenses by dropping acoustic and magnetic mines from the air into the harbor in an effort to cut down the outflow of oil to Japanese forces elsewhere. The defenders had sown more mines and constructed obstacles in the shallows and had emplaced numerous guns in the hills. Even though the Japanese here could count on no surface and little air support, they appeared prepared to make any would-be invader pay dearly.

But Allied amphibious forces had by now attained such power and precision that apparently no beachhead could hold out against them. Allied air forces, correctly estimating the situation at Balikpapan, attacked the new beachhead prior to invasion for a solid month, expending 3,000 tons of bombs. On June 17 the Seventh Fleet support vessels arrived off Balikpapan and began their bombardment. By D-day they had fired at the shore defenses 38,000 rounds of shell, 114,000 rounds from automatic weapons, and 7,300 rockets. Meanwhile motor minesweepers had swept the approaches, and underwater demolition teams had blasted holes through the obstructions. The minesweepers, working in water too shallow for close gunfire support, took the brunt of the Japanese fire. Only three sweepers were hit, but three others, in dodging enemy shells, ran into mines and were blown up.

So thorough and effective was the preparation for the Balikpapan invasion that on July 1 the assault troops, in 17 waves, went ashore without suffering a single casualty. In the high interior however the invaders as usual met stiffening resistance. For a week the cruisers remained off shore to provide fire support, expending 23,000 more rounds of shell. There followed two additional weeks of attack and counterattack before the last of the Japanese defenders had been killed or had fled the area. By that time the invasion forces had advanced some 50 miles to the north, seizing oil wells and refineries. Australian losses for the entire operation were 229 killed. Seventh Fleet losses were seven killed in the damaged and destroyed minesweepers.

With the completion of the Borneo campaign, General MacArthur planned to advance on Java. This time however the Joint Chiefs of Staff called a halt to his southward drive. All available Allied strength was to be concentrated for an invasion of Japan, for which MacArthur was to command the ground forces.

## The Capture of Iwo Jima

We must now backtrack a few months to observe the activities of Nimitz' Central Pacific forces, which were again operating independently of MacArthur's Southwest Pacific forces.

In late November 1944, B-29's of the 21st Bomber Command, based on Saipan, had begun raiding the Tokyo area. The results from the Allied point of view were less than satisfactory because the big bombers were operating under severe handicaps. The 3,000-mile round trip required them to cut their bomb loads from a possible ten to three tons. Lack of fighter support obliged them to make fuel-consuming climbs to around 28,000 feet, an altitude from which precision bombing was impossible. Enemy bases in the Volcano and Bonin Islands, lying midway between the southern Marianas and Japan, further cut down the effectiveness of the bombers by warning Tokyo of their approach and by sending up fighters to attack them en route. Capture of an island in the Volcano-Bonin group would not only enable American aircraft based there to put an end to this nuisance but would also provide a base for fighter planes and medium bombers within attack radius of Japan, a way station for B-29's in need of refueling, a refuge for damaged bombers, and a base for air-sea rescue. To obtain these obvious advantages, the

Joint War Planning Committee in Washington began drawing up plans for the capture of Iwo Jima in the Volcanoes almost as soon as the decision was made to invade the Marianas. In early October 1944 the Joint Chiefs directed Admiral Nimitz, after providing fleet cover and support for MacArthur's invasion of Luzon, to proceed in early 1945 with the capture of Iwo Jima, and also of Okinawa in the Ryukyus.*

Because the situation on Leyte had obliged MacArthur to postpone his invasion of Luzon from December 20, 1944 to January 9, 1945, Halsey was not able to deliver the Fast Carrier Task Force to Spruance at Ulithi until near the end of January. As a consequence, the Iwo assault was deferred till mid-February, with the invasion of Okinawa to follow six weeks later. This was tight scheduling, but further delay was out of the question because planning was already under way for a massive invasion of Japan in the fall, and the success of this invasion depended in large measure upon long-sustained air operations involving both Iwo Jima and Okinawa.

To direct the new operations, Nimitz, newly promoted to fleet admiral, shifted from Pearl Harbor to advanced headquarters on Guam. Under Admiral Spruance, the Central Pacific Force again became U.S. Fifth Fleet. Vice Admiral Marc Mitscher resumed his command of the Fast Carrier Task Force, back to its old title of Task Force 58. The Fifth Fleet now had two amphibious forces, the Third and the Fifth, with Vice Admiral Richmond Kelly Turner in over-all command as Commander Amphibious Forces Pacific Fleet. Lieutenant General Holland Smith was in over-all command of the corresponding III and V Amphibious Corps, with the title General Fleet Marine Force Pacific.

After the Fifth Fleet invasion of the Marianas in the summer of 1944, the Japanese had taken for granted that the Americans would eventually try to capture one of the islands of the Volcano-Bonin group and had selected Iwo Jima as the probable target because it provided the best terrain for airfields. So on this tiny volcanic ash heap they established a garrison of 14,000 army and 7,000 naval personnel, nearly all highly trained combat troops. Able Lieutenant General Tadamichi Kuribayashi, in over-all command of the island's defenses, set out to make Iwo the most formidably defended eight square miles in the Pacific. In achieving this goal he was abetted by the terrain. The broad northeast end of the island was a plateau of lava, for the most part tortured into fantastic hills and ravines and falling off into steep escarpments at the shoreline. At the opposite end stood an extinct volcano, 550-foot-high Mt. Suribachi. These two heights flanked the only possible landing beaches, along the tapering waist. On the heights Kuribayashi concentrated his artillery

---

* To allow Nimitz some freedom of action, the Joint Chiefs' directive specified only "one or more positions" in each of the two island groups, but it was understood that Iwo and Okinawa were the preferred targets.

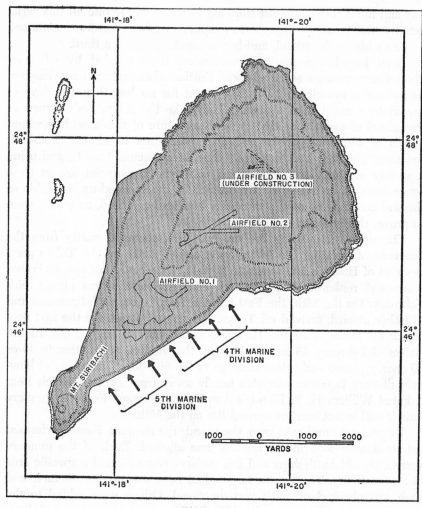

141°-18'   141°-20'

N

24° 48'   24° 48'

AIRFIELD NO. 3
(UNDER CONSTRUCTION)

AIRFIELD NO. 2

AIRFIELD NO. 1

24° 46'   24° 46'

4TH MARINE
DIVISION

MT. SURIBACHI

5TH MARINE
DIVISION

1000    0    1000    2000
YARDS

141°-18'   141°-20'

IWO JIMA

where it could enfilade the beaches and the ridge between. On the high
ground he set up more than 400 pillboxes and blockhouses, interconnected
by passages tunneled through the lava.

For 74 consecutive days, B-24's of the Seventh Air Force, also operating out of the Marianas, raided Iwo in preparation for the coming
assault. The raids however achieved no important effect other than to
stimulate the defenders to greater exertions in their underground bur-
rowing. Pinpoint precision was required to hurt Kuribayashi's type of
defenses, and high-level bombing was not noted for precision, particularly where, as in the Bonin-Volcano area, haze or cloud cover is almost
continuous. In an effort to isolate Iwo, marine-operated B-25's made

day and night sorties against shipping in the area. Despite all this aerial activity, the Japanese brought in supplies to Iwo as before, maintained two airfields on the island, and began construction on a third.

Even hard-bitten marine commanders were startled by what air photo-reconnaissance revealed about Kuribayashi's preparations. Assigned to make the assault on Iwo, they asked for no less than ten days of preparatory naval bombardment. They, like the Navy, had learned in the school of experience that rapid expenditure of shells, with resultant clouds of obscuring smoke and dust, could not knock out well-built defenses. The fleet had to take its time, locate actual targets, and using a variety of shells and trajectories, endeavor to pinpoint fire at close range from different angles. Unfortunately, the speeded-up timetable of the war could allow only a three-day bombardment and, as events were to prove, this was not enough.

The delay in opening fire on Iwo Jima stemmed partly from the necessity of isolating the island by a carrier strike on the Tokyo area. Because of Halsey's late return to Ulithi, TF 38 could not rest its crews, rearm and replenish its ships, and reach Japanese waters before mid-February. On the 16th, the Fast Carrier Task Force, with Spruance and Mitscher aboard, arrived off Tokyo and sent in planes for the first fleet attack on Japan since the Halsey-Doolittle raid of early 1942. In the strikes of February 16 and 17, bad weather limited destruction to 40 or 50 enemy planes and minor damage to the airfields. The raids did however distract Japanese attention briefly away from Iwo, on which Rear Admiral William H. P. Blandy's Amphibious Support Force of gunnery vessels and escort carriers opened fire on the 16th.

Despite rain and mist over the island, the Support Force performed extraordinarily well in the limited time allowed. Each of the gunnery vessels, six old battleships and five cruisers, was assigned a specific area of responsibility. The known targets had been mapped in advance, and each was checked off as it was destroyed. Others were added to the control map as they were discovered. Though the Japanese had from the beginning returned the American fire and early on Febuary 17 hit a battleship and a cruiser, Kuribayashi's heaviest coast defense batteries were holding their fire until the actual invasion in order not to reveal their location. But when, in mid-morning of the 17th, underwater demolition teams moved toward the east coast beaches accompanied by twelve LCI gunboats, the defenders must have assumed that the assault had begun. At any rate, the heavy batteries now opened up, putting nine gunboats out of action and damaging the other three. The old *Nevada* began counterbattery fire against the new targets at once, and the other gunnery ships soon followed suit. On the 18th the Support Force shifted fire so as to concentrate on the landing beaches, but this was probably a mistake, for the Japanese, in conformity with current doctrine, had left the beaches and the area between the two citadels only lightly defended.

Throughout the naval bombardment, the escort carrier aircraft did valuable service in spotting gunfire and in dropping napalm bombs to burn off concealing vegetation and camouflage. Neither their 500-pound general purpose bombs nor their 5-inch rockets had the power to knock out the heavier Japanese emplacements, but the rockets because of their accuracy proved formidable weapons against less well protected enemy positions. High-level bombers from the Marianas joined the softening-up operations but were generally defeated by cloud cover and achieved negligible results.

Following the raids on Tokyo, TF 58 turned back to join the bombardment of Iwo. At the same time Rear Admiral Harry Hill's Attack Force approached, bringing the assault troops under Major General Harry Schmidt USMC, commanding general of the V Amphibious Force. Also with the Attack Force were Secretary of the Navy James Forrestal, who came as an observer, and Lieutenant General Holland Smith, in over-all command of the expeditionary troops, including garrison.

On D-day, February 19, Vice Admiral Turner took personal command of the Amphibious Support Force. The gunnery vessels now shifted from slow destructive fire to fast neutralizing fire in order to drive the defenders underground. After more than a hundred Task Force 58 planes had roared over the island, firing rockets and machine guns and dropping general purpose and napalm bombs, the fleet resumed the naval bombardment, throwing up clouds of dust that obscured the sun. Already nearly 500 landing craft, carrying eight battalions of the 4th and 5th Marine Divisions, were moving to the line of departure. At 0830 the first wave, 68 armored amphibians, headed for the beach. The naval guns thereupon shifted fire to provide a rolling or box barrage ahead of and on the flanks of the landing force, while more than 50 LCI gunboats advanced to furnish close support.

The momentum attained by this powerful assault was expected to carry the first waves well beyond the beach, but at the shoreline they were brought to a virtual halt by an unforeseen obstacle. The shore, rising steeply from the water, was composed of volcanic ash so soft that the treads of many of the amphibians sank in without taking hold. Succeeding waves of landing craft could not be beached at all. Many were thrown broadside to the shore and swamped. Newly arriving craft had their screws damaged or their bottoms stove in by the wreckage of earlier arrivals.

The marines who succeeded in scrambling ashore began crawling up a series of terraces toward the island's spiny ridge. For a while the heavy fleet bombardment kept the Japanese relatively quiet. But after the barrage had passed over, the defenders gradually recovered, opening fire first with machine guns and mortars and then with heavier guns. As the marines reached the first terrace, they came under intense rifle and machine gun fire from pillboxes on the central ridge. Nevertheless they doggedly climbed the second terrace, taking heavy losses, and advanced from shell crater to shell crater. Tanks and heavy weapons were slow to arrive in support, chiefly because many of the LST's, LSM's, and other craft bringing them in, unable to beach themselves or to find purchase with their anchors in the soft ash, collided and added to the confusion at the shore line.

The marine right wing, nearest the northeast plateau, remained pinned down through the 19th. The center, after putting several pillboxes out of action with flamethrowers and 75-mm. tank guns, got as far as Airfield No. 1. The marine left surged across the narrows, isolating Mt. Suribachi. All this the invaders accomplished under continued heavy fire from the flanks, and with no other cover than sparse vegetation and depressions in the churned up ash. The cost was high; of the 30,000 marines put ashore the first day, more than 2,400 were casualties by nightfall.

On February 20, marines of the center captured Airfield No. 1, those on the right began to penetrate the high ground to the northeast, and the regimental combat team on the extreme left began the assault on the mountain. The capture of Suribachi required nearly three days of blasting or burning out pillboxes and sealing up interconnected caves with grenades, flamethrowers, rockets, and demolition charges. On the morning of the 23rd the volcano was surrounded, and a patrol reached the summit and raised the American flag.* Meanwhile the 4th Division and two regiments of the 5th Division had pivoted to the right and begun the assault on the plateau. As the battalions that had suffered the most casualties were relieved, the 3rd Marine Division, in reserve, began to be committed, moving in between the other two divisions.

Throughout the advance into the northeast plateau area, which involved fighting among crevices, gullies, ledges, and caverns, the fleet added call fire to the barrage from the American artillery ashore. In the course of the campaign, the support ships fired nearly 300,000 rounds of shell, with a weight of more than 14,000 tons. At night the ships reduced opportunities for Japanese infiltration by starshell and searchlight illumination. Carrier air support was unusually effective, particularly during the first four days while TF 58 stood off Iwo Jima. Coordination of the various supporting arms reached a new high, reflecting improved com-

---

* Toward noon the marines raised a second and larger flag, visible to the entire island and a source of inspiration to all the Americans. Newspaper photographer Joe Rosenthal took a picture of the second raising, producing the most frequently copied and reproduced of all war photographs.

munication procedures and sound training based on experience. Nevertheless most of Kuribayashi's well concealed strong points had to be taken one at a time by infantry with close-range tank support.

The expected counterattack from Japan came in the late afternoon of the 21st, when some 20 kamikazes escorted by fighters appeared over Iwo Jima and struck at the carriers of the Amphibious Support Force, to which the heavy carrier *Saratoga* was attached for night operations. The suicide planes crashed into five ships. Three were only moderately damaged, but the *Saratoga,* hit by three aircraft and as many bombs, was wreathed in flames and had a huge underwater hole in her hull. Though she was at length saved by expert fire fighting and damage control, she suffered nearly 300 casualties and was out of action for the rest of the war, undergoing extensive repairs. The two kamikazes that struck the escort carrier *Bismarck Sea* started fires that set off her ammunition in a series of rending explosions, one of which blew off her stern. Abandoned, she rolled over and sank. Of her crew, 350 were lost.

Instead of the estimated five days, the capture of Iwo Jima required nearly a month of vicious fighting and mutual slaughter. The island was declared secured on March 16, but on the 25th hidden Japanese troops came forth and made a final attack. At length however all the enemy garrison except 200 prisoners of war were killed. This time casualties among the assault forces exceeded losses among the defenders; on the island and in the fleet 19,000 Americans were wounded and nearly 7,000 were killed or died of their wounds. "Among the Americans who served on Iwo Island," said Fleet Admiral Nimitz, "uncommon valor was a common virtue."

The stepped-up campaign against Japan got under way even before the captured air fields on Iwo were usable, for on February 25 bombers and fighters from Task Force 58 cooperated with 200 B-29's in a massive raid on Tokyo. The B-29's succeeded in burning out two square miles of the enemy capital, while the carrier aircraft, attacking military targets, destroyed about 150 Japanese planes. From off Tokyo TF 58 shaped course southwest to raid and photograph Okinawa. It then proceeded to Ulithi to replenish for the next invasion.

## The Okinawa Campaign

Shortly after the American conquest of Saipan, Admiral Spruance had suggested the capture of Okinawa, 350 miles southwest of Japan. Okinawa in American hands, he pointed out, would provide airfields to supplement the bomber bases about to be established in the Marianas. The Joint Chiefs of Staff at that time rejected Spruance's suggestion, for plans were being drawn up for an invasion of Formosa. The plan for Formosa however was canceled by the decision to invade the Philippines because

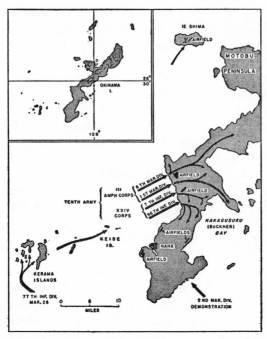

**OKINAWA**

there were not enough troops in the Pacific theater to occupy both. But whereas Luzon was as good as Formosa as a base for interdicting Japanese communications with the Southern Resources Area and for staging an invasion of the home islands, it was too far away from Japan to provide airfields for effectively bombing Japanese industrial centers. So the Joint Chiefs, reverting to Spruance's proposal, decided that they had enough troops to capture Okinawa. In October 1944, as we have seen, they issued orders for the capture of both Iwo Jima and Okinawa.

To support and cover the new assault, TF 58 departed Ulithi in mid-March 1945, with Spruance in strategic and Mitscher in tactical command. Spruance knew that the fast carriers would not return to base for many weeks. The conquest of Okinawa, much the largest island invaded by the Central Pacific forces, would entail an extended campaign involving many troops. The supply problem would be formidable, requiring a steady stream of shipping into an area that was within easy attack range of Japanese airfields on Formosa, in China, in the Ryukyus, and in Japan. Kamikaze attacks could be expected. American airfields would of course be established as quickly as possible on Okinawa, but flyers operating from these would have their hands full supporting the troops. They could not also protect the logistic shipping. That would be the main task of aircraft from the big carriers, which accordingly would have to remain off Okinawa until the island was secured or the threat from the air had been greatly lessened.

To pave the way for the invasion, Task Force 58 on March 18 and 19 launched a series of massive raids on the airfields of Kyushu, southernmost of Japan's home islands, and on the dwindling Japanese fleet in the Inland Sea. This time Japanese aircraft counterattacked, bombing the carriers *Enterprise, Yorktown, Franklin,* and *Wasp.* Only the *Franklin* was seriously damaged. Two bombs penetrated to her hangar deck while she was launching aircraft and set off fires and explosions that took the lives of more than 800 of her crew. No other ship in World War II, and possibly in history, suffered as extensive injuries and yet remained afloat. Saved by an extraordinary feat of damage control, the battered *Franklin* headed under her own power for the United States and a major repair job. These preliminary raids also cost the Americans 116 planes, but they damaged several enemy warships and did so much damage to installations and communications on Kyushu that the Japanese were unable to strike back again in force for nearly three weeks.

On March 23, after refueling, TF 58 began the pre-assault air strikes on Okinawa. On the 24th Rear Admiral Morton L. Deyo's Gunfire and Covering Force of old battleships, cruisers, and destroyers and Vice Admiral Lee's new battleships from TF 58 began the preparatory naval bombardment. Deyo's force in its support capacity was a part of Rear Admiral Blandy's Amphibious Support Force, but Admiral Spruance, suspecting that the Japanese might attempt a surface counterattack, had organized it as a detachable command to counter any such threat.

While the softening up of Okinawa was in process, an amphibious attack force including troops of the 77th Infantry Division carried out an inspired piece of planning by seizing the Kerama Islands, 15 miles west of southern Okinawa. These tiny islands were lightly held, for the Japanese considered them of little use to an invader. But to the Americans the Keramas were invaluable because they provided a sheltered anchorage where a seaplane and a logistic base could be set up. Into the Kerama anchorage on March 27 steamed the first of the tenders, oilers, repair ships, ammunition ships, and other auxiliaries of Service Squadron 10 to begin servicing the fleet. Thus was established a floating base for replenishment and light repairs right in the area of operations, supplementing Service Squadron 6, which remained underway to the southeast. The Kerama attack force also unexpectedly removed a serious threat to shipping by capturing some 350 depth-charge-carrying powerboats such as had menaced the fleet at Lingayen Gulf. Following the invasion of the Keramas, a field artillery group landed on the Keise Islands, still nearer Okinawa, and emplaced 155-mm. guns on the Japanese flank.

During the preliminary operations, aircraft from TF 58 and from escort carriers in Blandy's Amphibious Support Force flew 3,000 sorties in the Okinawa area, and the gunnery vessels fired 5,000 tons of shell. As minesweepers cleared 3,000 square miles off the Okinawa coast, the support ships moved in ever closer, achieving increasingly effective results. After the mines were cleared, underwater demolition teams reconnoitered the selected invasion beaches on the west coast and blew out of the water about 2,900 wooden posts that the defenders had set up as obstacles to landing craft. Involved in the final preparations, besides the gunfire and rocket vessels and the carrier aircraft of the Fifth Fleet, were bombers from the Marianas, the Philippines, and Western China. Task Force 58 covered the approaches from Japan, and at the other end of the line the British Pacific Fleet, designated Task Force 57, covered the approaches from Formosa and kept the intervening islands neutralized by cratering the airfields.

Newly arrived via Sydney and Manus under the command of Vice Admiral Sir Bernard Rawlings RN, the British fleet included four carriers, two battleships, five cruisers, and ten destroyers—about the strength of one task group of TF 58. Though the British carriers had nearly the same displacement as American *Essex*-class carriers, they could accommodate only about half as many planes, their logistic force was not designed to service them in long-sustained campaigns,* and their closed-in hangars slowed operations and proved uncomfortable in tropical waters. In the Okinawa campaign however their armored flight decks gave them a special advantage, rendering them less vulnerable to kamikaze attack than the contemporary American carriers with wooden flight decks and armored hangar decks.

Admiral Turner's Joint Expeditionary Force, assembled from such distant points as Espiritu Santo, Guadalcanal, San Francisco, Seattle, Oahu, Leyte, and Saipan, arrived off Okinawa on schedule in the early hours of D-day, April 1. In the force were 1,300 ships bringing 182,000 assault troops. These included the III Amphibious Corps, composed of the 1st and 6th Marine Divisions; and the XXIV Army Corps, comprising the 7th and 96th Infantry Divisions. These two corps made up the U.S. Tenth Army, commanded by Lieutenant General Simon Bolivar Buckner, Jr. USA. Three more infantry divisions were available as reserve forces: the 27th, as floating reserve; the 81st, as area reserve; and the 77th, after it had captured the Keramas and Ie Shima off the Okinawa west coast.

Awaiting the invasion on Okinawa were about 100,000 defenders, of whom 67,000 were regular Imperial Army troops and the rest were naval personnel and Okinawan draftees. Lieutenant General Mitsuru Ushijima, the army commander, had prepared his defenses in accordance with current Japanese doctrine. All Okinawans whose services could be spared by the armed forces had been transported to Japan or ordered into northern Okinawa. The main defense force took position in a natural citadel of steep hills and narrow ravines in southern Okinawa northeast of Naha. This position they rendered even more defensible by siting mutually supporting artillery to cover all approaches and by linking pillboxes, caves, blockhouses, and other strong points together with trenches and tunnels. About the main citadel they established smaller outlying bastions in concentric rings to slow down the invader's advance. On

---

* From April 20 to May 3, at the height of the Okinawa campaign, the British fleet was obliged to retire to Leyte for replenishment. During its absence, escort carriers of Blandy's Amphibious Support Force took over the task of covering the southwest approaches to Okinawa.

Ushijima's orders, the Japanese guns held their fire throughout the American preparatory bombardment so as not to disclose their positions to naval gunners. On his orders also, no troops were to be wasted in any attempt to stop the Americans at the beachhead, which he correctly estimated would be on the west coast north of Naha. A regiment of Okinawans would man the hills overlooking the beach, but these were to serve only as a delaying force, retreating before the invaders and joining the rest of the defenders in their prepared positions. The general plan was to maintain the defense as long as possible, exposing the invasion forces on land and sea to a prolonged period of attrition, chiefly by Japanese air power.

On the morning of April 1, after the heaviest neutralizing fire unleashed on any beach in the Pacific, the Tenth Army began going ashore. At the same time, in a needless attempt to draw defending forces away from the beachhead, a Demonstration Group including the 2nd Marine Division staged a mock landing on the southeast coast.

The Tenth Army met only sporadic small-arms and mortar fire. In the course of the day, 50,000 soldiers and marines went ashore, and advance elements seized two airfields. By noon of April 2 the invaders had thrust across to the east coast. Then, while most of the XXIV Corps wheeled right for an advance to the south and the 1st Marine Division secured the area opposite the beachhead, the 6th Marine Division advanced up the long northeast axis of the island. In northern Okinawa the marines met only scattered resistance until they entered the rugged hills of the Motobu Peninsula. Here the enemy fought back for several days. Capture of the peninsula provided high elevations for bombardment in support of an assault on nearby Ie Shima, which the 77th Division invaded in order to obtain another airfield. By April 18 the marines had secured all of northern Okinawa but continued to patrol the coasts on the lookout for possible counter-landings.

Meanwhile the XXIV Corps, reinforced by the 27th Infantry Division, had penetrated the outer defenses in the south and had come up against the main Japanese citadel. This they attacked on April 19 but were bloodily repulsed. Thereafter the battle remained relatively stalemated for several days while American fleet guns and shore artillery blasted away in vain against the enemy stronghold. Around May 1, the American front was reorganized to put fresh troops in the line. The 27th Division relieved the 6th Marine Division in northern Okinawa, and the III Amphibious Corps took over the west flank in southern Okinawa. The 77th Division, having completed its conquest of Ie Shima, relieved the 96th Division, which rested for ten days and then relieved the 7th Division for ten days of rest. The Japanese, who had had neither rest nor relief, counterattacked on May 4 but were thrown back. Toward the end of May, the Americans, closely supported by fleet guns, began to outflank the enemy citadel by advancing down both coasts. The defenders, to avoid being surrounded, thereupon began withdrawing under cover of rain to a new defense position in the southern tip of the island.

Because planning for the Okinawa operation was largely completed before heavy kamikaze raids developed in the Philippines, the Fifth Fleet commanders had not anticipated large-scale Japanese suicide attacks at Okinawa. They nevertheless took due precautions. Admiral Mitscher stationed radar picket destroyers for early warning around TF 58. Admiral Turner set up around Okinawa a double ring of radar picket stations, patrolled early in the campaign typically by a destroyer and two well-armed amphibious vessels. On Okinawa, the Keramas, and Ie Shima the army emplaced antiaircraft batteries as quickly as possible, and from captured airfields marine fighter groups soon began to operate.

From the beginning, Japanese bombers and suicide planes made sporadic attacks on the American ships off Okinawa. On March 31 a kamikaze crashed into Spruance's flagship *Indianapolis*, releasing a bomb that penetrated several decks and blew two holes in her hull. While Spruance transferred his flag to the old battleship *New Mexico*, the *Indianapolis* was patched up in the Kerama anchorage and then headed for Mare Island Navy Yard for extensive repairs. On April 4 a crashing kamikaze so mangled a destroyer-transport that she had to be sunk. By April 5 Japanese bombers and suicide planes had succeeded in damaging 39 naval vessels, including two old battleships, three cruisers, and an escort carrier. These raids however were mere preliminaries to the general counterattack which the Imperial Army and Navy, acting for the first time in really close concert, launched on April 6. On the morning of the 6th a Japanese reconnaissance plane sighted TF 58 east of Okinawa. Shortly afterward 355 kamikaze pilots in old aircraft rigged for suicide attack began taking off from airfields in Kyushu. Some headed for TF 58, others for the shipping off Okinawa.

First and most persistently attacked by the kamikazes were the outlying picket vessels, which early in the campaign generally had only their own guns to protect themselves. In mid-afternoon of the 6th, suicide planes swarmed down on the destroyer *Bush* on picket patrol north of Okinawa and made three hits. The destroyer *Colhoun*, patrolling the adjacent station, rushed to support the damaged *Bush* and was herself crashed by three kamikazes. Both destroyers began to sink. An alert combat air patrol and long-practiced countermeasures prevented the enemy aircraft from reaching TF 58 that day, but about 200 reached the Okinawa area. Here most of the attackers were disposed of by fighter planes and by antiaircraft fire so intense that a hail of falling shell fragments caused 38 American casualties. Nevertheless the enemy planes damaged 22 naval vessels, sank a destroyer-transport and an LST, and demolished two loaded ammunition ships, leaving the Tenth Army short of certain types of shell.

Meanwhile the second phase of this wholesale suicide attack got underway as the giant battleship *Yamato,* the light cruiser *Yahagi,* and eight destroyers emerged from the Inland Sea propelled by the last 2,500 tons of fuel oil in Japan—just enough for a one-way passage to Okinawa. Due to arrive at the island at dawn on the 8th, they were to beach themselves there and fire at the American forces until all the Japanese ships had expended their ammunition or been destroyed. But

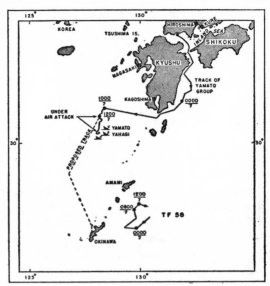

LAST SORTIE OF THE IMPERIAL JAPANESE
FLEET, APRIL 6–7, 1945

two American submarines patrolling off Kyushu sighted the Japanese force before dark on the 6th and flashed a warning. Admiral Spruance thereupon alerted Admiral Deyo's battleship force to prepare to carry out its covering function. Deyo was to let the Japanese ships come south, too far for retreat into a Japanese port and beyond easy protection from Kyushu airfields. Then at the appropriate time on April 7 Deyo's force was to advance and take them under fire. But Admiral Mitscher had no intention of leaving the enemy ships to be dealt with by the surface forces. Before dawn on the 7th he began leading TF 58 northward for the kill. A little after 0800, his search planes relocated the enemy force steaming westward, and Kerama-based PBM's kept it under surveillance as it changed to a southerly course. At 1000 Mitscher launched his air groups. Two hours later the carrier planes struck the enemy in overwhelming force, sending down the *Yamato,* the *Yahagi,* and two destroyers and so damaging two other destroyers that the surviving vessels sank them before returning to base.

On April 7 a kamikaze at last penetrated the TF 58 air patrol and crashed into the deck of the carrier *Hancock,* killing 43 men. By nightfall, suicide planes had damaged four more naval vessels. The April 6-7 raid was only the first of ten general kamikaze attacks launched against the fleet and shipping off Okinawa. Smaller-scale suicide and conventional air raids occurred nearly every day. An additional suicide device used in the April 12-13 raid and in subsequent attacks was the *Oka* (cherry blossom),* a winged, rocket-propelled bomb that was released from

* Called *Baka* (foolish) bomb by the Americans.

the undercarriage of a bomber and then guided into the target by a pilot.

For nearly three months the Fast Carrier Task Force remained east of Okinawa patrolling a 60-mile-square area, while its planes supported the troops ashore, combatted enemy aircraft, and executed antisubmarine patrols. Task groups left the patrol area from time to time to refuel. They also moved north six times to strike at Kyushu airfields, but blanketing the fields as had been done at Luzon was out of the question because there were too many, they were too scattered, and they were too well protected by antiaircraft batteries.

Though the kamikazes continued to find most of their victims among the radar pickets and the ships off Okinawa, the fast carrier force took its share of hits. Admiral Mitscher lost a large part of his staff and had to shift flagships twice in three days as the carriers *Bunker Hill* and *Enterprise* were successively hit and put out of action by crashing kamikazes. Southeast of Okinawa the British task force also came under persistent kamikaze attack. All four British carriers were hit, but all were able to continue operations.

The American aviators and ships' crews obtained some relief as vessels were sent back to Ulithi or elsewhere for repair, upkeep, or overhaul. The Fifth Fleet Commanders however remained at the scene of operations until the strain they were under became almost unendurable. At last Admiral Nimitz, toward the end of May, took the unprecedented step of changing the command in the midst of a campaign. Halsey relieved Spruance, McCain relieved Mitscher, and Hill relieved Turner, whereupon the Fifth Fleet again became the Third Fleet. Halsey was not happy to remain off Okinawa in what appeared to him a purely defensive role, but he quickly perceived that he had no choice. He continued the tactics inaugurated by Spruance, but urged that American air power based on Okinawa be built up as rapidly as possible so that the Fast Carrier Task Force, now again called TF 38, could be relieved of its covering and support duties.

At the time of the change of command, the Americans, steadily improving their techniques, had got the kamikaze menace nearly under control. They had supplemented their surface radar pickets with picket planes, strengthened the surface pickets with additional destroyers and amphibious vessels, and provided the more exposed picket stations with their own combat air patrols. They had set up radar stations in northern Okinawa and on offshore islands that they seized for the purpose. The smaller and more maneuverable American ships had learned to present their beams to diving kamikazes for maximum fire power and to work up speed in order to present a difficult target problem to diving suicide planes, which generally came down so fast that air pressure froze their controls.

The kamikazes, on the contrary, could develop no body of data on which to base improvements because none who went into a final dive ever returned to base to report his experiences. Moreover the nature of the Special Attack Corps had undergone change. All the willing glory seekers had been expended, and Japanese aviators were now being coerced into giving up their lives. Among these unwilling suicides there was a growing feeling that they were making a useless sacrifice because Okinawa was already obviously lost. Pilots began returning to base claiming that they could not locate any enemy ships. One pilot vented his resentment at being sent to his death by strafing his commanding officer's quarters as he took off.

By June 10 the decline in kamikaze attacks, coupled with the build-up of air power on Okinawa and the successes of B-29's operating against Kyushu out of China and the Marianas, had created a situation that permitted TF 38 at last to be released from Okinawan waters. When the fast carrier force arrived at Leyte Gulf on the 13th to prepare for a series of July attacks against Japan, it had been at sea 92 days.

Gunfire support ships and escort carriers remained off Okinawa till the Japanese southern bastion had been taken. The island was declared secured on June 21. The next day General Ushijima and his chief of staff acknowledged defeat by ceremoniously committing suicide. Mopping-up operations continued however until the end of the month. By then practically all the defending forces except 11,000 prisoners of war had been killed. American naval guns, shore artillery, and aircraft had also killed some 24,000 Okinawan civilians who had the misfortune to be near Japanese troops or installations. For the invaders too the campaign had been costly. Nearly 13,000 Americans had been killed, of whom 3,400 were marines and 4,900 navy. In the fleet most of the casualties among ships and men were the result of enemy air attack, chiefly by suicide planes. By air attack alone 15 naval vessels were sunk, none larger than a destroyer, and more than 200 were damaged, some beyond salvage. This costly sacrifice had purchased a position for bringing air power to bear heavily upon the industrial centers of southern Japan and a base for completing the blockade of the home islands and for supporting an invasion of Kyushu.

## The Japanese Surrender

On June 22, 1945 Emperor Hirohito of Japan at a meeting of his Supreme War Council gave utterance to what others in authority had been unwilling or afraid to state officially: Japan must find a way to end the war. It was high time. Clouds of American bombers were turning Japan's cities into ashes. The strangling blockade was bringing the nation's production of war materials to a standstill. Hunger was stalking the land. In April the Soviet Union had made the ominous announcement that it would not renew its Neutrality Pact with Japan. In May the surrender of Germany had dispelled the vain hope that some decisive weapon might yet be obtained from that quarter, and at the same time released the combined forces of the Allied world for operations against Japan. Okinawa, the last Japanese outpost, had fallen to the Americans.

Ending the war was not simple. Powerful factions in Japan and in the armed forces abroad favored a war to the bitter end, and neither the rulers nor the people would accept a peace that did not preserve the imperial system. Negotiations therefore had to be carried out in secret, and terms short of "unconditional surrender" had to be obtained. Since of the major powers only Russia was even ostensibly neutral with respect to the Pacific war, it was appropriate that peace feelers be extended through Moscow. The Supreme Council hoped also by bringing the Soviet government into the negotiations to obtain a new neutrality commitment from Russia in exchange for concessions in Manchuria. But when the Japanese ambassador in Moscow approached the Soviet foreign office on the subject of peace terms, he found the Russians disposed to stall. At the July conference of the victors over Germany held at Potsdam, Premier Stalin at first said nothing to President Truman or to Prime Minister Churchill about Japan's request for mediation.* The Russians evidently had no intention of helping the Japanese get out of the war until they themselves could get into it and thereby share the fruits of victory.

But President Truman knew about the peace feelers, for American intelligence was reading the coded radio messages passing between the Japanese foreign minister in Tokyo and the Japanese ambassador in Moscow. On July 26 the governments of the United States, Britain, and China gave Japan her answer in the Potsdam Proclamation, which specified that for Japan "unconditional surrender" was to apply only to the armed forces. The Proclamation further stated that Japan was to be stripped of all her territorial gains and possessions except the four home islands, and that points in Japan would be occupied until a "peacefully inclined and responsible government" had been established in line with the people's desires expressed in a free elction. Nothing was said about the fate of the Emperor or the imperial system because the Allied governments had not yet made up their minds on that point. Two days after the Proclamation was issued, Stalin at last informed his colleagues of the Japanese request for terms.

The Potsdam Proclamation came a little too suddenly for the Japanese Cabinet, for they had not taken steps to prepare the Japanese people for surrender, they had not received the hoped-for commitment from the

* Clement Attlee replaced Churchill as British Prime Minister before the end of the Potsdam Conference.

Soviet Union, and they had not settled disagreements among themselves. The chief stumbling block however was the failure of the Proclamation to spell out what the Allies intended to do about the Japanese Emperor.

While the Russian leaders were stalling and the Japanese leaders were procrastinating, the Americans and the British were actively planning an invasion of Kyushu for November 1945, with an assault on Honshu and an advance into the Tokyo Plain to follow in March 1946. On July 16, 1945, the world's first man-made atomic explosion was set off at Alamogordo, New Mexico, and within a few hours the erstwhile Fifth Fleet flagship *Indianapolis*, newly repaired from the battering she received off Okinawa, was en route from San Francisco to the Marianas with the first military atomic bomb. Bombers from Okinawa and the Marianas were now appearing over Japan in waves of 500 or more, burning out vast areas in Japan's major cities. On July 10, Task Force 38 had raided airfields near Tokyo. From this date on, with a single break, the Third Fleet carrier force paraded up and down the Japanese coast till the end of the war, bombing and bombarding with virtual impunity while Japan hoarded her aircraft to throw back the expected invasion. On July 17, Halsey's 105 men-of-war were joined by 28 British warships, designated Task Force 37. This combined fleet, the most powerful striking force in history, then raided the naval bases at Yokosuka on Tokyo Bay and at Kure on the Inland Sea, sinking or heavily damaging the remnants of the Imperial Japanese Fleet. On July 30, the Third Fleet ended the first phase of its intensive operations against Japan with a raid on airfields and factories in central Honshu. On this date also, the *Indianapolis*, having delivered her bomb to Tinian, touched at Guam, and then headed for Leyte, was sunk in the Philippine Sea by a Japanese submarine with the loss of nearly 900 lives.

Japan waited a little too long for a commitment from the Soviet Union, for the Americans at length interpreted the continued Japanese silence as a rejection of the Potsdam Proclamation. On August 6, a B-29, taking off from Tinian, flew over Japan and dropped an atomic bomb that seared and flattened most of the city of Hiroshima. The Russians now realized that if they were to get into the war at all, it must be soon. On August 8 the Soviet foreign minister at Moscow handed the Japanese ambassador his long-awaited answer. It was a declaration of war. Within a few hours the Red Army marched into Manchuria. On the 9th another atomic bomb, dropped from an American bomber, devastated the city of Nagasaki. Also on the 9th the Third Fleet, having ridden out a typhoon, returned to Japanese waters and raided airfields in northern Honshu and Hokkaido. On the 10th Russian forces entered Korea.

These startling events both ended the procrastination of the Japanese government and solved one of its most difficult problems. Until then the imperial councilors had been at a loss how to present the facts to a nation long deluded with propaganda. There was a strong chance that any attempt to surrender would precipitate mutiny in the armed services and civil war among the people. But the power and mystery of the new bomb, the swift advance of the Red Army, and the resumption of Third Fleet raids persuaded all but the most hotheaded that further resistance was useless. Shortly after midnight in the morning of August 10, Emperor Hirohito rose with deep emotion before his Supreme Council and advised immediate acceptance of the Potsdam Proclamation. The Cabinet unanimously agreed but only on the condition that the imperial system remain unimpaired. This decision they forwarded via Switzerland and Sweden to Washington, London, Moscow, and Chungking. On receipt of the Japanese decision, America Secretary of State James Byrnes, acting on behalf of the Allied governments, drafted a reply accepting the condition but imposing two stipulations: that during the occupation the Emperor must submit to the authority of the Supreme Allied Commander in Japan, and that the Japanese people should decide the Emperor's ultimate status through free election.

While the Allies were considering the Japanese condition and the Japanese were considering the Allied stipulation, the Third Fleet raided northern Honshu again and struck at the Kurils. It then turned south and on August 13 once more attacked Tokyo. On the 14th the Japanese Cabinet, again on the Emperor's advice, accepted the Allied stipulations. On August 15, when one carrier strike was already over the Tokyo area and another had just been launched, the Third Fleet received the order to "cease fire."

On September 2 aboard the battleship *Missouri* in Tokyo Bay, with ships of the Third Fleet standing by, the Japanese foreign minister, acting for the Emperor, the Government, and Imperial General Headquarters, signed the instrument of surrender. General of the Army Douglas MacArthur then signed the acceptance as Supreme Commander for the Allied Powers. Fleet Admiral Chester Nimitz next affixed his signature as Representative for the United States. He was followed by Representatives for the United Kingdom, China, the Soviet Union, Australia, Canada, France, the Netherlands, and New Zealand.

Soon afterward General MacArthur moved into headquarters in Tokyo to direct the occupation.

# Index

All ships are noted as to nationality and type. Officers are listed with nationality and highest rank associated with their names in this book, but grades within ranks are not supplied. All military units are United States unless otherwise noted.

## Abbreviations

### Nationalities

| | | | | | |
|---|---|---|---|---|---|
| Am | American | Du | Dutch | Nor | Norwegian |
| Aust | Austrian | Fr | French | N.Z. | New Zealand |
| Austr | Australian | Ger | German | Pol | Polish |
| Br | British | It | Italian | Ru | Russian |
| Can | Canadian | Jap | Japanese | U.S. | United States |

### Ships

| | | | |
|---|---|---|---|
| AGC | Amphibious command ship | CL | Light cruiser |
| AKA | Attack cargo ship | CLC | Cruiser command ship |
| AM | Minelayer | CV | Aircraft carrier, heavy |
| AMS | Minesweeper | CVE | Aircraft carrier, escort |
| APA | Attack transport | CVL | Aircraft carrier, light |
| APD | Destroyer transport | DD | Destroyer |
| AR | Repair ship | DE | Destroyer escort |
| ARS | Repair ship, submarines | DL | Destroyer leader |
| AV | Seaplane tender | DMS | Destroyer minesweeper |
| BB | Battleship | IX | Unclassified ship |
| CA | Heavy cruiser | mer | Merchant ship |
| CB | Battle cruiser | SS | Submarine |